# HASKALAH AND HASIDISM IN THE KINGDOM OF POLAND

# THE LITTMAN LIBRARY OF
# JEWISH CIVILIZATION

*Dedicated to the memory of*
LOUIS THOMAS SIDNEY LITTMAN
*who founded the Littman Library for the love of God
and as an act of charity in memory of his father*
JOSEPH AARON LITTMAN
*and to the memory of*
ROBERT JOSEPH LITTMAN
*who continued what his father Louis had begun*

יהא זכרם ברוך

'*Get wisdom, get understanding:
Forsake her not and she shall preserve thee*'

PROV. 4: 5

*The Littman Library of Jewish Civilization is a registered UK charity
Registered charity no. 1000784*

# HASKALAH AND HASIDISM IN THE KINGDOM OF POLAND

◆

## *A History of Conflict*

◆

### MARCIN WODZIŃSKI

*Translated by*
SARAH COZENS

*Assistant translator*
AGNIESZKA MIROWSKA

**The Littman Library of Jewish Civilization**
in association with Liverpool University Press

The Littman Library of Jewish Civilization
in association with Liverpool University Press
4 Cambridge Street, Liverpool L69 7ZU, UK

www.liverpooluniversitypress.co.uk/littman

Managing Editor: Connie Webber

Distributed in North America by
Oxford University Press Inc., 198 Madison Avenue,
New York, NY 10016, USA

First published 2005
First published in paperback 2009

Catalogue records for this book are available from the
British Library and the Library of Congress

ISBN 978-1-906764-02-9

Publishing co-ordinator: Janet Moth
Design: Pete Russell, Faringdon, Oxon.
Copy-editing: Laurien Berkeley
Index: Bonnie Blackburn
Typeset by Footnote Graphics, Warminster, Wilts.

Printed in Great Britain by
CPI Group (UK) Ltd., Croydon, CR0 4YY

*To my parents*

*This translation was funded by*

THE INSTITUTE OF POLISH PHILOLOGY
UNIVERSITY OF WROCŁAW

*and by*

THE FOUNDATION FOR POLISH SCIENCE

# Preface and Acknowledgements

THIS BOOK was first published in Polish in 2003. Since then research in the field has continued, new ideas have been developed, and many new studies have appeared. For all these reasons it was necessary for me to review critically the typescript of the English edition and make appropriate changes to reflect the latest research and the development of my own thinking. Some additional changes were introduced as a result of criticisms expressed both in reviews of the Polish edition and in private discussion, and for these I am deeply grateful, particularly to Adam Galos, Wiesław Puś, Ryszard Rubinkiewicz, Shaul Stampfer, Jerzy Tomaszewski, Theodore R. Weeks, and Wacław Wierzbieniec.[1] Parts of this book have been also published in English as separate articles in *East European Jewish Affairs* (parts of Chapter 5), *Gal-ed* (sections of Chapters 3 and 4), *Jewish Social Studies* (parts of Chapter 2), and the *Journal of Jewish Studies* (parts of Chapter 6).[2] The editors of these publications, and particularly Professor David Engel, helped me in correcting many mistakes and in developing ideas. This edition also differs from the Polish one in that it includes a number of passages explaining and clarifying the Polish context for the benefit of English readers who are not familiar with its detail. Finally, bearing in mind that most readers will not have easy access to the sources I cite, I have added thirteen more documents to the six originally contained in the appendices; these are both illustrative of the ideas I analyse and useful for the independent study of maskilic–hasidic relations in the nineteenth-century Kingdom of Poland.

*

This book could not have been written without the extensive help of numerous people and institutions. To them I want to express my deepest gratitude. I should like to thank the Yad Hanadiv Foundation for granting me a generous fellowship at the Hebrew University of Jerusalem; the Center for Research on the History and Culture of Polish Jews, Hebrew University of Jerusalem, for granting me the

[1] Of the reviews, see Jerzy Tomaszewski, 'Maskile, chasydzi, misnagdzi i niektórzy inni', *Midrasz*, 6 (2003), 48–9; Wacław Wierzbieniec, *Kwartalnik Historii Żydów*, 55/3 (2004), 419–22; Wiesław Caban, *Studia Judaica*, 7/1 (2004), 185–9.

[2] These were 'Jakub Tugendhold and the First Maskilic Defence of Hasidism', *Gal-ed*, 18 (2001), 13–41; 'How many *Hasidim* were there in Congress Poland? On the Demographics of the Hasidic Movement in Poland during the First Half of the Nineteenth Century', *Gal-ed*, 19 (2004), 13–49; 'Good Maskilim and Bad Assimilationists, or Toward a New Historiography of the Haskalah in Poland', *JSS* 10/3 (2003–4), 87–122; 'Language, Ideology and the Beginnings of the Integrationist Movement in the Kingdom of Poland in the 1860s', *East European Jewish Affairs*, 34/2 (2004), 21–40; 'Neither Hatred, nor Solidarity: Integrationists and Hasidim in Congress Poland in Light of *Jutrzenka* and its Circles (1861–1863)', *Journal of Jewish Studies*, 56/2 (2005).

status of Fellow during my stay in Jerusalem; the Mordechaj Anielewicz Centre for the Research and Teaching of the History of Polish Jews, University of Warsaw, for accepting me as its Fellow; and the Institute of Polish Philology, University of Wrocław, for enabling the research and writing of this book. A Professor Bernard Choseed Memorial Fellowship of the YIVO Institute for Jewish Research in New York allowed me to carry out supplementary research, which turned out to be invaluable for this English edition. I should also like to thank the institutions that gave me access to their collections: the University Library in Wrocław; the State Archives in Kielce, Lublin, and Radom; the University Library and National Library in Warsaw; the Central Archive for the Old Files in Warsaw; the Central Archives for the History of the Jewish People in Jerusalem; the National and University Library in Jerusalem; the YIVO Institute for Jewish Research in New York; and the American Jewish Archives in Cincinnati.

I owe special thanks to two people: Professor Jerzy Woronczak and Professor Moshe Rosman. The tireless assistance of the late Professor Woronczak shaped me as a historian of Polish Jewish history and helped me on the difficult path to intellectual maturity. Professor Rosman inspired me to take a new, more critical, look at both my studies and myself. I hope that both of them have found in the present book a spark of the understanding of history that they endeavoured to breathe into me, and that they have felt that their efforts are not completely wasted. I should also like to thank David Assaf, Israel Bartal, Glenn Dynner, Shmuel Feiner, Chaim Gertner, Jakub Goldberg, John D. Klier, Michael Silber, Shaul Stampfer, Jerzy Tomaszewski, Scott Ury, Theodore R. Weeks, Shmuel Werses, and others too numerous to mention. Their suggestions and opinions inspired me to revise critically many parts of this study. I also owe much to the help and friendship of Rina Benari and Rivka Parciack. Last but not least, I thank my parents for their never-ending encouragement, and my wife Agata and son Antek for their patience, and their tolerance of my numerous and time-consuming absences while I worked on this book.

I am deeply grateful to the many people who made the present English edition possible. Ada Rapoport-Albert and Shaul Stampfer supported the idea of translating the book into English and persuaded others to make the effort to read, evaluate, and recommend it for publication. I am most grateful to the Institute of Polish Philology, Wrocław University, and the Foundation for Polish Science for funding the translation. I should also like to thank all the staff of the Littman Library of Jewish Civilization, especially Connie Webber, Ludo Craddock, Janet Moth, Laurien Berkeley, and Bonnie Blackburn, and the translators Sarah Cozens and Agnieszka Mirowska, who did much more than I could have hoped to improve the text and prepare it for publication. Sections of Chapters 3 and 4, which have been published in *Gal-ed*, were also excellently translated and critically edited by Professor David Engel, to whom I am most grateful, as I am to Arno Pomerans, who masterfully translated parts of the appendices. I hope they will all find the resulting publication a worthy reflection of their efforts.

M.W.

# Contents

# Note on Transliteration and Place Names

THE transliteration of Hebrew in this book reflects consideration of the type of book it is, in terms of its content, purpose, and readership. The system adopted therefore reflects a broad approach to transcription, rather than the narrower approaches found in the *Encyclopaedia Judaica* or other systems developed for text-based or linguistic studies. The aim has been to reflect the pronunciation prescribed for modern Hebrew, rather than the spelling or Hebrew word structure, and to do so using conventions that are generally familiar to the English-speaking reader.

In accordance with this approach, no attempt is made to indicate the distinctions between *alef* and *ayin*, *tet* and *taf*, *kaf* and *kuf*, *sin* and *samekh*, since these are not relevant to pronunciation; likewise, the *dagesh* is not indicated except where it affects pronunciation. Following the principle of using conventions familiar to the majority of readers, however, transcriptions that are well established have been retained even when they are not fully consistent with the transliteration system adopted. On similar grounds, the *tsadi* is rendered by 'tz' in such familiar words as bar mitzvah, mitzvot, and so on. Likewise, the distinction between *het* and *khaf* has been retained, using *h* for the former and *kh* for the latter; the associated forms are generally familiar to readers, even if the distinction is not actually borne out in pronunciation, and for the same reason the final *heh* is indicated too. As in Hebrew, no capital letters are used, except that an initial capital has been retained in transliterating titles of published works (for example, *Shulhan arukh*).

Since no distinction is made between *alef* and *ayin*, they are indicated by an apostrophe only in intervocalic positions where a failure to do so could lead an English-speaking reader to pronounce the vowel-cluster as a diphthong—as, for example, in *ha'ir*—or otherwise mispronounce the word.

The *sheva na* is indicated by an *e*—*perikat ol*, *reshut*—except, again, when established convention dictates otherwise.

The *yod* is represented by *i* when it occurs as a vowel (*bereshit*), by *y* when it occurs as a consonant (*yesodot*), and by *yi* when it occurs as both (*yisra'el*).

Names have generally been left in their familiar forms, even when this is inconsistent with the overall system.

Thanks are due to Jonathan Webber of Birmingham University's Theology Department for his help in elucidating the principles to be adopted.

As for the spelling of the place names, so complicated and ideologically loaded in eastern Europe, I have given the Polish form for localities in Congress Poland and other territories of contemporary Poland. There are two exceptions: the first is those cities that have well-known English names (Warsaw, not Warszawa; Breslau, not Wrocław—although I have used Kraków); the second is the names of hasidic courts, of which the Yiddish version differs markedly from the Polish one. Here I give both names, Polish then Yiddish: Góra Kalwaria (Ger), Mszczonów (Amshinov), Opatów (Apta). Other hasidic sites are given only Polish names—Kock, not Kotsk (which would be only a minor difference of spelling). Names of other localities (Ukrainian, German, Belarusian, Lithuanian, etc.) are given in either their Yiddish, Polish, or (if they have one) their English form.

# Figures

# Tables

# *Abbreviations*

| | |
|---|---|
| AGAD | Archiwum Główne Akt Dawnych, Warsaw |
| AmL | Akta miasta Lublina (1809–1874) |
| APK | Archiwum Państwowe w Kielcach |
| APL | Archiwum Państwowe w Lublinie |
| APR | Archiwum Państwowe w Radomiu |
| AŻIH | Archiwum Żydowskiego Instytutu Historycznego, Warsaw |
| *AZJ* | *Allgemeine Zeitung des Judentums* |
| *BŻIH* | *Biuletyn Żydowskiego Instytutu Historycznego* |
| CAHJP | Central Archives for the History of the Jewish People, Jerusalem |
| CWW | Centralne Władze Wyznaniowe, AGAD |
| *Izr.* | *Izraelita* |
| *JE* | *Jewish Expositor and Friend of Israel* |
| *JI* | *Jewish Intelligence* |
| *JSS* | *Jewish Social Studies* |
| *Ju.* | *Jutrzenka* |
| KRSW | Komisja Rządowa Spraw Wewnętrznych, AGAD |
| KWK | Komisja Województwa Kaliskiego, AGAD |
| *KŻP* | *Kwartalnik poświęcony badaniu przeszłości Żydów w Polsce* |
| *MGWJ* | *Monatsschrift für Geschichte und Wissenschaft des Judentums* |
| *MI* | *Monthly Intelligence* |
| *PSB* | *Polski Słownik Biograficzny* [Polish Biographical Dictionary], 42 vols. to date (Kraków, 1935– ) |
| RGR | Rząd Gubernialny Radomski, APK |

# Introduction

THE conflict between representatives of the Jewish Enlightenment (the Haskalah) and its rival hasidic movement has, with justification, been seen in the historical literature as one of the most important debates to occupy Jewish society in central and eastern Europe in the modern age. This may explain the conviction among researchers that the subject has already been sufficiently explored and explained, and that the present state of knowledge is satisfactory. Indeed, the earliest studies devoted to this question made their appearance at the dawn of modern Jewish historiography. Almost every work on the history of nineteenth-century east European Jewry discusses it, while the writings of the better-known ideologists of the maskilic movement, particularly Joseph Perl, Judah Leib Mieses, Jacob Samuel Byk, and Eliezer Zweifel, contain countless references to it.[1] There have also been numerous studies devoted to figures such as Baruch Schick, Manasseh of Ilya, and Moses Berlin, who, while perhaps less influential in the world of the Haskalah, are nevertheless of interest by virtue of their attitude towards hasidism.[2]

However, a closer reading of such studies reveals that the overwhelming majority of references to the 'age-old hostility' of enlightened Jews to hasidism are based on stereotypes that often obscure a proper understanding of the sources. Also, surprisingly few analyses of the attitude of 'progressive' circles towards hasidism go beyond an examination of individual views, making more widely contextualized studies the exception: those by Raphael Mahler, Shmuel Werses, and Shmuel Feiner stand out among the few attempts at a more general presentation of the

---

[1] For Perl's attitude towards hasidism, see Mahler, *Hasidism and the Jewish Enlightenment*, 121–68; Rubinstein, 'Hahaskalah vehahasidut'; Perl, *Uiber das Wesen der Sekte Chassidim* (see the introd. by Avraham Rubinstein); Werses, 'Ketav pulmus maskili ganuz bigenutah shel hahasidut'; id., 'Bein metsiut lebidyon'. On Mieses, see Friedlander, 'Hasidism as the Image of Demonism'; id., 'The Struggle of the Mitnagdim and Maskilim against Hasidism'. On Byk, see Werses, 'Bein shenei olamot'. On Zweifel, see Feiner, 'Hamifneh beha'arahat hahasidut'; Wiederkehr-Pollack, *Eliezer Zweifel*.

[2] On Baruch Schick, one of the harbingers of the Haskalah in eastern Europe, and his attitude towards hasidism, see Fishman, *Russia's First Modern Jews*, 118–19; Salmon, 'Al pulmus keneged hahasidut'. On Manasseh of Ilya, another early maskil, see Barzilay, 'Acceptance or Rejection'. On the Russian 'learned Jew' Moses Berlin, see Lurie and Zeltser, 'Moses Berlin and the Lubavich Hasidim'. On Ruben Braudes, see Weinfeld, '"Ish hasidi" shel re'uven asher brodes'. An interesting study of Micha Josef Berdyczewski and his attitudes towards hasidism is to be found in Werses, 'Hahasidut be'olamo shel berdits'evski'.

issue.[3] Yet, for all their many and varied strengths, these studies are themselves incomplete in many respects. First, they focus almost exclusively on the Galician Haskalah, as if the conflict in question did not stray beyond the boundaries of the Habsburg empire. This trend can be illustrated by Mahler's interesting monograph on the history of the Haskalah and hasidism in Galicia and the Kingdom of Poland. In the section devoted to Galicia, Mahler paints a relatively rich (if somewhat tendentious and Perl-centred) picture of anti-hasidic attitudes and views, but in the section dealing with the Kingdom of Poland the subject is allocated just a few general sentences, and Mahler even suggests that such attitudes did not in fact exist in the Congress Kingdom.

Secondly, the authors of the more recent studies, such as Werses and Feiner, focus on the 'classical' texts of the Galician anti-hasidic maskilim—mainly those of Perl and Mieses, but also on those of their contemporaries Nahman Krochmal, Solomon Judah Rapoport, and Isaac Erter. The hostile views of Menahem Mendel Lefin of Satanów, considered to be the father of the Galician Haskalah and the inspiration for its anti-hasidic attitudes, have also aroused interest.[4] To an extent, this approach can be justified, as Lefin, Perl, and Mieses can all be seen as representing the epitome of anti-hasidic phobia. The motif of the fight with the hasidic movement occupies an important place in their works, and the accusations they level at hasidism are particularly fierce. However, this concentration by researchers on a relatively small group of Galician maskilim can give the impression that an anti-hasidic obsession was the only, or at least the overwhelmingly predominant, attitude towards hasidism in the enlightened Jewish camp, and a natural consequence of this has been the tendency to present the writings of defenders of the hasidic movement, such as Jacob Samuel Byk and Abraham Kohn, as unusual and innovative. Without questioning the accuracy of this viewpoint (excellently justified by Shmuel Werses) in the Galician context, we should nevertheless look closely at the validity of its underlying assumptions: can the attitudes and opinions of Perl and Mieses be deemed to be truly typical, and Byk's views exceptional? If the answer is yes, one must ask: typical for whom, and where and when? What was the relationship between the polemic against hasidism and other aspects of the philosophy of the maskilim of the time? Was it always, for everyone and everywhere, the most important issue, or were there significant geographical variations, or differences over time? Feiner mentions various attitudes to hasidism on the part of the maskilim of Galicia and other territories of the Habsburg empire that were the result of differences in the social standing of the individuals concerned,[5] and

---

[3] See Mahler, *Hasidism and the Jewish Enlightenment*, and the original Hebrew version of the book, *Haḥasidut vehahaskalah*; Werses, 'Haḥasidut be'einei sifrut hahaskalah'; id., 'Tofaot shel magiyah vedemonologiyah'. Feiner, *Haskalah and History*, esp. 91–115, 306–17, is very valuable and, to date, the most comprehensive study of the subject.

[4] See Chapter 1 for Lefin and his attitude towards hasidism.

[5] Feiner, *Haskalah and History*, 73.

it is reasonable to assume that there were similar divergences in opinions and attitudes in other places and at other times. Were opinions on hasidism in the 1890s the same as those prevailing in the 1820s or 1830s? Was the anti-hasidic obsession of the leaders of the maskilim shared by the wider circle of their supporters, those who are referred to in Mordecai Zalkin's studies as the 'social backbone of the Haskalah'? And what was the real significance of the opinions voiced in the Galician maskilic camp on the hasidic issue?

The same questions should be put to researchers examining the attitude of the Haskalah towards hasidism in the Russian empire, who have concentrated almost solely on the crucial publications of the 1870s and, more specifically, on Eliezer Zweifel's treatise *Shalom al yisra'el* (Peace to Israel). Again, without wishing to undermine the validity of Shmuel Feiner's observations, we should consider whether his thesis has universal application, and whether the breakthrough in attitudes towards hasidism it documents was common to all maskilic circles in eastern Europe (or at least in Russia).

There is a further reason why our knowledge of the conflict between the maskilim and the hasidim seems incomplete: the historical literature reveals a predominant interest in the ideological dimension of the dispute and, consequently, in the ideological declarations and polemical works of leaders of both groups—particularly Lefin, Perl, and Mieses. Clearly, the anti-hasidic works of leaders of the Haskalah had a significant impact on the ideology of their supporters: numerous examples show how widely these works were read, commented on, and used. Nonetheless, even a cursory examination of several local skirmishes in the hasidic–maskilic war unambiguously reveals that the conflict at community level, where representatives of the two groups were in daily contact, was not shaped by ideological debates, publications, or even tabloid polemics, but grew along the lines of any typical conflict, where the original cause of the dispute is forgotten as hostilities escalate and the battle develops a momentum of its own.[6] We can see from this that the anti-hasidic enlightened ideology is not enough to explain the conflict's true nature or the mechanisms underlying the course of hundreds of local disputes in east European Jewish communities. In addition to ideology, we therefore have to examine the day-to-day expression of the conflict in Jewish communities, the sphere of daily contact between supporters of the opposing parties. Research into the ideological development of the conflict between supporters of the Haskalah and of hasidism has been enhanced by some detailed analysis of these disputes, from their earliest phase in the 1820s to their advanced form at the start of the 1870s. The results shed considerable light on the true nature of the dispute.

By way of summing up, I can say that, even though numerous studies mention various important aspects of enlightened attitudes towards hasidism, our knowledge of this field is still somewhat static and fragmentary because the point of refer-

---

[6] Theoretical model of differentiation, introduced by Gregory Bateson, in Bauman, *Globalization*, 30–1.

ence is the anti-hasidic writings of the Galician maskilim Perl and Mieses, and the turn towards hasidism is exemplified by Russian representatives of the moderate Haskalah, particularly Zweifel. For over a century scholars have developed the concept of a hostile attitude towards hasidism on the part of enlightened Jews of central and eastern Europe on the basis of two chronologically and territorially specific cases, which, irrespective of their importance, do not permit a proper understanding of the structure of the conflict, nor of its evolution and internal dynamics. Even more significant is the fact that such an approach also prevents us from understanding why hasidism occupied such a prominent place in the ideology of the maskilim (if indeed it did), and what the real function of anti-hasidic polemic was in the philosophies and strategies of Jewish supporters of modernization.

It was these questions that led me to examine the attitude of the maskilim, and their successors, towards the hasidic movement in the broadest possible time-frame—that is, from the first enlightened comments concerning hasidism at the end of the eighteenth century to the demise of the Haskalah and its successors at the start of the twentieth century—and to ask the widest range of questions in the broadest possible context. I not only asked myself what it was that enlightened Jews had thought and said about hasidism; I also considered the whole range of issues outlined above. What was the connection between the views voiced on hasidism and other aspects of the ideology and strategy of the Haskalah? To what extent and in what ways did the polemic against hasidism reflect other social conflicts in Jewish society in the nineteenth century? To what extent did it reflect actual changes in Jewish society in eastern Europe and, in particular, how was it connected with the evolution of hasidism itself? Did hasidism truly become one of the obsessions of maskilic circles? If it did, why and when did it happen? What were the expressed and—more interestingly—the hidden functions of this anti-hasidic polemic? What did the average representative of the modernizing camp mean when he said or wrote 'hasid', and did the word always have the same meaning for all representatives of this camp?

The available materials have not always offered complete answers to all of these questions. Some findings, especially in the area of the social development of hasidism and the natural context of the ideas I examine, have had to remain preliminary, because a broader consideration of the issues would exceed the scope of this book. All the same, having posed our questions, we can seek credible answers, at least in the main areas of this study.

The subject is also significant in another sense. Examining the attitude of modernizing circles towards hasidism, I cherished the hope not only that I would succeed in reconstructing a fragment of an important ideological conflict in nineteenth-century Jewish society, but also that I would contribute to a wider understanding of the origin and development of social phobias and of stereotypical images of the adversary, and to an explanation of the significance of these processes in the creation of group identity. The subject is all the more topical because the prejudice of secular society in modern-day Israel against ultra-Orthodox circles is an important element of the social life of that country, and stems directly from the ideas and events on which this book focuses. Moreover, we can take it that the nature of these phobias is not far removed from similar phenomena in many other contemporary societies.

Some words of explanation are necessary concerning the geographical boundaries of this study. Although the issues it examines are characteristic of the whole maskilic movement in central and eastern Europe, I have restricted my research to central Poland, politically corresponding to the Duchy of Warsaw and its successor, the Kingdom of Poland (the territorial differences between them are immaterial for this book). Although this contradicts my stated aim of treating the subject as broadly as possible, the specific nature of the Polish version of the Haskalah, and its evolution against the background of Galicia, Russia, and the countries of central Europe, has made it unavoidable.[7] Because of the specific path taken by Jewish modernization in central Poland (one which differs from that taken in Galicia and Russia), the group whose views are the subject of analysis here can only be referred to in a general sense as the Haskalah camp. In fact, there were two groups, rather than one, that is, the Haskalah of the first half of the nineteenth century (discussed in Chapter 2) and its immediate successors in the second half of the century (Chapter 5). The Jewish traditional Enlightenment camp disintegrated in the Kingdom of Poland considerably earlier than it did in Galicia and the Russian empire, and by the late 1850s and early 1860s the circles were already splitting into opposing groups: the Hebrew pro-Russian maskilim, the radical assimilation wing, and the Polonized integrationists.[8] Although only the first of these (which was the least numerous) could be covered by the term 'Haskalah' in its strictly understood definition,[9] the last will also—and in fact to a greater extent—be a focus of interest.

This is, first, because the epigones of the Hebrew Haskalah in the Congress Kingdom did not adopt a clear stance towards hasidism almost until its dissolution, while the Polish Jewish circles of integrationists keenly entered the maskilic

[7] In accordance with the terminology of 19th-century literature as well as contemporary Jewish historiography, I use the term 'Poland' and 'Polish' for the Kingdom of Poland (so-called Congress Poland) only, and not for other provinces of the former Polish–Lithuanian Commonwealth. Similarly, 'Polish Haskalah' means 'Haskalah in the Kingdom of Poland'. In cases where the term 'Poland' is used otherwise, it will be annotated. (The only exception to this is in discussion about Polish culture, which always refers to the broader category.)

[8] See Mendelsohn, *On Modern Jewish Politics*, 16–17, for a discussion of terminology appertaining to modernist sections of Jewish society and the difference between 'assimilation' (i.e. a drive for the total abandonment of Jewish identity) and 'integration' (i.e. an endeavour to create a modern version of Jewishness). In my use of the term 'integrationist', I follow Mendelsohn's suggestion that 'integration' be used for the mainstream movement, while 'assimilation' has been reserved for those who explicitly sought to erase any major traces of their Jewish origins.

[9] I have followed the definition suggested by Feiner, 'Towards a Historical Definition of the Haskalah'.

debate surrounding the hasidic issue and in this way upheld the views of the earlier maskilim. A second, and more important, reason is that the integrationists were the immediate continuers of the ideas of the Polish Haskalah, and ideologically were halfway between the traditional ideas of the Jewish Enlightenment and post-Haskalah ideas. In other words, their views (including their stance on the hasidim) were very close to those of the east European Haskalah, especially of its radical factions of the second half of the nineteenth century.[10] Thirdly, and most important of all, it is of interest on account of the fact that, from the late 1850s, the integrationists were the group of modernizing Jews who were dominant in the Kingdom of Poland, and who were the immediate successors of the maskilic camp.

Despite the crisis, which began to intensify in the 1880s, the integrationist camp in the Congress Kingdom endured until the beginning of the twentieth century. Its end took the form not of a spectacular collapse, but rather of a lingering, drawn-out, and painful process of atrophy and decay. The new Zionist and left-wing internationalist groups—and the various shades of assimilationists and those represented by the Yiddish press—which replaced it came from outside the Haskalah tradition and were often fiercely critical of it. Their separation from the enlightened past was evident in a number of ways. Significantly, one of the clearest signs of abandonment of the ideology of the Haskalah and of entry into the world of post-Haskalah values was the renunciation of the polemic with hasidism and an acceptance of the hasidic movement, which was characteristic, for example, of the writings of Micha Josef Berdyczewski.[11] The end of the maskilic camp (and its integrationist continuation) thus also marks the boundaries of this study.

Like the overall development of the Polish Haskalah, the attitude to the hasidic movement of Jewish supporters of enlightenment in central Poland differed from the attitudes of Russian and Galician maskilim, and from views voiced by Jewish supporters of integration in Bohemia, Germany, and Hungary. In this sense, the results of this research constitute a 'case study' and cannot be directly transposed to observations concerning the Haskalah in Galicia or the Russian empire. This preserves the integrity of the defined territorial boundaries of this study. Besides, it does not seem to require any special explanation that the Haskalah in Poland cannot be described using the same comparative measures as might be applied to the Haskalah in Brody, Vilna, Odessa, or Berlin. The mono-ethnic national culture, the significant scale of the Polish state's independence, its dynamic educational traditions, and the high-level participation of educated representatives of the Jewish community in state institutions distinguished Poland from the remaining centres of eastern Europe. Poland differed also from the countries of so-called central

---

[10] Shmuel Werses calls the representatives of the integrationist movement who collaborated in the years 1860–80 with *Jutrzenka* and *Izraelita* the 'radical Haskalah'; see Werses, 'Hasifrut ha'ivrit bepolin', 166. For a broader discussion of this matter, see Chapter 5.

[11] See Feiner, 'Kayonek hanoshekh shadei imo', 81; and also for the broader characteristics of the post-Haskalah.

Europe (for which Prussia was always the model) by virtue of her weaker economic development and the lower legal status of her Jewish population, and, more significantly, because of the existence of a dense concentration of traditional Jews who opposed the emancipation process. These factors suggest that the Haskalah in the Kingdom of Poland must have assumed its own characteristic forms and prove that there were numerous dissimilarities and distinguishing characteristics, which are, after all, completely understandable. Bearing these differences in mind, I hope that this study will not only contribute to an understanding of the relations between the Haskalah and hasidism in central Poland, but will also provide an analogy for studies of these relations in other countries of eastern Europe and shed new light on the history of the Haskalah in Galicia, Russia, and Hungary. Ultimately, there were far more elements in common than there were differences, and the latter were often of secondary significance. It is my opinion that the similarities should be emphasized here, because analysing all the followers of the idea of Jewish enlightenment in Poland, Galicia, Russia, Hungary, and Bohemia (whether we call it Haskalah, Haskaloth, or anything else is of secondary importance) seems important to a proper understanding of the history of that movement in Poland and, more generally, in central and eastern Europe. Polish Jewish modernizers viewed themselves as representatives of the Haskalah and traced their ideological lineage back to the circles of Moses Mendelssohn. This awareness found expression on several occasions in activities that would be incomprehensible if taken out of a maskilic context. Similarly, a proper understanding of the Haskalah in eastern Europe seems difficult, if not impossible, without taking into account Jews living in the Kingdom of Poland. It should be remembered that (after Jews in the Ukraine) they constituted the second greatest concentration of Jews in nineteenth-century Europe, and exceeded the Jewish populations of Lithuania, Belarus, and Galicia not only in actual numbers, but also in terms of their proportion of the country's general population and their particularly high urban concentration. In 1830 the 390,400 Jews living in the Kingdom of Poland constituted 10 per cent of the general population; in 1827 they constituted 35.3 per cent of the urban population, a figure that had increased to 46.5 per cent by 1865.[12]

Some explanation of the source basis of this study is due. My aim was not only to analyse attitudes towards hasidism among a few famous representatives of the Haskalah in Poland (members of the so-called 'maskilic republic of writers'), but also to look into the ideas, concepts, and prejudices of a broad section of the maskilim among Polish Jews. I was interested in the origin and evolution, but also in the

---

[12] For example, at the same time (1830) in Galicia there lived *c.*250,000 Jews, i.e. 6 per cent of the total population. In the Russian Pale of Settlement, i.e. in the Lithuanian, Belarusian, and Ukrainian provinces, the Jewish population in 1838 numbered *c.*1,030,000. There is a good summary of the demographic data for the Congress Kingdom in the 19th century in Eisenbach, *Z dziejów ludności żydowskiej w Polsce*, 137–43, 254–302. Still the best, though heavily biased, work on the subject is Wasiutyński, *Ludność żydowska w Polsce*.

social absorption and functioning, of these ideas. An analysis of popular Polish and Polish Jewish periodicals led me to conclude that, in shaping public opinion in the wider sphere of 'progressive' Jews in Poland—both maskilim and their successors in the second half of the nineteenth century—the most influential source was the popular press. Their opinions were not shaped by the great historiographers, such as Heinrich Graetz or Simon Dubnow, but rather by weeklies, monthlies, calendars, pamphlets popularizing sciences, etc. This is important both because it in some way defines the nature of the movement and its intellectual scope, and also—and more practically—because it allowed me to reconstruct quite precisely the development of the ideas, opinions, and motifs central to this study. As a result, the most significant resources for this study have been Polish Jewish periodicals (*Dostrzegacz Nadwiślański, Jutrzenka, Izraelita, Varshoyer Yidishe Tsaytung, Hatsefirah*), and related sources, such as leaflets and pamphlets. Unfortunately there are few Jewish publications and periodicals in Poland for the early nineteenth century, so I extended my search for sources to Polish periodicals (*Pamiętnik Warszawski, Kurier Warszawski, Korespondent Warszawski, Gazeta Codzienna, Gazeta Polska, Gazeta Warszawska*), German Jewish periodicals (*Allgemeine Zeitung des Judentums, Orient, Israelitische Annalen*), British missionary periodicals (*Jewish Expositor and Friend of Israel, Monthly Intelligence, Jewish Intelligence*), and, above all, archival resources. The last of these groups turned out to be especially important.

# ONE

# The Beginnings: Anti-Hasidic Criticism in the Last Years of the Polish–Lithuanian Commonwealth

DURING the second half of the eighteenth century the states and communities of central and eastern Europe experienced a period of ideological ferment and political, economic, and social transformation. These new ideas were most clearly formulated by the ideologists of the Enlightenment, whose influence permeated everywhere, from royal courts to hitherto marginal groups, including the Jewish community.

Although the early Jewish Enlightenment began to develop simultaneously in a number of European centres, from London to Königsberg to Trieste, it is a philosopher from Berlin, Moses Mendelssohn, who is generally recognized as the father of the Haskalah. For many decades the Haskalah, especially in its Berlin version, became for Jewish society in central and eastern Europe synonymous with progressiveness, emancipation, and liberalism.

In the Polish–Lithuanian Commonwealth the major centre of Enlightenment ideology was the court of King Stanisław August Poniatowski, who made several attempts to rescue the declining Polish–Lithuanian state—efforts that were ultimately unsuccessful. In 1772 three neighbouring powers, Russia, Prussia, and Austria, annexed about 29 per cent of the Commonwealth's territories along with about 37 per cent of its population. Although in this first partition the territories lost to Poland–Lithuania were its most highly developed and those on which its economy most depended, the Commonwealth was still a huge state with considerable potential. During 1788–92, the time of the Four-Year Sejm, or parliament, new attempts were made to reform the state, and this time the reforms were much more far-reaching and courageous, with the Sejm passing several laws of central importance for the state. Of these the most significant was the constitution, the first in Europe and preceded internationally only by that of the United States. The reforms, however, were crippled by the intervention of the neighbouring powers, which in 1795 finally dismantled the Commonwealth.

Among the issues addressed by these reforms was that of the 'Jewish question'.[1]

---

[1] For the most general and up-to-date survey of the situation of the Jews in 18th-century Poland–Lithuania, see Hundert, *Jews in Poland–Lithuania*; see also Weinryb, *Jews of Poland*; Mahler, *Divrei*

During the second half of the eighteenth century the status of the Jews became one of the most important topics of public debate in the Commonwealth, both for ideological (though not necessarily antisemitic) and for more general demographic, economic, and social reasons. The major concern lay in the fact that the ideologues of the Polish Enlightenment opposed organization of the state along religious lines, while the Jews were the only estate, or quasi-estate, distinguished solely by religion. It was thus natural that enlightened reformers should endeavour to remove Jewish autonomy and aim for closer integration of the Jews into other sections of society.

The demographic reasons for the debate were somewhat more complex. During the eighteenth century the Jewish population of the Commonwealth increased from under 200,000 around 1675 to c.750,000 in 1764, at the time of the first census. This was not only the largest concentration of Jewish people in the world, but it also outnumbered by far any other Jewish centre of the period. Demographic growth among Jewish people was much faster than among other groups so that within a century they grew from around 3 per cent to around 7 per cent of the total population. Moreover, because the Jewish population was unevenly distributed, in some areas, especially in the towns in south-eastern territories, the demographic explosion was especially visible, and this must have increased competition with the Christian burghers and heightened social tensions more generally.

These demographic and social factors coincided with internal changes in Jewish society. Among the most important of these was a gradual decrease in the competence of the *kahal*s, the traditional Jewish authorities. This arose out of a rapid deterioration in their financial situation and their growing indebtedness (these debts were eventually paid off by the whole community), and a decline in the moral authority of the rabbinate and other communal institutions. The fall in 1764 of the Council of Four Lands (Va'ad Arba Aratsot), the parliament of Polish Jewry, further accelerated the disintegration of Jewish social institutions in the Commonwealth. Despite considerable efforts, it proved impossible to maintain its activity informally after the Council had been abolished. From that time Polish Jewry lacked any central or regional representation, or its own internal authorities, and this quickly resulted in the further break-up of Jewish life.

The eighteenth century also brought unrest and upheaval in the sphere of Jewish religious life. The popularization of kabbalistic ideas caused a fundamental change in the religious life of east European Jews, especially in its popular expressions. Throughout the century the followers of the heterodox doctrine of Shabateanism had remained active. Although traditional historiography has overestimated

*yemei yisra'el*, ii. 269–330; id., *History of Modern Jewry*, 279–313. On the 'Jewish question' and reforms, see Eisenbach, *Emancypacja Żydów*; Zienkowska, 'Citizens or Inhabitants?'; Michalski, 'Sejmowe projekty reformy'; Gelber, 'Żydzi a zagadnienie reformy Żydów na Sejmie Czteroletnim'; Ringelblum, 'Projekty i próby przewarstwienia Żydów'. For general information on the Jewish demography in the 18th-century Polish–Lithuanian Commonwealth, see Mahler, *Yidn in amolikn Poyln*; Eisenbach, *Z dziejów ludności żydowskiej w Polsce*; see also Stampfer, 'The 1764 Census of Polish Jewry'.

this doctrine in terms of its influence and the number of its adherents, it is clear that traditional Jewish society, especially the rabbinic elite, perceived crypto-Shabateanism as a serious danger, and this led to widespread suspicion and periodic witch-hunts. The real threat came with eruption of the Shabatean movement of Jacob Frank in the 1750s, which resulted in 1759 in the mass conversion to Catholicism of about 2,000 Frankists. At the same time, another Jewish mystical movement emerged among Polish Jews. This was hasidism.

## THE MITNAGEDIM

Opposition to hasidism is almost as old as the hasidic movement itself. However, it was not the supporters of the Jewish Enlightenment ideology, the maskilim, but representatives of the rabbinical elite who were the first to begin an organized wave of opposition. Their hasidic opponents therefore called them 'mitnagedim' (Hebrew: 'opponents').[2]

Among the wealth of mitnagdic polemical literature there are repeated accusations against the hasidim relating especially to their neglect of talmudic studies and their lack of respect for the learned, the establishment of their own prayer halls (*shtiblekh*), changes to the liturgy and the time for saying prayers, changes to the methods of ritual slaughter (*sheḥitah*), their alleged connections with Shabateanism, their eccentric and debauched behaviour, avarice among the tsadikim, and fraudulent miracles. From time to time other accusations surfaced, such as the abuse of tobacco and deviations from traditional dress, and sometimes slanders were fabricated and used for polemical advantage. In literature aimed at the non-Jewish reader the hasidim were also accused of inciting hatred against Christians and of active hostility towards the government and the state.

However, the latter accusations were relatively marginal. What mobilized the rabbinate to make its first major pronouncement against the hasidic movement was the challenge to traditional Jewish values manifested by the hasidic attitude to talmudic studies and prayer.[3] Contrary to these dominant and deeply entrenched convictions, the hasidim did not recognize the study of religious law as the highest form of religious activity and the best means of serving God: that place was reserved for prayer. Furthermore, supporters of the new movement publicly criticized talmudic studies, deriding those with a religious education and undermining

[2] Although historiographical literature on the early stages of the conflict is quite comprehensive, the arguments put forward by the anti-hasidic opposition to date have not been comprehensively studied. An annotated collection of sources published in Wilensky, *Ḥasidim umitnagedim*, is a vital contribution to this field. Some of the works that best summarize the anti-hasidic polemics of the mitnagedim are Wilensky, 'Hassidic Mitnaggedic Polemics'; Wertheim, *Law and Custom in Hasidism*; Nadler, *Faith of the Mithnagdim*; Hundert, *Jews in Poland–Lithuania*.

[3] See Wilensky, 'Hassidic Mitnaggedic Polemics', 261–6; Nadler, *Faith of the Mithnagdim*, 151–70, for greater detail.

the prevailing social order. Their opponents among the mitnagedim responded
not only by emphasizing the damaging religious and social consequences of these
actions, but also by pointing out that to diminish the significance of religious studies was effectively to reject the power of religious law, and was hence out-and-out
heresy.[4] The lack of religious education among hasidic leaders, starting with the
founder of the movement, Israel ben Eliezer (Ba'al Shem Tov, the Besht), was said
to be the reason for such a contemptuous attitude towards religious studies, and
criticism of the Besht as an ignoramus became a recurrent motif in the literature of
both the mitnagedim and the maskilim.[5] Based on the contrast between the educated
as true religious leaders and the uneducated 'hasidic charlatans', hasidic leaders
were accused of fraudulent studies and practices. The doctrine of unity with the
tsadik during prayer, false miracles, a materialistic attitude, and the attendant economic exploitation of the Jewish poor by extracting *pidyonot hanefesh*, payments
for 'the redemption of souls',[6] were purportedly examples of this.

Accusations levelled at the hasidim were theological and halakhic, as well as social
and even economic. The mitnagedim criticized the hasidim because of the extraordinary importance they ascribed to prayer, valuing it above talmudic studies.
Alterations to the liturgy and to the times for saying prayers, the doctrine of 'raising alien thoughts' (the role the tsadik played in sanctifying the thoughts of his
supporters), the mediation of the tsadikim in prayer, eccentric movements and
gesturing during worship, and the practice of separating themselves from the
community through the formation of their own *minyanim* (prayer groups) and
*shtiblekh* (prayer halls),[7] all provoked a negative reaction. The hasidim exchanged
the Ashkenazi liturgy commonly in use in eastern Europe for the Sephardi liturgy
or, more specifically, adopted the modified Sephardi prayer book of Isaac Luria
(*Nusaḥ ha'ari*). There was no controversy over the orthodoxy of this prayer book, as
this rite had been practised for at least a century by elite pietist groups, including
the most renowned mystical congregation, that of Brody. However, the mitnagedim accurately perceived a threat to the authority of tradition in hasidic customs
and, even more importantly, an attempt to undermine communal authority. Prayers
using an alternative ritual were a pretext for the hasidim to establish their own
prayer halls (which could be either individual houses or rooms), and to exempt
themselves from community obligations. Hence they would achieve an autonomy
that would go far beyond differences in the prayer book. But the economic conse-

---

[4] For example, *Zamir aritsim*, in Wilensky, *Ḥasidim umitnagedim*, i. 45: 'evil and sinful people . . . who
act against Torah, Gemara, *poskim* [halakhic decisors] and commentaries'.

[5] e.g. Israel Löbel's best-known anti-hasidic pamphlet, *Sefer vikuah*, in Wilensky, *Ḥasidim umitnagedim*, ii. 290; id., 'Glaubwürdige Nachricht', 309.

[6] See Wilensky, *Ḥasidim umitnagedim*, index, s.v. *pidyon*.

[7] Jacobs, *Hasidic Prayer*, provides an important study of hasidic prayer. See also Wilensky, 'Hassidic
Mitnaggedic Polemics', 248–53; Nadler, *Faith of the Mithnagdim*, 50–77. See Wertheim, *Law and
Custom in Hasidism*, 128–214, for a detailed description of the hasidic liturgy and its distinctive features.

quences of such actions were also pointed out, since the absence of the hasidim from the community synagogue effectively meant a fall in income from the reading of the Torah and from collection boxes, from seat hire, and even from community taxes and additional contributions. This argument had already been raised in 1798 in the protocols of the Vilna *kahal*, and it recurred frequently in the nineteenth century in complaints by the community boards against the *shtiblekh*.[8]

Controversy concerning hasidic prayer was also aroused by such innovations as impassioned recitation aloud of prayers by the whole community, and unconventional behaviour such as rocking, clapping, sudden interruptions, and the repetition of fragments of prayer, and the failure to observe the halakhically prescribed times for prayer. All these changes were viewed as a clear violation of religious law, and, unlike the controversy surrounding the Sephardi prayer book, they placed a question mark over the orthodoxy of hasidism. It is not surprising, then, that almost all the rabbinical writings consistently called hasidism a sect and placed it beyond the bounds of 'orthodox' Judaism. Although the hasidic leaders produced historical examples of loud recitations and gesticulations during prayer, and protested the impossibility of maintaining specific hours for prayer in the face of the need to be inwardly prepared for it, all such arguments were rejected. Their opponents considered examples such as that of King David dancing before the Ark of the Covenant to be exceptions and that they could not justify the introduction of such innovations as an everyday form of prayer. Israel Löbel, one of hasidism's most vehement critics, also accused the hasidim of not beginning their services at the correct time because once they were in the prayer hall, they wasted time in pointless gossip.[9] It was suspected that their non-conformist behaviour during worship was a device to ascribe great piety to themselves, or simple religious exhibitionism. This was viewed not only as a sign of arrogance, but also as a perverse attempt to impress ordinary people in order to gain new followers. To emphasize the fraudulence and hypocrisy of these practices, early opponents denied the hasidim even the title *ḥasidim* (Hebrew: 'the pious') and called them *mithasedim* ('sanctimonious hypocrites'), or 'Karlinites' (after Aron of Karlin, one of the hasidic leaders), or *kitajowcy*, 'men of silk', from the Polish *kitaj*, a fabric made of fine silk or cotton

---

[8] See Wilensky, *Ḥasidim umitnagedim*, i. 208–9, for the Vilna protocol. Jewish communities and private individuals raised very similar complaints in the territories of the Kingdom of Poland: Chęciny in 1818; Łask in 1820; Suwałki, Chmielnik, and Radzyń in 1821; Raczki and Złoczew in 1822; Szydłowiec in 1826; Włocławek in 1827; Pyzdry in 1828; Częstochowa and Pilica in 1830; Radomsko in 1831; Włocławek again in 1835; Lublin in 1836; numerous towns of the Augustów Province (*gubernia augustowska*) in 1844; Piotrków in 1845; Łomża and Łuków in 1851. Twice the government of the Congress Kingdom (1827 and 1839) attempted to address this issue. According to this law, hasidic prayer halls could be set up only after a special tax equal to the loss in the communal incomes caused by the establishment of the *shtibl* had been paid to the community. See AGAD, CWW 1411, pp. 66–74; 1871, pp. 321–4; APK, RGR 4405, pp. 6–8; APL, AmL 2419, pp. 85, 90.

[9] Israel Löbel, *Sefer vikuaḥ*, in Wilensky, *Ḥasidim umitnagedim*, ii. 273; see also Wilensky, 'Hassidic Mitnaggedic Polemics', 250.

worn by the hasidim. Later, Russian sources called them *skokuny* ('jumpers'), a comment on their unconventional movements during prayer.

However, of all the controversial modes of behaviour, it was the turning of somersaults that was most frequently mentioned. This was particularly prevalent among the followers of Abraham of Kalisk and Hayim Haykel of Indura, who turned somersaults in the synagogue and even on the streets as an expression of religious ecstasy.[10] This custom met with criticism even within the hasidic camp. It was strongly condemned by Shneur Zalman of Lyady, the founder of the Habad school and one of the most important of the third-generation hasidic leaders. However, he, too, was accused of eccentric behaviour—namely, of ecstatic dancing unbecoming to a religious leader.

The mitnagedim also mentioned other supposed violations of good conduct and morality—the most serious being imputations of homosexual practices.[11] These and similar accusations were intended to be used against hasidism not only as evidence of immorality, but also as proof of antinomian tendencies and thus of obvious heresy.

The accusation of primitive materialism completed this picture of the hasidim as immoral heretics. In particular, hasidic criticism of traditional, ascetic pietistic practices laid them open to charges of hedonism. Hasidic monistic materialism was diametrically opposed to the beliefs of leading mitnagedim, who maintained a dualistic, ascetic criticism of earthly pleasures. To them, the act of eating or drinking was not the religious act that it was for the hasidim, but rather an unavoidable physiological necessity and an obstacle to religious perfection.[12] Hasidic celebrations were seen as an idolatrous cult of the loaded food platters and the adulation of luxury. Accusations of tobacco and alcohol abuse, or simply of drunkenness, accompanied these charges.

The innovations introduced by the hasidim in relation to *shehitah* were also a major point of contention, though, in spite of the number and strength of these accusations, the nature of the controversy has never been clear.[13] These changes did not infringe halakhic rules, and some critics of the hasidim, including the more famous ones, such as Elijah ben Solomon Zalman (the Gaon of Vilna), and Hayim of Volozhin, were very careful about raising this accusation. For the butcher's knife to be fit for *shehitah*, according to the hasidim, it had to be as smooth as it was

[10]   See Wilensky, 'Hassidic Mitnaggedic Polemics', 257–9, on the unusual behaviour of the early hasidim. See also Jacobs, *Hasidic Prayer*, 56, 170, and Dubnow, *Toledot hahasidut*, 132, on the performing of somersaults.

[11]   Wilensky, 'Hassidic Mitnaggedic Polemics', 257.

[12]   Nadler, *Faith of the Mithnagdim*, 84–7.

[13]   Controversies over the hasidic *shehitah* have attracted considerable interest in historiographical literature on hasidism. The best study of the subject, which convincingly explains the nature of the conflict, can be found in Stampfer, 'Lekorot mahaloket hasakinim hamelutashot'. For the social aspects of hasidic ritual slaughter, see Shmeruk, 'Mashma'utah hahevratit shel hashehitah hahasidit'. See Wilensky, 'Hassidic Mitnaggedic Polemics', 253–7, for the significance of *shehitah* in anti-hasidic polemics. See also Wertheim, *Law and Custom in Hasidism*, 302–15.

strong, straight, and sharp. This requirement was problematic when it came to iron blades. The very thin, polished blades introduced by hasidic butchers met with opposition because it was suspected that, during slaughter, they could easily become jagged, with the result that the butchered animal would be non-kosher. Worse still, hasidic knives, being so sharp, were hazardous for the inspectors checking them. Although there was no halakhic basis to the mitnagedim's opposition to hasidic *sheḥitah*, they did not hesitate to pronounce meat from hasidic slaughter ritually unclean.

Accusations levelled at the hasidic *sheḥitah* usually related to economic and social questions: the waste of money if the meat was proved to be non-kosher as a result of damage to the blade during slaughter, the dismissive attitude of the hasidim to the traditions of their forebears, the way they represented themselves to the Jewish masses as extraordinarily pious, and their aspiration to set themselves apart, 'for even in the butchering of beast and fowl for the kosher they differ from the [other] Jews, saying that they alone eat kosher meat'.[14] Suspicions of Shabatean tendencies, or simply doubts about the religious integrity of hasidic butchers (which was understandable during a time of major conflict), led the mitnagedim to predict dire consequences for the entire Jewish community in the event of the appointment of hasidim as ritual slaughterers. Ritually unclean meat sold by a butcher as kosher meat meant ritual uncleanliness for all those who had eaten it— potentially the entire community. David of Maków described an inquiry into a butcher who, on the recommendation of a hasidic *magid* (preacher), represented a non-kosher beast as being kosher, causing the entire community to sin. This example was used to justify further accusations, particularly since such incidents occurred repeatedly in other communities.[15]

Reported cases of violations of religious law strengthened suspicions of heterodoxy among the hasidim, and particularly of their connections with the doctrines of the false seventeenth-century messiah Shabetai Tsevi. David of Maków and Israel Löbel, the foremost critics of the hasidim, did not directly accuse them of belonging to the Shabatean sect, but it appears from numerous allusions that they perceived in hasidism a continuation of the activities of Shabetai Tsevi and Jacob Frank, and they predicted that the spread of hasidism could have consequences equal to the catastrophe of Shabateanism.[16] The fears of the mitnagedim were constantly fuelled by the living memory of Jacob Frank (barely sixteen years had

[14] AGAD, CWW 1871, p. 106. See Katz, *Tradition and Crisis*, 208, for a discussion of separation from non-hasidic society as the most important aspect of the hasidic *sheḥitah*.

[15] See David of Maków, *Shever poshim*, in Wilensky, *Ḥasidim umitnagedim*, ii. 138–9; see also Wilensky, 'Hassidic Mitnaggedic Polemics', 256.

[16] Wilensky, 'Hassidic Mitnaggedic Polemics', 259–61. See also the numerous allusions to Shabateanism and Frankism in the writings of David of Maków and Israel Löbel in Wilensky, *Ḥasidim umitnagedim*, ii, index. It was only Avigdor ben Hayim, the rabbi of Pińsk, who explicitly and openly accused the hasidim of belonging to the Frankist sect and of connections with the heresies of Shabetai Tsevi; however, his allegations were based on his personal conflict with the Pińsk hasidim.

elapsed between the ban (*ḥerem*) placed on him in Brody in 1756 and the ban placed on the hasidim in the same town in 1772), and by the fascination that kabbalah held for both hasidism and Shabateanism.[17] Suspicions of Shabatean tendencies were aroused by the role of the mystical in hasidic doctrine. Although interest in kabbalistic speculation was not foreign to the mitnagedim either, their basic objection was to the hasidic tendency to disseminate these ideas widely and to elevate the importance of ecstatic mystical practices to the detriment of existing theoretical, theosophical thought. This was particularly so because, in the mitnagedim's pessimistic and elitist view of human nature, they did not believe it possible for a proper spiritual level to be reached by a wider group of Jews.[18]

In summary, the mitnagedim expressed their opposition to the growing hasidic movement in a number of ways and made numerous accusations against it. However, it is clear that this opposition did not arise out of fundamental theological and doctrinal differences since many of the practices of Beshtian hasidism, particularly for those ascetic, pietistic groups close to the Gaon of Vilna and other rabbinical critics, were not an entirely new phenomenon. Rather, their objections were founded upon a diametrically opposing view of human nature, as well as a different vision of religious expression and its attendant socio-religious ideas.[19] The mitnagedim, many of whom had practised the old form of 'pre-hasidic hasidism' themselves,[20] did not question the value or the significance of kabbalistic studies and mystical experiences, nor did they deny the halakhic legality of many hasidic innovations. However, attempts by the new group to popularize these mystical studies and practices traditionally restricted to small circles of initiated mystics did arouse fundamentalist opposition. Convinced of the degeneracy of the contemporary generation, the mitnagedim did not believe that such experiences could become the preserve of the wider Jewish masses. Thus they suspected that this populism had undeclared, and probably hostile, aims, and they strongly opposed it. This basic divergence of opinion related less to doctrine itself than to its social functioning. The religious exhibitionism of the hasidim, and their anarchic ecstatic practices, were viewed by their rabbinical critics not simply as distasteful and deceptive, but as dangerous: the hasidim introduced and sanctioned behaviour

---

[17] The putative affiliations with Shabateanism are one of the most comprehensively studied aspects of hasidism. Dubnow, *Toledot haḥasidut*, 24–34; Scholem, 'Hatenuah hashabta'it bepolin'; Rubinstein, 'Bein ḥasidut leshabta'ut'; Liebes, '"Ha-Tikkun ha-Kelali" of R. Nahman of Bratslav', are all essential reading matter on this subject. A new and interesting contribution to the field (although, in my opinion, an unsuccessful one) is Doktór, 'Mesjańskie widzenie Beszta', and especially id., *Początki chasydyzmu polskiego*.         [18] Nadler, *Faith of the Mithnagdim*, 29–49.

[19] Ibid. 171–5. Interesting attempts to explain rabbinical opposition to hasidism can be found in Hasdai, 'The Origins of the Conflict between Hasidim and Mitnagdim'; Schochet, *The Hasidic Movement and the Gaon of Vilna*; Piekarz, 'Meni'ei hamahalokot harishonot al haḥasidut'. For an essential study re-examining the origins of hasidism, its attitude towards tradition, and the origins of rabbinical opposition, see Rosman, *Founder of Hasidism*, esp. 36–9.

[20] See Rosman, *Founder of Hasidism*, 27–41: 'Hasidism before Hasidism'.

that was destructive to religious unity and they challenged traditional behavioural norms. The threat to the socio-religious and economic order was thus the chief and recurring argument in anti-hasidic polemics. Although arguments of this type were not the only source of opposition, in terms of social categories the mitnagedim occupied the position of conservative defenders of the existing system of values and the prevailing socio-religious and economic order, rejecting the new hasidic movement as a destructive force. Even if some of its critics recognized positive elements in hasidism (for example, its group cohesiveness and its widespread philanthropy), they could not reconcile themselves to its social 'subversiveness', for which there could be no justification.

## THE FIRST VOICES OF THE HASKALAH

The first maskilic voices to criticize the hasidic movement were heard at almost the same time as those of the mitnagedim, or perhaps, as some historians suggest, slightly earlier.[21] In his *Nezed hadema*, published posthumously in 1773, Israel Zamość (*c.*1700–72), one of the pioneers of the Haskalah and the teacher of Moses Mendelssohn, strongly condemned the 'drunkards of Efraim' for their arrogance and gluttony, and for succumbing to their passions and mystical fantasies. He criticized keenly a number of hasidic customs, for example, that of *shirayim*, or eating the leftovers from the plate of a tsadik,[22] the abuse of alcohol to induce ecstasy, and excessive merriment ('every day is a feast day').[23] These criticisms were consistent with those of earlier polemicists from Vilna and Brody, but they were narrower, in that they were limited to moral aspects rather than including the broader socio-religious and doctrinal questions that were the focus of mitnagdic opposition. This is because hasidism itself was of marginal importance and evidently not a serious social problem to Israel Zamość. It was the keen interest in this passage in later research literature that gave it significance, but in fact it constituted only a small part of a more general attack on different moral excesses.

It would be almost twenty years before the publication of the next Haskalah texts dealing with the hasidim. At the beginning of the 1790s Salomon Maimon's *Lebensgeschichte* appeared, as did an essay by Menahem Mendel Lefin of Satanów

---

[21] See Graetz, *Geschichte der Juden*, xi. 594; Dubnow, *Toledot hahasidut*, 77; Piekarz, *Bimei tsemihat hahasidut*, 320–38; Nadler, *Faith of the Mithnagdim*, 29–30, 202, on the putative criticism of hasidism in the writings of one of the harbingers of the Haskalah, Solomon of Chełm. It appears extremely doubtful whether the mystical group described by Solomon of Chełm was identical to the hasidim.

[22] See Wertheim, *Law and Custom in Hasidism*, 252–4, for more on the custom of *shirayim*.

[23] Extensive extracts from *Nezed hadema* and a discussion of Israel Zamość's attitude to hasidism can be found in Mahler, *Divrei yemei yisra'el*, iv. 26–30, 160–3. See also Dubnow, *Toledot hahasidut*, 118; Liberman, 'Keitsad hokerim hasidut beyisra'el'; Scholem, 'Hapulmus al hahasidut'; Zinberg, *History of Jewish Literature*, ix. 234–5.

dedicated to the reform of the Jewish masses in Poland, both of which dealt more broadly with the hasidic movement.[24]

There is clear evidence in their works that both Maimon and Lefin knew of the condemnation of hasidism by the communal leaders in Vilna and Brody in 1772 and of the literature on this subject. Both also belonged to the elite group of young adepts of religious knowledge who were engaged in learning at the time, so that not only were they aware of the arguments in rabbinical circles against hasidism but they were part of the milieu in which the public bans against it had originated. It may be assumed that they would have taken part in the debate surrounding the new movement and that this debate would have had a particular impact on young people immersed in religious studies. In his autobiography Maimon confirms that hasidic propaganda was aimed especially at these young students as it was they who were most keenly interested in religious life.[25] Thus, one would expect Maimon and Lefin's texts to make extensive reference to the arguments they recalled from their youth.

Meanwhile, both of these texts were surprisingly independent of the stand taken by earlier mitnagedim in their debate with hasidism. Admittedly, both Maimon and Lefin shared with the rabbinical elite a highly critical attitude towards the hasidic movement, and both were convinced that it was an unlawful successor to the Judaic tradition and a threat to the Jewish people, but the similarities between the views of the maskilim and mitnagedim ended here.[26] While the mitnagedim criticized hasidism from a conservative viewpoint as being a threat to the established socio-religious and economic order, for the maskilim this was the one point at which they perceived convergence in their aims with the alleged programme of hasidism. Unlike the mitnagedim, they saw hasidism rather as an obstacle to reform than as a threat to tradition and the social order.

The originality of the views of Lefin and Maimon was influenced by personal factors. It is certain that rabbinical criticism of hasidism was not the sole source of information about the new movement for either of them; their knowledge derived above all from personal experience. Lefin lived in Satanów, Podolia, until 1780 and then in Mikołajów, on the border of Volhynia, where hasidism had been making considerable progress for a number of decades. Maimon, on the other hand, has left a detailed description of his contacts with the court of the Great Magid, Dov Ber of Międzyrzecz Korecki, the leader of the second generation of hasidim. Ultimately, both authors had certain goals when writing their texts and this was the most significant factor shaping their attitude towards hasidism in the literature discussed

[24] Maimon, *Lebensgeschichte* (the citations follow, whenever possible, the only available abridged English translation, Maimon, *Autobiography*); Lefin, *Essai d'un plan de réforme juive en Pologne*.

[25] See Maimon, *Autobiography*, 173.

[26] For the similarities and differences between these ideologies, see Feiner, *Haskalah and History*, 91. A radical view of the discrepancies between the maskilim and mitnagedim was voiced by Nadler, *Faith of the Mithnagdim*, 130–1.

here. Hasidism was not the sole, or even the main, subject of their works. Although it played an important role, their anti-hasidic criticism cannot be read in isolation from the context and their overall message. For these authors, hasidism was used deliberately as an element in a broader literary strategy whose function is easy to identify.[27]

## FROM LITHUANIA TO BERLIN: SALOMON MAIMON

Salomon Maimon (1754–1800) was born and bred in Lithuania, where he received a traditional rabbinical education. His brief contact with secular education prompted him to leave the territory of the Polish–Lithuanian Commonwealth and seek a proper education, travelling via Königsberg, Stettin, and Poznań, and arriving in Berlin in 1779. There, after many changes of fortune, he gained the recognition of the Berlin maskilim centred around Moses Mendelssohn. Maimon's penetrating analyses of the philosophy of Immanuel Kant brought him renown, but his major claim to fame in the history of the Jewish Enlightenment is as the author of the first autobiography tracing the road from the world of the Polish Jewish small-town settlement (*shtetl*) to the ideals of the Haskalah.[28] This was emphasized by his publisher, Karl Philipp Moritz, who drew attention to Maimon's 'impartial' description of Judaism and the significance of that description for plans for the reform of Jewish society in eastern Europe. According to Maimon and the Berlin exponents of the Enlightenment who supported this work, his autobiography was intended as a reliable and detailed description of Jewish life in the Polish–Lithuanian Commonwealth, which could act as the primary resource in projects for the reform of Polish Jews. For the author, however, it had another, more personal, function. It was intended as evidence of his belonging to the world of Western civilization and to distance himself from the barbaric East: to emphasize the gulf of civilization separating the narrator from the world he presented.[29]

The Jewish community in Poland that Maimon presented was made up of a productive and basically honest people who, however, were oppressed by fanaticism and social backwardness. The Jewish masses were 'like an ass groaning under two burdens—its own ignorance and the religious superstitions accompanying it as well as the ignorance and superstitions of those in power'.[30] According to Maimon, the Mosaic religion, since the collapse of the Jewish state, was increasingly

---

[27] Some interesting comments on Lefin's literary strategies appear in Sinkoff, 'Strategy and Ruse in the Haskalah of Mendel Lefin of Satanow'.

[28] See Feiner, 'Solomon Maimon and the Haskalah', for the evolution of Maimon's attitude towards the ideology of the Jewish Enlightenment.

[29] More on the subject appears in Robertson, 'From the Ghetto to Modern Culture', esp. 21–2 (on the significance of the hasidic motif). More on the problems of German Jewish identity in Maimon's autobiography can be found in Schulte, 'Salomon Maimons *Lebensgeschichte*'. See Librett, 'Stolen Goods', for more on the problems of Maimon's cultural identity.

[30] Maimon, *Autobiografia*, vol. i, p. vii.

moving away from the ideal of the natural and rational religion it had once been, and playing a significant role in causing and maintaining Jewish backwardness. Thus, in his autobiography Maimon devoted considerable space to a description of Judaism and its institutions. He presented his religious upbringing in great detail and derided the Talmud and talmudic studies. He described the neglect of Hebrew language studies and denigrated the Yiddish language; exposed in detail distasteful aspects of his own marriage, and derided the custom of matchmaking and contracting marriages; and was particularly critical of the widespread ideal of devoting oneself to religious studies, which, he maintained, had made an industrious people a nation of idlers. He defined kabbalah as a system that had changed from being about knowledge of influences on nature written in symbolic language to the 'art of raging reasoning' where the key to the symbols had been forgotten.[31] Two movements presented by Maimon—traditional ascetic hasidism and the 'new hasidic sect'—were to serve as practical examples of this kabbalistic madness.

In a chapter on Beshtian, i.e. new, hasidism,[32] Maimon first discussed the basic differences between hasidism of the old and new type and pointed to the anti-ascetic attitudes of the new movement and to the persistent nature of the battle between the two sides. He compared the attempts at hasidic reform with the earlier endeavours of Jesus and Shabetai Tsevi. This motif was known from the writings of the mitnagedim. In Maimon's case, however, unlike that of David of Maków or Israel Löbel, this comparison indicated a positive aspect of hasidism and its reformist aspirations. Hasidism criticized traditional Judaism for its extreme ascetic religiosity and for the abuse of rabbinical knowledge, which had degenerated into lifeless legalism and spiritually bankrupt ceremoniousness. According to Maimon, 'Rabbi Joel (not Israel) Balschem', who was the founder of the new movement, was a quack and a charlatan who won the acclaim of the rabble with 'kabbalistic hocus-pocus'. His students had added to their standard repertoire—fraudulent miracles and healing—the ability to locate 'lost' objects, which they had stolen earlier. Maimon characterized hasidism as a secret society with a complex, hierarchical structure, the product of an aristocratic conspiracy of kabbalists with secret religious and political aims. (The shady nature of these aims is a theme reminiscent of the criticisms made by the mitnagedim discussed earlier.) Hasidic learning was based on the idea of *devekut*—turning one's thoughts from everything but God. Adherents of hasidism used strange movements and cries to help themselves achieve a state of religious ecstasy. Maimon stressed, however, that for many adherents this training was intellectually unattainable; they shuffled along with a pipe in their mouth for days at a time and, when asked what they were doing, replied, 'Why, we are thinking about God!' This soon led to various excesses such as physiological

---

[31] For more on Maimon's views on the kabbalah and hasidism, see Schulte, 'Kabbala in Salomon Maimons *Lebensgeschichte*'.

[32] Maimon, *Autobiography*, 166–79, 'On a Secret Society, and therefore a Long Chapter'. It actually is one of the longest chapters of the book.

functions being performed in public, nudity, indulgence, and a lack of respect for the rabbis, all of which showed the weaknesses of the new movement and led to its collapse.

Examples of hasidic abuses, swindles, and ideological flaws were complemented by Maimon's own experiences from the court of the Magid of Międzyrzecz, where the author had spent time probably at the beginning of the 1770s (the Magid died in 1772). Maimon arrived there, having been influenced by the propaganda of wandering emissaries of hasidism, and was initially enthralled by the apparent miracles and by the profundity of the tsadik's mind. Newly arrived guests were craftily questioned on various details by the tsadik's attendants and were then surprised by his knowledge. Dov Ber appeared dressed in white (a kabbalistic sign of favour) and aroused admiration both by his ability to weave biblical quotations given to him into a single sermon and by his perspicacity. Ultimately, though, Maimon saw all this as a simple ruse and Dov Ber as a barbaric swindler. Soon he recognized that the teachings of the Magid gave no satisfaction, and he left his court.

Maimon paid special attention to hasidism in his memoirs not because of the significance of the hasidic episode in his life but because it suited the goals he had set himself for his book. First, though he had no direct knowledge of early, ascetic hasidism, he had personally experienced the new hasidic way. Although he admitted that his contact with hasidism had been only fleeting, and that his knowledge of the structure and doctrine of the new movement had been a matter of deduction rather than experience, the presence of the 'long chapter' in his autobiography was justified. His personal experiences were an important advantage—they gave his descriptions credibility and the accusations he levelled became standard in the subsequent anti-hasidic literature of the Haskalah. Secondly, Maimon maintained that 'in our times, when so much is said both *pro* and *contra* secret societies, I believe that the history of a particular secret society . . . should not be passed over'.[33] This was particularly the case because hasidism related to the contemporary concerns of readers and, more importantly, was illustrative of arguments in Maimon's work. As a secret society, it was both alien and hostile: it was anti-rational (hence, in conflict with the fundamental values of the civilized world of the West) and secretive (hence, consciously concealing its political aims). It was precisely these qualities that allowed it to be presented as the complete embodiment of an alien Jewish world existing in eastern Europe. Maimon consciously exploited the interest in sects and secret societies whose aim was supposedly to gain control of the world—an interest which was widespread during the period of the French Revolution—comparing hasidism with the notorious Bavarian Illuminati sect. Thirdly, according to Maimon (and he may be supported in this by anti-hasidic literature of the mitnagedim), the hasidic movement had been very popular in his youth. Although Maimon (erroneously) believed it had quickly and almost completely disappeared, the ease with which it had spread justified its being seen as a

---

[33] Ibid. 168.

distinctive phenomenon and as being important to an understanding of the nature of eastern Jewry. For Maimon, hasidism was the quintessence of anti-rational traditional Judaism, and it was criticism of this that formed the basis of his entire work. Fourthly, Maimon perceived hasidism as an attempt to reform the Jewish masses and, although that attempt had proved unsuccessful or even detrimental, it showed that irreversible changes had already taken place in Jewish society in Poland, and this, after all, was one of the most important features of the programme of the Haskalah. Maimon believed that, in its initial phase, the new movement had accomplished some of the aims of that programme, focusing on the spread of education among the masses and on coming to grips with the ills of Judaism. Thus, it was a first attempt at reform and the east European precursor of the Jewish Enlightenment.

Such an ambivalent approach to hasidism came easily to Maimon because he believed that it was an outdated phenomenon that no longer constituted a threat. The picture that emerges from his autobiography is one of an elite secret society that gained the upper hand over the hasidim of the old type at the outset (and was therefore somewhat larger than the other group), which had the potential to control the entire Jewish population of Poland, but which had ultimately been eradicated. This eradication was 'brought [about] especially by the authority of a celebrated rabbi, Elijah of Vilna, who stood in such great esteem among the Jews that scarcely any traces of the society can now be found'.[34] Quite obviously, Maimon, unlike Lefin and Calmanson, was unaware of the situation regarding Eastern Jewry at the time; the picture he created was probably relevant to Lithuania in the mid-1770s (when Maimon left the Polish–Lithuanian Commonwealth) but was totally irrelevant to the 1790s, when his work appeared. It must have been especially incorrect with regard to Podolia and Volhynia, where hasidism had emerged as a social force to be reckoned with, and the home of Mendel Lefin, the second of the Haskalah authors to speak out on this issue.

## FROM PODOLIA TO GALICIA: MENDEL LEFIN

The French-language publication *Essai d'un plan de réforme ayant pour objet d'éclairer la nation juive en Pologne et de redresser par là ses mœurs* appeared anonymously, probably at the end of 1791 or the beginning of 1792, in Warsaw. Its author, Menahem Mendel Lefin (1749–1826), came from Satanów in Podolia. From 1780 until 1784 he lived in Berlin, where he made the acquaintance of Moses Mendelssohn and the Berlin Haskalah circles.[35] After returning home, he settled in Mikołajów in

---

[34] Maimon, *Autobiography*, 179.

[35] Essential data on Lefin's life can be found in Gelber, 'Mendel Satanower der Verbreiter der Haskala in Polen und Galizien'; Weinlos, 'Mendel Lefin-Satanower'; Josef Klausner, *Historiyah shel hasifrut ha'ivrit*, i. 224–53; Mahler, *Divrei yemei yisra'el*, iv. 71–82; id., *History of Modern Jewry*, 588–601; Levine, 'Menahem Mendel Lefin', 1–58; Sinkoff, 'Tradition and Transition', 14–48.

the Proskurów Administrative District, and it was there that he met Prince Adam Kazimierz Czartoryski, who became his patron as well as taking him on as a teacher of algebra for his children. From that time on Lefin was almost constantly connected with the Czartoryski court, and he spent most of his time in their residences in Sieniawa, Puławy, or Warsaw. It seems likely that it was Prince Czartoryski who encouraged Lefin to put forward a project to reform the Jewish masses when the Four-Year Sejm debated the issue in 1791. However, as Lefin himself stated, the major factor in his decision to participate in the Sejm's work was that he wished to assist in the projects of a number of Polish politicians, particularly of Hugo Kołłątaj. According to Lefin, these politicians, for all the unquestionable nobility of their purpose and goodwill, were nevertheless incompetent when it came to matters concerning Jewish society, and their plans were ultimately unsuccessful.[36] The voice of somebody versed in Jewish relations and simultaneously interested in the successful introduction of reforms seemed very necessary.

Lefin's *Essai* was written in the form of a draft of a two-part Act in 106 paragraphs, this form being very typical of the period.[37] The first part, comprising forty-eight paragraphs, was devoted to a description of the Jewish religion and its institutions, while the second part introduced the reform plan. According to Lefin, 'religion is the most powerful and active force of the Jewish nation',[38] so any reform of the masses had to include religion in its approach. As opposed to Maimon (who perceived Judaism as the road to degeneration), Lefin presented the history of the Jewish religion as a history of rational reflection centred first on the Talmud and then on Maimonides. According to Lefin, its ultimate form was the idea of Moses Mendelssohn, who 'cleared the way marked by Maimonides'. However, as Lefin wrote, this healthy stronghold of religion was threatened by 'pious ignorance' and mystical trends, the cornerstone of which was the Zohar, a kabbalistic forgery attributed to Simeon bar Yohai, a teacher of the mishnaic period. The kabbalistic trend was allowed to gain in strength even further because the followers of rational Judaism undermined their own position. The students of Maimonides were so enthralled with the Greek philosophical works that they treated their Hebrew legacy with contempt and ultimately fell into a state of doubt and unbelief, which added fuel to the arguments of their opponents and pushed the Jewish people into a state of isolationism. In his own times Lefin saw a similar threat in the activities of radical maskilim centred around the Haskalah publication *Hame'asef*.

[36] Lefin's manuscript is quoted and discussed in Gelber, 'Mendel lefin-satanover'. See also Sinkoff, 'Strategy and Ruse in the Haskalah of Mendel Lefin of Satanow', 98–9. The most comprehensive description of the debate on the 'Jewish question' during the Four-Year Sejm can be found in Eisenbach, *Emancypacja Żydów*, 70–124.

[37] The *Essai* has been summarized and discussed on a number of occasions; see e.g. Gelber, 'Żydzi a zagadnienie reformy Żydów na Sejmie Czteroletnim', 331–4; id., 'Mendel lefin-satanover', 271–5; Max Erik, *Etyudn*, 142–3; Mahler, *Divrei yemei yisra'el*, iv. 73–5, 266–8; Sinkoff, 'Strategy and Ruse in the Haskalah of Mendel Lefin of Satanow', 97–101; Levine, 'Menahem Mendel Lefin', 183–4; van Luit, 'Hasidim, Mitnaggedim and the State'.

[38] Lefin, *Essai d'un plan de réforme juive en Pologne*, 410.

Instead of continuing where Mendelssohn had led the way, they began to criticize the rabbis and became involved in conflict with their own people, thereby losing any chance of influencing them.

The most dangerous creation of kabbalistic visionaries was believed by Lefin to be the new sect of the followers of the Zohar, which, because of its effect on the fertile imaginations of the young, almost dominated Polish Jewry. The sect of new zealots (and there is no doubt that Lefin had the hasidim in mind) attributed to their leaders the power to perform miracles and even to absolve sins. They scorned religious study and ridiculed the rabbis. The war between the new visionaries, who 'wanted nothing more than to drive out reason completely', and the old rabbis, who defended the remnants of rational thought, ended in the defeat of the latter, who, pressured by the hasidim, were ultimately forced to seek their favour. The hasidic leaders attracted converts from traditional Judaism with the splendour of their courts, which they owed to the sumptuous gifts of the numerous pilgrims flocking to them. By the use of spies and because of the persecution of adversaries, and their rabbis in particular, the hasidim controlled their native Podolia as well as Ukraine, Volhynia, and part of Lithuania, although many Lithuanian towns successfully resisted them. Wielkopolska (Greater Poland) and Germany remained free of hasidic influence. Even in Warsaw there was a large group of adherents of hasidism, which was visited from time to time by leaders of the movement.

In the second part of his work Lefin focused less on hasidism and instead outlined his plans for reform, some of which are discussed below. Reform plans were to be carried out with the help of the rabbis who had been deprived by the hasidim of their old authority. Rabbis who gave their approval to works promoting education were to be appointed by the government as district rabbis with a wide-ranging sphere of competencies, such as the right to censor books and to anathematize. It was also proposed that state-funded Jewish schools should be established, teaching in Polish in Warsaw and other cities. The graduates of these schools were to pass on to the masses the education they received at school by becoming assistants to district rabbis. In addition, they would be encouraged to enter into dialogue with the adherents of hasidism and challenge their belief in miracles, as such debates could encourage hasidic leaders to turn to rational argument. Satirical publications that subtly ridiculed hasidic beliefs and their preposterousness, without ridiculing their leaders and without acrimony, could be helpful in this fight. The fanaticism of the hasidic leaders could possibly even be used to spread the reforms; for example, references to religious rules governing flour for matzot could encourage tsadikim to steer their supporters towards work to produce that flour, hence into agricultural activities. Similarly, care in maintaining the law forbidding the combination of linen and wool in fabrics (*sha'atnez*) could result in hasidim working in the textile factories. Other tools of reform that were not aimed exclusively at the hasidic movement were the spread of the sciences (particularly astronomy, as advised by the Talmud), the simple teaching of religious truths devoid of 'artful coxcombry and mystical ornamentation', support being given to rational religious studies, a ban on charlatanry, and enforced work for beggars.

Analysing Lefin's attitude to the hasidim, one must remember that the aim of this work was to engage in battle with hasidism itself, as much as to reform the Jewish masses in Poland in general. Despite that aim, hasidism became the principal threat, and in fact the only threat, to the process of modernization of Jewish society to be identified. There seem to have been many reasons for this. First, his own moderation, and his renunciation of radicalism among both the 'mystical zealots' and the radical advocates of the Haskalah (see the criticism of anticlerical pronouncements in *Hame'asef*), persuaded him to take a stance closer to that of the mitnagedim, who continued to be in the majority. In addition, as has already been mentioned, Lefin spent a large part of his life in Podolia, where the hasidic movement had been developing since the 1750s (or even the 1740s), and this would have strongly influenced him in this and many other respects.[39] Lefin's own religious perspective also reinforced his criticism of hasidism. It established Judaism as the most important, if not the sole, driving force in the history of the Jewish people. As a result, manifestations of religious life held special significance in Lefin's argument. For him, hasidism was the embodiment of kabbalah, and therefore represented one of two competing trends in Judaism. The dissemination of rationalistic thought must therefore have been for him synonymous with the fight against opposition in its most threatening manifestation. The fact that the *Essai* was a political publication must also have influenced its militant tone: Lefin was using political tools to describe Jewish society and its current condition and he must have ascribed political aspects to hasidism that would have added strength to his criticism of the movement. Hillel Levine's thesis, that the intensity of the anti-hasidic polemic of both Lefin and the maskilim in his milieu resulted from the immediacy of the problems confronting both the maskilim and the hasidim, seems convincing. After all, the situation of these two groups was in some ways very similar—both were minority groups in deep conflict with the majority, and both were highly ideological.[40]

The project announced by Lefin in Warsaw was the first published criticism of hasidism in the Polish–Lithuanian Commonwealth. It was therefore quite paradoxical that it was almost totally ignored in Poland and made very little impression either on the debate on the 'Jewish question' during the Four-Year Sejm or on attitudes towards hasidism. Later, in the Kingdom of Poland, the sole advocate of Lefin's plan was Abraham Stern, and it is difficult to find any other reference to it in either the publications or the activities of the Polish maskilim.

The fact that Lefin has been virtually forgotten is singularly striking, given his popularity in Galicia, where his views, including those on the fight against hasidism, had a decisive influence on the entire first generation of Galician maskilim, including Joseph Perl, who was the most prominent of the anti-hasidic polemicists.[41]

---

[39] For more on this, see Sinkoff, 'Tradition and Transition', 14–48.
[40] See Levine, 'Menahem Mendel Lefin', 179–81.   [41] See Feiner, *Haskalah and History*, 91–3.

This might have resulted from the fact that Lefin did not stay in Warsaw long after publication of his *Essai*. In fact, he left the city shortly after the collapse of the Four-Year Sejm and took up residence on the Belarusian estate of Joshua Zeitlin, a wealthy Jewish merchant and patron of the maskilim. After 1808 he moved to Galicia, where he formed close contacts with local supporters of the Haskalah, particularly Perl and Nahman Krochmal. Thus it was the close personal contacts of some twenty years' standing and his subsequent anti-hasidic activities, rather than the publication dating back to the Four-Year Sejm, that had a bearing on the influence Lefin had on the Galician maskilim and his lack of influence in Poland.[42]

The fact that the *Essai* was just one of many voices in the political debate on the future of the Jewish community in Poland during discussions in the Four-Year Sejm also doomed it to oblivion. Historical events—the Targowica Confederacy, the war of 1792, the second and third partitions, and the loss of independence—meant that it was not long before the entire debate lost its topicality. In addition, the image of hasidism, which was based on observations from Podolia, was quite exotic in the eyes of Warsaw's educated circles and was certainly not relevant to local conditions in the central and western provinces of the Polish–Lithuanian Commonwealth. Despite Lefin's assertions about the existence of hasidic 'gangs' even in Warsaw, local Jewish and Polish reformers simply did not believe that the hasidim were a threat[43] since the movement itself was never particularly visible in that part of the Polish territory and it was the traditional and all-powerful *kahal* that appeared to be the most dangerous opponent of all.

The final and perhaps most important reason, even if not directly so, for Lefin's lack of popularity in central Poland was the general incompatibility of two world-views—the views held by Lefin and his followers (who would subsequently be at the centre of the Galician Haskalah) and the views of the maskilim of central Poland. In very general terms, Lefin's outlook, including his attitude towards hasidism, sprang from a strictly religious view of the world. Thus, hasidism, for Lefin, appeared to be an ideological and religious threat. The Polish maskilim had a completely different perception of it. The most important point in their programme related to social questions (education and productivization) and, to some degree, political matters (legal status), whereas religious issues—which were so central for Lefin—were seen to be important only where they had a bearing on social life. Fundamentally, for the Polish maskilim, the world was viewed through the prism of social categories (see the next chapter). Admittedly, it was also possible to treat hasidism as a threat to society, and religious-ideological categories were not entirely

---

[42] See Levine, 'Bein hasidut lehaskalah'; Sinkoff, 'Tradition and Transition', 131–56; id., 'Benjamin Franklin in Jewish Eastern Europe', on the anti-hasidic polemics in *Heshbon hanefesh*. See Zinberg, *History of Jewish Literature*, ix. 237, on *Der ershter khosid*. See Weinlos, 'Mendel Lefin-Satanower', 349–52; Werses, 'Be'ikvotav shel hahibur *Mahkimat peti*', on *Mahkimat peti*. See Sinkoff, 'Tradition and Transition', 156–69, on *Masaot hayam*. See Shmeruk, 'Al ekronot ahadim shel tirgum mishlei lemendel lefin', on the translation of the book of Proverbs.

[43] See e.g. Czacki, *Rozprawa o Żydach i karaitach*, 106–7.

unknown to the maskilim in the Kingdom of Poland; but the general difference in viewpoints did not encourage the maskilim to set out in pursuit of Lefin, whose diagnosis and prescription seemed quite inappropriate to them.

## THE COMMONWEALTH S FIRST MASKIL: JACQUES CALMANSON

As far as we are aware, Jacques Calmanson (1722–1811) was the first advocate of the Haskalah associated with central Poland and Warsaw to speak out on the hasidic question. Solomon Jacob, son of Kalman (or Hirsh), originated from Hrubieszów, where his father was probably the rabbi. As far as is known, Calmanson received a broad education, studied medicine in Germany and France, knew French, German, and Polish[44] in addition to the Jewish languages, and travelled on a number of occasions around Germany, France, Turkey, and Russia. He settled in Warsaw (at 2478 Mylna Street) and was for many years King Stanisław August Poniatowski's doctor. He was also active in public life, drafting a memorandum on changes to the Jewish taxation system, translating Hebrew and Yiddish texts on plans for the reform of the Jewish population, and mediating between Jewish representatives and the priest Scipione Piatolli during work on amendments to the legal status of Jews in Poland during the Four-Year Sejm. In recognition of his services, Calmanson received a pension from a masonic lodge and from the king. When the king died, he received a pension from Ludwik Gutakowski, a well-known freemason and outstanding politician associated with Stanisław August. He spent the rest of his life in Warsaw, as a resident of one of the local Catholic monasteries.[45]

Unlike Lefin, Calmanson did not leave behind a rich literary heritage. His one known text, *Essai sur l'état actuel des Juifs de Pologne*, was a treatise on the project to reform Polish Jews, which was published in 1796 and addressed to Karl von Hoym, the Prussian minister governing new territories annexed from Poland. His *Essai* did influence the changes the Prussians made to the status of the Jewish population in central Poland in 1797 (in the so-called Judenreglement). Its Polish translation, in which Calmanson had considerably expanded on the original text, was printed and distributed in an edition of the translator, Julian Czechowicz.[46] According to Calmanson, the French text had been written far earlier, during the

---

[44] Shatzky ('Avraham Ya'akov Stern', 206) erroneously claimed that Calmanson did not know Polish. For proof of his fluency in Polish, see his letter, AGAD, Rada Stanu i Rada Ministrów Księstwa Warszawskiego, 216, p. 1 (copy in CAHJP, HM3667).

[45] Data on the life of Calmanson are very few, the most valuable source for these being Radomiński, *Co wstrzymuje reformę Żydów*, 21–2, 44. Some interesting information can also be found in Ringelblum, 'Baytrogn tsu der geshikhte fun di doktoyrim in Poyln', 128–9; Shatzky, *Geshikhte fun Yidn in Varshe*, i. 130 ; Eisenbach, *Emancypacja Żydów*, 99, 574 n. 172.

[46] Calmanson, *Essai sur l'état actuel des Juifs de Pologne*; id., *Uwagi nad niniejszym stanem Żydów polskich*.

period of the Four-Year Sejm, and formed part of the debate in which Mendel Lefin had come out so strongly against the hasidic movement.[47]

The structure of Calmanson's treatise was very similar to that of Lefin's *Essai*, but it was far more detailed. It began with a short history of the Jews, with chapters on their religion, the aristocracy, the clergy, and the communal institutions. The second part of the work was devoted to considerations on the reform of Jewish society. In accordance with the predominant views of the time, Calmanson suggested that the autonomy of the Jews should be limited (although he did not wish to abolish the *kahal*) and that the ban, the rabbinate, and the institution of *shtadlanim* (intercessors between the Jewish community and the non-Jewish authorities) be abolished. This was an attempt to topple the hegemony of the religious–financial aristocracy, which was perceived to be the greatest enemy of the Jewish people and the source of all evil among Jews. According to Calmanson, it was also necessary to reform the burial societies and to forbid the wearing of traditional Jewish dress and other signs of separatism. This was all intended to form part of the introductory stage of reform. To carry it through to its end, the author proposed the establishment of national Polish-language schools for the Jews, which would teach secular subjects and the rudiments of ethics. He also suggested changes to the language of the liturgy and to basic religious texts. His reform programme concluded with suggestions to limit the freedom to marry before the age of 18 and to bring laws regarding Jewish artisans into line with those governing their Christian counterparts. The Polish version contained an addendum in which the author included comments on marriage, dress, beards and sidelocks, bathing, kosher laws, ritual slaughter, and agriculture, as well as on beliefs associated with dreams. This work, then, was a detailed treatise on Jewish history, religion, rituals, and customs, in addition to which it contained a detailed programme for the reform of Jewish society in Poland. The underlying thesis of this programme was very similar to other proposals coming from Berlin and Polish Haskalah circles in the same period.

The first chapter of Calmanson's work was devoted to religion, since according to the author, an understanding of the beliefs and customs of the Jewish community was necessary if the reforms were to be a success. The chapter was divided into five paragraphs, which discussed in order the general principles of the Jewish religion, as well as the Karaite, hasidic, and Frankist sects, and the ban. One paragraph of interest, 'Concerning the Sect Named the Choside, or Zealots, the Bigots',[48] presented the hasidim as a sect known only to Polish Jewry which had been formed just twenty years earlier, in the 1770s, in Międzybóż, Podolia. Accord-

---

[47] AGAD, Rada Stanu i Rada Ministrów Księstwa Warszawskiego, 216, p. 1: 'During this celebrated Sejm, which worked so wholeheartedly for the good of the people, I started on my project to transform these idlers, of whom there are so many in our country [i.e. Jews], into industrious inhabitants of this country.'

[48] See Appendix 1. The French original, which is somewhat shorter than the Polish version, was published in Graetz, *Geschichte der Juden*, xi. 595–6.

ing to this text, its founder was a fanatical rabbi (the author does not refer to the Besht by name), who declared himself a prophet and deluded the gullible masses who craved fantasy. He also maintained that he could heal the sick by the power of kabbalah and, using these means, gained numerous followers and fame. This sect, 'which endures even now', rejected the teaching of religious law and made ignorance a virtue, all of which added up to a convenient justification for the idleness of the hasidim. The only teaching the hasidim respected was that of kabbalah, but even in this their leaders were ignoramuses who kept alive the belief in their mystical knowledge among adherents only as a means of controlling them easily and 'to assert their right to the property of new adherents'. The hasidim lived in a property-based communal system, which those at the higher level naturally controlled to their advantage. Calmanson emphasized strongly the thread of economic gain to condemn the tsadikim and to contrast them with the honest naivety of the simple masses:

one should pity their lack of enlightenment, the good but misplaced faith of these uneducated, gullible souls who believe that they are serving God with this insane fanaticism, whereas, in fact, all their efforts simply make them vulnerable to the eccentricity of a number of cunning zealots, in whom they have, and will continue to have, heavy-handed despots.

The motive of economic gain had appeared even earlier in the writings of the mitnagedim, but it was Calmanson who first made it a major feature in the description of hasidism and extrapolated from it a strongly defined division between swindling exploiters and the good, but deceived, masses. This view was eminently relevant to the basic thesis of the treatise on the exploitation of the simple masses by the Jewish aristocracy, as well as the need to liberate Jewish society from the rule of the despotic 'doctors'. Thus, according to Calmanson, hasidism was simply another embodiment of the general Jewish conflict between the religious and financial elite and the common people. What is more, Calmanson explained, in his opinion it was not the most dangerous form that that conflict took. Significantly, criticism of the economic structures of hasidism and of financial exploitation by the tsadikim was soon one of the most regular threads of maskilic criticism of the hasidim, and appeared in almost all its publications in eastern Europe.[49]

The paragraph Calmanson devoted to hasidism ended with an appeal to the government to take positive steps against 'this spreading pestilence', which 'has already infected almost all the synagogues' faster than had seemed possible only a few years before. Hasidic fanaticism was all the more dangerous because it was founded on the conviction of the hasidim that they were fighting under the banner of religion for a just cause. Calmanson believed that, in time, hasidism could become a major threat not only to Jewish society but to the entire country.

Since Heinrich Graetz published the French version of Calmanson's text in the

---

[49] For more on this, see Bartal, 'Le'an halakh tseror hakesef?'

nineteenth century, it has been used as an example of the vehement criticism of hasidism among the first east European maskilim, thus providing evidence of the early origins of this conflict. In Dubnow's time it was seen as an illustration of 'the viciousness of the war' between the Haskalah and hasidism.[50] However, this thesis, which is still held even today, appears to be founded on a lack of understanding of the fundamental meaning of the work, even if only because the author made a clear distinction between an evil, swindling leadership and the good, but naive, adherents of the new sect. Unlike Lefin, Calmanson seems, if anything, to have pitied rather than despised the hasidim. Equally ambiguous is his attitude to their interest in kabbalah. Calmanson wrote that even the tsadikim were unfamiliar with kabbalistic learning, but, unlike Lefin or Maimon, he did not condemn this fascination with anti-rationalistic kabbalistic studies; rather, he spoke of it with a certain amount of respect.

The introduction of these qualifications does not, of course, mean that Calmanson's picture of hasidism was necessarily positive; on the contrary, hasidism was consistently criticized in his work. But the misinterpretation of his supposedly aggressive anti-hasidic attitudes comes from a superficial reading of this criticism, in which a two-page paragraph about hasidism has been taken out of the context of the seventy-page work. In reality, Calmanson presented hasidism more as a curiosity than as a real social threat. While he warned of the potential danger to the country of the fanatical nature of the movement and of its rapid growth, this is all fairly mild in comparison with the charges levelled at traditional Jewish institutions and in particular at the whole of the religious aristocracy. This is consistently referred to in the treatise as the greatest plague and the cruellest exploiter of the Jewish people. In the treatise, 'the doctors', or the learned, are seen as ruling by the terror they instilled in an ignorant and gullible Jewish population, particularly by use of the ban. Hasidism, therefore, was only one of the elements of Jewish social life to be criticized. It was not viewed as the most dangerous, and it remained very much in the shadow of the most powerful enemy—the *kahal* and the rabbinical elite.

In addition, an accurate understanding of Calmanson's accusations against hasidism requires us to compare them with his depiction of other sects, to which he devoted a large portion of his book. According to Calmanson, the Jewish sects that existed in the Polish–Lithuanian Commonwealth constituted the best evidence of the decline of the Jewish community since they represented deviations from pure Mosaic principles. He wrote about three such sects, ranking them in order of significance and degree of fanaticism. He began with a relatively amicable description of the Karaites, followed by a critical depiction of hasidism, and scathing criticism of the Frankist movement. A short paragraph on the Karaites described them as simple men, uneducated but honest. Unfortunately, Calmanson noted, their lovable

[50] See e.g. Graetz, *Geschichte der Juden*, xi. 71, 218–19, 595–6; Zinberg, *History of Jewish Literature*, ix. 235–6; *Encyclopaedia Judaica*, v. 64; Schiper, *Przyczynki do dziejów chasydyzmu w Polsce*, 37–8.

simplicity was the result not of an honest heart but of a lack of intellectual enlightenment. The section on Frankism is four times as long as the paragraph about hasidism, comprising half of the chapter on the Jewish religion. In it, Calmanson declared that 'this sect is quite numerous, especially in Warsaw',[51] whereas he wrote of hasidism only that it 'is spreading with greater enthusiasm than could have been predicted from its feeble beginnings'. The author consistently described Frankism as the most dangerous eruption of religious fanaticism and the most powerful example of the errors to which anti-rationalist religious views were liable to lead: 'for the coming generations, the history of Frank will serve as everlasting testimony to where passion may lead when allied with fanaticism in minds set alight by a religious imagination'.[52] Calmanson strongly emphasized the sect's economic base, the greed of Jacob Frank, and his swindling and exploitation of the members of the sect. His belief that the Frankist sect was more numerous and more dangerous than hasidism was no doubt the result of the existence of a powerful Frankist community in Warsaw,[53] and this is why Calmanson came to estimate such a low figure for the adherents of hasidism and casts light on how we should interpret his anti-hasidic criticism. In reality in 1759 the total number of Frankist converts stood at fewer than 2,000.[54]

Some preliminary conclusions may be also drawn from Calmanson's lack of familiarity with his subject matter. Unlike other parts of his book, the paragraph devoted to hasidism is lacking in detail and full of errors. The only information concerning the doctrine of the hasidim relates to their alleged glorification of indolence and of kabbalah. This leads us to believe that the author knew little about them and that his knowledge was, in any case, second- or third-hand. This is not to be taken as evidence that there were no hasidim in Warsaw or that such information was unobtainable: we know that there were hasidic groups in Warsaw at the time, just as there were in other towns in central Poland.[55] In addition, Calmanson must have personally known Shmul Zbitkower, one of the patrons of the hasidim, because they mixed in the same royal circles. It must therefore be presumed that hasidism was simply not a major topic of conversation in Warsaw's Haskalah circles and that the level of interest in the hasidim and knowledge of their sect (albeit incorrect) was simply proportional to society's perception of their significance. If this is so, we may conclude that the first generation of Polish maskilim viewed hasidism as a fairly insignificant curiosity, rather than as a threat to Jewish society in Poland.

[51] Calmanson, *Uwagi nad niniejszym stanem Żydów polskich*, 20. The French text does not contain the phrase 'especially in Warsaw' (*osobliwie w Warszawie*), suggesting, perhaps, that this was a translator's interpolation.  [52] Ibid.

[53] On this community, see Doktór, 'Warszawscy frankiści'.

[54] Doktór (ibid. 197–8) offers this as a likely figure. An interesting, albeit uncritical, survey of variations in the sources concerning Frankist numbers (from 1,000 to 24,000) is offered in Mieses, *Z rodu żydowskiego*, 12–15.

[55] See Ringelblum, 'Khsides un haskole in Varshe'; Schiper, *Przyczynki do dziejów chasydyzmu w Polsce*, 19–27; Rabinowicz, *Bein peshishah lelublin*, 21–100; Dynner, 'Men of Silk'.

## CONCLUSIONS

The history of subsequent maskilic polemics on the subject of hasidism in the Kingdom of Poland (and, to some extent, the history of the Haskalah in eastern Europe) is, broadly, the history of the reception of these works by Salomon Maimon, Mendel Lefin, and Jacques Calmanson. Although Maimon's comments on hasidism were frequently cited by the next generation of maskilim, what was quoted from his literary legacy was highly selective. Later authors did not refer substantially to his speculative comments concerning the power structure of the hasidic sect or the philosophical context of their doctrine. Instead, they quoted facts and anti-hasidic arguments from those extracts that described his personal experiences. Thus, Maimon's text figures as first-hand experience, as opposed to an analysis, of the hasidic movement. His speculations all too frequently lacked any connection with social reality or were simply erroneous, while a philosophical analysis of hasidic thought did not form a part of the canon of attitudes towards this movement. However, these interpretations were compatible with the more general aims of the author and editor of the autobiography. Both emphasized the 'neutrality' of its description and its significance to plans to reform Jewish society in Poland and treated the work as a form of eyewitness account. Indeed, Maimon's text functioned among both Jewish and Polish supporters of Jewish reform as a model of the current state of Jewish society in Poland and it was cited, even as late as the twentieth century, as evidence of the backwardness of this people 'in the face of fanatical paralysis of the hasidic masses'.[56]

With Lefin the situation was different. For several reasons his project was not particularly popular in Poland. First, the very nature of the publication condemned it to an early death. Secondly, Lefin left the Warsaw maskilic environment too soon to make a lasting impression. Thirdly, his *Essai* described a situation that was little understood in central and western Poland, where hasidism was neither particularly visible as a social force at the time, nor a fundamental threat to projects for reform. The mixed reception of Lefin's views seems indicative of a crucial distinction between the attitudes to hasidism of the Haskalah in the Kingdom of Poland and in Galicia, where there was an essential difference in world-views. Lefin's combative attitude won him a large circle of followers in Galicia, whereas in central Poland attitudes like his made no headway in the period of the Four-Year Sejm and later during the Duchy of Warsaw and the Kingdom of Poland, with Abraham Stern the sole anti-hasidic polemicist there for a long time.

It was Calmanson, the least known of the three, who had the greatest influence on the views of the Polish Haskalah towards hasidism. He was quoted and referred

---

[56] Thus wrote Leo Belmont in 1913; see Maimon, *Autobiografia*, vol. i, p. xi. In the 19th century Maimon was cited as an authoritative source in, *inter alia* [Antoni Eisenbaum], 'O Rabinach', *Rozmaitości*, suppl. to *Korrespondent Warszawski*, 5 (1822), 46; Niemcewicz, *Lejbe i Sióra*, i. 121.

to in relatively numerous texts, particularly at the time of the first debate on the 'Jewish question' in the Congress Kingdom in 1818–22. He referred to his own *Essai* at the beginning of 1808, when he sent a copy with commentary to the State Council of the Duchy of Warsaw, with 'the hope that now, if the state were to return to its former self, the government would definitely undertake the reform of the Jews'.[57] It was not only the Polish maskilim who were influenced by Calmanson's ideas, but also people prominent in various government spheres involved in the reform of Jewish society; for example, Jan Alojzy Radomiński and Julian Ursyn Niemcewicz.[58] There was nothing unusual in this since Calmanson was the only early critic of the Polish hasidim to be active in central Poland for a prolonged period and he remained in close contact with prominent Polish politicians. The fact that the majority of Jewish supporters of modernization had had experiences of the hasidim similar to those described by Calmanson was also important. They viewed them as dangerous fanatics, but as no more numerous or fanatical than the adherents of other mystical movements. If anything, they viewed them as less of a threat than many of those institutions of traditional Jewish society in Poland that formed a central point of interest and criticism for enlightened Jews. The arch-enemy was the *kahal*.

[57] AGAD, Rada Stanu i Rada Ministrów Księstwa Warszawskiego, 216, p. 1 (copy in CAHJP, HM3667).

[58] See e.g. Radomiński, *Co wstrzymuje reformę Żydów*, 21–2, 63–4; Niemcewicz, *Lejbe i Sióra*, vol. i, pp. x–xi, 121–2. See also anonymous reports by the Jewish Committee on Hasidism in Mahler, *Haḥasidut vehahaskalah*, 488–91 (app. 14(3)), and 391 n. 26. The influence of Calmanson's views is discussed in the following chapters.

# Characteristics of the Haskalah in the Kingdom of Poland, 1815–1860

THE first maskilim to have been active in the territories of central Poland or to have come from the area and been active in the central provinces of the old Polish–Lithuanian Commonwealth (mainly in Warsaw) appeared in the 1780s and 1790s. They included Israel Zamość, Zalkind Hourwitz, Elijah Akord, and Issachar Ber Falkensohn, as well as Mendel Lefin and Jacques Calmanson.[1] However, it is probably not accurate to speak of the Haskalah as a social movement in this period either in the territories of central Poland or in any other area of eastern Europe. Rather, these were isolated groups of individuals connected with growing commercial centres, such as Shklov and Brody.[2] The Haskalah as a visible social movement, though still not large, only emerged in central Poland in the period of the Congress Kingdom, that is, after 1815. This was not a matter of chance. One of the most important factors to accelerate the expansion of the Haskalah movement in Poland was the 'Jewish politics' of the state, as well as the very close links between the new maskilim and the administration of the Kingdom of Poland. This symbiotic relationship with state institutions proved to be the most important feature of the Haskalah in Poland, as was the co-operative relationship in the Russian empire between the Russian maskilim and the tsarist administration in the next generation.[3]

## WHAT WAS THE KINGDOM OF POLAND?

The reasons for this state of affairs can be traced to the unique political and social situation in the Duchy of Warsaw and the Kingdom of Poland alluded to earlier. Some basic points should be mentioned here. There is still an anachronistic conviction in current research into nineteenth-century Jewish history in eastern Europe that the Kingdom of Poland was an integral part of the Russian Pale of Settlement, and was much like the remaining provinces in the western part of Imperial Russia (setting aside relatively insignificant differences in the structure of its nationalities and in the legal situation). This is a legacy of the old Russian Jewish

[1] See Etkes, 'Leshe'elat mevasrei hahaskalah', on the forerunners of the Haskalah in eastern Europe, and also those from central Poland.

[2] For Shklov, see Fishman, *Russia's First Modern Jews*; for Brody, see Gelber, *Toledot yehudei brodi*, 173–257.  [3] See Stanislawski, *Tsar Nicholas I and the Jews*, 51–4, 106–9, 118–22, 187–8.

historiography of the Dubnowian school, which quite imperialistically viewed all of eastern Europe's Jews as Russian. The political agendas inherent in these views are long since dead, and yet the attitude persists. Historians either omit to mention the existence of the Kingdom of Poland at all[4] or else they quote facts about central Poland and fail to explain that these facts do not originate in the Russian Pale of Settlement, but in a different political unit.[5] Alternatively, if they refer to the Kingdom as a separate entity—or even pay considerable attention to it—they treat its past as if it were a part of the history of the Jews of Russia.[6] These attitudes are encountered equally among those researching the Jewish Enlightenment,[7] and it therefore seems reasonable to describe some of the essential political features of the Kingdom of Poland.

The new Kingdom of Poland, also known as the Congress Kingdom, was founded on the basis of a decision of the Congress of Vienna in 1815, which effectively confirmed the founding principles of the constitutional Napoleonic Duchy of Warsaw, on the ruins of which it arose. There was admittedly a personal connection between the Kingdom and Imperial Russia, but the autocratic ruler of Russia was a mere king in Poland (official documents never referred to him as the tsar) and his authority was limited by the constitution. The powers of the king were limited also by certain prerogatives of the Sejm, the Administrative Council, and the viceroy, as well as by the independent nature of the judicial system. The Sejm's legislative powers were themselves limited (for example, it had no right to frame laws), but it did monitor the functioning of the government and bestowed immunity upon members of parliament, which was a new and important prerogative in Europe. The government was wholly appointed by the king and was accountable to him, but the constitution also introduced the principle of ministerial legal responsibility. For royal decrees to become law, they had to be countersigned by the minister responsible for that portfolio. Thus the Kingdom of Poland was a 'semi-independent entity' ruled by independent organs of state, with its own territory, and its own emblems and borders, in which its inhabitants had Polish, not Russian, citizenship, as well as wide-ranging civic freedoms. A separate and independent school system, judiciary and legislature (which also applied to the Jews), monetary system, and even army meant that the Kingdom had an entirely Polish character. Polish was the sole official language (correspondence with St Petersburg was in French), and state functionaries had to be citizens of the Kingdom. Although there were exceptions to this rule (for example, Grand Duke Constantine was the head of the Polish army and Senator Nikolai Novosiltzoff was the tsar's

---

[4] The most prominent example of this appears in an otherwise excellent study by Stanislawski, ibid.

[5] e.g. Lederhendler, *The Road to Modern Jewish Politics*, 59, 102, 118.

[6] See e.g. Klier, *Russia Gathers her Jews*, 170–81; id., *Imperial Russia's Jewish Question*, 145–58.

[7] An example of the former is Patterson, *The Hebrew Novel in Czarist Russia*. The most up-to-date examples of the latter, more popular treatment, are Zalkin, *Ba'alot hashaḥar*; Feiner, *Haskalah and History*.

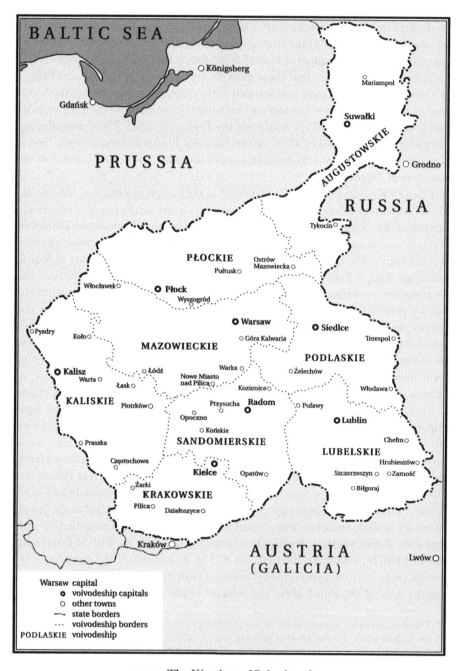

**FIG. 1.** The Kingdom of Poland, *c.*1830

special envoy), these occurred only in individual cases and do not imply any subordination of the state apparatus to Russian officials. The existence of a legal liberal opposition, something unprecedented in the Russian empire, provides evidence of the independence of the Congress Kingdom, as does the independent nature of its judiciary. This was most apparent during the parliamentary court of 1827, when, despite the pressure brought to bear by Grand Duke Constantine and Tsar Nicholas I, the court found the leaders of the conspiratorial Society of Patriots not guilty.[8]

This wide-ranging independence of the Kingdom of Poland, however, was not particularly long-lived. The first attempts to limit constitutional freedoms were made almost from the moment the Kingdom came into being (for example, with the introduction of censorship, which was in conflict with the constitution), but a general withdrawal from the 'liberal experiment' occurred following the events of 1831. After the suppression of the November Uprising, Tsar Nicholas overthrew the constitution and began the process of circumscribing autonomy, gradually restricting the competence of the central organs of government in Warsaw and transferring a part of their function to St Petersburg. Despite these measures, the Kingdom retained a considerable degree of independence and fairly broad powers in internal matters until the overthrow of the uprising in 1864.

What is particularly significant here is that the Kingdom of Poland also maintained considerable independence in its policies regarding the Jewish population. The best-known instances of this independence are the rejection of Senator Novosiltzoff's liberal project to manage the Jews in Poland (drawn up with the personal recommendation of Tsar Alexander I), the rejection of plans for Jewish conscription (introduced several years later during the period of limited Polish autonomy following the 1830–1 Uprising), and the fiasco of later attempts to standardize Polish and Russian legislation concerning Jews.[9] Until the First World War the political situation of Jews in the Congress Kingdom remained significantly different from that of Jews in the Russian empire, and all this had a tremendous influence on the situation of all sectors of Jewish society in Poland. For example, the differences between the conscription system in Russia (where the draft was brought in in 1827) and in Poland (where a much less rigid system was introduced later, in 1843) greatly influenced the outlook and political ideas of the Jewish populations in Poland and Russia respectively.[10] The same is true of the passing of the Act to emancipate

---

[8] A brief introduction to this subject is to be found in Kieniewicz, *Historia Polski 1795–1918*; id. (ed.), *Polska XIX wieku*. A good example of the contemporary state of research and attitudes is to be seen in Chwalba, *Historia Polski 1795–1918*, 257–87, 319–84.

[9] A complete collection of reports on the Novosiltzoff project can be found in AGAD, I Rada Stanu Królestwa Polskiego, 283. A critical analysis of this project and the Polish politics involved appears in Eisenbach, *Emancypacja Żydów*, 179–96. See ibid. 316–22 on attempts to bring Polish and Russian laws covering Jews into line in the 1840s.

[10] For a comprehensive account of the effects of conscription on Jews in Russia, see Stanislawski, *Tsar Nicholas I and the Jews*, 13–34; Litvak, 'Literary Response to Conscription'.

Polish (but not Russian) Jews in 1862, and the failure to implement the so-called May Laws in Poland, which limited the rights of Russian Jews from 1881 onwards.

Some of these legislative differences made the Kingdom more attractive to the Jewish population; others did not. What increased its attractiveness to the modernizing sector of the Jewish community was its more general features—those that were not necessarily directly connected with Jewish affairs. Contrary to the negative picture painted by a number of historians, the Congress Kingdom was relatively modern (by eastern European standards) and efficiently run, and this gradually put an end to its economic backwardness. Until 1832 at least (that is, until the full development of the Polish Haskalah) it was led by well-known liberals, or rather, ex-liberals, former Polish Jacobins, leaders of the patriotic progressive party from the period of the Four-Year Sejm, and prominent figures in the Enlightenment movement, or simply freemasons. Appointing himself in this period as the leader of a liberal Europe, Tsar Alexander I gave the position of viceroy to a former Jacobin and Napoleonic general, Józef Zajączek. One of the leaders of the patriotic party, a well-known mason and anticlerical, Stanisław Potocki, was appointed Minister of Education, and various other functions in the upper echelons of the hierarchy were performed by the radical Enlightenment writers and commentators Stanisław Staszic and Julian Ursyn Niemcewicz. The influence of freemasonry was extremely strong, particularly the light of the widespread belief that Alexander I and his brother Grand Duke Constantine (head of the Polish army) supported freemasonry. Of sixteen ministers serving in the Kingdom in the period 1815–30, at least ten were members of masonic lodges. Numerous senators and senior state officials, for example, all the presidents of voivodeship commissions between 1818 and 1821, were members of lodges. For the whole of that period the Grand Master of the Great Polish East was the Minister of Education, Stanisław Potocki.[11] Religious barriers began to break down as Jews were accepted into masonic lodges; they also began to frequent literary salons, and their presence in professional societies and participation in the money market also increased.[12] Well-known activists and patrons of the Haskalah, including Samuel Müchheimer, Natan Glücksberg, Jakub and Józef Epstein, and Antoni Eisenbaum, were freemasons.[13]

   This appeared to give the Kingdom of Poland a modern, liberal profile; but in reality, Poland demonstrated that these 'distinguishing characteristics' were a far

---

[11] Hass, *Wolnomularstwo w Europie Środkowo-Wschodniej*, 280–1.

[12] The areas of social integration were comprehensively described by Eisenbach, *Emancypacja Żydów*, 251–93.

[13] Hass, *Wolnomularstwo w Europie Środkowo-Wschodniej*, 282; id., 'Żydzi i "kwestia żydowska" w dawnym wolnomularstwie polskim'; Eisenbach, *Emancypacja Żydów*, 274–8. See AGAD, KRSW 6630, fo. 87, for Eisenbaum's alleged membership of a masonic lodge. More on the Jews and freemasonry can be found in Katz, *Jews and Freemasons*; although, unfortunately, Katz ignored eastern Europe in his study.

cry from genuine modernism and liberalism. The viceroy Józef Zajączek proved to be a conservative and weak politician, and the majority of the 'liberal' politicians soon abandoned their earlier views, with those few who remained faithful to them being forced to step down. It soon became obvious that this was not a state that was particularly well disposed towards Jews. The first signal of this was the king's suspension for ten years, until Jews became more 'civilized', of the full civil rights granted to them in the constitution of the Duchy of Warsaw. In the Kingdom of Poland the constitution did not give such rights to the Jews at all, plainly stating that civil rights were due to all Christian subjects of the state. Historians have rightly maintained that the stability of the former class structure and the strength of influence of the conservative land-owning nobility were impediments both to the development of liberal ideas in Polish society and to attempts to emancipate the Jewish people. Despite this, the characteristics of a liberal, anticlerical, legitimate state with modernizing and secularizing tendencies were definitely close to the ideals of the maskilim and increased the attractiveness of the state, particularly as even those laws that were most distressing to the Jews (e.g. the removal of their right to retail alcohol) were not necessarily viewed by the maskilim as hostile. Likewise, radical arguments and proposals on the 'Jewish question' in Poland did not in any way alarm Jewish advocates of modernization. One must remember that even the very critical attitudes towards traditional Jewish society at this time were consistent with the general principles of the Enlightenment tradition[14] of which the maskilim considered themselves to be the heirs. In addition, the radical suggestions of Polish politicians and writers such as General Wincenty Krasiński, Stanisław Staszic, and Walerian Łukasiński (enforced productivity, radical changes in the education system, the overthrow of the authority of the *kahal*, limitations to the 'destructive influence of the Talmud', the battle with separatism in dress and language, etc.) were in step with the programmes of many Haskalah ideologists. Thus, with relatively few exceptions (e.g. the notorious proposal that the Jews be driven out to 'the borders of Great Tartary'), the criticisms levelled by Polish political writers and commentators against traditional Jewish society were not necessarily taken by the maskilim to be unambiguously hostile. This is clearly borne out by Jewish statements made in the dispute of 1818–20 (on which more will be said later), which emphasized the good intentions of most of the Polish polemicists, including those who made highly restrictive proposals. That Jewish support for such radical plans was by no means transitory is borne out by the fact that even seventy years after the debate, Hilary Nussbaum, the well-known integrationist, defined the projects of these Polish writers and politicians as 'redolent of civilizing tendencies and civic aspirations'.[15]

---

[14] Hertzberg, *French Enlightenment and the Jews*, 268–313.

[15] Nussbaum, *Historia Żydów*, v. 382. See also Samuel H. Peltyn, 'Z przed lat 70-ciu', *Izr.* 24 (1889), 428–9, 438–9; 25 (1890), 3–4, 14–15. Similarities between the Christian and maskilic criticisms were also noted by Katz, *Tradition and Crisis*, 226–7.

## WHO WERE THE MASKILIM OF THE
## CONGRESS KINGDOM?

The Kingdom of Poland was attractive to the Jewish advocates of modernization not simply because of its generally modern character, but more because the state initiated the reform of the Jewish people and itself employed a wide cross-section of Jews in these reforms. In fact, all the leading maskilim were officials in various government institutions, particularly in their 'Jewish' sections. Jakub Tugendhold (1794–1871) worked in the Elementary Schools Inspectorate, the Censorship Committee for Hebrew Books, the Warsaw Rabbinical School, and many other state commissions. He also managed the interdenominational cholera hospital, sat on the Citizens' Committee of the municipal council, and was involved in numerous charitable organizations. Abraham Buchner (1789–1869) was a teacher of Hebrew and biblical studies at the Rabbinical School, and consultant for the education authorities. Abraham Paprocki (1813–52), Jakub Centnerszwer (1797–1880), and Antoni Eisenbaum (1791–1852) taught at the same school; the latter also published a government-sponsored weekly and translated for the state secret police. Ezechiel (Stanisław) Hoge (1791–1860) was a consultant for the Government Commission for Religious Denominations and Public Enlightenment (i.e. the Ministry of Education), and after his baptism he became secretary of the Jewish Committee and private secretary to Stanisław Staszic, who at that time was a minister and chairman of the Warsaw Society of the Friends of Learning. The Warsaw maskil Jan Glücksberg (1782–1858) became Secretary of the Advisory Chamber of the Jewish Committee and the State Attorney for Jewish Divorce Proceedings in the Supreme Court. His brother Natan Glücksberg (1780–1831) was an official typographer at the Royal University of Warsaw and the publisher of many government publications. Abraham Jakub Stern (1762–1842), who worked in the Elementary Schools Inspectorate, the Censorship Committee for Hebrew Books, and the Advisory Chamber of the Jewish Committee, but who resigned from his position as director of the Rabbinical School, was particularly active in government circles. In addition, a number of less well-known maskilim, such as the Warsaw municipal doctors Benjamin Rosenblum (1815–89) and Moses Studencki (1806–76), the voivodeship surgeon in Kalisz, M. Schönfeld, a translator for the Kalisz Voivodeship Commission, Jakub Bursztyński (1790–1852) from Częstochowa, and the correspondent to the Advisory Chamber of the Jewish Committee in Płońsk, Joseph Frenkel, were all associated with various government departments. The participation of educated east European Jews in the state administration, or, more precisely, in those branches responsible for the 'civilizing' of the Jewish people, was of course unexceptional. The same occurred in Galicia and also in Russia, though somewhat later. However, the Austrian authorities withdrew from an alliance with the Galician maskilim very early on, and friendly relations between the Russian government and representatives of the Russian Haskalah came about only in the 1840s. What is interesting is that the fruit of this alliance was the birth in the 1860s of a Russian Jewish intelligentsia with a very similar profile to that of the maskilic circles in Poland a generation earlier.[16] This might indicate that the characteristics of the Haskalah in Poland were not so far removed from those of other groups of maskilim in Russia or Galicia, but, because of its different socio-political context, the group evolved at a different pace.

Thus, the most active members of the maskilim in the Congress Kingdom were, almost without exception, those who were centred around the government institutions that were entrusted with 'civilizing' the Jewish masses, or around other government and public institutions. The group was partly made up of the descendants of German supporters of the Jewish Enlightenment (such as Tugendhold and Buchner, who were second-generation maskilim) and of maskilim of German origin (such as Schönfeld). There were also people who, because they had travelled or studied abroad (usually in the German territories), had received a secular education and therefore had access to public institutions (such as Stern and Centnerszwer). The first maskilim to receive formal education (e.g. Antoni Eisenbaum and Abraham Paprocki) and those who had been educated 'independently' (e.g. Ezechiel Hoge) also belonged to this group. It was thus a very diverse group.

In addition to these leaders of the Haskalah movement, the ideology of the Jewish Enlightenment had already acquired a large circle of followers by the time of the formation of the Congress Kingdom. This circle was made up of both less active proponents of the Haskalah and passive supporters, as well as of wealthy patrons whose fortune and favour became an important instrument of social influence. This group was far more numerous than the elite Haskalah 'republic of writers', and it formed the core of the Jewish Enlightenment in Poland and determined its strength.[17] Although it would be difficult to call its representatives maskilim in the true sense of the word, they defined themselves as supporters of the Enlightenment and of progress. Most of all, though, they had personal and institutional connections with the leaders of the Haskalah movement and sympathized with them ideologically. These people were mainly wealthy merchants, industrialists, bankers, and 'tax farmers' responsible for collecting the taxes imposed on Jews by the state, and suppliers of military provisions; in other words, the circles giving rise to the new Jewish bourgeoisie that were exposed to daily contact with the external, non-Jewish world and were subject to its influence. These circles were new not only because the bourgeoisie had existed for a comparatively short period, but also because a significant proportion among them had originated not

---

[16] For rapprochement between the Russian Haskalah and the tsarist authorities, see Stanislawski, *Tsar Nicholas I and the Jews*, 51–4, 118–22; on languages, ibid. 115–18.

[17] The most important social study of the Haskalah is that of Zalkin, *Ba'alot hashahar*. For the social structure of the Haskalah movement in Poland, see id., 'Hahaskalah hayehudit bepolin'. For the Haskalah in Kraków, see id., 'Hahaskalah hayehudit bekrakov'.

from the former oligarchy of the *kahal*, but either from families that had made their money during the Napoleonic wars or from the new affluent settlers from Prussia, Silesia, and Bohemia. The group also included the Warsaw doctors who had been the co-founders of the Polish Haskalah from its beginnings at the end of the eighteenth century, such as Eliasz Akord (d. 1811), Joseph Wolf (b. 1766), and Jacques Calmanson.

The support, or at least the interest, expressed by a broad spectrum of supporters of the Jewish Enlightenment took a variety of forms. These ranged from acceptance of the external manifestations of modernization, via subscriptions to Haskalah books and periodicals, financial backing for various initiatives, and participation in Jewish self-government and charitable institutions, to active literary, or more frequently journalistic, output. On occasions, Mathias Rosen (1804–65) and Eleazar Talgrün (d. 1857), for example, in addition to their social and charity work, turned to creative activity of this kind. Others, such as Jakub Epstein (1771–1843), contented themselves with passive support of modernizing Jewish circles or with philanthropic works. It is impossible to measure the impact these groups, with their varying degrees of involvement, had on Enlightenment ideology. However, it is possible, for example, to compare the number of subscribers to Haskalah works in Warsaw with figures for other centres in the Russian empire. Such a comparison reveals that the interest in Haskalah Hebrew publications in Warsaw was comparable with that in Berdichev, Vilna, and Odessa, the largest centres of the Jewish Enlightenment in Russia.[18] It should also be noted that at that time Warsaw was a major centre of Haskalah publishing. From the end of the eighteenth century to 1862 about 100 publications in Polish or German by the Polish maskilim appeared in print, as well as about 200 Hebrew-language publications promoting Enlightenment ideology (approximately 20 per cent of all Hebrew books published there). These included classical Haskalah works such as the annotated Bible translated by Mendelssohn, and the works of Shalom Hakohen, Mendel Lefin, Herz Homberg, and Naftali Herz Wessely.[19] Haskalah publications also found numerous subscribers in the smaller cities, such as Kalisz, Częstochowa, Włocławek, and even Działoszyce, Praszka, and Opoczno.

## INSTITUTIONS OF THE HASKALAH:
## THE MASKILIM AS A SOCIAL GROUP

One qualification must be made here regarding maskilic publications in Warsaw: most were written by authors who lived outside the Kingdom, mainly in Russia, so cannot be counted as part of the literary output of the Polish Haskalah. That significant numbers of maskilic publications were printed in the Kingdom nevertheless indicates that conditions in Warsaw were particularly favourable. Unlike those in

[18] Zalkin, 'Hahaskalah hayehudit bepolin', 408–9.
[19] See Werses, 'Hasifrut ha'ivrit bepolin', 163.

the Russian territories, publishing houses in Poland were not dominated by the hasidim, and were therefore accessible to maskilic authors. In addition, censorship in Warsaw, through the influence of Stern and Tugendhold, was sympathetic to maskilic Hebrew literature. This favourable influence of the publishing houses and the censorship office in regard to the Polish maskilim extended far beyond the borders of Congress Poland.

This brings us to the question of maskilic institutions, which played a vital role in bringing cohesion to the Polish maskilim as a social group. Tugendhold, Stern, Buchner, and others established many formal or informal bodies to institutionalize their contacts. These ranged from the very formal Jewish community boards, to charitable and municipal institutions, to completely informal salons and social gatherings.

In the case of the Jewish community boards (*dozory bóżnicze*), the maskilim in Warsaw succeeded in placing a representative on the community board at the time that it was established (1821) and the *kahal* dissolved (1822). The maskilim had a decisive voice on the board between 1839 and 1855, and succeeded in transforming it into an institution that supported maskilic ideology.[20] Likewise, followers of the Jewish Enlightenment were active and visible on community boards in the large provincial cities, such as Kalisz, Płock, and Włocławek, as well as in the medium-sized and small towns, such as Opoczno and Praszka.[21]

Advocates of the Haskalah also dominated other institutions, such as the boards of the Jewish Hospital and Orphanage in Warsaw, and the board of the Jewish Hospital first in Kalisz and thereafter in other cities.[22] Hospitals and other social welfare institutions particularly attracted the Polish maskilim, partly because they fell within the sphere of the movement's social interests and partly because they enabled the quiet propagation of maskilic ideology. Warsaw's Jewish Orphanage had a school with a typically maskilic syllabus: the children studied crafts in addition to religion and Hebrew (both courses were based on original biblical texts), Polish, German, Russian, mathematics, and drawing.[23]

One of the important institutions of the maskilic movement in Warsaw was to be found in the 'German' synagogue on Daniłowiczowska Street. From the moment of its establishment in 1802 it had been a central meeting place for nearly all

---

[20] Although historical literature on the Warsaw Jewish community is quite extensive, no real study of the Jewish community board has been done. So far, the best studies on the subject have been published by Shatzky, *Geshikhte fun Yidn in Varshe*, i. 264–81; ii. 139–60, 175–92. Basic archival sources for the Warsaw community board in the years 1839–55 can be found in AGAD, CWW 1724–1726.

[21] For Opoczno and the hasidic opposition to Pinkus Eliasz Lipszyc, a local maskil and deputy of the Jewish community board there, see AGAD, CWW 1501, pp. 3–25, and Chapter 4 of this volume; on Praszka, see AGAD, CWW 1557, pp. 15–32.

[22] For Warsaw, see Nussbaum, *Szkice historyczne*; for Kalisz, see Beatus, *Rys historyczny*; for Piotrków, see AGAD, CWW 1411, pp. 550–7; for Hrubieszów, see AGAD, CWW 1602, pp. 272–5.

[23] See Tugendhold, *Słowo w swoim czasie*, 3–5. See Lewin, 'Beit hayetomim' for the pedagogical activities of the orphanage.

Warsaw's modernized Jews. Despite its name, these Jews did not necessarily come from Germany but they maintained German cultural traditions.[24] For more than half a century it was the informal headquarters of the Polish Haskalah. It was a place where many initiatives and plans were conceived and carried out, and where numerous members of the group received moral and financial support, and the wealth of quite a number of the congregation, such as Isaac and Mathias Rosen, Jakub Epstein, and Samuel Kronenberg, had a social impact. It was only in the 1840s that a similar synagogue was established in Łódź.

The institutions set up by the government to 'civilize' the Jewish people in Poland need to be seen in the context of those bodies that institutionalized the maskilim as a social group. These were the Censorship Committee for Hebrew Books, the Advisory Chamber of the Jewish Committee, and educational institutions such as the elementary schools established in 1820 by Jakub Tugendhold and the Warsaw Rabbinical School, which was founded in 1826. Their importance to the maskilim working in these institutions was twofold. First, it enabled them to influence and co-operate on government projects to reform Jewish society in this optimistic period when it was believed that their aim was to improve the social conditions of the Jewish people. Secondly, it allowed them to be both financially and socially independent of traditional Jewish society, which was still dominant and often viewed maskilic activities with fear, if not contempt. The Rabbinical School, in particular, played a major role as a centre for the propagation of integrationist ideology (although it was not always maskilic), and as an institutional base for most of the above-mentioned maskilim—Eisenbaum, Buchner, Paprocki, Centnerszwer, and, later, Tugendhold. The 1,209 graduates of this school established a very strong social foundation for the Haskalah in the Kingdom of Poland.[25]

In addition, the Polish maskilim, like their peers in the rest of eastern Europe, maintained contacts through a network of informal clubs, salons, cultural gatherings, and, above all, correspondence, which was the most important means of propagating maskilic ideology and maintaining personal relations. The term 'literary republic of writers', which was typically employed to describe these informal relations, might seem inappropriate in the case of the Polish maskilim as only a few of them were genuinely writers; most confined their activity to journalism, translations, or compilations of textbooks. However, their correspondence was the most important means of personal contact both between the maskilim in Poland and with other proponents of the Jewish Enlightenment throughout eastern and central Europe. Again, Jakub Tugendhold may be used as an example. He maintained contacts with, and was held in high regard by, almost all the maskilim in Warsaw and numerous enlightened personalities in Poland, Germany, and Russia (espe-

[24] Zilbersztejn, 'Postępowa synagoga na Daniłowiczowskiej'.
[25] See Lewin, 'Beit hasefer lerabanim bevarsha', and Polonsky, 'Warszawska Szkoła Rabinów', for the Rabbinical School as a centre of the Haskalah and of integrationist ideology.

cially Vilna). These included his brother Wolf Tugendhold, Isaac Ber Levinsohn (Ribal), Isaac Marcus Jost, Leopold Zunz, Shalom Hakohen, Feivel Schiffer, Solomon Ettinger, Moses Frankfurt (Mendelssohn), Alexander Zederbaum, and Samuel Joseph Finn.[26] His correspondence with Ribal indicates a particularly close relationship and mutual respect. This is evidence of the fact that the Polish maskilim were a typical social group that interacted on several levels: the objective level (they had common goals and means), the subjective level (in terms of their self-awareness as a group), and the behavioural level (represented by the frequency of contacts within the group). Tugendhold, Stern, Buchner, and the others referred to themselves as members of maskilic society, which showed a strong collective identity. They also maintained social contacts, undertook numerous collective initiatives, co-operated on a number of projects, established a number of formal or semi-formal bodies to institutionalize their interactions, and participated in the 'maskilic literary republic of writers'. Their contacts with Russian maskilim were particularly vital, but the strongest unilateral influence came from the German Jewish Enlightenment movement and its successors.[27]

## THE GEOGRAPHY OF THE POLISH HASKALAH

Warsaw was the largest, oldest, and most important Haskalah centre in the Kingdom of Poland.[28] The city was where the majority of the representatives of the two main social groups that made up the core of the Haskalah—the Jewish functionaries and those who had connections with state institutions, and the emerging bourgeoisie—converged. The number of arrivals from Berlin, Breslau (Wrocław), and Königsberg was greater than from elsewhere and meant that Warsaw Haskalah circles had an obviously German origin, which resulted in strong ideological and personal links with Prussian Enlightenment centres. Despite this, the association of Haskalah circles with state institutions meant that the acculturation process and that of linguistic assimilation occurred at a faster rate in Warsaw than elsewhere. In the first years of the Kingdom's existence, Polish, not Hebrew or German, became the literary language and, frequently, the language of everyday use. Antoni Eisenbaum wrote in 1822 of 'the local Jews called Germans' and that 'their children speak Polish only and, in many homes, Polish has already become their

---

[26] On Ribal, see Weinryb, 'Toledot ribal', and Zinberg, *History of Jewish Literature*, xi. 54, 59, 64; on Jost, Weinryb, 'Aus Marcus Jost Briefwechsel', and CAHJP, PL/82 (Jost's letters); on Zunz, Weinryb, 'Zur Geschichte des Buchdruckes', 288, and Shatzky, 'Arkhivalia', 727–8; on Shalom Hakohen, Landau, *Short Lectures*, 116, 125, and Shalom Hakohen, *Pierwsza wskrzeszona myśl o istnieniu Boga*, introd.; on Frankfurt Mendelssohn, Werses, 'Hasefer *Penei tevel*', 210; on Zederbaum, Łastik, *Z dziejów oświecenia żydowskiego*, 190–1; on Finn, *Hakarmel*, 1 (1861), 317–18.

[27] Weinryb, 'Zur Geschichte der Aufklärung bei den Juden'.

[28] On the Haskalah in Warsaw, see Kats, 'Varshe der tsenter fun haskole'; Shatzky, *Yidishe bildungspolitik*, 16; Zalkin, 'Hahaskalah hayehudit bepolin', 404–9; Guesnet, *Polnische Juden im 19. Jahrhundert*, 285–95 (mainly on the institutions of the Warsaw Haskalah).

mother tongue'.[29] This accelerated Polonization of Jewish Enlightenment circles in Warsaw made the further development of the Haskalah in the entire Congress Kingdom a foregone conclusion.

Warsaw was also exceptional with regard to the number and economic strength of these maskilim, and particularly for the influence they gained in community institutions and in state institutions responsible for the reform of the Jewish people. This meant that the Warsaw maskilim, unlike supporters of the Enlightenment in more isolated localities, were not exposed to constant battles for survival and could begin to function socially and attempt to carry out the Haskalah programme as early as the beginning of the nineteenth century. They were therefore strangers to the frustrations suffered by their peers from smaller centres, who were alienated and deprived of any opportunity to influence community life.

Zamość and its environs was second to Warsaw as a centre of the Haskalah.[30] The earliest representatives of the Haskalah there were Solomon of Chełm and Israel of Zamość, east European pioneers of the Haskalah. After the partitions many Jews from Zamość who had strong ties with Galicia (which had incorporated the town between 1772 and 1809) remained under the influence of the local Haskalah; thus numerous maskilim, even once they had left their native Zamość, Szczebrzeszyn, or Hrubieszów, founded a group quite different from those in other centres of the Kingdom of Poland. The best-known members included Arie Leib Kinderfreund and Efraim Fishel Fischelsohn, who were born in Zamość, and Solomon Ettinger, who had also lived there; Abraham Jakub Stern, a native of Hrubieszów; and Faivel Schiffer and Jacob Reifman, residents of Szczebrzeszyn, as well as Leib Szper, who came from the town.

Other important Haskalah centres in the Kingdom of Poland were Płock, Kalisz, Częstochowa, Łódź, and Włocławek—all large or medium-sized towns at the time. Enlightenment circles in Kalisz were particularly active, and made their appearance from the first years of the Congress Kingdom. However, Haskalah circles were also active in many small communities, such as Działoszyce, Opoczno, Praszka, Żarki, Pyzdry, and Pułtusk.[31] British missionaries attempting to convert Jews to Christianity spoke of numerous enlightened (*aufgeklärte*) opponents during their activities, not only in the larger centres (e.g. Warsaw, Włocławek, Lublin, and Częstochowa), but also in small towns and villages, which were unknown to literary sources as Haskalah centres (e.g. Żarki, Puławy, Opatów, Tykocin, Władysławów, Koło, Biłgoraj, and Suwałki).[32] It is particularly interesting that

[29] Z. [Antoni Eisenbaum], 'O wychowaniu młodzieży żydowskiej', *Rozmaitości* [suppl. to the daily *Gazeta Korrespondenta Krajowego i Zagranicznego*], 5 (1822), 32. This was corroborated by later journalists; see e.g. Nussbaum, *Szkice historyczne*, 93.

[30] See Shatzky, 'Haskole in Zamość', Mahler, *Hasidism and the Jewish Enlightenment*, 233–8, on the Haskalah in Zamość.                          [31] See Zalkin, 'Hahaskalah hayehudit bepolin'.

[32] On Warsaw, see W[ilhelm] Ferdynand Becker, 'Rev. F. W. Becker's Further Proceedings at Warsaw', *MI* 4 (1833), 132; on Włocławek, J[an] G[ottfried] Lange, 'Letter from Mr. J. G. Lange', *JI* 5 (1839), 118; on Lublin, AGAD, CWW 1458, pp. 274–5; on Częstochowa, AGAD, CWW 1458,

the maskilim there were often the most passionate defenders of the Talmud and of rabbinic tradition, and more than once were called upon by other Jews to assist in disputes with the missionaries. This indicates that they saw themselves as the defenders of the religious traditions of Judaism, a view also held by some of the traditional adherents.

It was not simply a matter of coincidence that a significant number of these places were situated on the western border of the Kingdom. The example of diminutive Praszka (whose population in 1827 was 1,659, including 541 Jews) is very telling. Its community board opposed the nomination of an 'unenlightened' rabbi in 1828 on the grounds that he might impede the development of the Enlightenment in a settlement 'which lies on the very border and which already has quite a number of residents who have already been civilized and cleansed of their previous wrongdoing'.[33] There is frequent reference in the official correspondence of members of other communities from Praszka to the fact that this congregation had already been 'civilized and enlightened more than the others'.[34] This was apparently attributable to the settlement's location on the border, where it had regular contact with enlightened German Jews and education in public schools. The fact that in the whole of the voivodeship of Kalisz, the region most strongly influenced by the trend towards modernization, only forty-three Jewish pupils were enrolled in the 1822–3 school year in the public state elementary schools provides a truer picture of the minimal reach of this education.[35] These 'more polished' Jews from these areas usually emphasized the more external manifestations of 'civilization', such as changes in dress, language, and customs, and it is possible to surmise that this was merely a cosmetic change as opposed to a deep-seated transformation in the spirit of the Haskalah, although one might encounter there writers and active propagators of Haskalah ideology. Działoszyce, a small town in the voivodeship of Kraków (where the Jewish population in 1827 was 1,267 out of a total of 1,735), was interesting, if exceptional, from the point of view of the sphere of its activities. It boasted an exceptionally large number of subscribers to Haskalah publications, as well as the writer Isaiah Tugendhold, his sons Jakub and Wolf, and the prominent Enlightenment activist Eliasz Moszkowski. In 1861 the Jewish com-

pp. 472, 568; on Żarki, AGAD, CWW 1458, p. 397; on Puławy, AGAD, CWW 1458, p. 452; on Opatów, [Jan] Waschitschek, 'Journal of Mr. Waschitschek', *JI* 3 (1837), 83–4; on Tykocin, [Jan Gottfried] Lange, [Jan] Waschitschek, 'Journey of Messrs. Lange and Waschitschek', *MI* 4 (1833), 139–40; on Władysławów, 'Poland: Report Made to the General Consistory of the Evangelical Confession in the Kingdom of Poland, by the Missionaries of the London Society for Promoting Christianity amongst the Jews, for the Year 1838', *JI* 5 (1839), 66; on Koło, 'Poland: Annual Report of the Missionaries in Poland Made to the General Consistory of the Evangelical Confession in the Kingdom of Poland', *JI* 6 (1840), 72; on Biłgoraj, L[udwig] Hoff, 'Extracts of Two Letters from the Rev. L. Hoff', *JE* 14 (1829), 98; on Suwałki, AGAD, CWW 1458, pp. 183–4.

[33] AGAD, CWW 1557, pp. 15–32.   [34] AGAD, CWW 1470, pp. 120.
[35] More on this appears in AGAD, KWK 700, pp. 48–61 (copy in CAHJP, HM2/6010).

munity in Działoszyce brought in an 'enlightened' rabbi, Abraham Seelfreund.[36] In the larger areas of population, modernizing circles even attempted to establish (usually unsuccessfully) Jewish state schools for 'children of the Mosaic faith', modelled upon the Warsaw elementary schools. In Praszka and Częstochowa, Daniel Neufeld[37] succeeded in setting up private schools, and Jews in Kalisz, under the direction of Dr Schönfeld and the merchants Filip Schneer and Hirszel Malarz, attempted to open a Jewish grammar school in 1820. A year later in Kalisz, Jakub Bursztyński announced a project to found a Polish-language elementary school.[38]

## IDEOLOGY AND PROGRAMME

It is not correct to speak of a unified Polish Haskalah programme and ideology since the movement was made up of people of such varied and often conflicting views, such as the conservative and anti-rationalist Tugendhold, and Buchner, a vehement proponent of rationalism. The situation was complicated by the radicalism of Jewish groups centred around Antoni Eisenbaum (including Abraham Paprocki, Synaj Hernisz, and Szymon Goldfluss), who in the 1820s were already campaigning for total integration and were rejecting Haskalah ideology. Eisenbaum wrote that Jews in Germany owed less to Mendelssohn (who was universally revered as the father of the Haskalah) than to Israel Jacobson (1768–1828), the radical advocate of religious reform.[39] This radical orientation encountered a violent reaction from the moderate wing of the Haskalah, and the divisions deepened with the passing of time. Eisenbaum's party became more extreme, while his opponents assumed a more conservative position. In addition, the maskilim were divided not only ideologically, but by personal animosities, so that conflict became widespread. Jakub Epstein and Eleazar Talgrün denounced Tugendhold, not because of their differences in outlook, but to protect their group's financial affairs. In turn, Tugendhold made accusations against Epstein, not because of ideological differences, but because of personal ill will. Jan Glücksberg and Tugendhold tried to prevent an epitaph in Polish being placed on the grave of Antoni Eisenbaum, not because they opposed the use of the language (which in fact they promoted), but because they disliked him.[40]

Despite these difficulties, some of the most characteristic elements of their ideology and programme, which nearly all the maskilim of Poland had in common, can

---

[36] AGAD, KWK 700, pp. 48–61.     [37] See Shatzky, 'Biografye fun Daniel Neufeld'.

[38] On attempts to establish a grammar school for Jews in Kalisz, see AGAD, KWK 699, pp. 1–181; on the Bursztyński project, see AGAD, KWK 699, pp. 182–6; 700, pp. 48–61.

[39] Z. [Antoni Eisenbaum], 'Uwagi nad artykułem p. Hering', *Gazeta Codzienna*, 2679 (1839), 4.

[40] Talgrün's denunciation appears in AGAD, CWW 1725, pp. 47–8; for an anonymous denunciation that was written or inspired by Jacob Epstein, see ibid. pp. 318–23. More on the conflict surrounding Eisenbaum's inscription can be found in Kandel, 'Napisy nagrobkowe'; Schiper, *Cmentarze żydowskie w Warszawie*, 122.

be easily identified. In fact, their programme, as set out in both Polish and Hebrew literature, was neither particularly original nor did it fundamentally differ from similar programmes put forward by Jewish supporters of the Haskalah in Prussia, Russia, and Galicia. Its main points can be summarized as follows: the dissemination among Jews of universal values and a disdain for separatism; the opposition to some institutions of traditional Jewish life and with manifestations of separateness; a secular education programme and a productivity programme; and an ideology based upon loyalty to the state and to the monarch. Alongside these proposals, which aimed at transformation and modernization of Jewish society, the protection of Jewish identity (through the promotion of the Hebrew language, the Bible, and historical awareness) and a fight against pseudo-enlightenment and religious indifference also played an important role in the ideology of the Polish maskilim.

## *Education*

As was the case all over eastern and central Europe, the maskilim of the Kingdom of Poland were convinced of the inability of Jewish society to adapt to the demands of the modern world. They were aware of the morbid condition of Jewish society and of the flaws in many of its chief institutions. They were also aware of the need for a fundamental transformation of all Jewish society in both religious and moral spheres and in the area of secular relations. Like the other maskilim, the Polish supporters of the Haskalah recognized the fact that education, interpreted as the entire educational process, was a basic tool for change. Tugendhold stated that education

leads us out of a degraded bestial state, it revives and it disseminates those elevated and excellent strengths buried within us; it stifles and ousts bad habits, encourages us to embark upon the roads of virtue that lead us to our genuine destiny; in a word, it is . . . the torch of uprightness, light and learning for the entire human race.[41]

Its ultimate aim was to transform young Jews 'into righteous and useful members of society'.[42] This interest in educational programmes resulted from the involvement of the Polish maskilim in government institutions aiming to reform the Jewish people, which enabled them to participate in these educational projects. One outcome of this—and one of the negative consequences of the Haskalah's symbiosis with government institutions—was the predominance of particular types of maskilic writing, such as catechisms, moral tracts, textbooks, and extracts from religious texts and prayer books. Original Hebrew literature constituted only a small fraction of their literary output, and was far outweighed by functional texts that were often of minuscule literary value. This was particularly the case with Polish texts, where literary works were all but absent.[43]

[41] Tugendhold, *Modły*, 6.  [42] Tugendhold, *Słowo w swoim czasie*, 11.
[43] See Werses, 'Hasifrut ha'ivrit bepolin', 164.

The Polish maskilim introduced no new ideas into the Haskalah's programme of education. Following Naftali Herz Wessely's theories, they focused on two areas: religious knowledge and secular knowledge (*torat ha'adam*), simultaneously emphasizing the need for the harmonious acquisition of both.[44] Religious knowledge was interpreted as the study of ethics, complemented by rudimentary Hebrew language and grammar, and a knowledge of Jewish history and classical religious literature, particularly the Bible, and Hebrew poetry. Their attitude towards the Talmud was also generally positive, although collections of talmudic and rabbinical quotations published by them were aimed at replacing talmudic studies with a superficial knowledge of quotations and basic moral precepts.[45] However, this was not generated by anti-talmudic sentiments. The maskilim were convinced that a talmudic education played too great a role in the curriculum of Polish Jews, and the elimination of talmudic studies was simply seen as a means of restoring educational balance. As a matter of fact, the Talmud itself was attacked only by a few representatives of the radical wing of the modernizing camp. Such criticism was usually associated with strong criticism of a *ḥeder* education (private religious school) and of the status of the rabbi in traditional Jewish society. Antoni Eisenbaum, a leader of the radical fraction of the 'enlightened class',[46] gave a detailed description of the alleged absurdities of the Talmud, the *ḥeder*, and rabbinical power. Abraham Buchner likewise became well known for his anti-talmudic treatise.[47] However, statements of this kind were peripheral to the Polish Haskalah.

The study of secular subjects was intended to focus on Polish and German, mathematics, astronomy, geography, and history, and on a study of crafts and agriculture, these abilities being vigorously promoted by the maskilim of the Kingdom of Poland. A familiarity with these subjects, particularly with astronomy, was presented not only as a vital preparation for life in the modern world, but also as a religious obligation, testified to by the most eminent of talmudic authorities.[48]

Considerable importance was attached to the study of vernacular language. A knowledge of Polish or German was intended to lead to the gradual disappearance

---

[44] See e.g. Buchner, *Katechizm religijno-moralny*, 121. For the educational programmes of the Polish maskilim, see Shatzky, *Yidishe bildungs-politik*; Borzymińska, *Szkolnictwo żydowskie w Warszawie*, 54–7; Lewin, 'Batei hasefer ha'elementariyim'.

[45] See Buchner, *Kwiaty wschodnie*, introd.

[46] Z. [Antoni Eisenbaum], 'O wychowaniu młodzieży żydowskiej', *Rozmaitości*, 5 (1822), 27–34. One can assume from Abraham Buchner's note (*Prawdziwy Judaizm*, 165–6) that the articles signed 'Z' were written by Eisenbaum. Buchner wrote that from 1821 all texts on Jewish matters published in *Korespondent*, *Gazeta Warszawska*, *Gazeta Polska*, and *Gazeta Codzienna* that were signed 'Z' or 'E' or were anonymous had been written by Eisenbaum.

[47] Buchner, *Der Talmud in seiner Nichtigkeit*. A partisan view of the anti-talmudic leanings of some of the Jewish reformers in the Kingdom is presented in Mahler, *Hasidism and the Jewish Enlightenment*, 218–19.

[48] The religious significance of a secular education was highlighted by the Berlin Haskalah; see Barzilay, 'The Ideology of the Berlin Haskalah', 4.

of Yiddish, which was condemned (although not unanimously) as a bastard dialect of German and one of the symptoms of Jewish separatism.[49] German and Polish had equal status in the educational programmes. In numerous educational projects the benefits of a knowledge of German were underlined: it was of assistance in commerce, and it was easily absorbed by Jewish children who were already familiar with its 'jargon' (i.e. Yiddish). However, the ultimate goal of this education was the acquisition of the 'language of the country', i.e. Polish. This was perceived as the best means of integrating Jewish society with other social groups.[50] The importance attached to the Polish language was reinforced by its widespread use by the Polish maskilim themselves—a subject to be discussed below.

## Productivity: The Social Focus of the Polish Haskalah

The interest of the Polish maskilim in agriculture and crafts was equally important to their programme. Poets composed pastorals extolling the delights of rural life, and the authors of religious compilations testified that work on the land was the most important calling of the Jewish people and the one occupation approved by the patriarchs and the divine lawgiver, Moses. Long lists of biblical figures and talmudic scholars daily labouring on the land or at a craft were supposed to provide evidence not only that such occupations were open to Jews, but that they were sanctified by religious tradition.[51] Jewish agricultural colonies in the Chersson region were described with approval and, just as the joys of rural life were praised, so too was agriculture presented as the ultimate solution to the social problems of Jews in Poland.[52] In 1825 a Polish maskil, Moses Łaski, composed an economic treatise (which was never published) based on physiocratic theories and stressing the importance of Jewish agricultural colonization for both Jewish well-being and the economic development of the whole country.[53] Jan Glücksberg, the author of a treatise on the state of the Jews in the Kingdom of Poland, actually directed most of his attention to the lack of success of the colonization plans, and viewed the mistakes of the government's agricultural policies as one of the main reasons for the poor state of Jewish society.[54] Leib Szper from Szczebrzeszyn and Solomon Marcus Posner from Warsaw were the positive heroes of maskilic stories. The former settled Jewish farmers on his land; the latter founded renowned Jewish

[49] More on the attitude towards Yiddish and other languages can be found in Mahler, *Hasidism and the Jewish Enlightenment*, 229.

[50] See Stanislawski, *Tsar Nicholas I and the Jews*, 115–19, who writes about the purely pragmatic preference for the use of the German language of the Russian Haskalah, which was paralleled by very similar attitudes expressed by the Polish maskilim.

[51] 'Moses did not want to make Israelites merchants, but he wanted to turn them into peasants': Buchner, *Prawdziwy Judaizm*, p. xxiii. See also id., *Katechizm religijno-moralny*, 119–20; Tugendhold, *Modły*, 67–77; id., *Skazówki prawdy i zgody*, 76–94.

[52] Antoni Eisenbaum, 'Rozmaitości', *Dostrzegacz Nadwiślański*, 2 (1824), 245–8; 2 (1824), 254–6.

[53] See Weinryb, 'Letoledot hade'ot hakalkaliyot'. See also Mahler, *Hasidism and the Jewish Enlightenment*, 228.    [54] Glücksberg, *Rzut oka na stan Izraelitów w Polsce*.

industrial–agricultural colonies in Kuchary in the voivodeship of Płock.[55] Agricultural colonization projects were also revived in many of the projects submitted by the maskilim to the authorities of the Kingdom of Poland. In April 1830 Jakub Tugendhold and Ezechiel Hoge, an ex-maskil who converted to Christianity and later returned to Judaism, went to the government with a proposal to found an artisans' school for middle-class and poor Jewish young people and to establish a fund for Jewish students in an agronomic school. Young people would study carpentry, ironwork, wheelwrighting, and weaving—areas in which Jewish participation was low.[56] Tugendhold presented the government in October 1836 with another project for a Jewish school of crafts and stressed that the success of Jewish agricultural colonization would depend solely on exempting settlers from the special Jewish taxes. This is the only example in Tugendhold's considerable legacy in which he allowed himself to criticize the government's policies in relation to Jews.[57] Tugendhold even stated that the chances of success for any programme aiming at the moral reform of the Jewish people depended exclusively on progress made in directing Jews towards agriculture and some trades, and that in turn depended on the creation of favourable legal conditions.[58]

In 1840 Solomon Marcus Posner, an 'enlightened' mitnaged close to the maskilim,[59] established a project dear to the Haskalah to develop agricultural settlements. A group of Warsaw maskilim, supported by prominent Orthodox and hasidic leaders, appealed in 1841 for Jews to settle in the countryside.[60] In 1842 the maskilim were particularly politically active in connection with plans for new regulations in the area.[61] In 1845 Eliasz Moszkowski, a maskil from Działoszyce, applied to the Government Commission for Internal and Religious Affairs with a project for rural resettlement, and a year later founded two agricultural settlements—Łabędzie and Ksawerów—with his brother.[62]

As Raphael Mahler noted, interest in agricultural colonization and programmes

[55] See e.g. Buchner, *Prawdziwy Judaizm*, 160–7; A.W., 'Odpowiedź na "Uwagi p. Z. nad Artykułem p. Hering"', *Gazeta Codzienna*, 2705 (1840), 3–4; 'Polen. Warschau' [correspondence], *Der Orient*, 4 (1843), 15. On Leib Szper from Szczebrzeszyn, see F. S—ki, [correspondence], *Kurier Warszawski*, 245 (1835), 1263–4. On Posner, see Gelber, *Hayehudim vehamered hapolani*, 17–22, and suppl.; Różański, 'Dzieje osad żydowskich we wsi Kuchary', 31–49.

[56] AGAD, CWW 1416, pp. 37–43.

[57] Tugendhold, *Modły*, 76–7. Projects to free Jewish agricultural settlers from the special Jewish taxes were proposed as early as 1812 by the Ministry of Internal Affairs of the Duchy of Warsaw; see AGAD, Rada Ministrów Księstwa Warszawskiego, 165, pp. 35–45.

[58] Jakub Tugendhold, 'Odpowiedź na artykuł w Nrze 174 Kuriera Warszawskiego z dnia 25 Lipca', *Gazeta Warszawska*, 131 (1821), 1887–8.     [59] AGAD, CWW 1419, pp. 62–78.

[60] An appeal signed, *inter alia*, by Solomon M. Posner, Jakub Epstein, Isaac Rosen, Jakub Tugendhold, and rabbis Hayim Dawidsohn, Shyia Muszkat, Isaac Kalisz of Warka, and Isaac Meir Alter of Góra Kalwaria (Ger) appears in AGAD, CWW 1436, pp. 324–5, and is reproduced in Gelber, *Hayehudim vehamered hapolani*, 38–9; Frenk, Zagorodski, *Di familie Dawidsohn*, pp. xii–xx.

[61] See the series of correspondence 'Zeitungsnachrichten. Russland und Polen', *AZJ* 6 (1842), 743–6.     [62] AGAD, CWW 1436, pp. 213–23; Shatzky, *Yidishe bildungs-politik*, 94–5.

for Jewish productivity was markedly greater among the Polish maskilim than among advocates of the Haskalah in neighbouring countries.[63] The first, and most obvious, reason for this, as indicated by Mahler, was the particularly strong connection the Polish maskilim had with government institutions dealing with this and similar matters. This, of course, led to their involvement in the projects. However, from the number and content of the Haskalah projects (which were frequently critical of the politics of the government and which frequently got a less than positive reception from the government), it would appear that the maskilim were significantly more interested in the agricultural programmes than were the authorities and that the inspiration was provided to the government by the maskilim, rather than vice versa. Explaining their involvement, the maskilim themselves indicated that agricultural settlements and greater Jewish involvement in the 'heavy' trades and crafts were the simplest means by which to deflect tension between Jewish and Christian factions and to build bridges of a non-religious nature. Abraham Grossglück, an economist at the Jewish Hospital in Warsaw, even maintained that cultivating the soil was a universal means of honouring God as well as being a quasi-religious act that joined all people of the earth.[64] Other writers maintained that physical work in the fields was the best way of showing one's love for the homeland and one's ties with it.

However, the decisive factor for there being such a great interest in projects to develop Jewish agriculture and industry was the acute social awareness of many of the most prominent Haskalah ideologists in Poland; significantly, none of them was associated with the radical wing of the Haskalah. Admittedly, the unbalanced social and occupational structure of Poland's Jewish population, its increasing impoverishment, and its difficulties in adjusting to the new social and legal order were not problems that were confined to the Congress Kingdom; they were to be encountered in nearly all areas of the former Commonwealth. However, it was in the Kingdom more than elsewhere that these problems were reflected in the activities and writings of Jewish proponents of the Enlightenment. The rural colonization and trade development projects were actually major indicators of the Polish maskilim's social involvement.

It should be emphasized, however, that this was neither the sole, nor the most important, maskilic response to the problems pervading Jewish society. Equally important were their pronouncements against abuses committed by the *kahal*s, as well as campaigns to reduce the Jewish community's tax burden (for example, the tax on kosher meat), attempts at a fair distribution of those taxes, tax relief for the worst-off, and, above all, numerous charitable undertakings and publications dedicated to promoting widespread charity. These works were second only to educational texts in Haskalah literature in Poland. In the case of the Polish maskilim,

---

[63] Mahler, *Hasidism and the Jewish Enlightenment*, 228. On productivization projects among Russian maskilim, see Zalkin, 'Economic and Occupational Aspects of the Jewish Enlightenment', 223–8.

[64] Grossglück, *O powadze majestatu*, 42 (p. 28 in the Hebrew section).

social activity did not equate with social radicalism—quite the opposite. Social criticism was virtually absent from these writings, and where it appeared, it was exceptionally well camouflaged. The activities they proposed were of a very limited nature and the programme was cautious and conservative, a natural consequence of the strong links between representatives of the Haskalah and government institutions. The maskilim of the Kingdom of Poland sought ways of improving the situation of the Jewish population without suggesting more radical changes to the existing social structure. Despite this, their activities led on more than one occasion to tension and conflict with the affluent patrons of the Haskalah. The worst was a long-lasting 'war' rife with denunciations, which took place in 1837–42, between Jakub Tugendhold and his followers, who were defending the 'poverty-stricken class', and Jakub Epstein and his followers from the Jewish bourgeoisie, who were defending the economic status quo.[65]

However, the modest nature of these social initiatives, which were so important to the maskilim, seems not to have arisen out of a servile wish to placate the government. The pressure they applied to the agricultural programmes—frequently against the government's wishes—provides proof that the opposite was true. The moderate nature of the proposed changes was, if anything, a reflection of the pragmatism of the leaders of the Polish Haskalah, who, on principle, took the prevailing social conditions into account and avoided urging extreme solutions that were doomed to failure. The maskilim's silence on military service, which was enthusiastically received by many supporters of the Jewish Enlightenment in other eastern European countries but hated by the Jewish public, was typical. Their restraint in this matter is striking when contrasted with their intervention in agricultural projects, particularly given that the two government initiatives came about almost simultaneously.

## Criticism of the Kahal

As mentioned earlier, several of the pronouncements and activities of the Polish maskilim that attempted to reform the organization of Jewish community life found their way into the current of social criticism—particularly criticism of the *kahal*. The *kahal* was accused of numerous financial improprieties, the unjust allocation of conscription and kosher taxes, the misuse of religious institutions for personal financial gain, and persecution of the more enlightened individuals. It was also seen by the maskilim as the foundation stone of Jewish separatism, the quintessence of a 'state within a state', and the greatest obstacle to Jewish integration with the rest of society. An anonymous brochure published in 1820 by Pinkus Eliasz Lipszyc, a wealthy merchant and maskil from Opoczno, violently attacked the 'three ills' of Jewish society—the *kahal*, the rabbinate, and the burial societies—citing them as the most important, if not the sole, reason for the oppression of the Jewish masses in Poland.[66] The abolition of the *kahal* system in 1822 was greeted

---

[65] See AGAD, CWW 1724, pp. 424 ff., 1725.　　　　[66] Lipszyc, *Prośba czyli Usprawiedliwienie*.

with approval by both the most radical and the most conservative supporters of modernization. Eisenbaum announced that the times had passed when a *kahal* officer would force poor petitioners away from the doors of the *kahal* session, behind which the members of the *kahal* would drink alcohol and smoke tobacco bought with money from the poor. 'Brothers in faith! It was not the government which was oppressing you, no. It was our brothers. It was the members of the *kahal*.'[67] However, it was the extent of the criticism that distinguished the conservative and radical modernizers. Those maskilim who were more traditional confined their criticism to the economic activities of the *kahal*, criticized abuses in the allocation of dues and taxes, and voiced their indignation at the immoral extortion conducted by the burial societies. However, these accusations were in no way linked with plans to limit the religious autonomy of the Jewish community, and there was certainly no intention of abolishing the purely religious function of the *kahal*.[68] For the radical reformers, an attack on socio-economic ills was inextricably linked with criticism of the *kahal*'s religious function and undertakings to abolish the burial societies and the rabbinate, together with its prerogatives—the rabbinical court and the power to pronounce bans. The radicals accused the rabbis of ignorance, of submitting to pressure from dishonest members of the *kahal*, of entering into shady dealings with them, and of making a mockery of the Jewish religion itself by exploiting it for dishonourable purposes. Eisenbaum even stated that the function of the rabbinate was completely superfluous, that many communities managed perfectly well without a rabbi and that the one function of the rabbis was 'passing judgement in regard to the kitchen', that is, decisions concerning matters of *kashrut*.[69] Even stronger accusations were aimed at the *ḥadarim*, which were accused of spreading ignorance and superstition, and at the burial societies, which

[67] Z. [Antoni Eisenbaum], 'Zniesienie Kahałów: (Artykuł nadesłany)', *Rozmaitości*, 5 (1822), 10–12.

[68] Izakowicz Cudek [Jakub Tugendhold], 'Odpowiedź Moskowi Jankielowi', *Rozmaitości*, 5 (1822), 21–2; Izaakowicz [Jakub Tugendhold], 'Do Moszka Jankiela', *Rozmaitości*, 5 (1822), 34–6. In an anonymous denunciation written in 1840, the author accused Tugendhold, *inter alia*, of having published in 1820 anti-Jewish articles in *Rozmaitości*, a supplement to the daily *Korrespondent Warszawski*, that were signed with the pen-name 'Moszek Jankele' (AGAD, CWW 1725, p. 318). However, it was Julian Ursyn Niemcewicz, and not Tugendhold, who used this pen-name, and this is confirmed in the table of contents for *Pamiętnik Warszawski* for 1815. It seems reasonable to assume that the anonymous author was mistaken, attributing articles signed by Moszek Jankiele to Tugendhold instead of articles engaging in debate with Moszek Jankiele, which were signed with the pen-name Izaakowicz Cudek. In addition, the views of 'Izaakowicz' corresponded with views expressed by Tugendhold on other occasions; 'Izaakowicz' was well informed about the new Jewish community board in Warsaw and sympathized with its new government-appointed deputies (Tugendhold was at that time a secretary of the community board and was closely linked with the new deputies); and the editors of *Rozmaitości* (5 (1822), 21) annotated the 'Izaakowicz' article with a footnote: 'Piece submitted to the editors, truly written by one of the Israelites'.

[69] [Eisenbaum], 'O Rabinach', *Rozmaitości*, 5 (1822), 37. The expression, originally Zalkind Hurwicz's (see Hurwicz, 'Usprawiedliwienie czyli Apologia Żydów', 116), was taken by Eisenbaum from Niemcewicz, *Lejbe i Sióra*, 119.

were accused of demoralization, hindering the progress of the Enlightenment, greed, and exploiting human misery and naivety.

## The Battle with Separatism

According to the maskilim, in addition to the pathological socio-occupational structure, the other source of Polish Jewry's misfortunes was the fatal separatism of Jewish society itself. This view was shared by those in favour of modernization all over eastern Europe. The external manifestations of this separateness were the differences in clothing, language, and customs with which representatives of the Haskalah consistently battled. However, what they recognized as being most dangerous were those deeply entrenched convictions that fuelled a belief in the inferiority of the Christian world and the religious sanctioning of Jewish separatism. It was emphasized that, by cutting itself off from Christians, Jewish society would limit the opportunities for present and future generations to solve underlying social problems related to its failure to adjust to the changing conditions of the outside world and to the untenable socio-occupational structure. These ills could only be solved by integration with, and participation in, economic, cultural, and social life in non-Jewish society. It was also indicated that the antipathy shown towards Christians by Jews created a reciprocal feeling on the part of the Christians towards Jews and their religion, and that this worsened the position of Jews. Religiously oriented writers also noted that this discredited Judaism, and they went to considerable lengths to convince Jews and Christians alike that there was no religious justification for Jews to take a hostile stance towards Christians and that, if anything, it ran counter to the precepts of Judaism. Tugendhold published a treatise in three languages (first in Polish and Hebrew, and then in Yiddish) in which he stated that the expression *akum* (idolater),[70] and any religious connotations inherent in that expression, were not references to Christians but only to pagans. He also acknowledged that his work was aimed at two groups of readers: Christians and Jews.[71] The intention was to persuade Christians that the negative stance of some Jews towards them emanated not from the nature of Judaism, but only from the fanaticism of some of its less enlightened followers. For Jews, the text was intended as a testimony to the immorality of such anti-Christian attitudes and the way in which they conflicted with religious precepts. It was also intended to bring about a change in such reprehensible behaviour. Thus it was both an apologetic and a moralistic work. In order to broaden its social influence, Tugendhold sought two rabbinical approvals (*haskamot*), such as were traditionally used to support Jewish religious texts and to testify to the righteousness of the author's work. In this case, the approvals were dispensed by the eminent scholars (both mitnagedim) Hayim Dawidsohn of Warsaw and Judah Bachrach of Sejny. The

---

[70] *Akum* is an abbreviation of *Oved kokhavim umazalot*, 'worshipper of the stars'.
[71] Tugendhold, *Skazówki prawdy i zgody*.

treatise was supplemented with a study by the 'modern, honourable, and enlightened talmudist' Solomon Marcus Posner, who proved that 'contemporary nations (especially Christian ones), after they had rejected repugnant idolatry, worship the real God and follow praiseworthy morals'.[72]

Other authors used similar strategies. Abraham Buchner testified that God's commandments applied to Jews and non-Jews alike. Furthermore, it was necessary to behave with even greater integrity towards people of other faiths than towards Jews, because a sin committed against a co-believer would be attributed by the injured party to the perpetrator, whereas a sin committed against one of another faith would be attributed to the religion of the perpetrator. Thus, it would become a transgression not only against one's fellow man, but against the name of God. The chosen nature of Israel gave one not the right to rule over others, but merely the obligation to pay special tribute to God; hence, this was being chosen not to rule, but to serve.[73] Buchner also stated that even the idolater was a fellow human and that a Jew was obliged to show him brotherly love. Brotherly love for a non-Jewish person was actually one of the main themes of the writings of Buchner, who frequently detailed different aspects of it: a ban on receiving stolen goods, swindling, and particularly stealing from those of another faith; the principle of love of one's homeland; the obligation of loyalty to one's monarch; the need to undertake productive activities, etc.[74]

## Monarchism and Patriotism

Of all the obligations to the outside world, it was monarchism in particular that occupied a prominent place in the ideological programme of the eastern European Haskalah, including the Kingdom of Poland. The principle of fidelity to the monarch was taken from the talmudic maxim 'The law of the country is the law' (*Bava kama* 113*a* and elsewhere), which, contrary to rabbinical tradition, received absolute sanction.[75] Other talmudic sayings, such as 'royal authority on earth is akin to royal authority in heaven' (*Berakhot* 58*a*) and that man should pray for it because, were it not for authority, people would devour one another (Mishnah *Avot* 3: 2) were equally popular. Of course there can be no doubt that the loyalty to the monarch frequently emphasized by the maskilim of the Kingdom of Poland was as strong as that demonstrated by their counterparts in Galicia and Russia. The honour accorded the monarch sometimes went so far that he was attributed with semi-divine qualities: 'the supreme father of the land spoke: "let the unfortunate be cared for", and so it came to pass'.[76] Abraham Grossglück, the author of a theological treatise on the religious obligation of love for the monarch, even testi-

---

[72] Ibid. 56.     [73] Buchner, *Doresh tov*, 12*a*–*b*.

[74] Ibid. 3*a*, 24*b*–25*a*; id., *Katechizm religijno-moralny*, 13, 32, 80–1, 92; id., *Prawdziwy Judaizm*, pp. i–xx; id., *Kwiaty wschodnie*, pp. xx–xxi.

[75] See Lederhendler, *The Road to Modern Jewish Politics*, 61–8, on the limitations of this law.

[76] Tugendhold, *Słowo w swoim czasie*, 1.

fied that earthly rulers were proof of the existence of God: 'Monarchs are appointed by decree of God Himself, they are endowed with but a particle of His greatness and the appointed are God's Representatives here on earth and as such are visible evidence of the Holiest Ruler of all time.'[77] Since they are imbued with a particle of divine majesty, monarchs are superhuman creations and the nature of their spirit 'far more elevated than the spirit which breathes life into each man created in the image and likeness of God'.[78] Very similar theories were expressed by one of the leading Warsaw maskilim, Moses Tannenbaum.[79] The most superhuman qualities were naturally attributed to the ruler in panegyric poems in Polish and Hebrew composed by a number of Polish maskilim, including Herman Saphirstein, Abraham Stern, Feivel Schiffer, and Isaiah Tugendhold (father of Jakub and Wolf).[80] In this sense, the programme of the maskilim in the Congress Kingdom was an ideal reflection of similar views held by the Haskalah in eastern and central Europe, which adapted the old political principle of the 'royal alliance' with the monarch.[81] This is even more striking when one notes that the monarchism of the Polish maskilim emerged in political conditions that were very different from those in absolutist Galicia or Russia.

The one feature that typified the monarchism of the Polish maskilim was that they combined the idea of fidelity to the ruler with the principle of love of homeland, which, in the case of the 'semi-independent' Kingdom, was accompanied by serious ideological and political consequences (although this was not a revolutionary attitude and did not imply a withdrawal of loyalty to the monarchy). Ezechiel Hoge clearly stated: 'Until the coming of the Messiah, every Israelite should view the country in which he was born and raised as his homeland.'[82] Similar statements could be found in other Haskalah catechisms. During the 1830–1 Uprising, Jakub Tugendhold stated that love of Zion did not preclude a love of Poland as a homeland, for the former was uncertain in terms of time and was distant, whereas a love of Poland could manifest itself daily:

[77] Grossglück, *O powadze majestatu*, 3.    [78] Ibid. 35.

[79] Tannenbaum, *Mata'ei mosheh*. More on the monarchical views of Moses Tannenbaum can be found in Mahler, *Hasidism and the Jewish Enlightenment*, 222–7.

[80] Saphirstein, *Mowa*; Stern, *Hymn i modlitwa*. Isaiah Tugendhold, *Rzecz w języku Hebrajskim*. A dedication appears in the copy of this anonymous essay in Warsaw University Library (4g.18.7.3). It reads: 'w dowód głębokiego uszanowania składa J. Tugendhold Członek Sekret[arz] Komitetu Cenzury do Ksiąg i Pism Hebr[ajskich]' (Presented as a mark of deep respect, J. Tugendhold, Member and Secretary of the Censorship Committee for Hebrew Books and Periodicals). This seems to confirm Tugendhold's involvement, while the title explains that the brochure was written by a Hebrew author in a small town, subsequently translated into the Polish by his son. This indicates the authorship of Jakub Tugendhold's father, Isaiah.

[81] On the political ideology of the Haskalah, see Biale, *Power and Powerlessness*, 103–9; Sorkin, *The Transformation of German Jewry*, 63–78. On the 'royal alliance', see Yosef H. Yerushalmi, *Lisbon Massacre*, 35–66; Lederhendler, *The Road to Modern Jewish Politics*, 17–19. More on maskilic loyalty can be found in Mahler, *Hasidism and the Jewish Enlightenment*, 53–8.

[82] Hoge, *Nauka religii*, 76.

*Gratitude* and *understanding* call out to me: the earth from which you drew life and nurture, the soil upon which your forebears found refuge centuries ago, where the dusts of generations of your forefathers lie, where you yourself, your parents, kin and brothers in one faith enjoy the safety of body and possessions, beneath the shield of general law they can perform their rituals and have a means by which to live; that should be, and is, your *homeland*.[83]

This strongly emphasized theme survived the catastrophe of the November Uprising and recurred in the writings of the Polish maskilim and their successors throughout the nineteenth century.

### Preservation of Jewish Identity

The postulate of rapprochement with the surrounding non-Jewish population, which was so important to the maskilim of the Congress Kingdom, was not identifiable with the assimilationist tendencies of which they would later be accused. These tendencies were interpreted as an aspiration to reject totally the world of Jewish values. In reality, they were quite the opposite. Side by side with programmes fighting the outward manifestations of separateness and projects to promote psychological and occupational adaptation to external conditions and to oppose antipathetic attitudes towards Christians, an equally important, if not the single most important, element of the programmes was the protection of Jewish identity. This aimed at reinforcing the status of the religion and religious values in the lives of the Jewish population in Poland. According to the maskilim, the campaign was to be fought on two fronts, because the 'hardened fanatics' who had poisoned Judaism with their calamitous prejudices and fallacies were as great a threat to the religion as were the freethinkers who completely eliminated religion from their own lives and from society. The campaign against the 'religiously corrupt' pseudo-maskilim was Tugendhold's obsession. His numerous works defended the status of the religion and its significance for the social order, and testified to the immortality of the spirit and the socio-religious obligations that stemmed from it, such as the sacred nature of Judaic traditions. Similar pronouncements warning against the disastrous consequences of a superficial education and the weakening of religious ties are attributable to many other maskilim, such as Edward Hering, Abraham Stern, and Eleazar Talgrün.[84] The warnings increased in the 1840s and 1850s, when a radical option of the modernizing camp, represented by Antoni Eisenbaum and his circle, gained strength.

The publication of numerous works of Hebrew classical literature, collections of ethical maxims from Jewish religious literature, support for knowledge of the Hebrew language, the Bible, and the history of the Jewish people, all of these activities were designed to strengthen religious tradition. The Polish maskilim published the original versions of classical Hebrew texts of rabbinical traditions as well as their Polish translations. One major undertaking was the publication of

---

[83] Tugendhold, *Dumania Izraelity na warcie*, 4.
[84] Lowenstein, *Berlin Jewish Community*, 95–103; Feiner, 'The Pseudo-Enlightenment'.

Mendelssohn's Bible with annotations (the *Bi'ur*), the most significant work of the Berlin Haskalah. Financially, the undertaking was almost disastrous for the publisher Teodor Toeplitz. However, such losses had been taken into account at the planning stage, because the main aim was the dissemination of knowledge of the Bible unaccompanied by corrupted and fanatical commentaries.[85] As in the case of the Berlin Haskalah, the catechisms were the basic means of popularizing a purer version of Judaism. The chief objective was the preservation of what, according to the maskilim, was authentic Judaism, the battle for which was waged as much against the degeneracy of fanaticism as against religious indifference and assimilation. Thus, the catechisms were intended to teach the 'main principles of our religion and to save it, if not from decline, at least from corruption'.[86] Admittedly, there was no consensus on what constituted the 'main principles of religion'. Some, like Antoni Eisenbaum, advocated fundamental transformation of rabbinical Judaism. The vast majority, however, defended traditional rabbinical forms of Judaism, with the Talmud and Oral Law as their guiding principles. In numerous reports for the Polish government, Tugendhold, Stern, and even Hoge (before his conversion) defended halakhic rulings and Jewish religious law, declaring them absolutely binding on the Jewish people.[87] Attempts by Stern, and later by Tugendhold, to implement traditional religious training with an emphasis on the Talmud and rabbinical supervision in the Warsaw Rabbinical School attested to a predominantly conservative attitude towards religious matters among the Polish maskilim.[88]

Historical awareness was to be supported by various stories and poems based on accounts of well-known figures from rabbinic literature. From a literary viewpoint, most such works had no value whatsoever. A number of characters who symbolized that aspect of Jewish religious tradition which the maskilim recognized as the depository of authentic Judaism, such as the great medieval rationalist Maimonides and the father of the Jewish Enlightenment Moses Mendelssohn, enjoyed considerable popularity. The popularization of the thoughts of Maimonides was the work of Buchner,[89] himself a fervent rationalist, while Mendelssohn found his greatest follower in the person of Tugendhold.[90] Few works were devoted to more recent history. Of those that were, the most popular was the Hebrew adaptation of Marcus Jost's works by Shalom Hakohen, which was widely distributed in the Kingdom of Poland, thanks to the efforts of Tugendhold.[91] Abraham Paprocki, the author of the first textbook in Poland on the history of the Jews, wrote of the significance of history to Jewish identity:

---

[85] See AGAD, KWK 699, pp. 391 ff. For more on the translation, see Bałaban, 'Polnische Übersetzungen und Editionen der Werke Moses Mendelssohn'.        [86] Homberg, *Ben yakir*, introd.

[87] See e.g. AGAD, CWW 1408, pp. 8–23; 1409, pp. 242–4, 262–4; 1411, pp. 358–61; 1420, pp. 104–13; 1448, pp. 396–9; 1675, pp. 2–14.

[88] Kandel, 'Abraham Stern a Szkoła Rabinów'; Sawicki, 'Szkoła Rabinów w Warszawie', 247–8, 261–74.        [89] See Buchner, *Hamoreh letsedakah*.

[90] See Mendelssohn, *Fedon*, here Mendelssohn's biography; Tugendhold, *Obrona Izraelitów*, introd.

[91] See Shalom Hakohen, *Koreh hadorot*, 2.

If, in general, every person should have a knowledge of history, it is indeed vital that the Israelites gain knowledge of the history of their forebears. In historical accounts, one not only finds examples of a specific exercise of one's obligations and social virtues, of loyalty and obedience to the monarch, but one also becomes convinced that this all flows from religious principles and that it is upon these that human happiness depends.[92]

## DOES LANGUAGE MAKE A MASKIL?

Although, as we have seen, the Polish maskilim praised and cultivated the Hebrew language, a major part of their literary output, including some of the texts defending Jewish identity, were actually written in Polish and not Hebrew. This radically differentiated the Polish Jewish Enlightenment from the maskilim in Galicia and the Russian empire and turned out to be of great consequence for Jewish historiography. Raphael Mahler claimed that the Duchy of Warsaw and the Congress Kingdom were areas in which the Jewish Enlightenment movement did not develop, because cultural, national, and religious assimilation took its place.[93] This was the most extreme expression of a thesis that divided the Jewish modernization movement into two factions, consisting of 'good maskilim and bad assimilationists'.[94] Some of the factors that Mahler cited as a deterrent to the Haskalah were the lack of a suitable metropolis to act as a natural maskilic centre; the unattractiveness of Polish aristocratic culture; antisemitism; the low intellectual level and incompetence of Polish officials of all ranks; the enmity shown towards Jews by the Polish state itself; the backwardness of the Polish economy and associated lack of a broadly based bourgeoisie (a natural ally of Enlightenment ideas); and a high percentage of conversions in circles that had traditionally supported the Haskalah. All this was taken to mean that the insignificant number of maskilim who remained in the Kingdom of Poland were not interested in Polish culture and gravitated towards the German language and culture. Those who were drawn to Polish language and culture, however, did so for their own benefit, and this was in itself 'a conspicuous indication of a tendency to extreme assimilation, which was a far cry from the aims of the Haskalah movement'.[95] Mahler named Jakub Tugendhold, Abraham Buchner, Ezechiel Hoge, Antoni Eisenbaum, and Abraham Paprocki as belonging to the ranks of the 'suspect assimilationists'.

The linguistic argument was of singular importance to Mahler, as an analysis of the writings of the 'bad assimilationists' and the 'good maskilim' led him to

---

[92] Paprocki, *Krótki rys dziejów ludu izraelskiego*, pp. i–ii. See Feiner, *Haskalah and History*, for the role of history in the maskilic conception of Jewish identity.

[93] Mahler, *Hasidism and the Jewish Enlightenment*, 203–12. See also id., *Divrei yemei yisra'el*, vi. 92–3; id., *History of Modern Jewry*, 363–8.

[94] For other prominent writings of this type, see Dubnow, *History of the Jews in Russia and Poland*, i. 384–9; Hirszhorn, *Historia Żydów w Polsce*.

[95] Mahler, *Hasidism and the Jewish Enlightenment*, 204.

conclude (rightly) that the ideological programmes of both groups were, in effect, identical. However, this challenged Mahler's thesis concerning the existence of two competing trends in Jewish modernization in Poland and forced him to search for a criterion that would ultimately prove their dissimilarity. Furthermore, Mahler not only accurately established that the declared programmes were identical; he also noted that the 'maskilic' camp, in his view, was so weak that it drew back from putting into action its own slogans, thereby leaving this sphere of activity to the 'assimilationists'. Thus, it was not the 'maskilim', but the 'assimilationists', who carried out the programme of the Haskalah, and therefore to deny them the honorific title 'maskilim' was all the more incomprehensible.[96] For Jacob Shatzky, another prominent historian of Polish Jewry, the situation was simple: the title 'maskil' was based purely on moral judgement. Tugendhold could not be a maskil because he was a 'careerist and cynical opportunist, who in his naivety had created an institution and in addition was a great coward and taker of bribes', and Eisenbaum was a two-faced collaborator with the tsarist secret police in Warsaw.[97] Mahler added a little sophistication by introducing the final criterion, which permitted clear classifications and a distinction between the 'assimilationists' and the 'true maskilim'. That criterion was language.

From the epithets Mahler attributed to 'assimilationists', it is clear that the language criterion was simply a poor pretext for his value judgements. Still, the very argument that love and popularization of the Hebrew language was one of the chief characteristics of the Haskalah programme is extremely significant, as historians of this movement were predominantly (although not exclusively) accustomed to treating literary works written in Hebrew as maskilic literature. In effect, the linguistic argument is a strong one because even a cursory glance at the literary works of the modernizing Polish Jews in the nineteenth century shows that a large number were written in Polish, although some did appear in Hebrew, Yiddish, German, and French. It is this very use of Polish that seems to have played a prominent part in the exclusion of these works from the research of modern historians of the Jewish Enlightenment—even among those historians who recognize and have helped to point out the traps inherent in modern historiography with regard to national provenance.

However, by making the language criterion an absolute, the historians of the Haskalah in Poland have themselves fallen into a certain trap. After all, the significance of Hebrew does not necessarily mean that it was the sole language of the maskilic 'literary republic of writers'. Israel Bartal has emphasized bilingualism as an identifying characteristic of east European maskilim.[98] In analysing the atti-

---

[96] Mahler, *Hasidism and the Jewish Enlightenment*, 229–33.

[97] Shatzky, 'Yidn un der Poylisher oyfshtand fun 1831', 362–4.

[98] Bartal, 'From Traditional Bilingualism to National Monolingualism'. It is also significant that the Hebrew language plays a rather minor role in Feiner's new definition of the Haskalah (see Feiner, 'Towards a Historical Definition of the Haskalah', 219).

tudes of Polish Jewish 'assimilationists' towards the Hebrew language, not only the relative dominance of Polish (compared to Russian maskilic texts in Russia, or even German maskilic texts in Galicia) needs to be taken into account, but also the place of Hebrew in the education programmes advocated by Tugendhold and other 'assimilationists', and their ideological attitude to the language.

First, although Polish-language texts predominated, the literary output in Hebrew of the authors mentioned above was relatively extensive and interesting. The appearance of both Polish and numerous Hebrew texts in the literary legacy of these writers is enough to prove their close relationship with the Haskalah. Abraham Buchner and Abraham Stern published the majority of their works in Hebrew, and only a limited number in Polish and German. Tugendhold, who specialized in translations and compilations, regularly published in both Polish and Hebrew not only textbooks, prayer books, and catechisms, but works with literary aspirations such as the biblical poem of the maskilic poet Shalom Hakohen, and *Beḥinat olam* by the medieval poet and philosopher Yedaiah ben Abraham Bedersi.[99] Polish translations of classical Hebrew works featured in the literary output of other Warsaw maskilim, such as Stern. Hebrew verses, usually of a commemorative nature, were written by Tugendhold and Stern, but also by less prominent figures such as the scribes of provincial communities Herman Saphirstein, Samuel Berson, and Loewy S. Feilchenfeld.[100] Some of the lesser Polish maskilim contributed to the Hebrew maskilic periodicals in Vienna;[101] others, including Tugendhold, planned to establish a similar Hebrew maskilic periodical in Warsaw.[102]

Stern, Tugendhold, Buchner, and their associates voiced their attachment to the Hebrew language on several occasions, emphasizing its beauty, and also its significance for the religious identity of Jews, for a necessary understanding of religious principles, and for the personal development of every Jew. For example, Buchner wrote that the importance of Hebrew lay in the fact that it was in this language that God created the world, conveyed his prophecies and commandments, and related the history of the Jewish people to the adherents of Judaism. Thus, a good knowledge of the language was necessary to maintain Jewish tradition, and also to develop intellectually, since a good knowledge of the rules of the language would engender rational thought in a person.[103] Henryk Liebkind preceded his

---

[99] Shalom Hakohen, *Pierwsza wskrzeszona myśl o istnieniu Boga*; Yedaiah ben Abraham Bedersi, *Beḥinot olam*.

[100] Tugendhold's poems in Werses, 'Hakitsah ami', 33; [Jakub Tugendhold], 'Zagadka', *Kalendarz dla Starozakonnych w Królestwie Polskim na Rok 5585* (1825), 32. References to many other poems can be found in Wierzbieniec (ed.), *Judaika polskie z XIX wieku*, nos. 1094–1191.

[101] See Wachstein, *Hebräische Publizistik in Wien*, 71, 81–2, 108, 188, 190, 212–13.

[102] Weinryb, 'Tsu der geshikhte fun der Poylish-Yidisher prese'.

[103] Buchner, *Otsar leshon hakodesh*, 4b–5b. Mahler claimed with reference to Buchner that 'There is no mention in his program of the Haskalah of slogans for the fostering of the knowledge of Hebrew and the Bible nor of the study of *languages and wisdom*'. See Mahler, *Hasidism and the Jewish Enlightenment*, 217.

Polish translation of prayers with a defence of the beauty and significance of the Hebrew language.[104] Equally typical was the 110-page review of the Hebrew dictionary by Luigi Chiarini, which Stern and Tugendhold had written in a defence of the purity of the language and of its future students.[105] Tugendhold also published a history of the Hebrew language and literature. In this, alongside some original ideas concerning the similarities between the Semitic and Slavonic languages, he extolled Hebrew as the mother of languages and the repository of divine revelations, praising its beauty and divine wisdom:

> There is no element that the Hebrew language lacks in order to render it the adornment of eloquence. On the contrary, it abounds in all manner of forms and elegant modes of syntax and it is when something does not belong to the earthly realm that this language is singularly rich in treasure, those particular adornments of inspiration by which it outclasses all other tongues.[106]

This piece concluded with praise for the maskilic revival of the Hebrew language and literature, and Tugendhold named Moses Mendelssohn, Moses Hayim Luzzatto, Naftali Herz Wessely, Solomon Dubno, Salomon Maimon, and others among the restorationists. Even more eloquent were the words of praise for the Hebrew language directed by Tugendhold to Feivel Schiffer:

> Would that all the Lord's people would know their sacred tongue, would that they should understand it perfectly, for the worth of every nation lies in its language and its writing. . . . The Hebrew language is our forefathers' legacy to us. Into it, all the unique treasures of our sacred faith are absorbed; all the bonds of brotherly love are forged by means of it; within it are stored the treasures of solace for our souls which are bowed down and our spirits which are sorrow-laden; and by it our exalted hope is engraved with the finger of God.[107]

Buchner and others wrote very similarly in praise of the Hebrew language.[108]

In summary, Hebrew maskilic writings were not a rarity among these (or many other) authors, and the attitude towards Hebrew was undoubtedly positive. If one were to evaluate them on the basis of their Hebrew-language output alone, they would undeniably be viewed as fully fledged maskilim, totally in step with other followers of the ideology in eastern Europe. However, this view is untenable since their Hebrew writings constituted only a part of their literary activity, accom-

---

[104] Liebkind, *Modlitwy dla Izraelitów*, pp. ii–iii.

[105] Stern and Tugendhold, *Recenzja dzieła pod tytulem: 'Słownik hebrajski'*, esp. introd.

[106] Tugendhold, 'Krótki rys historii języka i literatury hebrajskiej', 4–5. A shorter edition of this essay appears in Tugendhold's introduction to Shalom Hakohen, *Pierwsza wskrzeszona myśl o istnieniu Boga*, 5–20. Jakub Tugendhold's brother Wolf also wrote about the similarities between Slavonic and Semitic languages; see Stanislawski, *Tsar Nicholas I and the Jews*, 115.

[107] Mahler, *Hasidism and the Jewish Enlightenment*, 232. Naturally, Mahler commented on this quotation, stating: 'Even Tugendhold the assimilationist alluded to the connection between the Hebrew language and hopes for the future.'

[108] A[braham] Buchner, 'O Izraelitach z powodu artykułu pana Zonaras w N. 123 Pow. Sz. Kr.', *Gazeta Polska*, 148 (1830), 4; 149 (1830), 3–4.

panied, as it was, by a huge number of Polish publications. Why is this so? And does it negate their membership of the elite maskilic club, even though the ideology expressed in these texts was purely maskilic? In order to answer these questions, one must look for the reasons that led them to write in Polish. Without this context, we can understand very little.

## WHY IN POLISH? THE POLISH HASKALAH AND ITS POLISH CONTEXT

When asking why these authors wrote in Polish we must first take into account the differences between the Congress Kingdom and the territories of Galicia and the Russian empire, which provide us with a model of the Hebrew Haskalah. Taking into consideration the differing legal, national, social, economic, and cultural systems, both from the point of view of the Polish Christian majority and from the point of view of the Jewish minority, one would not expect the Haskalah in Poland to assume a similar form, particularly with regard to language, as its counterparts in Galicia, Ukraine, Belarus, or Lithuania. As Mark Baker rightly observed, multi-ethnic states and cultures (such as those in eastern and central Europe, like Austria and the western provinces of the Russian empire) tended to seek a universal language in order to create common ground in terms of intercultural communication and to allow the development of cultural partnerships that would override particular ethnic divisions. For the maskilim living in western Russia and Galicia, that language was, of course, Hebrew, and in some places German. However, wherever a mono-ethnic national culture predominated, modernization processes in Jewish society led to linguistic assimilation with the native population. Examples of such linguistic assimilation in mono-ethnic states were eighteenth-century Germany, the Netherlands, and England, and the Kingdom of Poland in the nineteenth century.[109]

The fact that the young Kingdom of Poland included in its structure a relatively broad cross-section of educated Jews and that integration also followed at other levels must have been a significant factor in the linguistic assimilation of the Polish maskilim. As mentioned, a great majority of the maskilim mentioned above were officials in various government institutions. This involvement of the most active maskilim with state institutions would certainly have induced them to use the language of the state and to participate in that country's public life. However, in the case of central Poland, the pressure was all the more intense in that the Duchy of Warsaw and the Congress Kingdom were states that were far more protective of their Polish national character than might have been expected, given the extent of their 'semi-independence'. This further distanced the Kingdom of Poland from Russia and Austria, which, for obvious reasons, rejected the idea of national state-

---

[109] Baker, 'The Reassessment of Haskala Ideology', 239.

hood and viewed the state essentially as a monarchy. Polish education and national symbols, and the official use of the Polish language, were promoted by the new government, which was acutely aware of the threat to the nation's existence as a consequence of the trauma of the partitions. Such programmes were closely compatible with the integrationist ideals of the Haskalah and encouraged the participation of the maskilim in Polish public life; although, of course, for Polish officials it was not the Jewish people who were the most important object of their politics.

Because Enlightenment traditions were very influential among the elite sections of the state, the Kingdom of Poland was later than other central and east European states to experience the conservative reaction so typical of the period following the Congress of Vienna. Unlike Russia, and particularly Galicia, the Polish official apparatus from the first years of the Kingdom's existence sought allies in the upper, educated echelons of Jewish society above all, and perceived the maskilim, or at least enlightened Jews, as their potential allies. In Galicia support for the maskilim in their struggle with hasidism was withdrawn as early as 1806; this occurred only in the 1840s in the Kingdom of Poland. Equally, at the local level, officials of various ranks more than once resorted to using the advice and services of the provincial Jewish intelligentsia, particularly in matters concerning the 'civilizing of the Jewish people' and thus matters of central significance to the Haskalah. The most intriguing Jewish consultant I know of, Dr M. Schönfeld, was adviser to the Voivodeship Commission in Kalisz in the 1810s and 1820s.[110] Functions of the same kind, those of an unofficial 'learned Jew', were performed on other occasions by well-known Warsaw maskilim. We may draw similar conclusions concerning the relatively close links between the 'learned Jews' and the official apparatus from the subscription lists of Polish-language works of the maskilim, particularly those of the very well-connected Jakub Tugendhold. Of 480 subscribers to the bilingual Polish–Hebrew edition of a poem by Shalom Hakohen, only 170 were Jews (these were mainly the Warsaw bourgeoisie, in addition to a number of well-known maskilim such as Adolf Bernhard, Pinkus Lipszyc of Opoczno, Mathias Rosen, and Abraham Stern), whereas 282 surnames were those of senior government officials. Several Catholic bishops appeared on the list, as well as several representatives of the Polish aristocracy, the well-known writer of children's literature Stanisław Jachowicz, the outstanding scholar and lexicographer Samuel Bogumił Linde, and so on. Similar ratios and names—including those of Viceroy Zajączek, Senator Novosiltzoff, and Julian Ursyn Niemcewicz, the eminent writer—could be found on subscription lists for the translation of Herz Homberg's *Ben yakir* (106

---

[110] See AGAD, Komisja Województwa Kaliskiego, 702, 704 (copy in CAHJP, HM2/6010–6012). See Kandel, 'Komitet Starozakonnych'; Eisenbach, *Emancypacja Żydów*, 193–6, 258–60, concerning the representation of the provincial Jewish intelligentsia on the Advisory Chamber of the Jewish Committee.

officials out of 169 subscribers), the translation of Moses Mendelssohn's *Phaedon* (153 officials out of 382 subscribers), and *Beḥinat olam* by Yedaiah ben Abraham Bedersi (69 officials out of 184 subscribers).[111] This appears to be evidence not only of the close personal links that Tugendhold had with senior state officials, and of their predisposition to the charitable works which such subscriptions were supposed to support, but also of a more generalized goodwill towards the Jewish 'civilizing' endeavours that gave rise to such initiatives.

These factors must have brought the Polish maskilim closer to the state, and above all to the Polish language. However, the ultimate incentive, which figured prominently as a reason for the high percentage of maskilic literary works written in Polish during the Congress Kingdom, was certainly the phenomenon of public, especially political, life. This forced maskilic writers to turn to polemic and apologetic forms of journalism, and hence those forms of expression that, even in the traditional Jewish world, used non-Jewish languages. As is well known, the Haskalah followed earlier Jewish literary practice whereby works for internal Jewish consumption were published either in Hebrew or in Yiddish, whereas apologetic and polemical works, whose potential readership was primarily Christian, were in a 'world' language, that is, one comprehensible to the society around them.[112] Samuel Joseph Finn, a well-known maskil from Vilna, praised Tugendhold for 'saving the glory of Israel', precisely because he defended Jews in the language of the wider society.[113] Hence, since the overwhelming majority of publications by the Polish maskilim were didactic, apologetic, or polemical, or simply political essays, their texts were inevitably written in a language comprehensible to the Polish polemicists. The appearance of Polish-language publications at successive stages of the debate on the 'Jewish question' to coincide with antisemitic statements and with government educational campaigns provides a model of the theory of the connection between the language of a publication and the nature of its social function. Thus, we can see that the first wave of publications appeared in 1818, during the sitting of the First Sejm of the Kingdom of Poland, when Jewish reforms were to be debated. An animated discussion on the social position of Jews in the Kingdom of Poland had been taking place since 1815, and it now gathered even greater momentum, with a series of pamphlets on the subject appearing. Two works by Polish maskilim appeared at this time: Jakub Tugendhold's *Jerobaal* and Pinkus Eliasz Lipszyc's *Prośba czyli usprawiedliwienie się ludu wyznania Starego Testamentu* (Petition or Self-Justification of the People of the Old Testament Faith) were a direct response to criticisms of Jewish society levelled by writers and com-

---

[111] Homberg, *Ben yakir*; Yedaiah ben Abraham Bedersi, *Beḥinot olam*; Shalom Hakohen, *Pierwsza wskrzeszona myśl o istnieniu Boga*; Mendelssohn, *Fedon*. The subscription lists are not numbered. There are a significantly lower number of names of Polish clerics to be found on the subscription list for Buchner, *Kwiaty wschodnie*.     [112] See Sorkin, *The Transformation of German Jewry*, 81–2.
[113] [Samuel Joseph Finn], *Hakarmel*, 1 (1861), 317–18.

mentators and particularly to the virulently anti-Jewish ideas put forward by the anonymous author (in fact Gerard M. Witowski) who advocated sending the Jewish people to the Tatarstan steppe. Inevitably, replies to these and other accusations by Polish antisemites were in the language in which the original accusations had been made.[114] Both of these Jewish declarations received an animated response and were commented on in almost all the publications covering the great debate, which lasted until 1822.[115]

More Polish-language publications of the maskilim in the Kingdom of Poland appeared in the first half of the 1820s, commissioned by government agents. They were predominantly textbooks and catechisms of the Jewish religion that were printed either simultaneously in Polish and Hebrew (more rarely in Yiddish) or completely in Polish. They included Jakub Tugendhold's *Siedem modlitw na siedem dni w tygodniu z hebrajskiego* (Seven Prayers, 1823), his translation of Herz Homberg's *Ben yakir* (1824), Ezechiel Hoge's *Nauka religii dla młodzieży Izraelitów* (Religious Studies for Israelite Youth, 1822), and *Modlitwy Izraelitów* (Prayers of the Israelites, 1822), as well as a dictionary and history textbook by Natan Rosenfeld.[116] The appearance of these and similar texts was, of course, directly related to the activities of the Polish educational authorities and their plans for the Jewish population, particularly the establishment of government elementary schools for Jewish children in Warsaw in 1820. The administration was actively involved in promoting and distributing these publications, campaigning for subscriptions, and sending out numerous free copies.[117] An important aspect of these government plans was its sponsorship of the Polish Jewish weekly *Dostrzegacz Nadwiślański* (*Der Beobachter an der Weichsel*), published by Antoni Eisenbaum simultaneously in Polish and in German in Hebrew transcription, and the establishment of the Warsaw Rabbinical School.

A series of polemical and apologetic works from the end of the 1820s was provoked by the activities and publications of Luigi Chiarini. The best-known of these reactions appeared in the review of Chiarini's dictionary published by Stern and Tugendhold mentioned above, in the press articles of these and other authors, and in the translation of *Vindiciae Judaeorum* by Manasseh ben Israel, which was accompanied by an extensive introduction by Tugendhold himself. This introduction addressed the accusation of Jewish use of Christian blood in religious

---

[114] Witowski, *Sposób na Żydów*; Tugendhold, *Jerobaał*; Lipszyc, *Prośba czyli Usprawiedliwienie.*

[115] The debate of 1818 has been described many times, the most comprehensive descriptions being those of Gelber, 'She'elat hayehudim bepolin bishenot 1815–1830'; Mahler, *Divrei yemei yisra'el*, v. 167–72, 292–3 (here there is important information on the authorship of some anonymous essays); and Eisenbach, *Emancypacja Żydów*, 165–223. Interesting, hitherto unknown, reactions to Tugendhold's booklet were also published, e.g. 'O Żydach w Polszcze', *Rozmaitości*, 1 (1818), 97–100; 'Wojna o Żydów', *Rozmaitości*, 1 (1818), 86–8.

[116] For a full list of the Jewish textbooks from the years 1817–64, see Shatzky, *Yidishe bildungspolitik*, 224–8.

[117] See AGAD, KWK 699, pp. 236–75, 378–477; APL, AmL 2415; 2158, pp. 45–70, 81–6, 153 ff.

ceremonies and it was a direct response to Chiarini's publication, which had resurrected that accusation.[118]

Texts from the time of the November Uprising of 1830–1 mainly contributed to the renewed debate surrounding the reform of the Jewish population and the Jews' patriotic obligations towards the Polish state; e.g. *Dumania Izraelity na warcie w pierwszych dniach grudnia 1830* (Reflections of an Israelite Mounting Guard in the First Days of December 1830) by the indefatigable Tugendhold and another polemic attributed to Jan Glücksberg, as well as a whole series of articles printed in the insurgent press.[119]

The collapse of the uprising in 1831 paralysed Polish Jewish public life and the journalism associated with it for many years. The next wave of publications by the Polish maskilim appeared only at the beginning of the 1840s, but it did not recapture the dynamic nature of the pre-uprising era. The next dynamic period came during the great 'Polish–Jewish fraternity' from 1861 to 1863, but that lies outside the framework of the history of the Haskalah in the Kingdom of Poland.

## CONCLUSIONS

In many ways, the Haskalah in the Kingdom of Poland was a movement similar to others in eastern Europe, but it also retained many unique features. In terms of its similarities, the programme of the Polish maskilim was fundamentally in sympathy with the ideological foundations of the entire east European Haskalah. Educational plans and the struggle with Jewish separatism occupied a particularly important place, but so too did the maintenance of Jewish identity through the cultivation of the Hebrew language, Jewish literature, and historical awareness. The maskilim from the Kingdom also formed part of the east European Haskalah, as they participated on equal terms with the maskilim from Galicia and the Pale of Settlement in the Haskalah 'republic of writers', a correspondence network linking Jewish supporters of modernization from all over the area.

However, along with the obvious similarities and connections, there were also relatively numerous distinguishing characteristics. These determined the separate path of development taken by the Haskalah in the Kingdom of Poland and meant that many of the ideas assumed a different form from those in Galicia and the Russian Pale of Settlement. Differences in the programme were attributable to the Kingdom's specific legal, social, cultural, and even economic context. The opportunity to participate in the government project for Jewish reform and the genuine

[118] The most comprehensive description of the writings and activities of Luigi Chiarini and of the debate surrounding him can be found in Raskin, *Ks. profesor Alojzy Ludwik Chiarini w Warszawie*. See also Ages, 'Luigi Chiarini'.

[119] Basic information on Jewish subjects in the Polish press of that period appears in Schiper, *Żydzi Królestwa Polskiego w dobie powstania listopadowego*. Important amendments can be found in Shatzky, 'Yidn un der Poylisher oyfshtand fun 1831'.

influence which many maskilim brought to bear on these projects meant that Jewish supporters of modernization in the Kingdom were particularly interested in the socio-political aspect of Haskalah ideology and in putting it into action. As a result, they paid considerable attention to the productivity programme and to changes in the socio-occupational structure of the Jewish population in Poland, while neglecting areas of theory or religion that occupied so much space in the literature of the Galician maskilim.

The most obvious distinguishing characteristic of the Polish Haskalah was the predominance of literature in the Polish language. Those maskilim who were influential in government institutions aiming at Jewish reform took the opportunity to become involved in the activities of those institutions, which, of course, meant that they had to use Polish. The Polish government pushed for the popularization of a national language and the maskilim willingly succumbed to these pressures, because their aim was fundamentally in agreement with the Haskalah ideal of rapprochement with the Christians, which would enable their educational projects to be carried out. The intense interest in the 'Jewish question' from the Polish public, and the subsequent waves of debate, which also attracted supporters of the Haskalah, influenced the popularity of the Polish language. At the same time, however, the Polish maskilim nurtured the Hebrew language and emphasized its importance to Jewish identity, and the number of Hebrew publications that appeared at the time is proof that the maskilim's stance on the Polish language was neither straightforward nor unconditional.

The unique features of the Haskalah in the Congress Kingdom that distinguished it from similar movements in other eastern European countries also influenced the significant difference in the attitudes of the Polish Haskalah to hasidism. The socio-political interests of the Polish maskilim meant that questions of a purely ideological and religious nature did not occupy their attention to any degree. Consequently, polemics of a religious nature with the hasidim—which had been so important to Mendel Lefin and his Galician students—were virtually unknown in central Poland. The social structure in the Kingdom differed from that of Galicia in that its links with the rabbinical elite were considerably weaker, and this played an important role. Whereas many of the Galician maskilim were rabbis (e.g. Solomon Leib Rapoport and Tsevi Hirsh Chajes) or people connected with rabbinical circles, there were few such connections in the Congress Kingdom and the state officials and leaders of the Haskalah had a low level of religious education. Therefore, it is not surprising that the traditional anti-hasidic rabbinical polemics that had made a decisive mark on the attitudes of the Galician maskilim and shaped many of their arguments had virtually no influence on the opinions of the modernizing Jews in the Congress Kingdom.

It also seems that the difference in attitudes towards the hasidim had more prosaic reasons, which may even have been of primary importance. In the first half of the nineteenth century, hasidism on central Polish soil was still not as strong as it was in Galicia, Podolia, and Volhynia. This is why the greatest opponent in the struggle to transform Jewish society as perceived by maskilim was the *kahal* and not the hasidim. Moreover, hasidism may even have been perceived as a potential ally in the fight with the unlimited powers of the rabbinate and the *kahal*. For the majority of the Polish maskilim who were active in the first half of the nineteenth century, it was, therefore, a marginal issue. Although the hasidim were never particularly liked, neither did they elicit an especially hostile reaction. It was only at the end of the 1830s that the hasidic movement began to take on significance in the eyes of the maskilim, but even then the demonization of the movement could not be considered commonplace. Contrary to widespread historiographical lore, hasidism in the constitutional period of the Kingdom of Poland was a peripheral problem and not always an unambiguously negative one. Yet its first defenders made their appearance in the 1820s. It would be difficult to overestimate the importance of this fact. A comparison of the attitudes and literature of the Polish maskilim with equivalent publications and activities of the maskilim of Galicia or the lands of the former Commonwealth that had been annexed by Russia provides evidence that the anti-hasidic obsession attributed by historiography to the entire east European Haskalah was in fact just one of a variety of attitudes towards the new movement on the part of the supporters of modernization in this region. As such, it leads us to a relativistic view of the Galician 'model of Haskalah'. Hostility towards hasidism and its growth was neither universal nor the only attitude among proponents of the Haskalah, and Jacob Samuel Byk, the Galician maskil who came out in its defence, was not an 'apostate', because he had ideological allies in the neighbouring Kingdom of Poland.

The history of these views and attitudes in the first half of the nineteenth century is examined in the following two chapters.

# THREE

# The Development of Anti-Hasidic Criticism among the Maskilim of the Congress Kingdom, 1815–1830

A TELLING silence of more than twenty years' duration had elapsed between Jacques Calmanson's criticism of the hasidic movement in 1796 and the first anti-hasidic comments made by the maskilim of the Kingdom of Poland. Under Prussian rule and during the period of the Duchy of Warsaw, not one voice was heard on the subject of hasidism from Jewish Enlightenment circles in central Poland, even though the Prussian and Austrian authorities had taken an interest in its existence in both the Sandomierz and Kraków voivodeships as well as in Mazovia as early as 1798 and 1799 respectively.[1] This could be partly explained by the fact that the Haskalah was just emerging and lacked strength at this stage, and that there was therefore little evidence of any Jewish Enlightenment literature in this period or of any activity on the part of the maskilim. Alternatively, this apparent silence could be attributable to chance, or to the fragmentary nature of the sources that have survived. However, the history of the development of the attitude of the maskilim towards the hasidim in the opening years of the Kingdom of Poland known as the constitutional period (1815–30) provides proof that this silence was not merely a matter of chance. This reticence is particularly striking when contrasted with the keen interest shown in the general situation of the Jews, which was evident in the Kingdom from its beginnings. From 1815 the 'Jewish question' was one of the main topics of public debate, preoccupying writers and statesmen throughout the whole period. The state's most prominent politicians—Stanisław Staszic, Julian Ursyn Niemcewicz, Stanisław Potocki, Józef Zajączek, Adam Jerzy Czartoryski, and Wincenty Krasiński—voiced their opinions on the status of the Jewish community and its reform. Representatives of the Jewish community, such as Pinkus Eliasz Lipszyc, Jakub Tugendhold, and Antoni Eisenbaum, also participated in the great debate, which lasted from 1818 to 1822. Moreover, other Polish maskilim were involved in a variety of activities aimed at 'civilizing' the Jewish people, such as attempting to establish new communal institutions representing Enlightenment values, or sending reports and memoranda to the state authorities. The most active of these maskilim included Eisenbaum, Tugendhold, Ezechiel

[1] AGAD, Sekretariat Stanu Królestwa Polskiego, 199, pp. 253–8, 462–3.

(Stanisław) Hoge, Abraham Stern, and Dr M. Schönfeld. The hasidic issue is either completely absent from their views, or features marginally. Only one Polish maskil, Abraham Stern, gave it prominence in his public activities.

## THE DEMONIZATION OF HASIDISM: FRIEDLÄNDER, RADOMIŃSKI, NIEMCEWICZ

Significantly, the first voices to speak out about hasidism came not from the local maskilim, but from Polish Christian writers and from the well-known leader of the radical wing of the Berlin Haskalah, David Friedländer (1750–1834).

Friedländer's treatise on the situation in the Jewish community in the Congress Kingdom was commissioned by the bishop of Kujawy, Franciszek Malczewski, and was one of many views in the ongoing dispute over the legal regulation of this situation.[2] In January 1816 Malczewski approached Friedländer on behalf of the State Council (Rada Stanu) with a request that he comment on the reform bill. Within two months Friedländer had presented his extensive report (published in 1819), in which he proposed far-reaching changes to the traditional educational and schooling system by the introduction of compulsory Polish lessons, compulsory changes to dress, and radical limitations on the autonomy of the *kahal*. He listed hasidism as one of the impediments to the educational development of Polish Jews. Friedländer based his observations on Salomon Maimon's autobiography (in other words, on obsolete data originating from outside the Congress Kingdom), on contributions by an unknown, and poorly informed, source, and possibly also on his own observations from Greater Poland (Wielkopolska). Like Maimon, Friedländer contrasted the old ascetic hasidim with the new anti-talmudic sect, describing the teachings of this sect as an incomprehensible mixture of kabbalistic, mystical, and Neoplatonic ideas devoid of any structure or system. According to Friedländer, the hasidim had no printed books, or even manuscripts, and respected no authority other than that of their chosen leaders, known as *magidim* or *ba'alei shem*. These leaders typically engaged in miracle-working, amulet-trading, communing with the dead in the afterworld, and achieving a state of mystical ecstasy. According to Friedländer, the tsadikim were loathed by non-hasidic Jews, although little in their lifestyle justified this hatred. What lay at its root was rather the fact that the mitnagedim perceived hasidism as a threat to their position, particularly given that the movement was gaining thousands of new supporters among women and, Friedländer also suggested, among non-Jews, although this last was a misinterpretation on his part of visits to tsadikim by Christians seeking cures or other miracles. According to Friedländer, the tsadikim were very generous and charitable. However, this generosity emanated not from their own pockets, but from the purses of their wealthy followers. The authorities had not paid any heed to the existence

---

[2] See Eisenbach, *Emancypacja Żydów*, 174–5.

of the hasidim thus far because there had been no major conflicts between them and the mitnagedim. In addition, no government had ever taken an interest in the internal problems of Jewish society. In reality, a close examination of this movement had become an issue of prime importance, according to Friedländer. In previous centuries, the hasidim had been encountered in many countries, but now only existed in the Kingdom. Even in Greater Poland, e.g. in Poznań and Leszno, where kabbalists could still be encountered among the rabbis and talmudists, the hasidic sect was non-existent, because mystical doctrines were not able to win wider support among the Jewish subjects of Prussia. Because of the abolition of 'Jewish streets' (i.e. the lifting of limits placed upon Jewish settlement) and owing to daily contacts with the non-Jewish community, the Jews of this province were ready for reform. Thus, hasidism constituted a serious political issue particularly affecting the Congress Kingdom.[3]

Friedländer's knowledge of hasidism was very superficial and often completely erroneous. Suffice it to say that, although sixty-six hasidic titles had appeared in a total of 161 editions by 1815, Friedländer wrote in 1816 that there had been no hasidic publications.[4] Also, like his assessment of the general situation of Polish Jewry, his assessment of hasidism lacked historical context, and the focus on contemporary political issues was one-sided. He used the existence of hasidism, which had been discussed in his report, as one of the arguments to support his conviction concerning the need to emancipate Jewish society in the Kingdom completely and at once. Despite their banal and superficial nature, Friedländer's observations on the hasidim became an important source in the following years, influencing the opinions of journalists participating in the discussion, and the opinions of writers from Polish Haskalah circles.

However, before the latter began to voice their opinions, two influential Polish writers, Jan Alojzy Radomiński and Julian Ursyn Niemcewicz, joined the debate. Both were closely connected with government circles in the Kingdom of Poland during the constitutional period.

Radomiński (1789–1864) had been a high-ranking government official for many years. During the period under discussion he had worked as head of the Department for Public Education in the Government Commission for Religious Denominations and Public Enlightenment, and as a political writer he was keenly interested in the situation of Jews in Poland. His erudite essay devoted to the reform of Jewish society was written in a positive tone, although he consistently emphasized that reform was necessary because of the low moral standards inherent in Jewish society.[5] Responsibility for this state of affairs lay both with Poles, who had enslaved this community, and with the elders of the Jewish communities, who had exploited their poor. The tone of Radomiński's diagnosis bore a resemblance to other Enlightenment reform projects, and drew particularly on Calmanson's works. In

---

[3]  Friedländer, *Über die Verbesserung der Israeliten im Königreich Pohlen*, 38–42.
[4]  See Dynner, 'Men of Silk', 348.          [5]  Radomiński, *Co wstrzymuje reformę Żydów*.

the section devoted to hasidism (see Appendix 3), he made liberal use of Calmanson's writings, often quoting him, as well as Friedländer and Israel Löbel. The latter's anti-hasidic lampoon, which was published in *Sulamith* in 1806, convinced Radomiński of the particular threat posed by the perverse and antisocial teachings of hasidism.[6] One might say that Radomiński's case serves as a warning against excessively meticulous use of all the available sources. Like Israel Löbel, he described the teachings of this 'reptilian tribe' in the following manner:

there exists the strictest possible prohibition on improving their minds in any way whatsoever; indeed, were they to emerge, they would be stifled and destroyed; the more a sinner sins, the nearer he draws to the deity; those who govern wield the power to absolve not only the grossest sins that have been committed, but also those sins that are about to be committed because of the sinner's predisposition and will; all sins can even be rewarded in certain circumstances, etc.[7]

Thus the hasidim were viewed as the epitome of perversity and the greatest threat to reform plans, because their exceptional zeal in spreading the new teachings allowed the sect to grow at an alarming rate. Although the hasidim comprised the worst aspect of Jewish society, their popularity was proof of the low moral state of the whole Jewish people, in that they were capable of accepting such disgraceful and antisocial teachings. Accordingly, even if Jews were to have been given their own country that very day, their moral decadence and antisocial attitude would not have augured well either for the improvement of their living conditions or for instant moral reform.

Radomiński's work provides us with a good example of the exaggerated interpretations made by Christian writers who had used maskilic and rabbinical sources criticizing hasidism. Accusations that appeared in Israel Löbel's works in a purely polemical function became, in Radomiński's work, objective proof of the depravity of the whole Jewish community, which was acknowledged even by Jews themselves. Hasidism, which was alluded to in passing by Calmanson and Friedländer as an example of extreme fanaticism, epitomized the demoralization of the whole population and constituted the greatest impediment to the attempted reforms, according to Radomiński. Interestingly, Radomiński, who was relatively well acquainted with Jewish problems, did not take up the accusations which Calmanson aimed against Frankism (in Calmanson's view, Frankism was the worst catastrophe to be visited on Polish Jews), because he was aware of its gradual disintegration. While less enquiring Polish writers and journalists still tended to frighten their readers with the legions of Jacob Frank's treacherous followers,[8]

---

[6] Israel Löbel, 'Glaubwürdige Nachricht', 308–33. For more information on the German pamphlet that formed the basis for the article, see Michael, 'R. yisra'el lebel vekuntreso hagermani'.

[7] App. 3; Radomiński, *Co wstrzymuje reformę Żydów*, 65.

[8] See e.g. 'O Żydach w Polszcze', *Rozmaitości* [suppl. to *Gazeta Korespondenta Krajowego i Zagranicznego*], 1 (1818), 89–91; Janowski, *O Żydach i judaizmie*. In his ignorance, Wincenty Krasiński believed that the two sects shared common origins: 'When the new converts gathered around Frank,

Radomiński, who had scrupulously read Israel Löbel's works, saw the same kind of threat in hasidism. However, he did not build his work around a criticism of this movement, just as the struggle with hasidism was not viewed in his work as the only, or even a particularly important, remedy for the situation of the Jewish people. Despite his catastrophic visions of hasidic depravity, Radomiński retained a sober perception of the extent of this phenomenon, and his anti-hasidic criticism constituted only one of his many comments on the state of Jewish society.

Although it was the most erudite of all publications concerning the Jewish debate of 1818–22, Radomiński's text did not enjoy great popularity, either among Christians or among Jewish participants in the debate, and his comments therefore had little impact. The only person to refer to his writings with approval on a number of occasions was one of the most prominent Polish writers and politicians of that time, Julian Ursyn Niemcewicz (1757–1841).

Niemcewicz's attitude to Jews and Judaism was ambivalent. Despite his indisputable interest in their tribulations and his declared goodwill, he was deeply distrustful and suspicious, and his criticism frequently acquired an openly anti-Jewish character, which included typically ethnic and religious prejudices.[9] This can be illustrated by his well-known antisemitic story *Year 3333*, his polemics concerning Jewish community boards, and his behaviour towards Abraham Stern, whom Niemcewicz praised in his writings as an enlightened Israelite and an example to be followed, but to whom he never spoke at the meetings of the Warsaw Society of the Friends of Learning, which both regularly attended.[10] His suspicious attitude towards the Jews was fuelled by the literature on the hasidim to which he had access. Therefore it is not surprising that he chose to portray the hasidim as the epitome of all evil and depravity in Jewish society. The romance *Lejbe i Sióra czyli Listy dwóch kochanków* (Leibe and Siora; or, the Letters of Two Lovers), the first Polish novel devoted to Jewish society, depicts the fight between a number of noble individuals and the ruthless, depraved, and unfeeling mass of Jews who are completely under the control of the hasidim.[11] Jankiel, their leader, is

Izrael Hirszowicz, the rabbi of Międzybóż, established in Poland a new sect which follows the teachings of Moses Maimonides, a Jew from Alexandria in Egypt. Frank was afraid of the influences of this new sect, so he established a society of which he declared himself the hereditary leader.' See 'O Żydach w Polsce: Tłumaczenie nowo wydanego w Warszawie w francuskim języku dziełka przez pewnego jenerała polskiego, posła na Sejm', *Rozmaitości*, 1 (1818), 31.

[9] For Niemcewicz's attitude towards Jews and his publications on this subject, see Borowy, 'Z historii równouprawnienia Żydów'; Brandstaetter, 'Moszkopolis'; Panas, *Pismo i rana*, 7–12; Janion, *Do Europy*, 101–25 (here there are interesting comments on Niemcewicz's vision of hasidism); Goldberg, 'Julian Ursyn Niemcewicz wobec polskich Żydów'; Piotrowski, 'Kwestia żydowska w twórczości Juliana Ursyna Niemcewicza'.

[10] Niemcewicz, *Lejbe i Sióra*, i. 122; Kieniewicz, 'Assimilated Jews in Nineteenth-Century Warsaw', 177.

[11] Although the novel has been already the subject of several literary analyses, the best study of the hasidic issue so far is the master's dissertation by Cecylia Wastrakówna, '*Lejbe i Sióra*'. See also Sienkiewicz, 'Między romansem a rozprawą: *Lejbe i Siora* Juliana Ursyna Niemcewicza'.

the embodiment not only of moral depravity and idiocy, but also of physical ugliness. He is comical rather than frightening in his ferocity and fanatical blindness. Failing to find a wife, he tries to create a child (in Polish *bachor*, 'brat') by using magic—an attempt which exposes his moral and intellectual poverty. In the novel the hasidim repeatedly assure one another that only the followers of Judaism have a real soul, that it is right to cheat Christians because they are not real people, and that anything lost by a Christian belongs to a Jew. They also conspire against Christians, and against disobedient Jews; they cheat and smuggle, drive the Polish peasant to drink, deprive him of his property through all manner of devices, and lead him into a physical and moral state of decline. Niemcewicz thus endowed the hasidim with all those traits that traditional anti-Jewish journalists and a large number of enlightened reformers deemed to be signs of the moral depravity of the entire Jewish population. For this writer, hasidism became the embodiment of Jewish evil. This might be considered a literary device, because hasidism never again performed such a function in any of Niemcewicz's works, although he did not avoid the Jewish theme. However, the demonization of hasidism was not an accident, but rather seemed to be the logical consequence of having read certain works, which the author himself named as the basic sources of his information about the Jewish world: those of Calmanson, Israel Löbel, Friedländer, and, above all, Radomiński, whom Niemcewicz referred to repeatedly and with approval.

Thus by 1822 hasidism already appeared in Polish literature as the demonic embodiment of all the worst traits of Judaism, and although it was many years before Polish writers or journalists used hasidism as the central motif in their depiction of the world of Polish Jews, hasidim appeared many times, even if only peripherally, as the most fanatical, dangerous, and blinkered branch of Judaism. An extreme example of this was a modified version of an accusation of ritual murder, according to which 'there is one sect, that of the hasidim, who . . . crave the blood of Christian children for their rituals'.[12] Admittedly, the allegations of ritual murder were unknown to Niemcewicz, but the general tenor of anti-hasidic criticism was such that it made an accusation like this possible. Anti-Jewish writers soon took advantage of opportunities such as this, with Luigi Chiarini leading the way.[13]

## THE POLISH HASKALAH IN THE DEBATE OF 1818–1822: ANTONI EISENBAUM

Jewish writers were not particularly impressed with the opinions voiced by the Polish writers Radomiński and Niemcewicz. It is not surprising, therefore, that Niemcewicz's novel, although it was in step with the general style of the Jewish debate of 1818–22, received a frosty reception from Jewish Enlightenment circles,

---

[12] Wodzicki, *Wspomnienia*, i. 204.
[13] Chiarini, *Théorie du Judaisme*, i. 355–7. See the next chapter for more on this.

**FIG. 2.** Antoni Eisenbaum (1791–1852)
Muzeum Narodowe w Warszawie, MNW (Gr. Pol.) 79374

possibly because a demonic portrayal of any followers of Judaism—even the hasidim—struck the Polish maskilim as inappropriate and hostile. With a view to discrediting Jakub Tugendhold in the eyes of the Jewish community board of Warsaw, Józef Chaim Halberstam accused him of supplying Niemcewicz with materials for his novel *Lejbe i Sióra*. Tugendhold, although he usually took pride in his contacts with influential Christians, deemed it necessary to deny this allegation.[14] Only Antoni Eisenbaum, who was the most radical of the Jewish reformers in the Kingdom of Poland, quoted extracts from Niewcewicz's romance; but it should be pointed out that these quotes were not about hasidism.

[14] AGAD, CWW 1723, pp. 220–4. See also Natan Glücksberg's opinion on the novel *Lejbe i Sióra* in Tatarzanka, 'Przyczynki do historii Żydów w Królestwie Kongresowym', 290.

**FIG. 3.** Simha Bunim of Przysucha (1765–1827)
Yitshak Alfasi, *Gur: Hameyased ba'al ḥidushei harim: Ḥayav, maḥashavato vetorato*
(Tel Aviv, 1954), p. 32, illus. 3

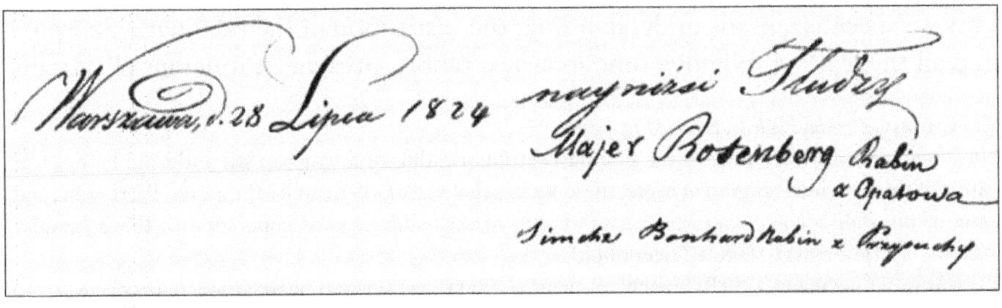

**FIG. 4.** The Polish signatures of tsadikim Me'ir of Opatów (Apta) (1760–1831) and
Simha Bunim of Przysucha on the petition to the Government Commission for
Religious Denominations and Public Enlightenment
AGAD, CWW 1871, p. 117

However, this frosty reception did not mean that the Polish maskilim approved of the hasidim. Quite the contrary: like Niemcewicz, Haskalah publications described hasidism as an extremely negative phenomenon. Yet Jewish writers differed markedly in their assessment of the scale of this movement, in terms of both its popularity and its resulting dangers. Of the three Jewish journalists whose works were published during the 1818–22 debate, Pinkus Eliasz Lipszyc did not even mention hasidism,[15] Tugendhold made one obscure critical allusion that may have referred to hasidism,[16] and it was only Eisenbaum who devoted a few sentences to this movement in his article about Polish rabbis. The hasidic motif in his work served as an illustration of the most wretched backwardness, superstition, and fanaticism. In the article, which criticized the ignorance of the rabbis, the tsadikim of Kozienice and Przysucha (probably Moses of Kozienice and Simha Bunim of Przysucha) served as an illustration of the use of devious medical practices. Likewise, the hasidic belief in metempsychosis was intended as an illustration of the superstitiousness of the class of rabbi kabbalists ('Balc [*sic*] szem', i.e. *ba'alei shem*) who were particularly popular with the followers of the sect of the zealous (*hasidim*). Hasidism was described here in just one sentence: 'the sect consists of the most superstitious Jews, with the most pernicious principles'. Further criticism only referred to the rabbis (and not necessarily the hasidic rabbis). In the entire account Moses of Kozienice and Simha Bunim of Przysucha (see Fig. 3), who were the most famous tsadikim in the Kingdom, served only as examples of the degenerate nature of the rabbinate but did not occasion any comments about the movement they led. In any case, Eisenbaum did not view the tsadikim as a particularly offensive example. As far as he was concerned, the embodiment of extreme fanaticism was Berek Boruchowicz, a non-hasidic kabbalist, *ba'al shem*, and deputy rabbi of Białystok, who had endeavoured in 1818 to drive an evil spirit, a dybbuk, out of a 12-year-old boy in Warsaw.[17] A series of Eisenbaum's articles was devoted to criticism of the three institutions most hated by the radical wing of the Haskalah: the Jewish community boards, the *heders*, and the rabbinate. Hasidism was not included in this list, and Eisenbaum mentioned it only in passing. This was because, in his understanding, the institution of the rabbinate incorporated all the leading religious functionaries: rabbis, preachers, itinerant charlatans

---

[15] Lipszyc, *Prośba czyli Usprawiedliwienie*.

[16] Tugendhold, *Jerobaal*, 6: 'these singularly stubborn idols of fanaticism stir and trouble the clear waters of this precious religion of mine, these waters that were ladled out by the sacred Patriarchs; and some of my Polish co-religionists are wandering in the wilderness of superstition'. For a broader analysis, see Wodziński, 'Jakub Tugendhold'.

[17] [Antoni Eisenbaum], 'O Rabinach', *Rozmaitości*, 5 (1822), 43–5. The passage on Boruchowicz is a verbatim reprint of the report sent by an anonymous maskil to the Warsaw police in 1818 (see AGAD, CWW 1424, pp. 1–10; copy in CAHJP, HM2/6863). The report has been published in Wodziński, 'Dybuk'. Considering that Eisenbaum was familiar with a confidential police report and that he quoted from it without mentioning the source, one might conclude that either he personally, or one of his closest associates, was the author of the report.

(*ba'alei shem*), and even the tsadikim.[18] Undoubtedly, this was an echo of Calmanson, who also regarded the 'leaders of hasidism' as yet another incarnation of the rabbis' power.

Eisenbaum devoted even less attention to hasidism in the first periodical for Polish Jews, *Dostrzegacz Nadwiślański* (*Der Beobachter an der Weichsel*), which he edited and which was published thanks to government subsidies in 1823–4. Articles about Jewish customs and sects mentioned the ancient hasidim, Essenes, Pharisees, or Karaites, contemporary groups of itinerant preachers, moralizers, and even itinerant penitents, but they failed to mention the new Beshtian hasidism.[19]

This was typical not only of Eisenbaum's writings, but also of almost all the statements by the Polish maskilim during the constitutional period. In their criticism of social and religious relations in Jewish society, the maskilim directed their accusations against the Jewish community boards, and sometimes against the rabbinate or a burial society, but if the hasidic movement happened to be mentioned, criticism of it was completely secondary to the struggle with the traditional institutions of the Jewish community. Calmanson's works were particularly important in this context. His treatise on the reform of the Jewish people was frequently read and quoted from, so this author's attitude to hasidism (which he viewed as a hostile, but peripheral, force) must also have been a significant source of inspiration for the Polish maskilim. It is interesting that, on the basis of sources similar to those used by Niemcewicz (Friedländer, Maimon, Calmanson, and the contributors to *Hame'asef*), Eisenbaum came to create an extremely different picture, in which criticism was focused on the Jewish communities and the rabbinate, and hasidism was a completely marginal issue.

## THE KALISZ VOIVODESHIP: PRELIMINARY INQUIRIES AND REPORTS

Two reports written for the Voivodeship Commission in Kalisz in 1820 provide an excellent example of a similarly reticent attitude towards hasidism. The Kalisz voivodeship authorities availed themselves of the services and opinions of Jewish modernizing circles, and invited them to co-operate with them in their attempts to 'civilize' the Jewish population. The Commission's president particularly valued Dr M. Schönfeld, the local provincial surgeon, a member of the Mineralogical Society in Jena, a contributor to the German Jewish periodical *Sulamith*, the author of a number of educational projects, and an active maskil. The president of the

---

[18] Z. [Antoni Eisenbaum], 'Zniesienie Kahałów (Artykuł nadesłany)', *Rozmaitości*, 5 (1822), 10–12; id., 'O wychowaniu młodzieży żydowskiej', *Rozmaitości*, 5 (1822), 27–34; id., 'O Rabinach', *Rozmaitości*, 5 (1822), 37–46.

[19] [Antoni Eisenbaum], 'O sektach żydowskich które dawniej istniały i po części jeszcze istnieją', *Dostrzegacz Nadwiślański*, 2 (1824), 53–6; 2 (1824), 61–4; id., 'Niektóre wiadomości o nowszych obyczajach Izraelitów', *Dostrzegacz Nadwiślański*, 2 (1824), 213–16.

Voivodeship Commission consulted him on private Jewish prayer houses, school reforms, and the scope of rabbinical power, to name but a few topics.[20] Schönfeld's views and arguments concerning religious issues proved, however, that he was neither particularly knowledgeable (quite the opposite, in fact) nor impartial with regard to the issues in question. His was one of the first reports on hasidism.

In May 1820 the elders of the Jewish community in Łask complained to the Voivodeship Commission about the new sect that had emerged during the war (i.e. the Napoleonic wars, 1806–13), whose members prayed in a separate prayer hall and did not attend the synagogue (see Appendix 4).[21] The elders of the *kahal* requested that the Commission forbid the sect to organize separate services and argued that (*a*) Judaism forbade the organizing of services outside the synagogue, (*b*) by not attending the synagogue, sect members were unable to find out about new government directives announced there, and (*c*) by failing to attend the synagogue prayers, they reduced the income of Jewish communities from the collection boxes and readings of the Torah. The Voivodeship Commission asked for Schönfeld's opinion on 'whether the Mosaic faith allows Israelites to establish private prayer sites for holding services other than in the main synagogue'. In a lengthy report Schönfeld refuted, one by one, all the arguments of the elders of the Jewish community, claiming that (*a*) Jews could hold services not only in the synagogue, but in any other place, as well as in any language, (*b*) government directives could be announced just as well in private locations as in the main synagogue, (*c*) Jews should not be condemned for wanting to break free from the financial oppression and exploitation of the Jewish community's oligarchy (see Appendix 5).[22] According to Schönfeld, the elders of the Jewish community were, after all, interested in nothing other than maintaining financial control over the Jewish community, while the leaders of the Jewish community 'made known their intention of making the faithful pay money; that is, contributions'. By the same token, he called attention to their other alleged failings, their deceitfulness, and their falsification of the true and pure Jewish faith. The establishment of the hasidic *shtiblekh* thus provided Schönfeld with an opportunity to criticize the management and customs of the Jewish community boards while ignoring hasidism altogether. It is not known whether he deliberately ignored the hasidic issue, or whether, in fact, he did not understand that this was the main thrust of the complaint of the Jewish community board in Łask. In any case, the establishment of a prayer hall by the new sect did not prompt any anti-hasidic reaction in Schönfeld, so the polemic with hasidism cannot have been of any major significance to him.

The Voivodeship Commission sent Schönfeld's report, with a set of docu-

[20]  See AGAD, KWK 702 (copy in CAHJP, HM2/6012). Some information on Schönfeld appears in Bero, 'Z dziejów szkolnictwa żydowskiego w Królestwie Kongresowym', 79; Shatzky, *Yidishe bildungs-politik*, 23; Sawicki, 'Szkoła Rabinów w Warszawie', 245.

[21]  AGAD, CWW 1555, pp. 6–8.

[22]  Ibid. 10–16; AGAD, KWK 702, pp. 5–12 (copy in CAHJP, HM2/6012).

ments, to the Government Commission for Religious Denominations and Public Enlightenment, requesting a decision. The Government Commission sought counsel in this issue with Ezechiel Hoge, who was a well-known maskil and the author of numerous memoranda submitted to the authorities of the Kingdom of Poland and who, in his youth, had been a supporter of the tsadik of Lublin, Jacob Isaac Horowitz.[23] As a former hasid, Hoge immediately spotted the hasidic context of the conflict, pinpointed errors in the religious sources quoted by Schönfeld, and rejected his conclusions, noting that

If Doctor M. Schönfeld has reasons to complain about Jewish supremacy in the town of Łask, he could be of service if he were to try to reduce their influence in a different way . . . not by replacing a mistake with an error. If I am correct, the conflicts between the Jews in this town originated with the followers of the so-called sect of hasidim, who wish to differ from common Jews, and who are known to be the most dangerous of the Jews in this country.[24]

The final decision of the Government Commission concerning this issue is not known. However, Dr Schönfeld's opinion with regard to the hasidic threat did not change, even after Hoge's report had been submitted. There was ample opportunity to demonstrate this in November of the same year.

At that time a fierce battle was being fought in the Jewish community of Częstochowa between a group of hasidim and the Jewish community over the right to use the *mikveh*, or ritual baths. Anti-hasidic opponents claimed that the baths were to be used solely by women and that the hasidic attempts to use them were contrary to religious law and decency. The hasidim attempted to prove that the baths belonged to the whole Jewish community, and that therefore everybody was entitled to use them. They complained that by being prevented from entering the baths, they were forced to bathe in the river Warta, which made them susceptible to frequent diseases in the autumn. (The whole affair took place in October and November.)[25] *Kahal* members, alarmed by their opponents' endeavours to involve the mayor in the issue, had the *mikveh* closed completely (which ultimately was as inconvenient for the hasidim as it was for their opponents). The crowd that gathered at the baths used clubs to drive out the hasidim and the policemen who escorted them. As a result, the mayor of Częstochowa and the Voivodeship Commission instituted an inquiry.[26] During the investigation the Voivodeship Commission approached

---

[23] For information on Hoge and his hasidic background, see the interesting, although not always reliable, essay by Frenk, 'Yekhezkel Hoge'. An English summary appears in Lask Abrahams, 'Stanislaus Hoga—Apostate and Penitent'. [24] AGAD, CWW 1555, pp. 17–20.

[25] Traditionally, ablution in the ritual bath (*mikveh*) is obligatory for all women after menstruation and for proselytes during the ceremony of conversion, as well as for ritually purifying dishes bought from non-Jews. The hasidim, however, following the customs of other mystical groups, made it obligatory for men preceding the sabbath and religious festivals. For more on hasidic customs of using the *mikveh*, see Wertheim, *Law and Custom in Hasidism*, 215–16.

[26] AGAD, KWK 702, pp. 4–45, 50–86; CWW 1542, pp. 4–12.

Schönfeld for his opinion concerning the hasidim and the possibility that they had a right to use the *mikveh*. Soon after, Schönfeld submitted a fourteen-page report, in which he presented the history and practices of hasidism as well as his views concerning ablutions (see Appendix 6).[27] A large part of the report quoted Friedländer verbatim. Schönfeld also used Israel Löbel's German article (printed in *Sulamith*, to which Schönfeld contributed). However, Schönfeld mistakenly referred to the author of the article, Israel Löbel, as the founder of hasidism, when in fact it was actually Israel ben Eliezer. Schönfeld compared the founder of hasidism to the infamous fraudster Alessandro Cagliostro. The motif is also present in Joseph Perl's well-known anti-hasidic treatise *Uiber das Wesen der Sekte Chassidim*, but Schönfeld is highly unlikely to have used this source. The comparison of the Besht with Cagliostro may have been commonly used in maskilic circles at that time.[28] Like Friedländer, Schönfeld asserted that hasidic teaching was an incomprehensible mixture of kabbalah, mysticism, and Neoplatonism, that the hasidim did not have their own books, that their manuscripts had possibly been concealed, and that they could freely choose their rabbis, who were called *magid* or *ba'al shem* and who typically engaged in miracle-working, amulet-trading, and communing with the dead. Upon the death of a leader, his favourite disciple would take over his position. The hasidim were hated by other Jews, despite a lack of any moral grounds for this hatred, because their influence was envied. Rounding off this general description, Schönfeld added that 'No hasidim can be found outside the Kingdom of Poland or Austrian and Russian Poland'. The report thus presented hasidism in a critical light, yet its tone was neutral and it was inconclusive.

The section devoted to the Częstochowa baths showed a different angle. There, Schönfeld clearly turned against the Jewish community (as a result of which he assumed a pro-hasidic stance), and acknowledged that the purification regulations were part of the religious laws of Judaism. Thus, if the hasidim wished to observe them strictly, purification could be recognized as an act that formed part of their rituals. The followers of hasidism had this right—all the more so because they observed ritual laws more closely than other Polish Jews, and their observation of purification regulations was even deserving of praise. Furthermore, there was nothing indecent in the use of the same baths by men and women, as each group could be allocated its own hours, so that the two groups would not encounter one another in the *mikveh*.

As was the case with Łask, the author of this report saw an adversary only in the traditional leadership of the Jewish community, but he remained neutral in relation to hasidism, finding there an ally in the fight with the all-embracing power of the Jewish communities. Evidently, in Schönfeld's opinion, hasidism did not constitute a major threat to the reform of the Jewish people, and the movement could be even useful as 'our enemy's enemy'.

---

[27] AGAD, KWK 702, pp. 73–86.          [28] Perl, *Uiber das Wesen der Sekte Chassidim*, 61.

The views held by Dr Schönfeld were not unusual. Apart from Eisenbaum, other Polish maskilim also shared them. For instance, Schönfeld's associate in Kalisz, Jakub Bursztyński (1790–1852), aimed all his accusations against the rabbinate, Jewish community boards, and traditional Judaism, and failed to mention hasidism at all in a campaign in 1821 to establish a private, secular school for Jews in this city.[29] Similarly, Ezechiel Hoge, despite his negative attitude towards hasidism in the opinion quoted above, did not write about hasidism in any of the other numerous memoranda, opinions, and petitions which he submitted to the authorities of the Kingdom of Poland, although he touched upon almost all the main subjects which arose in the debate on the reform of the Jewish people.[30] He criticized their practice of early marriage, their lack of productivity, the monopoly of power held by the Jewish community's elders, and rabbinical malpractices. In other words, he criticized those aspects that were usually attacked by the east European maskilim. However, hasidism was not mentioned here. In addition, Hoge even wrote respectfully of two students of kabbalah in a work published after his conversion, 'who understood this teaching and were interested in it alone', which was a clear allusion to tsadikim he knew.[31]

A similar stance in the conflict with hasidism was taken in 1823 by the Jewish community board of Warsaw and the Censorship Committee for Hebrew Books. Both institutions were controlled at that time by Haskalah supporters. In October 1823 the Voivodeship Commission of Kalisz addressed a letter to the Government Commission for Religious Denominations which stated that some Jewish community boards (apparently, those of Łask and Złoczew) had complained about co-believers who prayed in private prayer halls instead of attending the public synagogue, thereby reducing the income of Jewish communities. Referring to an old custom, the Jewish community boards requested permission to collect on Rosh Hashanah (the New Year) and Yom Kippur (the Day of Atonement) such taxes as would force co-believers to attend services in the synagogue of the Jewish community, and not in clandestine *shtiblekh*. The Voivodeship Commission, having no directives in this matter, asked the Government Commission to decide, and this commission turned the matter over to the Jewish community board of Warsaw and the Censorship Committee. The opinion of the first institution was signed by the Jewish community board members Józef Chaim Halberstam and Natan Glücksberg, as well as by the secretary of the Jewish community board, Jakub Tugendhold. The latter two were Haskalah activists, while Halberstam vacillated between the mitnagedim's camp and the conservative Haskalah. They unanimously claimed that, according to Jewish law each Jew had the right to pray anywhere, provided

---

[29] AGAD, KWK 699, pp. 182 ff.

[30] See e.g. AGAD, Sekretariat Stanu Królestwa Polskiego, 199, pp. 428–32; Protokoły Rady Administracyjnej Królestwa Polskiego, vol. xii. p. 88; CWW 1409, p. 44; 1410, pp. 4–5; 1411, pp. 16–19; 1416, pp. 37–43; 1431, pp. 79, 150–1; 1663, pp. 114–15; 1723, pp. 28–35; 1780, pp. 6–7.

[31] Hoge, *Tu Chazy*, 101.

that a *minyan* (a group of ten men necessary for the conduct of public prayer) gathered. Since all Jews paid synagogue contributions, irrespective of whether they came to the synagogue or prayed at home, there was no need to force anybody to attend the synagogue. Moreover, as the letter of the Voivodeship Commission mentioned voluntary contributions, all the less reason to resort to any form of pressure. The following week a similar opinion was handed down by the Censorship Committee.[32]

The question of the monopoly of Jewish communities on the place of prayer was one that elicited an ambivalent response from the maskilim, because granting Jewish community boards the right to license prayer sites could make it difficult not only for the hasidim but also for the maskilim to establish such places of prayer. Although they had no reason for fear in Warsaw (where they controlled the Jewish community board), the threat was real in many other places, such as Łask, Złoczew, Łódź, and even Kalisz.[33] Nevertheless, the way that the hasidic context of the whole issue was ignored is striking here, and marks a distinct departure from the contemporary anti-hasidic attitudes of the maskilim in Galicia (who at that time were publishing denunciations of hasidism) and of later supporters of the Haskalah in the Kingdom. Clearly, the Polish maskilim still did not see the hasidic movement as a threat serious enough for them to change their policy against Jewish community leaders and turn their criticism against the hasidic *shtiblekh*.

## THE GOVERNMENT INQUIRIES OF 1818–1824 AND ABRAHAM STERN'S ROLE

The first maskil to engage in the fight with the hasidim in the Kingdom of Poland was Abraham Jakub Stern (see Fig. 5), a conservative maskil, mathematician, and inventor widely respected both by Christians and by all Jewish circles.[34] Stern was not only the first critic of hasidism in the Kingdom to make a clear accusation against this movement, but also the first and, for a long time the only, Polish maskil for whom the fight with hasidism constituted one of the main inspirations for his public activities.

In 1818 the State Council of the Kingdom of Poland decided to allow the establishment of the Rabbinical School. The educational authorities requested the bishop of Płock, Senator Adam Prażmowski, and Abraham Stern, who was highly respected in government circles, to prepare projects for this school. In government circles Stern was envisaged as the future head of the school. In his project he opposed the introduction of secular learning in the seminary, advocated that its traditional character be maintained, and emphasized the need to appoint trust-

---

[32] AGAD, CWW 1433, pp. 216–19, 260–2.

[33] AGAD, CWW 1712, pp. 37–73 (copy in CAHJP, HM2/6874).

[34] The one critical, but tendentious, biography of Stern can be found in Shatzky, 'Avraham Ya'akov Stern'.

FIG. 5. Abraham Jakub Stern (1762–1842)
National and University Library in Jerusalem, Shvadron Collection

worthy teachers of impeccable character. Thus, according to Stern, the Rabbinical School was to be a modern, reformed yeshiva (talmudic academy), modelled on similar institutions in Germany. In the project he gave prominence to the school's basic mission—that of fighting off hasidic influences. Describing the principal's duties, he wrote that 'the head will be obliged to ensure that no mystical teaching, which is called kabbalah in Hebrew, takes place, either in the Central School or on Polish soil in general, either in schools or in private homes. The head will also be obliged to strive to have all mystical books removed from the libraries of all Jewish communities.'[35] Thus, by managing the Rabbinical School, Stern endeavoured to

[35] Sawicki, 'Szkoła Rabinów w Warszawie', 248. See also AGAD, I Rada Stanu Królestwa Polskiego, 436, pp. 852–66; Lewin, 'Beit hasefer lerabanim bevarsha'.

gain influence in the country's whole educational process, as well as control over all Jewish libraries, both public and private, thereby counterbalancing the influence of any threatening mystical movements, and particularly hasidism. The connection with Lefin's ideas is clear here. In the 1791 project to reform Polish Jewry, Lefin had suggested that government-appointed regional rabbis be granted similar rights and considered censorship a useful tool in the fight with hasidism.

In 1818 Stern also had the opportunity to speak against hasidism for the second time, this time in connection with 'the case of the hasidim' (*sprawa chasydymów*), a long-standing government inquiry into the existence and possible legality of this movement. It commenced on 1 June 1818, when the Voivodeship Commission of Płock informed the government that the local police had closed a hasidic prayer hall. The Minister for Religious Denominations and Public Enlightenment, Stanisław K. Potocki, requested further details concerning the new sect, to which the Voivodeship Commission replied that the sect seemed to be dangerous and deserving of the government's attention, and that the 'men of silk' (i.e. the hasidim) 'differ in their practices from other Jews and they mutually loathe one another, and they are so numerous that in nearly all of the towns in this voivodeship, they have separate prayer houses'.[36] The Government Commission, alarmed by these accounts from Płock, decided to inspect the new phenomenon more closely. To these ends, they called upon Ezechiel Hoge and Abraham Stern, who were then the most highly esteemed Jewish advisers, 'to inform us how the men of silk sect differs from others and whether its members do not or cannot come to common prayers in synagogues'.[37] Unfortunately, Hoge's opinion has not been preserved, but one can inevitably conclude that it did not favour the hasidim.[38] Stern presented his report on 29 September 1818. For many years this lengthy text has been the best, and the most critical, depiction of hasidism written in Polish Haskalah circles (see Appendix 2).[39]

Stern began by explaining the terminology, introducing the etymology of the word *hasid*, and he went on to tell the story of 'an Israelite from Wallachia called Israel', who assumed the title of *ba'al shem*, that is, 'one who works kabbalistic wonders by calling on the various names of God and the angels'. The Besht was portrayed by Stern as a fraud, who lied to people about his alleged miracles and communing with God in order to gain influence, and, for better effect, introduced

---

[36] AGAD, CWW 1869, p. 7. See Wodziński, 'Rząd Królestwa Polskiego wobec chasydyzmu', for a more thorough description of the case in Płock in 1818.          [37] Ibid. 6.

[38] See AGAD, CWW 1871, p. 130. This report was described as 'Hoge's word against the hasidim's'.

[39] A copy of this report can be found in AGAD, CWW 1871, pp. 43–6; other copies also appear in AGAD, KRSW 6634, fos. 239–42 (copy in CAHJP, HM3635); KWK 702, pp. 137–41 (copy in CAHJP, HM2/6012). Mahler published an anonymous copy of the report found in AGAD, KRSW 6634, fos. 239–42 (Mahler, *Hahasidut vehahaskalah*, 477–81), and a comprehensive English summary (Mahler, *Hasidism and the Jewish Enlightenment*, 318–21), but he attributed its authorship to Abraham Buchner, claiming that Stern could not be so vicious. See Mahler, *Hahasidut vehahaskalah*, 374–6; id., *Hasidism and the Jewish Enlightenment*, 321–2.

changes into the ritual as well as various inappropriate forms of behaviour and ecstatic practices, such as handclapping, shouting, or swaying during prayer. Although the alleged miracle-workers attracted the uneducated, the majority of Jews despised the new sect, and the name 'hasid' had acquired an ironic connotation. Sometimes the hasidim were also called 'men of silk' (*kitajowcy*), from the word *kitaj*, the pure silk fabric used by followers of the Besht so that they could avoid contact with fabric consisting of a mixture of wool and linen fibres (*sha'atnez*), which was forbidden by the Jewish religion. After the Besht's death his students had popularized the teachings of hasidism, in which a prominent place was given to the *pidyon*, a donation customarily paid to the tsadikim by supplicants. The castigation of the *pidyonot* and the financial exploitation of naive people by hasidic 'ringleaders' (*herszty*) was probably the most recurrent motif in Stern's report. According to him, hasidism spread mainly because it encouraged superstitions, it had an increasing network of emissaries, and it took advantage of the naive, of women, young people, and the wealthy. He maintained that, when they arrived in a town, the hasidim would try to open their own prayer hall there, so that they could more easily entice the young people with their excesses and indecent behaviour. Next they would win over the women and the wealthy, who from then on would approach the tsadik with all their religious, family, or financial problems. Using their contrived system of trickery, the hasidim would coax naive people into believing in their leaders' infallibility. Further on, Stern described the custom of the third sabbath meal, pilgrimages to the more influential tsadikim, and the aversion to secular teaching. The Jewish people in Poland despised hasidim, but had no means at their disposal to oppose their expansion. This is why, in the conclusion, Stern appealed to the Government Commission to forbid the hasidim to establish separate prayer halls, and to force them to attend services in the common synagogue.

Stern's report was the first text by a Polish maskil to be based on a good knowledge of rabbinical anti-hasidic polemics and to quote a whole spectrum of accusations from mitnagdic writings aimed against the new movement. Stern seems to have used mainly Hebrew texts written by Israel Löbel and David of Maków, that is, the classic writings of the mitnagedim, although influences from early maskilic works are also noticeable. The particularly strong emphasis placed on the economic exploitation in hasidic communities points to Calmanson as its source. However, Stern placed this economic criticism of hasidism against the broader context of moral and religious arguments, and various fragments of the text—particularly those concerning hasidic morality—are based on his own observations. All of this results in a completely black picture of hasidism, in which he did not see a single virtue. Stern could not match Joseph Perl in his knowledge of the hasidim, but he resembled him in his extremely negative attitude to this movement and his unequivocal condemnation of it.

On the basis of Stern's report, the Government Commission (or, more precisely, Staszic in lieu of Potocki) decided that gathering for prayer in private homes

contravened police laws and could no longer be tolerated. This finding was sent to
the Voivodeship Commission. However, the decision was not long-standing; soon
after, the viceroy, General Józef Zajączek, became involved in the issue and
requested a new report on the case. On 24 November 1818, at the meeting of the
Administrative Council, he acquainted himself with Staszic's report and, quoting
'freedom and independence for all denominations', he acknowledged the right of
the hasidim to gather for prayer separately.

Thus ended the first act of 'the case of the hasidim', but the effects of Stern's
report endured. An inquiry into this affair was revived on 20 September 1823 after
a denunciation by the head of Parczew's police, Colonel Dulfus, concerning what
he believed to be an illegal gathering of hasidim for prayer in a private home.[40]
Dulfus sent the report to Zajączek, and the latter ordered an inquiry into the matter. Among the numerous reports, at the beginning of 1824 a letter came from the
Censorship Committee, signed by Adam Chmielewski, Józef Chaim Halberstam,
and Abraham Stern. The members of the Committee (with only Jakub Tugendhold's signature missing) informed the Government Commission that a similar
inquiry had already been conducted in 1818 and that Stern had prepared an appropriate report, in which 'all that concerns this sect has been explained reliably and
precisely, without omitting even the smallest details'. Consequently, they decided
to present the government with the report of 1818, which they attached to their
letter.[41] However, the Committee, or, as it turned out later, Stern himself, did not
stop at that. In the covering letter attached to the report, it explained the difference
between the name given to a member of the 'society' in the singular (*chasid, chusyt*)
and in the plural (*chasidim, chusyci*, or *chasydymy*), which had hampered the government's identification of the hasidim, and it then contrasted the mitnagedim with
the hasidim, claiming that the latter were not a sect, and therefore they should not
be legitimized as a separate denomination:

Members of this sect, or, rather, society, do not differ in any way from the other adherents
of the Jewish religion and they have no separate religious rules to govern them, nor can they
have them. Those who believe the Chusites, or hasidim, to be a separate branch of the
Jewish faith, governed by special rules and religious laws in the same way that the Christian
religion has separate branches, are in error. It is simply a free gathering under the guise of
piety, which leads to idleness, delusion, deceit, enticement of the gullible and the less sens-
ible and to the rejection of all that is decent and moral, likewise to the ruin of all the praiseworthy aims of the government in relation to the education of the young; each leader is
governed in this regard according to his fancy. The members of this society come and go at
any time, according to their visions, as they wish, without any previous religious ceremony.
A father can belong to the society while his children do not, or vice versa. What results from
this is that all obstacles to this gathering at least do not impair any branch of the religion,
which would have to receive government protection.[42]

[40] See Wodziński, 'Sprawa chasydymów'; Mahler, *Hasidism and the Jewish Enlightenment*, 315–32.
The essential collection of sources for this case appears in AGAD, CWW 1871, pp. 1–218.
[41] AGAD, CWW 1871, pp. 43–6.                                                    [42] Ibid. 41–2.

Further on Stern informed the government that the new sect had influence over almost all voivodeships in the Kingdom of Poland and that this menacing 'society' was gradually expanding. Finally, he called for immediate action to be taken. He advised against the use of drastic measures, instead advocating the introduction of a strict prohibition on gatherings in separate prayer halls as well as the imposition of a ban on secret meetings and pilgrimages to tsadikim. In his opinion, it was particularly important to counteract the formation of hasidic *shtiblekh*:

> in the towns and the hamlets these sect members, the hasidim, or Husites, are to be found; they try to have a private building or a separate school in which to conduct services, pretending that they have differently established forms of prayers for the Polish, Lithuanian, Czech and Moravian Israelites, which have been used since time immemorial and they want to pray in the same manner as did once the Spanish Israelites; however, social assignations of a shady nature are their main aim . . . in which case it is appropriate that the government not permit them to have separate schools or private buildings in which to conduct their services, but that those wanting to pray participate in ordinary public services and with other Israelites in accordance with the old custom.[43]

Stern's report was effective once again. The Government Commissions turned the matter over to the viceroy and, on 15 March 1824, General Zajączek forbade the hasidim to pray in separate halls, introduced a ban on pilgrimages and clandestine meetings, but at the same time recommended that force be avoided in the execution of this law. Thus, he did everything that Stern had suggested.[44] The decision was sent to all voivodeship commissions.

However, Stern's victory also turned out to be short-lived. Following a series of protests by influential supporters of hasidism, the viceroy ordered another inquiry to determine whether the movement really constituted a threat. Finally, specially appointed deputies (again led by Staszic) ruled that 'there is no need whatsoever to persecute them', and the viceroy decreed that 'the sect of Jewish hasidim, that is, the men of silk, are not, in actuality, ruled by laws which are in defiance of moral norms, but they wish to have their own synagogues only in order to be separated from other Jews', and therefore they were to be tolerated.[45] At the same time one of the officials at the Department of Religious Denominations concluded that Stern's views, although they contained numerous serious accusations worthy of investigation, were not completely reliable, as the author was hostile to hasidism 'to the point of obduracy'. Solomon Marcus Posner was allegedly equally ill disposed to hasidism, but his opinions concerning the issue have not been preserved.[46]

Stern continued to take action against hasidism in the following years. As a

---

[43] Ibid. 47.

[44] AGAD, KRSW 6634, fo. 249 (copy in CAHJP, HM3635); CWW 1871, pp. 52–3; repr. in Mahler, *Haḥasidut vehahaskalah*, 484–5.

[45] AGAD, KRSW 6635, fo. 6 (copy in CAHJP, HM3636); repr. in Mahler, *Haḥasidut vehahaskalah*, 491; Wodziński, 'Sprawa chasydymów', 241.

[46] AGAD, CWW 1871, pp. 124–9.

member of the Censorship Committee for Hebrew Books, he was known for his exceptionally hostile attitude towards hasidic books and for promoting maskilic publications.[47] In 1830 he published another opinion unfavourable to the hasidim (see Appendix 8).[48] The government deputy for the Olkusz district had the synagogue in Pilica closed down as structurally unsafe. When the Jewish community board ordered contributions for renovations, the local hasidim in the upper two taxation brackets refused to pay, insisting that they did not attend the synagogue anyway. The community board therefore asked the government to forbid the hasidim to hold 'secret meetings and similar gatherings of the hoi polloi in inappropriate places . . . so that on no account could the sect of the hasidim hold prayers and services in any house other than the synagogue, as their proper place'. As usual, the Government Commission did not take a stance in this matter, but asked the Jewish Committee for an opinion. (The Jewish Committee, or Komitet Starozakonnych—literally, 'Old Testament believers'—was a government institution established to plan the reform of Jewish society.) The Committee's reply, signed by Assessor Stefan Witwicki, pointed to the regulations of 1827, which had legalized private prayer halls. This was, however, accompanied by a separate note, signed by the head of the Committee, Ignacy Zaleski, and a member of the Advisory Chamber (Izba Doradcza) of the Jewish Committee, Abraham Stern, which read as follows:

In the opinion of the Jewish Committee, religious law grants people of this faith the right to pray both in private homes and in synagogues if 10 persons gather. However, as the issue concerns the renovation of the synagogue, which has been closed for reasons of safety, and because exempting the sect of the hasidim would make such a difference that the poorer classes would be unable to afford to pay their required contributions, it would seem necessary to make all Jews without exception contribute to the costs, but to allow them the freedom to choose whether they pray in the synagogue or in private houses. Surely both the Prussian and Austrian authorities forbid Jews to pray in private homes for no other reason than to ensure that everybody, without exception, pays their contribution in similar cases.[49]

At this time Stern also opposed the hasidic practice of separating themselves from the religious community, although, in the face of the government decision of 1827, he could no longer dispute their right to gather for prayer in private homes.

Stern's aggressiveness seems to have differed markedly from the stance taken by other maskilim in the Kingdom of Poland. The official mentioned in the context of the inquiry of 1824 (possibly Radomiński) wrote that Stern's and Posner's negative views ran counter to the opinions of Natan Glücksberg and Juda Leib Bauererz, who were both known to the government for their enlightened views, and who 'do not claim that the hasidim are worse than other Jews, but that they perform many good deeds'.[50] It must be emphasized, however, that the differences between Stern and other maskilim were not founded upon a greater or lesser degree of liking for

---

[47]  Shatzky, 'Avraham Ya'akov Stern', 216.

[49]  Ibid. 18.

[48]  AGAD, CWW 1472, pp. 16–18.

[50]  AGAD, CWW 1871, pp. 124–9.

hasidism (which none of the sides had), but on their perception of the degree of significance this socio-religious grouping had and the possible need to oppose it. Like Stern and Posner, Bursztyński, Glücksberg, Eisenbaum, Hoge, and Schönfeld all castigated 'superstitious fanatics', even if, for tactical reasons, they saw some virtues in them. But unlike Stern, the above-mentioned maskilim agreed with Calmanson that hasidism was a marginal issue and was not deserving of particular interest. In contrast, Stern as early as 1818 perceived the movement as a serious threat not only to the Enlightenment, but also to Judaism as a whole, and declared open warfare.

The difference between Stern's attitude and that of the other maskilim of the Kingdom is all the more significant because Stern's views were relatively similar to the anti-hasidic obsessions of the Galician maskilim at the time, who were mainly Mendel Lefin's students. When Stern presented his critical opinions of the hasidim to the authorities of the Kingdom, the most prominent Galician maskilim reported the hasidim to the provincial government in Lemberg (Lwów) and to the central imperial authorities in Vienna, while Joseph Perl submitted further memoranda and plans to fight 'the plague of hasidism'.[51] Hasidism and its ideology also began to occupy an increasingly important position in the literary works of Galician Haskalah supporters. The texts written by Perl and by Judah Leib Mieses were particularly aggressive in this respect.[52] The difference in the attitude towards hasidism in Galicia (where it was extremely critical) and in the Kingdom of Poland (where it was less harsh) is striking.

Incidentally, it is worth noting that the difference in the above-mentioned attitudes manifested itself in the border city of Kraków as well. Although Kraków is usually associated with Galicia, it only belonged to the Habsburg monarchy between 1793 and 1809. From 1809 to 1815 it formed part of the Duchy of Warsaw, and from 1815 to 1846 (the period in question) it was the autonomous Republic of Kraków, which was under the protectorate of the three occupying powers. After 1846 the city returned to Galicia, but until 1846 the greatest political and cultural influence in Kraków was that of the Congress Kingdom and the Polish king (i.e. the Russian tsar). Naturally, this also influenced the Kraków Haskalah, which was, in fact, closer in nature to the Jewish Enlightenment in Warsaw than to the Jewish Enlightenment in Lwów or Vienna. In the little-known work *Schreiben eines Krakauer Israeliten an seinen Christlichen Freund auf dem Lande, die Chassidim betreffend* (Letter of a Kraków Jew to his Christian Friend about Hasidism) its anonymous author stated that hasidism was not a dangerous mystical sect, but quite the opposite: it attempted to free the Jewish people from the oppression of the rabbis' perverted legalism. The hasidic movement was, in fact, analogous with

[51]  See Mahler, *Hasidism and the Jewish Enlightenment*, 121–48.

[52]  For anti-hasidic literature in Galicia, see Werses, 'Hahasidut be'einei sifrut hahaskalah', 91–109; Feiner, *Haskalah and History*, 91–115, 306–17; Mahler, *Hasidism and the Jewish Enlightenment*, 149–68.

the Haskalah and Moses Mendelssohn's reforms in Germany, although it had been forced to assume the camouflage of kabbalism because of the east European context. According to the author, to view hasidism as a threat was completely unjustifiable.[53] The letter was actually addressed to non-Jewish readers (evidence of which can be seen not only in the title, but also in the language and structure of the publication) and may have been apologetic in character. Yet the underestimation of the threat of hasidism and the assumption of an attitude similar to that of the Polish maskilim is a particularly striking aspect of the work. Thus it appears that hasidism was ignored not only in the Congress Kingdom, but also at times in neighbouring Kraków.

To return to Stern, it may be assumed that the similarity between his views and the ideology of the Galician Haskalah was not a matter of coincidence. Born, brought up, and educated in Hrubieszów, he spent the thirty-seven years of his life that were the most important to his intellectual growth as a subject of the Habsburg monarchy and an inhabitant of Galicia, which in 1772–1809 also encompassed Zamość lands. It therefore seems natural that in the following years as well, as a subject of the Duchy of Warsaw and the Kingdom of Poland, Stern remained in the circle of intellectual influences of the Galician Haskalah, with whose representatives he maintained contact.[54] Lefin's influence was very clear. It was evident in the various solutions Stern adopted: not only in his general definition of hasidism, but also in some of his detailed proposals, such as the question of granting special rights to the head of the Rabbinical School to censor hasidic publications or the avoidance of drastic measures in the fight with this movement.

We cannot rule out the possibility that the harshness of Stern's anti-hasidic polemic also stemmed from the fact that hasidism was particularly widespread on his home soil at that stage, and that Stern saw more clearly the threats it brought than did the other Polish maskilim. British missionaries wrote in 1829 that the vicinity of Zamość was dominated by hasidism, while in the remaining areas of the Kingdom of Poland its influence was barely noticeable.[55] If this was true, Stern's harsh assessment of hasidism is far more understandable.

## WHY DID THE POLISH MASKILIM IGNORE HASIDISM?

The above explanation, pointing to the Galician origins of Stern's ideas, opens another, much wider-ranging question, which is fundamental to an understanding of the entire ideological profile of the Polish Haskalah. One might ask the question: why was it that the prevailing attitudes towards hasidism in the Kingdom and in Galicia differed so much? What was the source of these differences and what was the reason for such a low level of interest in hasidism on the part of the Polish maskilim between 1815 and 1830? The easy answer is the close dependence on the

---

[53] *Schreiben eines Krakauer Israeliten.*          [54] See e.g. Kupfer, 'Merahok umikarov'.
[55] See L[udwig] Hoff, 'Extracts of Two Letters from the Rev. L. Hoff', *JE* 14 (1929), 138, 140.

German version of the Jewish Enlightenment. For the Berlin maskilim, hasidism was merely one of the marginal manifestations of Jewish fanaticism in eastern Europe, one that lay at the extreme edge of the civilized world. It was interesting only as an example of the cultural backwardness of their east European co-religionists, as seen in the autobiography of Salomon Maimon. Even though the Polish maskilim came into contact with hasidism much more frequently than did Moses Mendelssohn or Naftali Herz Wessely, this was not sufficient to allow them to define their own attitude to the complex problems of the surrounding world. A large part of the literary output of the Polish maskilim consisted of imitations or simply translations of the writings of the Berlin Haskalah. It would be difficult to expect to find there anything in the way of more original reflections on the socio-religious situation of the Polish Jews. For a long time the maskilim of Congress Poland availed themselves only of the methods and ideas that had been worked out by the German Haskalah. The confrontation with hasidism was not one of them.

Such an answer, however, seems less than satisfactory. No matter how dependent the Polish maskilim were on the Berlin Haskalah, surely, in one way or another, they must have reflected some of the features of their own environment. Thus, the question regarding the reasons for such a low level of interest in hasidism can be formulated somewhat differently: was the low level of interest in hasidism in any way connected with features of this movement specific to the Kingdom of Poland?

One first must consider the characteristics that differentiated hasidism in the Kingdom of Poland from hasidism in other regions of eastern Europe. Historians researching Polish hasidism have pointed out quite correctly that some features of hasidism came to the Kingdom relatively late. These included the flamboyant gestures of the 'regal way' of hasidism, the hereditary dynasties of the tsadikim, and the extensive use of magical and mystical practices that were so characteristic of the hasidic movement in Russia and Galicia.[56] Significantly, since it was these features that were particularly repellent to maskilic critics of hasidism, Polish hasidism might well have appeared to the maskilim as being less degenerate and abhorrent. In addition, other features specific to Polish hasidism might have softened the anti-hasidic criticisms of the local maskilim. Strong ties between the Polish tsadikim and the emerging economic elite, as well as the personal involvement of many tsadikim in economic activities, made them more open to non-traditional society, more rational and socially oriented.[57] Possibly the best example was the tsadik Isaac of Warka, who, in the guise of a traditional *shtadlan* (intercessor), engaged in very 'worldly' and modern political enterprises to protect the well-being of the

---

[56] For a description of the characteristics of Polish hasidism, see Aescoly, *Haḥasidut bepolin*; Rabinowicz, *Bein peshiṣḥaḥ lelublin*; Rubinstein, 'Reshitah shel haḥasidut bepolin hamerkazit'; and especially Dynner, 'Men of Silk'.

[57] See Dynner, 'Men of Silk', ch. 2, for the connections the Polish tsadikim had with the Warsaw financial elite.

Jewish people in Poland.[58] Thus the Polish manifestation of hasidism might have seemed less distasteful to the maskilim. Indeed, some Polish maskilim stated as much. Jakub Tugendhold drew a distinction between the fanatical hasidic leaders from Ukraine and the far less harmful and pious Polish tsadikim (see Appendix 15). Likewise, Daniel Neufeld (one of the leading Polish Jewish integrationists) contrasted the Galician charlatans with the Polish rationalistically driven tsadikim, and reserved special praise for Menahem Mendel of Kock and Isaac Meir Alter of Góra Kalwaria (Ger). Thus it would appear that the 'worldly' and rationalistic features of Polish hasidism made this movement more acceptable to the Polish maskilim and that they genuinely expressed their appreciation of the direction Polish hasidism had taken. However, the importance of this positive perception should not be overestimated, particularly in relation to the first two decades of the nineteenth century. Such a positive re-evaluation of the Polish tsadikim—as opposed to their Galician or Russian counterparts—came relatively late. The earliest such account of Menahem Mendel of Kock appeared in 1838 and it was written by an anonymous Galician maskil.[59] Tugendhold's opinions were made known only in 1857 and Neufeld's in 1861. That earlier reports did not differentiate between Polish, Galician, and Russian hasidism is quite understandable, given the low level of knowledge of hasidism and its internal divisions displayed by maskilim engaged in the dispute, such as Dr Schönfeld or Antoni Eisenbaum.[60] Without an in-depth knowledge of the movement, how could they possibly have made a distinction between the differing forms of hasidism? Moreover, the positive re-evaluation of Polish hasidism in the 1860s was not responsible for the lack of interest in fighting the movement or for the decrease in criticism of the movement. Quite the opposite was true. The same Neufeld who had contrasted the Polish rational tsadikim with the Galician fanatics was preoccupied with the hasidic issue and elevated it to the level of a major ideological problem for the integrationist movement in Poland. In fact, the period of positive re-evaluation of hasidism in Poland was also a time when criticism of the movement was widespread (see Chapter 6). Thus, the lack of criticism by the Polish maskilim from 1815 to 1830 bore no similarity to the positive re-evaluation of hasidism in the 1860s. Any attempt to project the positive attitudes towards hasidism expressed in the 1860s on to the period preceding the 1830s lacks solid foundations and the connection between the objective features of Polish hasidism and the perception of this movement by the maskilim becomes far more problematic. Therefore, qualitative argu-

[58] For more on Isaac, see Assaf and Bartal, 'Shetadlanut ve'ortodoksiyah'; Wodziński, 'Hasidism, *Shtadlanut*, and Jewish Politics'.

[59] 'Charakteristik der jüdischen Sekten in Galizien', *AZJ* 2 (1838), 384.

[60] A good example was provided by Antoni Eisenbaum, who cited both Israel of Kozienice and Simha Bunim of Przysucha as examples of fraudulent tsadikim who profited from the supposed healing of infertile women. The former was actually renowned for his healing practices, and the latter was famous among the hasidim for his rationalistic approach. See [Antoni Eisenbaum], 'O Rabinach', *Rozmaitości*, 5 (1822), 42.

ments (i.e. those pointing to the ideological and social characteristics of the movement) as an explanation of the striking restraint shown by the Polish maskilim, even though valid, seem to lack substance.

If the qualitative reasons seem unsatisfactory, should one perhaps seek quantitative explanations? In other words: how large (or how small) was the hasidic movement in the Congress Kingdom around 1830 and how could it have influenced the maskilic perception of hasidism in Poland?

These are surprisingly difficult questions, as very little has really been done to estimate the numbers involved in hasidism—not only in the Kingdom of Poland, but throughout eastern Europe.[61] Historians usually view the hasidic movement as one of the most significant social phenomena in the history of Polish Jewry during the eighteenth, nineteenth, and twentieth centuries. However, historical studies determining the actual extent of the hasidic influence usually resort to generalizations that suggest that there was a significant number of followers of hasidism by the final decades of the eighteenth century. A closer look at the data from Congress Poland indicates, however, that these numbers were much lower in the first half of the nineteenth century than those usually estimated, and much lower than in Galicia (eastern Galicia in particular), Podolia, or Volhynia.[62]

Let us start with estimates from the period under consideration. Jan Alojzy Radomiński, a government official and a writer with a keen interest in the Jewish question, wrote the following about hasidism in Poland in 1820:

the sect has now spread to all of the provinces of our country, and there is hardly any place from which it is absent and where it is not still gaining new supporters.

But although Israel Löbel had counted almost 40,000 of them at its founder's death, about 15 years after the sect had been established, that is, around the year 1780, I do not want to estimate this figure [now], leaving it to the reader's discretion to guess easily [the extent of] their increase over the passage of time.[63]

Around the same time Julian Ursyn Niemcewicz wrote in a similar fashion about hasidism, also citing Israel Löbel.[64] These accounts, of course, like the great majority of other, similar descriptions, are second- or third-hand versions, which often draw uncritical conclusions from the catastrophic predictions of rabbinical and maskilic anti-hasidic polemicists, for example from the publications of Israel Löbel, David Friedländer, and Joseph Perl, and are thus not of significant value to this investigation. For example, Radomiński, who in 1820 could not even guess at

---

[61] One of very few such attempts is Stępniewska-Holzer, 'Ruch chasydzki na Białorusi'.

[62] The development of the hasidic movement in central Poland has recently been considered in Dynner, 'Men of Silk', 13–25. Despite there being much interesting material in this work, in my opinion it does not provide persuasive evidence for the author's thesis that hasidism experienced a sudden, rapid growth in central Poland in the second decade of the 19th century. In the event, none of the figures cited by Dynner confirms a large number of hasidim at that time, and Dynner did not draw any strong conclusions concerning their number. For more on this issue, see below.

[63] Radomiński, *Co wstrzymuje reformę Żydów*, 66.      [64] Niemcewicz, *Lejbe i Sióra*.

the hasidim's numbers, declared in 1824, after he had become familiar with official documents relating to the movement, that they amounted to 'a few tens of thousands' and constituted a non-threatening minority.[65] In 1822 the Civil Council (Rada Obywatelska) of the voivodeship of Sandomierz announced that 'a few dozen Jews have been brought to the public gaols, who testify that there is still a much larger concentration of those evildoers [*Złoczyńcy*], all of whom have secret connections'.[66] It seems highly likely that the reference was to the hasidim. These estimates were also based upon widespread assumptions and were clearly intended to provide an argument in favour of the proposed Jewish reforms.

One of the most interesting sources with reference to the religious tendencies of the Jews in the Congress Kingdom, including the development of hasidism, are the reports of the London Society for Promoting Christianity amongst the Jews. The British missionaries were possibly the only educated non-Jewish observers who took an interest in Jewish religious life in Poland, and they left a relatively large number of reports on the subject. For this reason, their reports are an invaluable source of knowledge, despite their obviously partisan character. The missionaries frequently made reference to particular hasidic individuals or groups whom they encountered in the course of their missionary travels; typically their texts speak of 'several individuals and one of the Chasidim'. In the period under consideration they spoke of the hasidim in Warsaw, Końskie, Wyszogród, Terespol, Ostrów Mazowiecka, Nowe Miasto nad Pilicą, Kozienice, Goździków near Przysucha, Sienno (in the voivodeship of Sandomierz), Włodawa, and Żelechów. Their interest in the hasidim was all the greater since they regarded them as being particularly stubborn defenders of Judaism whose conversion would make an enormous impression on the entire Jewish population. Some missionaries deliberately sought out the hasidim in the towns they visited in order to engage them in debate; they even made use of hasidic songs and textual interpretations in their missionary work.[67] Nevertheless, despite their marked interest in hasidism, during the period under study the missionaries mentioned only two places in which the hasidim constituted a majority of the inhabitants, and that was out of dozens of accounts of missionary activity in over 100 locations in central Poland.[68] These places were Przysucha and an area called 'Zamrose' (more than likely Zamość).[69] Indirectly, we are able to

[65] See AGAD, CWW 1871, pp. 124–9.   [66] AGAD, KRSW 6634, fos. 214–17.

[67] 'Two hundred to two hundred and fifty Jewish families live in this place [Żelechów], and among them many Chasidim. I was particularly encouraged by this information'; W[ilhelm] Ferdinand Becker, 'Extracts from the Journals of Messrs. Becker and Bergenfeld', *JE* 13 (1828), 262. See also 'Extracts of Missionary Journals from Warsaw', *JE* 14 (1829), 418–19, 454.

[68] The reports from the Congress Kingdom were published regularly in the society's bulletin, *Jewish Expositor and Friend of Israel*, from 1822 until the bulletin ceased publication in 1831.

[69] On Przysucha, see L[udwig] Hoff, 'Journal of Mr. Hoff', *JE* 10 (1825), 28–9. On 'Zamrose', see id., 'Extracts of Two Letters from the Rev. L. Hoff', *JE* 14 (1829), 138, 140. The information on 'Zamrose' may be doubtful, because it was based upon the testimony of an anonymous 'so-called enlightened Jew'; it was thus not first-hand information.

draw a conclusion about the significant numbers of hasidim (although they were not necessarily a majority) from a report about Kozienice which indicated that the hasidic prayer house was filled to overflowing while only a few people prayed in the community synagogue.[70]

Obviously, the information provided in these reports is imprecise, and firm conclusions cannot be drawn from it. There are two reasons for such caution. In the first place, it can be safely assumed that the missionaries were not always acquainted with the true religious situation among the local Jews. Secondly, there is always an element of uncertainty in arguments based on silence: the fact that hasidim were mentioned as a majority in only two places does not necessarily mean that they did not constitute a majority elsewhere. Nevertheless, given the missionaries' great concern for religious questions, it seems safe to assume that their estimates, even if not precise in every case, remain the best source available on the subject and that they generally reflect the situation of hasidism in Poland at the time. Moreover, the opinion that the hasidim in Poland were relatively few in number is not only implicit in the many reports that mention nothing of their numerical strength, but was confirmed explicitly by certain British missionaries. In their report on a visit to the Russian Pale of Settlement the missionaries Alexander M'Caul and Ludwig Hoff indicated that the hasidim predominated in those territories, *in contrast to the situation in Congress Poland*. Describing the hasidic ban (*ḥerem*) on missionary books issued by a tsadik from 'M'. (most likely the Apter Rebbe, Abraham Joshua Heshel of Opatów, who lived in Międzybóż towards the end of his life and died there in 1825), Hoff added, 'This hostile feeling continued the whole way to the Polish fortress, that is, wherever Chasidism had *any* influence. On entering the Kingdom of Poland, matters were immediately reversed.'[71] Not only does this sentence indicate that the Congress Kingdom was free of the hasidic dominance that characterized Russia, but it even suggests that the hasidim lacked any influence at all in Congress Poland. Similarly, Hoff reported from Ożarów that 'Chasidism is *beginning* to spread there and the Chasidim have a Rabbi, who is now gaining status as one of their most famous wonder-workers, for the Rabbis of Przysucha, Abt [Opatów], and Meshibesh [Międzybóż], have died with-

---

[70] W[ilhelm] Ferdynand Becker and Miersohn, 'Journal of Messrs. Becker and Miersohn', *JE* 13 (1828), 185. See also W[ilhelm] Ferdynand Becker, 'Journal of Rev. W. F. Becker', *JE* 11 (1826), 229.

[71] Alexander M'Caul and L[udwig] Hoff, 'Journal of Messrs. M'Caul and Hoff', *JE* 10 (1825), 145; my emphasis. The word 'fortress' may refer to Zamość, or it may have been used in error instead of the word 'frontier'. The latter reading is suggested by the context. Also see ibid. 142 for hasidic dominance in the Russian lands. In 1826 one of the English missionaries, E. Henderson, reported that in 'Russian Poland' (the term used in British missionary publications for territories of the former Polish–Lithuanian Commonwealth that had been incorporated directly into Russia, exclusive of the Congress Kingdom) and the European parts of the Ottoman empire, the hasidim had already become a majority in the local communities. Henderson, *Biblical Researches and Travels in Russia*, 236, cited in Dynner, 'Men of Silk', 298.

in a year of one another.'[72] In other words, in spite of the successes of the tsadik of Ożarów, Arie Leib (d. 1837), hasidism had only just begun to spread in the town. The missionary immediately added that 'a great number of the Jews there oppose the idolatry of the Chasidim'. According to Hoff's description, the 'great' anti-hasidic opposition decidedly outweighed the small number of adherents of that movement.

Unfortunately, the reports of the British missionaries, rich in information as they are, do not include estimates of numbers. Nor do we know upon what M'Caul's and Hoff's statements regarding the complete lack of hasidic influence were based. However, three extremely valuable reports from the government's Jewish Committee complement the picture. In the first, from 1827, the Committee informed the tsar's adviser in the Polish Kingdom, Nikolai Novosiltzoff, that Jews in the Kingdom were divided into sects known as 'rabbanite' and 'talmudic', along with a very small number of hasidim.[73] Although we do not know what the Committee understood by a very small number or how accurate the information in its possession was, the wording of the document suggests that the hasidim were an insignificant minority, and thus confirms the missionaries' impression. That same year the Committee, in its report on the need for the Talmud to be translated into French, stated that, of the 5 million Jews worldwide, the Samaritans, Karaites, and hasidim constituted 1 million or fewer.[74] What this meant was that the Committee's estimate was that the total number of hasidim constituted less than 20 per cent of the Jewish population worldwide. However, this information is extremely imprecise, because it does not suggest what the estimate would have been for the Kingdom of Poland. A more precise estimate for the Kingdom was given in a report of 23 June 1834 prepared for the Government Commission on Internal and Religious Affairs and Public Enlightenment. The report was ordered by Viceroy Ivan Paskevich in connection with denunciation of hasidism by maskilim from Krzemieniec and a subsequent investigation initiated by the Russian government.[75] The government wanted to know, among other things, 'how many Jews [*Starozakonnych*] belong to this sect?' The Committee responded that 'the number of hasidim in the Kingdom of Poland can be counted only approximately, but certainly it does not exceed the twentieth portion of the Israelite people in the Kingdom, although recently there has been significant growth in the number of its adherents.'[76] Who supplied the Jewish Committee with this information or what motives he might have had to make the number of hasidim appear lower or higher than it was is unknown. It is highly likely that the figures came from the Committee's Advisory Chamber (Izba

---

[72] Hoff, 'Extracts of Two Letters from the Rev. L. Hoff', *JE* 14 (1829), 96; my emphasis.

[73] Mahler, *Hasidism and the Jewish Enlightenment*, 332–3.

[74] AGAD, Kancelaria Senatora Nowosilcowa 626, pp. 52–3.

[75] Lederhendler, *The Road to Modern Jewish Politics*, 95–6.

[76] AGAD, CWW 1871, pp. 245–50. The government commission duplicated the information supplied by the Jewish Committee in the report sent to the viceroy; see ibid. 251–61.

Doradcza), in which the various Jewish groups (hasidim, mitnagedim, and maskilim) were represented in such a way as to allow one to assume that the data were gathered and reported in a relatively objective fashion (although the reporters did not necessarily possess accurate knowledge of the actual situation).[77] Moreover, as the Committee's estimates did not deviate from other figures reported at the time, they cannot have been completely divorced from the true state of affairs.[78] If anything, they were somewhat obsolete, reflecting the situation not in 1834 but before 1830.

Confirmation is also to be found in an 1862 description of the activities of 'the hasidic leaders' (*naczelników chasydowskich*) by Daniel Neufeld (1814–74), the well-known Jewish advocate of integration, editor of the Jewish weekly *Jutrzenka* and an undisputed expert on hasidism. Until 1860 Neufeld had lived in provincial towns that were within the orbit of the hasidic movement; he studied the hasidim closely and was fascinated by their folk religiosity. 'Before 1830,' he noted, 'these charlatans had been a rarity in Poland; the most illustrious and devout of men behaved unscrupulously towards them, because their followers were unjustly accused of being sectarians who were a danger to society.'[79] An indication of what Neufeld meant by 'a rarity' (*dziwowisko*) is found in an article he wrote about hasidism three years earlier, in which he observed that the persecution of the hasidic movement 'only brought about an increase in its numbers and strength, to the point where at present hasidism must be regarded as a fait accompli numbering as many as 800,000 adherents'.[80] To what did the figure 800,000 refer? It could not have referred to the Kingdom of Poland, where in 1859 there were approximately 600,000 Jews in all. Hence it may be assumed that it included all of the east European territories where the hasidim were to be found, including not only the lands of the former Polish–Lithuanian Commonwealth, but also Hungary, Bukowina, Bessarabia, New Russia, Moravia, and even Upper Silesia and the Duchy of Poznań. In other words, in 1862 Neufeld recognized that the hasidim, who were then at the height of their influence, comprised less than one-third of the Jewish population in the lands in which they were influential. Thus, before 1830, when

---

[77] The Advisory Chamber of the Jewish Committee was dominated by partisans of the Haskalah, who enjoyed the support of the authorities there. Nevertheless, they had to take into account the opinions of the other Jewish groups. Many times the chamber, on its own initiative, spoke out in defence of the traditional Jewish community. See Kandel, 'Komitet Starozakonnych'. For examples of the opinions of the Advisory Chamber defending traditional Jewish religious law and society, see AGAD, CWW 1409, pp. 1802 ff.; 1411, pp. 66–74, 81–90, 98–125; 1416, pp. 19–24; 1417, p. 100 ff.; 1504, pp. 63–75; 1508, pp. 41–53; 1708, pp. 4–27; 1779, pp. 5–17; 1784, pp. 52–65.

[78] This was how Mahler evaluated the figures: Mahler, *Hasidism and the Jewish Enlightenment*, 334–7. The report has been published (in Polish) in the Hebrew version of the book; see Mahler, *Haḥasidut vehahaskalah*, 506–8.

[79] [Daniel Neufeld], 'Urządzenie konsystorza żydowskiego w Polsce. IX: Dozory Bóżnicze', *Ju.* 2 (1862), 362. The comment concerning 'unjust accusations' no doubt refers to the investigation directed against the hasidim by Stanisław Staszic between 1818 and 1824.

[80] Neufeld, 'Chassyd', 171.

the hasidim were 'a rarity', their number must have been estimated as being far lower than 30 per cent, and most likely a single-figure percentage.

The only source from the constitutional period of the Kingdom of Poland to provide estimates that were significantly higher than any of those cited to this point came from the hasidim themselves. In 1824 Alexander (Zusya) Kahana (1795–1837), an influential hasid from Warsaw and a close associate of the tsadik Simha Bunim of Przysucha (1765–1827), addressed a letter to Viceroy Józef Zajączek asking him to withdraw the order of March 1824 which outlawed hasidism.[81] Kahana spoke in the name of all hasidim in Congress Poland, arguing that hasidism was not a marginal sect but that it constituted 'almost one-third of all Jews'.[82] It may be assumed that this figure, even if it was far from suggesting that the hasidim predominated numerically, was inflated. Alexander Kahana's aim was to prove that the hasidic movement was very widespread, and he therefore had good reason to overestimate the numbers. Thus it appears even from this source that the number of hasidim in 1824 was considerably lower than 30 per cent of the Jewish population.

The estimates we have vary from 'a rarity' (Neufeld) and 5 per cent (the Jewish Committee) to one-third of the Jewish population (Kahana). The lower estimates seem the more likely, both because of the reliability of their authors and in the light of the numbers discussed below.

Statistics derived from contemporary sources are of crucial significance to an estimate of the number of hasidim in the Kingdom of Poland. Such statistics allow us to establish realistic figures for nineteen cities and thirteen Jewish communities, on the basis of which we can build up a picture of the situation in the remaining *c.*300 Jewish communities that existed at the time. Figures for 1820–9 came from Częstochowa, Płock, and the voivodeship of Podlasie. While the available figures derive from only a small sample, we nevertheless have good reason to believe that they are representative and reliable. First, the statistics were not gathered in a tendentious manner (at least as far as we are aware), but derive from reports by various authors from various regions and were compiled with a variety of purposes in mind. It is therefore difficult to imagine that the authors would all have distorted the data in the same manner. Secondly, the information from various widely dispersed locations is quite consistent in nature and is in step with the estimates made by Neufeld and the Jewish Committee. Finally, it is from a wide range of communities, including towns in which there were no hasidim at all, towns where opponents of the local hasidim fought them actively, and towns regarded as powerful centres of the movement, where contemporary sources noted the existence of strong hasidic communities. For example, the data from the voivodeship of

---

[81] For details, see Wodziński, 'Sprawa chasydymów'; a French translation, published without the knowledge or consent of the author, appears in *Tsafon: Revue d'études juives du Nord*, 29 (1997), 35–58; see also Mahler, *Hasidism and the Jewish Enlightenment*, 315–32.

[82] AGAD, CWW 1871, pp. 88–90; repr. in Wodziński, 'Sprawa chasydymów', 232.

Podlasie encompass a spread-out and diverse region of seventeen towns, most of which had Jewish communities. Two communities, Sokołów and Żelechów, have been noted in the literature as major hasidic centres,[83] and the presence of a large number of hasidic adherents in Żelechów is confirmed by the reports of the British missionaries.[84] Moreover, in 1824 Abraham Stern, who was the most powerful critic of hasidism in Poland, mentioned the voivodeship of Podlasie as being one of six voivodeships under hasidic influence. Thus we can safely assume that support for hasidism here approximated that in the other voivodeships.[85]

## Częstochowa

The oldest available statistics are from 1820, from correspondence concerning the struggle referred to above between the hasidim and their opponents over the use of the local *mikveh*. The anti-hasidic opposition, concerned about the way in which their adversaries were lobbying the town mayor, wrote, *inter alia*, in the name of 'the hundred-odd families of the local synagogue . . . that several dozen superstitious characters [*zabobonników*] have thrown off the yoke of heaven (as a result of which even some of our most prominent members are looking to move abroad)'.[86] The information about 'several dozen superstitious characters' appears to be reliable considering that petitions from the hasidim from Częstochowa were signed by a maximum of fourteen people, always the same ones, who probably constituted all, or almost all, of the local hasidic settlement.[87] The percentage of hasidim in the entire Jewish population of Częstochowa in 1820 can thus be determined by dividing fourteen into the number of Jewish families known to have been living in the town at the time. According to a communal tax roll from 1822, there were 388 Jewish households. Subtracting from this number the female taxpayers (fifteen widows) and families living in nearby villages, we are left with a total of 259 Jewish families in Częstochowa proper.[88] If all fourteen signatories of the hasidic petitions were the heads of households, hasidic families would have constituted 5.4 per cent of Częstochowa's Jews. However, it seems fairly certain that not all of the signatories were heads of households. This is indicated, for example, by the fact that the names of only nine of the fourteen appear on the tax roll (the others may have been the adult dependent children of heads of households, sons-in-law being supported by their wives' families, older parents living with their married children, domestic servants, etc.). Thus, the percentage of hasidim among the Jews of Częstochowa in 1820 was, most likely, even lower than 5.4 per cent.

In the course of an investigation into episodes of violence accompanying the

---

[83] See e.g. Schiper, *Przyczynki do dziejów chasydyzmu w Polsce*, 22–3; Rabinowicz, *Bein peshishah lelublin*, 97–100; Dynner, 'Men of Silk', 58–64. One of the first hasidic *rebbes*, Levi Isaac (later known as Levi Isaac of Berdichev), accepted a position in Żelechów in the mid-1770s.

[84] W[ilhelm] Ferdinand Becker, 'Extracts from the Journals of Messrs. Becker and Bergenfeld', *JE* 13 (1828), 262; AGAD, CWW 1457, p. 469.          [85] AGAD, CWW 1871, p. 42.

[86] AGAD, KWK 702, p. 27.          [87] Ibid. 37.          [88] AGAD, KWK 713, pp. 3–33.

fight over the *mikveh*, a questionnaire was distributed in which one of the questions asked of the leaders of the hasidim and mitnagedim was 'How long has the hasidic sect [*sekta kitajowców*] been in existence in Old Częstochowa?' The hasidim Berek Kochin and Józef Gajfler answered that 'they have been conducting separate prayer services for 16 years'. Two representatives of the *kahal*, Lewek Kohen and Saul Landau, stated in response to the same question that 'it has been 10 years, but it is closer to five years since they began to conduct separate prayer in a private home'.[89] Notwithstanding the differences between the testimonies, it seems reasonable to surmise that the first hasidim appeared in Częstochowa between 1804 and 1810, while a separate hasidic *minyan* was established only around 1815.[90]

## Płock

Some information regarding the number of followers of hasidism also appeared during the first stage of the 'Case of the Hasidim' in 1818 in Płock. The Voivode-ship Commission had reported that 'the hasidim [*kitajowcy*] separate themselves from other Jews by their rituals and in return arouse hatred; but there are many of them, and in almost all towns in the voivodeship they maintain separate prayer houses'.[91] The Government Commission subsequently learned from hasidic infor-mants in Płock that, in addition to the two official synagogues, the hasidim had established for themselves 'a third, resembling a school, dedicated more to prayer and religious study, which has existed peacefully for 10 years'.[92] Thus, according to those closest to the situation, a hasidic prayer house was established in Płock in 1808. Unfortunately, the records contain no information on the size of the hasidic community.[93]

Inferences regarding the development of hasidism during the following ten years can be drawn from the official correspondence generated in the wake of the next controversies concerning the hasidim in Płock. In 1822 the hasidim managed, apparently by criminal means, to win approval for the establishment of their own

[89] AGAD, KWK 702, pp. 38, 41.

[90] It should be noted that in subsequent years also the number of hasidim in Częstochowa remained at a very low level. According to Jakub Bursztyński (1790–1852), the interpreter for the Provincial Commission in Kalisz and one of the most active of the Częstochowa maskilim, there were 20–25 hasidic families in the town in 1841 out of 400 Jewish families altogether (5–6.25 per cent). According to him, this low number was the result of the fierce struggle waged by the Jewish community against hasidic influence. J[akub] B[ursztyński], 'Russland und Polen: Czenstochau', *AZJ* 5 (1841), 567. Archival sources support Bursztyński's claim; see e.g. AGAD, KWK 702, pp. 214–17. The city is therefore not representative of the process of growth of hasidism in the Kingdom of Poland.

[91] AGAD, CWW 1869, p. 7.                                          [92] Ibid. 10.

[93] The hasidic documents are signed by ten people 'in the name of all'. On that basis Dynner, 'Men of Silk', 104, states that the hasidic community in Płock must have been quite large at the time. In the light of the example from Częstochowa, however, in which fourteen people signed in the name of a community numbering 'several', it is not at all certain that the community in Płock numbered more than ten members. There is no document available to confirm or refute either conclusion. On Często-chowa, see above.

'school' or synagogue, although it never came into existence because of general opposition to a separate hasidic *shtibl*.[94] In a controversial move in 1829 the Jewish community board nominated Alexander Kahana (who had represented the hasidim in their correspondence with the authorities over the March 1824 order outlawing hasidism) for the position of rabbi, and the Voivodeship Commission ratified the nomination.[95] Kahana's opponents protested to the Government Commission for Religious Denominations and Public Enlightenment, arguing that he was a hasid and a usurer and for that reason was not fit to serve as the rabbi of a non-hasidic community. They proposed in his place Abraham Rafael Landau (1789–1875), the rabbi of Ciechanów, who, curiously enough, was himself a hasidic sympathizer who became a well-known tsadik later in life.[96] The Government Commission sought the opinion of the Advisory Chamber of the Jewish Committee, which determined that Kahana was indeed a hasid and that his appointment as rabbi in Płock was inappropriate, given the marginal nature of the hasidic movement in the Płock Jewish community (see Appendix 7).[97] At the same time the municipal administration forwarded information about the town's hasidim, indicating that 'there are at most 40 Jews in Płock who belong to this sect'.[98] Three of Landau's supporters—Wolf Bimberg, Abraham Kronenberg, and Jakub Lichtenstein—gave a somewhat higher, but still remarkably low, figure:

As to the number of Chussidem, which is very small in Płock, the fact is that the best information is in the possession of the municipal administration, which has a general list. Nevertheless, we mention [the following] to support our argument. There are over 600 families of the Mosaic faith resident in Płock, of which the families of those hasidim who pay taxes and contribute to communal funds make up no more than 10; there is an equal number of others, for there are 10 families which are so poor that they cannot be summoned to pay tax and community dues.[99]

From this description it appears that there were approximately twenty hasidic families living in Płock in 1829, of which half belonged to the fifth fiscal category (the poorest, who were exempt from taxes). In other words, according to this source, the hasidim amounted to barely 3.3 per cent of the local Jewish population. Obviously, the authors of the document would have wanted to give as low a figure as possible for the number of hasidim in order to support their contention that a hasidic rabbi would not enjoy sufficient support in the community. However, their estimate was greater than that made by the municipal administration, which had obviously been based upon data from other sources. Thus, even if the figures

---

[94] AGAD, CWW 1666, pp. 6–10.

[95] See Michelson, 'Kuntres mareh kohen', 5 (separately paginated), for the controversy surrounding the nomination of Alexander (Zusya) Kahana as rabbi of Płock. See Grynszpan, 'Rabanim', 93–6; Boim, *Harabi rebe bunem mipeshishah*, i. 275–82, for more general information on Rabbi Kahana.

[96] AGAD, CWW 1666, pp. 219 ff.  [97] Ibid. 268–9.

[98] Ibid. 278. The document stated that the hasidim 'have rented a separate location in which orgies regularly take place'.  [99] Ibid. 292.

provided were artificially low, the actual number of hasidim still would not have amounted to more than 10 per cent of the community.

Two motifs are significant in these testimonies. The first is the mention of 'non-hasidic' communities. The existence of non-hasidic communities implies the existence of hasidic communities—meaning, presumably, communities in which the hasidim maintained a decisive presence among the Jewish population. The existence of both types of community as early as 1829 suggests that the distribution of hasidim in the Congress Kingdom was an uneven one and that, side by side with the powerful centres (where, no doubt, the famous tsadikim resided), there were numerous communities where the hasidim played no perceptible role. This is not surprising, after all. Confirmation that it was the case comes from a report by the Government Commission for Religious Denominations and Public Enlightenment, according to which the entire voivodeship of Augustów was free of the hasidic influence.[100] Confirmation is also found in Abraham Stern's report of 1824, in which he noted that the centre of Polish hasidism was the voivodeship of Sandomierz and that the hasidic influence extended to five other voivodeships as well—Lublin, Mazovia, Płock, Kraków, and Podlasie. The voivodeships of Augustów and Kalisz were not mentioned, which suggests they were in Stern's opinion free of hasidic influence.[101]

Hasidic communities were not necessarily those in which the hasidim constituted a numerical majority. Indeed, numerous testimonies speak of situations in which the opposite was the case. Observers emphasized cases where the hasidim managed to dominate the collective consciousness and to impose their will on the community even though they were a minority. There were places where, as a result of their high social profile, effective use of patronage, or greater determination than that of other groups, they succeeded in representing themselves as the sole true representatives of Jewry.

The second, noteworthy motif is the fact that both sides in the controversy over the appointment of the communal rabbi put forward hasidic candidates, even though one of the competing groups presented itself as openly hostile to the hasidic movement. Landau, the candidate of the anti-hasidic faction, had much to recommend him: his fame as a scholar and ascetic, his family ties to the Płock communal oligarchy (his father-in-law, Dan Landau, had been one of the most influential figures in Płock Jewry), the personal contacts made in the course of his studies with Rabbi Arieh Leib Zunz of Płock, and his leadership of the local yeshiva.[102] Therefore, it would appear that candidates for rabbinical positions in communities where support for hasidism was quite weak could be selected independently of, or even

---

[100] AGAD, KRSW 6634, fo. 238. The report was reprinted in Mahler, *Haḥasidut vehahaskalah*, 475–6.

[101] AGAD, CWW 1871, p. 42. As we know, Stern's assumption was wrong, which can also be deduced from the above documents about the hasidim in the towns of the Kalisz voivodeship, Często-chowa and Łask.    [102] See *Pinkas hakehilot polin*, iv. 358–72.

in spite of, their displays of sympathy towards the movement. Whether or not a candidate was himself a hasid or not was clearly not a primary criterion in the choice of a rabbi. Indeed, such was the case in nearby Pułtusk, where 'the inhabitants of the Mosaic religion, who belong to both hasidic and talmudic sects, live, but the absence of conflicts between these two sects has been confirmed both by the community board and by the mayor; where the election of the rabbi is concerned, both sects work together'.[103] A similar situation was also noted in Radomsko (where the hasid Hayim Klugerman became rabbi in 1811 and the tsadik Solomon Rabinowicz, in 1835, even though a hasidic leader noted in 1831 that the town contained only 'a few fellow hasidim'[104]) and in Maków (where in 1851 Isaac Meir Alter, whose hasidic sympathies were well known, was put forward as a compromise candidate for the local rabbinate in order to avert conflict between 'the hasidim and the talmudists').[105] Scholarly reputation was more important than hasidic affiliation.

In Płock in 1829 the Government Committee appointed Alexander Kahana as rabbi. The ministerial authorities were not interested in negotiating between conflicting factions, so they declared that Kahana was neither a hasid nor a usurer.

## The Podlasie Voivodeship

The most extensive information on numbers of hasidim came from the voivodeship of Podlasie in 1823 and 1824. The particular value of this information lies in the fact that it referred to a territory encompassing seventeen towns, most of which had Jewish communities and at least one of which, Żelechów, was an old hasidic centre. The information was collected by various sources—town magistrates, Jewish community boards, and district authorities—in conjunction with 'the case of the hasidim', which had been set off by a denunciation in Parczew, Podlasie Voivodeship. Zajączek ordered the Government Commission for Religious Denominations and Public Enlightenment to investigate. In turn, the Commission requested the voivodeship commissions, the Jewish community board in Warsaw, and the Censorship Committee for Hebrew Books for further information about the sect. It received the most detailed responses from Podlasie, where the voivodeship authorities instructed all local mayors and Jewish community boards to investigate the hasidim. These reports are deserving of closer study.

---

[103] AGAD, CWW 1661, p. 296.

[104] The figure was most certainly deliberately underestimated, because the hasidic leader in Radomsko, Majer (Meir) Braudes, sought to lower the tax on Torah reading that had been levied on the town's hasidim. See AGAD, KWK 702, pp. 218–22. For additional evidence that the hasidim in Radomsko were a minority with no influence on decisions concerning the synagogue even up to 1851, see AGAD, CWW 1562, p. 42.

[105] AGAD, CWW 1661, pp. 287–93. Alter declined the offer. Similar situations have been noted in towns outside the Congress Kingdom, such as Pińsk in Russia and Nikolsburg in Moravia. On Pińsk, see Nadav, 'Toledot kehilat pinsk', i. 191–5; on Nikolsburg, see Nosek, 'Shemuel Shmelke Ben Tsvi Hirsh ha-Levi Horovits'.

The mayors of Stężyca, Stoczek, Garwolin, Laskarzew, Maciejowice, Parysów, Osieck, and Adamów reported, in one-line notes, that there were no hasidim in their towns.[106] In the cases of Laskarzew and Stężyca, these reports were certainly true, as no Jews at all lived there at the time. In addition, the report from Maciejowice seems very reliable because even in 1846 there were no hasidim in the town.[107] Some of the others arouse an element of doubt. For example, the mayor of Osieck wrote that 'because they are so shrewd, as everyone knows, it is impossible to learn about their rites'. Reports from the towns in which mayors and district commissioners discovered groups of hasidim were somewhat more detailed. The district commissioner for Biała stated that

the sect of the hasidim [*Husidymów* or *Hussytów*] exists in the following towns of the district: In Sokołów they number 100 people and have leased a house in the town for their prayer services. In Biała they number 15 people and have leased a house for their prayer services. In Terespol they number five people and have also leased a house as a synagogue.[108]

The report also contained an interesting summary of hasidic doctrine, which shows that the commissioner had some idea of what he was describing. The district commissioner in Siedlce reported that 'the Jewish sect known as hasidim exists in the towns of Węgrów and Kosów; the former has up to 30 families, the latter has up to 10 persons only'.[109] The mayor of Żelechów presented a detailed description of hasidic teachings, but with regard to the number of hasidic adherents in his town, he noted laconically, 'according to the information we have obtained, among the believers in the Old Testament, the sect of the hasidim has reached up to 60'.[110] The relative accuracy of the description of hasidic doctrine here makes the rest of this report credible.

The sources of the data regarding the number of hasidic adherents are known in the cases of Łuków, Siedlce, and Parczew. The mayor of Łuków stated, 'on the basis of information obtained from Jews and from converts to the Catholic faith, I have the honour to report that in the town of Łuków, of all the Jews in Łuków, approximately 20 are hasidim [*Hussytów*]'.[111] The mayor appears to have attached great importance to checking the sources of his information, with the result that his figures appear to be fairly reliable. The interrogation of Abram Dawidowicz Kohen (in whose home the local hasidim congregated) yields the number of hasidim in Siedlce. He is on record as having stated that 'there are up to 30 of us in the sect who pray regularly, but any Jew is permitted to come and pray together with us'.[112] Of course, the witness may not have been telling the truth, but it is difficult to imagine any reason why he would want to reduce the size of the group to

[106] AGAD, CWW 1871, pp. 26–33.

[107] AGAD, CWW 1457, p. 472. This is what local Jews told the British missionaries. It seems to have been reliable information, because they had no reason to conceal the existence of the hasidim, and in many places the missionaries had no difficulty in tracing them.

[108] AGAD, CWW 1871, pp. 37–8.

[109] Ibid. 35–6.          [110] Ibid. 24–5.          [111] Ibid. 22–3.          [112] Ibid. 9–10.

which he belonged, especially since he was trying to prove the longevity of the sect in Siedlce. He claimed that it had been in existence 'since Austrian times' (i.e. 1795–1806), and he was obviously interested in presenting the group as being large and influential, as his words suggested.

The most detailed information, which was based upon three different sources, came from Parczew, where a thorough investigation was undertaken in the wake of the denunciation by Colonel Dulfus. The mayor, the magistrate, the Jewish community board, and the leaders of the local hasidim testified unanimously to the existence of two hasidic groups in the town.[113] The first, which was older and more peaceful, consisted of followers of the tsadik of Radzyń, Jacob Simon Deutsch (d. 1826), while the second, which had been punished several times by the mayor and town police for making disturbances at night, followed Simha Bunim of Przysucha. According to the mayor and magistrate, the first group 'for a long time has not exceeded a few dozen people', whereas the second group was said to consist of 'perhaps 20 Jews'. The estimates provided by Abram Mandelkier and Baruch Apelboim, who were both members of the community board and opponents of the hasidim, were quite similar. They noted that there had been hasidim in the town 'since long ago' (*od dawnych czasów*) and that 'a few dozen Jews belong to each of the two groups'. The local hasidic leaders, Ayzyk Szteyn, Szmul Sukiennik, Herszek Erps, and Berek Erlich, counted twenty people in the second group. The consistent nature of the information given by the three sets of informants, who represented conflicting interests, makes it extremely reliable. It does not confirm the reliability of the other reports, particularly those from the towns in which no hasidim were reported (where it is possible that the mayors had little interest in carrying out a thorough investigation). What it does prove, however, is that at least some of the information was collected correctly in towns in which the investigation was carried out. In addition, the numbers in this reliable report from Parczew are similar to those in other towns and considerably lower than those for the hasidic centres in Żelechów and Sokołów. This fact could be an indication that the information collected really did reflect the general state of hasidic influence in the Kingdom of Poland.

Altogether, the figures from the seventeen towns show a total of 430 hasidim in the voivodeship of Podlasie.[114] According to the census of 1827 (the census closest to the 1823–4 investigation), the total number of Jews in these towns was 14,231, meaning that the hasidim made up approximately 3 per cent of the local population. There is some doubt about the figures from the 1827 census, however, as they

---

[113] Ibid. 11–21.

[114] In Węgrów only the number of families is given. For the purposes of this study, a family is assumed to consist of five people. Data collected by the Government Commission for Religious Denominations and Public Enlightenment during the years 1827–30 show that the average size of Jewish families in the voivodeships of Mazovia and Podlasie ranged between 3.92 and 5.15 individuals (AGAD, CWW 1439). It should be noted, however, that even if the number of family members was assumed to be higher, this would not change these statistics since, together with the rise in the total number of family members, the

differed significantly from those recorded in the Jewish population rolls compiled by the synagogue governors in 1830.[115] Nevertheless, even the most dramatic adjustments of the figures will not change the general impression that the hasidim formed a very low percentage of the communities investigated. Indeed, the percentage may have been even lower than the available data suggest. The reports from the Siedlce and Biała districts failed to mention the situation in nine communities (Łomazy, Kodeń, Piszczac, Konstantynów, Sarnaki, Janów, Łosice, Mokobody, and Mordy) in which the 1827 census recorded a total of 4,977 Jews. We do not know whether the local officials simply did not discover any hasidim there or whether they did not seek them out (see Fig. 6). If the former was the case, the relative number of hasidim in the voivodeship must be significantly reduced. Moreover, the reports from Węgrów, Kosów, Żelechów, Siedlce, and Parczew spoke of there being 'up to' a certain number of individuals; they are thus the maximum figures and some of them—for example, those for Parczew—may need to be scaled downwards.

On the other hand, we do not know whether the data from towns other than Węgrów reflected the total number of members of each hasidic household, only the head of each household, or perhaps all adult members of each household who regularly took part in hasidic prayer services. The last of these possibilities seems the most likely. Estimating that there were, on average, 1.25 adult men per hasidic household (including the head of each household and a second adult male—a son or son-in-law—in every fourth household) means that, to obtain a true estimate of the total number of hasidim, it is necessary to multiply the official figures by 4 (5:1.25). This maximum estimate, together with a minimum estimate, is presented in Table 1. The estimates range from 3 to 8.9 per cent. Even if we assume that the figures include only one head of each five-person household, the percentage of hasidim in the Jewish population of the voivodeship of Podlasie did not exceed 11 per cent. However, this figure seems unlikely. We may legitimately assume that not every man who attended the hasidic *shtibl* represented an entire family. There were a considerable number of adult males (i.e. over 13 years old) who had not established their own families, and they were likely to be counted with the hasidim. Families were often divided between the hasidim and mitnagedim, with hasidism appealing to younger men and to women.[116] Therefore, it is more than likely that the best estimate is somewhat lower than 10 per cent.

number of adult males would rise too, so the proportions and the final statistics relating to hasidim would not change. For the size of Jewish families in Poland in the 18th century, see Mahler, *Yidn in amolikn Poyln*, i. 182–4. Mahler uses an average of 6 individuals per household, but this number is somewhat greater than the number of people in a family, because it may include domestic servants, shop assistants, students, etc.

[115]  AGAD, CWW 1439, pp. 194–288.

[116]  This was particularly emphasized by Menahem Mendel Lefin; see Sinkoff, 'Tradition and Transition', 113–16. Also Polish maskilim, e.g. Abraham Stern and Eliasz Moszkowski, complained about the way that hasidism appealed especially to women and young people. See Mahler, *Haḥasidut*

FIG. 6. Distribution of hasidim in the voivodeship of Podlasie in 1823,
according to official reports

One additional aspect is the question of the accuracy of the definition employed
in the reports of a 'hasid' discussed above. It seems reasonable to assume that most
of the numbers of hasidim given in Table 1 were based on the number of males fre-
quenting the local *shtibl*. However, is it not legitimate to assume, one might argue,
that, in addition to a solid core of hasidim (i.e. those who regularly visited a hasidic

*vehahaskalah*, 477–80; AGAD, CWW 1436, pp. 215–33. In Parczew the community board reported in
1824: 'those who join them [the hasidim] take items, or money, from their father or wife and they
spend it together [with the hasidim]; such are the negative outcomes, as well as the fact that other children no longer obey their parents'.

**Table 1.** Hasidim in the voivodeship of Podlasie, 1823

| Town | Total Jewish population (1827[a]) | No. of Jewish families (1830) | No. of hasidim (1823) | % of hasidim in Jewish population (est.) (1823) | |
|---|---|---|---|---|---|
| | | | | Minimum[b] | Maximum |
| (1) | (2) | (3) | (4) | (5) | (6) |
| Adamów | 108 | 21 | 0 | 0 | 0 |
| Biała | 2,091 | 415 | 15 | 0.7 | 2.9 |
| Garwolin | 141 | 385 | 0 | 0 | 0 |
| Kosów | 315 | 147 | 10 | 3.2 | 12.7 |
| Łaskarzew | 0 | 0 | 0 | 0 | 0 |
| Łuków | 2,023 | 674 | 20 | 1.0 | 3.9 |
| Maciejowice | 337 | 87 | 0 | 0 | 0 |
| Osieck | 102 | 23 | 0 | 0 | 0 |
| Parczew | 1,079 | 294 | 40 | 3.7 | 14.8 |
| Parysów | 220 | 48 | 0 | 0 | 0 |
| Siedlce | 2,908 | 391 | 30 | 1.0 | 4.1 |
| Sokołów | 1,186 | 484 | 100 | 8.4 | 33.7 |
| Stężyca | 0 | 0 | 0 | 0 | 0 |
| Stoczek | 0 | 0 | 0 | 0 | 0 |
| Terespol | 1,019 | 250 | 5 | 0.5 | 2.0 |
| Węgrów | 1,436 | 379 | 30[c] | 7.9[d] | 7.9 |
| Żelechów | 1,266 | 466 | 60 | 4.7 | 19.0 |
| Total | 14,231 | 4,064 | 430 | 3.0 | 8.9 |

[a] The census closest to the 1823–4 investigation.
[b] Col. 4 divided by col. 2.
[c] No. of families. For calculation of the total this figure has been multiplied by five.
[d] Calculation based on the number of families (col. 3).

*Sources*: AGAD, CWW 1871, pp. 9–38; 1439, pp. 194–288; Wasiutyński, *Ludność żydowska w Polsce*.

*shtibl*), there would have been numerous individuals who visited hasidic courts and prayer halls only occasionally, who were not strongly tied to the hasidic dynasties and yet who were closely associated with hasidism? Reliable data from later periods confirm the existence of such quasi-hasidim. It is impossible to deny the existence of such quasi-hasidim in the first three decades of the nineteenth century, although we have no direct information confirming their existence either. One can assume that, even if they did exist, they could not have been too widespread during this period. Numerous local conflicts between the non-hasidic majority and hasidim, such as the altercations in Częstochowa, Łask, and Płock described above, indicate that the divisions between the two factions were quite often clear-cut and that hasidism in many localities was still a dissident movement. As sharp divisions restrict transitory options, the Kingdom of Poland could not have been a particularly favourable environment for such quasi-hasidic choices before the 1830–1 Uprising. This is not to say that hasidic and non-hasidic communities were strictly segregated and that there were no areas of contact. As we have seen, a hasidic candidate could easily have been elected as community rabbi in a non-hasidic community, if his fame as a talmudic scholar was sufficiently great. In addition, famous tsadikim, like any other miracle-worker, were frequently visited by many ordinary Jews. However, this should not be interpreted as an expression of any strong hasidic sympathies, because massive pilgrimages to famous tsadikim were made mainly to seek medical help or out of sheer curiosity.[117] After all, Christians visiting a tsadik could not have been suspected of harbouring hasidic tendencies and we have a considerable number of testimonies confirming such visits.[118] Equally, one can hardly believe that Jewish crowds visiting British missionaries during their missionary travels were aspiring to be converted.[119] In addition, those who occasionally visited a famous tsadik for medical help were often faced with local community conflicts between the hasidim and the non-hasidic majority when they returned to their communities and had to make a clear choice for one or the other option. As many of these clashes were of a financial nature, it was virtually impossible to remain indifferent to them. This, in turn, significantly limited the possibility of transitory quasi-hasidic affiliations. Areas of contact did not necessarily encourage one to assume a semi-hasidic position therefore. It would appear that such quasi-hasidism was more frequently encountered only during the later stage of the hasidic conquest, when the movement had turned its attention to Jewish community institutions. In the Kingdom of Poland this only came about in the 1840s (see the following chapter). In summary, we might assume that there were Jews with a hasidic leaning who did not adhere to any specific hasidic court, who did not visit the *shtiblekh* regularly, and who did not openly manifest their hasidic sympathies, and that this was the reason why they were not included in the numbers delivered to the authorities by the local mitnagedim, Jewish community boards, or by converts. Still, it is safe to assume that, in the period under consideration, these quasi-hasidim did not constitute a large group and their existence would not have distorted the general picture of a relatively low number of adherents of hasidism.

## CONCLUSIONS

None of these figures can be taken entirely at face value. Nevertheless, they provide an approximation of the size of the hasidic movement in the Kingdom of

---

[117] See e.g. [Antoni Eisenbaum], 'O Rabinach', *Rozmaitości*, 5 (1822), 42; 'Die Gemeinde Lublin', *AZJ* 5 (1841), 474.

[118] See e.g. Friedländer, *Über die Verbesserung der Israeliten im Königreich Pohlen*, 40; Segel, 'O chasydach i chasydyźmie', 680; Grochowska, 'Srul Rabi Bal-Szim', 50–3; Chajes, 'Baal-Szem-Tow u chrześcijan', 445–7, 557–65. See also Cała, 'The Cult of Tzaddikim among Non-Jews in Poland'.

[119] Missionary reports have often revealed great interest in their activities on the part of the local Jewish population, yet a lack of any tangible effects from their activity. See e.g. L[udwig] Hoff and G. Wendt, 'Extracts of a Letter from Messrs. Hoff and Wendt, Missionaries in Poland', *JE* 8 (1823), 449; W[ilhelm] F[erdynand] Becker, 'Journal of Messrs. Becker', *JE* 11 (1826), 227.

Poland during the 1820s. The data for Częstochowa, Płock, and the voivodeship of Podlasie, the 1834 estimates by the Jewish Committee, and Daniel Neufeld's account (published in 1862) all point to approximately similar percentages. Therefore, it seems likely that they could be applied to the entire Kingdom, in which case, the adherents of hasidism in Congress Poland would have numbered between 3 and 10 per cent of the Jewish population. A figure closer to the upper limit seems more likely, especially given the pace at which the hasidic movement grew during the following decades. Obviously, there would have been centres with a significantly higher percentage of hasidim at this time. In Sokołów, for example, the hasidim had three prayer houses on the properties of Jojna Hurwec, Moszek Ajzenberg, and Dawid Jankielowicz, as well as their own facilities for kosher slaughtering.[120] In Łask the percentage of hasidim in the town's Jewish population in 1828 appears to have reached 25 per cent.[121] There surely would have been larger concentrations of hasidim in the towns that served as the headquarters for the tsadikim, e.g. Kozienice, Radzyń, Opatów, and Żelechów. Yet even in these centres the numbers of hasidim were not considerable. The hasidim made up less than 20 per cent of the Jewish community in Żelechów in 1824. The pilgrimage to Meir Rotenberg (who was one of the most important tsadikim of his generation) in Stopnica numbered 'hundreds of Jews from near and far' in 1819, yet later, at the height of his fame, only about 200 hasidim came from out of town to his court in Opatów on the sabbath and 500–600 on religious festivals.[122] Even if we were to assume that an equal number of followers of the *rebbe* lived in Opatów, the hasidim would still have not constituted a decisive majority of the town's Jews, who numbered 1,377 in 1827.[123] Confirmation of the rather small scale of the pilgrimages (small compared to the figures known from the early twentieth century) comes also from other sources.[124]

---

[120] AGAD, CWW 1871, pp. 102–6; CWW 1786, pp. 8–20.

[121] AGAD, KWK 700, p. 283. Łask had been known to be a centre of hasidic activity from at least 1820; see e.g. AGAD, CWW 1555, pp. 4–20; KWK 702, pp. 4–14.

[122] Majmon, 'Luźne kartki'; AGAD, KRSW 6635, fos. 16–17; Mahler, *Haḥasidut vehahaskalah*, 495–7.

[123] The hasidic court of Shneur Zalman of Lyady was famous for its size. He instructed his followers not to visit him more than once a year. See Etkes, 'Darko shel rabi shneur zalman', 334–41; Loewenthal, *Communicating the Infinite*, 47–8. The usual interpretation notwithstanding, the order might have been issued not because the tsadik had too many followers, but because of the tendency of the Habad school he founded to give hasidism a more speculative, less popular character. This interpretation is supported by the fact that the order was issued together with his book the *Tanya*, which was supposed to be a widely accessible spiritual guide.

[124] A report by a maskil from Działoszyce, Eliasz Moszkowski, in 1845 (i.e. after twenty-five years of significant hasidic growth) stated: 'Upwards of several hundred men, women, and children, and even entire families, come on the sabbath from distant regions of the [Congress] Kingdom to the *rebbe*s; on holidays they number in the thousands.' See AGAD, CWW 1436, pp. 215–33 (see App. 11). Similar figures are recorded for pilgrimages outside the Congress Kingdom. In 1826 about 1,000 hasidim came to the court of Israel of Ruzhin, about 3,000 to Przemyślany in 1839, and over 3,000 to Sadagóra

If these numbers appear suspiciously low, the reason is the anachronistic projection of the situation in the second half of the nineteenth century back onto the first half of the century. In the constitutional period (1815–30), hasidism was still a small-scale movement (although it was not marginal) and was treated as such by the maskilim of the Kingdom. It should be stressed that hasidism did increase its sphere of influence in the period under consideration. The hasidim did become more visible in nearly all the Jewish communities in the Kingdom. We may even be able to assume that the uneven distribution of the movement resulted in the total dominance of hasidism in some areas. Still, the maskilim were remarkably moderate in addressing these processes. It seems legitimate to believe that their perceptions did not completely lack a realistic assessment of the state of affairs, especially given that the figures we have available prove that the hasidic movement was not still a decisive power in Congress Poland. Therefore, it seems that the maskilim were, in a sense, correct in seeing the real danger as being to the progress of education in traditional *kahal* institutions, rather than in this new mystical movement. Alarmist descriptions of hasidism by Radomiński and Niemcewicz, and the aggressive anti-hasidic actions undertaken by Stern, who was one of the most influential Jews in Congress Poland (and, allegedly, by Posner), could not and did not change the generally tolerant attitude of the majority of Polish maskilim towards that movement. Admittedly, this 'tolerance' was the product of their historical setting, which restrained the maskilim from displaying their intolerant tendencies, rather than of an idealistic conviction regarding the virtues of tolerance. Even so, their 'lack of intolerance' was one of the most significant features of the ideological profile of the Polish maskilim.

One should also point out that there were other factors that softened the anti-hasidic criticism of the Polish Haskalah. Of these, the more rationalistic profile of Polish hasidism, its social concerns, unobtrusiveness, and more 'democratic' organization, must have been the most important. The Polish hasidim appeared to be less harmful and less abhorrent than their Galician or Ukrainian co-believers. Also, the ideological dependence of the Polish maskilim on the Berlin Haskalah could conceivably have hampered the development of independent criticism, so that the Polish maskilim might have felt less inclined to attack it wholeheartedly. Still, it seems that the deciding factor for the low level of interest in the hasidic movement shown by the Polish maskilim was the relatively low number of adherents of hasidism and their limited influence. Polish Jewish followers of the Enlightenment turned their interest to hasidism only in the 1830s and 1840s, when hasidism enjoyed remarkable growth and considerably expanded its sphere of influence. It was at that stage that the maskilim realized that the 'dark fanatics' might really be a dangerous enemy.

on Yom Kippur in 1844. Assaf, *The Regal Way*, 157, 352 n. 5, regards these figures as inflated. In 1846 Jews in Warka reported to the British missionaries that more than 4,000 hasidim had arrived in this town to celebrate Rosh Hashanah. See AGAD, CWW 1457, p. 575.

# FOUR

# *Growing Interest, Growing Conflict,*
# *1831–1860*

THE collapse of the November Uprising, the downfall of constitutional government in the Kingdom of Poland, and ongoing unification with the Russian
empire brought obvious changes to the situation of society as a whole, and to the
situation of Jewish society, including the hasidim and supporters of modernization.[1] Both groups grew rapidly in the period between the November and the
January uprisings. At the same time it was a period in which the 'Jewish policy' of
the Polish government underwent a perceptible re-evaluation, gradually moving
away from its plans to 'civilize' and Polonize the Jewish population, and instead
endeavouring to preserve the status quo and social stability. This change of policy
considerably weakened the position of Haskalah supporters, who no longer constituted an important ally for the Polish government. At the same time the shift in
policy created a favourable environment for the development of the hasidic movement (see the discussion on pp. 126–35), which was now able to claim legitimately
that it was maintaining public order. The result was that interest in hasidism
increased among the Polish maskilim, as did hostility on both sides.

## GROWING INTEREST IN HASIDISM

The publication in the late 1830s and the early 1840s of a number of texts discussing hasidic issues written by Polish maskilim was an indicator of a gradual
growth of interest in hasidism. A few were literary texts, but these were considerably outnumbered by journalistic pieces. For example, hasidism was often mentioned in narratives concerning Jewish communities in Poland, especially those from
the provinces, in the German Jewish periodical *Allgemeine Zeitung des Judentums*.
In the first years of its existence the periodical displayed a keen interest in religious
issues and the day-to-day life of Jews in eastern Europe, so accounts from Warsaw,
Kalisz, Częstochowa, and the Free City of Kraków featured relatively often.[2]
Attitudes towards hasidism in these texts were extremely varied, and the periodi-

[1] See Eisenbach, *Emancypacja Żydów*, 316–22, for the summary of the 'Jewish politics' of the government of the Congress Kingdom in the period of unification (1831–64).

[2] See e.g. 'Krakau' [correspondence], *AZJ* 4 (1840), 665; 'Krakau' [correspondence], *AZJ* 5 (1841),

43.

cal itself did not adopt a clear policy in this respect. The Warsaw correspondent Dr Józef Bernstein wrote a completely objective report on the growth in significance of this 'large party' and its role in the election of the chief rabbi of Warsaw, Hayim Dawidsohn.[3] Similarly neutral was the description of Anna Waldenberg's school for Jewish girls.[4] A completely different tone was used in relation to the hasidim by an anonymous correspondent who was closely connected with the Rabbinical School (possibly Antoni Eisenbaum). In this emotional and antagonistic piece of writing, the hasidim were accused of preventing the intellectual and economic growth of Polish Jews.[5] Yet another attitude to hasidism was that displayed by the moderately oppositionist author of a correspondence concerning the smoking of tobacco in the *beit midrash*. The author was possibly Jakub Tugendhold.[6] This and other accounts were undoubtedly written because of the growing interest in the movement, which could be observed in German Jewish periodicals (particularly in *Allgemeine Zeitung des Judentums* as well as in *Der Orient* and *Israelitische Annalen*) in the late 1830s and the early 1840s.[7] The phenomenon was two-sided: hasidism was increasingly frequently mentioned in the Jewish press because an increasing number of accounts of it were coming from eastern Europe; these, in turn, were the result of the growing importance of hasidism in those German Jewish publications that were read there. The Polish maskilim usually published their works in *Allgemeine Zeitung des Judentums* (with the exception of Chaim Zelig Słonimski and Jacob Reifman, who regularly wrote for *Der Orient*). Their opinions of hasidism were usually based on the essay *Der Chassidismus in Polen*, which was published in the journal in 1839–40. This work was considered to be a reliable source of information about the hasidim in the Kingdom of Poland, even though it dwelt entirely on its earlier doctrine and, like the articles in the two other periodicals, omitted to mention issues such as the social structure, morality, and everyday life of the hasidim in Poland. This was not surprising, given that the article was written by the maskil Julius Barasch of Brody (1815–63), who, being at that time a young student of medical science in Berlin, could not have had a great knowledge of hasidism in the Kingdom.[8] This indicates

---

[3] See J[oseph] B[ernstein], 'Zeitungsnachrichten. Russland und Polen. Warschau' [correspondence], *AZJ* 3 (1839), 361.

[4] L., 'Russland und Polen. Warschau' [correspondence], *AZJ* 4 (1840), 494–5.

[5] 'Die Rabbinerschule', *AZJ* 4 (1840), 330–6.

[6] 'Russland und Polen. Warschau' [correspondence], *AZJ* 4 (1840), 649–51.

[7] See e.g. 'Der Chassidismus in Polen. 1. Artikel', *Der Orient*, 2 (1841), 46–8, 55–6; 'Orient. Jerusalem' [correspondence], *Der Orient*, 4 (1843), 121–2; 'Die Gallizischen Rabbinen', *Israelitische Annalen*, 1 (1839), 238–9, 246–7, 253; 'Getreues Bild von der Beschaffenheit der Israeliten in Polesie, Lithauen und Reußen', *Israelitische Annalen*, 2 (1840), 261–3, 269–71, 278–9, 294–6.

[8] Julius Barasch, 'Der Chassidismus in Polen', *AZJ* 3 (1839), 618–20, 631–2, 650–1; 4 (1840), 245–6, 378–90, 394–6, 577–9, 588–94. The article was published under the nom de plume 'Julius Marcussohn B——', which was explained only in 1858 by Ludwig Philippsohn, 'Der Chassidismus', *AZJ* 22 (1858), 713. 'Poland', as used in the title of the article, is a generic term and differentiates Polish hasidism from medieval *hasidei ashkenaz*. Had 'Poland' in the title had a geographical meaning, the main focus of interest would have been hasidism in the Kingdom of Poland or, even more broadly,

how poorly informed the Polish maskilim must have been about the issue of Polish hasidism.

Even Jakub Bursztyński wrote extensively about the 'hasidic plague' in the early 1840s. While, as mentioned in the previous chapter, his prolific correspondence with the provincial authorities during 1821 included not a single acknowledgement of the existence of hasidism, twenty years later, in his report from Często-chowa to the German Jewish press, he proudly listed the successes of the enlightened community in fighting this 'epidemic' and reported that 'the poison brought to Poland from Ukraine 50–60 years before' had done less damage in Częstochowa than in other communities, and that the hasidim in Częstochowa, who were the followers of the tsadik Issachar Ber of Radoszyce (1765–1843), were some of the most moderate. In the author's opinion, this was the result of the war with hasidim that had been fiercely fought by the whole Jewish community.[9]

Such an openly hostile style was typical of correspondents from the provincial towns and cities. For example, an author from Kalisz made a hostile allusion to the hasidim while reporting their opposition to the Jewish Hospital, the director of which was a local maskil, Ludwig Mamroth.[10] A Lublin correspondent devoted a comparatively large amount of space to the hasidim, although he simultaneously claimed that there were few of them in that city. He stated that the tsadikim were consulted not only by a handful of hasidim, but also by the mitnagedim, because Jews in Lublin had practically no access to any medical facilities. Thus, fraudulent miracle-workers provided the only form of health care to the poor masses. Like-wise, the hasidic *beit midrash* was primarily a popular place for gossip (*Schwatzhaus*), rather than for prayers or religious studies (*Lehrhaus*).[11]

The most fruitful source of information about the attitudes of contemporary maskilim towards hasidism is an interesting debate centred on the controversy sur-rounding Jewish education in Poland. Opinions were published in *Korespondent*, *Gazeta Poranna*, *Gazeta Codzienna*, and *Allgemeine Zeitung des Judentums* in the years 1839–40. The debate was started by a young merchant and maskil from Warsaw, Edward Hering (1818–88).[12] Voicing his opinion on the progress of education, he gave the chief credit in this respect to the Rabbinical School and elementary schools that had been operating in Warsaw since 1820. However, he acknowledged that some contribution, albeit involuntary, had also been made by the hasidic sect, which had facilitated the progress of 'the light of civilization'

in the territories of the former Polish–Lithuanian Commonwealth. The same holds true for the above-mentioned articles published in *Der Orient*.

[9] J[akub] B[ursztyński], 'Russland und Polen. Czenstochau' [correspondence], *AZJ* 5 (1841), 567–8.

[10] 'Russland und Polen. Von der polnischen Gränze' [correspondence], *AZJ* 5 (1840), 310.

[11] 'Die Gemeinde Lublin', *AZJ* 5 (1841), 408–10, 446–7, 474–5, 534–6.

[12] Edward Hering, 'Rzut oka na stan oświaty Izraelitów w Polsce', *Gazeta Poranna*, 286 (1839), 3–4; 288 (1839), 3–4; also in *Korespondent*, 279 (1839), 3–4; 281 (1839), 3–4. Some information on Hering can be found in Guterman, *Perakim betoledot yehudei polin*, 180–2.

among the fanatical Jewish masses by liberalizing the general principles of traditional Judaism.[13] He described it in one inordinately long sentence:

Even the sect of the hasidim, the sect whose true basis and growth have not been explained
clearly, the sect which has so greatly departed from its original meaning through its activities, which is scorned by almost more than half of its 'almost co-believers', and which seeks
in debauched behaviour some small compensation for its strict adherence to rules, through
this libertinism and the liberality of its rules, inadvertently contributes to the breaking
down of this age-old barrier which has prevented the light of civilization from reaching
those who combine religion with fanaticism and call each and any novelty contemptible,
even those that have long been known, not giving even a thought to the benefits such a
novelty might bring.[14]

Hering observed that, despite all their faults, the hasidim were capable of selfless
acts and higher feelings, for example 'respect and love . . . sacrifice and a scorn for
both privilege and money'. This made them strong, and gave the hasidic leaders
unlimited power over their followers. However, it also rendered a hasid potentially
'more perceptive and more willing to be exposed to the impressions of education',
and there was hope that 'with time, out of this stagnating pool, one day a clear
stream will flow forth'. Naturally, Hering hastened to add that it was not his intention to applaud the hasidic sect, because its good acts were performed inadvertently,
and even ran counter to the will of the hasidim.

More than any other text of the period, this article illustrated the appalling lack
of knowledge the Polish maskilim had of hasidism. Hering realized this and wrote
about the hitherto unexplained sources of the strength of this movement, and formulated the first theories concerning the issue. Both the fact that Hering undertook
to reflect on hasidism and that he attempted to integrate his reflections into the
more general educational plans were innovative. At the same time, however, his
opinions concerning the hasidim, and particularly their libertinism and debauchery, indicated that their author had little idea of the real attitude of the hasidim to
ritual law, and that his opinions were based upon superficialities (probably on
David Friedländer's treatise) rather than on thorough observation. What is of
interest is that he used exactly the same generalizations and even the same adjec-
tives to describe hasidism as had been used in maskilic literature since the end of
the eighteenth century.

Another, equally meaningful, event was the reaction to Hering's hypothesis that
the hasidim might inadvertently turn out to be favourable to progress. Izaak Emes
(probably a nom de plume) rejected all of the theses contained in Hering's article
and focused on the hasidic issue.[15] He rejected the belief that liberalizing ritual

---

[13] The same opinion was reiterated in the 1870s by the Russian maskil Abraham Ber Gottlober. See
Feiner, *Haskalah and History*, 316.

[14] Edward Hering, 'Rzut oka na stan oświaty Izraelitów w Polsce', *Gazeta Poranna*, 286 (1839), 4.

[15] Izaak Emes, 'Uwagi nad artykułem: "Rzut oka na stan Izraelitów w Polsce"', *Gazeta Codzienna*,
2668 (1839), 3–4; 2669 (1839), 3–4.

regulations would lead the hasidim to enlightenment, because the hasidim had replaced ritual with blind faith in the tsadikim, in whom they had boundless trust and who, in their opinion, wielded the power to influence divine will. He believed that the hasidim were tainted with hatred for all those Israelites who did not share their views. Blind faith even blighted their appearance: 'Their gait and posture, and even their everyday speech, all bear the stigma of their ignorant view of the world. Enemies of burgeoning enlightenment, they secretly curse its worshippers.' By luring frivolous young people, hasidism was growing in strength day by day. Faith in the tsadikim had the potential to be used as a civilizing tool, but only if the tsadikim themselves were willing to encourage this civilizing effect. Meanwhile, the leaders kept their followers in a state of fanaticism and ignorance so that they might benefit more easily from this.

An article written by Emes quoted nearly all of the accusations to have appeared in maskilic criticisms of hasidism, which at that stage were still virtually absent from maskilic literature in the Congress Kingdom, but which were widespread, for example, in Galicia. The hasidim were described as ignorant and fanatical adversaries of enlightenment who fought their opponents with great hatred; their leaders deliberately kept their followers in a state of ignorance because they benefited financially from their lack of enlightenment. Emes rejected all the attempts that had been made to reflect upon the development of the movement. He referred to Hering's thesis as completely erroneous; the sole aspect of the thesis that aroused respect was Hering's ignorance ('it must be said of the author that he displays little knowledge of this zealous religious sect'), because this was proof of just how distant Hering was from the phenomenon. It appears that the virtue of ignorance in this matter was exceptionally widespread. Deviating briefly from the press debate, we may quote the example of Abraham Buchner, who, in advertising subscriptions to his work *Kwiaty wschodnie* (Flowers of the East), stated that it had been ordered 'by the Reverend Rabbi Israel of Warka'.[16] One of the most famous, and indisputably the most active, tsadikim of this generation, the rabbi of Warka was known under his second name, Isaac. Abraham Paprocki, who taught history at the Rabbinical School, had an equally superficial knowledge of the hasidim. There is no mention of hasidism in the Kingdom in his first Polish course book on Jewish history, and the cursory notes on the beginnings of the movement and religious relations in the western provinces of the Russian empire were copied verbatim from Marcus Jost.[17] The discrepancy between accounts (even where they were reprints) of the religiosity of the Russian hasidim, and a complete lack of any information about the hasidim in the Kingdom of Poland, are striking here.

Others who commented on Hering's article were equally poorly informed. Antoni Eisenbaum accused the author of ignorance and was appalled at the fact

---

[16] A[braham] Buchner, 'Prospekt na dzieło *Kwiaty wschodnie*', *Gazeta Codzienna*, 2994 (1840), 1–2.

[17] Paprocki, *Krótki rys dziejów ludu izraelskiego*, 285–7, 315–18.

that Hering should think that the hasidim might—even inadvertently—raise the level of education among Jews:

It is beyond me to understand how Mr H. expects the hasidim to spread enlightenment among Jews. Can Mr H. name even one hasid who would send his son to school or make him an apprentice? Has he ever seen an Israelite engaged in a craft who, on subsequently becoming a supporter of this school, would still pursue his trade? Has he detected in their behaviour any small trace of approaching civilization, or in their tidiness, morality, dress, etc.? In my view, the sect hinders the dawning of enlightenment among Polish Israelites. Its leaders will try to prevent even the smallest beam of light from reaching their followers for ever. Otherwise, what use would their false promises have and what would become of their authority?[18]

Thus Eisenbaum reiterated the traditional anti-hasidic accusations in the belligerent form that he favoured, and barely touched upon Hering's main thesis. He was not willing to change his attitude to hasidism, or even consider its positive aspects, because, had he acknowledged the role the hasidim had played in spreading enlightenment and their readiness to accept it, he would have had to place less emphasis on the role of the Rabbinical School which he headed (the article extolled its virtues) and also admit his failure in educating the followers of hasidism. Eisenbaum evidently took Hering's article personally and felt offended.

Yet, regardless of this confrontation with Hering, Eisenbaum's views had undergone a significant transformation. While, in the 1820s, his early texts had completely ignored hasidism, in the late 1830s he readily admitted that the movement constituted an important problem, although as yet he did not see the need for deeper reflection. The change in perceptions of the importance of hasidism was even clearer in the next voice to be heard in this discussion. More than likely, this also belonged to Eisenbaum or to one of his close associates. The author claimed that hasidism was the main threat to the progress of 'civilization' among Polish Jews, and that its success constituted the main barrier to the spread of enlightenment.[19] This opinion was also shared by other participants in the debate.[20] After twenty years of little more than a peripheral presence in Polish maskilic literature, hasidism was beginning to emerge as one of the main problems in the modernization of Polish Jews, although the growth in interest still did not reflect a greater knowledge of the issue. What had also not changed was the perception of hasidism (which had been unstintingly hostile since the end of the eighteenth century), the arguments used against it, and the programmes (or rather the lack of them) under way to fight it, while the one attempt to reflect on the phenomenon (that of Edward Hering) had met with the openly hostile reactions of offended, established 'progressives'.

[18] Z. [Antoni Eisenbaum], 'Uwagi nad artykułem p. Hering', *Gazeta Codzienna*, 2678 (1839), 3.

[19] 'Die Rabbinerschule', *AZJ* 4 (1840), 330–1, 333.

[20] A.W., 'Odpowiedź na "Uwagi p. Z. nad Artykułem p. Hering"', *Gazeta Codzienna*, 2705 (1840), 3–4; See J[oseph] B[ernstein], 'Zeitungsnachrichten. Russland und Polen. Warschau' [correspondence], *AZJ* 4 (1840), 89–90.

## THE *THEATRE OF THE HASIDIM* OF
## EFRAIM FISCHELSOHN

A very interesting, if somewhat isolated, example of the use of the hasidic motif in literature was the play written by the maskil Efraim Fishel Fischelsohn from Zamość in the late 1830s or early 1840s and published posthumously. Little information about Fischelsohn himself is available. He lived in Lublin and Zamość, where he befriended Joseph Zederbaum and Solomon Ettinger, and he wrote both in Hebrew and in Yiddish.[21] The play *Teater fun khsidim* (The Theatre of the Hasidim), which has survived in manuscript form, involved a typical dispute, which was not adaptable for the stage, between an enlightened protagonist, Leib Philosopher, and a group of hasidim from Bełz.[22] The discussion takes place in a hasidic *beit midrash* in Kielce,[23] where Leib, a merchant from Kraków, studies traditional Hebrew texts (Maimonidean, of course). Enlightened, but faithful to his religion and tradition, he quotes typically maskilic arguments against hasidism, proves its irrationality, and depicts the parasitic life of the tsadikim, who financially exploit the poorer Jews. Leib supports his rational arguments with references to a wealth of rabbinical literature, with the aim of persuading the reader of his erudition. Leib's polemicists do not enter into any factual discussion with him, but instead invite him to visit a tsadik and to drink alcohol (of course, Leib abstains), and attempt to make him see the greatness of the tsadik with tales of his miracles, the visits of his soul to heaven, and his extraordinary teaching. Yet, ultimately, they turn out to be shiftless, devious, and dull-witted parasites, gluttons, and ignoramuses, as illustrated by their attitude both to their enlightened co-believers and to Christian circles. The criticism of the devious practices used by the hasidim with regard to non-Jews occupies an important place in the discussion. The debate, of course, culminates in the maskil's triumph, and with students from the yeshiva (the traditional talmudic academy) hearing of it and siding with Leib, and castigating the hasidim as 'beggars and monstrous scoundrels'.

Fischelsohn's text was the first maskilic literary work in the Kingdom of Poland to use the motif of hasidism, and also one of the few literary texts written within Polish maskilic circles in the 1840s. But its originality did not end here. *Teater fun khsidim* was allegedly the only literary dispute between a hasid and a maskil to give the impression of being a likely record of hasidic propaganda activities. The debate was couched in terse, colloquial language, often interspersed with vulgarisms,

---

[21] Scarce biographical data on Fischelsohn can be found in Zinberg, *History of Jewish Literature*, ix. 182–3.

[22] The drama was published only in 1929; Fischelsohn, 'Teater fun khsidim'. See a discussion of it in Borodianski, 'Araynfir-shtudye tsum *Teater fun khsidim*'.

[23] It should be noted that at that time not only was there not one single *beit midrash*, but there was also not one Jew living in Kielce, a fact that Fischelsohn must have known. Thus literary Kielce was a mythical never-never land.

which were used in equal measure by both sides (Leib called the tsadikim 'thieves, bastards and scoundrels').[24] The difference between the two sides lay not only in their arguments, but also in their diametrically opposing world-views. Thus it would seem that, notwithstanding the author's sympathy for Leib's arguments, he attempted to create as faithful a representation as possible of both sides in the conflict. Finally, the fact that the text was written in Yiddish is worth mentioning, because the use of this language was still not popular among the east European maskilim.

All these features of Fischelsohn's text point to its close relationship with the writings of Solomon Ettinger, who also lived in Zamość. He was the most prominent poet to write in Yiddish in the first half of the nineteenth century and he occasionally turned to hasidic themes.[25] In addition to the writers being friends and living in the same town, there is no doubt that, like other maskilim in Zamość, both were strongly influenced by the Galician Haskalah, and particularly by the works of Menahem Mendel Lefin. In Ettinger's case, this has been corroborated by written sources, whereas in Fischelsohn's case it can be inferred from his preserved work. Lefin's strategy (one also adopted by his disciples) was carried out literally in *Teater fun khsidim*: Lefin preferred literary to political debate[26] and, both in promoting Haskalah ideology and in engaging in conflict with hasidism, he tended to use Yiddish. Fischelsohn's text also provided evidence of some literary connections with contemporary Galician writers, for example with Joseph Perl's satires. Likewise, the structure showed some similarities with that of a philosophical dialogue between an alleged supporter of enlightenment (Rabbi Solomon of Chełm) and the medieval philosopher Maimonides, used by Judah Leib Mieses in his anti-hasidic satire *Kinat ha'emet* (The Zeal for Truth).[27] The connections with Perl's anti-hasidic publications were even more pronounced in the unpublished foreword to the play.[28] The narrator of the Hebrew text is a hasid, who explains that *Teater fun khsidim* is, in fact, a hasidic text and is to be studied by the hasidim in order that their beliefs should be strengthened. In addition, the readers of the play were to reject the arguments of the enlightened Leib, no matter how convincing they might seem. This was a typically deceptive device, which was similar to that of Perl's epistolary novel *Megaleh temirin* (Revealer of Secrets),

[24] Fischelsohn, 'Teater fun khsidim', 658.

[25] See e.g. Salomon Ettinger, *Sheydim*, in id., *Ale ksovim*, 256–9. A mention of hasidic motives in Ettinger's writings can be found in Mahler, *Hasidism and the Jewish Enlightenment*, 236–7.

[26] On Lefin's literary strategies, see my comments in Chapter 1; for a more detailed analysis, see Sinkoff, 'Strategy and Ruse in the Haskalah of Mendel Lefin of Satanow'.

[27] On Mieses's anti-hasidic satires in *Kinat ha'emet*, see Friedlander, 'Hasidism as the Image of Demonism'; id., 'The Struggle of the Mitnagdim and Maskilim against Hasidism'; Werses, 'Hahasidut be'einei sifrut hahaskalah'; Feiner, *Haskalah and History*, 96–104.

[28] Borodianski only published the summary; see Borodianski, 'Araynfir-shtudye tsum *Teater fun khsidim*', 633–4. The manuscript of the introduction has been preserved in the YIVO Archives, RG 87: Simon Dubnow Collection 996, pp. 75716–22.

written in the form of letters between hasidim. Connections with Perl's novel were emphasized by the inclusion of a 'hasidic' letter concerning a similar subject in the foreword.

Thus Fischelsohn's ideological, and even stylistic, connections with the Galician Haskalah were evident. Efraim Fischelsohn of Zamość was the first maskil in the Congress Kingdom to have devoted so much attention to hasidim since Abraham Stern of Hrubieszów, who had made hasidism one of the most important objects of his public activity in the second and third decades of the nineteenth century. The fact that both maskilim were connected with the Haskalah school in Zamość (which ideologically was known to be closely allied with Galicia) could not be simply a coincidence.

## REFORM PROJECTS: ELIASZ MOSZKOWSKI

The growth of interest in the hasidim was also occasioned by the appearance of the first projects to reform Jewish society to take into account the existence of this movement. This was a novelty, because, in the wealth of literature referring to the 'Jewish issue' and numerous reform projects of the second and third decades of the nineteenth century, hasidism was mentioned only in passing, and, moreover, by Christian writers as a rule (such as Niemcewicz and Radomiński). Abraham Stern was an exception here. In the 1840s maskilic reform projects also began to deal with the hasidic question much more extensively. For example, Benjamin Rosenblum, a doctor from Warsaw, proposed a number of religious reforms in his short work, under the pretext of discussing Jewish hygiene. Although his work was not openly hostile towards traditional circles, Rosenblum proved, point by point, the need for fundamental changes to take place in circumcision, ritual baths, the *ḥeder*, the synagogue, etc. Interestingly, he also mentioned the hasidim, saying that, because of their lack of hygiene, the hasidic baths constituted a threat to the whole population—that of contracting venereal disease—and that hasidic houses of prayer, in which 'rocking to and fro and ill-tempered shouting' was common, were a danger to the health and lives of their regular visitors.[29]

A memorandum concerning improvements to the situation of Jews in Poland was also written at this time by Eliasz Moszkowski, an influential entrepreneur and maskil from the small provincial town of Działoszyce.[30] The proposal, which Moszkowski put before the Government Commission for Internal and Religious Affairs in 1845, contained plans to reform Jewish schools, ways of counteracting vagrancy, begging, and luxury, improvements in certifying marital status, the establishment

[29] Rosenblum, *Uwagi nad teraźniejszym stanem starozakonnych*.

[30] See Kozłowska, 'Z dziejów przedsiębiorczości żydowskiej w Małopolsce', on the economic activities of Moszkowski. See Shatzky, *Yidishe bildungs-politik*, 40, 94–5; APK, RGR 4010, on his public activities, and on his and his children's charitable activities, see Menahem David Krzenski, 'Działo-szyce' [correspondence], *Hatsefirah*, 18 (1891), 577.

of charitable funds, and an extensive programme to fight hasidism (see Appendix 11).[31] Criticism was levelled at the tsadikim in particular. Moszkowski depicted them as frauds who strove to preserve superstitions and fanaticism and who used the most despicable means possible 'because this gives them the power to inveigle money'. He stated that the tsadikim also spread religious intolerance, superstition, magic spells, and hatred of the authorities, and that they forbade Jews to send their children to Christian schools, or even to enlightened Jewish teachers. Thus, it was not that all hasidim were enemies of enlightenment, but only their leaders, 'as they are well aware that the more enlightenment spreads among Jews, the more their wicked sect will decline and disappear'.

Other aspects denigrated by the author of the memorandum were hasidic morality, pilgrimages to 'leaders', idleness, debauchery, and drunkenness in the courts of the tsadikim and in hasidic *shtiblekh*, as well as the financial bankruptcy to which they exposed their own families by taking their most precious household items as presents to the tsadikim. He also criticized mayors who did not counteract the spread of depravity and fanaticism in their towns, but, on the contrary, drew benefits from the fact that the tsadikim who lived in their towns attracted the hasidim to visit them. He therefore advised that a total ban be imposed upon hasidism, that any pilgrimages to the tsadikim or gatherings in halls of prayer be prohibited, and that the hasidim be forced to attend the public synagogues. He believed that the tsadikim should be subjected to 'a punishment fitting frauds and debauchers', while mayors supporting the tsadikim should be threatened with fines or even dismissal.

Both the portrayal of hasidism and the suggested methods of fighting the hasidim clearly drew upon the ideas of Abraham Stern, yet they were considerably more radical. Stern feared making martyrs of the hasidim and therefore advocated that drastic methods should be avoided, whereas Moszkowski claimed that decisive pressure should be applied. There was also a significant change in the language used in descriptions: it became emotive, full of strong epithets and undisguised hatred. Moszkowski's memorandum was a perfect example of this demonization of hasidic leaders:

These leaders . . . when they manage to win a certain number of supporters, mediators and assistants, immediately assume the title of *rebbe*, that is, leader [*naczelnik*], and, using their devious and allegorical teachings, try to instil in them the worst ignorance, superstitiousness and religious hatred, because this gives them the power to inveigle money, and to spread and strengthen their ruses with fortune-telling, magic spells, and their ability to treat illnesses, chronic ailments and mental disorders, and also with claims that their machinations can nullify government decisions, delivering culprits and frauds from punishment, and all this allegedly through the use of talismans, etc. . . .[32]

---

[31] AGAD, CWW 1436, pp. 215–33. See also AGAD, KRSW 6630, fo. 81.
[32] AGAD, CWW 1436, p. 217. See App. 11.

Although it was never published, the memorandum became relatively well known, because the Government Commission asked several influential people for their opinions on this issue. Most opinions were unfavourable to Moszkowski. Mathias Rosen, the most influential leader of Warsaw Jewry, emphasized that the memorandum was written in good faith, but that it was naive and unrealistic (see Appendix 12).[33] For example, in Rosen's opinion, descriptions of pilgrimages to the tsadikim were exaggerated, as the 'clandestine meetings' did not differ in any aspect from Christian pilgrimages and were purely religious acts. Exerting pressure would only make martyrs of the hasidim and, moreover, would win them supporters. Rosen suggested that the war with this group could be adequately fought by strict adherence to existing regulations governing the movements and records of the Jewish population—regulations that were not fully adhered to at the time. Rosen emphasized, however, that this would be a temporary measure, because, if the 'hasidic issue' was to be resolved properly, Jews needed to be fully emancipated. This was a clear reference to the views of David Friedländer, who had claimed as early as 1816 that the existence and development of hasidism in Poland was a political issue and that it was the result of the less than optimal legal situation of Jews living there.

A similar stance towards Moszkowski's project was adopted by the Jewish community board of Warsaw, including prominent maskilim such as Jan Glücksberg, Abraham Wienawer, and Jakub Rotwand.[34] It would appear that, despite their overt dislike of this 'pernicious sect', Polish maskilim had no desire to approve openly repressive means; nor did they demonize hasidism.[35] At the same time, however, maskilic circles did not create their own programme to fight hasidism, and they were practically helpless in the face of its development.

## A NEW STAGE OF HASIDIC EXPANSION

The gradual growth of interest in the hasidim in Polish maskilic works appearing in the 1830s and 1840s had two main causes. The first was the growth of the importance of hasidism itself, and the second was the associated increase in the number of local conflicts between the supporters of the two groups. The hasidim had been involved in a relatively large number of community conflicts in the 1820s, yet these had been with traditional Jewish society or its senior representatives on the Jewish community boards, and they had fought for the right to establish their own *shtiblekh* to use some shared community facilities (for example, the *mikveh*), or not to

---

[33] AGAD, CWW 1436, pp. 238–54.   [34] Ibid. 316–19.

[35] It might be that the Polish maskilic opinions concerning Moszkowski's project were an indirect reaction to a very heated controversy surrounding the possible deportation from Sadagóra in Bukovina to Russia of the tsadik Israel Friedman of Ruzhin. The opinions of the east European maskilim were divided into two camps: those who unequivocally condemned the tsadik and those who defended a hasidic leader who was being persecuted by the tsarist government. See Assaf, *The Regal Way*, 132, 147.

pay some synagogue taxes and contributions. In these conflicts the hasidic community was perceived by maskilim to be a group of dissidents, a minority by definition, defending their right to autonomy in Jewish community structures, fighting against the repression and pressures imposed by the majority. As such, they did not constitute a vital problem in the eyes of the maskilim and sometimes they even succeeded in winning maskilic support, as we have already seen in cases in Łask and Częstochowa.

The 1830s, and the 1840s in particular, brought a visible change. There was increasing evidence that the hasidim aspired to gain control of some community institutions, to force upon the entire community solutions that would be of benefit to the hasidim, and even to gain full control over the Jewish community boards.[36] There were also conflicts surrounding the appointment of rabbis and elections to community boards, in which the hasidic or anti-hasidic sympathies of the candidates were becoming more important than the actual qualifications of the candidates. For example, in 1852 in Hrubieszów the mitnagdic faction supporting Rabbi Josek Gelernter complained that the hasidim wanted to remove the rabbi from his post only because he was not a hasid.[37] This proves that, at that time, the hasidic faction considered itself to be strong enough to promote its own candidate, even against the will of significant sections of the community. Several years before, a hasidic candidate could have been appointed rabbi only if he had been supported by the non-hasidic majority.

Definitely the most important reason for these changes was the obviously increasing influence and numerical proliferation of followers of the hasidic movement. Indeed, reports by correspondents in Warsaw and Kraków published in the *Allgemeine Zeitung des Judentums* confirmed that the maskilic reporters were increasingly aware of hasidic influence and perceived this group as a growing force. These feelings were already predominant in the 1840s. One of these reporters (possibly Antoni Eisenbaum) suggested in 1840 that the hasidim comprised two-thirds of all Jews in Poland (did he mean Congress Poland or the Commonwealth?), even though it is clear from articles that these estimates had very little in common with actual numbers and that their function was polemical. The role of these estimates was to justify the policies of the modernizing camp and to demonstrate the impossibility of bringing about rapid change in conservative communities.[38] The hasidim also exaggerated their number at times for similar purposes, as in 1855, when they claimed that they numbered some 6,000 heads of households in Warsaw (that is, approximately 30,000 individuals)—or three-quarters of the

---

[36] e.g. in Piątek in 1852 and 1860; see AGAD, CWW 1716, pp. 73 ff.; KWK 3224.

[37] AGAD, CWW 1602, pp. 237 ff.

[38] 'Die Rabbinerschule', *AZJ* 4 (1840), 331. This is not to say that the hasidim could not make up two-thirds of the population in a given location. Such appears to have been the case in Hrubieszów in 1852; see AGAD, CWW 1602, pp. 272–5, 417–20. The hasidic majority in Hrubieszów was reported as early as 1847 by the British missionaries; see AGAD, CWW 1457, p. 723.

city's Jewish population.[39] The only official source to suggest that the hasidic population may have been as large as that was an 1857 report for the district of Mława, which gave a figure of five-sixths of the Jewish community associated with the movement.[40] Most of the other reports from *Allgemeine Zeitung des Judentums* and most government sources were more circumspect. Typical were descriptions of the hasidim as a 'large party', or a 'substantial part of the community', or the observation that 'they increase in number and strength, so that all the country is flooded with darkness, superstitions and prejudices', so that 'even in Warsaw they reside in significant numbers'.[41] Whatever their tone, all these accounts emphasized the ongoing growth of the hasidic movement, some even mentioning that 'the hasidim [*Husyci*] have begun to dominate'.[42]

In addition, the British missionaries of the London Society for Promoting Christianity amongst the Jews became increasingly aware of the influence of the hasidim. As mentioned in Chapter 3, missionaries in the earlier period only sporadically mentioned hasidic opposition, and then it was only in Przysucha and in the area of Zamość that they noted a hasidic majority. Even in the early 1840s they made few comments about the hasidim. In the mid-1840s and in the 1850s the tone of their accounts became increasingly alarmist, and they named a relatively large number of Jewish communities in which they had noted the dominance (though not necessarily a quantitative one) of the hasidim. Between 1844 and 1854 (after which date they were expelled from the Kingdom) they visited 229 Jewish settlements (some of them on a number of occasions) and noted a hasidic majority in fifteen of them, located primarily in the province of Lublin (mainly in the area of Zamość, in which hasidic dominance had been already reported in the 1820s), in the area of Łódź, and in localities where famous hasidic dynasties were based. These were Brzeziny, Działoszyn, Hrubieszów, Izbica, Kock, Końskowola, Piotrków, Raciąż, Tomaszów Mazowiecki, Turobin, Uchanie, Warka, Warta, Zambrów, and Zduńska Wola (see Fig. 7).[43] Warka was called the 'hasidic capital', with nearly all the Jewish inhabitants being hasidim. In many other communities, e.g. Biała Podlaska, Przedbórz, and Żelechów, the missionaries reported significant hasidic influence, although not a numerical majority.

The 'predominance' or 'influence' of which most of these and other missionaries' reports spoke may, however, have been relative, and connected with a strong hasidic civic presence and tight organization rather than with absolute numerical

[39] AGAD, CWW 1730, pp. 94–111. Possibly this number included not only the hasidim, but all the traditional Jews in Warsaw.

[40] AGAD, CWW 1441, pp. 85–91. The information provided is unclear.

[41] See J[oseph] B[ernstein], 'Zeitungsnachrichten. Russland und Polen. Warschau', *AZJ* 3 (1839), 361; 'Krakau', *AZJ* 4 (1840), 665; 'Krakau', *AZJ* 5 (1841), 43; AGAD, CWW 1436, p. 216; 1871, p. 286.

[42] AGAD, Centralne Władze Oświatowe, 33, p. 24 (report of Abraham Buchner, 2 June 1859).

[43] AGAD, CWW 1457, pp. 166, 463, 515, 525, 567, 575, 723, 727; 1458, pp. 409, 521, 565–6, 586, 762, 778, 834, 838.

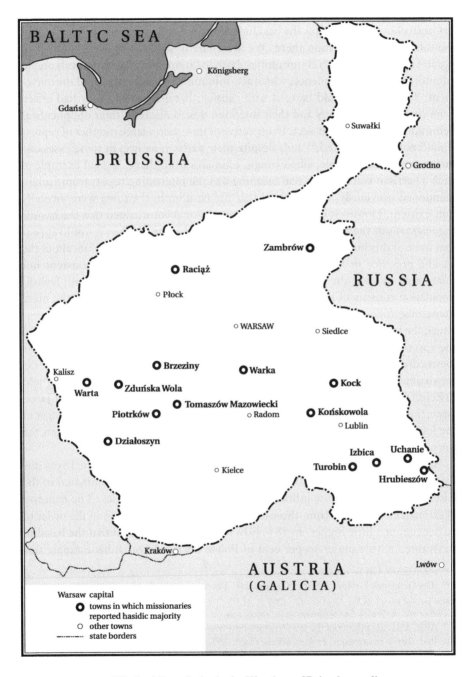

BALTIC SEA

○ Königsberg

Gdańsk ○

○ Suwałki

PRUSSIA

○ Grodno

Zambrów ○

○ Raciąż

○ Płock

RUSSIA

○ WARSAW    ○ Siedlce

Kalisz ○    ○ Brzeziny    ○ Warka

○ Warta    ○ Zduńska Wola    ○ Kock

○ Tomaszów Mazowiecki

Piotrków ○    ○ Radom    ○ Końskowola

○ Lublin

○ Działoszyn

Izbica    Uchanie

Turobin ○ ○    ○

○ Kielce    Hrubieszów

Kraków ○

Lwów ○

AUSTRIA
(GALICIA)

Warsaw capital
○ towns in which missionaries
   reported hasidic majority
○ other towns
·········· state borders

**FIG. 7.** The hasidic majority in the Kingdom of Poland according to
missionaries' reports, 1844–1854

superiority. There is the previous example of the very limited power of the hasidim in Częstochowa: in the 1840s the hasidim comprised approximately 5–6 per cent of the total Jewish population there. We are aware of a relatively large number of reports from other Jewish communities, both in German Jewish periodicals and in administrative correspondence, which also minimized the significance of the movement. True, these should be read with caution, because usually they had arisen from community conflicts and their intention was to discredit their opponents as being adherents of a fringe sect. Irrespective of this, such a large number of reports should not be overlooked,[44] and, despite their partisan nature, in some cases one might draw quite reliable, albeit rough, estimates from them. A good example of such a partisan voice and its real meaning was the interesting report from Lublin mentioned previously, which stated that the hasidim in the town were virtually non-existent. However, elsewhere the same author acknowledged that the hasidic *beit midrash* was the most crowded prayer house in Lublin.[45] Thus it would appear that none of this information was reliable, given that other available data about the hasidic presence in Lublin suggested that they were neither non-existent nor numerous. In 1865 the Jewish community board stated that the 'local [Jewish] population consists of two synagogal associations, of which one (by far the more numerous) follows German ritual, and the second—the kabbalistic–Portuguese ritual; the latter association consists of the so-called hasidim'.[46] Simultaneously, of the 1,411 seats in Lublin's synagogues only 92 (6.5 per cent) were located in the 'besmedresz de chasidim', which could accommodate no more that 180 people, i.e. approximately 8 per cent of the Jewish population.[47] In another hasidic stronghold in Żelechów the influence of the local tsadik, Joshua Asher (1804–62), son of Jacob Isaac, the 'Holy Jew' of Przysucha, was too limited to protect him from the anger of the local lessee of tax collection Israel Elbaum, or from being expelled from the town. The tsadik ended his days as the rabbi of the hamlet of Parysów.[48]

Nevertheless, it is clear that the period from the 1830s through to the 1850s saw the continued growth of the number of hasidic adherents, and culminated in the hasidim achieving genuine influence in many Jewish communities. The majority of estimates and figures from these decades indicated a proportion in the order of 30 per cent or a little higher. In 1839 Edward Hering maintained that the hasidim constituted a little under 50 per cent of Polish Jewry, although his estimate was

[44] e.g. AGAD, CWW 1632, pp. 110–19; 1684, pp. 63, 117–18, 125; 1730, p. 335; 1788, pp. 52–4.

[45] 'Die Gemeinde Lublin', *AZJ* 5 (1841) 409, 446. This report from Lublin was cited by Mahler as the ultimate proof of the considerable power of the hasidic movement in this town; see Mahler, *Hasidism and the Jewish Enlightenment*, 242, 380 n. 139.

[46] APL, AmL 2415 (letter of the Jewish community board to the mayor, 21 Sept./3 Oct. 1865).

[47] Ibid. (list of synagogues, 27 Jan., 8 Feb. 1852); APL, Rząd Gubernialny Lubelski Adm., 1725, pp. 268–9. Although the hasidic *shtiblekh* might have existed alongside the recognized synagogues, the case of the Kozhenitser *shtibl* established by Krajndla Sejdenwajsowa shows they were neither numerous nor easy to establish. See AGAD, CWW 1610, pp. 547–50, 596–606, 611–28; 1611, pp. 47–63, 172–89, 200–5.          [48] AGAD, CWW 1800, *passim*.

very approximate.[49] Somewhat lower estimates were given in the conflict over taxes paid by hasidim in Włocławek. A list of all those called to read the Torah in the hasidic *shtibl* in Włocławek in 1837 contained only nineteen names, which made the Jewish population of the town as low as 12.4 per cent (again, based on the assumption that 1.25 adult males should be counted as a family of five).[50] However, the local lessee of tax collection did not agree with the list and demanded that the tax be increased to 150 zlotys , i.e. 29 per cent of the annual tax levied on Torah scrolls in the Jewish community in Włocławek. The hasidim appealed, claiming the esti-mate was far too high. Thus the estimates varied between 12 per cent and 29 per cent. It should be remembered, however, that Włocławek was famous as a strong-hold of modernizing Jews, so the influence of hasidism might indeed have been weaker there than on average. The numbers supporting the hasidim were also similar in Pilica. In 1835, during elections of a rabbi, the non-hasidic candidate, Shaul Spira, received 93 votes (83.8 per cent), while a hasidic one, Meir (Majer) Eybeszyc, received only 18 votes (16.2 per cent), mainly from the two highest cate-gories of taxpayers, thus the wealthiest ones.[51] Simultaneously, in 1849 during the rabbinical elections in Rypin, the non-hasidic candidate, Hersh Guttentag, gained 98 votes (77.2 per cent), while a hasid, Icek Bytenfeld, had only 53 votes (27.8 per cent).[52] In both cases, clashes over the hasidic origin of one of the candidates were so strong that they ensured that his hasidic tendencies were the most important issue to divide the voters. In 1840 Rafał Goldman from Międzyrzec represented 400 people in a defence of the hasidic custom of smoking tobacco in the prayer house. Assuming that the 400 were all adult hasidic males (which is almost cer-tain), the hasidic population of Międzyrzec came to approximately one-third of the town's Jews.[53] In Łomża about half of the Jewish population attended any of nine private prayer houses instead of the community synagogue, but not all of the private prayer houses were necessarily hasidic.[54] Of the 490 adult Jewish men who participated in public worship in the hasidic centre of Tomaszów Lubelski in 1857, 150 (approximately 30 per cent) prayed in the hasidic *shtibl*.[55] The same year

[49] Edward Hering, 'Rzut oka na stan oświaty Izraelitów w Polsce', *Korespondent*, 279 (1839), 4.

[50] See AGAD, CWW 1734, p. 224. In 1837 in Włocławek there were 612 Jewish inhabitants; see Gruszczyńska, 'Początki osadnictwa żydowskiego we Włocławku', 29.

[51] See AGAD, CWW 1472, pp. 96–7.

[52] See AGAD, CWW 1684, pp. 62–4, 90–3. In 1849 in Rypin there were approximately 900 Jewish inhabitants, i.e. approximately 180 families; 151 voters would constitute almost all the members of the community with the right to vote (male heads of family).

[53] AGAD, CWW 1780, pp. 50–2. The entire Jewish population of Międzyrzec was 3,012 in 1827 and 4,437 in 1857.

[54] AGAD, CWW 1827, pp. 16–39. The numbers could be quite inaccurate, because some of the worshippers may have been women.

[55] AGAD, CWW 1617, pp. 121–2. There may have been additional hasidim who attended the com-munity synagogue. The Jewish population of Tomaszów Lubelski in 1857 was 2,090, suggesting that the 490 men may have constituted the entire number of adult male Jews.

in Goworów (in the province of Płock) one-third of the Jewish population was reported to be praying in the hasidic *shtiblekh*.[56]

In 1858 the editor-in-chief of *Allgemeine Zeitung des Judentums*, Ludwig Philippsohn, claimed that in all of eastern Europe the hasidim constituted a grouping that was equal in number to two other movements, i.e. the non-hasidic Orthodox movement and the 'enlightened' movement, but that the hasidim were superior to them in terms of their energy and organization.[57] An estimate of 30 per cent seems reasonable, particularly as it is backed up by information provided by Daniel Neufeld.[58] However, Philippsohn's observation, repeated later by others reporting on hasidism,[59] pointed not only to the numerical increase and the actual size of the hasidic movement, but also to a very important feature of this movement and its expansion. The followers of hasidism, even if they did not constitute a majority in a given community, managed to dominate the community with their exceptional social involvement and better social organization, and also because of the aggressiveness and ruthlessness of their enterprises. It partly explains why, in the 1830s and 1840s, when they still could not claim a real majority, they started to play a dominant role in the community life of Polish Jews. This raises the question why the decisive turning point in the growth of hasidic influence came when it did. An exhaustive answer to this question lies beyond the scope of this study.[60] It should be observed, however, that the growth of the hasidic movement in the 1830s and 1840s did not represent a huge, quantitative leap. A three- or fourfold growth from below 10 per cent during the 1820s to around 30 per cent during the 1840s (that is, within the space of twenty to twenty-five years) actually represented a slowing of the pace of growth during the previous period, when the hasidim increased from a negligible minority (possibly around 1 per cent) at the beginning of the century to around 10 per cent at the end of the 1820s. What happened between the 1820s and the 1840s was not that the hasidic conquest gained momentum, but rather that the number of hasidim reached a critical mass which allowed them to become an active force in Jewish community life.

It is difficult to explain why that critical mass stood at 30 per cent and not at 10 per cent. First of all, it must be remembered that hasidic influence was not evenly distributed; 30 per cent was an average figure, but in some communities the hasidim remained a small minority (as in Częstochowa and Włocławek) or were non-existent, while in others they may have constituted an absolute majority as

---

[56] AGAD, CWW 1696, pp. 21.

[57] Ludwig Philippson, 'Der Chassidismus', *AZJ* 22 (1858), 714.

[58] Somewhat lower numbers, namely 300,000, were given by an anonymous Vilna maskil in 1840. See 'Rußland. Wilna', *Der Orient*, 1 (1840), 22.

[59] See e.g. W.A., 'Increase of Chasidism', *JI* 25 (1859), 138–40; Jezajasz Chudy, 'U źródeł zastoju', *Izr.* 43 (1908), 321–3.

[60] The most recent work on the subject is that of Glenn Dynner, 'Men of Silk'. However, his conclusions about the numerical increase of the hasidim seem unconvincing to me (see the previous chapter).

early as the 1820s. Such examples came from several small communities, such as Przysucha, Raków, and Białobrzegi, in which the 'dark spirit of hasidism reigns over almost all the Jewish population'.[61] The semi-democratic nature of the Jewish community's administration also worked to the advantage of the hasidim. With the exception of Warsaw, which had its own electoral system, Jewish community boards were elected by all Jewish taxpayers, who were divided into five curias weighted according to the amount of taxes paid. In communities in which the hasidic movement included an appropriate number of well-to-do residents, one-third of the votes would have been sufficient to elect a community board with hasidic leanings. Numerous sources (such as those from Piątek, Włocławek, and Rypin) indicated that, during the period in question, the hasidic movement was indeed of particular interest to competing members of the financial elite.[62] This must have favoured the increase in hasidic influence. The election of a hasidic rabbi was somewhat more difficult, because the election of rabbis was more democratic: all adult males voted, voters were not divided into curias, and all votes counted equally. Nonetheless, even in this case, a well-organized bloc of 30 per cent, or even fewer, could have been sufficient to force the election of its candidate as long as the remaining 70 per cent were not united against the bloc.

In addition, during the 1830s and 1840s certain factors came into existence that led the hasidim to seek an active role in community administration. In the previous phase of the movement's development, its followers had been interested in the broadest possible autonomy, which included the opportunity to establish their independent prayer houses, but also to break free of the community tax burden imposed on all the other members of the community. Steps taken by the Polish government during the 1820s inadvertently aided this trend. In 1822 the old community administrative boards (*kehilot*) were abolished and replaced by community boards (*dozory bóźnicze*), which had no power or authority.[63] These boards were not only weak but highly unpopular, and their lack of popularity encouraged dissident tendencies. In many communities, despite pressure from the state, the local administration was unable to find three people who would be willing to join a community board. In 1826 the government was forced to offer financial privileges to

---

[61] AGAD, CWW 1458, p. 521. For Przysucha, see Ludwig Hoff, 'Journal of Mr. Hoff', *JE* 10 (1925), 28–9; for Raków, G. Wendt, 'Kielce. Letter from the Rev. G. Wendt', *JI* 1 (1835), 242; for Białobrzegi, J[an] Lange and S[iegmund] Deutsch, 'Journal of Mr. J. Lange and Mr. S. Deutsch', *JI* 1 (1835), 115.

[62] See AGAD, CWW 1472, 1632, 1684, 1716, 1734; KWK 3224. These documents contradict the long-standing image of hasidism as a popular or 'proletarian' movement conveyed in Dubnow, *Toledot haḥasidut*; Mahler, *Hasidism and the Jewish Enlightenment*; and Dinur, 'The Origins of Hasidism'. This image has been the subject of criticism for some time. See e.g. Rosman, 'Social Conflicts in Międzybóż in the Generation of the Besht'. For observations on the connection between hasidism and the Jewish financial elite in Poland, see Dynner, 'Men of Silk', 116–73.

[63] See Schiper, 'Samorząd żydowski w Polsce', on the status of the Jewish community boards after 1822.

those who would accept a position as a member of a community board. In addition, owing to the retraction of the order outlawing hasidism, after 1824 the hasidim became the only Jewish group whose right to establish prayer houses and to conduct their religious affairs (and effectively all others) without restriction was guaranteed. As one can imagine, the hasidim took full advantage of these rights. At times there were even complaints that a group calling itself a hasidic one was not truly such but consisted, instead, of pretenders who were trying to exploit the movement's relatively advantageous legal position.[64]

By contrast, during the following phase these factors diminished markedly in importance, whereas others contributed to making active participation in community life more attractive; especially for the purpose of helping tsadikim win positions as community rabbis. This change came about partly because of further reforms in community structures, partly because of changing government policies towards dissident Jewish religious movements, and partly because of transformations within hasidism itself. In the first place, the salary of the town rabbi, which was guaranteed by the government, became increasingly attractive, because the traditional sources of income for tsadikim, such as fees for conducting special rites or proceeds from the sale of amulets, or specific 'hasidic taxes' (*pidyonot*, *ma'amadot*),[65] began to dry up in the face of the increasing fragmentation of the hasidic leadership and growing competition within its ranks. Secondly, after 1846 the only way to avoid paying the exorbitant fees charged for wearing traditional Jewish attire was to occupy the post of rabbi or Jewish religious official, and after 1850 only rabbis and deputy rabbis were allowed to wear such attire.[66] The most common anti-hasidic charge coming from traditional (not maskilic) circles during the 1840s–1860s was that hasidic candidates for religious office sought such positions only in order to be able to wear traditional Jewish attire.[67] Ultimately, a rabbinical position became a means to avoid military conscription, which was made mandatory for Polish Jews in 1843. Not only could a rabbi not be drafted, but he could also exempt one or more rabbinical students from the military draft. As a result of these factors and more traditional ones (the desire to have a say in the distribution of community funds and patronage or the hope of obtaining a sinecure from the community), during the 1840s the hasidim in the Congress Kingdom began to mount a campaign to take over community institutions.

[64] Such was the case, for example, in Włocławek. See AGAD, CWW 1788, *passim*.

[65] See Assaf, 'Money for Household Expenses'; id., *The Regal Way*, 285–309, on *pidyonot*, *ma'amadot*, and generally on the financial aspects of the hasidic courts.

[66] See Kirszrot, *Prawa Żydów w Królestwie Polskim*, 271–2; Israel Klausner, 'Hagezerah al tilboshet hayehudim'. A good bibliography on this subject can be found in Assaf, *Derekh malkhut*, 277 nn. 94–5; Assaf and Bartal, 'Shetadlanut ve'ortodoksiyah', 75–6 nn. 22 and 23.

[67] See e.g. APL, AmL 2258; AGAD, CWW 1613, pp. 210–12. Opponents of the hasidic candidate for the post of rabbi in Łęczna wrote of him: 'Because he wanted to wear Jewish attire, he managed to gather some support for the position of deputy rabbi from the lower classes as well as from a few individuals from the higher class; thus he will be allowed to wear Jewish attire.' For yet another aspect of

This did not mean that the hasidim unequivocally began to dominate Jewish communities in the Congress Kingdom from the 1840s onwards. Although there were 'hasidic' communities, i.e. communities that were completely controlled by the hasidim, the majority appointed their Jewish community board members from the traditional, non-hasidic and non-maskilic elite, and a decided majority of rabbis and their assistants were not connected with the hasidic movement. Those members of the financial and rabbinical elite who were indifferent or hostile to hasidism still controlled most institutions in the Kingdom's Jewish communities, so, as a rule, the hasidim managed to elect no more than one of three Jewish community board members. Thus, the basic change that took place in the balance of power in Jewish society hinged not so much on the hasidim's assumption of power as on their obviously increasing aspirations to play an influential role in the community. This led to an intensification in the conflict between the hasidim and their opponents, on the part of both the traditional Jewish elite and the supporters of the Haskalah.

Yet, for the Haskalah, the growing significance of hasidism was much more important than the statistical increase in the number of its supporters. The interest in Jewish community institutions and the intense social involvement of hasidism reported by Philippsohn made this movement the natural rival of the Polish Haskalah, with its strong social agenda and its aspirations fundamentally to transform existing social interactions. The maskilim saw in hasidism an adversary in the fight for the souls of what they perceived as the passive Jewish masses. Thus it is barely surprising that the hasidic movement soon progressed from being an ignored sect to the role of one of the major threats to the modernization of Jewish society. That attitudes evolved so quickly was attributable also to the fact that the period following the Uprising saw an increase in the number not only of hasidim, but also of supporters of modernization, who had been endeavouring since the 1830s to spread their influence to a greater number of communities in the Kingdom of Poland. This made conflict inevitable.

## CONFLICT IN DAILY LIFE: ANATOMY OF DISSENT

The power struggle between the hasidim and the maskilim has been one of the more frequently recurring themes in traditional Jewish historiography. Numerous skirmishes have been described in a number of historical works of varying integrity, and particularly in the local histories or 'memorial books' put together by Jewish groups since the Second World War. Yet probably the majority of these accounts were based on unreliable testimony rather than on analysis of reliable sources. To illustrate: the opposition to the enlightened rabbi of Kalisz, Tsevi Hirsh Chajes (1805–55), was attributed in literature to the hasidim. In reality, however, the

the hasidic involvement in Jewish communal life connected with its climb to power, namely hasidic infiltration of traditional *havurot*, see Petrovsky-Stern, 'Hasidism, Havurot, and the Jewish Street'.

opposition came from the circles of reform supporters and supporters of a radical preacher from Germany, Natan Streisand, who accused Chajes of an alliance with the hasidim.[68] Thus, some instances of the conflict between the Haskalah and the hasidim that are backed by primary source documentation do need to be reconstructed if we are to establish the actual, rather than supposed, nature of the conflict. This applies also to the arguments and strategies adopted by both sides. Four cases—from Opoczno, Warta, Łódź, and Warsaw—are presented below. These cases were based upon numerous denunciations and government reports sent to provincial and central authorities in the Kingdom.

The first local conflicts between the supporters of hasidism and the advocates of Jewish enlightenment of which we have documentary evidence took place in the 1830s. However, it is possible that some cases had occurred earlier, in the previous decade. In the 1830s the Haskalah was still represented by individuals, rather than by larger organized groups. In Opoczno, Pinkus Eliasz Lipszyc was the only influential member of the Jewish community board. Lipszyc was possibly the author of a pamphlet, *Petition or Self-Justification of the People of the Old Testament Faith* (1820), that targeted Jewish community boards, and was also a prominent supporter of the ideology of enlightenment. Curiously, he simultaneously maintained contact with leaders of the hasidic movement.[69] Owing to his wealth and excellent connections, Lipszyc occupied key positions in the community power structure and considerably influenced Jewish life in Opoczno. In 1830 the hasidim, under the protection of the wealthy Temerl (Berek Sonnenberg's widow), intervened with the Government Commission for Religious Denominations and Public Enlightenment, accusing Lipszyc of numerous frauds and embezzlements.[70] The conflict was provoked by the hasidim in an attempt to remove their adversary from the Jewish community board and to discredit him in the eyes of government institutions by using as their tools denunciations and interventions with the authorities. The Government Commission ordered an inquiry, which did not find the accused guilty, so the attempt proved ineffective. Soon, however, the Voivodeship Commission of Sandomierz announced that Lipszyc had withdrawn from running for a new term of office on the Jewish community board because of the public persecutions and insults to which he and his wife had been subjected on Rosh Hashanah in the synagogue.[71] Public harassment as a hasidic method of fighting with their modernizing opponents would also feature later.

The conflict in Opoczno, in which the hasidim took action against their

---

[68] Traditional opinions on the conflict between Tsevi Hirsh Chajes and hasidim in Kalisz can be found in Bet-Halevi, *Toledot yehudei kalish*, 182. See AGAD, CWW 1445, *passim*, on the conflict between Chajes and Streisand.

[69] Lipszyc, *Prośba czyli Usprawiedliwienie*; some additional information on the interactions between the tsadik of Kozienice and Lipszyc can be found in Alfasi, 'Toledot yehudei opotshno', 25.

[70] See Dynner, 'Men of Silk', 150–9, for the role played by Temerl in hasidic circles in Poland and her patronage. See also the hasidic point of view in Boim, *Harabi rebe bunem mipeshisḥah*, ii. 585–94.

[71] AGAD, CWW 1501, pp. 3–25.

'enlightened' rival, was rather unusual for the 1830s. At that time the reverse was more common: individual maskilim attempted to discredit their hasidic adversaries as being supporters of backwardness and fanaticism, and they undertook individual interventions against their growing influence. This may be illustrated by a campaign organized by Mendel Zahlbergier and a member of the Jewish community board, Jakub Piotrowski, which targeted the hasidic candidate for the post of rabbi of Warta in 1835. Instead of Moszek Nechymia Katz, who was the candidate of 'the hoi polloi of the fourth and fifth classes of taxpayers', Piotrowski and Zahlbergier nominated Jakub Szwajcer, a graduate of the Warsaw Rabbinical School in 1831, who was in fact the only graduate of the school ever to apply for the position of rabbi.[72] Piotrowski portrayed the hasidic contender for the post as one of the spiteful, fanatical, and restless party of the rabble, whereas Szwajcer's supporters belonged to the first and second classes of taxpayers, and thus to the financial elite. He denigrated Katz as being an ignoramus who lacked the necessary qualifications for a rabbi and who had no knowledge of any language, not even Hebrew. He also claimed that Katz had assumed judicial authority, and adjudicated in conflicts between those who turned to him. The Voivodeship Commission ordered a re-election in which Moszek Nechymia Katz gained 106 votes and Szwajcer seventeen.[73]

The election results could not have come as a surprise to Piotrowski (although obviously not all of Katz's 106 votes could have come from the hasidic party). After all, his accusations did not appeal to the will of the majority, but only to the opinions of the 'civilized' and affluent members of Jewish society. This motif was a recurrent one in community conflicts between the Polish maskilim and the hasidim. Supporters of the modernizing option presented their movement as being superior, better-educated, wealthier, and, above all, as carrying out the government's 'civilization' plans. Surely, then, that is how they must have perceived themselves. Their ideological adversaries, the hasidim, brought a different vision of social order into being. However, they were not genuine adversaries, but a pack of fraudulent rogues with low morals; a collection of 'citizens who could be termed a rabble'; an uncouth, violent, fanatical, and ignorant mob. The belief that the opponents of modernization inevitably possessed such characteristics resulted

---

[72] Adam Penkalla ('Rabbis in the Radom Province', 78–9) also mentions Rubin Dawidowicz Międzyrzecki, rabbi of Opoczno, and Samuel 'Molewer', rabbi of Radom, as graduates of the Rabbinical School in Warsaw. Penkalla erroneously based his claim on examination certificates issued by the Rabbinical School. From the 1840s such certificates were issued to all rabbinical candidates in the Kingdom of Poland, not only to the graduates of the school. See APR, RGR I 4359, p. 1146; RGR II 4130, pp. 9–10. In addition, the list of all the students of the Rabbinical School (see *Z dziejów gminy starozakonnych w Warszawie*, 123–35) omitted to mention these names and the latter of the rabbis mentioned by Penkalla was not 'Molewer', but Samuel Mohilewer (1824–98), a graduate of the Volozhin yeshiva, from 1868 rabbi in Radom, one of the founders of the Zionist movement, who, of course, never studied in the Warsaw Rabbinical School.

[73] AGAD, KWK 710; CWW 1571, pp. 16–21.

from the fundamental premisses of the Haskalah movement, that if anybody attempted to contradict the historical determinism of enlightenment and rejected the sole means of saving the Jewish masses from ruin, lack of this very enlightenment had to be the reason. But surely the experience of everyday encounters with the hasidim, who willingly resorted to the crudest methods of social combat and ruthless group pressure, played a more significant role than this theoretical premiss. Inevitably, the result was that the hasidic opposition was perceived as a brutish mob devoid of any scruples or morals. This, in turn, led to increasing antipathy and aggression, and, with time, to the demonization of the opposition. By the late 1830s the attitude to hasidism had reached the level of delegitimization; that is, the hostility was such that the opponent was not even viewed as a human being.[74] Significantly, this local hostility is apparent from documentation in government archives, but not from the maskilic literature of the period; simply, the extent of the threat that hasidism posed had not yet been fully internalized.

The degree of hostility in community conflicts was well illustrated by events in Łódź from 1848 onwards. The rejection of traditional Jewish attire by proponents of modernization in Łódź and other departures from tradition, such as the shaving off of beards and sidelocks, sending children to the Russian-language *Realschule*, or living outside the Jewish district, resulted in hasidic persecution of this small group. The persecuted maskilim stated clearly that the hostility they had suffered came not from the entire traditional community, but only from the hasidic sect. The combative methods used by the hasidim included public mockery and ridicule, insults, shoving and jostling, knocking off headgear not in the traditional Jewish style, damaging non-Jewish attire, canvassing against participation in services with 'progressives' and preventing them from praying in the synagogue, imposing excessive community contributions on them, or inflating burial fees. As a result, eleven individuals, led by Icek Seidenman, a wealthy cotton merchant,[75] applied to the Government Commission for Internal and Religious Affairs to have their own prayer house (which had already been functioning for a number of years) legalized. In addition, they sought punishment of their persecutors, the inclusion of two representatives from the 'civilized' Jews on the Jewish community board, the appointment of delegates from all income groups to set community contribution rates, and the introduction of strict monitoring of synagogue expenses.[76] On the basis of the subsequent inquiry (see Appendix 13),[77] the city council of Łódź advised the Warsaw provincial authorities to legalize the prayer house and to exert pressure so that at least one representative of the 'civilized' Jews could be included on the Jewish community board for the next term of office. The provincial author-

---

[74] See Bar-Tal, 'Delegitimization', on delegitimization as an extreme form of social conflict.

[75] On Seidenman, see Missalowa, *Studia nad powstaniem łódzkiego okręgu przemysłowego*, i. 113, 117, 271, 274; Friedman, *Dzieje Żydów w Łodzi*, 59, 153, 213, 282, 300; Puś, *Żydzi w Łodzi*, 199; Walicki, *Synagogues and Prayer Houses of Łódź*, 37.

[76] AGAD, CWW 1712, pp. 38–73 (copy in CAHJP, HM2/6874)          [77] Ibid. 52–65.

ities, in referring the matter to the Government Commission, agreed with the first proposal of the city council but ignored the second.

The direct reason for applying to a government institution seems to have been the threat to the existence of the 'civilized' prayer hall as a result of conflict with the lessee of communal taxes for the reading of the Torah.[78] However, protection against hasidic persecution was just one of the objectives of the complaint. The remaining proposals—to include representatives of the modernization option on the Jewish community board and to allocate community contributions under their supervision—were equally important. Seidenman and his supporters complained that their lack of influence on community matters was unjust on two counts: first, because they observed 'principles appropriate to the spirit of the times and the will of the enlightened government'; secondly, because 'almost a majority of the community's income is contributed by the latter'.[79] The amount paid in contributions and taxes did not, of course, imply a great number of supporters of modernization (they probably did not exceed a small percentage of the Łódź community), but was a result of their high financial status. Once again, then, wealth, education, and general 'civilization' in line with 'the paternalistic intentions of the magnanimous [government] authorities' lay at the root of their demands. The compatibility of the adopted method of 'civilization' with government projects was a frequently recurring motif in maskilic accusations and petitions in their fight with the hasidim. Compliance with the will of the government was aimed at winning government support for the maskilim, because the authorities represented a strategic ally for the supporters of modernization. While the traditional community could bring a wide range of pressures to bear, and could even expel or ostracize renegades, the maskilim had virtually no means of exerting pressure. Accusations and denunciations were one of the few methods available to them in their fight with hasidic influences, and the goodwill of the government provided their only chance of success. The maskilim believed that their anti-hasidic interventions would prove successful because they were convinced that in abandoning all manifestations of Jewish separateness they had complied with the will of the government, so that the government would therefore be interested in supporting their case.[80] Yet this belief had already become outdated by the 1840s. The Polish government had lost any concern it had had for Jewish reform in the previous decade, and all it was interested in from the November Uprising onwards was the maintenance of law and order in communities and an efficient means of exacting taxes. The governor of Lublin even wrote that the authorities should ensure that 'under the pretext of civilization, the progressive Jews are not accorded greater care by the authorities, as in this way the less wealthy hasidim might feel repressed'.[81] Thus it was in vain that the

---

[78] For more on this, see Walicki, *Synagogues and Prayer Houses of Łódź*, 37–40.

[79] AGAD, CWW 1712, p. 49.

[80] See Lederhendler, *The Road to Modern Jewish Politics*, 86–110, on the importance of government support for the maskilim in the Russian empire.     [81] APL, AmL 2419, p. 237 (dated 1866).

maskilim from Łódź sought an ally in the Government Commission in their struggle for influence in the community.

The frustration and sense of repression apparent in Seidenman's complaint were rooted in the maskilim's belief that they were predestined to occupy prominent social positions despite their obvious isolation from the community. These two themes were present in provincial press reports throughout the second half of the nineteenth century, and the accusers mainly blamed the hasidim for this abnormal state of affairs. Interestingly, the hasidim did not wield power in the communities in question (although the Jewish community board mostly sided with the hasidim, despite not being hasidim themselves). However, the leaders of the Jewish community board, dominated by the non-hasidic, traditional financial and rabbinical elite, were completely ignored in the dispute, while the maskilim persisted in claiming that those circles were passive and could be controlled only if the hasidic opposition was crushed. The hasidim were presented as the only group that was actively opposing the influence of the 'enlightened' members of the community, and maskilic criticism was aimed against them. Such a stance was justifiable in a sense, as hasidism was, in fact, the best-organized, most united and active faction, and one that could inflict genuine pain on its adversaries by using the above-mentioned methods of harassment, petitioning, and so on, even if in reality it had very little power. It was also no coincidence that this aspect of the conflict between hasidism and the Enlightenment emerged only in the 1840s since it was not until then that the conflict with hasidism was seen at community level. This was surely a consequence of the way in which the two groups, which until the 1830s had been too weak and had ignored one other, had developed. In the 1830s maskilim aspiring to positions of power in the community encountered resistance from a new force, that of the organized hasidic community, which was soon perceived by them as synonymous with all the misfortunes that had befallen Jewish society. Those modernizers aspiring to positions of power suffered greater disillusionment, which sprang from their unsatisfied craving for power as well as from their inability to carry out their own programme. To blame hasidism for their own failures was, of course, to oversimplify the situation (just as their belief in the neutrality of the remaining groups was particularly mistaken). Yet at most these maskilim, isolated as they were, and lacking any influence in the community, could only be witnesses to the successes of the hasidim, and so they directed all their bitterness against this group. Anti-hasidic denunciations thus served a therapeutic purpose. It must be noted, however, that hasidism was not only an enemy by proxy. It was the most active opponent of maskilic circles, and soon became the main rival in the fight for control of the souls of the community.

In Warsaw by the 1840s, and even more so by the 1850s, the situation had assumed a different appearance. Maskilim from the capital had found various ways to influence community life, either via those institutions that promoted maskilic ideology and which they controlled, or through the Jewish community board itself, which was controlled from 1840 to 1856 by supporters of the modernizing option—first Mathias Rosen and later Jakub Tugendhold, Mathias Berson, and Jan Glücksberg. The conflicts between the maskilim and the hasidim in Warsaw therefore took on a completely different pattern from those in the provinces, and denunciations to the government authorities were usually made by the hasidim and not the maskilim.

A typical conflict between the hasidim and the Haskalah in Warsaw may be illustrated using a well-publicized dispute over a hearse.[82] In Warsaw, as in the whole of eastern Europe, modified coal carriages were used to take bodies to the Jewish cemetery. 'More civilized' members of the community thought it improper, and thus in 1848 one of the wealthy members purchased a sumptuous hearse. Although traditionalists said that the hearse was 'non-Jewish', the modernizing party nevertheless succeeded in introducing it as part of the burial rites. Jakub Rotwand (1825–1913), the secretary of the Jewish community board and the author of the new cemetery regulations, was particularly active in this regard. The new hearse was boycotted by the traditionalists, and transport of a corpse by the modernizing members of the community was declared a public scandal because the driver—seated on the hearse, not walking beside it—had his back turned to the deceased, which was considered to be extremely insulting. Hasidim from Warsaw, led by Chil David Erlich, Shyia Prywes, and Israel Gesundheit, commenced a campaign appealing to the municipal, provincial, and central authorities to ban the driver from travelling on the hearse, and presented the authorities with a whole series of criminal charges against Jakub Rotwand and 'Rotwand's party' (*partia rot-wandzistów*). After two drawn-out inquiries, the accusations against Rotwand were dismissed, and the decision over whether the driver was to sit on the hearse or walk beside it was left to the family of the deceased.[83] Interestingly, in his petitions to the authorities, Chil Erlich accepted the label of fanatic that was applied to the hasidim, but stressed that, of the two opposing parties, it was they, and not the modernizing party, who were loyal to the state and monarch. Rotwand's supporters were depicted as a group of hedonists, atheists, libertines, and frauds, who counted no more than a few dozen members, and Rotwand himself was accused by Erlich of low origins, ingratitude, and hypocrisy. Rotwand was said to gorge himself on non-kosher meat on Yom Kippur and steal community funds earmarked for aid for the poor.[84]

In this conflict it was the hasidim who appealed to the authorities. Andrault, the mayor of Warsaw, emphasized in a report from the inquiry that complaints against Rotwand had been submitted solely by the hasidim and that it was their revenge on Rotwand for having become involved in changing the cemetery regulations in

---

[82] See Krakowski, 'O cmentarzu i służbie pogrzebowej', 58–9; Nussbaum, *Szkice historyczne*, 76–90; Guesnet, *Polnische Juden im 19. Jahrhundert*, 303–25.

[83] See AGAD, CWW 1729, pp. 235–45, 253–8, 261–76, 494–513; 1730, pp. 94 ff.

[84] See AGAD, CWW 1730, pp. 94–110.

connection with the new burial instructions and the ultimate dissolution of the burial society.[85] Not feeling threatened, the maskilim from Warsaw had not engaged in a polemic with the hasidic arguments, but had only sought a favourable solution to the problem of the hearse and the cemetery regulations. This kind of attitude to the matter was directly connected with the strong influence they had in the Warsaw community. At the same time they launched a whole series of campaigns in other forms, for example, an attempt to raise the first tombstone with an inscription in Polish in the Jewish cemetery, soon thereafter an attempt to oblige all Jews to have the identifying elements on tombstones written in one of the European languages, and a successful attempt to exempt the synagogue in Daniłowiczowska Street from the control of the Jewish community board, as well as an ineffective change of electoral law concerning community authorities in 1855.[86] Thus it seems that it was the possibility of being communally active and their successes in this respect that diverted the Warsaw maskilim from interventions with the authorities and from community arguments. Also, owing to their social and financial security, their conflicts with the hasidim were not as dramatic as those in Opoczno, Warta, or even Łódź. This already heralded the changes that would soon take place in the early 1860s in the Warsaw circles of the modernizing Jews, when the clash with hasidism was no longer a question of a struggle for existence, but became a central ideological problem.

## THE FIRST MASKILIC DEFENCE OF HASIDISM:
### JAKUB TUGENDHOLD

However, the change of attitude towards hasidism on the part of the Jewish modernizing circles in Poland did not occur suddenly or unexpectedly: it had its forerunner in the Kingdom of Poland as early as the 1820s. Jakub Tugendhold, one of the most influential and active members of the Warsaw Jewish community, and one of the first of the 'progressive' Jews to defend hasidism, even outside Poland, appears to have played a key role in this change in attitude.[87] The attitude was contemporaneous with the well-known 'apostasy' of Jacob Samuel Byk, and preceded

---

[85]  AGAD, CWW 1729, pp. 271–2.

[86]  See Guesnet, *Polnische Juden im 19. Jahrhundert*, 403–10, for the controversies that resulted from this election.

[87]  For biographical notes and a description of Tugendhold, see my article 'Jakub Tugendhold'; see also Mahler, *Haḥasidut vehahaskalah*, 253–4; id., *Hasidism and the Jewish Enlightenment*, 410. Interesting details can be found in Nirnstein, *Proverbia Salomonis*, 1–7 (the source seems to be reliable, as the author was the subject's nephew and, while writing the biography, had access to the personal papers of Tugendhold); see also Samuel Henryk Peltyn, 'Ś.p. Jakób Tugendhold (wspomnienie pośmiertne)', *Izr.* 6 (1871), 130–1; Schiper, 'Początki haskali na ziemiach centralnej Polski', 324; Levinson, *Toledot yehudei varsha*, 117–18; *Z dziejów gminy starozakonnych w Warszawie*; Isaiah Tugendhold, *Divrei yeshayahu*; Shatzky, *Yidishe bildungs-politik*, 236–7.

FIG. 8. Jakub Tugendhold (1794–1871)
Joachim Nirnstein, *Proverbia Salomonis: Przysłowia Salomona. Wyjątek z Pisma świętego z hebrajskiego tekstu spolszczył wierszem* (Warsaw, 1895)

the publications of Eliezer Zweifel (primarily *Shalom al yisra'el*), which heralded a change of approach towards hasidism among the moderate Haskalah of the Russian empire by almost fifty years. The works and activities of Byk and Zweifel are relatively well known today,[88] but those of Tugendhold, whose role in the Kingdom of Poland in the 1820s and the 1830s was somewhat similar to that of Zweifel, have not been properly studied. This might be because it is difficult to compare the intellectual contribution that these writers made to the revision of attitudes towards hasidism. Whereas Eliezer Zweifel dealt extensively with hasidism, it was merely one of a number of subjects with which Tugendhold dealt, and then only marginally so. Tugendhold's significance was not, however, based on his

[88] For Jacob Byk, see Werses, 'Bein shenei olamot' (in the footnotes numerous references to earlier literature on Byk, mainly by the same author, can also be found). For Eliezer Zweifel, see Wiederkehr-Pollack, *Eliezer Zweifel*; Feiner, 'Hamifneh beha'arakhat haḥasidut'. See also Zweifel, *Shalom al yisra'el*.

literary activities but rather on the influence that his works and his activities brought to bear on the younger generation of Warsaw's modernizing Jews.

Tugendhold's first comments on hasidism, albeit indirect and marginal, appeared in a pamphlet which he wrote in his youth—*Jerobaał czyli mowa o Żydach* (Jerobaal; or, Treatise on the Jews)—and which was published in 1818 in connection with the public debate on the 'Jewish question' that was taking place at the time. A flood of articles, pamphlets, leaflets, and press articles appeared as a result of the approaching session of the First Sejm of the Kingdom of Poland. In accordance with previously announced plans, the First Sejm was to discuss the social and legal status of the Jewish population. The young Tugendhold's *Jerobaał* was a fiery riposte to accusations against the Jewish community made by the anonymous author of the pamphlet *Sposób na Żydów czyli środki niezawodne zrobienia z nich ludzi uczciwych i dobrych obywateli* (Dealing with Jews; or, Sure Methods by which They Can Be Made into Honest People and Good Citizens), which was published some time earlier, probably by Gerard Witowski.[89] In an extensive discussion of the religious and social conditions of Polish Jews, Tugendhold acknowledged that 'fairly stubborn idols of fanaticism stir and trouble the clear waters of this precious religion of mine, drawn up by the sacred Patriarchs; and that some of my Polish co-religionists are straying in the wilderness of superstition', and then he immediately added that 'in the course of those dark ages, fanaticism prevailed among the Israelites and later grew even more intense as the result of the rise of superstition'.[90] Undoubtedly, both statements referred to hasidism, while the language and style of the accusations could be linked directly to other anti-hasidic texts of the contemporary Haskalah. At that time Tugendhold's stand on hasidism in no way differed from the opinions that were being voiced by Warsaw's modernizing Jews, with whom he was closely associated, and they were typical of his era. One could hardly expect originality from a 24-year-old writer who, in the very first sentence of his polemic, apologized for his youthfulness and lack of a proper education.[91]

Six years later, in 1824, his views had developed, and Tugendhold engaged for the first time in a full-scale defence of hasidism. This was in relation to the government investigation into the legality of the 'sect of the men of silk or hasidim' and their religious practices. It should be remembered here that the report of the Censorship Committee for Hebrew Books, in which Abraham Stern so harshly criticized hasidism, was signed by Stern, Chmielewski, and Halberstam, but not

[89] Witowski, *Sposób na Żydów*. Estreicher and other Polish bibliographers attribute *Sposób na Żydów* to Wincenty Krasiński. However, an analysis of the text contradicts this. According to Jacob Shatzky, the pamphlet was written by Ksawery Klemens Szaniawski (Shatzky, 'Avraham Ya'akov Stern'), while Nathan Gelber attributed it to Gerard Witowski (Gelber, 'She'elat hayehudim bepolin bishenot 1815–1830', 119). See also Mahler, *Divrei yemei yisra'el*, v. 292–3. For a broader treatment of the 1818 debate, see Gelber, 'She'elat hayehudim bepolin bishenot 1815–1830', 106–43; Eisenbach, *Emancypacja Żydów*, 173–212.        [90] Tugendhold, *Jerobaał*, 6, 19.

[91] More comprehensive analysis of the attitude towards hasidism expressed in this booklet, see my 'Jakub Tugendhold', 26–9.

by Tugendhold. In July 1824, when the hasidim were petitioning the government to annul the decree banning hasidism, the Government Commission for Religious Denominations and Public Enlightenment summoned Jakub Tugendhold in his capacity as censor to explain the 'scandalous passages' in a Jewish book, the title of which is unknown to us. One can conclude from Tugendhold's explanation that the publication in question was a prayer book of the Ashkenazi rite, in which one of the passages aroused the suspicions of the Government Commission that it might spread religious intolerance. The Government Commission also took the opportunity to ask Tugendhold whether that book was also used by the hasidim. In reply, Tugendhold submitted an extensive report in which he defended the hasidim. In explaining the book, Tugenhold presented the following answer:

The above prayers are not used by the hasidim but by the so-called *highly pious* class [*klassę tak zwaną bardzo nabożną*], who are predominantly zealous talmudists and who are usually opposed to the hasidim. Even regular, daily prayers are said by the hasidim at a much later time than by other traditional Jews. The reason for this is that one must be physically and morally prepared for such a solemn activity as worshipping the Highest Being.

The present circumstances force me to present my own opinion; my convictions as to the insolent intolerance displayed almost exclusively by those exceedingly devout, zealous talmudists, who are opposed to hasidism: a large number of the hasidim in Poland should attract the attention of the High Government, for the hasidim, who are distinctive for their praiseworthy unity and mutual brotherly bonds, who do not allow themselves to be subjugated by the zealous talmudists, deserve the noble favour of the High Government with regard to their beneficial enlightenment. I dare to conjecture that if the High Government should undertake a general reform of Jews, it should begin with the class of zealous talmudists, who would surely prove more stubborn than the others.[92]

In the next part of the report Tugendhold also explained the circumstances in which the report of the Censorship Committee for Hebrew Books, signed by Stern, had been made, as well as his own attitude towards that report:

I had wanted to present these brief comments on the hasidim, together with various other additions, to the Government High Commission six months ago in the reply of the Committee for Censorship to the Government High Commission in response to their question on the hasidim. However, when just a few members of the Committee, and particularly one [i.e. Abraham Stern], contrary to all precepts of formality and order, decided to present his own arbitrary opinions, which were not the product of any meeting and hitherto had not been forwarded by him to the files of the committee, and he submitted them to the Government High Commission without the knowledge of several other members, I was unable to act upon this matter.

The significance of Tugendhold's words did not only lie in the fact that his report was one of the factors that led to the resumption of the investigation into the 'case of the hasidim' and resulted in a settlement beneficial to the hasidim, in that they were

[92] The original document by Tugendhold has been lost; excerpts of the report are to be found in AGAD, CWW 1871, pp. 162–4.

granted freedom of religion in the privacy of their homes. What seems more crucial was that this was the first appeal by a Haskalah representative in defence of the hasidic movement—an appeal that was both innovative and courageous[93] and, in the long term, was very important to the change of attitude of the Polish modernizing Jews towards the hasidic movement. Here Tugendhold contrasted the hasidim, who were pious, noble, and obedient to the government, with the intolerant, insolent, and arrogant 'zealous talmudists', i.e. the mitnagedim. This was a very unusual reversal of the accusations that were levelled mainly against the followers of hasidism by their opponents from the circles of the mitnagedim. Furthermore, according to Tugendhold, the real threat to the reform of the Jews in Poland was not the hasidim but the mitnagedim, and the government thus should protect the hasidic movement and direct its efforts at reform to the intolerant 'zealous talmudists'.

Tugendhold's reply may have been an emotional reaction to Stern's unfortunate arbitrary pronouncement, which, on behalf of the entire Censorship Committee for Hebrew Books (and thus also on behalf of Tugendhold), expressed a very negative opinion of hasidism and called for a ruthless war to be fought against it. Tugendhold not only contradicted Stern's accusations but also diverted the government's suspicions away from hasidism to the mitnagedim, who were favoured by Stern. This was, then, a personal conflict between two civil servants from the Committee for Censorship. Thus it seems obvious that, by turning the government's attention to the intolerance of the mitnagedim, Tugendhold's aim was merely to provide a diversionary tactic to deflect the government's attention away from any possible plans to reform the hasidim by raising the case of the mitnagedim. It was not an attempt to direct those reforms at the mitnagedim, because Tugendhold was highly critical of any government attempt to intervene in the religious affairs of Judaism. His manoeuvre proved fully effective. However, more important than his personal animosities towards Stern and the mitnagedim whom he supported was the fact that Tugendhold's defence of the hasidic movement was consistent with the views found in his writings. He defended hasidism as a righteous, noble, and valuable, even if not flawless, religious movement within Judaism. This distinguished Tugendhold's position from that of Schönfeld or Eisenbaum, who accepted hasidism as a tactical ally but were unwilling to recognize that the hasidim possessed any virtues.

Another interesting pronouncement in defence of hasidism was contained in a few sentences devoted to the movement by Tugendhold in the introduction to his translation of *Obrona Izraelitów* (The Defence of the Israelites), published in 1831 in Warsaw. This treatise by Manasseh ben Israel, written in 1656, was devoted to the defence of Jews against the accusation of using the blood of Christian children for religious rites. Tugendhold's very extensive introduction to the translation focused on polemics on that subject presented after Manasseh ben Israel's work

[93] The criticism, and even persecutions, that Tugendhold encountered in return for his wooing of the 'ignorant, fanatical Jews' are mentioned in Shatzky, 'Der kamf arum geplante tsaytshriftn far Yidn', 66.

had already been written, and to which the author had therefore not been able to reply. One variation on the accusation of using Christian blood stated that the blood was not used by all Jews but only by some Jewish sects. Tugendhold noted that modern, 'enlightened' antisemites, including the priest Professor Luigi Chiarini, whom Tugendhold abhorred, 'now state that the concept of the requirement of blood for religious rituals by traditional Jews is a secret known only to a certain number, to a certain sect'. Tugendhold rebuffed the accusation by asserting that contemporary Judaism had no sects. Developing this thesis, he mentioned several historical Jewish sects—the Pharisees, Sadducees, Essenes, Shabateans, Karaites, and Frankists—and added that they had all long since ceased to exist (which in the case of the crypto-Shabateans and the Karaites was incorrect), and that most of the Frankists had converted to Christianity.

> The hasidim who exist today cannot be regarded as a *sect*, if one considers the true meaning of that term in relation to the essence of religion. For these hasidim do not deviate in any way from the fundamental laws and regulations of the Old Testament, the Talmud, or other subsequent works that are respected by the nation of Israel for their religious value. Indeed it is the duty of every hasid to obey all such laws and regulations much more scrupulously than their law requires.[94]

Then Tugendhold recalled that the name 'hasid' was derived from the Hebrew word *ḥasid*, or 'pious', and that 'hasidim is the plural form'. He also mentioned that it would be absurd to assume that the hasidim, whose aim was to become particularly devout and to 'zealously fulfil all the religious regulations', would use blood for any ritual, since they observed and obeyed more scrupulously than any others the religious laws forbidding Jews to 'murder, to use even the smallest particle of blood, or to use any substance that may cause fermentation during their festival of Passover'.

This defence of hasidism had two dimensions. The first was an external one, namely the defence against the accusation of using Christian blood. There was a genuine need for such a defence, for in eastern Europe in the first decades of the nineteenth century there were indeed assertions that there was a sect at the heart of Judaism that used Christian blood for its rites. For example, in 1828, three years before the publication of *Obrona Izraelitów*, Tsar Nicholas I actually ordered a search of hasidic homes for books that exhorted the followers of hasidism to commit ritual murder,[95] and in 1830 Luigi Chiarini made such an accusation in Warsaw. This belief soon became increasingly widespread.[96]

[94] Tugendhold, *Obrona Izraelitów*, pp. xxiii–xxiv. See also the authorized German translation, *Der alte Wahn*, 14.

[95] Khiterer, 'Tsensory i tsensura evreyskikh religyoznych knig v Rosii', 10. On 18 March 1835, in a commentary on the verdict in the famous blood libel of Velizh, Tsar Nicholas I acknowledged that those who had already spent nine years in prison were innocent. Nevertheless, he wrote: 'Numerous examples of similar murders . . . go to show that among the Jews there probably exist fanatics or sectarians who consider Christian blood necessary for their rites'; see Dubnow, *History of the Jews in Russia and Poland*, ii. 83.

[96] In 1840 Stanisław Wodzicki, former chairman of the Senate of the Free City of Kraków, stated in his memoirs that such murders were committed by the hasidim and that such a crime had taken place

The second, far more interesting, dimension lay in Tugendhold's claim that hasidism did not have the characteristics of a sect; that, in terms of its doctrine, it did not differ from other groups within Judaism; and that it was completely legitimate and on a par with the other religious currents, the mitnagedim and the maskilim. It would be difficult to overestimate the significance of this truly revolutionary statement, which, it should be remembered, Tugendhold formulated in 1831. Unlike other previous statements by Jewish Enlightenment writers, he did not attempt to exclude hasidic doctrine from the heart of true Judaism. He recognized the hasidim as being equal co-religionists in Judaism, who were subject to the same religious commandments and, in some respects, he even pointed out their merits. These included their special piety and their yearning to adhere scrupulously to the religious commandments.

Over the following years Tugendhold often repeated the view he had put forward in his introduction to *Obrona Izraelitów*. In his writings as well as in his various activities, he emphasized the unity of Judaism and he viewed any potential criticisms of the hasidic movement as being arguments 'within the family'. This became particularly evident when, from the 1840s, he began to direct the edge of his criticism against 'religious rationalism', or indifference, which he perceived as a far graver threat than hasidism to the internal unity of Judaism. By comparison, hasidism, although it was somewhat fanatical and even alien to the attitudes of a moderate maskil, was by no means dangerous.

Tugendhold strictly maintained this attitude in his later works. In 1844 he published the bilingual Polish and Hebrew *Skazówki prawdy i zgody*, or, *Koshet imre emet* (Admonitions about Truth and Harmony), a short work of a religious nature in which he attempted to prove that the term *akum* (idol-worshippers) did not apply to Christians, and that the spirit of Judaism was full of tolerance and even respect for believers of other monotheistic religions. On this occasion he repeatedly made reference to those characterized by their 'mean conceit', 'ignorance and fanaticism' without ever naming the hasidim as such. At the same time, when mentioning kabbalah, he averred that it was full of deep, mystical knowledge 'which used to resonate with a certain saintliness', and that it had preserved the precious religious traditions of Judaism through the ages. Hasidism, he claimed, was the rightful heir to this tradition. His conclusion was important, inasmuch as it proved once again that he considered hasidism to be the rightful heir to a religious tradition in Judaism. Even his critical comment that 'nowadays many followers of that teaching, partic-

on his estates in Olkusz in 1787; see Wodzicki, *Wspomnienia*, 203–4. It provided a basis for the idea that the very first accusation of ritual murder had already been raised against the hasidim in 1787 (Goldberg, 'Julian Ursyn Niemcewicz wobec polskich Żydów', 150; Dynner, 'Men of Silk', 93). However, Wodzicki wrote his memoirs in 1840, and there is no reason to suppose that in 1787 he held the opinions expressed at this late date. In addition, Wodzicki did not suggest that he had held those views during the investigation in Olkusz in 1787. It seems likely that his opinion was influenced by the blood libel in Damascus (which was being widely debated in 1840), in which the accusation that the crime had been committed by 'Jewish fanatics' became widespread; see Frankel, *The Damascus Affair*, 208–11, 264–70.

ularly among the hasidim, have distanced themselves from the proper aims of that teaching, and create in its name the most shallow and strange explanations' did not detract from his statement.[97]

Tugendhold prepared a similar, moderately critical statement about hasidism in 1840—with Stern, curiously enough. A resident of Międzyrzec Podlaski, Moszko Taitelberg, had submitted a proposal to the Government Commission for Internal and Religious Affairs to prohibit hasidim from smoking tobacco inside the area of the *beit midrash*.[98] At the same time the Commission received a letter from Rafał Goldman, who represented the hasidim of Międzyrzec. Citing numerous religious sources, Goldman demanded the legalization of smoking in the *beit midrash*. The minister asked for Tugendhold's opinion on the matter,[99] and in a very extensive report he categorically rejected the demands of the hasidim and pointed out the influence this incident could have on 'curbing the fanatical liberty of this so-called sect of hasidim, which is spreading in Poland, and thereby on the prevention of conflicts and arguments which oftentimes have taken place between the supporters of this sect and other Israelites who do not belong to it' (see Appendix 10).[100] He called Goldman's explanation 'veritable hasidic prattle' and suggested that the Commission issue a general statement prohibiting the smoking of tobacco in the *beit midrash*, 'in order to place, in the country as a whole, something of a restraint upon the fanatical liberty and conceit of this sect which oftentimes vexes the simple pious class of Isra[elites] and disturbs the peace in communities, and whose supporters, even those youthful in years, so compulsively smoke tobacco that oftentimes they enter the *beit midrash* during a service with a pipe'.[101] This view resulted from consultation with Hayim Dawidsohn, the chief rabbi of Warsaw, and Abraham Stern, whose note of approval was attached to the report.[102] The Government Commission accepted Tugendhold's suggestion and prohibited the smoking of tobacco in the *beit midrash*, which, naturally, did not prevent the hasidim from breaking the law on this account.

This opinion is particularly telling in relation to comments made in 1824 in which Tugendhold defended the hasidim from the persecution of the 'zealous talmudists'. In 1840 the side being attacked and that being defended had changed places, but the strategy remained the same. Tugendhold once again came out against the 'aggressor', against a group that aspired to gain advantage at the expense of a competing ideological group. This, then, was the strategy of defending all of the choices available in Judaism and their unassailable right to an equal place in the Jewish community. Tugendhold defended the hasidim against the mitnagedim and the mitnagedim against the hasidim, the maskilim against the hasidim and

[97] Tugendhold, *Skazówki prawdy i zgody*, pp. x, xviii, 101.

[98] AGAD, CWW 1780, pp. 34–5. Fragments have been quoted in Borzymińska, *Dzieje Żydów w Polsce*, 61–2.     [99] Ministerial note in AGAD, CW 1780, p. 37; letter by Goldman, ibid. 50–2.

[100] Ibid. 38. Fragments of Tugendhold's opinion appear in Borzymińska, *Dzieje Żydów w Polsce*, 62.

[101] AGAD, CWW 1780, p. 44.     [102] Ibid. 47.

even the hasidim against the maskilim. As Bernhard Weinryb (possibly the fore-most authority on Tugendhold's life and works) has noted, the post of Warsaw censor was treated by Tugendhold as an opportunity to defend all sectors of Jewish society in Poland and Jewish people as an entirety.

An interesting episode from 1853 also sheds light on the nature and background of Tugendhold's pro-hasidic activities. The Polish central authorities had received an anonymous letter accusing the hasidim of using a prayer book that contained a prayer cursing the tsar and the government. In response, Tugendhold prepared a report defending the hasidim. For his main argument, he referred to a similar case from 1837, in which Jews reciting the *Melekh evyon* were accused of cursing the tsar and the government. This investigation had ended with a report that was also prepared by Tugendhold, in which he declared that traditional Polish Jews were innocent in using the prayer since it did not curse the tsar. In both cases, the government accepted his arguments and did not force Jewish communities to withdraw the prayer book containing the poem *Melekh evyon*.[103] What is interest-ing about the case is that Tugendhold's defence of both cases was virtually identi-cal, even though in the first case the accusation was levelled at all traditional Jewry, and in the second only at the hasidic community. The defence of the hasidim was not an expression of any special predilection for the hasidic movement, but rather one element in the total defence of the Jewish people and every group existing within it. This attitude was a constant hallmark of all of Tugendhold's actions.[104]

In 1858 Ludwik Lubliner, who was ill disposed towards Tugendhold, mentioned the close relationship the Warsaw censor had with the local hasidim. Reviewing the report made by Tugendhold for Tsar Alexander II in 1857, Lubliner stated that Tugendhold's animosity to religious reforms resulted from the fact that he 'allowed himself to be led by the hasidim'.[105] It was well known that Tugendhold's

---

[103] Weinryb, 'Zur Geschichte des Buchdruckes', 284, 298.

[104] During the 1862 sitting of the Warsaw Censorship Committee, Czerskier and Tugendhold applied to have banned a publication of the maskilic book by Shalom Jacob Abramovich, also known as Mendele Mocher Seforim (1835–1917), entitled *Limedu hetev* (Study Diligently). In their opinion, the book slandered the hasidim: 'The author calls them foes of the Bible, people deprived of the fear of God, immoral, licentious drunkards, who claim to be pious and holy; they like not wisdom, but debauchery, plunder and robbery; good deeds they despise.' Tugendhold and Czerskier noted that 'there are, among them, numerous genuinely pious and moral people'; Weinreich, 'Mendele-dokumentn', 365. The committee declined their application.

[105] Lubliner, *Obrona Żydów*, 10: 'That same Tugendhold who, seeking to portray himself as an ardent patriot during the revolution, published in the Warsaw papers the thoughts of a Jew standing guard, and then returned to his post as censor, allowed himself to be guided by the very same hasidim against whom he had protested so zealously in 1831, and, with their persuasion, he recently presented to the tsar (who had been wanting to introduce reforms that would be favourable to the Jews) a report stating that *Jews do not want any reform, that they are very happy in the present political situation*. If Tsar Alexander II had had an opportunity to read one of the German newspapers ridiculing Tugendhold, he would probably have favoured him with a dismissal (honorary, of course) for his false report instead of the Order of St Andrew, which our dear censor had craved for so long.' Possibly Lubliner was

anti-rationalistic attitudes had a far deeper ideological basis than was suggested by the vindictive Lubliner; however, this does not alter the fact that at the time Tugendhold's links with influential members of the hasidic community in Warsaw were growing stronger, and that he was closely connected with the leader of the Warsaw hasidim, Rabbi Isaac Meir Alter, the tsadik of Góra Kalwaria (Ger), known as the Gerer Rebbe.[106] At that time the tsadik of Góra Kalwaria was very active in the life of Warsaw's Jewish community, and he was also popular and respected by the 'progressives'.[107] In 1858 relations between Tugendhold and Rabbi Isaac Meir Alter had become so close that the Gerer Rebbe would visit Tugendhold asking him to intervene with the government. One such visit was connected with the government's education plans, which were carried out by Warsaw's integrationists. The visit was described by Marcus Jastrow, the newly arrived preacher at the 'German Synagogue' in Warsaw, who was present at the meeting.[108] These contacts also continued later on. When, in 1859, the government took various initiatives to reform the Jewish community in Poland, 'the hasidim, having found out about these negotiations and fearful of changes that might support education, employed the good services of the Censor and Director of the Rabbinical School, Jacob Tugendhold'.[109] Tugendhold proved useful, as he managed to convince Pavel Muchanov, the Minister of Education, to replace the project of the liberal representatives of the Jewish community with his own, which was more advantageous to the traditional sector of Jewish society.

Thus, in his later years Tugendhold was a conservative maskil who defended traditional Jewish society from what he perceived to be excessively radical changes in socio-religious life, which potentially could lead to a weakening of the Jewish community and its religion. During an investigation into a journey made to the Zamość area by the Volhynian tsadik Abraham Twersky of Turisk (1806–89), Tugendhold harshly criticized the excesses of the 'royal' tsadikim from the Ukraine—'roguish fanatics who, pretending to work wonders, take advantage of the credulousness of unenlightened persons of the Mos[aic] fai[th] and inveigle contributions out of them under the pretext of interceding with the Heavenly Lord to alleviate some ailment' (see Appendix 15).[110] At the same time, however, he felt compelled to add that 'In the Kingdom of Poland, there are a few such fanatical

referring to an article published in *Der Orient* in 1844 by an anonymous 'Warschauer', but which was unanimously attributed to Chaim Zelig Słonimski. See Ein Warschauer, correspondence, *Der Orient*, 45 (1844), 351–2; see also Shatzky, 'Der kamf arum geplante tsaytshriftn far Yidn', 67.

[106] Nussbaum, *Szkice historyczne*, 73.

[107] See e.g. Daniel Neufeld, 'Wiadomości bieżące', *Ju.* 3 (1863), 152; id., 'Bibliografia', *Ju.* 3 (1863), 7. For more on the role of the Gerer Rebbe, Isaac Meir Alter, in the pre-uprising period of 1861–3, see Kandel, 'Kariera rabiniczna cadyka Icie-Majera', 131–6; Shatzky, *Geshikhte fun Yidn in Varshe*, iii. 356–62.          [108] Jastrow, 'Bär Meisels', *Hebrew Leader*, 15/25 (1870), 2.

[109] Marcus Jastrow's letter to Jacob Raisin (n.d.) can be found in the American Jewish Archives in Cincinnati. See also the American Jewish Archives, Marcus Jastrow Biographical Notes 26; Shatzky, *Geshikhte fun Yidn in Varshe*, iii. 359.          [110] AGAD, CWW 1446, pp. 137–8.

leaders, but, living a pious life and not imposing themselves with their demands, they are far less pernicious than strangers such as Tweryskier, who usually practise their art with brazenness.'

It should be borne in mind that Tugendhold was not an apologist for the hasidic movement; that he repeatedly expressed unfavourable and critical opinions about that movement; and that he invariably accused its adherents of fanaticism and ignorance. Furthermore, the originality of his defence of hasidism did not necessarily lie in the ideas he expressed, since in those days similar views could be encountered among non-hasidic traditionalists, and even among the Polish public. Moreover, during the late 1820s Jacob Samuel Byk, a Galician maskil who was a little older than Tugendhold, went so far in his pro-hasidic revisionism that maskilic contemporaries who not long before had been his colleagues plainly accused him of 'apostasy' to the hasidic camp. Tugendhold never allowed his opinions to become so radical. Rather, his 'revolutionary attitudes' hinged on the fact that he was the first modernizing Jew who had dared not only to express them, but subsequently to spread and defend them to victory. Ultimately, that proved to be the most important issue.

## CONCLUSIONS

In the period between the uprisings both of the competing ideological options saw an increase in growth, and subsequently the enmity between the Haskalah and hasidism gained momentum both as an ideological struggle and in daily conflicts within the Jewish community. The shape the conflict took was the result mainly of daily life in the community, rather than in the literature and in ideological arguments. Although a differing vision of the world, and the place of Jewish society in that world, formed the basis of the conflict, the local struggle between the hasidim and proponents of modernization was played out against a background of daily annoyances and insults, not intellectual altercations. The most obvious motive of the conflict was the desire of both competing factions to seize power, or at least influence, within the community. It caused an increase in aggression towards the opposing side which became ruthless conflict (particularly on the part of the numerically superior hasidim), and in time resulted in an antipathy that bordered on demonization. Curiously, Haskalah literature of the period rarely reached such a level of hostility. Although the subject of hasidism was addressed increasingly in journalism in the Kingdom of Poland, and the first literary text devoted entirely to the struggle appeared at that time, interest in the movement was far from being obsessive. In reality, the attitudes of the Polish maskilim of the time varied widely. The more antagonistic texts derived from the circles of the radical modernizers who congregated in the Rabbinical School (the leading role here being played by Antoni Eisenbaum). Maskilim from smaller centres, in which the daily conflicts and pressures exerted by the hasidic group were far stronger than in Warsaw, were similarly hostile towards the hasidim. At the same time the more moderate maskilim (for example, Edward Hering) made the first attempts to come to grips with the hasidic phenomenon and even to include these reflections in their more general educational programmes. Generally speaking, the growth of interest in hasidism was not accompanied by a growth in knowledge, and, according to some maskilim, ignorance of the subject was a virtue.

Jakub Tugendhold's attitude towards hasidism was innovative among modernizing Jews. Tugendhold treated hasidism as one of the legitimate sectors of Judaism and persistently endeavoured to limit social tensions between all sectors of Jewish society. Tugendhold's voice was an isolated one in the 1820s, but it found its way into the consciousness of moderately integrationist Jewish circles in the Kingdom of Poland in the next generation. His means differed from those of Byk, whose ideas were commonly rejected and failed to bring any visible changes into the social dimension, and, ultimately, Tugendhold's ideas were victorious. In the 1850s and 1860s, there was a clear change among Warsaw's modernizing Jews from the confrontational attitudes which had been prevalent in the 1840s. It is true that the change was but one aspect of the general ideological transformation within the modernizing camp, and it was perfectly harmonious with the general direction that the entire process took. Furthermore, the integrationists of *Jutrzenka* and the *Izraelita* never quoted Tugendhold as their ideological patron (probably because he represented a radically different political option) and some of them—particularly Jastrow—wrote about him very critically.[111] However, the similarity between the views on hasidism expounded by Tugendhold and the opinions presented a few dozen years later by Neufeld, Jastrow, and their younger colleagues was so striking that, in principle, there could have been little doubt that it was Tugendhold's ideas (even if not Tugenhold himself) which decided the ultimate shape of their ideology. On the other hand, the fact that Tugendhold's final efforts and the most important publications in that field by Neufeld or Jastrow came at exactly the same time (the early 1860s), and the fact that a considerable number of the young members of the integrationist movement were students at the Rabbinical School directed by Tugendhold, indicate that these were direct influences.

[111] Jastrow, 'Bär Meisels', *Hebrew Leader*, 15/25 (1870), 2; 16/3 (1870), 2; Krakowski, 'O cmentarzu i służbie pogrzebowej', 60.

# FIVE

# The Twilight of the Haskalah and the Dawning of Integration

THE major changes in the structure and legal position of Jewish society in Poland coincided with the so-called Polish–Jewish fraternity, the renowned rapprochement between the Polish and Jewish intelligentsia that occurred in the period preceding the 1863 Uprising. However, these changes had been preceded, in the late 1840s to the early 1860s, by a social and, above all, ideological shift that, while not as yet wide-ranging, was spectacular.[1] It was probably at this time that a new group emerged from among the young followers of the Haskalah, the students of the Warsaw Rabbinical School, the liberal bourgeoisie, and the new representatives of the Jewish intelligentsia. This new group began to dominate the Jewish modernization movement in the Kingdom of Poland from the mid-1860s onwards, and it was this new Jewish intelligentsia that Hilary Nussbaum saw as the main engine of the social changes that had been taking place since the 1850s among Jewish supporters of modernization, mainly in Warsaw:

Educational resources such as *Jutrzenka*, *Izraelita*, and the Jewish Orphanages run by the Warsaw Charitable Society marked new trends in the 1860s. However, the most spectacular, the most visible feature of this period, was the rise of the first generation of young Israelites—physicians, lawyers, biologists, philologists—who dedicated themselves to the specialist, higher-level, and honourable professions; they became the spirited citizens of the country, supporters of general education, and the most effective force for progress among the wider circles of their co-religionists.[2]

The process had begun earlier. Initially, in the early 1840s, small modernizing circles gained influence on the Jewish community board of Warsaw, and systematically increased their sphere of influence in the 1850s. In 1852 the 'German' synagogue in Daniłowiczowska Street, which for half a century had been the centre of one of the most prominent Haskalah circles in Warsaw, gained a rival, the 'Polish' synagogue, to which mainly the younger people gravitated, i.e. the second generation of the Warsaw Haskalah. (The other liberal synagogue, at the Rabbinical

---

[1] An interesting, though outdated and tendentious, study of the state of the integrationist movement during this period can be found in Nussbaum, *Historia Żydów*; id., *Szkice historyczne*. See also Gelber, *Die Juden und der Polnische Aufstand 1863*. Of the newer studies see Eisenbach, *Kwestia równouprawnienia Żydów*, 241 ff.; id., *Emancypacja Żydów*, 468–513; Opalski and Bartal, *Poles and Jews*, 12–37.  [2] Nussbaum, *Szkice historyczne*, 174.

School, was short-lived and not particularly influential.) In 1854–7 a series of conflicts swept through the Jewish community in Warsaw concerning both the introduction of a new hearse, in line with the ideas held by the integrationists, and the first Polish inscription on the tomb of one of the most radical leaders of the Jewish modernizing group in Poland, Antoni Eisenbaum.[3] The events heralded an end to the concept of modernization in the spirit of the Haskalah, and saw the leading representatives of the 'progressive' group turning towards a greater degree of integration with the surrounding Polish culture. Samuel Henryk Peltyn, one of the active participants in these events and later the editor-in-chief of *Izraelita*, remembered this period as the *Sturm-periode* of the new group.[4]

## MASKILIM, INTEGRATIONISTS, AND ASSIMILATIONISTS

With the growth of the modernizing camp in the 1850s and the 1860s, a clear division emerged within the camp. Three main groups were already distinguishable by the late 1850s: a relatively weak group comprising both the traditional maskilim, who wrote only in Hebrew, and some members of the earlier disbanded group from the wealthy middle classes and the Warsaw bourgeoisie with their pragmatic pro-German sympathies; a group of radical assimilationists, often accused, justifiably, of religious indifference and of renouncing Judaism; and a moderate group aiming at hegemony, who promoted pro-Polish acculturation while wishing to preserve the status of Judaism and religious traditions.[5]

The first of these groups was made up chiefly of maskilim who wrote mainly in Hebrew, had pro-German cultural tendencies, and rejected the dominant pro-Polish integrationist movement, seeking ideological allies among the Russian or Galician maskilim and the Russian authorities, rather than among the Polish Jewish proponents of modernization. This relatively small group, which challenged the pro-Polish stance of the Haskalah in the Congress Kingdom, had been in existence since the beginning of the nineteenth century, with its first known centre in the literary salon of Moses Tannenbaum (1795– 1849).[6] During the second half of the century the ideological course taken by this group did not coincide com-

---

[3] See Guesnet, *Polnische Juden im 19. Jahrhundert*, 303–31, for the considerable importance of changes in the burial customs and ceremonies to the modernizing segments of Jewish society. For more on the conflict over Eisenbaum's tombstone, see Kandel, 'Napisy nagrobkowe'; Schiper, *Cmentarze żydowskie w Warszawie*, 122.

[4] Judaita [Samel Henryk Peltyn], *Projekt reformy w judaizmie*, 44–5.

[5] More on the Jewish 'assimilation' factions and camps in 19th-century Poland can be found in Cała, *Asymilacja Żydów*; id., 'The Question of the Assimilation'. See also Kieniewicz, 'Assimilated Jews in Nineteenth-Century Warsaw'; Lichten, 'Notes on the Assimilation'.

[6] For a discussion of Tannenbaum and his salon, see Mahler, *Hasidism and the Jewish Enlightenment*, 222–9.

pletely with the direction the mainstream of the Jewish modernization movement
in Poland was taking, although, of course, the boundaries of the two groups were
frequently and easily crossed. Representatives of the integrationist movement
reached out to Haskalah literature and made appeals to its readers, while the traditional maskilim wrote and published in the Polish language or in Hebrew periodicals and defended the ideals of the Polish–Jewish fraternity and of 'a Pole of the
Mosaic faith'. Israel Weissbrem serves here as a good example.[7]

The most important forum for the later Haskalah in the Kingdom of Poland was
*Hatsefirah*, the first Hebrew weekly in the Congress Kingdom. The periodical was
established at the beginning of 1862 by Chaim Zelig Słonimski (1810–1904), to be
discontinued but later resurrected by him, and it gained enormous influence in
the circles of the Jewish intelligentsia and had the largest circulation of the east
European weeklies in Hebrew at that time. This indicates that it was the Hebrew
moderate supporters of modernization, who were represented in the Kingdom by
*Hatsefirah*, who had the broadest social backing, although it was not until the 1890s
that they were as active as the integrationists. *Hatsefirah* showed minimal interest
in the Polish and Polish Jewish environment (although privately Słonimski was
drawn to the Polish language and culture), but was ostentatiously loyal towards
the Russian empire and maintained a policy of non-involvement. These elements
were particularly striking when compared with the fervent patriotism of the two
remaining groups of the modernizing movement.[8] The pragmatic orientation was
reflected in its practical programme, named 'Organic Work', conveying the idea of
grassroots activity for the improvement of the community at large.[9] However, very
similar ideals could also be encountered outside *Hatsefirah*, in other, more traditional forms of expression, for example, in Haskalah religious-moral treatises and
popular history texts. Allegiance to the Hebrew language and traditional Haskalah
values, such as loyalty to the monarchy and strong cultural identification with
Hebrew, increasingly distanced representatives of this group from the integrationist movement. Differences of opinion and even out-and-out conflicts mirrored
similar developments in the Russian empire, with the division into moderate and

---

[7] See Baker, 'The Reassessment of Haskala Ideology', 227–8, for the political views of Israel
Weissbrem.

[8] See Cała, *Asymilacja Żydów*, 33–48; Fuks, *Prasa żydowska w Warszawie*, 103–23, for the strategy
of popularization of the sciences and the apolitical direction of *Hatsefirah* before Sokołów's editorship.
Interesting comments on the attitude of the periodical towards the dilemmas of Polish versus Russian
loyalty are to be found in Baker, 'The Reassessment of Haskala Ideology', 226–7.

[9] The above-mentioned division of the Jewish 'progressive' camp in a way reflects the two directions in the Jewish 'assimilation' in Poland described by Ezra Mendelsohn—namely, a pragmatic and
a Romantic one. At the same time, however, it proves that pragmatism and Romanticism were two of a
number of elements dividing this group into two competing camps. See Ezra Mendelsohn, 'A Note on
Jewish Assimilation in the Polish Lands'. Ela Bauer correctly traced the influence of the Polish positivist ideology to the second of the *Hatsefirah* editors, Nachum Sokołów. See Ela Bauer, 'Nahum
Sokolow'.

radical Haskalah.[10] It may be assumed that in both cases the impetus for the changes came from the 'post-Sevastopol détente' and a palpable intellectual revival in the empire after the death of Tsar Nicholas I and rise to power of his successor, Alexander II.

At the other extreme, the representatives of the radical pro-Polish assimilation movement, who strove to obliterate all signs of Jewish separateness, were as far removed from the integrationists as were the above-mentioned offshoots of the Haskalah. In reality, the 'movement of radical assimilationists' was more of a rhetorical concept than a genuine social movement sharing common views and aims that had been institutionalized in some form, unlike the moderate integrationist movement and the traditional Haskalah. The concept was conjured up by their adversaries to refer to both those who steered towards radical renunciation of Jewish tradition for ideological reasons and those indifferentists who were devoid of ideals and who drifted away from Judaism and its moral teaching out of sheer laziness or for material gain. The second group was referred to in Galician and Russian maskilic periodicals as the pseudo-Haskalah.[11] Radical assimilationists in the Kingdom of Poland were labelled using very similar terms by their moderate adversaries: 'backward progressives', 'fanatical progressives', 'pseudo-progressives', 'pseudo-progressive ultras', or 'progressive reactionaries'.[12] This once again points to similarities between the pro-Polish integrationists and Haskalah groups in other centres of the east European Haskalah. In the mid-1870s the very term 'progressive' had become so overused that the editors of *Izraelita* began to replace it with the terms 'the right-thinking' or 'the enlightened class'. Whatever the case, if the alarmist appeals of moderate integrationists are anything to go by, the radical group was quite large in the 1860s and 1870s, and its ranks were becoming progressively larger, although, of course, we have no statistical data on the size of this or any other group.[13] Unfortunately, little is known of the group because its lack of a clear ideology and its amorphous character, and the fact that it did not have its own press section, meant that it remained 'silent'. As a result, most of the available information about it comes from its rival *Jutrzenka*, and later from *Izraelita*. These two publications were equally ill disposed towards religious indifferentists, and one suspects that information concerning the group's size and influence could have been exaggerated or even fabricated to further the arguments of the moderate integrationists in their disputes with the traditional camp. However, the frequency

[10] See Feiner, *Haskalah and History*, 274–95, for information on the clash between moderate and radical Haskalah in Russia.        [11] See Feiner, 'The Pseudo-Enlightenment'.

[12] Samuel H. Peltyn, 'Z życia: Pogadanki tygodniowe', *Izr.* 3 (1868), 90–1; Izrael Leon Grosglik, 'Listy Młodego Ex-Chasyda', *Izr.* 4 (1869), 262; H. N[eumanowicz], 'Przyczynki do listów ex-chasyda', *Izr.* 4 (1869), 311; Samuel H. Peltyn, 'Optymizm i pesymizm', *Izr.* 9 (1874), 319; id., 'Nasze Drogi', *Izr.* 21 (1886), 157.

[13] For some of the statistical aspects of Jewish assimilation and acculturation in Warsaw, see Corrsin, 'Aspects of Population Change and of Acculturation'. See also Endelman, 'Jewish Converts in Nineteenth-Century Warsaw'.

with which the debates with indifferentism recurred in these journals is a sign that the radical assimilationists (or, if their existence is disputed, the very idea of radical assimilation) were actually seen as a serious, possibly even the most serious, obstacles to real progress.[14]

Considerably more information is available about the views of the moderate wing of the modernizing camp, which I refer to as the integrationist group. A number of factors are responsible for this. Most importantly, the group was distinctive from the 1860s on, if not for its numbers, at least for its social involvement. In order to understand its views better, we should bear in mind that this particular group published two periodicals, first *Jutrzenka*, and later *Izraelita*, 'around which all of the progressive Israel of Warsaw congregated'.[15] The defining characteristics of this group are its radical and ideological gravitation towards the Polish language and Polish culture, its strongly cohesive tendencies encompassing all the factions of Jewish society, and an increasing interest in religious issues, including debates with hasidism. It was this group that began to dominate modernizing Jewish circles in the Kingdom of Poland, and its dominance continued until the end of the nineteenth and beginning of the twentieth century.

## FROM THE POLISH LANGUAGE TO A POLISH IDENTITY

The transformation of Jewish modernizing circles in Poland in the second half of the nineteenth century appears to have been mainly a result of the trend towards Polonization already observable among the first generation of maskilim in the Kingdom of Poland, that is, Abraham Stern, Jakub Tugendhold, Ezechiel Hoge, and Natan and Jan Glücksberg. Yet, however strong this linguistic integration might have been, among the older generation pro-Polish sympathies were, as a rule, utilitarian in nature. These sympathies were perceived as a local, Polish version of integration with a wider European culture and a convenient way of promoting the Haskalah ideology, or even influencing government projects to 'reform the Jewish people'. Moreover, they were associated with the typically maskilic interest in Hebrew writings, with a modicum of the religious and social conservatism characteristic of the moderate Haskalah (at which Stern and Tugendhold excelled), and finally—and most significantly here—with their attachment to the German language and culture. The last factor, although in fact coincidental, was

---

[14] During the period in which *Jutrzenka* and *Izraelita* were published, several dozen extensive programmatic articles were devoted to the dispute with religious indifferentism; see e.g. S[onia] Trachtenberg, 'Pia desideria', *Ju.* 3 (1863), 103; 'Listy żydowskie. List VIII: Izaak do Redaktora Jutrzenki', *Ju.* 3 (1863), 137–8; Samuel H. Peltyn, 'Indifferentyzm religijny', *Izr.* 1 (1866), 41–3; id., 'Rzut oka na sprawy Judaizmu w roku ubiegłym', *Izr.* 5 (1870), 1–3, 9–11; id., 'Optymizm i pesymizm', *Izr.* 9 (1874), 319–20; Adolf Jakub Cohn, 'Bezbarwni', *Izr.* 11 (1876), 249–50. On the controversies about the importance of religion and the direction of the religious reforms among Jews in the Congress of Poland, see Guterman, 'Hapulmus bekhitvei-et yehudiyim bepolin'.

[15] Judaita, *Projekt reformy w judaizmie*, 44.

for the Polish maskilim one of the defining elements of their maskilic identity. This inclination towards the German language was not strictly an ideological choice and in no way did it conflict with their Polish sympathies, but rather it resulted from a natural propensity towards one's mother tongue or the language of intellectual initiation. It is hardly surprising that in the milieu of the Warsaw, Łódź, and Kalisz bourgeoisie (which often originated from Prussia), as well as of the Warsaw and Łódź Jewish intelligentsia (educated for the most part in German schools and from German texts), links with this culture remained alive until the 1850s.[16] These cultural links were also maintained through influences such as personal ties between the most prominent Polish and Prussian maskilim, and even by seeking the assistance of mediators from Berlin in solving Warsaw's problems.[17]

The situation altered radically in the next generation, which had been brought up with a growing attachment to the Polish language and the Polish *raison d'état*. The choice of the Polish language (or even Polishness) was not simply the choice of a way to integrate with European culture. For many representatives of this group, Polish was the natural language of communication and the only language of their culture. Antoni Eisenbaum had already observed this in 1822.[18] The group of Jews who used Polish, not Yiddish or German, on a day-to-day basis was relatively large (or at least noticeable) by the 1840s, and observers constantly emphasized its growth.[19] In 1839 Eisenbaum and Joseph Bernstein, a physician and maskil from Warsaw, estimated it at one-third of the Jewish population in Poland, which was undoubtedly an exaggeration.[20] The Polish language had an emotional value for many Jews, and this was well nourished by contemporary Romantic ideals. The events of the 1850s and the early 1860s, manifesting ever stronger pro-Polish integration among modernizing Jewish circles, were thus a natural and inevitable consequence of the direction chosen by the generation of their fathers in the 1820s and the 1830s. It was this generation of maskilic fathers who published mainly in Polish as opposed to Hebrew, who devoted much attention to learning and disseminating this language, and who carefully maintained relations with Polish circles. Ironically, the strategies adopted for a typically maskilic defence of the values of the Jewish world led to an integration that went far beyond the ideals of the Haskalah

---

[16] See Guesnet, *Polnische Juden im 19. Jahrhundert*, 298–300, for the role of the German language as an element of identity and social position. It is interesting that in a volume devoted to the study of the influences of the German model on the directions of the Jewish Enlightenment in other European countries and regions, not a single passage is devoted to the Kingdom of Poland (Katz (ed.), *Toward Modernity*).　　　　　　　　　　　　[17] See Weinryb, 'Zur Geschichte der Aufklärung bei den Juden'.

[18] Z. [Antoni Eisenbaum], 'O wychowaniu młodzieży żydowskiej', *Rozmaitości* [suppl. to *Gazeta Korrespondenta Krajowego i Zagranicznego*], 5 (1822), 32.

[19] See e.g. Liebkind, *Modlitwy dla Izraelitów*, p. iii.

[20] J[osef] B[ernstein], 'Warschau' [correspondence], *AZJ* 4 (1840), 89–90; Z. [Antoni Eisenbaum], 'Uwagi nad artykułem p. Hering', *Gazeta Codzienna*, 2678 (1839), 3. In 1897 only 13.7 per cent of the Jews in Warsaw declared Polish as their mother tongue. However, these figures should not be taken at face value.

and often amounted to fundamental assimilation, a consequence of which was the renunciation of many of the ideals and values that they had defended.

This evolution from a Haskalah outlook to an integrationist ideology can be observed in the example of the attitude towards Hebrew. For the previous generation, it was a sacred language and its importance to maskilic identity was indisputable. While accepting the fact that Polish had to replace Hebrew in some of its functions, the maskilim protested, *inter alia*, against eliminating Hebrew from schools and from prayer, and scrupulously maintained their knowledge of the language.[21] While Hebrew was still important to the generation of young integrationists, Polish had already become their first language, the language of their identity. For Neufeld, Nussbaum, Peltyn, and Bersohn, Hebrew was a necessary tool for learning religious principles properly and for studying Holy Scripture, and they regarded it as their religious duty to advocate the learning of Hebrew. At the same time, however, they claimed that people's knowledge of Hebrew was so poor that, in order to promote the idea of 'progress', one had to use the language of the country. Neufeld also stated that Hebrew writings on current issues were 'a discussion behind closed doors'. Every Jew

values something written in a language comprehensible to his Christian neighbour completely differently, for here, the discussion becomes a public one and is read by those in broader spheres and higher circles. It affects him all the more strongly, seeing that his neighbour listens to the discussion; the Jew takes it to heart, avoids being inconsistent, justifies, defends, if he can, his principles, concedes, having recognized that there are some he cannot defend because he would not want his people or his faith to suffer on account of a lack of dignity or respect.[22]

Thus, Hebrew no longer constituted an autonomous value for the younger generation. Instead, it had become a genuine obstacle to the modernization of Jewish society. Hilary Nussbaum wrote in a similar vein about learning it with a mixture of respect and annoyance. While underlining the significance of Hebrew for Jewish religious traditions (he himself wrote Hebrew poetry), he pointed out that its rightful place was among other dead languages and that it was 'a language for intellectuals, and not for ordinary mortals'.[23] While, according to him, it was important to study the language, prayer and religious instruction should be conducted solely in Polish. 'A handful of real connoisseurs of Hebrew-rabbinical literature' should aim to incorporate its treasures into Polish writings and in this way promote it among the followers of Judaism, at the same time making knowledge of Hebrew unnecessary.[24]

One step in this direction was made when a 'Polish' synagogue was established in Nalewki Street. It employed Izaak Kramsztyk (Kramstück) as its first preacher, and he delivered his sermons in Polish. The Nalewki prayer house was the initia-

---

[21] See e.g. Tugendhold, 'Krótki rys historii języka i literatury hebrajskiej', 22–3.
[22] Neufeld, *Or torah*, 3.
[23] Nussbaum, *Leon i Lajb*, 24. See also Judaita, *Projekt reformy w judaizmie*, 127.
[24] Nussbaum, *Szkice historyczne*, 169.

tive of a small group of graduates from the Rabbinical School. By 1860 its member-ship had dropped to under 100, and the synagogue committee ran into financial difficulties.[25] Nevertheless, the synagogue very soon proved to be part of a more widespread movement and a visible sign of a change in attitude within the whole milieu. The young integrationists who gathered there soon gained significant influence in Jewish society in the Kingdom of Poland. Kramsztyk himself epito-mized the new type of Jewish integrationist, or (in their own terminology) 'Pole of the Mosaic faith'. Born in Warsaw in 1814 into a family of poor merchants, he studied at the Warsaw Rabbinical School from 1832, where he later taught religion and Talmud. In 1852 he became the preacher in the new 'Polish' synagogue. In the pre-uprising period of Polish–Jewish fraternity he entered the ranks of national martyrs when he led Jewish patriotic demonstrations with the chief rabbi of Warsaw, Baer Meisels, and a preacher from the 'German' synagogue, Marcus Jastrow. After his arrest on 9 November 1861 he was imprisoned in the Warsaw Citadel, and was later the only one of the three imprisoned leaders to be sent to the dungeons in Bobruisk. He was released in 1862, and the next year he was exiled to the province of Saratov, where he remained until 1867. On his return, he took up publishing and literary activities, which were, of course, conducted solely in Polish. He died on 23 September 1889 in Warsaw.[26]

The establishment of the 'Polish', 'progressive' synagogue with sermons in Polish was only one of a long list of signs of the gradual Polonization of this group. In 1855, after lengthy pleadings with the authorities and conflicts with the commun-ity's traditional majority, the hitherto 'German' synagogue became independent of the Jewish community board and assumed the name of 'the synagogue in Daniłowiczowska Street' (the government authorities did not agree to the name 'the normal synagogue').[27] Soon the board of the synagogue stopped using German in protocols and religious instruction, replacing it with Polish. In 1858 the syn-agogue in Daniłowiczowska Street appointed Marcus Jastrow as preacher. As a condition of his appointment, he was required to learn Polish immediately. On his arrival in Warsaw, Jastrow already had a rudimentary knowledge of the language, and by 1859 he was able to preach in Polish. From this time onwards the 'German' synagogue became one of the strongest ideological centres of pro-Polish linguistic assimilation.

[25] See AGAD, CWW 1731, pp. 659–67.

[26] For more on Kramsztyk, see Kramsztyk, *Kazania*, vol. i, pp. i–v; Wein, 'Kramsztyk, Izaak'; Gelber, *Die Juden und der Polnische Aufstand 1863*, 83–5; Shatzky, *Geshikhte fun Yidn in Varshe*, iii, index.

[27] See AGAD, CWW 1728, pp. 182–97; 1729, pp. 1–75, for information on the transformation of the 'German' synagogue. A brief history of the synagogue in Daniłowiczowska Street is presented in Zilbersztejn, 'Postępowa synagoga na Daniłowiczowskiej'; see also Guterman, 'The Origins of the Great Synagogue in Warsaw'; id., *Mehitbolelut lele'umiyut*. Some comments on the ideological dilemmas of the integrationist Jews in Poland are to be found in Kozińska-Witt, 'Żydzi—polscy? niemieccy?'

Interestingly, the growth in the significance of the Polish language to Jewish society could also be observed at that time in the traditional sector of this group, which was directly concerned with rapprochement between the leaders of the Orthodox group and the leaders of the liberal movement. This process of Polonization culminated in the appeal by Orthodox rabbis, including the chief rabbi, Baer Meisels, and the Gerer Rebbe, to every Jewish religious teacher 'to try to introduce Polish language teaching, using a native Pole with an excellent command of this very language as the teacher'.[28] The Gerer Rebbe appealed in 1863 for Jews to use Polish in drawing up the documents for the halakhically required sale of *hamets* (bread or leavened dough) to non-Jews for the duration of Passover.[29] But neither then nor at any later time did Polish supersede Yiddish as the language of everyday communication for the Jewish masses, and the significance of the pro-Polish declarations of hasidic leaders waned considerably in the period of post-uprising disillusionment. However, the transformation that took place in Jewish society as a whole was decisive for the ideological development of Jewish integrationist circles, in which Polish became an integral part of one's identity. Unfortunately, no reliable statistics are available from the period in question; the first census to take language criteria into account was not conducted until 1897. According to the census data, a mere 0.4 per cent of Warsaw Jews claimed German as their mother tongue, while 13.7 per cent claimed Polish.[30] An overwhelming majority still spoke Yiddish; however, the use of Polish was gradually spreading among the so-called progressive classes. This was not simply a manifestation of the pragmatic acquisition of the local language (as in the case of the earlier maskilim), but a significant cultural choice that determined the identity of the whole integrationist camp in the Kingdom of Poland.

## POLISH PATRIOTISM

The adoption of Polish as the language of sermons and prayer and, generally, as the language of everyday communication was important because it meant that Polish was no longer simply a sign of adaptation to the environment and a convenient means of communicating with the non-Jewish world. From the late 1850s onwards sermons preached in both 'progressive' synagogues, and works by Daniel Neufeld, Marcus Jastrow, Aleksander Kraushar, Hilary Glattstern, and many others express the view that the use of Polish was merely an external sign of a fundamental change in identity that was taking place among the circles of the young integrationists.

---

[28] *Ju.* 2 (1862), 381, cited in Borzymińska, *Szkolnictwo żydowskie w Warszawie*, 219–20.

[29] 'Wiadomości bieżące: Suum cuique', *Ju.* 3 (1863), 152. The Polish emigrant press devoted considerable attention to these events; see Shatzky, *Geshikhte fun Yidn in Varshe*, iii. 359.

[30] The two other languages were Yiddish (83.7 per cent) and Russian (2.2 per cent); see Corrsin, 'Aspects of Population Change and of Acculturation', 131. Interestingly enough, Polish was declared less frequently in Łódź; the statistics for Łódź were: Yiddish 93.6 per cent, Polish 4.1 per cent, Russian 1.2 per cent, German 1.1 per cent. See Janczak, 'Struktura narodowościowa Łodzi', 49.

FIG. 9. Marcus Jastrow (1829–1903)
National and University Library in Jerusalem, Shvadron Collection

The principle of unity with the Polish nation came to the fore at that stage, to be followed by that of Polish patriotism. Neufeld even claimed that, by adopting the Polish language, one served the chief aim: the 'amalgamation of individual, autonomous races and tribes into one social structure', that is, complete social and cultural, though not religious, integration with the Polish nation.[31] The renunciation of the principle of 'the golden alliance' with the monarchy and alignment with one party in the ethnic conflicts, particularly with the Polish *pritsim* (Yiddish for 'noblemen') and their culture, which was then at the height of Romantic frenzy, was not only at variance with the fundamental ideas of the traditional Haskalah, but also so completely contrary to its rationalist and loyalist foundations that it met with an angry reaction from all too many eastern European maskilim.[32]

One of the most fervent adherents of this new integrationist movement, whose hallmark was ostentatious Polish patriotism, was Marcus Jastrow (see Fig. 9). He was a Germanized newcomer from the province of Poznań, in Prussia, and a preacher at the synagogue that until recently had been called the 'German' synagogue. Despite a relatively short stay in the Kingdom of Poland (a mere six years), he became one of the most important protagonists in the events of that period. Born into a family of merchants in Rogoźno in the Grand Duchy of Poznań, he

[31] Neufeld, *Or torah*, 2.

[32] See Baker, 'The Reassessment of Haskala Ideology', 221–49, for the reaction of the Hebrew maskilic press to the January Uprising and Jewish involvement in the uprising. See also Borzymińska, *Szkolnictwo żydowskie w Warszawie*, 298–9. More on the reaction in Jewish literature can be found in Opalski and Bartal, *Poles and Jews*, 78–97.

attended a Protestant grammar school in Poznań in 1844–52, after which he went on to study in Berlin and Halle, completing his doctorate in 1856. With the assistance of Heinrich Graetz, he was appointed to the position of preacher in the 'German' synagogue in Warsaw in August 1858. He was an active supporter of the Polish revolutionary movement in 1861, for which he was soon imprisoned in the Warsaw Citadel and then, as a Prussian subject, expelled from the Kingdom of Poland. Following a short stay in Mannheim, he returned to Warsaw, where he remained until the failure of the Uprising. After a few months spent in Breslau, he moved to Worms, where he led the Jewish community for the next two years. In 1866 he accepted the position of rabbi of the Rodeph Shalom community in Philadelphia, a congregation of Jewish immigrants from Germany. In the United States, Jastrow became involved in a debate with the radical reformist movement, siding with the historical school, a forerunner of the Conservative movement. In 1876 a serious illness forced him to curtail his public activities, and during the long period of recovery he concentrated on his *magnum opus*, a two-volume talmudic-midrashic dictionary. He retired in 1892, leaving an abundant collection of writings, including several volumes of sermons, the dictionary, some longer works, and numerous articles on history and politics.[33]

Commenting on the events of 1858–61 and his radically pro-Polish stance, Jastrow explained: 'I believed it my duty to address my co-believers, who are considered to be Poles, in the Polish language, and to introduce into the house of the God of Israel this treasure which is so precious for all who still remember Poland's past and who still believe in its rebirth.'[34] This statement clearly illustrates the ideological link between the Polish language and the identity of 'my co-believers who are considered to be Poles' which lay at the root of the ideological shift. In addition, Jastrow himself showed how rapid this process was in his own case. Further on, explaining the circumstances in which he and the chief rabbi of Warsaw, Baer Meisels, were arrested and exiled from the Kingdom of Poland, he wrote: 'After three months of suffering, I and my venerable friend Meisels had to leave the country whose borders I had crossed as a stranger and left as a native!'[35] It would be difficult to find a more eloquent example than that of Jastrow, who in 1861, after a three-year stay in Warsaw, declared himself to be a Polish patriot.

Meanwhile, another 'progressive' preacher, Izaak Kramsztyk, spoke very similarly in a sermon preached during a service for those who had died in Warsaw during the demonstrations of 27 February 1861:

There, where the first rays of sun shone upon us as upon newborn children, where the first days of our lives in newborn innocence passed in those tender maternal embraces, there, brothers, there is that land we should call our homeland. There, where our youthful strength

---

[33] American Jewish Archives in Cincinnati, Marcus Jastrow's biographical notes. The best description of the Polish episode in the life of Jastrow can be found in Eisenbach and Kozłowski, 'Jastrow, Marcus'. See also Gelber, 'Dr mordekhai (markus) yastrov'; Friedland, 'Marcus Jastrow and *Abodath Israel*'.          [34] Jastrow, *Kazania*, 7.                    [35] Ibid. 9.

developed, where our activities and effectiveness grow, where hope smiles on one's youthful years, where our minds were taught to comprehend, our hearts to feel, there, brothers, there is the country we are obliged to love. . . . Let us, therefore, unite in love for our country with the rest of our fellow citizens of differing faiths, let us follow them on the road to enlightenment and civilization, on the road of learning and tolerance. Let us honour God in the sacred speech of our forefathers, but in civil life let us adopt the speech of the country. Let us endeavour to remove all the obstacles that have divided for many centuries the inhabitants of the one country, the children of the one earth.[36]

Kramsztyk's example illustrates the interesting development of this idea. A collection of sermons contains his speeches from 1852 onwards. However, the above quotation was the first ever passage in which he unambiguously and unconditionally referred to Poland as the homeland of Polish Jews. While sermons from earlier years emphasized the need to learn Polish and conform to local customs, theirs were more practical, integrationist proposals than patriotic declarations of their attachment to Poland. Thus it seems that the relationship was more complex than it appears in Jastrow's declaration. The identity transformations taking place in the modernizing camp from the 1850s onwards drew this movement closer to the Polish viewpoint and eventually led to its participation in the pre-uprising events of 1861–3. However, the culmination of the idea of Polish patriotism and a relationship with Poland as their native land took place later, in the context of the rapprochement known as the Polish–Jewish fraternity (and it should be remembered that the initiators of this movement on the Jewish side included not only integrationists, but also some Orthodox Jews). But the fraternity was largely a phenomenon of young Jewish integrationists in the Kingdom and it influenced their ideological choices.

The new ideas seem to have embraced a relatively broad spectrum of Jewish youth. One indirect proof of this symptomatic evolution from Haskalah loyalism to pro-Polish patriotism lies in the subsequent revisions to what was at that time the most popular Jewish catechism, written by Jakub Elsenberg (d. 1886). He was a teacher at the Rabbinical School and an inspector of Jewish elementary schools, who also worked for *Gazeta Warszawska*. He was also a prolific writer of textbooks for Jewish children and young people. His catechism was published in 1846 and followed the example of earlier texts by Hoge, Buchner, Tugendhold, and others. In it he included a chapter on the 'duties towards the monarch and the state', in which he explained that 'loyalty, obedience, respect and love are the subjects' obligations' towards the monarch, and also that 'His Royal Highness is to be regarded as the most gracious Father, whom God has endowed with some of His majesty to rule on Earth.'[37] This typically loyalist text fitted well within the principles of the Haskalah concept of loyalty to the monarchy and remained unchanged in subsequent editions in 1850 and 1854. Other texts written by Elsenberg were

[36] Kramsztyk, *Kazania*, 310. A good selection of pro-Polish Jewish manifestos from the years 1861–3 can be found in Eisenbach *et al.* (eds.), *Żydzi a powstanie styczniowe*.

[37] Elsenberg, *Droga wiary*, 60.

equally abundant in servile declarations.[38] However, the fourth edition of the catechism, issued in 1860 (the edition that appeared in the period of these ideological
transformations), contained an additional question, 'What are an Israelite's duties
towards his native country?', and the answer 'An Israelite should love his native
country, should respect its laws, should cater for all its needs, should foster its
well-being and glory, should down lay his life in its defence, and should pay taxes
according to his position and means.' The additional text did not carry any revolutionary proposals. Similar ideas could be encountered in Hoge's and Buchner's
catechisms as early as the 1820s and 1830s. However, the changes introduced
signalled a more fundamental transformation, for both Elsenberg and the whole
Jewish modernizing camp in the Congress Kingdom. This was because, alongside
the category of 'state' and 'monarch', there appeared the category of 'native land',
which, in the case of the Polish lands, was not synonymous with the ideology of
loyalty to the state. The 'native land' was Poland, and the 'state and monarch' was
the Russian empire. In 1863 the changes to the catechism went even further. Elsenberg not only removed the question concerning the attitude of the subject to the
head of state, but also replaced the actual word 'monarch' with the more democratic
'ruler' (*panujący*), thus dispensing with, or at least diminishing, the head of state's
divine splendour and supernatural sanction, and changing the ideological meaning
of the whole chapter.[39]

   This catechism illustrates an evolution of attitudes from Haskalah loyalism to
pro-Polish patriotism. The most telling proof of this evolution was the active participation of some young Jews in independence demonstrations, conspiracies, and
ultimately the January Uprising itself. However, illegal activity, although spectacular, always remained a marginal issue in both Jewish and Polish society, and it is
not through revolutionary acts that the degree of involvement of Jewish integrationists in new social movements should be measured. The fact that the pro-Polish
identity of the young integrationists was not limited to a narrow group of Warsaw
activists can be substantiated by the popularity of anti-tsarist principles in groups
even very remote from the insurrectionary movement and by the popularization of
such ideas, for example by promoting them in a catechism for children and young
people that had a wide circulation.

## NATIONALITY OR RELIGION?

Unsurprisingly the introduction of the ideals of Polish patriotism was associated
with rejection of the concept of a Jewish national community. The representatives
of the integrationist movement claimed that Jewish society was neither a nation,
nor even 'an ethnic community' (*wspólnota plemienna*), but merely a religious group.
Although in ancient times national ties existed among the Israelites, and some

---

[38] Elsenberg, *Modlitwy dla dzieci wyznania mojżeszowego*, 143–4.
[39] Elsenberg, *Droga wiary*, 4th edn.; id., *Przewodnik religijny*, 43–4.

common ethnic characteristics had been retained, the ties had long since lost their power to bind, because the fall of the Jewish state and centuries of dispersion had brought the Jews closer to the peoples among whom they lived, and had distanced them (in national but not in religious terms) from their co-believers in other countries. In 1857 Kramsztyk declared: 'We, my honourable co-religionists, have long since ceased to exist as a separate social structure on earth, have long since ceased to be called a people. In this respect we have become part of any people among whom we dwell.'[40] A little later, in 1868, the editor-in-chief of *Izraelita*, Samuel Henryk Peltyn, stated: 'The ties that once held [the Jewish people] together as one nation have long since been broken; today those who are scattered all over the globe are unified as one community only by their religion, their institutions and customs based on this religion.'[41]

Such a strong expression of Polish national identity was undoubtedly the result of the powerful influence of Polish Romanticism and the circumstances in which the ideology of Jewish integration took final shape. These circumstances hinged mostly on the well-known Polish–Jewish fraternity of 1861–3. In the turbulent pre-Uprising period the pro-Polish stance of assimilating Jewish society was greeted enthusiastically by most of the Polish intelligentsia, and this considerably aided the process. Although relatively soon after 1864 the paths of the Polish intelligentsia and the Jewish modernizing camps would diverge, and before long the *Izraelita* group would renounce the Romantic ideals of *Jutrzenka* and its editor-in-chief, Daniel Neufeld, the period of 1861–3 long remained a mythical 'golden age' for both groups.

However, for Jewish integrationists, the rejection of the idea of national identity did not mean breaking their ties with their co-religionists in other countries of the Diaspora. It is evident, for example, from Peltyn that integrationists in the Kingdom of Poland emphasized strongly that this unity was not of a national character, but that it was a strictly religious duty: 'This unity was embraced by our fathers at the foot of Mount Sinai and it has been passed on to their descendants, along with the Divine lessons imparted there.'[42] In addition to bearing out the concept of Jewry as a religious community, the emphasis on the religious nature of this unity helped to protect integrationists from the traditional antisemitic accusation of Jewish separatism, while the frequently quoted argument that the community was less unified than it should have been was used to prove that the accusation was groundless. However, despite being dangerously ambiguous, this premiss of religious unity was a very important element of the outlook of the modernizing Polish Jews and it constituted one of their distinguishing characteristics. Doubtless, it was attributable to their Haskalah roots and the links with the ideas of the Jewish Enlightenment, which remained strong and were characteristic of this generation.

[40] Kramsztyk, *Kazania*, 120.
[41] Samuel H. Peltyn, 'Rzut oka na nasze stosunki religijne, obecne i przyszłe', *Izr.* 3 (1868), 265.
[42] Kramsztyk, *Kazania*, 301.

A revival of religious ideals and unity among Jews matched the canon of principles of the Jewish Enlightenment movement exceedingly well, so their appearance in the programmes of the young integrationists, who were the immediate successors to the Haskalah, was not surprising. What was new and surprising, though, was the pressure that those secularizing circles placed on religious values. This must be viewed primarily as a consequence of the rejection of Jewish national identity and its replacement with an identity based on religion. Because, according to integrationists, faith was the sole criterion for belonging to Jewish society, its significance grew disproportionately and in some ways exceeded the function ascribed to it by traditional sections of society.

The growing significance of religious identity was also favoured by other factors, such as the importance of the 'God and homeland' atmosphere during the twilight of Polish Romanticism (which had a considerable influence on all integrationists). In addition, there was the fierce rivalry from those with overtly anti-religious or religiously indifferent attitudes, which increased in Jewish society in the second half of the nineteenth century and represented a serious threat to Jewish identity. The threat of mass desertion from Judaism by the assimilationists forced the leaders of the integrationist movement to place more emphasis on religious matters and to defend its core values more strenuously. Although in the 1860s and 1870s the number of conversions to Christianity in Warsaw reached a record low (only 7 per cent of all the conversions in 1800–1903), the conversion of members of some very influential Jewish families (the Blochs, Kraushars, Kronenbergs, Orgelbrandts, and Toeplitzes) was bound to arouse anxiety among moderate integrationists. In addition, however low these numbers might have been, the editors of *Jutrzenka* and *Izraelita* rightly observed that the increasing indifference towards religion could augur its eventual complete rejection. This observation was corroborated by a rapid growth in the number of conversions in the last two decades of the nineteenth century,[43] and by numerous accounts of 'pseudo-progressives' who were ashamed of their Jewish origins, which showed that such attitudes—even if not particularly common—must have been evident, if not blatantly obvious.

All the same, attitudes towards religion in the integrationist movement were highly ambivalent. Religious values certainly preoccupied the editors of *Jutrzenka* and *Izraelita* and were the subject of very lively and important disputes. At the same time, however, writers for these periodicals were willing to accept these religious values as relative, and questions of religious experience lay completely beyond the range of their interests. The author of a religious reform project, probably Samuel H. Peltyn, even maintained that ultimately Judaism would die out and that it would merge with other religions into a universal, non-dogmatic faith. At the time, however, it was an essential form of social organization and the only founda-

---

[43] Endelman, 'Jewish Converts in Nineteenth-Century Warsaw', 37, 40–8. See Guterman, 'Yahasam shel mitbolelei varsha lehamarat hadat', for a discussion of the attitudes of the so-called assimilationists (who were actually representatives of the integrationist movement).

tion of moral order, so it occupied an important, albeit solely utilitarian, social function.[44] This stance was particularly radical, but similar views were held by other members of this group. Paradoxically, the growth of interest in religious issues and the sense of religious identity was linked to questioning of its transcendental value and to its declining in status to that of a useful social function. Integrationists were unable to deal with this paradoxical attitude, and this was one of the major weaknesses that contributed to the continuing crisis that began in the late 1890s and ended with the group's break-up in the following decade. Religion and religious unity, when treated in a utilitarian manner, were not a firm foundation for group identity. This was particularly the case from the 1880s onwards, when the budding Jewish national movement put forward the challenging notion that what united the Jewish people was not necessarily faith, but their common nationality.

## FACE TO FACE WITH HASIDISM

Bearing in mind the core ideology of the integrationist movement—the revived role of religious identity and religious unity—it is not surprising that one of the most important factors in the self-determination of this group in the 1860s and the 1870s was their attitude towards tradition and traditional religious forms, and above all their attitude towards hasidism. The following is a discussion of the three basic groups' attitude towards hasidism.

### Assimilationists

The situation among radical assimilationists differed from that among integrationists. The issue of hasidism was as remote here as were all the other problems of Jewish society. Although in the late 1850s a long-term member of this group, Ozjasz Ludwik Lubliner, resorted to one of the most popular devices of anti-hasidic rhetoric—comparing the hasidim to the Jesuits—his was a fringe opinion, and he was using it to attack Jakub Tugendhold, whom he wholeheartedly loathed.[45] According to Lubliner, 'each religion has its Jesuits; even Jews have them. Hasidic fanatics, the enemies of light, who carefully nurture old prejudices and superstitions, are nothing but Jewish Jesuits, Jewish bigots.' The comparison itself is interesting, as it also appears in other assimilationist writings and is a leitmotif of polemical writings; for example, attention had often been drawn in sixteenth-century Protestant writings to the similarity between the threatening role of the Jews and that of the Jesuits.[46] In the eighteenth century Chrétien Malesherbes, counsellor to the French king Louis XVI, named Jews and Jesuits in his report as two allegedly secret organizations (*status in statu*).[47] The antisemitic connotations of the Jesuit theme did not prevent assimilated Jewish contributors from adopting

---

[44] Judaita, *Projekt reformy*, 44.   [45] Lubliner, *Obrona Żydów*, 10, 24.

[46] See Tazbir, 'Conspiracy Theories'. For similarities in the anticlerical and anti-Jewish polemics, see id., 'Żydzi w opinii staropolskiej', 227.   [47] See Poliakov, *The History of Anti-Semitism*, iii. 149.

it in the intra-Jewish dispute with hasidism. An anonymous informer from Warsaw wrote that, 'under the guise of religion, the perfidious and ungodly burial society, just like those Jesuits, resists the approaching enlightenment and, acting to its own advantage, blinds unenlightened Israelites with fanaticism, so that they can dupe them more easily and seize their fortunes'.[48] At the same time hasidic sources were also using the Jesuit motif, and referred to their Haskalah adversaries Tugendhold and Jan Glücksberg as 'Jesuits despised by all'.[49] *Izraelita* referred to hasidism as a 'veritable Jesuitism of the Mosaic faith',[50] and its advocates were presented as hypocrites, wolves in sheep's clothing, who resorted to trickery and ruses to achieve their ignoble aims. The comparison also appeared in Jewish literature outside Poland, and in Protestant and Orthodox countries it assumed an additional, anti-Catholic face: the hasidim (or, more broadly, Orthodox Jews) were the Catholics of Judaism, and 'the most hypocritical of the hasidic leaders, Nahman of Bratslav, is a Jewish Ignatius Loyola'.[51]

However, the most typical attitude towards hasidism among other radical assimilationists was one of complete indifference. This is not surprising since they avoided any subject connected with their Jewish origins, and the existence of the 'fanatical and unenlightened' hasidim, if not particularly painful, must have been at least troublesome to them. Whatever the case, there are few manifestos that describe the attitudes of this group in relation to challenges to their view of the world.

## The Traditional Maskilim

It is understandable that the assimilationists were embarrassed by the perseverance of this 'medieval fanaticism' and that they endeavoured to ignore hasidism. However, the paucity of opinions on the hasidic issue coming from the camp of the traditional maskilim (who initially gathered around Moses Tannenbaum, and then, in the period in question, around Chaim Zelig Słonimski and his *Hatsefirah*) may appear surprising. In the first half of the nineteenth century Hebrew writers in Poland published virtually nothing concerning their opinions of the growing importance of the hasidim in the Congress Kingdom and seem to have been indifferent towards the movement. Interestingly, even Abraham Buchner, who openly and harshly criticized hasidism and pointed out the threats it constituted in his memorandum to the director of the Warsaw Education District,[52] otherwise either completely ignored hasidism or mentioned it only in passing in his many works.[53] It was only later, in a volume containing a commentary on the book of Psalms pub-

---

[48] AGAD, CWW 1727, pp. 180–1.                                              [49] Ibid. 945–6.

[50] Henryk Lichtenbaum, 'Reforma judaizmu. III', *Izr.* 42 (1907), 454; Jezajasz Chudy, 'U źródeł zastoju', *Izr.* 43 (1908), 322.

[51] Schapiro-Memel, 'Ein jüdischer Pater Loyola'. See also Feiner, *Haskalah and History*, 301–2.

[52] AGAD, Centralne Władze Oświatowe, 33.

[53] Mahler (*Hasidism and the Jewish Enlightenment*, 25, 395 n. 11) found such passages in Buchner, *Doresh tov*, 16a, 25a, 37, 39, 54.

lished in 1854, that Eleazar Talgrün dared to voice a rebuke. Talgrün criticized the hasidim chiefly for their renunciation of old religious practices, and the whole accusation was based on the comparison of the old and new paths of piety (*hasidut*).[54] The old, traditional piety consisted of purity, moderation, holiness, fear of God, and humility, and could be attained only when all of these criteria were met. Talgrün stated that the contemporary, false hasidim wanted to achieve piety without any effort, making a display of virtues they did not have and thinking that it was sufficient to go to the ritual baths like the others and wear Rabenu Tam *tefilin*.[55] In the past Rabenu Tam *tefilin* had been worn only by the most pious, whereas now everybody was wearing them. In Talgrün's opinion 'those fools' changed the traditionally sanctioned times for prayer as they pleased and believed that in this way they would achieve spiritual greatness and become mystics, like Isaac Luria, the sixteenth-century kabbalist. His criticism was thus limited to rituals and customs, and he completely disregarded the social aspect of hasidism, which was the main point of contention for the maskilim of the time. In this respect, his criticism was similar to that of Israel Zamość in a text published nearly a century earlier. In addition, hasidism was only one of many phenomena criticized in Talgrün's writing, and his mild tone of admonition remained in stark contrast both to the virulent attacks on hasidim launched by Haskalah circles in Galicia and to the keen interest in the hasidic issue displayed in the writings of Jewish advocates of integration in the Kingdom, who were Talgrün's contemporaries.

A similarly moderate attitude towards hasidism was displayed by Słonimski, who actually did not publish a single text in *Hatsefirah* dealing broadly with this subject until the late 1880s, although he did publish anti-hasidic opinions in other Hebrew periodicals, for example, in connection with Eliezer Zweifel's revisionist work *Shalom al yisra'el*.[56]

Słonimski's actions were completely in accordance with the general policy of *Hatsefirah*, which avoided conflict with traditionalists and strove to promote Haskalah ideals by fostering popular knowledge of the natural sciences, history, and technology. Admittedly, there were occasional mentions of the hasidim and hasidism: for example, a description of the school established by the hasidic leader Aron of Chernobyl included a caustic reference to Kobryń, a hasidic town but not a town of compassion (a pun on the words *hasid* and *hesed*), and the story of a riot instigated in 1879 by followers of the local hasidic leader in Aleksandrów, who were harassing an alleged assailant who was a follower of the Gerer Rebbe, the two groups being in bitter conflict.[57] Similar records providing details from the life of

[54] Talgrün, *Tokhahat musar*, 9b–10a, 14b–15a. See also Mahler, *Hasidism and the Jewish Enlightenment*, 234.

[55] For Rabenu Tam *tefilin* and the hasidic customs connected with them, see Wertheim, *Law and Custom in Hasidism*, 120–3. See ibid. 215–16 for the ritual bath.

[56] Feiner, *Haskalah and History*, 306.

[57] Mordecai Weinstein, 'Rusland: Chernobyl', *Hatsefirah*, 2 (1875), 338–9; Meir Josef Pomerants, 'Kobrin', *Hatsefirah*, 6 (1879), 132; L.B., 'Varsha', *Hatsefirah*, 6 (1879), 324.

the hasidic province were published later.[58] However, as a rule, these were not editorials but simply letters sent in by provincial maskilim. Moreover, the number of letters and the form they took, and even their attitude towards hasidism (which was very unclear and ambivalent), were clearly at variance with the fervour of the disputes concerning the hasidic movement that appeared at that time in *Jutrzenka*, *Izraelita*, and even some Polish periodicals.[59]

The policy of *Hatsefirah* seems to be represented by the attitude of David Jaffe from Disna (in the province of Minsk), who disagreed with the Haskalah weekly *Hamagid* in a lengthy letter calling for a fair appraisal of the strengths and short-comings of hasidism. According to Jaffe, who as a young man had been a hasid him-self, the hasidim surpassed the maskilim in many respects: they were more unified, helped one another, showed magnanimity, and were interested in the affairs of the country. He believed that this was not the case with contemporary maskilim, for whom the Haskalah was just an empty word, and who, for the most part, epito-mized egoism and a lack of higher feelings. And the fact that the hasidim travelled once a year to visit their tsadik was 'not a sin after all'. Far worse was the fact that the maskilim were no better than the hasidim, but that, in their criticism of the hasidic movement, they provided arguments for antisemites, such as Hipolit Lutostanski, who claimed that there was a sect among the Jews whose aims were detrimental to humanity.[60]

On the surface Jaffe's views, which were apparently supported by the editors of the periodical, were very similar to earlier and current opinions held within the Warsaw integration camp of Neufeld and Grosglik (to be discussed in the next chapter), which questioned the superiority of the modernizing camp over the hasidic masses and called for a re-evaluation of attitudes towards this group. How-ever, the similarity was only superficial. The pro-hasidic stance of Neufeld and Grosglik was accompanied by simultaneous criticism of certain aspects of hasidism, a keen and growing interest in this movement, and the inherent belief that rap-prochement with hasidism must ultimately lead to internal reform undertaken by the hasidim themselves, so that, while retaining what was valuable, it could adapt to the demands of the contemporary world, thus effectively ceasing to be hasidism. Jaffe had intended exactly the opposite in his letter: he called for the debate on hasidism to be toned down and for statements on the issue to cease. So, although Jaffe and Neufeld's arguments were almost identical, their conclusions were dia-metrically opposite.

[58] See e.g. 'Talna', *Hatsefirah*, 7 (1880), 77; Izhak Meir Shvarzman, 'Międzybóż' [obituary of Abraham Joshua Heshel], *Hatsefirah*, 7 (1880), 308; 'Lublin', *Hatsefirah*, 8 (1881), 29; 'Grodzisk', *Hatsefirah*, 18 (1891), 768.

[59] From the 1880s notes relating to hasidism, usually of a hostile nature, started to appear in the Polish daily press, e.g. in *Kurier Warszawski*, and their number steadily increased. It appears that this was connected with a wave of antisemitism, in which hasidim figured as a symbol of the most fanatical and despised Jews. See the next chapter for more on this subject.

[60] David Jaffe, 'Disna' [letter], *Hatsefirah*, 7 (1880), 28–9.

A good example of the ambivalence of traditional Hebrew Haskalah circles can be seen in the work of Israel Weissbrem (1838–1915), a little-known and somewhat second-rate Hebrew writer from Warsaw who was connected with *Hatsefirah* and its circle.[61] In 1888 Weissbrem published a long social novel, *18 agorot* (Eighteen Coins), which was devoted entirely to the issue of hasidism.[62] The plot was set around two families of followers of the hasidic leader from the (probably fictitious) town of Szyfkowa, or Shifkova, their marital plans, and the machinations of the closest advisers to the hasidic leader. The entire novel was generally critical of hasidism, and the lesson that one of the tsadik's 'henchmen' (low-ranking assistants) taught a new disciple—that to be a hasid it was sufficient to dress like a hasid, recite sacred texts without understanding them, and repeat the legends about the tsadik—was intended to prove its lack of intellectual substance. Yet, in contrast to its general view of the movement as a whole, the novel was ambivalent about individual hasidim. It did not introduce unequivocally negative characters (a pseudomaskil was one of the more pitiful characters), and most significantly the author did not make it clear whether the tsadik was actually aware of the immoral machinations of his henchmen or what kind of a person he himself was. This inconclusiveness seems intentional, particularly in that it matched excellently the tactics adopted by Słonimski, *Hatsefirah*, and the other maskilim associated with the periodical. The ambiguous attitude towards the hasidim is all the more striking because Weissbrem's novel was one of the very few longer Hebrew texts in the Kingdom devoted specifically to them.

Relations between the hasidim and the editors of *Hatsefirah* began to deteriorate quite by chance in the early 1890s. According to Słonimski, the antagonism began when *Hatsefirah* published articles concerning the celebrated conflict between London's chief rabbi Herman Adler (1839–1911) and the local hasidim from the radical strictly Orthodox organization Mahzikei Hadas, who were trying to control *shehitah* (ritual slaughter) in London. The conflict intensified when the London hasidim overstepped the limits by pronouncing a ban on Rabbi Adler.[63] This aroused the indignation of the general public, and *Hatsefirah* published letters of protest written by east European rabbis. According to Słonimski, the only reason that this stage of the conflict did not have any serious repercussions was that the hasidim bided their time, waiting for a better opportunity to attack. Such an opportunity arose at the end of December 1891 with the publication in *Hatsefirah* of an article providing evidence that the tale of the Hanukah miracle of the jug of

<hr>

[61] For more on Weissbrem, see Patterson, 'Israel Weisbrem'; id., *The Hebrew Novel in Czarist Russia*, index.    [62] Weissbrem, *Israel Weissbrem and his Work*.

[63] The most comprehensive, although somewhat partisan, account of the events can be found in Homa, *A Fortress of Judaism in Anglo-Jewry*. A more objective treatment of the subject appears in Gartner, *The Jewish Immigrant in England*, 209–14. *Izraelita* also commented on the affair; see T., 'Separatyści w Londynie', *Izr.* 27 (1892), 51–2.

olive oil saved from the Temple of Jerusalem was nothing more than a legend.[64] However, Słonimski's version of these events is full of inaccuracies, and he seems to have been attempting to justify his sloppy account, rather than describing the actual situation. In fact, a long letter from Rabbi Samuel Mohilewer condemning Mahzikei Hadas in London was published in *Hatsefirah* a day *after* the article about the Hanukah miracle appeared,[65] and further accounts on the subject were both few and infrequent.[66]

The war between Słonimski and hasidic circles had started at the end of 1891, and Słonimski's seditious text precipitated a major crusade on the part of hasidic movements, especially among Mahzikei Hadas circles in Galicia. According to Słonimski's account, a group of hasidim bought several copies of *Hatsefirah* and travelled to all the hasidic courts, organizing a boycott. Those who turned against Słonimski seem to have included not only the Galician hasidim, but also the Belarusian Habad (a hasidic faction that had formed around the Schneersohn dynasty of Lubavitcher *rebbes*), who published an appeal calling for people to cease to subscribe to *Hatsefirah*. Thus, the debate concerning the Hanukah miracle and the resulting conflict between Słonimski and the hasidim aroused keen interest and were widely commented upon.[67] Inevitably, many expressions of support for Słonimski appeared in *Hatsefirah*,[68] but other Haskalah and post-Haskalah periodicals, particularly those vying with this daily (for *Hatsefirah* had changed from a weekly to a daily), were rather critical. *Hamelits*, a Hebrew periodical appearing in Odessa, considered Słonimski's publication to be lacking in wisdom, and the undermining of a thousand-year-old tradition to be senseless. The editor of *Izraelita* did not refrain from pointing out that for thirty years the editor of *Hatsefirah* had been driven by popular demand and the cheap indulgence of Orthodox tastes. In Peltyn's words, at a time when *Izraelita* circles had been busy fighting off the influence of 'hasidic fanaticism', Słonimski's *Hatsefirah* had pursued a policy of winning hasidic readers, 'seeking peace with reactionaries and avoiding anything that could harm their beliefs'.[69]

The issue of the Hanukah miracle was frequently commented upon later. The fact that the debate involving Słonimski's theory persisted for a decade is proof of its animated character.[70] However, in terms of the history of relations between

[64]  Chaim Zelig Słonimski, 'Ma'i ḥanukah?', *Hatsefirah*, 18 (1891), 1123.
[65]  Samuel Mohilewer, 'Edut beya'akov', *Hatsefirah*, 18 (1891).
[66]  See e.g. 'Łódź', *Hatsefirah*, 18 (1891), 1132.
[67]  A good summary of the dispute and its literary career can be found in Werses, 'Mai ḥanukah'.
[68]  See e.g. Tsevi Perla, 'Nes minisayon', *Hatsefirah*, 19 (1892), 19; 'Ohev emet' [pseud. = Lover of Truth], 'Ha'emet veha'emunah', *Hatsefirah*, 19 (1892), 79.
[69]  The most interesting opinions on this affair to be published in *Izraelita* were Elkan, 'Za tydzień', *Izr.* 27 (1892), 27; Judaita [Samuel H. Peltyn], 'Nie tędy droga', *Izr.* 27 (1892), 33–5. Refer also to further polemics in Chaim Z. Słonimski, 'Odpowiedź', *Izr.* 27 (1892), 42–3; Judaita [Samuel H. Peltyn], 'Panu Ch. Z. Słonimskiemu', *Izr.* 27 (1892), 49–50. A comprehensive account can be found in Słonimski, *Malshinai beseter*.                    [70]  See Werses, 'Ma'i ḥanukah'.

the modernizing Polish Jews and the hasidim, this was, in fact, a belated episode of little significance, which served only to confirm how peripheral a place the hasidic issue occupied in *Hatsefirah*. Peltyn's accusations were valid in the sense that, during its almost thirty-year existence, the periodical had actually published extremely little about a movement that constituted one of the most important obstacles to the outlook of the Jewish Enlightenment and which was a contentious subject among many other Jewish modernizing groups. Słonimski, and later Nachum Sokołów, had persistently refrained from alienating their Orthodox and hasidic readers. Until 1891, when, by accident, relations radically worsened, *Hatsefirah* had been almost indifferent towards hasidism and had never adopted a clear position on the issue. Even during the most serious, and almost the only, dispute with the followers of Mahzikei Hadas, criticism of hasidism in *Hatsefirah* was kept within certain limits.

It was precisely at the time of this dispute that Słonimski and Sokołów were working in co-operation with Josef S. Bloch (1850–1923), a Jewish deputy to the Viennese parliament, and with Polish hasidim to clear the hasidic community in Ostrów Mazowiecka of the accusation of ritual murder. The whole affair had started with the publication of a well-known Viennese antisemite, Josef Deckert, who, on the basis of the testimony of the convert Paulus Meyer, had accused the hasidim in Ostrów, and by implication all hasidim, of committing ritual murder.[71] Meyer, who came from Ostrów, maintained that, as a student of the local hasidic leader Joshua b. Solomon Leib of Łęczna, he had participated in 1875 in the ritual murder of a Christian child and the subsequent bloodletting. The accusation, as was usual in the case of blood libels, caused an immediate reaction. Meyer's statement, accompanied by his photograph, was sent to *Hatsefirah*, where Słonimski and Sokołów ensured that the appropriate information on Meyer was gathered.[72] The daily published an unabridged version of the testimony, a summary of the case, as well as the text of an inscription on the tombstone of the tsadik Joshua b. Solomon Leib (who had died in 1873, two years before the alleged murder took place), and, most importantly, an appeal for information that could serve to discredit Meyer. In subsequent publications *Hatsefirah* verified the identity of the individuals mentioned by Meyer and kept readers up to date with preparations for the trial.[73] This information enabled Bloch not simply to undermine Meyer's credibility, but to prove beyond any doubt that he was in fact lying. Meyer withdrew his accusation and claimed that he had had nothing to do with the statement that had appeared in the press on his behalf, and that the signature had been forged. Deckert, however, maintained that he had received the text from Meyer himself. The libel case brought about by Bloch on behalf of the named beadles (*shamashim*)

---

[71] For a detailed account, including court protocols, see Bloch, *Erinnerungen aus meinem Leben*.

[72] See ibid. ii. 80.

[73] See e.g. 'Alilah nora'ah, mikhtav hamumar paulus me'ir', *Hatsefirah*, 20 (1893), 421–3; 'Alilat paulus me'ir', *Hatsefirah*, 20 (1893), 425–6, 433–4, 445–6, 450; 'Bein dam ledam', *Hatsefirah*, 20 (1893), 531; 'Mishpat paulus me'ir', *Hatsefirah*, 20 (1893), 726, 809–10.

of the hasidic leader, as well as his family, ended in a spectacular victory for the Jewish party. *Hatsefirah* published reports from Vienna daily, and the issue became one of its best-covered subjects.[74]

In this case, the fact that the editors of *Hatsefirah* took the side of the hasidic community was not surprising. It had always reported in detail and commented fully upon accusations of alleged ritual murder. In 1891, for example, there had been extensive coverage of a case in Corfu, and at the beginning of 1893 a case in the town of Kolin; and in 1900 there was the case of Hilsner, a man accused in Polna in Bohemia. Defence against antisemitic defamation was, after all, more important than any internal animosity, particularly where the most serious of accusations against Jews was concerned. It should be emphasized, however, that the editors of *Hatsefirah* did not concentrate on the hasidic affiliations of the leader and his beadles although the accusation clearly related to the myth of the 'fanatical hasidic sect' committing such murders. Słonimski and Sokołów stayed away from the general debate on this matter, although they could have followed the example of Tugendhold's apologetic text written more than sixty years earlier. Since they were not prepared to separate the term 'fanatical hasidism' into 'fanaticism' and 'hasidism', they were not in a position to extend their challenge to Meyer's specific accusations to a more general argument in which they could have defended the whole hasidic movement against blood libel. In my opinion, this demonstrates once again how little thought was given to hasidism by the camp of the traditional Hebrew Haskalah in the Kingdom of Poland.

## Integrationists

Thus in the second half of the nineteenth century the only Jewish circle in the Kingdom of Poland to focus on hasidism was a group of integrationists formed first around *Jutrzenka* and then around *Izraelita*. Hasidism occupied a special place in their landscape—one that was far more important than the place allocated to it by Haskalah writers in the first half of the century. In addition, unlike Abraham Stern and Eliasz Moszkowski, the young integrationists did not reduce the problem to the technical question of ridding themselves of 'a tumour' (although they shared this negative opinion), but they perceived the group rather as an ideological rival with which they had to fight for the control of souls. This was therefore the first time that hasidism had been viewed by Jewish modernizing society in the Kingdom as the greatest threat to the modernization of the Jewish people and as its chief ideological rival. This was the natural consequence of the growing significance of maskilic–hasidic conflicts in everyday life in the 1840s and the 1850s, as well as of an increasing emphasis on the shortcomings of hasidism in the literary output of the Haskalah.

---

[74] 'Mishpat alilat hadam bevien (Paulus me'ir vehaverav lifnei hashofetim)', *Hatsefirah*, 20 (1893), 814, 820, 823, 830–1, 835, 838, 842–3, 846, 850–1, 854–5.

Such a view of the balance of power in Jewish society clearly minimized the importance of what was still the largest group, the non-hasidic traditional Orthodox. Warsaw integrationists viewed the history of the Jewish people during the eighteenth and nineteenth centuries as a struggle to control what they saw as the passive Jewish masses (sometimes referred to as the mitnagedim, sometimes as *balebatim* or 'ordinary Jews'), a struggle that was fought between two rival forces: the 'progressives' and the hasidim. It is not therefore surprising that they devoted considerable attention to hasidism while ignoring the non-hasidic Orthodoxy. The integrationists generally agreed that the education of the mitnagedim did not represent a serious problem as the masses had already accepted some elements of secular knowledge, and many of them were obviously striving to improve their social position. They were seen as being hampered by the poor example of the hasidim and the pressure exerted by that movement. The key issue therefore seemed to be to weaken the influence of hasidism. The difference that integrationist circles saw between the mitnagedim and the hasidim is also evident in the different response to these two groups (as a rule, hasidism provoked far more of a reaction), and also in the consistent manner in which contributors differentiated between the 'reactionary' and the 'conservative' groups. It was the 'reactionary' hasidim, not the 'conservative' mitnagedim or the Orthodox camp in general, to which particular attention was paid and to which a disproportionately large amount of integrationist journalism was devoted.

This was new. The extremely aggressive attacks on hasidism that characterized the period of increase in local conflicts in the 1840s and the 1850s were not accompanied by any reflections on the movement (which was deliberately marginalized) and did not lead to any perceptible ideological debate. Although the young integrationists in the 1860s adopted much of the emotive anti-hasidic phraseology, they clearly tended to reject stereotypical and unambiguously negative views in favour of more balanced and nuanced views that to some extent redressed the attitude to hasidism. On the whole, they attempted to understand the phenomenon of hasidism, and it was this that marked the greatest change in the attitude of Jewish modernizing circles towards the movement in the Congress Kingdom. It should be reiterated that such a change was possible only after the balance of power had changed in the late 1850s and early 1860s. The major wave of Jewish intelligentsia that strengthened the 'progressive' camp reassured its representatives of their predominance, so that they ceased to perceive hasidism as a threat to the very existence of their group, and this in turn favoured a more balanced and pragmatic outlook.

It may be assumed that the process of moving away from the traditional unambiguously negative attitude towards hasidism was already under way in the 1840s and the 1850s when an early advocate of this position, Jakub Tugendhold, became highly influential within the Jewish community and soon afterwards became a director of the Warsaw Rabbinical School. Quite a number of the new integrationist generation were graduates of this school. Unfortunately, the lack of sources makes it impossible to trace this process of change before 1861. It was only with the establishment in that year of *Jutrzenka*, and the subsequent appearance of a whole series of publications written by writers connected with the periodical, that this phenomenon could be better understood. This, however, will be addressed in the next chapter.

## CONCLUSIONS

Paradoxically, the rapid growth of a Polish-speaking population in Jewish society and the development of emotional ties with the language (which came to be perceived as the mother tongue) were the result of the Haskalah's connection with the language and with state institutions during the constitutional period of the Congress Kingdom. The young generation of successors to the Haskalah had been brought up in the Polish language and culture and made Polish an important element of their identity as a group. The events that preceded the January Uprising of 1863–4 also accelerated the evolution of this linguistic and cultural identity into a Polish national identity. This became the natural path in the period of patriotic demonstrations and rapprochement with the Christian world.

At the same time, however, the integrationist movement had no intention of renouncing their Jewish identity: their search for identity focused mainly on religion. Their stance on religious issues was nonetheless patently inconsistent. On the one hand, they saw the renunciation of religious values as harmful to Jewish identity, laid strong emphasis on the significance of those values for their own ideology, and boldly defended the idea of religious unity. On the other hand, in the spirit of positivist philosophy, they restricted the meaning of religion to utilitarian and social issues, thereby reducing its spiritual and metaphysical role and perceiving it solely as one element in a social contract. Why were they therefore unwilling to adopt the position of the assimilationists, who replaced Judaism with a new, secular social contract, or even with accession to the dominant Christian surroundings? Clearly, this must have been because of the strong influence of the Haskalah, with its attachment to tradition and its emphasis on self-respect, in which the renunciation of one's origins was dishonourable. But it also seems that, contrary to all the declarations, religious unity had more than merely religious significance for the integrationists. After all, integrationist ideology was an attempt to construct a new, modern group identity with Jewishness as the central element of this identity. All the same, the 'progressives' had considerable problems defining it. Their close connection with the Polish language and gradual integration with Polish culture ruled out any definition based on cultural autonomy. Any assumption that such a concept would have been viable in the nineteenth century is, in any case, completely anachronistic. A definition based on the idea of membership of a Jewish nation as the basic element of Jewish identity was also inconceivable both because of the group's immersion in the Polish language and culture and because of the events preceding the uprising of 1863, which pushed them increasingly close to a Polish national identity. The situation was further complicated by the fact that Polishness itself was not clearly defined. Hungarian or Russian Jews could come to terms with their Hungarian Jewishness or their Russian Jewishness, and could build their 'Hungarian' or 'Russian' identity on the basis of state and culture, and their definition of 'Jewry' on the basis of their status as a people—during the last decades of the nineteenth century such a distinction between the two aspects of identity was often made. However, because there was no such thing as a Polish state, such a differentiation could not be made in Poland, so that definitions of Polishness had to be de facto stronger and also multidimensional. Polish Jewish integrationist circles strove to build a strong Jewish identity on the basis of the criteria available to them, in which religion came to the fore. Although it would soon turn out that this was not the best decision, it should not be seen a mistake, simply because in the mid-nineteenth century there were virtually no other options open to them. Overall, the group's significance and vitality, which could be observed up until the 1930s, prove that the decision was the best in the circumstances.

The increasing importance of religious identity makes it possible to understand why one of the subjects that most occupied the attention of the new integrationist movement was hasidism, the source of their most serious opposition within Judaism. Very soon, it became an integrationist obsession.

# SIX

# Hatred or Solidarity?
## Jewish and Polish–Jewish Fraternity in the 1860s

ONE of the most visible achievements of the new integrationist movement was the founding of Polish-language periodicals—first *Jutrzenka* (1861–3) and then *Izraelita* (1866–1915). The most active members of this new group were Marcus Jastrow (1829–1903) and Daniel Neufeld (1814–74), who was editor-in-chief of *Jutrzenka*. Both Neufeld's career and the life of his periodical seem quite illustrative of the nature of the movement. Neufeld was born in Praszka, a small town in the voivodeship of Kalisz in south-central Poland, where he received a traditional *ḥeder* education. As a 13-year-old, he enrolled in a provincial grammar school run by the Piarist Fathers in Wieluń. He seems not to have graduated from this school, possibly because of his involvement in the 1831 Uprising. From 1830 to 1860 he worked as a teacher in the Jewish school first in Praszka and then in Częstochowa. It was during this period that he began to be involved in public activity, and that he published his first poems in Polish and started work on his commentary and translation into Polish of the Bible.[1] But it was his collaboration with Orgelbrandt's *Encyklopedia Powszechna* (Popular Encyclopedia) in 1860 that took him to Warsaw and allowed him to make contacts with the leading integrationists in the city. It was at a meeting of autodidacts that the idea of a Polish-language periodical for Polish Jews was born and that he was offered the position of editor-in-chief of *Jutrzenka*.[2] As early as the 1830s and 1840s there had been a pressing need for such a periodical, so it was hardly surprising that *Jutrzenka* gained considerable support and that it became almost from the start a platform for the new integrationist movement.

The ideology and attitude of the integrationist movement in the Kingdom of Poland to the hasidim found full expression in *Jutrzenka*. The movement's attitude

[1] See Shatzky, 'Biografye fun Daniel Neufeld', on Neufeld's attempts to establish a Jewish school; the first of Neufeld's published poems appeared in Daniel Neufeld, 'Rymy męskie i żeńskie', *Gazeta Codzienna*, 146 (1841), 3–4; for his translation of the Bible, see id., *Or torah*, introd.

[2] For information on Neufeld's biography, see 'Daniel Neufeld', *Izr.* 9 (1874), 329–30; Shatzky, 'Biografye fun Daniel Neufeld'; Fuks, 'Neufeld, Daniel'. On Neufeld and the establishment of *Jutrzenka*, see Shatzky, 'Der kamf arum geplante tsaytshriftn far Yidn'; Fuks, *Prasa żydowska w Warszawie*, 45–8; id., 'Prasa żydowska w Warszawie XIX w. *Jutrzenka* (1861–1863)'; Daniłowicz, '*Jutrzenka*'; Broniewicz, '*Jutrzenka*'.

was part of its *raison d'être* and shaped its basic character and its activities. In their projects to reform traditional Jewish society in the 1860s, integrationists were faced with the burning issue of the place of the hasidic community in these projects. It was impossible to maintain silence on the issue of hasidism, either in appeals for religious solidarity or in discussions about traditional Jewish communities. The fact that moderate integration, which was the prevailing trend, was viewed as a happy compromise between the extremes of the hasidim and the radical assimilationists meant that the contributors to *Jutrzenka* often compared the two extremes. As a consequence, references to the hasidim were very frequent, although they were not always obvious. They were a litmus test of integrationists' sincerity in their attitudes towards hasidism: on the one hand, unity was openly expounded as an ideal; but on the other there was a distancing from the traditional Jewish community and a degree of support for reform. For this reason, an understanding of the attitude of the movement towards the hasidim could well provide a key to the ideological make-up of these integrationist circles.

One point worth noting is that until now scholars who have studied or even quoted from *Jutrzenka*'s texts relating to the hasidim (notably Jacob Shatzky) have failed to identify the central place occupied by the debate with this group. This is because of the coded language used by the editors and staff of *Jutrzenka*, and primarily by Daniel Neufeld. The expressions 'hasidim' and 'hasidism' were virtually absent from the columns of the weekly, although the hasidic question was discussed in almost every issue. Instead of these taboo terms, the editorial staff wrote of the hasidim as 'the exultant', 'the Kabbalah Party', 'supporters of the principles of the right', 'the pious', 'diehard adherents of mysticism', 'zealots', 'ultra-conservatives', and, most frequently, as 'reactionaries' and 'fanatics'. A certain pattern can be discerned here: the words 'hasidim' and 'hasidism' appeared almost exclusively in those accounts that defined the merits of hasidism, whereas euphemisms were used in critical texts. It may be concluded from this pattern that the aim of this code was to allay any criticism while avoiding tsarist censorship, thus assuaging social conflict and avoiding comments critical of any social group since to criticize a social group was to criticize the social order. The code was so effective that it misled not only the tsarist officials but also many historians. This was the case even though *Jutrzenka* often provided the tools to break the code it used and would certainly have been understood by readers of the time.[3]

## DIAGNOSIS

The community centred around *Jutrzenka* was unable to express openly its views about hasidism because the community was not unified, frequently vacillated, and

---

[3] Such comments can be found in both *Jutrzenka* and later *Izraelita*; e.g. 'the gang of drunkards that claim to be members of the sect of the pious (hasidim)' ('zgraja opilców, mieniących się być członkami sekty "cnotliwych" (chassydym)') (*Ju.* 2 (1862), 125); '[the party of] mystics, i.e. the hasidim' (*Ju.* 2 (1862), 328); 'the hasidim or, as some call them, conservatives, reactionaries' (*Izr.* 4 (1869), 230).

betrayed signs of internal conflict. Overall, the hasidim were objects of criticism in the columns of the periodical, and much of what was written about them was negative. In numerous articles charges levelled against the hasidim by earlier critics from Haskalah circles were quoted almost verbatim. One of these charges concerned the excessive use of tobacco and alcohol:[4] provincial correspondents frequently regaled the editors with descriptions of 'an ill-bred rabble, with no sense of personal dignity, for whom there is nothing more sacred than a brimming cup and a tobacco pipe'.[5] According to another writer, this rabble plunged itself into alcohol addiction out of despair, poverty, and awareness of the contempt directed at it.[6] Among other accusations levelled against the hasidim, and part of the traditional arsenal of the Haskalah's anti-hasidic literature, were those of rampant mysticism, compromising factional quarrels, terror tactics against non-hasidic Jews, and of course the spreading of fanaticism, deception, intolerance, naive faith in superstition, outlandish dress, language, and gestures, and undignified pilgrimages to the tsadikim. Reading between the lines of many of these charges, one senses the embarrassment that the hasidim caused their progressive co-religionists.

However, the most persistent charge to be raised against the 'hasidic authorities' (i.e. the tsadikim) by the editors of *Jutrzenka* was that they preyed on the naivety of their followers in order to extract financial gain from them. This accusation was strengthened by the conviction that in fact the leaders of the hasidim were keeping their followers in the dark simply in order to take advantage of them. In these judgements one clearly hears a belief in the goodness of the masses and the evil of the leaders, which might be a reflection of the Romantic views of some of the leaders of the integrationist camp, especially those of Daniel Neufeld. It is also worth noting that this belief formed the basis of one of the oldest anti-hasidic accusations. This had been expressed as early as 1796 in the works of Jacques Calmanson, and it later became one of the most common accusations, for example in Abraham Stern's denunciations. An anonymous author put forward this belief particularly graphically in *Jutrzenka*:

The black cavern of fanaticism—evil spirits gesticulating grotesquely grumble incomprehensibly; in the darkest corner of the cavern there lurks a vampire with broad, black wings, his face still smeared with the blood sucked from the victim, who has been anaesthetized by the air of the wings of his deceit, and, at his voice, the poor, emaciated sons of Israel from every city and village in the country of Poland approach, each of them carrying in one hand a knot with a gift for the vampire, the heavy sweat of the toiling, haggard wife, and in the other a cup that constantly fills itself with an abominable drink called, as if out of spite, aqua vitae instead of aqua mortis; from this cup the unfortunates drink in order to be oblivious of their impotence and their degradation, artificial joy forms on their brow, false colour on

---

[4] 'Czytelnia dla Żydów', *Ju.* 2 (1862), 255.

[5] Literally 'a brimming cup and a *lulka*': L[eopold] Lubelski, ['Wybryki Chassydów w Kaliszu'], *Ju.* 2 (1862), 125. This was the name adopted by the hasidim for the pipe used by the putative founder of the movement, the Besht.                              [6] 'Pro Memoria', *Ju.* 3 (1863), 121–3.

their pallid cheeks—these miserable pariahs descend from every town and village of Poland, cutting themselves off from all worldly pleasures, suicidally fighting off the magnanimous helping hand of their brothers in faith, which would draw them from this ordure, closing their eyes in fear that they may cease to be blind, blocking their ears for fear of the voice of conscience, they come from all cities and villages in Poland at the voice of the vampire from the cavern of darkness, at the voice of the prophets of Baal who have founded their mission upon the false authority supposedly obtained from the hands of the God of Israel in the words that centuries ago resounded in the Arab desert: 'Say to the sons of Israel: "Go!"', "Come forth with the *pidyonot*."'

But we return once more to these false prophets, once again we speak to them in the words of Isaiah: 'Why do you oppress my people?' What offence have these unfortunates caused you that you have determined to destroy them, to degrade them? What has this hospitable land done to you that you deprive it of the agricultural work of a substantial part of the people, whom you oppress on the road to wrongdoing? To whom do you close the gates to the shrine of learning? To whom do you bar the road to agriculture, to artisanry, to fair work? Whom do you ply with the poison of dreams of the absurd and harmful?

We have guessed at your ignoble intentions. Your decline will be the progress of your race. Social enlightenment will open the eyes of this people and they will cease to honour you as deities, seeing through your total emptiness.[7]

The vicious and apocalyptic tone of this passage was exceptional in the columns of *Jutrzenka*, but even the moderate Neufeld was sometimes known to direct stinging accusations against the hasidic authorities. In one text he presented dealings of a predatory nature as an inherent quality of hasidism, defining the movement as a mystical party 'held in deep spiritual darkness by authorities known as *rebbe*, who in various forms exact from their adherents offerings known as *pidyonot*, amounting to fabulous sums'.[8] Further on he explained,

The interest of these [hasidic] authorities is in banning learning and the study of local languages, even Hebrew, for they sense that if these sectarians look at any book whatsoever, it will open their eyes and they will become as God, distinguishing between good and evil, as a result of which they will cease to pay tribute to these authorities.[9]

Despite its strong wording, this account contained one positive element: it helped to define the programmatic difference between the integrationist camp and hasidism. The crucial issue was of course the approach to education. In the mind of the modernizing party, education was viewed as the panacea for all social problems. It was intended that education would miraculously convert traditional Jews into Poles of the Jewish faith, encourage them to forsake their ridiculous language, dress, and mannerisms, and, by doing so, make them equal as citizens to the Poles and lead to the 'merging of our people with the country'. Meanwhile, almost fifty years of effort were failing to produce the desired effect, and the resistance of hasidic circles

[7] 'Postęp (Znaczenie święta Paski)', *Ju.* 3 (1863), 134–5.
[8] Daniel Neufeld, 'Urządzenie Konsystorza żydowskiego w Polsce. VII: Gmina', *Ju.* 2 (1862), 328 (the article was also published as a pamphlet in 1862).          [9] Ibid.

was seen as the chief impediment to the integrationists' agenda. This diagnosis was a recurrent theme in the columns first of *Jutrzenka* and later of *Izraelita*. The intrigues of the tsadikim, who kept the Jewish people in ignorance for personal gain, were usually identified as the simplest explanation for such resistance. From time to time, however, deeper analyses of hasidic resistance to secular education appeared. Hilary Glattstern noted, for example, that the hasidim shunned secular learning because they viewed it as heresy and feared it as a tool that would lure them away from the true faith of their forefathers.[10] Another contributor asked, 'Oh, unhappy brothers. Why is it that you shut yourselves in dark hovels? . . . You fear the loss of your religion, your heritage from your forefathers, the evidence of long centuries of suffering and long centuries of triumph!'[11] As it was, the integrationists agreed that education would draw the hasidim away from their beliefs and that, 'imbued with civilization and learning, they would cease to be hasidim'.[12] One of the leading representatives of the modernizing movement, Izaak Kramsztyk, a preacher in the 'Polish' synagogue in Warsaw and teacher at the Warsaw Rabbinical School, even put forward a very detailed educational plan and indicated that history and the natural sciences would be most effective in the struggle with 'hasidic fanaticism'.[13] The difference between the integrationists and the hasidim lay in the fact that the latter viewed such a departure from tradition as a catastrophe, whereas for the 'progressives' it was their aspiration. However, what is significant is that, instead of suspecting the hasidim of self-interest and ill intent, the contributors to *Jutrzenka*, by confirming the existence of a threat from the indifferentists and the danger of a loss of faith, discerned the real apprehension of the hasidim and admitted that in some ways these fears were well founded. Another of the leaders of the integrationist camp, the preacher of the 'German' synagogue in Warsaw, Marcus Jastrow, also noted that the hasidic resistance to learning was actually in conflict with the spirit of Judaism, but that it resulted not from ill intent, but rather from a lack of understanding.[14] It is this that fundamentally distinguished the viewpoint of Jastrow, Neufeld, and their circle from the view taken by the earlier maskilim. Instead of universally and unequivocally condemning hasidism, Neufeld based his reflections on the differences in opinion, attempted to crystallize the fundamental points of divergence, and, in effect, devised projects to resolve the differences.

## SOLUTIONS

The solution was obviously education:

Only those educational institutions that are equipped as befits our epoch would provide the greatest and most appropriate remedial measures for the future destruction at their very

---

[10] See Hilary Glattstern, 'Rzut oka na redakcyję Jutrzenki', *Ju.* 2 (1862), 3–6.

[11] 'Oświata', *Ju.* 3 (1863), 81.

[12] [Daniel Neufeld], 'Listy żydowskie. List XIII: Redaktor Jutrzenki do Jędrzeja', *Ju.* 3 (1863), 178.

[13] Kramsztyk, *Kazania*, 325.                          [14] Jastrow, *Kazania*, 60.

core of all moral ills, and it is to this that all our efforts should be jointly directed and persistently applied for the common good, against all the difficulties encountered along the way.[15]

Neufeld, a teacher with thirty years' experience, emphasized that only sympathetic and patient teaching could gradually persuade the hasidim to accept secular knowledge. The emphasis on freedom of choice in participating in such education was accompanied by the admission that, in the struggle with the hasidim, 'various means, of a brutal kind that were not always in accordance with our view of the use of intervention', had been resorted to in the past.[16] This was obviously a condemnation of the ruthless means employed by the earlier maskilim in their struggle with hasidism. The same view was expressed by Ignacy Natanson in his public letter during the infamous Polish–Jewish war of 1859 (a heated debate over an antisemitic publication in the Warsaw daily *Gazeta Warszawska*), in which he wrote that compulsion ran counter to the original intention and that 'persecution and compulsion prevail, as do stubbornness and superstition'.[17] An illustration of this thesis, which appeared in *Jutrzenka*, was the tale of the Olympian gods who tried to induce a Polish hasid to forsake his ridiculous dress (see Appendix 16).[18] The efforts of Aeolus to divest him by force of his hat and cloak were frustrated because

violent means can sometimes have an effect, but only on weak minds. The youth whom we endeavour to improve has an unyielding character and that is why Aeolus did not defeat him. Is it possible to forbid him to look ridiculous on the outside if he so wishes, as long as his inner qualities command respect?

Only when a hasid is warmed by Phoebus,

with the benevolent heat of *enlightenment* [does he throw off his] fur cap and silk cloak, cut his long hair, [trim] his beard and moustache, [look] around and [see] all nature smiling at him . . . and Grzybów was Grzybów no more!

The district of Grzybów was the centre of Warsaw orthodoxy, so the end of Grzybów could have meant nothing other than the disappearance of hasidism. The tale must have been popular as it was published again several years later in *Izraelita* during the great debate on the alleged 'conversion to progressiveness' of the famous tsadik Dov Ber of Leovo.[19]

The contributors to *Jutrzenka* also noted that the education of hasidic communities could only proceed by good example on the part of representatives of

---

[15] L[eopold] Lubelski, ['Wybryki Chassydów w Kaliszu'], *Ju.* 2 (1862), 125.

[16] Daniel Neufeld, 'Listy żydowskie. List VI: Redaktor Jutrzenki do Izaaka', *Ju.* 3 (1863), 114.

[17] See Bartoszewicz, *Wojna żydowska*, 56, for more on the 'Polish–Jewish War'.

[18] 'Eol i Febus (Bajka)', *Ju.* 3 (1863), 1–2.

[19] Jakub Graff, 'Słówko z okoliczności listu otwartego b. przywódcy chassydów R. Beera Friedman', *Izr.* 4 (1869), 132.

modernizing circles, but religious indifference and the violation of precepts by some 'progressives' deterred the hasidim from the path of learning.[20] According to Neufeld, total political emancipation was one method by which hasidic circles could be attracted to education. It was only when the hasidim saw representatives of the other Jewish groups, and even their own children, availing themselves of the fruits of equal rights that 'they themselves would be attracted to education and realize that they had been deceived'.[21] This view of hasidism as an outcome of the disadvantageous political position of the Jews was clearly influenced by the opinions of David Friedländer, and had a very long and productive life in the writings of the maskilim in Congress Poland and in those of their successors.

Neufeld tied in Friedländer's beliefs with his own optimistic view that even at that time many representatives of hasidism had recognized the error of their ways and were waiting for a pretext to justify their desertion of the hasidic camp. Perhaps, then, in the future it would be necessary to introduce compulsory schooling to provide them with that pretext, but for the time being it was necessary to limit activity to a tactical alliance with the mitnagedim and to endeavour not to provoke the hasidim needlessly.[22] Neufeld pointed to the Jewish elementary school on Bagno Street in Warsaw as a worthwhile model. The relatively minor concession of allowing boys to wear traditional head-coverings in class led to a significant number of pupils being recruited from hasidic circles, which normally were not well disposed towards elementary schools supervised by secular institutions. Thus, there was the hope that what could not be achieved by force could be achieved by peaceful means, that victory over hasidism was possible, and that progress and education would triumph in the end.[23]

The call for accord and gestures of goodwill towards the hasidim had a practical purpose in *Jutrzenka* circles: to make the educational plans outlined above more acceptable to the hasidim. A statement to this effect was made by Izaac Kramsztyk, who asserted that peace and accord were necessary because they were beneficial to the education of traditional Jewish society.[24] However, in the understanding of Neufeld and Jastrow, accord with the hasidic camp was to serve a far broader purpose: it was to be the road to Jewish unification, embracing the integrationists as well as the hasidim and the mitnagedim. This all-embracing unity was an obsessively recurring theme, rooted in the growing recognition of the importance of reli-

---

[20] N[una] Nirnstein, correspondence, *Ju.* 3 (1863), 269: 'I consider that only when we show that we aspire to instil our national speech even in the fanatical sects of our people, if we complain about all violations of Mosaic law, and particularly the eating of non-kosher meat, if we celebrate the sabbath and we pray with greater piety than we have to date, then not only will the most obstinate fanatics of our faith abandon their misconceptions, but I am convinced that our compatriots from other faiths will be grateful to us for our sacrifice.' See also 'Listy żydowskie. List VIII: Izaak do Redaktora Jutrzenki', *Ju.* 3 (1863), 137. Similar theses appear in the sermons of Kramsztyk, *Kazania*, 304–5.

[21] Daniel Neufeld, 'Szkoły czy chedery', *Ju.* 3 (1863), 346.                        [22] Ibid.

[23] Daniel Neufeld, 'Szkoły elementarne wyznania Mojżeszowego w Warszawie', *Ju.* 3 (1863), 372.

[24] See e.g. Kramsztyk, *Kazania*, 123, 307.

gious identity, and, as a consequence, of religious ties in the modernizing camp in the 1860s. Above all, though, it was a response to the growth of interdenominational unity in the period of Polish–Jewish fraternity. Similarly, as Polish–Jewish unity was to be a condition of Poland's obtaining independence, so too was internal Jewish unification a way to equal rights for the Jewish people. Arguing for the need to unify the three religious parties—the hasidim, the mitnagedim, and the integrationists—within the pale of Polish Judaism, Neufeld was even moved to question the superiority of the 'progressives' over the remaining two groups:

Accord, then, accord at all costs, between our three religious parties, that is the main condition for the gradual merging of our people with the country. That accord is possibly best maintained through the tolerance that the three parties show one another. . . . Let the hasidim worship according to Portuguese ritual with their kabbalistic accompaniments; let them designate the time of worship according to their preferences as 8.00 in the morning or as 12.00, let them perform their rites of purification. None of this is in the least prejudicial to religion, morality or social obligations.

Who can prove, impartially and with abnegation of his own customs, which of the three liturgies is most pleasing to God! And so, what is the point of mutual persecution and degradation? Enough of these quarrels, of this suspicion of one another, of these unjustified accusations, all of which, after all, bring only suffering to the poor masses and profit for a few charlatans.[25]

Jastrow wrote in a similar vein. The main theme of his sermons in 1861 was that of general fraternity. In his introduction, in which he referred to the joint activity of the Orthodox rabbi Baer Meisels, the hasidic leader Isaac Meir Alter of Góra Kalwaria (Ger), and the rabbis of the integrationist communities (Kramsztyk and Jastrow himself), he explained: 'I cast out hatred and resentment from the bosom of those to whose aid I had been called, and the sons of Israel in the Kingdom [of Poland] learned anew to regard themselves as a unified entity, no matter how different their ideas of the ways to adore God and fulfil their religious obligations.'[26] He emphasized the equality of all factions of Judaism and the need for unity in 'dispersion and separation'.[27] Jewish internal unity, embracing all camps, including hasidism, was not only a political necessity and religious edict, but also the way of salvation for the Jewish people (whatever was understood by that concept).[28] The educative mission of the integrationists thus gained a new, eschatological dimension. Certainly, the unity advocated by Neufeld and Jastrow was not the same as a genuine brotherhood of two equal parties. It had rather a paternalistic character with a very strong pragmatic agenda intended eventually to convert the hasidim into civilized Poles of the Mosaic persuasion. Still, it was the first time that the modernizing circle had clearly expressed the conviction that the most faithful and

[25] Daniel Neufeld, 'Urządzenie Konsystorza żydowskiego w Polsce. VII: Gmina', *Ju.* 2 (1862), 329.
[26] Jastrow, *Kazania*, 5.  [27] Ibid. 35.
[28] See his comments on the exodus from Egypt (ibid. 34–5), and commentary on the eschatological vision of the prophet Ezekiel (ibid. 44).

backward followers of Judaism, namely the hasidim, were their real brothers in faith, even if they were not equal.

## CHARACTERISTICS OF HASIDISM

Here we come to a fundamental problem in the attitude of the modernizing camp. If the hasidim were a disreputable bunch, full of shortcomings, a fanatical mob under the influence of merciless swindlers and the main impediment to the programme to educate the Jewish people, how would it have been possible to form an alliance with them? An alliance was possible because, the contributors to *Jutrzenka* noted, the hasidim were not as unequivocally bad as would appear from the accusations levelled at them even in the columns of *Jutrzenka*. This was a radical reassessment. Jastrow maintained in one of the first issues of *Jutrzenka* that in the hasidim 'one also finds virtues worthy of emulation, which only need to be skilfully channelled'.[29] The deference shown the hasidim and their Warsaw leader by Jastrow was so great that it surprised even the Gerer Rebbe, Isaac Meir Alter, though later in his career Jastrow was very critical of the hasidim and of Alter himself.[30] Going even further in defence of the hasidim, Neufeld stated that they were idealists who were full of goodwill and concern for spiritual values combined with contempt for material well-being.[31] Neufeld also maintained that, contrary to widely held views, the hasidim were very open-minded and that some of them even wrote to *Jutrzenka*.[32] As an example of this exemplary openness, he pointed to the followers of the tsadik of Kock (the Kotsker Rebbe), 'who with intensive education retained their faith and were on the best path to reform'.[33] Other praiseworthy characteristics of the hasidim were their 'readiness to sacrifice everything for their ideals, their almost military discipline, which allows them to submit to their leaders, their spirit, which is free from cares about tomorrow, their dreamy disposition'.[34]

Sonia Trachtenberg similarly praised the merits of hasidism, maintaining that the hasidim were seized by ideas in which they believed and which they were prepared to defend. On the other hand, many members of the 'progressive' camp were hard-headed 'realists', scornful and cynical. Trachtenberg also maintained that the hasidim cultivated fraternity and unity while the indifferentists quarrelled and were internally divided. The former were generous and self-sacrificing, the latter petty misers, exemplified by the poverty suffered by the leader of the Russian Haskalah, Isaac Ber Levinsohn; the former were honest and frank, the latter prevaricators;

---

[29] Marcus Jastrow, Review of *Lejbe i Sióra*, *Ju.* 1 (1861), 28.

[30] Jastrow, 'Bär Meisels', *Hebrew Leader*, 15/25 (1870), 2; 16/4 (1870), 2; 16/5 (1870), 2. See also Shatzky, *Geshikhte fun Yidn in Varshe*, iii. 358–9.

[31] [Daniel Neufeld,] 'Przyjaciel zdrowia', *Ju.* 3 (1863), 98.

[32] [Daniel Neufeld,] 'Wybory członków Dozoru Bóżniczego Gminy Warszawskiej', *Ju.* 3 (1863), 44.

[33] Neufeld, 'Chassyd', 170.

[34] [Daniel Neufeld,] 'Listy żydowskie. List XIII: Redaktor Jutrzenki do Jędrzeja', *Ju.* 3 (1863), 178.

the former were the personification of life and hope, the latter represented stiff legalism and inertia.[35]

Two striking questions arise in relation to these views. The first is the Romantic contrast between idealism and realism. In the opinion of Trachtenberg, Neufeld, Glattstern, and others, idealism was unequivocally positive, while realism was prosaic and negative. In tune with Romantic ideas, they believed that simple folk— ordinary people, whether Jewish or Polish—represented the ideal, whereas the realist radical assimilationists represented a negative deviation from religious values. This seems to prove the existence of Romantic undercurrents in pro-hasidic revisionism among the community of Polish Jewish patriots before the January Uprising.

The second, possibly even more important, question concerns hasidism's confrontation with the growing camp of religiously indifferent radical assimilationists. For the moderate integrationists, hasidism was actually an infinitely better alternative than total religious indifference.[36] This means that the integrationists had begun to recognize the positive aspects of the hasidic movement and the role it played in maintaining some of the values of traditional Judaism. There are echoes here of the views of Jakub Tugendhold, though whether he had brought any degree of personal influence to bear is debatable. In fact, the development of the ideas of the integrationists might well have resulted from the conversion of indifferentists, including some of the prominent members of the Jewish community. Comparisons between hasidism and indifferentism appeared in the columns of *Jutrzenka* on more than one occasion, and it was always hasidism that turned out to be the worthier party.

This seems to reveal one of the central functions of the subject of the hasidim in the columns of *Jutrzenka* and among its circle. Emphasis on the differences between the integrationists and the radical assimilationists was intended to convince the traditional camp (though not necessarily the hasidim themselves) of the genuineness of the integrationist movement. The contributors to first *Jutrzenka* and then *Izraelita* claimed that, in religious terms, their position was closer to the right-wing, hasidic, rather than to the left-wing, indifferentist and assimilationist, camp. By claiming this, they strove to break down the barriers that separated them from the Orthodox camp and to prove that they were the only group that could defend Judaism against conversions or anti-religious assimilation. Neufeld reminded the followers of the Orthodox position that modernization and integration could not be halted, so that persistent opposition to any form of modernization would lead to growing indifference and more desertions from Judaism.[37] Thus, the goals of the hasidim, as well as the traditional non-hasidic orthodoxy and the integrationists, needed to be the same, and the two groups needed to co-operate in order to prevent indifferentist tendencies and to direct modernization towards

[35] S. Trachtenberg, 'Pia desideria', *Ju.* 3 (1863), 103.
[36] See also Feiner, 'The Pseudo-Enlightenment'.
[37] See 'Wiadomości bieżące', *Ju.* 3 (1863), 415.

forms that would preserve Jewish identity and the place of religion in the life of the Jewish people. The call for a coalition with the mitnagedim, or even with the hasidim, was motivated by a similar conviction about the need to fight a common enemy.

## DANIEL NEUFELD: IN PRAISE OF HASIDISM

As I have mentioned, it was Neufeld who went furthest in defence of the hasidim. On more than one occasion he praised their virtues and questioned the superiority of the modernizing camp. His exceptionally positive attitude towards hasidism probably resulted from a certain fascination with hasidic popular religiosity and his ethnographic interest in the popular beliefs of hasidism. This fascination was undoubtedly founded upon Romantic ideals. Neufeld was also one of a group of Polish Jewish publicists who were active in 1861–3. This group's pro-hasidic tendencies were noted—and even overestimated—by twentieth-century historiographers, who, no doubt, had been influenced by Jacob Shatzky.[38] It is worth remembering, however, that his fascination with hasidism was also evident to his contemporaries, and that he was viewed as an expert on hasidic issues by the Warsaw Jewish intelligentsia, to whom he lectured on the subject.[39]

Neufeld's hasidic concerns were most evident in an article published on the subject in *Encyklopedia Powszechna* (Popular Encyclopedia), edited by Samuel Orgelbrand.[40] In his introductory comments Neufeld was not particularly original: mostly he followed the writings of Salomon Maimon and David Friedländer. According to Neufeld, hasidism was a phenomenon that had existed within Judaism for years, and a hasid was one 'who does more in relation to God than religion itself demands of him'. Until the eighteenth century hasidism was not organized, and it was owing to the activities of the Besht (starting around 1740 in Tłuste and then in Międzybóż in Podolia) that it assumed the features of a social movement. The Besht had liberated hasidism from ascetic practices and imbued his followers with a commendable spirit of social activism. Of the numerous students and successors of the Besht, it was Menahem Mendel of Kock whom Neufeld cited, and whom he praised for instilling a spirit of criticism into hasidism and for his enthusiasm for education. The hasidic school of Kock, according to Neufeld, offered the best evidence that it was possible to combine profound faith (even the hasidic version) with an understanding of the need for reform and modern education. Neufeld also waxed lyrical on the subject of the Gerer Rebbe, whom he praised for continuing the most glorious traditions of his master, the tsadik of Kock, and was a 'man filled with talmudic erudition, contemptuous of charlatanry, a man who omitted kabbalah

---

[38] See Shatzky, *Geshikhte fun Yidn in Varshe*, iii. 359. For later comments, see e.g. Moshe Landau, 'Neufeld, Daniel', in *Encyclopaedia Judaica*, xii (Jerusalem, 1971), 1008; Biderman, *Mayer Balaban*, 20; Fuks, 'Neufeld, Daniel'; Rabinowicz (ed.), *The Encyclopedia of Hasidism*, 345–6.

[39] Shatzky, *Yidishe bildungs-politik*, 140–1.          [40] Neufeld, 'Chassyd', 169–77.

and mysticism completely from his scheme of things and who [intended] to lead Judaism to the same level as that at which the Besht left it'. These words of praise concerning the tsadikim of Kock and Ger are very significant because Neufeld knew them and many of their followers personally. He was not the first to have overestimated the innovative and reforming nature of Kock and Ger's version of hasidism. Even in 1838 an anonymous maskil from Brody had praised Menahem Mendel of Kock for his rationalist tendencies.[41] What was new in Neufeld's approach was that he was the first to attempt to learn about hasidism. By doing so, he could base his ideas and his criticisms about the group on knowledge, and not on clichés and stereotypes.

Having outlined the history of hasidism in his article, Neufeld explained how the hasidic court functioned as well as the principal activities of the tsadikim. He described hasidic prayer and a series of other hasidic practices (their tobacco pipes, alcohol, *mikveh*, charity, pilgrimages, etc.), and, finally, discussed the most important differences between the rituals of the hasidim and those of the mitnagedim. Among the merits of the hasidim listed by Neufeld, pride of place was given to their sense of fraternity and equality, their widely practised good works, mental alertness, courage, and openness, and their abhorrence of crime and wrongdoing. The article ended with a list of seventy-one popular maxims, hasidic proverbs, and quotations from hasidic books, which, according to Neufeld, constituted the basic premisses of hasidism.[42]

This highly interesting text was a combination of penetrating observations about hasidic people (and these observations were definitely Neufeld's own, from the time he had spent working in the provinces) and superficial, frequently imprecise or erroneous historical accounts taken from elementary works on hasidism. The introductory, historical part of the article was based primarily on information taken from Maimon, Friedländler, and Peter Beer's study of Jewish sects,[43] but subsequent paragraphs, devoted to hasidic rites and popular beliefs, were original. As distinct from earlier writers on hasidism, Neufeld devoted little attention to the beginnings of the movement and the basic principles of hasidism. For these, he referred to Peter Beer and Isaac Marcus Jost, both of whom had taken the works of Joseph Perl as the source for much of what they wrote. But, unlike many previous works on hasidism, these formed only a fraction of Neufeld's article. Instead, he provided first-rate ethnographic material, which was a reflection of his fascination with, and desire to examine, the true nature of the hasidic movement. The article was not free from accusations against the hasidim, especially against the Besht and anonymous 'reactionary' Galician tsadikim—accusations of this type were typical

---

[41] 'Charakteristik der jüdischen Sekten in Galizien', *AZJ* 2 (1838), 384.

[42] Its structure followed that of Jost, *Geschichte der Israeliten*, ix. 159–63. Some of Nahman of Bratslav's sayings quoted by Jost could conceivably have been paraphrased by Neufeld.

[43] Beer, *Geschichte, Lehren und Meinungen*, ii. 197–259. Neufeld also duplicated Beer's factual errors, e.g. that the first publication of the *Shivḥei habesht* had been in Berdichev.

of Haskalah writings on the subject. Primarily, however, the reader's attention was caught by observations about the positive aspects of the movement and the author's ability to capture the essence of its popular appeal. This is probably the first documentary evidence of the fascination with popular hasidism among secular Jews in the Kingdom of Poland.

Neufeld also appreciated the value of hasidism in another respect. He saw it as a Polish phenomenon, and accordingly recognized the hasidic movement in Poland as a Polish version of orthodoxy. In addition, Neufeld maintained that the Polish nature of hasidism would prove conducive to the Polonization of the Jewish people, and from that point of view could prove to be very positive. Neufeld wrote in the same spirit of the pro-Polish gestures of the Gerer Rebbe, seeing in them an unequivocally favourable omen.[44] The Polish tsadikim Mendel of Kock and Isaac Meir Alter of Ger were also, he believed, more enlightened than the Galician tsadikim, and generally carried out their enlightened ideas in the pale of hasidism.

What is interesting is that Neufeld's view that hasidism was a genuinely Polish phenomenon reflected the genesis rather than the contemporary state of this movement. This suggests that he saw Jewish history from a traditionally Polish perspective, or even in keeping with Polish Romantic mythology (Podolia and Volhynia as a part of the Polish lands, the myth of a mystical Ukraine, and so forth). His pro-hasidic leanings therefore had their roots in Polish Romanticism, which was completely in step with the ideological profile of this group.

On another level, Polish Romantic literature also had an influence. Between the publication in 1821 of *Lejbe i Sióra* by Julian Ursyn Niemcewicz and in 1878 of *Meir Ezofowicz* by Eliza Orzeszkowa, not a single work of Polish literature focused on hasidism, although Józef Ignacy Kraszewski's story of the Gaon of Vilna might be seen as an exception.[45] However, the hasidic issue was in a way present in Polish Romantic literature. After the publication of Adam Mickiewicz's *Pan Tadeusz* the traditional Orthodox Jew came to play an unequivocal role as the bearer of the positive values inherent in both Polish and Jewish society. Although Mickiewicz's hero Jankiel does not belong in this category, other traditional Jewish characters were easily recognizable to educated Jewish readers as being hasidic. For a reader familiar with the Jewish community, accessories such as the silk coat (*kitajowy lapserdak*), the fur hat (*shtrayml*), and a specific type of belt (the *gartl*) facilitated identification of these *kitajowcy*, as they were called in the first half of the nineteenth century. For Polish readers and writers these things were simply exotic; for the Jewish reader they could only be hasidic. Examples of this are the *arendator*

---

[44] See e.g. the appeal by Isaac Meir Alter to the Polish hasidim to write a traditional Passover contract for the selling of *ḥamets* (leavened dough or bread, which Jews are forbidden to have in their possession during Passover), in Polish only: 'Wiadomości bieżące: *Suum cuique*', *Ju.* 3 (1863), 152. For more on this, see Shatzky, *Geshikhte fun Yidn in Varshe*, iii. 359.

[45] See Kraszewski, *Wilno*, iii. 165; id., *Wspomnienia Polesia, Wołynia i Litwy*. A short description can be found in Żyga, 'Problem żydowski w twórczości J. I. Kraszewskiego', 156–7.

(lessee of tax collection) Abraham Ilski in *Pustelnik w Proniunach* (1858) and Rabbi Solomon in *Nowe pamiętniki kwestarza* (1862), both by Ignacy Chodźko.[46] Similarly, in *W przededniu* by Jan Zachariasiewicz (1863), Abraham in his silk coat was a positive Jewish character, and equally, he was recognizable as a hasid.[47] These and other hasidic figures in Polish Romantic literature represented the positive values of patriarchal Jewish society and were thus in conflict with the negative view of the movement that had predominated in earlier maskilic literature. In this way, new stereotypes replaced the old ones.

## THE ANATOMY OF CONFLICT: THE SEQUEL

This revision of attitudes towards hasidism did not take place without conflict. The most obvious manifested themselves between the Warsaw integrationists, who promoted the idea of the reconciliation of all Jews, and the 'progressives' of the old school, who often retained their attachment to Haskalah ideology and opposed an alliance with hasidism. In *Jutrzenka* and *Izraelita* the anti-hasidic position was most frequently put forward by contributors from the provinces, although similar opinions were occasionally heard from Łódź and Warsaw. Over the comparatively short period of the existence of *Jutrzenka* and throughout the 1860s and 1870s many adherents of Enlightenment ideology rejected the idea, which the periodical promoted, of a reassessment of attitudes towards the hasidim, but rather attacked them violently, and hasidism itself continued to appear, in these accounts, as the embodiment of all evil. The best examples of this are pieces of correspondence from Kalisz, in which their indignant author provided an account of drunkenness at the hasidic Purim celebrations and called the sect 'an uncouth rabble and ignorant riff-raff'.[48]

The difference in attitudes between Warsaw and the provinces, as well as provincial correspondents' dislike of hasidism, had the same roots they had had twenty years earlier. Unlike in Warsaw, in most provincial settlements there was an imbalance between the small and powerless modernizing communities and the considerably stronger, sometimes dominant (although not necessarily numerically superior) hasidic communities, which were applying the pressures and provocations mentioned above. For provincial members of the 'enlightened class', the fight with the hasidim was a fight for survival, and the hasidic movement was viewed not from the point of view of ideology, but on the basis of daily conflicts in their everyday dealings with the hasidim.

Another reason for this dislike was the continued frustration that sprang from

---

[46] Chodźko, *Pustelnik w Proniunach*; id., *Nowe pamiętniki kwestarza*. A comprehensive study of the subject can be found in Inglot, *Postać Żyda w literaturze polskiej*, 119–21.

[47] Zachariasiewicz, *W przededniu*, i. 28; cited in Inglot, *Postać Żyda w literaturze polskiej*, 154.

[48] L[eopold] Lubelski, ['Wybryki Chassydów w Kaliszu'], *Ju.* 2 (1862), 125; see also 'Pro Memoria', *Ju.* 3 (1863), 121–3.

the belief of the 'enlightened class' in their superiority over the 'ignorant' hasidim and their belief that 'individual right-thinkers' who 'come to the synagogue wearing Parisian hats' should be the ones to lead the Jewish religious communities; meanwhile, the fanaticism that held sway over the hasidic community prevented them from benefiting from these natural privileges—hence their hatred of this ungrateful and ignorant mass. Conflict of this type continued throughout the following decades.[49]

Finally, it should be mentioned that expressions of the hostility of the provincial modernizers were not confined to angry letters to the editor. As before, the conflict with hasidic circles took the form of everyday arguments concerning influence in the community, the appointment of a suitable rabbi or cantor, the right to a separate house of prayer, or, at least, the right to walk down the street peacefully. An interesting account of the conflict between the tsadik Moses Brukman (1794–1881) and the 'German' Jewish doctors from Piotrków sheds some light on the nature of this and many similar conflicts, which in equal measure shaped and were shaped by the attitude of modernizing circles towards hasidism (see Appendix 17). The affair took place in the period under discussion, i.e. the period of the January Uprising and the following few years, but the anatomy of the conflict differed little from that of the 1840s or 1850s.

Moses Brukman (also called Brukarz (Paver), or Hamartsef) took his nickname from the trade in which he had worked in his youth. In 1832 he settled in Piotrków, founded a *shtibl*, and began his career as a hasidic *rebbe*. He was particularly well known for exorcising dybbuks, selling amulets, and similar activities regarded as charlatanry.[50] According to hasidic accounts, the conflict between Brukman and two Jewish doctors at the Orthodox Hospital in Piotrków, Dr Stein and Dr Stanisław Szancer, began in 1864, when the tsadik refused to contribute to the fund for the insurgent national government and strongly opposed any Jewish support for the Polish uprising, and on this basis the doctors managed to persuade the insurgent government to issue a death sentence. However, one account of this and other persecutory actions seems to me to lack credibility. It was from this time that the denunciations by Jewish doctors of the tsadik's illegal medical practices began. They claimed that talismans sold by Brukman, to which he attributed healing properties, were contrary to Jewish law, harmful to the health of potential patients (who dispensed with conventional healing methods), and morally offensive as a form of economic exploitation of the naivety of the Jewish masses. Thus we again encounter the most common features of accusations used by the maskilim against the leaders of the hasidic movement, which could be discovered everywhere in the writings of the integrationist camp: the exploitation of the ignorance of the

---

[49]  e.g. 'Korespondencja: Kutno—w Czerwcu', *Izr.* 3 (1868), 190; 'Opoczno—w Maju', *Izr.* 3 (1868), 200.

[50]  Essential biographical information on Brukman can be found in Feinkind, *Gute Yuden in Poylen*, 176–83; Malts and Lau (eds.), *Piotrkov tribunalski vehasevivah*, 262–4.

masses, and even conscious attempts to act to their detriment; economic exploitation; and the distortion of Judaism. In 1867 the doctors finally succeeded in having the hasidic house of prayer closed, and brought a court case against Brukman. In the first instance, the court found Brukman guilty; however, in response the hasidim obtained a statement from the chief rabbi of Warsaw, Baer Meisels, that belief in talismans was not in conflict with Jewish law (although in the document Meisels distanced himself from their sale). A number of statements were presented testifying to Brukman's loyalty to the imperial authorities and to the innocuous nature of the talismans. The court of second instance and the appeal court exonerated the tsadik. However, the doctors were able to obtain the governor's backing for a decision to close the hasidic house of prayer and to impose a ban on all spurious healing practices. Even hasidic denunciations of the doctors for their part in the January Uprising, and their sympathies with it, failed to have the desired effect.[51] In this case, the attitude of the government was somewhat unusual since Jewish medical circles, particularly in Piotrków, were known for such sympathies, and a number of doctors from Piotrków had already been sent to Siberia for holding them.[52]

The conflicts between hasidism and the integrationists of the 1860s and 1870s thus took an identical course to earlier clashes, and, far from entering the elevated spheres of words and ideas, as the writers of *Jutrzenka* wished them to, they involved the traditional method of denunciation and slander, police intervention, and court hearings. In addition, the editors of *Jutrzenka* and the provincial maskilim were doing battle with a different enemy: while the Warsaw integrationists were carrying on a dispute with the tsadik Isaac Meir Alter, one of the intellectual giants of hasidism, the Jewish doctors in Piotrków were struggling with an uneducated charlatan whom even other tsadikim accused of being a fraud. Furthermore, the proponents of modernization in Warsaw had had at their disposal for several decades a number of institutions that had been putting their ideas into effect, and this influence within the community enabled them to see their plans put into practice. Outside Warsaw the maskilim were always an insignificant minority, and they were able to influence the life of their local communities only if they turned to the authorities for help. The simplest course was denunciation.

This difference proves once again that the picture of the hasidim presented by Neufeld and those supporters of 'progress' who gathered around him was an idealized one and was not widely accepted. *Jutrzenka*'s opinions on and visions of hasidism were shared only by a narrow circle of Jews in Warsaw and were foreign to most of the followers of integrationist ideology in provincial Poland. But this opposition to current attitudes and even to day-to-day experiences proves how

---

[51] AGAD, CWW 1411, pp. 550–9, 591–4.

[52] See Fijałek, 'Do zagadnienia szpitalnictwa żydowskiego w Piotrkowie', 54; Feinkind, *Dzieje Żydów w Piotrkowie*, 24. For more on the participation of the Jewish doctors in the January Uprising, see Ringelblum, 'Yidishe doktoyrim un mediker in oyfshtand fun yor 1863'; id., 'Reshime fun yidishe doktoyrim'.

intensely the young integrationists sought new means of social reconciliation and the rehabilitation of all levels of Jewish society. Neufeld was not unrealistic in his attitude towards hasidism; he did not retract his criticism of the movement (particularly of its leaders), but simply attempted to enhance it with reflections on the hitherto sidelined, positive elements of hasidism and thus augment the traditional black and white hasidic portrait with other, more varied colours. The developing relations between the leaders of the hasidic camp and the modernizing circles also proved that such attitudes were socially fruitful. Contrary to the picture created by hasidic hagiography of the tsadik Isaac Meir Alter of Ger as an uncompromising enemy of the 'progressives',[53] many events from the end of the 1850s proved that the friendly gestures of the integrationists were received well by the leader of the Warsaw hasidim and that they actually led to a major rapprochement between the two circles. One expression of this was the appeal by the Gerer Rebbe for the Polish language to be taught in the *ḥeder* (Jewish religious school), the appeal for documents for the sale of *ḥamets* to be in the Polish language, close contacts with Jakub Tugendhold, and participation in the committee for the planned reforms to Jewish education.[54] This period of rapprochement, although short-lived and limited to relatively small groups, was one of the more evident successes of the people associated with *Jutrzenka* and an event of epic proportions in the history of the relationship between two groups divided at the level not only of ideas, but also of social practices.

## CONCLUSIONS

*Jutrzenka* came to a quite sudden end. The weekly was closed down by the police on 23 October 1863 and Neufeld, suspected of supporting the Polish revolutionary movement, was exiled to Chelyabinsk. He returned to Warsaw in 1865, but was not permitted to continue his journalistic activities. Because of the repressive politics of the tsarist authorities, he vanished from public life.[55] The same happened to a significant majority of Jewish writers who had been active in the period 1861–3, following the overthrow of the uprising. They either maintained silence for a prolonged period or permanently left the Kingdom of Poland.

Even though it was active only for a short time, *Jutrzenka* and the writers associated with it wielded considerable influence. This has been acknowledged unanimously by both contemporary and later writers and historians. Their influence

[53] *Me'ir einei hagolah*, i. 65–6; see also Mahler, *Hasidism and the Jewish Enlightenment*, 313, 394 n. 481; Shatzky, *Geshikhte fun Yidn in Varshe*, ii. 101–10.

[54] On the position of the tsadik Isaac Meir Alter during the 'Polish–Jewish fraternity' and the January Uprising, see Kandel, 'Kariera rabiniczna cadyka Icie-Majera', 131; Shatzky, *Geshikhte fun Yidn in Varshe*, iii. 358–62. Important data on rapprochement between the tsadik and the Polish *pritsim* can be found in Bałaban, 'Żydzi w powstaniu 1863', 584–5. More generally, see also an interesting source in Kotik, *Journey to a Nineteenth-Century Shtetl*, 203–8.

[55] See Shatzky, 'Biografye fun Daniel Neufeld'.

extended to bringing about a realignment of the attitude of the modernizing camp towards the hasidim; in particular, it was not until the 1860s that hasidism was recognized as a major ideological problem and perceived to be the most serious enemy in the battle to emancipate and modernize Jews in Poland. Although the 'hasidic question' appeared in the writings of the Polish maskilim as early as the 1820s, it was not until four decades later that it became a major topic. By then, opinions on hasidism were very ambivalent. As earlier, hasidism was an object of severe criticism, but it differed from the earlier situation in that the contributors to *Jutrzenka*, instead of condemning the hasidic movement from the outset, conducted a debate with hasidism in a number of selected subject areas in which they saw a fundamental incompatibility of viewpoints. Above all, they perceived in hasidism a threat to their educational plans, and they identified that with socially and politically reactionary movements. In addition, the tsadikim were traditionally viewed as charlatans who profited from human ignorance and even kept the people in a state of ignorance. The integrationists did not renege on their educational plans, but they softened their position by admitting that the methods they had employed until now—the use of violence and resorting to the government for help—had been counter-productive. However, it did not alter the strong convictions held by Neufeld and other *Jutrzenka* writers that the hasidim needed to be educated and that learning would bring about the ultimate solution to the problem, i.e. the disappearance of hasidism.

But, alongside the voices of criticism, *Jutrzenka*'s writers increasingly expressed the positive features of hasidism, particularly their unrivalled unity, their caring for their families, their concern for religious education, and their wholehearted espousal of their ideology. Although similar views had been expressed before, and, simultaneously with *Jutrzenka*, the Russian maskilim had made themselves heard,[56] their efforts injected a new quality into Polish Jewish writing in the 1860s—an atmosphere that proved to be unexpectedly favourable to the hasidic movement. There appeared in Neufeld's and Jastrow's texts a quality that had been absent— elements of a solidarity with their hasidic 'brothers in faith' as well as considered and more nuanced assessments of the movement. This reflected a clear shift in their position: from the ignorance that had dominated the writings and activities of the maskilim in the 1820s and 1830s, and from the aggression of the 1840s, to the more conciliatory viewpoint, which Jakub Tugendhold alone had represented and which was now accepted by a broader sphere of integrationists. The change in stance was linked with the growth in the mood of solidarity in the pre-uprising period and with a strengthening of the modernizing camp, which had finally ceased to see in hasidism a deadly threat to its own existence. The positive features of hasidism also became clearer to integrationists at a time when religious indifference was on the increase; and this, according to the contributors to *Jutrzenka* and *Izraelita*, was a

[56] See e.g. Lurie and Zeltser, 'Moses Berlin and the Lubavich Hasidim', 60–2. More on this in Feiner, 'Hamifneh beha'arakhat haḥasidut'.

more serious threat to Judaism than 'ignorant' hasidism. With Neufeld, the most vehement defender of hasidism, there was also his ethnographic interest in popular faiths, and even a certain fascination with popular forms of religion. All this meant that hasidism began to be treated by the integrationist community as a complex and multifaceted phenomenon, inevitably not without its flaws, but also not without its positive traits, some of which might even provide an example to the integrationists. The reasonable conclusion to be drawn from this by the integrationists was that one should not seek opportunities to destroy hasidism violently and at all costs, but rather seek to establish areas of communication (or, at least, understanding) and to build an all-embracing Jewish cohesiveness. This led to the growth of interest in the subject of hasidism that became evident from the first issues of *Jutrzenka*, and such a development was hardly surprising. If, according to Neufeld, the mitnagedim were passive and there was no serious problem in winning them over, major efforts needed to be directed towards hasidism.[57] Thus, rapprochement with the hasidim was, for the integrationists, synonymous with rapprochement with all the traditionalists in Jewish society.

The reassessment of attitudes towards the hasidic movement among the moderate integrationist camp brought immediate, direct results in the pre-uprising period of Polish–Jewish fraternity and had a lasting effect. The first and most evident effect was the rapprochement between the Warsaw hasidim under the leadership of the Gerer Rebbe, on one hand, and the leaders of the integrationist movement on the other. It may be assumed that without this rapprochement the involvement of Isaac Meir Alter in the pre-uprising events and his pro-Polish declarations would have been impossible. The politics of solidarity with their hasidic brothers-in-faith in the period of Polish–Jewish fraternity from 1861 to 1863 undoubtedly lent authenticity to the solidaristic slogans of the integrationists, which embraced both the Polish nation and Jewish co-religionists of differing orientations.

But the effects of *Jutrzenka*'s activities and its altered attitude towards hasidism lasted far longer than the publication itself. Although the leaders of this group disappeared from the public scene in the Kingdom of Poland, and socio-political conditions underwent serious changes following the failure of the uprising, old and new representatives of moderate integrationism did not appreciably alter the central points of *Jutrzenka*'s programme. The integrationist paper *Izraelita*, founded in 1866, proved to be a faithful continuation of the abolished *Jutrzenka*, and it was actually *Izraelita* that, in the coming decades, would shape the attitudes of the moderate integrationist camp in the Kingdom of Poland, upholding revolutionary

---

[57] Although the analogy is not wholly adequate, a very similar belief, that the victory over hasidism would be a victory over the entire traditional Jewish camp, was held by the missionaries of the London Society for Promoting Christianity amongst the Jews. They deliberately sought out their adversaries, the hasidim, believing that a victory over them would be convincing to the whole of Jewry. This is proof that the hasidim were seen as the mainstay of Jewish orthodoxy, not only by the Jewish integrationists, but also by some Christians.

ideals in the post-uprising period and, in the same spirit, solidarity with the hasidic movement. Inevitably, in the fifty-year period of *Izraelita*'s activity, the views of its team and the community around it would undergo a gradual evolution, and already by the end of the 1870s these views were a long way from the optimism of the 1860s. What is important, however, is that *Izraelita*'s writers, especially Samuel H. Peltyn and Izrael Leon Grosglik, maintained *Jutrzenka*'s attitude towards hasidism, seeking common ground for understanding and ways to a peaceful solution to the 'hasidic question'. Although hasidism remained foreign in terms of its ideas, it ceased to be a deadly opponent with whom any kind of understanding would be impossible. Gradual rapprochement in questions that did not concern fundamental ideological differences finally led to the situation in which the creation of a coalition between the hasidim and the integrationists in the administration of the Warsaw Jewish community board, and later in the community of Płock, was possible. Even though these coalitions had only local significance and depended upon a combination of circumstances for their existence, it is also possible to recognize them, together with Eliezer Zweifel and his *Shalom al yisra'el*, which brought about the well-known rapprochement between the moderate Haskalah and hasidism in Imperial Russia, as the significant moment that ended the hostility between the Haskalah and the hasidim throughout broader areas of eastern Europe.

# SEVEN

# Waning Enthusiasm: Izraelita and the Moderate Integration Movement

ALTHOUGH *Jutrzenka* was discontinued by the tsarist police in 1863 and never re-established, those connected with it never ceased their efforts to publish a weekly to nurture its traditions. The weekly *Izraelita*,[1] which was established in 1866, carried on those traditions by employing the same journalists and by faithfully reproducing its integrationist ideals in a new period.

This came about mainly due to the efforts of Samuel Henryk Peltyn (1831–96), the founder and long-time editor-in-chief of *Izraelita*. Peltyn was born in Mariampol, in the voivodeship of Augustów (now in Lithuania), into an impoverished merchant family. There he received a traditional religious education but also educated himself in secular matters. In 1853 he moved to Warsaw, where he worked as a bookseller. From 1861 to 1863 he wrote for *Jutrzenka*, and in 1866 he revived it in a new form as *Izraelita*. Thanks to his efforts, *Izraelita* soon became the platform of the modernizing camp and he himself became its main ideologist and the undisputed leader of the moderate integrationists. Throughout his thirty years as a writer, Peltyn unceasingly promoted the idea of the social integration of Jews with Polish society and at the same time fought with the anti-religious tendencies of the radical supporters of assimilation. The most frequently recurring themes in his journalistic endeavours included an enlightenment programme for the lower classes of Jewish society, the strengthening of religious ties among modernizing Jews, and religious unity. Naturally, the hasidic issue was also one of the themes he discussed. On summing up the literary achievements of *Izraelita*'s leader, his successor, Nachum Sokołów, wrote that, in addition to maintaining the religious nature of integration, the fight with hasidic influences in Poland was the most important theme in Peltyn's career as a publisher, editor, journalist, translator, and man of letters.[2]

---

[1] For obvious reasons it was impossible to express open support for *Jutrzenka*. The periodical closed down because of its pro-revolutionary sympathies, so the editors of *Izraelita* referred to its predecessor only by way of hints and allusions. See e.g. Samuel H. Peltyn, 'Krańcowe kierunki religijne w judaizmie', *Izr.* 1 (1866), 27. More on the establishment of *Izraelita* can be found in Fuks, *Prasa żydowska w Warszawie*, 85–9; id., 'Prasa żydowska w Warszawie XIX w. *Izraelita*'.

[2] Good biographical notes on Peltyn appear in Fuks, 'Peltyn, Samuel Henryk'; id., *Prasa żydowska w Warszawie*, index; 'Bł. p. Samuel Henryk Peltyn', *Izr.* 31 (1896), 323–5. Important biographical

In some respects the texts devoted to the hasidic issue in *Izraelita* were even more interesting than those published in *Jutrzenka*. In reality, neither Peltyn nor any other writer for *Izraelita* was responsible for historical breakthroughs in attitudes towards hasidism, and their opinions frequently mirrored those of *Jutrzenka* and other opinion-forming circles of the period, especially those from German Jewish publications. However, hasidic subject-matter in *Izraelita* was considerably more daring than it had been in the texts published in 1861–3. The 'creative' terminology of *Jutrzenka* that aimed at concealing hasidism behind various euphemisms ('the exultant', 'the zealous', 'ultra-conservatives', 'the backward', 'fanatics', 'reactionaries') was still in use in *Izraelita*; however, articles using the term 'the hasidim' in preference to euphemisms began to appear more frequently. The hasidic subject-matter of *Izraelita* is all the more interesting because the weekly ran for fifty years, unlike *Jutrzenka*'s two years. Naturally, this resulted in both an abundance and a diversity of material. From its very first issue the journal published long editorials on the problem of educating hasidic circles, appeals to hasidic 'co-believers', extensive (but rarely original) studies devoted to the origins of the movement, anti-hasidic satires, faithfully reproduced hasidic tales, accounts of visits to tsadikim, and, above all, hundreds of letters from the provinces, short narratives, stories of incidents involving hasidim, and literary sketches.[3] Thus the periodical was a rich, if one-sided and tendentious, source of information on the everyday life of the hasidim in the Kingdom of Poland at that time.

## *JUTRZENKA*'S HERITAGE

The hasidim remained one of the main issues for *Izraelita*'s writers. Their existence and influence never ceased to preoccupy the leaders of the integrationist camp because of the latter's negative attitude towards traditional Jewish society with its different values and its other distinguishing features, which were offensive both to the Jewish 'progressives' and to the Polish public. The pressure exerted by the latter was particularly significant at that time. Polish journalism—both the 'young' liberal press and the more conservative periodicals—was still ruled by ideas that had emerged during the period of Polish–Jewish fraternity, so that the idea of the imminent social integration of Jews seemed not only indisputable, but also historically justified. However, this naive belief was contradicted by the facts. For Polish

notes may also be found in Nachum Sokołów, 'S. H. Peltyn: Wizerunek literacki', *Izr.* 31 (1896), 399–400, 407–8, 417–18, 425–7, 433–4; Shatzky, *Geshikhte fun Yidn in Varshe*, iii. 165–71 and index.

[3] The most interesting are the report on the funeral of Mendel of Warka ('Kronika krajowa i zagraniczna', *Izr.* 3 (1868), 192); the story of the visit paid to Hayim Halberstam in Nowy Sącz (Sanz) ('Odwiedziny cadyka w Sandecz', *Izr.* 4 (1869), 138–40); notes on the problems of the tsadik Samuel Aba of Żychlin ('Pogadanki', *Izr.* 8 (1873), 262–5); the account of the conflict between the tsadikim Abraham Jacob of Sadagóra and Menahem Mendel of Vishnits, which took place in Śniatyń ('Korespondencja', *Izr.* 10 (1875), 202–4); and a history of the origins of hasidism in Olkusz (Majmon, 'Luźne kartki').

writers, the repellently 'foreign' population of traditional Jewish society aroused annoyance and, within a short time, disillusionment as well. In the search for simple explanations, the 'civilized' strata of Jewish society were blamed, and accused of not making any effort educationally to enlighten their fanatical co-believers. When the weeklies *Jutrzenka* and *Izraelita* appeared, this criticism was levelled mainly at them, as they were regarded by the Polish press as the official representatives of the integrationist movement. This forced *Izraelita*'s writers to make constant references to the issue of the traditionalists, their own activities in relation to them, and their programme for social reform.

This programme was of course one of enlightenment. Like Neufeld, Peltyn was convinced of the remedial power of education and assumed that the Jewish issues in Poland could be resolved only through the comprehensive education of all Jewish society, by which means total integration could be achieved. The implementation of this programme was hampered by the hasidim and their fanatical hostility towards non-religious education. This made their existence and influence the focus of attention. The issue was particularly significant to Peltyn. Like *Jutrzenka*'s writers, he considered the mitnagedim to be ineffectual and defensive, and thus amenable to secular education. In his opinion, the only factor preventing the passive masses of mitnagedim from acquiescence was the pressure exerted by the 'backward fanatics', that is, the supporters of hasidism.[4] If their influence was to be eliminated, the effect on the non-hasidic masses would instantly be positive, and in time would lead to the final overthrow of hasidism, which would be isolated in its opposition. Peltyn thus believed, as Neufeld did, that the key to the happiness of all Jews in Poland lay in the enlightenment of the hasidim.

Neufeld and Peltyn were also united in their boundless optimism and their belief that ultimate victory was only a matter of time because that was the natural course of history. Progress was by definition inevitable. 'The very assumption that a river might flow backwards was regarded as nonsense.'[5] The integrationists were full of admiration for the emancipation and integration movements in western Europe and considered them to be a historical necessity, with the consequence that they took the imminent collapse of hasidism for granted and considered their position in their disputes with tradition to be unquestionably correct. Moreover, both *Jutrzenka* and the early issues of *Izraelita* claimed that the hasidim were already ripe for liberation from superstition, and that they were just waiting for a hand to be extended to them or for any opportunity to renounce their present faith and join the modernizing camp.

This claim was also connected with Peltyn's belief, inherited from *Jutrzenka*, in the significance of religious unity and the consequent need to seek common ground,

---

[4] See e.g. Samuel H. Peltyn, 'Postęp średnich klas społeczeństwa izraelskiego', *Izr.* 1 (1866), 9–10; id., 'Słówko do rodziców izraelskich', *Izr.* 1 (1866), 165. See also Izrael Leon Grosglik, 'Listy młodego ex-chasyda', *Izr.* 4 (1869), 262; L. N—ki, 'Korespondencja: Kutno—w czerwcu', *Izr.* 33 (1868), 189–90.        [5] Nachum Sokołów, 'S. H. Peltyn: Wizerunek literacki', *Izr.* 31 (1896), 417.

or at least to understand the phenomenon of hasidism. Unity of belief in the *Izraelita* camp meant that, once again, hasidism was the focus of interest for the journal.

The increasing impact of *Izraelita*'s criticism of the radical assimilationists sustained interest in the hasidic issue, although, as had been the case with *Jutrzenka*, the importance of the dispute, for integrationists, lay not so much in the dispute itself, but in other goals they hoped to achieve through it. It was anticipated that confrontation between the religious indifferentists and the hasidim would strengthen the position of the moderate wing of the modernizing camp and prove that this wing was the sole heir to the enlightened ideas of the Haskalah. Thus, *Izraelita*'s polemic was directed simultaneously at several issues that were believed to be a threat. Officially, it was aimed at the supporters of hasidism, but the radical assimilationists and the hasidim were depicted as being equally extremist and therefore similar ('extremes meet', as Peltyn wrote). Thus, the integrationists thought they could discredit the assimilationists at the same time, and force them to renounce the radical path of religious indifference. The same was to be achieved in the case of the supposedly neutral mitnagedim, who, if unwilling to form a coalition with extremist groups, would opt for an alliance with the integrationist movement.

However, although they were directly related to *Jutrzenka*'s programme, *Izraelita*'s views were not identical with the line that had been taken by Neufeld's journal. Neufeld's publications had represented little more than a simple expression of his own fascinations and the very specific circumstances of the 'Polish–Jewish fraternity' in the pre-Uprising period, as well as of the associated attempt to redefine the modernizing camp's stand on hasidism. In fact, *Jutrzenka*'s writers—especially Neufeld—believed that the combination of a more open attitude towards the hasidim, the positive example the writers themselves set, and their moderate educational activities would put an end to opposition from hasidic circles. However, Neufeld was not naive enough to view this plan as a cure-all. Peltyn, too, was fully aware of its shortcomings and, in the early years of the existence of *Izraelita* in particular, diligently sought new ways to resolve the 'hasidic issue'. Thus this interest in hasidism, bordering on obsession, was no more than an attempt to work out his own new position on the issue. The sudden termination of *Jutrzenka* precluded any chance of ever learning what the party and its attitudes would have been in the vastly different post-Uprising period. It is quite likely that the optimism of 1861–3 was doomed to failure, in any case. As fate would have it, however, it was their successors whom failure befell.

## PELTYN'S CREDO

Although hasidism remained a vital theme for Peltyn and his associates, coverage of the subject in *Izraelita* was patchy: there were clearly discernible periods of intensified interest and years in which the hasidim were almost absent from the

pages of the periodical. The first period in which the issue was intensively discussed were the years 1868–9. This may have been connected with the growth of
interest in the hasidic issue in German Jewish periodicals (numerous articles in
*Izraelita* were reprints or adaptations); with the appearance in *Izraelita*'s team of
a 'young ex-hasid', Izrael Leon Grosglik (in whose articles the hasidic issue frequently recurred); and certainly with the well-known anti-hasidic declaration of
the tsadik Dov Ber of Leovo (which was frequently referred to in the Jewish 'progressive' press) and his defection to the Enlightenment camp.[6] Comments on Dov
Ber's words published in *Izraelita* make it clear that his declaration had revived the
integrationists' belief in the approaching victory over hasidism. Moreover, the
tsadik's open letter was the only bilingual (Polish and Hebrew) text to be published
in the periodical in its fifty-year existence, which illustrates that the editors were
hoping not only to reach their regular readers (who did not have to be convinced
of the falseness of hasidic principles), but also hasidic circles.[7] In addition to Dov
Ber's letter and numerous commentaries on the matter, *Izraelita* published several
lengthy articles devoted to hasidism within the two-year period 1868–9, including
a satirical essay about its emergence, an account of a visit to the tsadik Hayim
Halberstam of Nowy Sącz (Sanz), a series of 'letters from a young ex-hasid' and
replies to them, one hasidic tale, and, most importantly, an editorial by Peltyn
entitled 'Hasidism, its Essence and its Attitude towards Rabbinism' (in fact Peltyn
also wrote most of the other articles).[8] The editorial is worth closer examination, as
in many respects it is an excellent example of the attitude towards the hasidic
movement in *Izraelita* circles.

Peltyn began by saying that hasidism, contrary to the statements of many of its
opponents, was not a sect and that it had not renounced any of the religious beliefs
common to the followers of Judaism. Nevertheless, it was a 'chronic evil' and a
'weakness' which had taken hold of a large number of Jews in Poland, and it had
become the most serious obstacle to the spread of 'any civilization, to any progress
in the areas of religion or education'. For this reason, the reader was obliged to
learn more about it in order to find some remedial measures against it. The article
was to serve this purpose.

Next, Peltyn considered the essence of religion and the reasons for the development of hasidism. According to him, hasidism was a short cut to religion: instead of
stimulating individual efforts to achieve the highest religious ideals, to approach
God, and to understand the mystery of existence, it provided intermediaries (the

---

[6] Studies of the subject include Horodezky, *Hahasidut vehahasidim*, iii. 124–54; Mahler, 'R.
Khayim Halbershtam', 297–304. On the literary career of the subject, see Assaf, *Derekh hamalkhut*,
458–9 n. 66. For the reactions of the press, see 'Analekten und Monatsbericht'; 'Mikhtav galui'. The
story was reported in *Izraelita* again in 1910; Leon Lichtenbaum, 'Cadyk—heretyk', *Izr.* 45/13 (1910),
7–8, 45/14 (1910), 6–7.

[7] 'List otwarty byłego naczelnika Chassydów r. Beera z Mołdawii', *Izr.* 4 (1869), 86–8.

[8] Samuel H. Peltyn, 'Chassydyzm, jego istota i stosunek do rabinizmu', *Izr.* 3 (1868), 193–4, 201–2,
217–19.

tsadikim) who absolved their supporters of any responsibility or obligation to improve themselves. Thus, it was 'a pursuit of ease, spiritual inertia, a means of seeking a scapegoat who could be blamed for one's own deeds'. However, reflection on the origins of hasidism led Peltyn to believe that the movement was rooted not in fanaticism and superstition, but rather in a noble attempt to reinvigorate Judaism. According to him, the Jewish faith, which had atrophied under its own formalism, was experiencing a crisis in the mid-eighteenth century as the dead hand of religious law had become an unbearable burden for believers, who had lost sight of its transcendental significance. 'A set form began to dominate, according to which religion became a simple set of exercises, rites, and traditions.' Like Heinrich Graetz (whose last volume of the history of the Jews appeared two years later and included a history of hasidism), Peltyn believed that Beshtian hasidism, just like the Haskalah which had emerged at the same time, was an attempt to extract some religious depth from this dead law, and thus was a noble and progressive attempt at religious reform. 'Despising form as a cheap device, [the Besht] delved for the idea pulsating beneath; and, spurning the mechanical execution of accepted conventions, he penetrated their very spirit, caring little for the external garb in which the spirit was clad.' Unfortunately, for want of rational tools, the Besht and his supporters had resorted to the realm of emotions, and this had pushed them towards mysticism, kabbalah, and the Zohar—well-known poisons of the Jewish soul. It was therefore not surprising that their laudable objectives had not been attained but had given rise instead to a cult focused on tsadikim, with many pernicious consequences.

Peltyn's short description of the institution of the tsadik began with a history of the Besht that was in fact an inaccurate précis of the work of Isaac Marcus Jost, whom Peltyn quoted without naming his source.[9] Further details, on sabbath feasts, on the foundations of the hasidic faith, and on the miraculous properties of the clothes of the tsadik, also derived from Jost's monograph. All this constituted a basis for reflection on the source of the power of the tsadikim and their influence on a wide cross-section of unwavering believers. Peltyn once again rejected maskilic criticisms of hasidism and—in contrast to Jost—acknowledged the tsadikim's genuine ability to satisfy the needs of the common people, and admitted that there was a mysterious quality to them. Moreover, apart from a few frauds, most tsadikim were people who were deeply and truly convinced of their own mission, 'endowed with superior powers of imagination, and—at the same time—energized by the adoration surrounding them, so that in the end they do become convinced of their divine powers, believing that their inspiration comes directly from God, believing in their personal relationship with Him, and hence also in the possibility of working wonders through their prayers'.

The final paragraphs of this lengthy study were intended to provide an antidote to the spread of hasidism. Peltyn believed the movement's power lay mainly in its

---

[9] See Jost, *Geschichte der Israeliten*, ix. 45–9. Numerous errors in quoting facts from Jost's book (e.g. 1740 as the date of the Besht's birth) indicate that Peltyn did not understand parts of the study.

vitality and in its ability to relate to genuine religious sentiment. In contrast to the cold rationalism of the indifferentists (i.e. the radical assimilationists) on the one hand and the equally spiritually empty adherence to set forms of the mitnagedim on the other, hasidism must have been attractive because it provided a genuine religious experience. The only way to bring it to an end would have been through a revival of ideals and fervent religious feelings 'just like the prophets used to live it, just like the Talmud teaches' among modernizing Jews. Only then could the integrationist camp be seen as an attractive alternative to hasidism; the hasidim would then renounce their world of superstitions and, inspired by a positive example, develop 'what is beautiful and useful in it'. These last words prompted Peltyn to list a long inventory of hasidim's virtues:

Sincere honesty, readiness to act when it comes to helping others, sensitivity to all that is good and elevated and, above all, a strong religious foundation; these are the qualities most often encountered in the hasidim. Hence, this rare willingness to make sacrifices for their own, this sincere fellowship, this laudable selflessness in their dealings with others . . . Finally, the reforming spirit that gave rise to hasidism, although it has gone astray, is still deeply rooted in it, so that it only needs a powerful guiding hand to guide this tendency onto a more enlightened path.

Of course, the hand was to be that of the Jewish modernizing camp.

In many places Peltyn's article was unoriginal and unconvincing. Those parts devoted to the Besht's history and the origins of hasidism show that he did not have the faintest idea about the history of the movement (though Peltyn introduced here the new idea of the Besht as an honest but naive reformer, and not a fraudulent deceiver), and the account of their customs, which was quoted from Jost, illustrates that he knew little about the beliefs and practices of his hasidic contemporaries. Moreover, unlike Neufeld's article, Peltyn's work did not reflect any genuine fascination with the subject. Rather, he based his information on the readily available monograph by Jost, although it was also rather superficial and repetitive (especially in regard to Joseph Perl, as well as Peter Beer). The misgivings with which he acknowledged the virtues of hasidism ('and why should we attempt to hide them') indicated that he felt ill at ease in his role as the defender of the movement. Yet the article was written and published, and its place in the journal proves how important it was to *Izraelita*'s agenda. It seems that at the root of this paradox lay the fact that Peltyn agreed with the thesis inherited from *Jutrzenka* concerning the crucial significance of solving the hasidic issue so that the integrationist movement could grow in the Kingdom of Poland. However, he was unable to form a clear opinion on this issue; or perhaps he simply had no personal opinion on the subject. The article—like many others from the 1860s—was based on the enthusiastic conviction, stemming from the *Jutrzenka* period, that a good example, patience, and gentle education must, in the end, bring down the walls of hasidism and lead to the victory of the 'righteous cause'. However, these naively optimistic views seem not to have satisfied Peltyn, and he sought his own answers to the issue of hasidism, which, in the final analysis, were not as positive. It may be for this reason that the ideas inherited from Neufeld eroded so quickly and so visibly over the following years.

## THE WAY TO RECOGNITION

Although Peltyn was certainly not an authority on hasidism, he had a methodical approach to the issue. Both the above-mentioned article and a number of other texts illustrate that he tried to understand the essence of the movement so as to answer the question 'How are the Jewish people to be freed from hasidic power?' In contrast to Hilary Nussbaum, for example (who will be discussed later), Peltyn regarded hasidism as a kind of historical necessity, born of the political and social situation of Poland in the eighteenth century. He perceived that the source of hasidism lay in the drive for reform and religious fervour, and he also acknowledged (albeit unwillingly) that there was a certain charm in the mysteriousness of kabbalah and an attractiveness in the brotherly unity that hasidim offered.[10] According to him, all of this increased the number of supporters of hasidism. Its attractiveness also derived from the fact that the movement was a reaction against enervating formalism and was an attempt to make the world a more spiritual place. It was a search for a mystical alternative to cold scientism on the one hand and outmoded religious laws on the other. According to Peltyn, in its essence it was not only a response to the erroneous ways of traditional Judaism, which the mitnagedim purportedly embodied, but also an anti-rational revolt against Mendelssohn's enlightened reforms. The hasidic faith gave a deeply religious sense to the life of ordinary people and their everyday activities, and thus it satisfied their natural need for a religious experience in a way that was accessible to any Jewish person. Because of it, each hasid felt as if he were 'a free member of the universe', while the mitnaged, bound by religious law, was 'an incapacitated slave of regulations'.[11] It may be assumed that *Izraelita*'s contributors praised the hasidic revolution as an attempt to revive religious ideals because they saw its objectives as analogous to the aims of their own group—namely, to loosen the strictures of the religious code and make it more spiritual in character. In this sense, they perceived hasidism as degenerate, and a bastardized precursor of their own movement. This surprising affinity, and the emphasis placed on the originally noble, reforming nature of hasidism, were important for the integrationists, as their task was to prove that, despite the fanatical and backward character of the movement, the powers of attraction it had for Jews were genuine, positive, and progressive by nature. This in turn gave rise to the hope that, with the use of an appropriate strategy to convince people of the failure of hasidic reform, it would be possible to attract the Jewish masses to the integrationist camp—the one group that could authentically carry out the programme of reform.

[10] See Samuel H. Peltyn, 'Krańcowe kierunki religijne w judaizmie', *Izr.* 1 (1866), 27.
[11] 'Beszt i jego następcy: Szkic biograficzno-humorystyczny', *Izr.* 4 (1869), 15.

Analogies between the first hasidim and the integrationists in *Jutrzenka* and *Izraelita* circles were, according to the latter, evident in another way. Just as hasidism was a response to the enervating formalism of traditional Judaism, which was, in fact, anti-religious, the integrationist movement was a response to the radical assimilationists' attempt to marginalize religious issues in the world of non-traditional Jews. Once again, the hasidim appeared to be closer to the moderate camp than were those assimilationists who were renouncing their Jewish identity.

*Izraelita* published a relatively large number of historical texts, with a view to enabling its readers to learn more about the hasidic movement and understand it better. A lengthy article on the origins of the movement, entirely based on *History of the Jews* by Heinrich Graetz, was accompanied by Peltyn's words: 'Bearing in mind that pathological historical phenomena develop and progress normally, and are deserving at times of reflection, we believe that our readers will not complain when we present them here with a more or less comprehensive history of this association.'[12] Almost all the other historical essays were devoted to the origins of hasidism, with the more extensive texts being reprints or adaptations of German Jewish (and later Russian Jewish) publications on the subject.[13] One of the most typical was an essay about the Gaon of Vilna and his opposition to the hasidim, in which his anti-hasidic stance was construed as support for the Haskalah and secular education.[14] A satirical history of the Besht, borrowed by Peltyn from the Viennese *Jahrbuch für Israeliten* (1867),[15] and a history of hasidism (again based on the work of Graetz), which were quoted in an account of a visit to the tsadik of Sadagóra,[16] were equally tendentious. All the articles revealed a limited knowledge of hasidism, and were full of stereotypical accusations and false information based on antiquated anti-hasidic literature, including Joseph Perl's views.[17] The medioc-

---

[12] 'Głośni a nieznani: Szkic historyczny', *Izr.* 12 (1877), 101.

[13] In addition to those mentioned above, see also Samuel H. Peltyn, 'Dzieje chasydyzmu: Jego nastanie, rozwój i utwierdzenie się', *Izr.* 25 (1890), 133–4, 145–6, 156–7, 164–5, 175–6, 185–6, 195–6, 204–5, 214–15, 235–6; id, 'Jak się u nas rozwijała schizma', *Izr.* 25 (1890), 442, 454–5, 466–7, 476–7, 489–90, 499–500. Both texts were based on Dubnow's study. See also Henryk Lichtenbaum, 'Chasydzi i rebowie', *Izr.* 40 (1905), 52–3, 62–3, 74–6, 86–8, 99–100, 110–11, which was a summary of Schechter, *Die Chassidim*.

[14] Zygmunt J. Justman, 'Rabbi Eljasz z Wilna, Gaon, i jego walka z chasydyzmem', *Izr.* 5 (1870), 370–2, 380–1. The legend of Elijah, Gaon of Vilna, as a precursor of the Haskalah reappeared in other articles, e.g. L., 'Korespondencja', *Izr.* 1 (1866), 310; Nachum Sokołów, 'Z dziejów zasłużonych', *Izr.* 31 (1897), 406. For more on the legend of the Gaon of Vilna as a pioneer of Haskalah, see Etkes, *Yaḥid bedoro*, 44–83; in English, see id., 'The Gaon of Vilna and the Haskalah Movement'; see also Nadler, *Faith of the Mithnagdim*, 127–50.

[15] 'Beszt i jego następcy: Szkic biograficzno–humorystyczny', *Izr.* 3 (1868), 414–16; 4 (1869), 1–3, 15–16, 30–2, 38–40. The article draws heavily on Szantó, 'Der Bescht und seine Nachfolger'.

[16] 'W stolicy cadyka (z niemieckiego)', *Izr.* 12 (1877), 278–80, 286–8, 294–6. This is a Polish abridged version of Hilberg, 'Der Rabbi von Sadagóra'.

[17] For example, accusations of economic exploitation of the hasidim by their tsadikim, of drunkenness, and of neglect of families. See e.g. Jakub Graff, 'Słówko z okoliczności listu otwartego b. przywódcy chassydów R. Beera Friedman', *Izr.* 4 (1869), 132; A. Trauenfels, 'Zarys stronnictw w

rity of the historical articles written by both Peltyn himself and by his associates indicates that interest in and knowledge of hasidism did not necessarily go hand in hand. A focus on the origins of hasidism (which is still of major interest to researchers) was understandable, because Peltyn could rightly assume that such an understanding would be synonymous with understanding the very essence of the movement. But his lack of reflection on his hasidic contemporaries proves that, unlike Neufeld, Peltyn was not genuinely interested in them, but that he perceived the whole issue in a purely utilitarian light as a problem that needed a solution, and pursued this solution accordingly, and not necessarily competently. Knowledge of hasidism and the hasidim interested him only as a means to winning a final victory over them. Thus, it is less than surprising that his attempt to acquire such a limited knowledge resulted in profound ignorance of the basic facts of the history of the hasidim and a lack of familiarity with contemporary hasidism; and thus in an inability to develop methods to deal with them that were constructive and realistic, and that would ensure ultimate success.

Their lack of knowledge of hasidism did not prevent the contributors to *Izraelita* from unanalytically expressing their beliefs, whether favourable or (considerably more frequently) critical. The views expressed by the journal in its early years did not differ very much from those published somewhat earlier in *Jutrzenka*. The only change was that they gained fuller expression owing to the sheer abundance of *Izraelita*'s output. Among the qualities that were the most vigorously and most frequently praised were hasidic unity and dedication, their remarkable involvement in all spheres of life, their enthusiasm, their unwavering belief in their ideals, their educational activity (religious, naturally), 'an elemental tendency to improve', 'a reforming zeal', and, above all, a rich spiritual life. The last was particularly important whenever hasidism was compared with the assimilation movement. In Peltyn's descriptions the religious indifferentists from the modernizing camp were living corpses, devoid of feeling, whose only occupation was counting money, and whose attitude to the surrounding world was full of cynicism. 'Gold is the only idol they worship.' In contrast to them, the spiritual hasidim were portrayed as seekers after the meaning of life. Although they had gone astray in their search, they were considerably worthier of respect than the indifferentists, who had freely rejected this quest. Hasidism brought true solace to the difficult lives of its supporters. On a number of occasions *Izraelita*'s writers praised the devotion with which the hasidim served their 'leaders' and helped one another, and praised them for the fervour of their prayers, and even for their respect for what was of value in tradition. The hasidim were also 'an example of the faithfulness and devotion that is laudable in hasidim, and worthy of being followed—for the benefit of other, and better, causes'.[18]

dzisiejszym judaizmie', *Izr.* 5 (1870), 176–7; H. N[eumanowicz], 'Przyczynki do Listów ex-chasyda', *Izr.* 4 (1869), 309; Pelai, 'Listy rabina z prowincji', *Izr.* 9 (1874), 205.

[18] Samuel H. Peltyn, 'Pogadanki', *Izr.* 8 (1873), 137.

With regard to the negative features of hasidism pinpointed by *Izraelita*, prominence was most often given to stories of exploitation of naive Jews by the tsadikim. This theme had thousands of versions and cropped up in almost every mention of the hasidim and was invariably present in accounts from the provinces. The mythology that grew up around these economic relationships (often involving exploitation) was based on the assumption that the tsadikim were the sole instigators of these dealings and that the hasidim were good, but naive and treacherously deceived by their leaders. The theme of *pidyon* (payments for the redemption of souls), and accusations—against the tsadikim of profiting financially from the faith of their supporters, and against the hasidim for their lack of productivity—were among the oldest of the anti-hasidic charges, yet they were the most prominent in *Izraelita*. Thus, the tsadikim were 'demi-gods', 'the almighty', 'God's governors on earth', 'false prophets', 'fraudulent governors'. In addition, 'the worshipper of the Besht is in the fullest sense of the word the slave of his *rebbe*, who—like Moloch in ancient times—swallows up the property, minds and souls of his worshippers'.[19] The witch-hunt against the tsadikim was so intense that in time the terms 'hasidism' and 'hasid' were increasingly frequently replaced by expressions such as 'the cult of the tsadikim', 'tsadikism', and 'worshippers of tsadikim', which had come to represent all that was negative in the hasidic movement. In the following years Peltyn took to writing about 'hasidism and the resulting tsadikism'.[20] *Izraelita* centred its criticism on some tsadikim specifically, and took every opportunity to discredit them. In 1874 Elijah Guttmacher of Grodzisk Wielkopolski, who was otherwise known for his modesty and selflessness, became the constant target of such attacks.[21] Peltyn did not even give credence to letters defending Guttmacher and extolling his virtues. More than likely, this was attributable to the fact that, in criticizing Guttmacher, he was influenced by German Jewish journals, for which a tsadik in the German empire was a deplorable innovation. At the same time, however, *Izraelita* praised some Polish tsadikim—especially Abraham Landau of Ciechanów—as virtuous scholars and selfless sages; even the fact that these men were hasidic leaders did not discourage such eulogies.[22] In the 1870s the journal (probably influenced by Graetz) introduced a distinction between the Besht—a naive

---

[19] 'Beszt i jego następcy: Szkic biograficzno-humorystyczny', *Izr.* 4 (1869), 15. This motif had been popular since the turn of the 18th century, having first been introduced into Polish maskilic writing by Jacques Calmanson (see Chapter 1).

[20] Samuel H. Peltyn, 'Dzieje chasydyzmu: Jego nastanie, rozwój i utwierdzenie się', *Izr.* 25 (1890), 133.

[21] *Izraelita*'s attitude towards Guttmacher was best expressed in Samuel H. Peltyn, 'Kosmopolityzm przesądu', *Izr.* 9 (1874), 98; id., 'Pogadanki', *Izr.* 9 (1874), 93, 107, 143–4, 158–9. For more on Guttmacher, see Bromberg, *Eliyahu gutmakher*.

[22] See e.g. Samuel H. Peltyn, 'Pogadanki', *Izr.* 7 (1872), 382; id., 'Pogadanki', *Izr.* 8 (1873), 198; 'Wspomnienie pośmiertne', *Izr.* 10 (1875), 64. See also notes on other hasidic leaders, e.g. Shaya Mushkat of Praga (*Izr.* 3 (1868), 76); Isaac of Warka (*Izr.* 3 (1868), 92); David of Mszczonów (Amshinov) (*Izr.* 9 (1877), 356); Judah Aryeh Leib Alter of Góra Kalwaria (Ger) (*Izr.* 40 (1905), 21).

reformer—and his successors, who corrupted their master's noble teaching (Neufeld and the maskilim regarded him merely as a fraud), and the few honest and great tsadikim and their fraudulent imitators from the provinces.

Criticisms of the institution of the tsadik particularly emphasized the subject of the impoverishment of hasidic families (from whom the tsadikim extracted every last penny as *pidyon*), and the negative influence of hasidism on the financial stability of these families, which were supported by the women while their shiftless husbands spent long days in *shtiblekh* or in the baths. It was also noted that it was damaging for fathers and husbands to spend most holidays away from their families, in the courts of their tsadikim. These two themes—lack of productivity and the lack of responsibility for one's family—were seen as being closely connected. *Izraelita*'s correspondent from Łódź sarcastically wrote:

It is understandable that a man who has so many connections in heaven and who is constantly surrounded by angels cannot care for such mundane matters as housekeeping, raising children, attending to trades or crafts; all this he leaves to his wife. She must think of everything, working day and night without a word of complaint, and if her husband returns home late at night, the poor woman is certain that he was in *beit midrash*, where he was studying God's law. If the head of the family is absent from home on the major religious festivals, his wife endures her loneliness with resignation and kisses her children with tears in her eyes.[23]

The hasidim were also reproached for drunkenness and tobacco abuse, for fanaticism of course, and for obscurantism, a lack of hygiene, indulging in mysticism (that is, in 'sick fantasy'), and 'a blinding of reason'. Often they were accused of hypocrisy, false piety, sloth, and of negatively influencing the mitnagedim and even undecided modernizing Jews. Less frequently they were accused of obstructing effective help for the poorer social classes and of indulging in 'merriment to the point of cynicism'. Finally, the most serious charge according to the 'progressive' Jews, was that of a hostile attitude towards enlightenment.

As was the case with *Jutrzenka*, Peltyn and his associates saw enlightenment as an antidote to the excessive influence of the hasidic movement, and one that would lead to its ultimate dissolution. Numerous contributors to *Izraelita* thus called for elementary schools to be established, in which hasidic children would be compulsorily taught secular subjects. Education would also include women, who, according to *Izraelita*, had thus far remained at home in hasidic households without any education whatsoever. A prerequisite for the effectiveness of the hasidic enlightenment process was the genuine involvement of modernizing circles and their delicate handling of the hasidim so as not to turn them against the whole idea of education. Like Neufeld, Peltyn acknowledged that the reprehensible behaviour, commonplace breaking of religious commandments, and disregard for religion displayed by many integrationists were the main reasons their programme lacked credibility

---

[23] Jakub Graff, 'Słówko z okoliczności listu otwartego b. przywódcy chassydów R. Beera Friedman', *Izr.* 4 (1869), 132.

among the hasidim. If they were to remedy this, their fight with hasidism would need to start with reform in their own camp and a reversal of the weakened state of religious principles in Jewish modernizing society. Peltyn did not even hint at how this could be done. His proposals were phrased broadly enough to imply that *Izraelita*'s circles had no programme of activities connected with the supporters of hasidism. Despite their best efforts, they did not succeed in going beyond *Jutrzenka*'s generalizations, thus manifesting their inherent inability to devise any concrete plan. *Izraelita*'s writers viewed the hasidim through the prism of typically maskilic prejudices, which could not be offset by the optimism inherited from *Jutrzenka*. Their lack of familiarity with the true nature of hasidism prevented them from seeing beyond their stereotypical views or departing from convention in their opinions. The whole issue was further complicated by the fact that the hasidic theme had become entangled in the debate between the moderate integrationists and the radical assimilationists, which gave rise to new myths and misunderstandings, and contributed substantially to blackening the image of hasidism. In such a situation it was impossible to develop a new programme.

## IZRAEL LEON GROSGLIK: 'LETTERS FROM A YOUNG EX-HASID'

Of all *Izraelita*'s plans to enlighten the hasidim, only one turned out to be truly original. It was proposed by Izrael Leon (Leib) Grosglik (1851–1904),[24] who came from a family of Warsaw hasidim. Through his own efforts, he learnt the Polish language and at the beginning of 1869 he began to write for *Izraelita*, where he soon became famous for his brilliant and significant articles. From 1870 to 1875, under the patronage of Herman Klüger, he regularly preached sermons in the 'progressive' synagogue in Nalewki Street (which had been known as the 'Polish' synagogue). From the beginning of 1873 he worked in the office of the Jewish community board, first as secretary in the *beit din* (rabbinical court), and later, until his death, as secretary of the board. He wrote at the same time for Polish journals and continued to write for *Izraelita*, which in later years (1902–4) he edited. He also published a series of notable texts in this journal, including a project for vocational evening courses at religious schools, a project for *ḥeder* reform, and a programme for a Jewish religious school.[25] Grosglik was also involved in extensive social work, and his participation in the aid committee for starving Jews in 'Babylonia and

---

[24] On Grosglik, see Shatzky, *Geshikhte fun Yidn in Varshe*, iii, index; 'Odgłosy: Jubileusz sekretarza gminy', *Izr.* 34 (1899), 467; 'B.p. Izrael Leon Grosglik', *Izr.* 39 (1904), 573–5.

[25] e.g. Izrael Leon Grosglik, 'Zachowawcza młodzież izraelska wobec kwestii kształcenia Żydów', *Izr.* 10 (1875), 263–5; id., 'Chedery i melamedy (Do zachowawczej braci)', *Izr.* 13 (1878), 277–9, 285–7, 293–5 (also as a separate booklet); id., 'Szkoła religijna', *Izr.* 13 (1878), 393–5, 401–3; id., 'Młodzież żydowska wobec sprawy szkół rzemieślniczych', *Izr.* 14 (1879), 299–301; id., 'Otwarcie szkoły rzemiosł przy szkołach Talmud-Tora', *Izr.* 14 (1879), 356.

Persia', which was organized by hasidim and mitnagedim alike, shows that, despite his defection to the integration movement, he remained on good terms with Orthodox Jews in Warsaw.[26] His colleagues from the office of the Jewish community board also emphasized his tolerance, respect for opposing views, and 'a deep attachment to all the constituent parts of the community'.[27] Genuine respect for the camp which he had abandoned continued to be the most characteristic feature of his writing in *Izraelita*, and this distinguished him from numerous of the weekly's other writers and activists from the integrationist camp.

Grosglik's first individual publication in *Izraelita* late in 1869 caused a sensation. This was a series of articles entitled 'Letters from a Young Ex-Hasid'.[28] Both the originality of his ideas and the authenticity of the narrative elicited strong reactions, debate, and even attempts in Jewish circles to imitate Grosglik's essay.[29] With only a few digressions, the text was wholly devoted to the issue of enlightening the hasidim.

Grosglik began by stating that the education of the hasidim presented considerably more difficulty than the education of the unenlightened strata in other societies. Unlike the members of other denominations, the hasidim were relatively well educated and intellectually advanced (even if narrowly so and in the wrong direction), and their attitude to secular education was extremely negative. The traditional teaching methods used in elementary schools were therefore ineffective, as hasidic parents would refuse to send their children to these institutions. There was a need to concentrate this educational effort not on children but on young people, because, despite the pressure exerted by their elders, they recognized the need for secular learning but lacked the opportunities to avail themselves of it. Both their traditional hasidic education and their social interactions completely isolated the young hasidim from secular learning and from their modernizing co-believers. In order to overcome this impasse, Grosglik believed that young people from the Enlightenment camp should be encouraged to meet their hasidic peers, because it was the 'progressives' who avoided the hasidim and not the other way round. 'Young hearts, they will find it easy to understand each other!' It was also felt that the young integrationists should devote some time to teaching their hasidic friends. What was important, however, was not education of the hasidim at any cost, but that their education should be practical. The intention was not to turn them from their religious values, but to have them retain the positive aspects of their faith and

[26] See Shatzky, *Geshikhte fun Yidn in Varshe*, iii. 168. See also the appeal by Moses Montefiore, 'Głód w Persji i Babilonii', *Izr.* 12/6 (1877), suppl.

[27] 'Odgłosy: Jubileusz sekretarza gminy', *Izr.* 35 (1899), 490.

[28] Izrael Leon Grosglik, 'Listy młodego ex-chasyda', *Izr.* 4 (1869), 229–30, 238–40, 255–6, 261–3, 303–5, 349–51 (also as a separate booklet).

[29] Of the polemics, see H. N[eumanowicz], 'Przyczynki do Listów ex-chasyda', *Izr.* 4 (1869), 309–11, 327–8; for the imitations, see N., 'Listy młodego nawróconego zacofańca', *Izr.* 11 (1876), 227–8; Henryk P., 'Córki ex-chasyda (opowiadania b. studenta galicyjskiego)', *Izr.* 11 (1876), 360–1, 368–9, 377–8. See also Shatzky, *Geshikhte fun Yidn in Varshe*, iii. 303.

knowledge, for example, their knowledge of the Talmud. Grosglik pointed to Germany as a negative example. There, he asserted, an uncontrolled rush for education had resulted in an epidemic of non-belief and indifferentism, while knowledge of the Scriptures, including the Talmud, had totally died out. According to Grosglik, the situation in the Kingdom of Poland could potentially be even worse. The hasidim would finally begin to study and then, 'having gained a taste of secular knowledge and encounters with the external world, they would be ready not only to completely renounce and discontinue their studies, but also to become even greater adversaries, and a change such as that would be the scourge of Judaism, and could turn out to be highly detrimental to society and learning'.[30] Grosglik therefore proposed that the hasidim should not be discouraged from their religious studies, which were actually very valuable ('For us, the Talmud is still, let me put it this way, live folk poetry, while in other places it has already become like a dried-up archaeological site'), and that secular education should simply complement those studies. 'Human life requires constant progress, but not necessarily a complete renunciation of the past. Only by combining one with the other can your intentions come to fruition.' Thus Grosglik believed that education should not be used to transform the hasidim into ordinary modernized Jews, but that it should make enlightened people of them, while preserving elements of their hasidic identity. Ideally, this could be achieved through talmudic studies complemented by secular learning in those areas in which it was necessary to an understanding of the Talmud. However, as there were no teachers capable of teaching it, it would be necessary to depend on friendly relations being maintained between young hasidim and integrationists and, whenever possible, to avoid behaviour insulting to Orthodox society; it would also be necessary to avoid, under any circumstances, becoming involved in religious disputes, because the young integrationists were ill prepared for them and could come to question the value of integration and progress.

The personal experiences to which Grosglik alluded so clearly in the title and which he emphasized a number of times in his argument formed the starting point of the text. His complaints about the tyranny of Orthodox parents and the avoidance of the hasidim by young integrationists rang particularly true. Yet it is difficult to avoid the conclusion that the extracts in which he described hasidic society and expressed his belief that the reign of hasidism was coming to an end, that there had been numerous defections, and that the movement was beginning to disintegrate, bore relatively little resemblance to the facts (as indicated by the polemicists), but that the image he presented of the declining hasidic movement stemmed rather from his own strong convictions and his urge to present himself as one example who would soon be followed by countless other hasidim (and was thus an attempt to justify his own choice). Thus, the hasidic world depicted by Grosglik

---

[30] Grosglik predicted a shift among young people of hasidic origin to socialist ideologies. This shift, which very much affected young people of hasidic origin, actually took place a quarter of a century after Grosglik's work was published. See Shatzky, *Geshikhte fun Yidn in Varshe*, iii. 367–71.

was an idealized world, and the 'rational hasidim' inhabiting it, who studied Polish grammar or read the maskilic Hebrew novels of Abraham Mapu and Isaac Erter at night instead of meeting with the tsadik, were undoubtedly the product of wishful thinking. However, what is worth noting is not whether the picture he painted was true or plausible, but that an 18-year-old boy who had recently left the hasidic camp and joined the ranks of the 'enlightened class' was brave enough to speak out in defence of the hasidic movement, and that it was a particularly daring defence and, in many respects, an original one.

The most interesting, and undoubtedly innovative, point of Grosglik's programme was the suggestion that the hasidim be 'civilized' without destroying completely their hasidic identity. Although Grosglik had formally broken with his hasidic past, his contacts with and very evident sympathies for the hasidim proved that he took his proposal very personally and tried to implement it in his own life. He was well disposed towards his 'friends of old in form, friends of today in feeling', and that achieved more than all the declarations that had been made by modernizing Jews in the Kingdom of Poland up until that time. Even the maskilim and their successors from the integrationist camp, such as Tugendhold or Neufeld, who were the most well disposed towards the hasidim assumed that the one solution to the hasidic issue was for the movement simply to disappear. Supporters of Enlightenment ideology believed that, in accordance with the laws of nature, hasidism would have to disintegrate and that this would take place because of the enlightenment of its supporters. Yet Grosglik not only questioned the historical necessity of such a solution, but even claimed that the unconditional capitulation of the hasidim would not be beneficial, as Jewish society would lose a number of the values that had long since been discarded by the modernizing Jews and were preserved only by the hasidim: he agreed with those mitnagedim who saw in hasidism an antidote to the plague of indifferentism and radical assimilation, which he regarded as being considerably more threatening to Judaism than hasidism.

Over the following years Grosglik developed his theses in numerous articles printed in *Izraelita*, and particularly in a series of essays entitled 'Talks' ('Pogadanki'), which he published during the first half of 1871. However, in contrast to many of his other projects, his ideas concerning hasidism never received popular acclaim and were never taken up by the editors or other writers. Even though they were given a more digestible form for the modernizing circles or interspersed with anti-hasidic clichés, they were not workable. Grosglik withdrew from editing and active co-operation with the journal in the second half of 1871, and although he sporadically wrote shorter articles, he only really returned to the journal in 1878. His views were thus more or less absent from *Izraelita* for several years. It seems not only that integrationist circles were unable to devise their own new programme for dealing with hasidism, adjusted to suit the changing times, but also that they were unable to accept Grosglik's innovative ideas—perhaps because of their originality.

## THE GREAT DISILLUSIONMENT

With the publication of 'Letters from a Young Ex-Hasid' and with the interest in the hasidic issue peaking around 1869, *Izraelita* increasingly rarely published long editorials devoted to hasidism. By 1870 mentions of the movement had been reduced virtually to short notes, reports from the provinces, or extracts from 'Talks', and these were edited in this period by Peltyn and sporadically by Grosglik. These contributions were quite varied, and even included letters praising the hasidim as enlightened people and admirers of Adam Mickiewicz's Polish Romantic poetry. However, with time the majority of the articles emphasized the negative aspects of hasidism (*pidyon*, pilgrimages to tsadikim, fanaticism) and scandals in which the tsadikim were implicated; for example, the court case and banishment from Chrzanów of David Halberstam, the local tsadik; the dispute between the tsadik Jacob David of Mszczonów (Amshinov) and God; the arrest of the tsadik Judah Pesah of Lipsko near Radom; and the illegal annulment of the marriage of a rich hasid from Płońsk.[31] In discussion of Grosglik's optimistic views, provincial correspondents emphasized the differences between the reforming nature of the Warsaw hasidim and the fanatical, ignorant face of hasidism in the provinces. They accused Grosglik of being out of touch with conditions outside Warsaw (which was true not only in Grosglik's case, but also in the case of the whole *Izraelita* team).[32] Increasingly, accounts came from provincial 'progressives' frustrated with the growing dominance of the hasidim and the removal of the 'right-thinking' from positions of authority in provincial communities. With time, suggestions that the issue of hasidic influences be resolved by involving the police re-emerged, and approval was voiced for the authorities' actions against *heder*s and *shtiblekh*.[33] Thus, the method of subtle means and persuasion, which had been advocated by *Jutrzenka* and Neufeld, completely vanished from *Izraelita*'s programme.

The 1870s seem to have seen Peltyn and his associates grow increasingly disillusioned about the possibility of enlightening the hasidim. Faith in the healing power of unity among all Jews and in the approaching victory of the integrationist camp over hasidism (an idea that had been inherited from *Jutrzenka*) turned out to be unfounded. Leaders of this camp, including Peltyn, were faced with the question of the reasons for the failure of their vision. In an impassioned appeal, directed rhetorically to 'our fellow hasidim', Peltyn accused them of having abandoned true Judaism for a cult led by debauched tsadikim which was inconsistent with halakhah. He also accused them of idolatry, blasphemy and paganism, madness and fanaticism, shiftlessness and naivety, and, most importantly, of exposing all

---

[31] On David Halberstam of Chrzanów, see A. W—ski, 'Korespondencja', *Izr.* 7 (1872), 330–1; on Jacob David of Mszczonów (Amshinov), see Samuel H. Peltyn, 'Pogadanki', *Izr.* 7 (1872), 381–2; on Judah Pesah of Lipsko, see Izrael Leon Grosglik, 'Pogadanki', *Izr.* 8 (1873), 21; for a report from Płońsk, see Samuel H. Peltyn, 'Temat do powieści. Z życia', *Izr.* 18 (1883), 210–12, 218–20.

[32] See H. N[eumanowicz], 'Przyczynki do Listów ex-chasyda', *Izr.* 4 (1869), 309–11, 327–8.

[33] e.g. Samuel H. Peltyn, 'Pogadanki', *Izr.* 11 (1876), 212; 'Kronika krajowa', *Izr.* 11 (1876), 222.

the adherents of Judaism to 'derision, disdain and disgust among enlightened nations'.[34] He stated that modernizing co-believers felt ashamed of the hasidim and that, for this reason, they should disappear so that Christian compatriots would no longer identify Judaism and its adherents with the gaberdine-clad hasidim and would be able to begin to view them as enlightened people deserving of equal rights and social esteem. 'A sense of shame prevents us from approaching them, as if we were ashamed in our own presence, and all the more so in the presence of Christians, in case they put us on a par with the gaberdine-clad rabble and treat us in a like manner.'[35] Once again, rhetoric about unity came up against a different reality and the fact that the desire of the 'progressives' to spread enlightenment was not necessarily for the good of the hasidim (as they frequently claimed), but for the improvement of their own social standing.[36]

Peltyn levelled even more serious accusations against the tsadikim, whom he perceived to be lacking in any merit whatsoever and who 'make of their piety, of their alleged miracle-working, in the words of our elders, *kardun lahtov bo* [an axe to chop with]—a craft, a profitable occupation that earns them a fortune, a fortune gathered from the last pennies of poor fathers and mothers'.[37] He explained with false concern that 'sometimes a bitter word of irony escapes our lips concerning your mistakes; but even this irony only expresses our deeply felt sympathy for you and our wish to see you enlightened, ennobled, happy'. The sympathetic sentiments had a singularly false ring, interspersed as they were with vehement accusations, insults, and expressions of shame with regard to his 'hasidic co-believers'. Peltyn's text was a prime example of those mistakes in the treatment of the hasidim against which Grosglik had so strongly warned: addressing the hasidim in an insulting manner, engaging them in religious polemics (and thereby displaying his own ignorance), and alienating himself from them by claiming that they brought shame to their modernizing co-believers. Peltyn could be certain that his appeal would not reach the hasidim. In reality, it was not even addressed to them, even if only because the author was aware that the hasidim, including those who knew Polish, did not read his journal. (Five years earlier, when he wanted a letter from Dov Ber of Leovo to reach hasidic readers, he printed it in Hebrew.) As usual, his 'civilized' compatriots, Jews and Christians alike, were his target audience. The emotive form of the appeal to 'fellow hasidim' simply expressed the feelings of shame, frustration, and intellectual helplessness which at that time had taken possession of the leaders of the modernizing camp with regard to the issue of hasidism. Peltyn was unable to present new ideological solutions to replace

---

[34] Samuel H. Peltyn, 'Do naszych braci chasydów', *Izr.* 9 (1874), 213–15.

[35] M., 'Nasz stosunek do braci zachowawczej, jakim jest i jakim być powinien', *Izr.* 21 (1887), 81 (the letter is critical of such attitudes).

[36] Shame as one of the reasons for the attitude of the 'progressive' Jews towards orthodoxy has correctly been pointed out by Guesnet, *Polnische Juden im 19. Jahrhundert*, 330–1.

[37] Peltyn, 'Do naszych braci chasydów', *Izr.* 9 (1874), 214.

*Jutrzenka*'s rejected and unrealistic ideas. Thus, he returned to the old repertoire of anti-hasidic polemics. According to him, the hasidim should simply disappear, but he knew neither how nor when that would occur.

Peltyn's anti-hasidic writings were further supported by similarly hostile contributions from the provinces. However, disillusionment and frustration culminated in an article by Adolf Jakub Cohn (d. 1906), a lawyer and man of letters, a reasonably capable writer, a regular contributor to *Izraelita*, and its editor from 1904 to 1906. Cohn wrote in 1876 that the hasidim were an irretrievably lost cause in relation to progress, and that there was no way that they could be transformed into civilized and socially useful people. While one could hope to enlighten the Orthodox non-hasidim, who might well become worthy members of Jewish society in the future, there was no such hope where the hasidim were concerned. Even if some hasidim were to defect to the modernizing camp (and there would not be many), they would do more harm than good there because their souls were completely and eternally tainted with their hasidic past:

And even among these dark masses sometimes, albeit rarely, there are those individuals who are endowed by nature with greater abilities, who, by their willpower, rise to the surface and occasionally gain some position and renown in the world. But these individuals, and those at the same level, still bear the stigma of their origins, delight in extremes, go from one polarity to another and exist not for Judaism at all. It is not so bad when they simply do not exist for Judaism—worse than that, they often inflict grave, even incurable wounds on the faith that nurtured them, on the learning that taught them to think. Look at the hosts of those who have slandered Judaism and its supporters at various times, who, conceited because of their social position and their alleged orthodoxy, have accused Jews of various imagined ideas and acts—and you will discover that nearly all of them were renegades, and belonged to the hasidim.[38]

Thus, according to Cohn, the situation was hopeless. The hasidic issue could not be solved through education and civilization, because the hasidic rabble was incapable of accepting them. Those few individuals among them whose innate intelligence enabled them to profit from a secular education and leave hasidism turned out to be degenerate renegades who were a danger to all Jewish society. Although Cohn refrained from drawing any conclusions, he gave the impression of one who simply wished that the whole hasidic camp would disappear and who was not totally averse to the antisemitic scheme to banish all gaberdine-clad Jews to the steppes of Tatarstan, as suggested some time before by Gerard Witowski.

It is difficult to pinpoint one clear reason for the modernizing movement's change in its view of hasidism and acknowledgement of the failure of its educational projects in the 1870s. Whatever the reason, their views had never been unreservedly positive (even in Grosglik's case), and their disillusionment did not necessarily constitute a radical change. Criticism of hasidism had become harsher—even if not so obviously—from the early 1870s. It may be assumed that

[38] Adolf Jakub Cohn, 'Nasi', *Izr.* 11 (1876), 81–2.

their disillusionment had been mounting since 1864, and that it gained an intensity that led to its sudden eruption in the 1870s. But none of the minor factors mentioned above could possibly have had such a decisive influence on Peltyn's views or those of *Izraelita*'s editors; rather, it was a combination of factors that was responsible for the change. Those factors that could have helped to intensify the sense of disillusionment included the anti-hasidic publications connected with the activities of Elijah Guttmacher of Grodzisk Wielkopolski. Although ostentatiously anti-German, *Izraelita* nevertheless listened to German Jewish views, and Peltyn's series of attacks on Elijah Guttmacher was directly connected with the articles in *Allgemeine Zeitung des Judentums*.[39] Another German Jewish publication critical of hasidism, and which influenced the journal's views, was *History of the Jews* by Heinrich Graetz. Its eleventh volume, which included a history of hasidism, was published in 1870. For the next twenty years every mention of the hasidic movement and its leaders included Graetz's views, and their influence should not be underestimated. Another important factor was the general strengthening of anti-clericalism in east European maskilic circles, which had been observable in Russia since the early 1870s. A more prosaic factor, however, was the growing significance of items written for *Izraelita* away from the editor's office, particularly in out-of-the-way localities. The unequivocally hostile attitude of provincial correspondents, whom the hasidim had offended by seizing positions of power in provincial communities, was finally heeded by *Izraelita*, and from the mid-1870s Peltyn depicted the provincial hasidim as the embodiment of evil and the source of all the misfortunes of Jews in Poland.[40]

The collapse of the old enthusiasm may also have been brought about by one of its architects, Marcus Jastrow. Although at that time his links with the Kingdom of Poland were no longer particularly strong, there is no doubt that his articles published in the United States would have been carefully read in Warsaw, especially those that described his recent Polish vicissitudes. The text devoted to Baer Meisels, in which Jastrow severely criticized hasidism and its leaders, must have made a considerable impression.[41] Jastrow not only contested the reliability of

---

[39] An article that caused a series of responses in *Izraelita* was 'Zeitungsnachrichten. Aus dem Posenschen', *AZJ* 38 (1874), 175–6. For reactions to Guttmacher's activities, see 'Zeitungsnachrichten. Aus dem Posenschen', *AZJ* 38 (1874), 263–4; 'Zeitungsnachrichten. Grätz', *AZJ* 38 (1874), 739; 'Vermischte und neueste Nachrichten'; 'Die Wallfahren nach Grätz'; 'Berichte und Correspondenzen'. Commenting on the aggressive reactions of the German press to Guttmacher, Peltyn noted with satisfaction: 'German works, referring to the pilgrims as an ignorant rabble who were supposed to have been so numerous that at the last railway station at Opalenica one might encounter daily several hundred of these wayfarers waiting for an opportunity to have access to the holy man, could not find the words to express their horror, which is all the greater for the fact that this phenomenon was hitherto unknown. What is particularly difficult is that Germans call themselves the propagators of a culture worldwide yet one often finds this ignorance and medieval backwardness in their own homes'; Samuel H. Peltyn, 'Pogadanki', *Izr.* 9 (1874), 93.

[40] See e.g. Samuel H. Peltyn, 'Optymizm i pesymizm', *Izr.* 9 (1874), 319. For information on the anticlerical mood, see Feiner, *Haskalah and History*, 295–306.     [41] Jastrow, 'Bär Meisels'.

the tsadik Isaac Meir Alter (with whom he had collaborated harmoniously ten years earlier), but also condemned the whole hasidic movement in strongly abrasive language, accusing it of being unenlightened and shiftless, and of spreading drunkenness.

It should be reiterated, however, that all these factors, and possibly others, were only of secondary importance. What must have been most important was the growing, and justified, belief that the strategy they had adopted in the early 1860s appeared to have been ineffective, so that the diagnosis that had been made then was no longer valid. At the same time, the leaders of the moderate integrationist faction were unable to devise a new strategy to replace those optimistic projects, and thus, in terms of ideology and rhetoric, the modernizing camp more or less returned to the anti-hasidic hysteria so characteristic of the enlightened writers of the 1840s and 1850s. This is especially significant in that the shift in their attitudes towards hasidism pre-dated the emergence of a new wave of ideological antisemitism and of the Jewish national movement, factors that could have drawn integrationists' attention away from hasidism, their traditional enemy.

## HILARY NUSSBAUM: A HISTORIAN'S HELPLESSNESS

An interesting expression of the ambivalence towards hasidism and ultimate disillusionment was that of Hilary (Hillel) Nussbaum (1820–95), one of the most active members of the integration movement, who was also a writer, a contributor to *Izraelita*, and an amateur historian.[42] He was typical of the 'second track' in Jewish historiography—the trend within Jewish historical works to promote maskilic values through popular knowledge of the Jewish past.[43] Like Neufeld and Peltyn, he was convinced that the way to reform hasidism was to gain an understanding of it, and he had been involved in the subject since his first works were published in 1880–1.[44] In his notes 'From the Files of a Veteran of the Jewish Community of Warsaw' (*Z teki weterana warszawskiej gminy starozakonnych*), published in 1880, Nussbaum put forward a number of observations on various aspects of Jewish communal life, including, of course, 'the sect of zealots'. He criticized hasidic customs, particularly pilgrimages to the tsadikim, their neglect of their families, time-wasting, living an idle life, disregard for many ritual forms, 'and, mainly, seeking supposed inspiration for prayer in alcohol and nicotine'.[45] But, at the same time, he drew attention to the reprehensible treatment of the hasidim by the 'progressive class', and the way in which they were being alienated from progress by the immoral behaviour and numerous petty halakhic offences committed

[42] For the most important biographical data on Nussbaum see 'P.' [Samuel H. Peltyn], 'Żałobnej karty: Hilary Nusbaum', *Izr.* 30 (1895), 376–7; Shatzky, *Geshikhte fun Yidn in Varshe*, index; Eisenbach, 'Nussbaum, Hilary'.

[43] On the 'second track' of Jewish historiography, see Feiner, 'Nineteenth-Century Jewish Historiography'.                     [44] Nussbaum, *Z teki weterana, passim*; id., *Szkice historyczne*, 114–39.

[45] Nussbaum, *Z teki weterana*, 91.

by the advocates of modernization. He also drew attention to the inability of most young integrationists to engage in religious debate with the hasidim and to win them over to their cause. The final proposal put forward in the pamphlet, made in the sympathetic tone adopted by Grosglik rather than in the disillusioned tone of Peltyn, was a call for mutual tolerance and greater respect for members of 'conservative' groups.

Attempts to find solutions to, or at least an understanding of, hasidism were also evident in the history of the Jewish community in Warsaw that Nussbaum wrote at this time.[46] In it Nussbaum depicted the origins of the hasidic movement using as sources Heinrich Graetz's *History of the Jews*, and also, in part, Israel Löbel. This section of the work was hardly original. However, while reproducing the historical facts as described by Graetz, Nussbaum provided his own interpretation of these facts, with an attempt to explain the mechanisms of hasidic expansion, an understanding of which was crucial to the ability to prepare an effective plan to reform the hasidim. Unlike Graetz, Nussbaum believed that solving the hasidic issue was not a historiographical problem, but a crucial and current social issue. His attitude towards hasidism was ambivalent. He criticized it severely, but he was also convinced that it was changing—or had changed— for the better, that hasidism was attempting a reform similar to that undertaken in Germany by Moses Mendelssohn. Graetz's observations concerning the parallel time-frames of the activities of the Besht and of Mendelssohn brought Nussbaum to the naive conclusion that, had Poland had Mendelssohn rather than the Besht, all Jews in Poland would have been maskilim. In his opinion, hasidism was therefore an attempt to escape fossilized rabbinism, and its ultimate shape was the result of pure accident or the self-interested machinations of its leaders. If only

a tiny breach in the fortress's wall of rituals, the first blow at the granite bedrock of the Talmud, had been made at the right time by a rational thinker . . . the seeds of enlightenment sown at the same time by Mendelssohn in Germany would have found fertile ground in Poland as well and, instead of the hasidic sect and the miracle-working tsadikim, we would have had a class of progressive Jews and spiritual leaders.[47]

Nussbaum was willing to acknowledge that there was some value in the kabbalistic doctrine of hasidism, but he believed that it had been misinterpreted by the tsadikim because of their covetousness, stupidity, and greed: 'Incomprehensible kabbalah, egoism, greed, impudence and haughtiness have given birth to the phenomenon of the tsadikim. Stupidity, gullibility, a streak of idleness and easy living have fuelled the hasidim.'[48] This position had more in common with Neufeld's views than with those of Graetz, as Graetz was hostile towards all forms of mysticism.

Yet Nussbaum's most interesting works were his chronicles about the Jews in Warsaw, including extensive notes about the hasidim in the town, from the late

---

[46] Nussbaum, *Szkice historyczne.*     [47] Ibid. 121.     [48] Ibid. 122.

1830s. As a long-time member of the Jewish community board and a well-known amateur historian, he gathered a wide variety of historical materials, which allowed him to provide an interesting and highly textured picture of relations in the Warsaw community at the time. This account did not often suffer from authorial bias and, for that, was all the more fascinating. Nussbaum achieved in practice what Peltyn had often proposed—to learn more about hasidic circles. He even turned to traditional rabbinical literature to complement his knowledge of the tsadikim in Poland (he was versed in Hebrew literature and composed Hebrew poetry). His knowledge led him to believe that most of the accusations aimed at the hasidim did not approach the heart of the matter, or were even false, and that they could play no part in reforming them. Characteristically, however, he devised almost no programmes for their enlightenment, and his projects of reform concentrated on 'conservative' rather than 'reactionary' members of Jewish society; that is, on the mitnagedim rather than the hasidim.[49] In this way, Nussbaum too acknowledged his helplessness in the face of hasidism, and he wrote in 1886 that

The mitnagedim put forward better material for the adoption of enlightenment and social graces, and it is mainly them that we have in mind when talking about influencing the reactionary class of Jews, whereas it is virtually impossible to speak of enlightening all of the hasidim, apart from those exceptional cases who saw through the deception of the miracle-workers and deserted them; there is a need here for the involvement of the state legislature . It is enough that the same chasm that exists between the progressives and the conservatives divides the mitnagedim from the hasidim.[50]

Thus even a relatively good understanding of the hasidic world did not help Nussbaum to find ways to reform it. His volume devoted to the history of Jews in Poland was published in 1890, and although it was very similar to his book on Jews in Warsaw of 1881 it quoted Graetz almost verbatim and completely ignored reforming elements among the hasidim.[51]

## NEW THREATS

The natural response to the growing disillusionment with hasidism that was observable in integrationist publications from the 1870s was a loss of interest in the issue. Although the subject never completely disappeared from *Izraelita*, it occupied less and less space in the journal from the late 1870s onwards, and was banished from correspondence and the weekly 'Talks'. During 1889–90 there was a short-lived revival of interest, stimulated, no doubt, by foreign publications about hasidism, including the innovatory works of Simon Dubnow in particular. (These were reprinted in *Izraelita* in 1890.) An interesting discussion also took place in

---

[49] See e.g. Nussbaum, *Leon i Lajb*; the educational and polemic activities of Leon were directed exclusively towards the enlightened mitnaged Leib, and not towards those 'followers of the *Shulḥan arukh* [*szulchanaruchistom*] gravitating towards hasidism'.

[50] Nussbaum, *Jakub Izraelowicz*, 74.          [51] Nussbaum, *Historia Żydów*, v. 285–306.

*Izraelita* in 1892 in connection with the 'storm in a jar of olive oil', as *Izraelita* called the controversial publication by the editor-in-chief of *Hatsefirah*, Chaim Zelig Słonimski, and the subsequent hasidic campaign against the journal mentioned in Chapter 5. However, hasidism no longer lay within the bounds of either Peltyn's or his team's interests, and the discussion with Słonimski illustrated that Peltyn, unlike Słonimski, was consciously striving to circumvent the subject. *Izraelita* considered the hasidic question a closed issue.

This corroborated the thesis that had already started to appear in *Izraelita* in the late 1860s, that hasidism was no longer the central social problem; its influence was waning; despite its apparent growth, it was losing its integrity and its end was near; the hasidim were defecting en masse from their sect; greater numbers of them were studying; and fewer 'worshippers of the tsadikim' were visiting their leaders. 'Nowadays, hasidic fervour has subsided, the friendship binding them has weakened and, finally, both their charitable works and mutual help have to some extent abated.'[52] This was supposed to be confirmed by numerous tales—literary and documentary—about boys leaving the 'worshippers of tsadikim' and seeking secular education. If these assertions sounded sincere if unconvincing in Grosglik's publications, in the case of Peltyn and Cohn they seemed even less straightforward since they were accompanied by disillusioned complaints about the spreading sect and the impossibility of transforming the hasidim into civilized members of society. Rather, it should be assumed that these writers removed the hasidic problem from the general sphere of their interests because they were unable to solve it, and in fact regarded it as irresolvable. In the late 1880s, when the issue was, for various reasons, less painful, Peltyn acknowledged that the modernizing camp had not found a solution to the problem and had simply abandoned the issue: 'In a way, we have already become accustomed to awareness of the misfortune that befell us and, because we are unable to find any remedy for the time being, we have almost ceased to mention it.'[53] The only proposal concerning the treatment of the hasidim to be made at that time (and it was in fact a declaration of helplessness) was to wait until hasidism had completely degenerated as the result of internal changes and in consequence ceased to exist: 'hasidism will crumble and fall as the result of internal processes rather than because of any external influence that may bring about its fall'.[54]

Apart from this disillusionment, the loss of interest in hasidism must also have been brought about partly because of objective social factors that diminished its importance. Two of these factors appear to have been particularly significant.

The first was the emergence of so-called modern antisemitism and its increasing presence in writings and social life in the Kingdom of Poland. The Warsaw pogrom of 25 December 1881 was a symbolic event, but for *Izraelita* circles the constant intensification of antisemitic views in the Polish press from the late 1870s was of

[52] Naftali, 'Listy zachowawczego żyda', *Izr.* 23 (1888), 290.
[53] Samuel H. Peltyn, 'Nasza obojętność', *Izr.* 24 (1889), 191.
[54] Samuel H. Peltyn, 'Światła i cienie—Rewolujący chasydzi w Łodzi', *Izr.* 19 (1884), 197–8.

even greater significance. The first antisemitic works of Jan Jeleński, the first anti-semitic periodical *Rola*, and finally the sudden eruption of antisemitic ideology in western Europe (especially Germany and Bohemia) were a tough test of the naive belief of modernizing Jews in the saving power of education, integration, and acculturation.[55] From the late 1870s the debate with antisemitism became *Izraeli-ta*'s most important theme, and religious discussions between Jews became secondary.

The marginalization of the theme of hasidism was not only determined by an automatic shift in interest connected with the rise of antisemitism. It was similarly a response to articles in the press that, since the 1870s, had increasingly used scenes from the life of the hasidim as illustrations of Jewish fanaticism and incorrigible backwardness, and as evidence of the failure of the policy of integration. These arguments were not only used by professional antisemites. In one of his harsher statements Bolesław Prus, the leading liberal writer of the period but one who was ambivalent about the Jewish community, identified all Jews with the hasidim, and claimed that Henryk Nussbaum, the eminent Polish Jewish intellectual who 'instead of walking in a dirty gaberdine and trousers which are always undone, dresses in a tidy manner and like a European', was not a real Jew.[56] Of course, *Izraelita*'s writers did not contest the backwardness of hasidism, and Peltyn even acknowl-edged that the movement was one of the factors responsible for the contemporary wave of antisemitism.[57] Nevertheless, integrationist writers strongly opposed all Jews being identified with hasidism, claiming that tales mocking the darkness of hasidism were based on false or even perniciously distorted narratives and had nothing at all in common with the true nature of the Jewish people.[58]

The second factor responsible for moving the discussion with hasidism from centre stage was the emergence of the ideology of modern Jewish nationalism. Zionism was a challenge for integrationists, and not only as one of rival ideologies fighting for the soul of the Jewish people. The 'progressives' had been engaged for a long time in this type of fight with the hasidim and the mitnagedim. Because it questioned the precepts of the integration policy of the modernizing camp, Zionism proved a greater challenge, especially since the criticism came from 'civil-ized' Jews, and this undermined one of the dogmas of their belief in progress—that education must inevitably lead to integration with the surrounding community. A rival ideology in non-traditional, secular Jewish society obviously belied this belief.

[55] Of the rich historiographical literature on the subject, see especially Weeks, 'Poles, Jews, and Russians'; Porter, *When Nationalism Began to Hate, passim*, esp. 160–82.

[56] Prus, *Kroniki*, ix. 220 (chronicle for 10 Oct. 1886). See also ibid. xi. 156. Prus's ambivalent atti-tude towards Jews has been mentioned by many historians, but the subject needs more detailed ana-lysis. See Blejwas, 'Polish Positivism and the Jews'; Szcześniak, 'Kreacje bohaterów żydowskich w twórczości Bolesława Prusa'; Friedrich, 'Bolesław Prus: Toward Zionism'.

[57] Samuel H. Peltyn, 'Dzieje chasydyzmu: Jego nastanie, rozwój i utwierdzenie się', *Izr.* 25 (1890), 133.

[58] A debate with Prus appears in [Samuel H.] P[eltyn], 'Żydem jestem', *Izr.* 21 (1886), 325.

In the first phase of the debate with the 'advocates of Zion' in the 1880s *Izraelita* was unable to devise an adequate language of discussion and attempted to use strategies tested in the fight with hasidism. A correspondent from Lemberg (or rather Polish Lwów) wrote about the Zionist organization Kadimah that 'hasidism, suffering a crushing defeat in its old form, has come back to life in the guise of the pseudo-progressive'.[59] In addition to the fact that this bears witness to their ideological helplessness in the dialogue with Zionism, it also provides the clearest evidence that, as far as the integrationists were concerned, these disputes with the nationalists literally replaced those with the hasidim. Examples of anti-hasidic strategies being transferred to a new adversary could be found later, for instance, when Theodor Herzl was referred to as a Zionist Dalai Lama. The term was a derogatory one in the minds of the modernizing writers and, starting with Menahem Mendel Lefin and Joseph Perl, was often used in maskilic writings to refer to leaders of the hasidic movement.[60] In this manner, the father of Zionism was placed on a par with the tsadikim, and the debate with Zionism replaced the debate with hasidic ideology.

At the end of 1880s Peltyn also became more conciliatory towards hasidim. The views of hasidism and its supporters that were sporadically voiced at this time became more balanced and less belligerent, and some tsadikim, for example, Judah Leib Eiger of Lublin, Isaac Friedman of Boyan, Judah Aryeh Leib Alter of Góra Kalwaria (Ger), and Elimelekh Shapiro of Grójec,[61] were described in favourable terms. Peltyn went so far along the path of peace as to print a letter criticizing those 'progressives' who had distanced themselves from the 'reactionaries' and the shame expressed by enlightened Jews for their contacts with the hasidim.[62] In a debate with a correspondent of the *Neuzeit* of Vienna, he also claimed that the greatest threat to the process of enlightening Polish Jews was not hasidism (as Aron had claimed in *Neuzeit*), but the 'icy indifference of those spheres from which one should be able to rely on a battle-cry to liberate Jewry'.[63] It would almost have been a return to the attitudes that had characterized *Izraelita* twenty years earlier were it not for the fact that Peltyn also published at the same time views that were diametrically opposite to these.[64] Despite these occasionally gentle and almost friendly

---

[59] Lwowianin, 'Korespondencja *Izraelity*', *Izr.* 19 (1884), 21.

[60] On Herzl, see S., 'Dalaj-lama syonizmu', *Izr.* 38 (1903), 136; on the Dalai Lama, see also Lefin, *Essai d'un plan de réforme juive en Pologne*, 419 (para. f); Perl, *Uiber das Wesen der Sekte Chassidim*, 31, 124. For the same theme in *Izraelita*, see Samuel H. Peltyn, 'Zwichnięta kariera (z życia)', *Izr.* 11 (1876), 103; Alfred Lor, 'Z teatru', *Izr.* 35 (1900), 329; Henryk Lichtenbaum, 'Z piśmiennictwa', *Izr.* 46/3 (1911), 8–9; B.E., 'Odgłosy: Potęga ciemnoty', *Izr.* 46/48 (1911), 3–4.

[61] 'B.p. Juda L. Eiger', *Izr.* 23 (1888), 46; J.W., 'Interwiew u cadyka', *Izr.* 24 (1889), 63–4; Elkan, 'Z życia', *Izr.* 24 (1889), 75–6; Elkan, 'Za tydzień', *Izr.* 27 (1892), 109.

[62] M., 'Nasz stosunek do braci zachowawczej, jakim jest i jakim być powinien', *Izr.* 21 (1887), 81.

[63] Samuel H. Peltyn, 'Nasza obojętność', *Izr.* 24 (1889), 21: debate with Aron, 'Zur Lage der Juden in Polen'.

[64] Samuel H. Peltyn, 'Nasi krańcowi szkodnicy', *Izr.* 30 (1895), 392–3; Judaita, *Projekt reformy w judaizmie*, 55–7, 81–2.

views, the diagnosis of hasidism remained crushing. *Izraelita*'s editor-in-chief did not believe that it was possible to educate the hasidim, and he compared them to the generation of Israelites who had left Egyptian slavery and who had to die out before new generations could reach the promised land of enlightenment and social integration. In this way *Izraelita* also managed to defend itself from charges made in the Polish press that 'progressive' Jewish circles did too little to enlighten their fanatical co-believers.[65] According to Peltyn, their enlightenment was simply impossible. Thus, the change discernible in publications concerning the hasidim from the 1880s was merely a change of rhetoric. Integrationist writers had no new ideas, and the moderate style of their writings was an expression of subsiding emotions and an underestimation of the significance of the issue rather than a significant evolution in their views. However, the change heralded further, more profound transformations that soon took place in the world-view of this group. The first sign of this was their waning dislike of hasidism at the end of the 1880s.

## CONCLUSIONS

The interest in the hasidic issue displayed by leaders of the integrationist camp who gathered around *Izraelita* may be characterized as a path that led from optimism through disillusionment to indifference. Publications from the first years of the weekly's existence reiterated the main theses of the integration camp from the early 1860s onwards. Peltyn and his associates were convinced that victory over hasidism was imminent, and that the methods to be used in the fight were voluntary education, intensification of intra-religious unity, and rapprochement between the young integrationists and the hasidim.

The most interesting programme for dealing with the hasidim was that put forward by Izrael Leon Grosglik, but the views most characteristic of *Izraelita* circles were those of Samuel Henryk Peltyn. Peltyn accepted *Jutrzenka*'s optimistic assumptions, but at the same time strove to understand the essence of the hasidic movement and to devise a more comprehensive position on it. Yet, contrary to expectations, the circle did not succeed in producing an adequate programme to deal with the 'hasidic issue'. History could not be shaped, and the course taken by events was not to the integrationists' liking. This led to their deep disillusionment and frustration. The hasidim once again became the target of unsubtle assaults, and the most prominent journalists of *Izraelita* rejected the optimistic ideas of the early 1860s and regarded the hasidic issue as one that could not be resolved.

Articles on hasidism began to disappear from the periodical a little later. This was officially justified by the theoretically diminishing influence of hasidism and the slow disintegration of the movement. In reality, it was merely a tactic to maintain silence on a subject painful both to the leaders of the integration movement who were published in *Izraelita* and to its rank-and-file supporters who read the

---

[65] Samuel H. Peltyn, 'Dla przyszłości!', *Izr.* 19 (1884), 81; id., 'Nasze Drogi', *Izr.* 21 (1886), 157.

weekly. Pent-up frustrations made themselves felt in various ways; for example, in publications touching on the subject of hasidism in the Polish press.[66]

Paradoxically, this tactic proved to be successful, mainly owing to the fact that from the late 1870s new social phenomena began to preoccupy *Izraelita*'s contributors and readers. The first of these was modern antisemitism, present on the political scene and in social life in the Kingdom of Poland from the late 1870s. The fight with antisemitism and the debate with hostile publications from *Rola* (and soon the majority of Polish periodicals) involved Jewish enlightened circles to the extent that there was no longer any place for a clash with the former 'enemy', hasidism. With the emergence of Zionism came the most serious ideological challenge to modernizing circles, and it focused integrationists' attention away from hasidism.

All this resulted in a change of attitude in the integrationist camp towards hasidism in the last decade of the nineteenth century. Although diagnoses of the issue were still very critical, and Peltyn believed that the only solution to the problem of hasidism would be the death of all its supporters, this period saw a considerable weakening of the verbal assaults, and even saw the publication of works praising the hasidim. This was accompanied by a growing scientific and literary interest in them. Although not reflected by any great increase in the number of publications on hasidism, this interest contributed significantly to a further thawing in relations with the movement. This was the beginning of changes that bore fruit only when *Izraelita* had a new editor-in-chief and a new ideology. At the same time the period marked the beginning of a radical reassessment of the approach to hasidism and the end of the integration movement.

[66] See e.g. Samuel H. Peltyn, 'Pogadanki', *Izr.* 9 (1874), 68, 304; 10 (1875), 329.

# EIGHT

# The Death of an Idea: Political, Historical, and Poetic Visions of Hasidism

## AN IDEOLOGICAL CRISIS IN THE INTEGRATION CAMP

The diminished significance of the hasidic issue to the ideology of the integrationist camp and the subsequently milder rhetoric in critical commentaries (though not in opinions) was mainly, as mentioned in the previous chapter, the result of objective social factors. These included the emergence of modern antisemitism and the conflict with nascent Jewish nationalism. However, these phenomena were only two among a whole list of factors that shaped the attitude of the 'progressives' to hasidism in the last two decades of the Congress Kingdom (or what remained of it). The evolution in attitude was also attributable to the internal change in philosophy which the integration movement itself was undergoing. In the mid-1890s the movement experienced a crisis that sounded the death knell for its philosophy, embedded as it was in the enlightened ideals of the Haskalah—itself a product of the late eighteenth century.[1]

The death of three leaders from the integrationist camp had considerable symbolic significance. Henryk Natanson (1820–95), the head of the Warsaw Jewish community board, Hilary Nussbaum, the journalist and social activist, and Samuel H. Peltyn, *Izraelita*'s editor-in-chief, died within months of one another in the years 1895–6. The demise of three such crucial figures surely left its imprint on the history of this group, though the philosophical crisis was related more to the wider ideological and cultural transformations taking place in Europe at the turn of the century. The emergence of Zionism, modern Jewish nationalism, was merely one of many signs that European societies—including the Jewish community—were embarking on a period of burgeoning modern political national identity.[2] The process of politicizing the Jewish population had already become widespread by the turn of the century, and almost all organizations and political parties—whether Bundists, Folkists, or Zionists—adopted the slogan of Jewish national revival. To

---

[1] For essential reading on the crisis of the integrationist movement, see Weeks, 'Poles, Jews, and Russians'.

[2] For literature on the beginnings of the Jewish national identity in Poland, see Tomaszewski, 'The Jews of Poland'. For a more general account of the *fin-de-siècle* contexts of this process, see Shavit, 'The "Glorious Century" or the "Cursed Century"'.

define the Jewish community as a nation was, of course, at complete variance with the basic ideological premisses of the 'Poles of the Mosaic faith' who—confronted with the appearance of these groups in the political arena—were helpless. Even worse, to engage in any debate with these new ideological rivals implied acceptance of the definition of a 'political' nation; that is, a nation that exists as an autonomous entity in political life. This was in marked contrast to the principal ideological premisses of the integrationists, who, apart from the short period of Polish–Jewish fraternity, had deliberately refrained from participating in political life until the mid-1890s, while their publication *Izraelita* was able to maintain the 'correct' line of positivist liberalism accompanied by deep-rooted political moderation. Repressive tsarist politics precluded political involvement so that any activity had to seem to be apolitical. Yet these constraints seem to have suited the integrationists, who attempted to unite all political persuasions under the flag of the modernizing camp. Within *Izraelita* even the debate with Zionism that was revived in the 1890s was not entirely political in character, but, rather, an extremely abstract ideological discussion. The sudden politicization of the Jewish world in the first years of the twentieth century enforced a radical change of strategy. However, the integrationists had no common policy; since they were not even a political organization, defined on the basis of common political aims, they were unable to meet the demands of the new epoch.

The ideological crisis among Polish Jewish integrationists was also brought about by the anti-positivist trends that became more prevalent in European culture at the end of the nineteenth century. Escalating criticism and the move away from positivist ideals was bound to impact upon the integration camp, whose ideology had grown out of this philosophy. Haskalah ideology, and later that of its successors, was based on a belief in the objective 'scientific' value of progress in science, technology, and civilization, which would inevitably lead to the overall betterment of humankind in all spheres, including the spiritual sphere. This belief was undermined by the escalation of decadent attitudes, a wavering belief in humanistic ideals, and increased pessimism, all of which were present at the end of the century. In Jewish society the political and social phenomena that particularly affected Jews and that did not fit the ideological framework of those who believed in progress, such as the sudden growth of modern antisemitism (and its extreme manifestation in the form of pogroms) and the birth of Jewish nationalism, were also responsible for shaking belief in progress. In the Kingdom of Poland the emergence of 'progressive antisemitism' and the assumption by leading positivist ideologists (particularly Aleksander Świętochowski) of attitudes hostile to Jews called into question the universal value of progress and the prudence of the positivist ideology.[3] The

[3] On 'progressive antisemitism', see Weeks, 'Polish "Progressive Antisemitism"'; on the ideological transformation of the leading Polish positivists and their shift towards antisemitism, see Golczewski, *Polnisch-jüdische Beziehungen*, 92–6; Cała, *Asymilacja Żydów*, 255–67; Opalski and Bartal, *Poles and Jews*, 98–103. For a representative transformation of Andrzej Niemojewski see Trześniowski, 'Biografia ideowa polskiego inteligenta'.

irrational trends that pervaded European ideologies at the end of the nineteenth century and that contradicted the enlightened belief in the primacy of the mind (the cornerstone of maskilic and integrationist beliefs) had an obvious influence on the crisis in integrationist philosophy.[4]

The first signs of the crisis appeared in integrationist circles while Peltyn was still alive. In the 1880s *Izraelita*'s writers were still greeting accounts of seances and an interest in spiritualism, mysticism, and magic with a mixture of amusement and feigned horror. However, it was not long before the attitude of Peltyn and others had changed to such a degree that the periodical started publishing articles devoted to the significance of mystical experiences to human spiritual development.[5] Being hostile to rationalism, the atmosphere of the *fin de siècle* took the edge off the resistance of Jewish modernizing circles to mysticism, including Jewish mysticism. This was all the more so since, even though they flew the positivist flag of scientism and rationalism, Peltyn and his supporters had never really abandoned the 'warm, religious sentiments' that had been an important element of its ideology, if not its identifying characteristic, since the birth of *Izraelita*.

The change in attitudes towards human extra-sensory experience deprived the critics of hasidism of an important argument in the dispute with this movement. Until that time hasidism had been regarded as the creation of Jewish mysticism and the essence of kabbalah ('this tumour on the body of Judaism'), which was sufficient explanation for all its shortcomings. This belief was manifest in the thesis held among integrationist circles that the Ba'al Shem Tov's ideals and objectives, although initially noble, had been perverted by the introduction of kabbalistic elements so that good intentions had led to deplorable results. The new attitude to mysticism made such an accusation pointless because hasidic mysticism—like any other—was no longer looked upon as unequivocally negative, so that holding it responsible for the shortcomings of the Jewish people was no longer axiomatic. This did not mean, of course, that kabbalah and hasidism had come to be regarded as being completely acceptable (Peltyn introduced numerous qualifications to his acceptance of mysticism), but one of the main charges against hasidism had lost its impact.

It was this new attitude towards hasidism that turned out to be the clearest sign of the end of maskilic ideology in Russia and the related integrationist philosophy in the Kingdom of Poland. In 1897 Micha Josef Berdyczewski announced that the new generation no longer nourished the hatred towards the hasidim that had typified the maskilim of old.[6] In fact, this meant not only the renunciation of former anti-hasidic sentiments, but also a departure from maskilic projects to fight hasid-

---

[4] The best study of the fall of the Haskalah in eastern Europe is Feiner, 'Kayonek hanoshekh shadei imo'.

[5] See, *inter alia*, R., 'Słów kilka o spółczesnym mistycyzmie', *Izr.* 27 (1892), 27; Samuel H. Peltyn, 'Niewyjaśniona zagadka', *Izr.* 27 (1892), 17–19; id., 'O spółczesnym mistycyzmie uwag kilka', *Izr.* 29 (1894), 35–6.    [6] Feiner, 'Kayonek hanoshekh shadei imo', 81; id., *Haskalah and History*, 346.

ism, or at least from those projects for the reform of the movement. This, in effect, constituted abandonment of the programme of Jewish enlightenment that had been so crucial to Haskalah ideology and a questioning of its superiority over the values represented by hasidism. Thus, the change in attitude reflected on the most fundamental philosophical premises. Until that time even those maskilim and integrationists who had been better disposed towards the hasidim (e.g. Eliezer Zweifel in Russia, and Daniel Neufeld and Izrael Leon Grosglik in Poland) had never questioned the principal ideological differences between their group and hasidism or the need for the enlightenment of the hasidic masses. In practice it meant that even the revisionist maskilim had been unanimous that hasidism would cease to exist, at least in the form it then took, as a consequence of historical processes, although some of its values were worthy of adoption by its enlightened successors. Even Grosglik believed that the hasidim—although they cherished those priceless treasures of Jewish tradition that had been lost by the modernizing class—needed to change fundamentally, and that their numerous strengths were outweighed by their even more numerous faults. The rejection of such views by the new generation, best represented by Micha Josef Berdyczewski, effectively signified the ultimate renunciation both of the Haskalah tradition and of the belief in the superiority of maskilic values over those of hasidism. From the late 1890s onwards sentimental attitudes that idealized the hasidim and their leaders began to prevail. There was also a growing interest in the movement as a repository of folk tradition, which was doubtless connected with the *fin-de-siècle* preoccupation with folklore. This admiration for hasidism was neither unqualified nor widespread, but even where hasidism was subject to criticism, the movement was seen in a completely different light—not as a reactionary force in need of enlightenment, but as a political adversary in the narrow sense, that is, as a creation hitherto unknown to maskilic journalism. The change in attitudes towards hasidism in the spheres of politics, historiography, and literature was thus the most obvious proof of the end of the maskilic idea of any fight against it.

## THE POLITICAL ASPECT OF HASIDISM:
### NACHUM SOKOŁÓW

Although the hasidic movement had had a clearly political function almost from its beginnings, it was not perceived by supporters of the Haskalah as a political threat until the end of the nineteenth century, even if the conflict with it had at times required the use of political weapons—mainly in the form of intervention with the authorities.[7] According to the maskilim, hasidism was the chief obstacle to enlightenment and the principal source of degenerate religious forms, but it bore none of the marks of a political movement. This position obviously suited the

---

[7] See Lederhendler, *The Road to Modern Jewish Politics*, 58–83, on the political context of the anti-hasidic campaign in Russia.

purposes of those extremely hostile maskilim who viewed hasidism as illegitimate and who, in describing the rival movement, not only denied its good intentions, but also questioned whether it had any function apart from the base motive of material gain. It was not until the late 1870s that Jewish modernizing circles in Galicia viewed hasidism as a political threat, after the establishment of the political organization Mahzikei Hadas by Simeon Schreiber, a rabbi from Kraków, and Joshua Roke'ah, a tsadik from Bełz. However, the wave of Galician anti-hasidic publications from that period did not reach the Kingdom of Poland,[8] and until the late 1880s practically the only journalist who observed the political activity of the hasidim in the Congress Kingdom was Wilhelm Feldman (1868–1919), then a young writer and contributor to *Izraelita*, himself from Lwów, in Galicia. But faced with a lack of political or social organizations representing Orthodox Jews in the Kingdom, Polish integrationists still regarded Feldman's accounts of the political counter-offensive of the hasidim as an exotic tale originating from beyond the Galician border.[9] Feldman's correspondence from Lwów, in which he fiercely attacked the hasidic leaders of Mahzikei Hadas,[10] remained incomprehensible to the readers of *Izraelita* and seems to have met with indifference.

All this changed when Nachum Sokołów (1859–1936) became editor-in-chief of *Izraelita* in 1896. Sokołów (Fig. 10) was a journalist of great political astuteness, who introduced the hasidic issue into the political discourse of integrationist circles in the Kingdom of Poland.[11] The change arose out of the transformation of the whole socio-political situation and the new awareness that accompanied it. The politicization of the election of the Warsaw Jewish community board in 1902, and later a whole series of events that were strictly political in character (the first projects for municipal self-government, the 1905 revolution, successive elections to the Russian Duma, etc.), forced integrationist circles to become involved in current events and to take a clearer political line. The modern mass politics that became part of the life of Jewish society at the turn of the century had a fundamental effect on the integrationist camp, while the turn towards politics created a shift in the debate on hasidic issues and was one of the striking developments in the treatment of the movement.

Nachum Sokołów observed the changes taking place in the social organization of hasidism and was aware that the movement was assuming a new shape—one more suited to the challenges of the approaching twentieth century. He perceived hasidism as a strictly political creation with well-defined social goals and a clearly

[8]  For the most representative Galician publications, see Warschauer, *W sprawie wiecu rabinów*; id., *Agitacje stowarzyszenia 'Machsike Hadas'*; Frühling, *Klątwa galicyjskich rabinów*.

[9]  Agudas Yisroel, the first hasidic political organization to be active in the Kingdom of Poland, was formally established only in 1912. See Bacon, *The Politics of Tradition*, 22–46, on the origins and formative years of Agudas Yisroel in the Kingdom of Poland.

[10]  See e.g. Wilhelm Feldman, 'Korespondencja "Izraelity"', *Izr.* 22 (1887), 5; id., 'Z piśmiennictwa', *Izr.* 22 (1887), 145.

[11]  On Sokołów's activities in *Izraelita*, see Stiftel, 'Sokolov veha'*Izraelita*'; Bauer, 'Nahum Sokolow'.

delineated sphere of influence, and thus departed from the established territory of apolitical anti-hasidic debate. This was in line with his more general views, as at that time he was seeking a new formula both for public activity and for a Jewish national ideology. According to Sokołów, the fight with hasidism could not be confined to the old methods of literary polemic, enlightenment programmes, and attempts to pacify the adversary. The hasidic issue was a question not of access to education by unenlightened Jewish masses, but rather of a struggle with an opponent with clear political aims. The battleground thus had to shift to more modern methods of political propaganda, electoral rivalry, and competition on the emerging scene of Jewish political life. In Sokołów's words, 'without a new programme, the usual criticisms of hasidism will become pointless moralizing' and would not bring about the desired effect. A fight of a political nature was to be the new slogan: a struggle with the political influences of hasidism in every possible place—in schools, in the Jewish community, in the (planned) municipal self-government, at state level. Sokołów thus called for an extensive alliance of anti-hasidic forces, which, united, would work to deprive hasidism of its influence, particularly its broad-ranging powers in community institutions. According to him, such an alliance (of a political nature—and therefore a novelty in itself) was possible between those members of the Jewish intelligentsia who were better disposed towards tradition and the more enlightened members of orthodoxy from the circles of the former mitnagedim. However, this required the involvement of Polonized intellectual circles, to whom Sokołów addressed numerous appeals.[12] At the same time he attempted to revive the old anti-hasidic stance of the mitnagedim, pointing to the damage hasidism had done to traditional Jewish circles (see Appendix 19),[13] and, in appeals for an extensive alliance between the intelligentsia and the mitnagedim, cited in support of his position the earlier rabbinical authorities, particularly Elijah, the Gaon of Vilna, with his anti-hasidic campaign of the end of the eighteenth century.[14] These activities, which were aimed at traditional circles, were accompanied by appeals to the other arm of the planned alliance, the Jewish intelligentsia, from whom he demanded greater emphasis on the national, Hebrew character to their movements and greater involvement in internal Jewish affairs. Sokołów even introduced the term 'Hebrew Haskalah', which was probably used for the first time in Polish-language works.[15] His image of divisions in the Jewish ideological scene

---

[12] See e.g. Sokołów, *Zadania inteligencji żydowskiej*, 4–5; id., 'Do pracy i zgody!', *Izr.* 34 (1899), 259–60; id., 'Błogostan nędzy', *Izr.* 35 (1900), 339–40.

[13] N[ahum] S[okołów], 'Zanik misnagdyzmu', *Izr.* 33 (1898), 449.

[14] See N[ahum] S[okołów], 'Z dziejów zasłużonych: Gaon Wileński, pionier oświaty i pogromca chasydyzmu', *Izr.* 32 (1897), 406.

[15] The positively weighted term 'Hebrew Haskalah' is used here in contrast to the negative term 'assimilation'. See Nachum Sokołów, 'Do pracy i zgody!', *Izr.* 34 (1899), 259–60. It should be noted that, despite the claims of traditional historiography, Sokołów treated Polish Jewish 'progressives' as members of the Haskalah movement, and not as 'assimilationists'. See Bauer, 'Nahum Sokolow', 117, 177. The situation changed only after Sokołów had stepped down from *Izraelita* and started to propagate Zionist ideology actively.

**FIG. 10.** Nachum Sokołów (1859–1936)
Museum of the Jewish Historical Institute, Warsaw, B-443/7-7

was very archaic in its terminology, using terms from the beginning, rather than the end, of the nineteenth century; but at the same time Sokołów imbued the old terms with a modern content of a markedly political nature, thus giving the old war between the hasidim and the mitnagedim a modern, political quality.

By the beginning of the twentieth century the belief in the political nature of hasidism was already widespread and had changed decisively the attitude to the movement of all active Jewish groups. *Izraelita* could repeat, in the style of the Yiddish journal *Fraynd*, that hasidism was by no means the angel of nostalgic tales written by Isaac Leib Peretz, but a dangerous demon in Jewish political life.[16] This conviction regarding the political nature of hasidism was reinforced by the establishment in 1912 of Agudas Yisroel, the first political organization of Orthodox Jews in the Kingdom of Poland.

[16] See Lektor, 'Z prasy żargonowej: O chasydyzmie', *Izr.* 46/3 (1911), 10.

FIG. 11. Abraham Mordecai Alter (1866–1948), the Gerer Rebbe,
one of the founders of Agudas Yisroel
Documentation Department, Jewish Historical Institute, Warsaw

## BEYOND THE MASKILIC HISTORIOGRAPHY OF HASIDISM

The reassessment of the attitude to hasidism in the ideology of the Jewish modernizing camp at the end of the nineteenth century and beginning of the twentieth can be observed in historiography and in more widely read Jewish historical publications in German, Russian, and Polish. A certain change in the attitude of Jewish historiography to the history of hasidism was already evident in the famous eleven-volume *Geschichte der Juden* (History of the Jews, 1853–76) by Heinrich Graetz, although—apart from the Romantic-idyllic elements present in the portrayal of the Besht—the work was very critical of the movement. However, Graetz's positive tone was noted by integrationists from *Izraelita* circles, whose observations proved considerably more accurate than those of Graetz's later critics, who chose to see him as the embodiment of enlightened anti-hasidic trends.[17] Graetz's thesis concerning the presence of noble elements in the origins of hasidism was readily accepted by Polish Jewish journalists because it was neither particularly new nor particularly surprising. The claim that hasidism had been a justifiable revolt against fossilized rabbinical formalism had already been introduced into maskilic writings in the late 1840s by a Lwów rabbi, Abraham Kohn, and a Romantic vision of the Besht had already been widely accepted in the late 1860s.[18] The first such text had appeared in *Izraelita* in 1868 and had been written by Peltyn himself.[19]

The next stage in the revision of Jewish historiographical attitudes towards hasidism was marked by Simon Dubnow's work *Toledot hahasidut* (History of Hasidism) published years after Graetz's monumental *Geschichte der Juden*. The work aroused some interest in integrationist circles, and large excerpts from the first volume of *Toledot hahasidut*, reprinted from the Russian periodical *Voskhod*, appeared in *Izraelita* as early as 1890. On this occasion Peltyn stated that 'it is high time . . . the history of the sprouting and growth of this weed on our soil was carefully examined'.[20] However, for a number of reasons Dubnow's monograph was not particularly popular with Polish Jewish integrationists. First, the beginning of the 1890s was a period when interest in hasidism in the publications of the integration movement was quite clearly on the decline. Secondly, the novelty of Dubnow's work lay mainly in the political implications of his view of hasidism, which remained outside the field of interest of most Jewish integrationists in the Congress Kingdom. Dubnow's lack of immediate success could also have been connected with the fact that, in the translation published in *Izraelita*, Peltyn had edited the text so much that the article lost much of its originality. It had been quite freely cut, and, rather than being an exact translation, was a reasonably faithful paraphrase of Dubnow's work, with Peltyn's own commentary appearing in several places. On the other hand, changes of this kind were common practice in *Izraelita* and other periodicals, and sprang not from any ill intention but from accepted editorial practice. This was unfortunate in the case of Dubnow's article because Peltyn, believing he had free rein with the format and content of the original text, shaped Dubnow's ideas into the usual patterns and terminology used by *Izraelita*

[17] See Graetz, *Geschichte der Juden*, xi. For more on Graetz's attitude towards mysticism, including hasidism, see Biale, *Gershom Scholem*, 19–25; Elukin, 'A New Essenism'; both authors, however, overemphasize Graetz's anti-hasidic views and neglect elements of his positive evaluation of the movement, such as the positive image of the Besht.

[18] See Kohn, 'Briefe aus Galizien'. For later publications see e.g. Horowitz, 'Chassidäische Silhouetten'; Szantó, 'Der Bescht und seine Nachfolger'.

[19] Samuel H. Peltyn, 'Chassydyzm, jego istota i stosunek do rabinizmu', *Izr.* 3 (1868), 193–4, 201–2, 217–19; id., 'Beszt i jego następcy: Szkic biograficzno-humorystyczny', *Izr.* 3 (1868), 414–16; 4 (1869), 1–3, 15–16, 30–2, 38–40 (based on Szantó, 'Der Bescht und seine Nachfolger').

[20] Samuel H. Peltyn, 'Dzieje chasydyzmu: Jego nastanie, rozwój i utwierdzenie się', *Izr.* 25 (1890), 133–4, 145–6, 156–7, 164–5, 175–6, 185–6, 195–6, 204–5, 214–15, 235–6; id., 'Jak się u nas rozwijała schizma', *Izr.* 25 (1890), 442, 454–5, 466–7, 476–7, 489–90, 499–500.

in articles devoted to hasidism. As a result, Dubnow's study was reduced to yet another, not particularly original, anti-hasidic account of the beginnings of the movement. It is also possible that Dubnow's ideas were too complex to be understood by Polish Jewish supporters of integration, and that Peltyn's paraphrasing was simply an attempt to make the text more accessible to Polish Jewish readers.

In terms of his philosophy, Dubnow was ahead of the integrationists of the Kingdom of Poland by a decade. At the turn of the century a group of young authors, literary critics, ethnographers, and historians emerged from *Izraelita* circles whose attitudes towards hasidism were far removed from those of Peltyn's and Nussbaum's circles, and who were considerably closer to their contemporary, Dubnow. Among the Jewish intelligentsia of the Kingdom of Poland it was the folklorists, particularly Beniamin Wolf Segel and Henryk Lew, who best articulated the change and saw the hasidic movement as a form of folk custom and a treasury of traditional folklore. Interest in the hasidic movement was seen by them as a typical manifestation of the modernists' obsession with folk customs and the related development of folklore studies. The need for studies of the Jewish people was voiced by both Polish and Jewish intellectuals of that period, and Polish ethnographers embarked upon a number of research projects. The growing interest in hasidism on the part of the Jewish intelligentsia was a direct result of these initiatives.[21] Similar trends were also observable at that time in Russia (such as the famous expedition to the *shtetlekh* (small Jewish towns) in the Pale of Settlement organized by S. Anski), the dual monarchy of Austria-Hungary, and the countries of western Europe. But it was not the intention of the young researchers to learn about hasidism in order to destroy or reform it, as had been the intention forty years earlier of even the integrationists who were well disposed towards hasidism. By the turn of the century any research into the history of hasidism was directed at learning about the spirit of the people and an understanding of their character—a people whose most representative group were the hasidim. Undoubtedly, in this respect one of the most important sources of inspiration for young ethnographers was Isaac Leib Peretz, the patron of the Warsaw circle of Jewish folklorists and author of the nostalgic *Hasidic Stories*.[22]

This new attitude was explained in 1897 by Beniamin Wolf Segel (1866–1931), one of the first Jewish folklorists in Poland and a journalist writing for *Izraelita*. Segel began by saying: 'I have always wished that one day there would come a teacher/historian in whose soul there was at least a spark of Renan's spirit, who would tell us the *inside* history of hasidism and its many directions, and who would depict for us the most prominent people in this movement' (see Appendix 18).[23] Thus far, historical and ethnographic studies (his own included) had been unsatis-

---

[21] For more on Jewish ethnography and its Polish inspirations at the turn of the century, see Goldberg-Mulkiewicz, *Ethnographic Topics Relating to Jews*, 9–25.

[22] For more on the influence of Peretz on Jewish folklore, see Kiel, '*Vox populi, vox dei*'.

[23] B[eniamin] W. Segel, 'Z piśmiennictwa', *Izr.* 32 (1897), 96–7.

factory for many reasons, so hasidism was still awaiting its historian. Segel levelled his harshest criticisms at Graetz:

Graetz, who devoted an entire chapter of the eleventh volume of his history to hasidism, dismissed it with a single, unflattering label which has been widely repeated: *hässlich*. But can this [dismissive attitude] truly explain the tremendous popularity and the nearly hundred-and-fifty-year existence of a movement which, unfortunately in such a terribly deviant form, has become so deeply ingrained in the spiritual organism of the Jewish people in eastern Europe?

Segel also criticized Dubnow, because his works, being 'strictly historical, deal more with the external manifestations and development of hasidism than with its internal substance'. Thus Dubnow was not the answer to Segel's dream of a Jewish Renan, although it was Renan's historical works that were Dubnow's chief inspiration.[24] According to Segel, the hostile attitude of modern Hebraic literature towards hasidism was partly justified, since maskilic writers, from Joseph Perl to Peretz Smolenskin, had known the hasidic movement in its declining form under the name of 'the cult of the tsadikim', so they could not perceive its strengths but saw only its weaknesses, considering it a threat to general education as promoted by the Haskalah. It had only been in recent years, when the power of the hasidim was past, that integrationist writers and historians had begun to develop an understanding of 'a whole store of profound philosophical and ethical reflections' stemming from the movement:

It is an interesting phenomenon that the present generation is far more objective and, in some cases, even sympathetic in its approach to this Jewish movement, a movement that has, after all, been deviant, and which has had disastrous effects. *Was im Liede soll auferstehen, muss im Leben untergehen* [Whatever is resurrected in song must die in life]. At present, when hasidism is nearing its end, when it holds on only by force of tradition and intellectual inertia, we, the younger ones, have begun to be interested in its poetic aspect, which has eased the lives of innumerable poor people, and in the contemplative and ethical elements which it contains and which even developed within it; we have begun to recall just how many powerful minds and astute personalities were caught up in its vicious circle, and that at its beginning hasidism was only a reaction against decaying rabbinism. It is child's play to ridicule it today; there is no need to fight it, because it is dying by sheer force of circumstance. Thus, viewing it as a historical necessity and a thing of the past, we prefer to *understand* its substance and its essence.[25]

Segel's text was an excellent illustration of what was now expected of hasidic studies. Hasidic power was on the wane, the fights were over, and the younger generation was beginning to view recent adversaries with a greater measure of sympathy. The clear line of demarcation between high ideals and debased results showed that Segel, like later researchers and apologists of the movement, was not seeking a com-

[24] Seltzer, 'The Secular Appropriation of Hasidism'.
[25] B[enjamin] W. Segel, 'Z piśmiennictwa', *Izr.* 32 (1897), 96–7.

plete vindication of the hasidim. The heritage of maskilic criticism persisted, but it now related to 'the period of errors and deviations' of late hasidism. Yet it was not these errors that Segel considered to be of prime importance. The emphasis placed on its strengths and achievements proved that he was prepared to make a far-reaching revision of critical opinion, and even to idealize the hasidic movement. Significantly, he made it clear that this tendency was widespread among his generation. Once the historical dispute with hasidism had been set aside, the younger generation decided that the movement was no longer dangerous as a social force and declared that it was time to learn about it.

Segel's folkloric works of that time proved that these were not merely platitudes. Both for Segel and for other Jewish folklorists, historians, and literary historians and critics of the period, hasidism was the subject of sympathetic, and sometimes intensive, study, the sole aim of which was to explain its mysteries.[26] *Izraelita* and Polish folkloric periodicals published numerous ethnographic accounts of hasidic rituals, beliefs, practices, and customs written by young Jewish folklorists from the *Wisła* group including Henryk Lew, Jerzy Or, Zygmunt Majer, and Regina Lilientalowa. A debut volume written by Martin Buber (1878–1965), with tales of Rabbi Nahman of Bratslav, also had a warm reception. This short collection soon became virtually the manifesto of neo-hasidism, an intellectual movement founded by Buber that aimed at a philosophical reinterpretation of hasidic doctrine.[27] It was greeted almost enthusiastically by Henryk Lichtenbaum, a contributor to *Izraelita*. Lichtenbaum praised Buber's work as 'a gem in the treasury of world literature', which portrayed the real nature of hasidism and its high ideals. He also noted that studies of the movement in western and central Europe were unencumbered by contact with its present-day manifestation, thus enabling them to take such an objective interest in its spirituality. In Lichtenbaum's view, Buber's virtue lay in the fact that he was able to draw a line between the high ideals of early hasidism and its present-day fraudulence and sectarianism, thanks to which the reader could become acquainted with the great works of the first masters without engaging in gloomy contemporary issues.[28]

---

[26] The most important work by Segel on hasidism was 'O chasydach i chasydyźmie'. See also id., 'Materiały do dziejów etnografii Żydów wschodnio-galicyjskich'; id., 'Wierzenia i lecznictwo ludowe Żydów'. Of Segal's more minor works to be published in *Izraelita*, see 'Z legend żydowskich: Potęga śpiewu. Z opowiadań chasydów', *Izr.* 33 (1898), 526–8; id., 'Legendy i opowieści ludowe', *Izr.* 34 (1899), 216–17, 224–5, 236–7, 248–50. A bibliography of the more important works by Segel appears in Weinig, 'Beniamin Wolf Segel'. For more on folkloric subject matter in *Izraelita*, see Goldberg-Mulkiewicz, *Ethnographic Topics Relating to Jews*, 19–25.

[27] Buber, *Die Geschichte des Rabbi Nachman*. For an analysis of Buber's interpretation of hasidism, see Scholem, 'Martin Buber's Interpretation of Hasidism'; Biale, *Gershom Scholem*, 43–7; Idel, 'Martin Buber and Gershom Scholem on Hasidism'.

[28] H[enryk] L[ichtenbaum], 'Z piśmiennictwa', *Izr.* 42 (1907), 52–3. The Polish translation of one of Buber's stories was soon published in *Izraelita*; see Martin Buber, 'Rabin i jego syn', *Izr.* 42 (1907), 160–1, 172–3.

Equally benevolent, if somewhat less enthusiastic, notes were published in *Izraelita* about other new publications in which hasidism was depicted as an embodiment of Jewish spirituality.[29] However, once again the vindication was not entirely unqualified. There was the recurrent motif of the dichotomy between the original ideal and the debased practices of contemporary hasidism, whose exist-ence could not in any way be justified. This distinction was emphasized at almost every opportunity, and interest in the history and essence of the movement was accompanied by condemnation of its present political activity. Henryk Lichten-baum, who wrote relatively frequently about hasidim, even said: 'Over the past years there has been a proliferation of works about hasidism. We anticipate that this revival of the movement in literature augurs its disappearance from life.'[30] Although the new generation of intellectuals was not interested in the weaknesses or the disappearance of hasidism, and Segel, Lew, and Lichtenbaum sought in it 'the closed petals of a mystical rose', attempts to gain a real understanding of the movement rarely went beyond rather superficial explorations, even on the part of the more committed journalists. Within a surprisingly short time, opinions con-cerning the positive elements of hasidism took the form of clichés according to which it 'was a *sui generis* positive movement . . . a popular protest against dry, soul-less rabbinism',[31] which had only been forced onto the decaying paths of ritualism by later rabbis. This dichotomy between past and present hasidism became an-other device to explain its unknown side and saved new contributors from having to learn about the movement since what was truly interesting and worth studying was eighteenth-century, and not modern-day, hasidism.

However, the integrationists' own perceptions of their non-judgemental atti-tudes, or even sympathy, towards hasidism should not, it seems, be taken at face value. There can be no doubt that, for numerous members of the third or fourth generation of Jewish modernizing circles, both hasidism and the whole Jewish traditional world were a distant issue, with which they had little or no personal contact. On the other hand, it seems unlikely that they genuinely believed in the ongoing decline of hasidism and its marginalization, especially since on a number of occasions they acknowledged the considerable popularity of the movement. Their attitude was simply a convenient ploy to dismiss the still unresolved prob-lem of hasidism by freeing integrationists from the obligation to become intellect-ually or emotionally involved in the issue. It became possible to reconcile an interest in the origins and doctrine of the movement with unremitting condemnation of its current political activity, and to maintain a distance without needing to provide answers to questions about the persistence of hasidism. Thus, Warsaw 'progres-

[29] See e.g. the reviews of Frenk's publications on hasidism: Beniamin Wolf Segel, 'Z piśmiennictwa', *Izr.* 32 (1897), 96–7; on Kahana, Lector, 'Z piśmiennictwa', *Izr.* 37 (1902), 182–3; on Bogratschoff, Henryk Lichtenbaum, 'Z piśmiennictwa', *Izr.* 43 (1908), 134; on Teitelbaum, id., 'Z piśmiennictwa', *Izr.* 46/3 (1911), 8–9.        [30] Henryk Lichtenbaum, 'Z piśmiennictwa', *Izr.* 43 (1908), 134.
[31] Henryk Lichtenbaum, 'Z piśmiennictwa', *Izr.* 46/3 (1911), 8–9.

sives' were able to perceive themselves as being completely liberated from the bonds of the past while also being able to retain old anti-hasidic prejudices.

## 'SINGING AND DANCING': THE HASIDIC TREND IN LITERATURE

The growth of historical and ethnographic interest in the hasidim was also clearly connected with the hasidic trend in literature that swept through Jewish and Polish Jewish writings at the end of the nineteenth and beginning of the twentieth centuries. The most prominent figure in this trend, both in literature and in folklore studies, was Isaac Leib Peretz (1852–1915), author of *Hasidic Stories*, written in 1899–1900.[32] Peretz's works lie outside the scope of this study because their author was not a supporter of the integrationist movement and because he consistently wrote in Yiddish (that is, for a completely different group of readers). Nonetheless, his tales left a significant mark on the ideological changes taking place in the integrationist movement and its successors as well as on attitudes to hasidism. It was no coincidence that these tales were first translated into Polish by the young Jewish folklorists from the *Wisła* group, who wrote regularly for *Izraelita*. The young ethnographers not only had their translations of Peretz's hasidic stories published, but, inspired by them, they themselves collected and published hasidic folk tales.[33] Hasidic themes soon also appeared in the Yiddish works of Sholem Asch (1880–1957) and their subsequent Polish translations in *Izraelita*.[34] The prevalence of translations from Yiddish, and from other languages as well,[35] resulted from the dearth of original literary works in the circles of Polish Jewish integrationists and their successors from the turn of the century. Translations of Peretz, Asch, and Zangwill were a substitute for their own writings, just as ethnographic collections and discussions of other authors' works replaced their own historical writings. Clearly, when they were experiencing a serious ideological crisis, modernizing Jewish circles in the Kingdom of Poland were not particularly prolific either intellectually or artistically.

The only area of literary interest in hasidism in which members of the movement left interesting original works was drama, more specifically, two plays by Wilhelm Feldman and Andrzej Marek. At the end of the nineteenth century the considerable growth of interest among the Jewish masses in modern secular

---

[32] For more on *Hasidic Stories* by Peretz, see Niger, *I. L. Perets*, 274–97; Glatstein, 'Peretz and the Jewish Nineteenth Century'; Wisse, *I. L. Peretz*; Roskies, 'Rabbis, Rebbes and Other Humanists'.

[33] See e.g. 'Z ludoznawstwa: Powieści i legendy ludu żydowskiego', *Izr.* 34 (1899), 560.

[34] See e.g. Sholem Asch, 'Piątek wieczór u Rebego (urywek z poematu "Miasteczko")', *Izr.* 42 (1907), 74–6; id., 'Przywitanie Rebego (urywek z poematu "Miasteczko")', *Izr.* 42 (1907), 98–100.

[35] See e.g. J. Zangwill, 'Baal-Szem (z cyklu "Marzyciele getta")', trans. Maria Feldmanowa, *Izr.* 36 (1901), 462–3, 475–6, 488–9, 499–500, 511–12, 522–3, 534–5, 545–6, 557–8, 570–1, 582–3; 37 (1902), 6–7, 12, 30–1.

culture was accompanied by an increasing demand for plays about Jews and for Jews, that is, plays in which Jewish society would be presented not as the object of vulgar mockery but as a genuine protagonist. After unsuccessful attempts to adapt the Yiddish repertoire to Polish open-air theatre, in 1897 the director of the Eldorado Theatre, Lucjan Dobrzański, commissioned Gabriela Zapolska, a well-known Polish writer, to write a Jewish play.[36] Staged in the same year, *Małka Szwarcenkopf* was a huge artistic and financial success, opening the way to a series of plays with a similar theme: *Jojne Firułkes* by Zapolska, the antisemitic *Sara Weisblut* by Teodor Jeske-Choiński, *Sądy Boże* (God's Verdicts) by Wilhelm Feldman, and the two hasidic plays mentioned above: *Cudotwórca* (*Cadyk*) (The Miracle-Worker (Tsadik)) by Feldman and *Chasydzi* (Hasidim) by Andrzej Marek.[37] As was customary in open-air theatre, these two plays were written partly in couplets and were staged as vaudeville, accompanied by 'singing and dancing'. This, of course, was a response to the current demand for 'authentic' Jewish folk-lore, which hasidism supposedly embodied.

Performed in 1900 and published a year later, Wilhelm Feldman's *Cudotwórca* (Fig. 12) was the rather banal story of the platonic love of Gabriel, a brilliant young talmudist, for the delicate, intelligent, and educated Perla, daughter of a wealthy hasid. Alter, Perla's father, resolves to give her in marriage to a young scholar and, following the tsadik's advice, chooses Gabriel. The latter is astounded, but consents. However, Perla firmly opposes the whole plan. Numerous hasidim witness the bitter conflict between her and the tsadik, who claims that the girl has been possessed by a dybbuk. He promises to drive the evil spirit away for a large sum of money, but Perla refuses to submit to the tsadik's unsubtle pressures. Then, in an aside, Gabriel expresses his admiration for the girl and enters into a secret agreement with her. Perla pretends to comply with the tsadik's will, but, on the sabbath before the planned wedding, Gabriel delivers a fiery sermon in the synagogue in which he reveals that the tsadik is a greedy fraud and that hasidism is a deviation from the true Jewish faith and the curse of the Jewish people. Gabriel's bold speech wins him the love of the beautiful Perla and the admiration of young talmudists, brings down the tsadik, and pricks the conscience of some of the hasidim. The enamoured woman says, 'With you will I work . . . fight . . . suffer!' and the curtain falls.[38]

The response of the Polish press to Feldman's play was reasonably positive,[39] although the author was criticized for a lack of realism and for creating stereo-types.[40] An anonymous *Izraelita* journalist even accused the hasidic playwrights of

---

[36] See Raszewski, 'Zapolska—pisarka teatralna', pp. lii–lxxv; Steinlauf, 'Polish–Jewish Theater', 100–12, for more on the circumstances surrounding the play.

[37] The best analysis of this 'literary fashion' in Jewish plays can be found in Steinlauf, 'Polish–Jewish Theater', 100–38.     [38] Feldman, *Cudotwórca*.

[39] See Rydel, 'Z teatru'; Sarnecki, 'Teatrzyki letnie'; Kempner, 'Ze scen letnich'; E.Z., 'Cudo-twórca'; Koneczny, 'Teatr krakowski'; Rabski, 'Z teatrów letnich', *Kurier Warszawski*, 80/190 (1900), 3.

[40] 'Zast', 'Przegląd dramatyczny'.

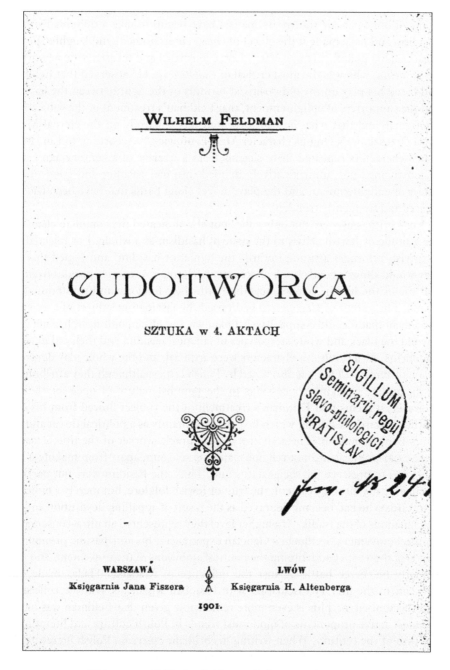

**FIG. 12.** Title page of Wilhelm Feldman, *Cudotwórca: Sztuka w 4. aktach* ('The Miracle-Worker: A Play in 4 Acts') (Warsaw, 1901)

capitalizing on the tastes of the rabble and of shallow mockery of the movement: 'some of our open-air theatre dramatists have begun to take a dubious liking to hasidism and have made it the object of cheap entertainment and laughter for the theatrical hoi polloi'.[41] It was Alfred Lor, a journalist and theatre critic who wrote for *Izraelita*, who was the most critical of *Cudotwórca*. He observed that Feldman had based his play on the old positivist formula of the fight between the hasidim and the supporters of enlightenment, that Feldman's treatment of the subject was unoriginal, and that what he had presented was 'a parody on the eternal Meir', Eliza Orzeszkowa's famous character Meir Ezofowicz.[42] According to Lor, Feldman's characters repeated 'trite slogans from a quarter of a century ago', were unconvincing, and unimaginatively divided into bad hasidim and good propagators of enlightenment, and the play 'moves along paths that have been hacked, cleared and frequently trodden'.

Lor's criticisms were not only valid, but also indicated the complete change in the attitude of Jewish critics to the issue of hasidism as a whole. Lor rejected the positivist, reformist attitude towards the 'ignorant hasidim' and hoped that the play would show 'a good chunk of ordinary life', tragic or comic episodes from the real life of the hasidic masses, together with their folkloric and mysterious elements. The author of *Cudotwórca* had raised the fascinating subject of a mystical movement that was still comparatively unknown, but, disappointingly, had not gone beyond the black and white stereotypes of fanatical hasidim and their enlightened opponents. As a result, his characters were artificial, and the whole play devoid of dramatic tension. This was also noted by Polish critics, although they attributed it to the author's making concessions to the populist nature of open-air theatre. However, it seems that Feldman's treatment of the subject flowed from his own attitude towards hasidism, which he perceived mainly as a political threat and not as a folk phenomenon. The activities of the miracle-worker of the title, a tsadik, were socio-political and not religious, and his sole aim, apart from making a fortune, was to preserve the social status quo. Thus, the hasidim were not part of a fascinating mystical movement, the fruit of Jewish folklore, but merely a bunch of drunkards who had become depraved as the result of appalling destitution and the machinations of the tsadik. At a higher level they represented an ultra-conservative political movement. Feldman's Galician experiences, his anti-hasidic pronouncements of the 1880s condemning the political ambitions of the movement, and particularly his fierce battle against the influence of Mahzikei Hadas made him resistant to the literary fascination with hasidism which his Warsaw colleagues had succumbed to. This is even more remarkable given that Feldman was one of the most active proponents of modernist trends in Polish culture and literature at the turn of the century. When writing his brilliant essays on Polish literature, he considered these forms of positivist literature to be anachronistic; however, when

---

[41] Lector, 'Z piśmiennictwa', *Izr.* 3 (1902), 182–3.

[42] Alfred Lor, 'Z teatru', *Izr.* 35 (1900), 329–31, 342–3.

confronted with the hasidic theme, he turned out to be unable to free himself from them.[43]

The other 'hasidic' play, *Chasydzi*, by Andrzej Marek (*c.*1879–1943), was written to compete with Feldman's *Cudotwórca*, and was also staged by open-air theatres in Warsaw. Commissioned by Wacław Gąsiorowski, *Chasydzi* was written in five days, and within a week was being staged at the Fantazja open-air theatre. The play was a literary and stage debut, so critics did not pay much attention to it. Even more unfortunately, the text was never published and the manuscript has not survived; thus information about the play is limited to fragmentary comments.[44] Only an anonymous reviewer of *Hatsefirah* has left a slightly more detailed summary.[45] The story was based on a motif almost identical with that of Feldman's: an educated girl, love, marriage plans, and hasidic circles. However, in contrast to Feldman's *Cudotwórca*, in *Chasydzi* there is no clear division into good and evil characters; in fact, the hasidim are not ideological adversaries, but appear mainly in order to enliven the scene with their dancing and singing.

The plot runs as follows. In a middle-sized town there lives a rich hasid named David Wagner, whose educated daughter Rebecca has refused to marry a tsadik from a nearby town. The matchmakers therefore suggest that Wagner should marry his daughter to a local maskil and doctor of medicine, Freiman. Wagner consents to this match, saying that, since his daughter must marry a maskil, it might as well be Freiman, because other candidates may be even worse. However, soon after the matchmakers have departed, Wagner's son, who is also the tsadik's son-in-law, arrives and announces that the whole family has fallen into disrepute because of the planned marriage to Freiman, who is the son of a heretic and reformer who tried to teach forbidden things to Jewish children and who defiled the Torah. Wagner swears that he was not aware of this and is ready to withdraw his consent, but the tsadik refuses to see him and the hasidim humiliate him. Angry, he returns home at exactly the moment when Freiman is paying the first visit to Rebecca. The young man instantly falls in love with Rebecca, and the father, annoyed with the hasidim, approves their match. The next act shows Wagner's house several months later, during Simhat Torah. Wagner is sadly reminiscing about the merry festivals spent in the company of other hasidim. Once again, he

[43] On Feldman's 'Jewish' dramas, including *Cudotwórca*, see Steinlauf, 'Polish–Jewish Theater', 118–24; Mendelsohn, 'Jewish Assimilation in Lvov'; Greń, *Rok 1900*, 274–90. Greń correctly pointed to the relationship between the plays' tendentiousness and their hasidic theme and, more generally, to Feldman's attitude towards hasidism. For more on the Jewish themes, including hasidic motives, in Feldman's writings, see Wróbel, 'Twórczość Wilhelma Feldmana'.

[44] See Steinlauf, 'Polish–Jewish Theater', for more on Andrzej Marek (Marek Arnshteyn). A fragment of this monograph has been published as Steinlauf, 'Mark Arnshteyn and Polish–Jewish Theater'. A good biographical note on Marek can be found in Zilbertsveig, *Leksikon fun yidishn teater*, v. 4414–67.

[45] T.W., 'Al hatsadikim ve'al haḥasidim (ḥizyonot al bimot hate'atron)', *Hatsefirah*, 27 (1900), 628–9. I have given here a broad summary of this article because it is the only description of the lost, hitherto unknown, play.

goes to the tsadik and invites him to his house. This time the tsadik allows himself to be persuaded and arrives with all his retinue, but insidiously suggests that Wagner should also invite his daughter's fiancé so that they might share the joy of the festival. During the conversation Freiman reveals his educational plans and his critical attitude towards the Talmud and Zohar, so the tsadik tells Wagner to throw him out and break off the engagement. And thus it is. Freiman returns home, and there we learn that he lives with his mother and Marta, an orphan taken in by them, who works hard in a factory to support all three of them as the doctor still cannot find work. Marta is recounting her meeting with the son of the factory owner, Szczerzyński, who has displayed great interest in her. Suddenly Rebecca, who has been cast out of the family home for refusing to marry the tsadik's son, enters. Freiman and Rebecca resolve to open a school for Jewish children in order to spread the ideals of the Haskalah. Another year passes, and during Yom Kippur, Rebecca begs her father for a reconciliation and for his blessing, but he refuses and calls her and Freiman wrongdoers and sinners. When the congregation enters the house of prayer, we see Marta leaning against the wall of the synagogue. The girl is listening to the cantor's voice but dares not enter because she has renounced Judaism. After a while Szczerzyński enters and we learn that Marta does not in fact love him and that she had converted to Christianity because she hoped to put some distance between herself and Freiman, for whom she feels a love that is not sisterly. Her hopes that she would start loving Szczerzyński in time had been in vain and now the girl is in a state of despair. Suddenly a fire starts in the synagogue and the congregation runs out of the building. The last to leave is Freiman, who had tried to extinguish the fire and rescue people. The crowd's anger and the rabbi's curse turn on him because he has profaned the festival by putting out the fire. Rebecca speaks out in his defence, the rabbi tells Wagner to silence her, but Wagner publicly announces that she is no longer his daughter because he has disowned her. Rebecca responds by calling Marta her sister, to which the crowd responds that she too will surely change her faith soon. In this way Freiman learns about Marta's conversion and, in a fury, attacks her. In the last act Szczerzyński tells the doctor that he has been unsuccessful in winning Marta's love and her hand in marriage because she still loves Freiman. Quite unexpectedly, the doctor suddenly abandons his enlightenment plans, leaves Rebecca and his mother, and elopes with Marta to a place unknown.

One critic, Gabriel Kempner, noted Marek's dramatic ineptness—his conspicuous references to other plays, his compositional weaknesses—but he also observed 'some honesty and passion that, nevertheless, permeates the play'.[46] The passion of the young author was also noted by others. In Alfred Lor's opinion, the work was a crucible of styles and genres, various themes and plots, poorly interwoven and interminable.[47] Irrespective of this, *Izraelita*'s reviewer acknowledged that the whole work was presented with a great feeling for mood, and that the

---

[46] Kempner, 'Ze scen letnich', 297.        [47] Alfred Lor, 'Z teatru', *Izr.* 35 (1900), 342–3.

author had skilfully incorporated 'modernist sentiments' and adeptly used poetry and subtlety side by side with terror and comedy. Lor thus acknowledged the superiority of Marek's play over Feldman's work, an opinion influenced by the attitudes of the two authors to hasidism. In contrast to Feldman's one-dimensional, stereotypical treatment, Marek's play depicted hasidism as neither unambiguously evil nor unambiguously good, but simply as providing a picturesque background to real life and genuine feelings. The play did not end in a victory of the hasidim over the maskilim, or vice versa, but in the triumph of true love over the artificial world of old ideological disputes. Marek thus lived up to the expectations of young Jewish critics, who wanted to see in hasidism a world of sentiment and mystery rather than an adversary to enlightenment programmes. Alfred Lor prefaced his review of Feldman's and Marek's plays with a characteristic comment:

The hasidim! . . . Indeed, in this word lie the trembling closed petals of a mystical rose; the word, like some echo from distant epochs, casts before our eyes some pensive ascetics with burning eyes and drawn faces! The hasidim are a land of rapture and fanaticism, intellectual backwardness and boundless devotion to one person, illustrating the idea of constant communion with the deity; a land of terrible prejudices and beautiful tales, it is a complete, original view of the world, with its historical basis, which advocates boundless optimism in its followers. The hasidim—they are a limitless ocean that has yet to be explored thoroughly, whose waves even now are in constant motion and from which it is not known what will emerge: maybe a new Atlantis, a land of wonders, dreams, and happiness, or perhaps a polyp with a hundred heads that will enfold all of Jewry with its thousands of arms . . .[48]

Thus, hasidism was (or at least was to be) for the young Polish Jewish intelligentsia an unknown and mysterious phenomenon, both fascinating and terrifying. This admirably suited modernist sentiments of the turn of the century. By being made less real in this way, it constituted an excellent *fin-de-siècle* literary theme. It had folk and mystical elements, it was immediate but unknown, full of contrasts, and, most importantly, it belonged to the world of the past; in other words, it was intellectually and emotionally safe. This vision surely corresponded with the level of knowledge of the Polonized intelligentsia, for whom the hasidism of Martin Buber's tales was more real than the surrounding world of the contemporary hasidim, of whom the young journalists of *Izraelita* simply had no understanding.

## CONCLUSIONS

At the start of the twentieth century the integration movement, which was successor to maskilic thought, was experiencing a serious crisis and gradual decay. One of the signs of departure from the old ideological line was, among others, the rapidly changing attitude to hasidism. The change was taking place in two opposite directions, both of which were unknown to previous generations of maskilim and their

[48] Ibid. 329.

successors. On the one hand, politically involved journalists such as Nachum Sokołów saw a new political threat in the hasidic movement and called for an alliance of all non-hasidic political forces against this group. On the other hand, from the mid-1890s it became more and more common to idealize the hasidic past, to see the movement as the fascinating creation of folk mysticism, a depository of authentic Jewish folklore, and above all an excellent literary theme. These two attitudes, although they seemed contradictory, frequently coexisted. Usually, they were evident in the belief that the good and beautiful teachings of the fathers of hasidism were later distorted by the tsadikim and had led to the contemporary degenerate form of the political movement.

The great interest in the origins of the movement was undoubtedly an attempt to escape contemporary reality and, at the same time, to escape the confrontational attitudes of the maskilim. This was obviously the result of changes in European writings that took place at the turn of the century in relation to the historiographic, philosophical, and literary portrayal of hasidism. The historical works of Dubnow and Solomon Schechter, and the 'hasidic' tales of Isaac Leib Peretz, Sholem Asch, and Martin Buber, were published and reviewed in *Izraelita*, and the nascent fashion for hasidism did not bypass the Kingdom of Poland. With Peltyn's death in 1896, a generation for whom the fight with hasidism was one of life's main missions died out. The young generation of secular Jews not only did not share the anti-hasidic fears and antipathies of their parents, but they also perceived hasidism with interest and sympathy as a museum of the Jewish nation's past. Of course, their sympathies were not unconditional and selfless. Their admiration of the philosophical and moral achievements of early hasidism and their praise for its leaders were always accompanied by condemnation of their stunted successors; but to relegate the hasidim to the past was to delegitimize their contemporary existence. Possibly, however, for the third and fourth generation of Warsaw 'progressives', the whole problem was actually so removed as to be lost in the mists of time. The young integrationists, especially in Warsaw, had never experienced the force of hasidic influence, so nothing marred their idyllic picture of the movement.

This, however, did not interfere with the intense debate with hasidism as a political movement. Yet the new journalists could permit such a glaring inconsistency because, as far as they were concerned, hasidism was just a fascinating literary theme and not the main ideological problem. Although hasidism still existed, and was even thriving, the 'hasidic issue' that had so bothered the maskilim and the integrationists belonged to the past.

# CONCLUSION

# Between Marginalization, Demonization, and Nostalgia

For a number of reasons, the development of the attitude of the Haskalah to hasidism in the Congress Kingdom is important to understanding the history of Jewish society, not only in this part of Poland but in the whole of eastern Europe. First, the striking differences between the attitudes of the Polish maskilim, the Galician supporters of the Haskalah, and the renowned critics of hasidism in Lithuania and Volhynia allow us to put in context the views of all these groups. The example of the Kingdom of Poland demonstrates that the struggle with the hasidic movement was not an obsession inherent to the entire east European Haskalah and an essential element of its ideology, but rather that it was the result of a confluence of many factors of an ideological and social, internal and external, nature. The breakthrough in attitudes towards hasidism associated with Eliezer Zweifel's views advocating reconciliation with the hasidic movement gains a completely new meaning in the context of similar declarations by Polish integrationists in the early 1860s. However, the significance of this breakthrough lies not so much in where it first occurred historically as in its usefulness as an analogy from which to draw lessons about the wider process taking place in modernizing Jewish circles in the Russian empire and the Kingdom of Poland. The similarities and differences in attitudes towards hasidism may be treated as a convenient starting point for more general studies of the Haskalah and hasidism in eastern Europe, the factors shaping them, and the characteristics that resulted from them.

The origins of the Haskalah in central Poland, later to become the territory of the Duchy of Warsaw and the Congress Kingdom, were not fundamentally different from those of the Haskalah movement in other areas of eastern Europe, even in regard to its reaction to hasidism. The maskilim who were active in central Poland were among the first maskilic critics of hasidism. Israel Zamość was apparently the first, followed by Mendel Lefin, who wrote his anti-hasidic project in Warsaw, and Jacques Calmanson, who was also active there. Nevertheless, it seems that, at the end of the eighteenth century and beginning of the nineteenth, anti-hasidic criticism was not an important element of Jewish Enlightenment ideology in Poland. In his *Autobiography* Salomon Maimon devoted a fairly prominent space to the history of hasidism while maintaining that the movement was already virtually non-existent. His highly abstract and erroneous description of its doctrine and organization showed how little Maimon knew about it. The care with which he described the 'neo-hasidic sect' was the result of complex literary strategies and a wish to shape the image of the world he was depicting, rather than the result of a belief in the objective significance of the movement to east European Jewry. Also, contrary to frequent claims in historiographical works, the hasidim were not an object of major interest to Calmanson. Close analysis of his text reveals that he considered the sect to be neither particularly fanatical nor dangerous, nor even numerous. According to him, the dangers of fanatical sectarianism were embodied not in hasidism but in Frankism, and for this reason he devoted considerably more attention to the latter movement.

Only the position of Menahem Mendel Lefin of Satanów could be called exceptional. From 1791 he was continuously involved in the dispute with hasidism and saw in it one of the main dangers to Jewish reform in Poland. It seems quite typical that Lefin's views left barely an imprint on the attitudes towards hasidism of other Polish maskilim (with the exception of Abraham Stern, whose views had been shaped by the Galician Haskalah). This was because of external factors: for example, the fact that, soon after the fall of the Polish–Lithuanian Commonwealth, Lefin moved first to Belarus and then to Galicia, where he attracted a large group of supporters. However, biographical details were of secondary importance. The clear differences in attitude towards hasidism that were observable between the Haskalah in Galicia and the Kingdom of Poland were an expression of more general ideological differences between these two groups of supporters of the Jewish Enlightenment. While the Haskalah in Galicia was shaped to a great extent by religious ideals and had a strong ideological basis, in the Congress Kingdom it was shaped mainly by its symbiotic relationship with state institutions, the opportunity to participate in numerous Jewish reform projects and public debates over the 'Jewish issue', and, indirectly, considerable pressure to integrate (including emphasis being placed on the use of the Polish language). These factors were particularly evident in the Duchy of Warsaw (1807–15) and in the constitutional period of the Kingdom of Poland (1815–30), but their results were also discernible later. They forced supporters of the Haskalah in the Kingdom to focus primarily on the practical aspects of their activities, on socio-political and economic changes. The attention that they devoted to productivization or to the political and legal situation was disproportionately greater than that devoted by maskilim from other regions of eastern Europe (some decades later similar trends would be observed among Russian maskilim and were the result of their alliance with the authorities). These factors were responsible for shaping the attitude of the Polish maskilim to hasidism. The hasidic movement was mainly seen not as representing an ideological challenge and a different world-view, but as a potential threat (or ally) to projects to reform the socio-economic system. It is not surprising, therefore, that the movement had been virtually ignored by the Polish maskilim until the 1830s.

Such a situation was possible because hasidism was still not a danger from the social and economic perspective. Its supporters in the Congress Kingdom represented less than 10 per cent of the Jewish population and their influence was still very minor. For this reason, almost all Polish maskilim saved their severest criticism for the traditional community institutions and completely ignored the hasidic threat. If they even mentioned the tsadikim and hasidism, they saw it as being just one form of traditional community structure (the concept was taken directly from Calmanson). Moreover, some maskilim—Dr Schönfeld of Kalisz serves as an excellent example—regarded hasidism as a potential ally in the fight with the all-powerful Jewish communal institutions and supported the dissenting activities of the movement.

The attitude to the hasidim only began to change in the 1840s, when their numbers reached one-third of the Jewish population and, in some communities, even represented the majority. Their particular type of social activism, their cohesiveness, good organization, and involvement in the community (Jewish communal institutions, the rabbinate, and voluntary associations) from the 1840s onwards made them the natural rivals of the supporters of the Jewish Enlightenment, particularly since the latter movement was at its peak at exactly the same time as hasidism. Confrontations mainly took place in community institutions and in the disputes of everyday life. Although both groups were still minorities, both aspired to gain power in the community, or at least to dominate some aspects of social life. In the case of the supporters of the Haskalah, this stemmed directly from their ideology. The maskilim used their better education, 'civilization', wealth, and sympathy with government policy to support their claims to power. However, the Kingdom's authorities had ceased in the mid-1830s to be interested in supporting 'civilizing' initiatives, and the relatively numerous interventions by the maskilim with the authorities did not achieve the desired results. Apart from Warsaw and a few larger cities such as Kalisz and Częstochowa, the maskilim failed to seize power in the community, or even to establish the kind of institutional basis that would enable them to carry out their programme. This led to disillusionment, growing frustration, and hostility towards hasidism, which was regarded as the chief obstacle and the only active adversary in the fight for power. This was particularly the case since the hasidim subjected their adversaries to daily harassment, which must have caused considerable pain to the supporters of the Haskalah. The 1840s saw a marked increase in the number of letters from the provinces to German Jewish newspapers, and especially in denunciations to the regional and central authorities of the Kingdom of Poland, in which hasidism was named as the primary problem facing Polish Jewry. These denunciations reiterated accusations and arguments that had been put forward for over half a century (hasidism as a form of exploitation of the masses and as a bastion of blind fanaticism, etc.). Yet for all the vehemence of these accusations, as a rule they were singularly lacking in intellectual rigour, while the authors' knowledge of hasidism was abysmal. Similarly, the participants in the press debate of 1839–40, Edward Hering, Józef Bernstein, Antoni Eisenbaum, and Izaak Emes, were equally poorly informed about the hasidim. The mid-century polemic best illustrated the compensatory nature of the debate: the fight with hasidism was a substitute for the maskilim carrying out their own programme and was intended to explain why the programme had failed to be carried out. Hasidism was blamed for all the misfortunes of the Jewish people, and accounts of it became more frequent, yet the maskilim consistently avoided the issue in their wider debates, in their overall reflections on hasidism, and in their attempts to find a systematic solution. The most frequent position was one of ignorance.

This phase of the conflict lasted until the early 1860s. The only maskil whose views differed significantly from the predominant attitudes of the period was Jakub Tugendhold, who had been defending hasidism as a legitimate form of Judaism since the 1820s. Although Tugendhold did not have any great sympathy for the movement, he consistently opposed delegitimizing it since this was, in his opinion, potentially dangerous for the whole Jewish world. The accuracy of his forecast was proved by the development of the myth of ritual murder, which assumed a new, refined form in the nineteenth century—by this stage it was not all Jews, but only the 'fanatic sect of the hasidim', who were accused of the crime. The accusation, which was especially common in the last decades of the nineteenth century, showed the danger that excessively radical anti-hasidic rhetoric posed for the whole Jewish community. Tugendhold not only openly disagreed with the accusation, but also claimed on many occasions that hasidism was not a sect and that its adherents were no more fanatical than other traditional Jews, and thus did not deserve to be singled out for condemnation.

However, a true breakthrough in the attitude towards the hasidim was attributed not to Tugendhold, but to a new generation of Polish Jewish integrationists who appeared on the scene in the early 1860s. It was these young intellectuals, who were mainly associated with *Jutrzenka*, who were the first to view hasidism as one of the principal ideological barriers to the whole Enlightenment—or post-Enlightenment—movement, not only as their chief adversary in the struggle for Jewish reform, but also as a challenge to their philosophy. This marked the culmination in the interest in hasidism among the Jewish supporters of modernization—the maskilim and their successors, the integrationists—in the Kingdom of Poland. The hasidic issue had never—either before or after—been so prominent in the ideological programme of the modernizing Jews in the Congress Kingdom, and had never had such significance to their identity as a group. Hasidism was one of two extremes (the other being the extreme assimilationists) between which the integrationists saw themselves as the happy medium and the only direction for Jewish society in Poland. Thus, hasidism acted as a justification for both the existence of the integrationist camp and its opposition to extreme forms of assimilation and religious indifferentism. At the same time, in the integrationists' eyes, a victory over hasidism (by force of argument, not the argument of force) was synonymous with ultimate victory over the entire Jewish traditionalist camp, the supporters of which, liberated from the fear of hasidic repression, would join the supporters of modernization en masse.

The statements and attitudes that came from *Jutrzenka*'s intellectuals concerning hasidism were ambivalent. Criticism of hasidism was frequent and very harsh: the tsadikim were accused of exploiting the naive, spreading drunkenness, and cultivating ignorance. At the same time, however, the *Jutrzenka* circle sought new levels of understanding and, most significantly, accepted hasidism as a partner in the dispute over the future of Jews in Poland. Praise for the positive features of the hasidim—their unrivalled unity, honesty, attention to religious instruction, charity, selflessness, and dedication to their own ideals—became more common. Leading this defence was Daniel Neufeld, who was fascinated by popular religious forms, questioned the superiority of the modernizing camp over supporters of the opposition, and called for unity with hasidic 'co-believers'. This aspect of integrationist ideology was surely a reflection of ongoing 'Polish–Jewish fraternity' and represented an attempt to transpose the Romantic ideology of unity onto intra-Jewish relations. Another significant factor must have been the strengthening of the position of the integrationist camp, which finally ceased to view hasidism as a threat to its existence and could thus afford to be on friendly terms with its adversary and begin to make an attempt to understand it.

None of this meant a renunciation by the integrationists of their criticism of hasidism, of their educational plans, or of their projected aim of transforming this group of Jews. Yet for the first time the debate moved from the everyday level of the struggle for survival and local disputes over power in the community to an ideological level, where the two sides could make their stand as equals. This represented a spectacular swing away from their earlier attitude, which was one of confrontation, delegitimization of hasidism, or at best of ignoring its existence, which had predominated in maskilic circles in the first half of the nineteenth century, to a position close to that of Tugendhold that sought a level of understanding and recognition of common values.

Nevertheless, *Jutrzenka*'s circles never managed to devise a cohesive programme concerning the 'hasidic issue', perhaps because the periodical lasted for only two years in the fraught period preceding the January Uprising of 1863 and many leaders of the integrationist movement left the country or were sent into exile. The group, however, endeavoured to revive the periodical and to rebuild itself, with its ideals and the directions of its research taken over by the weekly *Izraelita*, which made its appearance in 1866. *Izraelita*'s views on hasidism related directly to those of *Jutrzenka*, and *Izraelita*'s editor-in-chief, Samuel H. Peltyn, and initially sought common understanding and peaceful coexistence. This did not signify acceptance of the existing social order, but rather a belief in the impending victory over hasidism, which the integrationists would achieve through rapprochement using peaceful means, voluntary education, and good example. At the same time, the periodical carried on an active campaign to study hasidism and to become cognizant of its strengths and weaknesses. Some of the ideas, particularly those of Izrael Leon Grosglik, were unusually original. However, this idyllic period ended in the early 1870s when *Izraelita* began to be dominated by expressions of disillusionment with the persistence of hasidism. The analogy with post-uprising disillusionment and the intensifying misunderstandings in Polish–Jewish relations is striking. The frustrations of provincial 'progressives' returned to the journal's columns with redoubled force, and their content was very similar to the anti-hasidic opinions of the 1840s and 1850s.

There was a short-lived wave of publications hostile to the hasidim, but this subsided by the late 1870s—almost certainly an attempt to pass over a subject too painful for integrationist circles—but the significance of the debate with hasidism diminished considerably because of wider social and political changes taking place in public life in the Kingdom. From the start of the 1880s the lines of demarcation were running not within the Jewish world, between the supporters of the Jewish Enlightenment and the 'backward' traditionalists, but between Jewish society and the antisemites. The emergence of modern antisemitism had immense influence on the ideological transformation of the integrationist camp. It not only made the dispute with hasidism an issue of secondary importance, but it also reinforced the need for a united defence against mass attacks by enemies of Jewry. At times the defence also embraced hasidism, which struck a parallel with Jakub Tugendhold's activities half a century earlier.

Another factor that removed hasidism from the pages of *Izraelita* from the 1880s onwards was the emergence of modern Jewish nationalism. Integrationist circles showed themselves to be completely unprepared for ideological rivalry from the modernizing section of Jewish society, where thus far they had enjoyed almost total hegemony. Thus, in the fight with its new rival, *Izraelita* resorted to old anti-hasidic rhetoric: Zionists were called the new embodiment of hasidism, and Theodor Herzl a nationalistic Dalai Lama. In many respects, the debate with Zionism replaced the old ideological fight with the hasidic movement (*Izraelita* virtually did not enter into debate with the remaining Jewish nationalist groups).

Another breakthrough in terms of attitudes towards hasidism took place at the turn of the century, and at the same time marked the end of the integrationist movement. The social, political, and cultural changes that had been taking place across the world in the final decade of the nineteenth century and the first years of the twentieth century made their mark on the crisis and led to the ultimate disintegration of the integrationist movement. This was brought about by the ideological crisis within positivism, the appearance of ideologies questioning rationalism, fascination with esoteric doctrines, and so forth, and a new era of political mass movements in Jewish society, together with the accelerated development of a Jewish national identity. Similar changes were also taking place in the remaining countries of eastern Europe, where they again hastened the ultimate demise of the Jewish

Enlightenment movement. One of the signs of a departure from the old ideology by representatives of the Jewish secular intelligentsia was the abandonment of maskilic and post-Haskalah projects for the reform of hasidism, which had been one of the most important ideas of the Jewish Enlightenment for a large part of the nineteenth century. The most prominent representatives of this new trend were Simon Dubnow, Micha Josef Berdyczewski, Isaac Leib Peretz, and, slightly later, Martin Buber. In the Kingdom of Poland, with the exception of Peretz, the trend was represented mainly by folklorists from the *Wisła* group, contributors to *Izraelita*, and some other writers, including Andrzej Marek. The creators of the new Jewish culture not only renounced the fight with the hasidim, but also rejected the idea that a transformation of the hasidic movement was necessary. This attitude was somewhat analogous with the way in which the hasidim had been underestimated at the outset of the existence of the Kingdom of Poland. Representatives of the new trend attributed to hasidism various merits that were absent from the world of secular Jewry. In hasidism they saw a treasury of folk wisdom and uncorrupted Jewish folklore, folk mysticism, and, most of all, a fascinating literary theme. The only potential sphere of confrontation with hasidism was the political scene, yet this was also a significant innovation in attitudes to a movement that thus far had been viewed apolitically. It was possible to reconcile these contradictory attitudes by resorting to the old motif of the 'golden age', which had previously been used to criticize hasidism. Severe criticism of the political activities of contemporary hasidism was thus linked with idealization of its early leaders and their folklore. This notable interest in the past was undoubtedly an attempt to escape the reality of a lingering conflict that was not fully comprehensible to a majority of the young Jewish intelligentsia—the third or fourth generation of 'progressives'. It cannot be ruled out that the decreasing popularity of the hasidic movement, which was evident from the 1890s onwards, also contributed to a belief in the end of the hasidic world. Whatever the case, the Jewish intelligentsia at the beginning of the twentieth century saw hasidism, despite its persistence, as a closed chapter that belonged to the world of their forebears.

# *Appendices*

# 1. CALMANSON ON HASIDISM (1797)

From Jacques Calmanson, *Uwagi nad niniejszym stanem Żydów polskich i ich wydoskonaleniem* [Essay on the Current State of the Polish Jews and their Betterment](Warsaw, 1797), 18–19.

This pamphlet by Jacques Calmanson (1722–1811), one of the earliest maskilim in central Poland, was prepared as a contribution to the debate on the reform of Jewish society in Poland during the Four-Year Sejm (1788–92). However, it only appeared in print in 1796, in French, and then in 1797 in Polish. The following translation of a section of the chapter on the Jewish religion is from the expanded Polish edition.

## CONCERNING THE SECT NAMED THE CHOSIDE, OR ZEALOTS, THE BIGOTS

The sect, which is well known only to Jews in Poland, emerged no more than twenty years ago. Międzybóż, a town in Podolia, is its cradle. It owes its nature to a rabbi steeped in fanaticism, who, taking advantage of the gullibility of those people who have always been immersed in ignorance, who have always craved novelty and been astonished by anything that resembles a miracle, was so adept that he was considered a prophet among them. He claimed that he had the power to cure all diseases through kabbalah. This particular novelty initially aroused great adulation. The common people, attracted by one mere nothing and simultaneously repelled by another, eagerly ran to the fanatic's mud hut to regain their health, and although they could find nothing but errors in his teaching, the number of his followers nevertheless grew considerably.

The sect, which endures even now, rejects any teachings of the law; it treats a lack of learning as a matter of pride; the very lack of learning of which its supporters were earlier accused was seen as a fault and a vice and today it is made a virtue of, seen as beautiful, or at least suited to sloth; it knows only one teaching, that of kabbalah, but in this it shows neither reason nor restraint. It recommends a contemplative life as the only life for which man has been made; in public its followers pretend not to care for personal gain, but in private they do not hold with this belief. All their property is held in common and nearly always administered by their elders, of whom they think very highly and whom they even venerate with the title *the unerring*, which is rather for show than a reflection of the reality. Moreover, this kabbalistic skill, the profoundness and benefits of which their elders praise to the skies, and the secrets of which they carefully and prudently conceal from the crowd for their own gain, not only in order to preserve the relentless tyrannical power which they exercise over the minds of their followers, which is the sole rule and basis of their standing, but also to assert their right to the property of new adherents—I state that this same kabbalistic skill is an unfathomed mystery to them themselves. These two circumstances force one to wonder at how skilfully they abuse the misguided enthusiasm of simple folk. But, on the other hand, one should pity their lack of enlightenment, the good but misplaced faith of these uneducated, gullible souls who believe that they are serving God with this insane fanaticism, whereas, in fact, all their efforts simply make them vulnerable to the eccentricity of a number of cunning zealots, who are, and will continue to be, heavy-handed despots if the authorities do not contrive any effective means of eradicating this spreading pestilence.

Surely the authorities should take immediate and effective steps to put a check on the further spread of a sect so dangerous in its teachings, and even more dangerous in its effects; a sect that is spreading with greater enthusiasm than could have been predicted from its feeble beginnings, and which has already infected almost all the synagogues with its devastating poison. Why should not the country in which this reptile breeds, and not only Jews, fear its ferocity if there is no defence strong enough to withstand the folly of these dazzled zealots? Their fanaticism is all the more menacing for the fact that they, in good faith bordering on error, see themselves as fighting under the banner of religion, while they make it a priority to concern themselves with establishing and spreading their dogmas, which are as ungodly as they are terrible.

# 2. STERN'S REPORT (1818)

Abraham Stern (1762–1842), one of the leading maskilim in the Kingdom of Poland, prepared this report in response to the investigation into hasidism launched by the Voivodeship government in Płock in 1818. The report was commissioned from the Censorship Committee for Hebrew Books, where Stern acted as a censor, by the Government Commission for Religious Denominations and Public Enlightenment. It is in Polish, with a few phrases in Hebrew, and has been preserved in several copies in the archives of the central and provincial Polish authorities (AGAD, CWW 1871, pp. 43–6; KWK, 702, pp. 137–41; KRSW, 6634 ff., pp. 239–42). The following translation is from AGAD, CWW 1871, pp. 43–6.

To the high government commission for religious denominations and public enlightenment

In connection with the instructions handed to me concerning the sect called *ḥasidim* operating among the Israelite people in Poland, I submit the following explanation.

The Hebrew word in the singular form *ḥasid*, in the plural, *ḥasidim*, signifies a pious and devout man who observes all religious commandments, both ceremonial and moral, so strictly that he constantly does more than it is his duty to do, a duty common to all pious men, and always tends to do more good than is required by law. Such a devout man is characterized by a commendable piety, temperance, a refraining from any habits that could lead to depravity; he is characterized by humility, a love of others, and boundless charity. And, as a man with all these virtues is not easy to find, very few Israelites have earned the name of *ḥasid*.

No more than a few score years ago, an Israelite from Wallachia called Israel came to Podolia to the town of Międzybóż. He adopted the Hebrew name Ba'al Shem; that is, the one who works kabbalistic wonders by calling on the various names of God and the angels. He pretended that he could transport his soul to God at any time, and this communion with God revealed all secrets before him; namely, he knew how to cure all the ill and infertile people who turned to him, and how to improve the lot of the wretched with his judgement. This Israel Ba'al Shem bewitched a few persons from various places, and these became his followers and at the same time disseminators of wondrous fancies. With a view to ensuring greater esteem for this novelty among Israelites, he and his followers began to differ from other Israelites by way of celebrating the everyday service with an unusual clapping of hands, the most unbecoming leaping, and the wildest shouting. Having changed the form of praying common among Polish, Lithuanian, Bohemian, and Moravian Israelites, they also adopted a slightly different form once used by Spanish Israelites, pretending that this form was the surest gate through which prayer could enter heaven.

The common propensity of the simple people and the less rational members of society to listen to superstitions and tales of wondrous events drew to him some people who were ill or in some domestic trouble. Because they announced that through their extraordinary mystical deeds and fanatical ardour in prayer they remained in close communion with God and the angels, they assumed among themselves the name of *ḥasidim*. For all that, the Israelites despised them and their mystical teaching to such an extent that the name became an ironic epithet. In some places, they were called 'men of silk' [*kitajowcy*], owing to the fact that they did not dress in wool, but only in silk, for fear of finding a linen thread in the wool [which would be contrary to Jewish law], and so they wore only silk clothes.

After the death of the above-mentioned Israel Ba'al Shem, his followers dispersed in various directions and each of them made it known in his area that he had inherited from his leader the secret of working miracles. He taught and made it a requirement that each person coming to him with a request had first to give him *pidyon*, that is, ransom for the soul, and only then could such persons be assured that their request would be heard. Each of them strove to beguile and ensnare young people and less prudent Israelites, especially the rich and women. Thus, they took great pains to have their partisans in all towns and cities and for those to have a separate room or hall in which services could be held according to their custom, with them clapping their hands, leaping, and indulging in other indecencies, and in which their clandestine meetings in particular could be held, so that in this way they could all the more easily attract the young people to their company.

When one such ringleader [*herszt*] died, several replaced him from among the partisans, that is, his followers, proclaiming themselves leaders and behaving just like the ringleaders, breeding superstition and elevating fraud to the highest form of mastery.

The state and the conduct of the hasidim in the present time is such that they make it known among the Israelite rabble that, in one town or the other, there is this or that Israelite who, inspired by the holy spirit, sees everything; that through the communion of his soul with God he can change all things in the world with his utterances. To support their claims, they quote his fictitious miraculous deeds. At the news of this, naive people, especially women, approach this ringleader, either in person or through a messenger in writing, with a variety of questions: Should they become involved in this or that trade? Should they marry a given person, or not? Should spouses stay together or divorce? Some also come with requests: for fertility, for good luck in trade, for healing a sick person, for rescuing them from misfortune, for the recovery of a stolen item, for driving the devil, that is, an evil spirit, out of a person, for a favourable reply to a request to the authorities, for winning a court case. In the last two cases, some even take with them or send the particular piece of paper on which their request [to the authorities] or agreement will be written so that the pious ringleader will give his blessing to the paper. On each such occasion *pidyon*, that is ransom for the soul, must be given to the ringleader. The hasidim claim that whatever the ringleader says must come true, and simultaneously specify the condition that the supplicant must have absolute faith in the hasidim and their ringleader. These supplicants are standardly assured by the hasidic ringleader that their request will be heard, and when this does not happen and the deceived person grumbles, the hasidim come up with excuses: either the supplicant must have doubted their ringleader, or, since consulting him, he must have become a greater sinner than before.

With fraud and superstitions, they have gone even further: they use an unheard-of way to make the hasidim and those deceived by them leave their written requests on the graves of pious ringleaders. The son of the deceased or the successor to his leadership is in these cases an intermediary between the deceased and the supplicant and grants a hearing, but this must be preceded by *pidyon*, that is, ransom for the soul.

Such hasidic ringleaders abound in Poland in present times, each of them separately has his partisans in various places, and so some hasidim hold one in regard, while others believe another to be the most pious. Even though all hasidim have the common intention of deceiving, spreading superstitions, and dimming the light, hatred and quarrels often occur between the ringleaders themselves, each of them maintaining that the other is a rascal and a fraud.

In each town or city where there are several hasidim, they use any means at their disposal to hold clandestine meetings. This helps them to entice the young more easily. In such a place, various degenerate superstitions and immoral deeds breed;

idleness becomes natural there. Their clandestine meetings tend to be frequent, especially at the Farewell to the Sabbath, that is, *the third sabbath meal*; at that time they eat, drink, and sing songs. Their ringleader gives them nonsensical lectures on the Scriptures aimed at enhancing pernicious superstitions. After that they celebrate the evening service and again feast *melaveh malkah*—meaning the seeing off of the queen, which has an allegorical dimension: the *celebration of the coming sabbath*; their drinking, singing, and leaping commonly last until midnight, and often throughout the night. These hasidim try to persuade Jews that such behaviour leads to communion with God.

Of much greater significance are the clandestine meetings and gatherings of the hasidic ringleaders of a higher order; they come together from far and wide for a festival or for the sabbath, the richer travelling on wagons, the poorer walking. It often happens that the young people venture out without their parents' knowledge, and even clearly against their will, bringing with them *pidyon*, that is, ransom for the soul, both for themselves and for other people who are not present there, with the name of the supplicant and the subject of the request enclosed in writing. There, everything that happens is even more strange; mystical and kabbalistic splendour takes on a serious aspect. Each word uttered by the ringleader is inspired by the holy spirit (according to their claims) and is a sign that the same has been pronounced in heaven. A considerable number of young people stay there for several weeks and excel in idleness and superstition.

The entire mode of behaviour and the teaching of the hasidim during their clandestine meetings and gatherings are intended to prevent young people from acquiring any other teaching or skills than their religious and mystical teaching, and to instil repugnance for learning and craftsmanship to such a degree that they consider it an offence to read a scientific book, even though it is completely unrelated to religion, merely because it is written in another language and in other letters.

On the whole, the Israelites in Poland deplore the fact that these frauds and deluders each day spread more highly pernicious superstitions and try to draw young people away from enlightenment, but they have no power to remedy this wrong.

Having presented such an explanation, based on my own experience and beliefs, it appears to me to be necessary for the High Government Commission for Religious Denominations and Public Enlightenment to resolve: not to permit the hasidim in towns and cities to have separate rooms or halls in which to hold services, but to make them observe services together with other Israelites in synagogues according to the old custom and to ban strictly all their clandestine meetings and gatherings organized under any pretext.

Warsaw, this 29th day of September 1818

[signed] *Abraham Stern*

## 3. RADOMIŃSKI ON HASIDISM (1820)

From Jan Alojzy Radomiński, *Co wstrzymuje reformę Żydów w kraju naszym i co ją przyspieszyć powinno?* [What Is Hampering the Reform of Jews in Our Country and What Could Hasten It?] (Warsaw, 1820), 63–6.

This treatise, written in Polish, was published anonymously as a contribution to the debate over the reform of Jews in Poland, which lasted from 1818 to 1822. Its author, Jan Alojzy Radomiński (1789–1864), was a high-ranking government official greatly interested in Jewish issues, and his treatise turned out to be one of the most effective contributions to the discussion. The following extract translates the section devoted to hasidism. Numbered footnotes are original.

The greatest ill to the Jews and their societies has been, and is being, brought upon them by the various sects, each one more perverse than the other.[1] Of these, *the Sect of Zealots (hasidim)* appears to be the spawn of perversity, a plague disastrously engendered at the border of our country, that is, in Międzybóż in Ukraine between 1750 and 1765.

*Kalmanson* wrote strongly against it in his *Comments on the Present State of Polish Jews*, etc., often quoted here . . . *Friedländer*, in his work *Ueber die Verbesserung der Israeliten im Königreich Pohlen*, etc., mentions this sect in particular as one of the obstacles to the civilizing of the Jews in Poland, adding that it has existed in Poland for some centuries, though not as a sect, and at least not with such a considerable number of supporters.[2]

But here I would be glad to share with the reader information about this sect from the above-mentioned periodical *Sulamith* I. *Jahrgang* II. *Band*, card 308.* There its hideousness is painted in vivid colours, there are listed the horrible books which the leaders of this sect later published in Poland, their main content is depicted, from which for brevity's sake and so as not to offend reason, it is sufficient merely to quote: there exists the strictest possible prohibition on improving their minds in any way whatsoever; indeed, were they to emerge, they would be stifled and destroyed; the more a sinner sins, the nearer he draws to the deity; those who govern wield the power to absolve not only the grossest sins that have been committed, but also those sins that are about to be committed because of the sinner's predisposition and will; all sins can even be rewarded in certain circumstances, etc.

Indeed, such maxims directly contradict the laws of the Mosaic faith, and have brought upon themselves public castigation on the part of some rabbis, who have published various papers against this sect. But in the opinion of Israel Löbel, rabbi of Mohilev, and later deputy rabbi in Nowogródek in Lithuania, who is the author of the treatise discussed above [i.e. the article in *Sulamith*], these papers were merely protective measures to defend themselves from poison rather than direct attacks launched against the sect.

The lengths to which this man went in his concern for humanity are incredible:

despite the traps and dangers that threatened him wherever this reptilian tribe (*Otterbrut*, a term coined by the author) had its seat, he went to those places, preached and won converts, and gave away his Hebrew writings published in Warsaw in 1797 – one work entitled *Vikuaḥ* and another *Kivrot hata'avah* – exposing the ignoble principles that govern this sect. After numerous difficulties and sufferings, he proved that, in the parts of old Poland belonging to Russia and to the Austrian state, the clandestine meetings of this sect were banned and liable to severe punishment. And its leaders, escaping deserved punishment, moved to other parts of Poland, namely, to *Grodzisk, Nasielsk*, and *Stryków* (*Sulamith*, op. cit., p. 333).[3] For my part, as far as I know, I must add that the sect has now spread to all the provinces of our country, and there is hardly any place from which it is absent and where it is not still gaining new supporters.

But although Israel Löbel had counted almost 40,000 of them at its founder's death, about 15 years after the sect had been established, that is, around the year 1780, I do not want to estimate this figure [now], leaving it to the reader's discretion to guess easily [the extent of] their increase over the passage of time.

If other rabbis and the elders cared even half as much for the good of others as the person mentioned above, which has always been their duty, evil would never have taken root and spread to such an extent.

This sect, although it is the very worst and is hated by the Jews themselves, is gaining importance among them, because the well-known nature, way of thinking, and spirit of contemporary Jewry are anti-social, and that gives me reason to believe that, even if they were given a separate country, if their organization there were no different from what it is here now, they would be very wretched. Unfortunately, Jews completely lack pure morality, lack the willingness to work hard for their living, and lack a love even of their fellow Jews, and this is, after all, the very essence of the foundation of society.

---

[1] See *On the Reform of the Jewish People* by I. B. Wyszyński (Warsaw, 1818), p. 4.     [2] See page 38.
[3] See also *Histoire des sectes religieuses by Mr. Gregoire*, volume ii (Paris), pp. 337 ff.

* Israel Löbel, 'Glaubwürdige Nachricht von der in Polen und Lithauen befindlichen Sekte. Chasidim genannt', *Sulamith*, 1/2, no. 5 (1807), 308. MW.

## 4. THE ŁASK KAHAL'S COMPLAINT ABOUT A HASIDIC *SHTIBL* (1820)

**This complaint against a hasidic *shtibl* was delivered to the Voivodeship Commission of Kalisz by the *kahal* of Łask in 1820. It was written in good Polish, and signed in Hebrew. The translation is from AGAD, CWW 1555, pp. 6–8.**

To the Distinguished Commission of the Kalisz Voivodeship

During the worst times of war various vexations and irregularities have crept into our religion, so, with a view to preventing even greater disorder to those who come under its authority, the Łask synagogue feels obliged to state the following. Thus, according to the rites of our religion:

Firstly, services can only be held in the synagogue, and not in places inhabited, or even slept in, by members of society.

Secondly, those who hold services in various places cannot be informed about different official directives through announcements.

Thirdly, a matter that lowers the income of even the main synagogue:

(*a*) for the maintenance of hospitals and of the poor as well as to support/replenish other synagogal funds, in accordance with tradition, a collection box is placed at the entrance to the synagogue, so the more people who gather in the synagogue the higher its income;

(*b*) as Israelites also make voluntary contributions for the reading of the Torah, of the Ten Commandments and of other texts, when they do not gather in the synagogue, they do not make these contributions;

(*c*) the main synagogue thus has no alternative but to request a ban on the holding of services by Israelites in places other than the synagogue, unless with the special permission of the main synagogue, which is granted in some cases only according to the rites of our religion, but only under those conditions specified in the permission granted by former rabbis and the elders.

Requesting most humbly and trusting in the favourable outcome of our request, we remain the most humble servants of the Distinguished Voivodeship Commission.

The Elders of the Synagogue in Łask

[signed in Hebrew] that is *Abram Zorkowicz*
[signed in Hebrew] *Haiem Oszpi——n* [signature illegible]

Kalisz, this 7th day of May 1820

# 5. SCHÖNFELD'S REPORT ON A *SHTIBL* IN ŁASK (1820)

The opinion of Dr Schönfeld, one of the most influential maskilim in Kalisz, regarding a hasidic *shtibl* in Łask was commissioned by the Voivodeship Commission of Kalisz in response to the complaint from the local *kahal* (see Appendix 4 above) and forwarded to the Government Commission for Religious Denominations and Public Enlightenment. Because Schönfeld was not fluent in Polish, the report was supposedly written in German and then translated into the Polish by an anonymous translator. The preserved copy is badly corrupted, as the copyist(s) supposedly did not understand sections dealing with Jewish religious law. Many passages are barely comprehensible. The translation is from AGAD, CWW 1555, pp. 10–16.

Although the opinion requested of me concerning the private prayer halls in the town of Łask does not lie within my field, I still shall endeavour to satisfy the requirements of the High Commission, which honoured me with this request.

If, in the matter in question, I appear at times to be overly loquacious, I beg the reader to see the reason for this partly in the quotations, and partly in my ardour, with which I shall endeavour to explain to the High Commission the abuses committed by our Jews in their ceremonies, which are alien both to the Mosaic faith and to talmudism. . . .

Ad 1.  The elders of the synagogue in Łask have stated that Israelites can hold services only in the main prayer halls, that is, in synagogues. Which religious laws, or rather which books of Moses, served as a source for these elders? This was resolutely passed over. Both the Bible and Talmud allow each and every Jew to hold his prayers wherever he wishes. And so it is written in the second book of Mos[es] [Exodus] 20: 21: *Wherever you pray to me, I shall bless you.*—Also, in [*Shulḥan arukh*] 'Oraḥ ḥayim', chapter 90 §19, fo. 35*a*. Ibid., chapter 130 §4; chapter 49 §1; chapter 151 §12. In Hagai* this is clearly mentioned.

It has always been left to the free will of each Israelite, not only according to Moses, but also according to subsequent talmudists, that wherever he wishes, and as often as he wishes, he can reveal his feelings in prayer whenever he feels so disposed and whenever his heart requires consolation, and in any words which he deems appropriate ([*Shulḥan arukh*], 'Oraḥ ḥayim', chapter 101 §4. *Sotah* folio 33).[†] Yashi [*sic*] comment[s] *that any language* may express one's prayer, there is no need to seek evidence in the Holy Scripture, because prayer is none other than the affair of one's own heart and so it can be expressed in any speech one possesses.

A comparison (*ya'azor*) with Rabbi I[saiah?] Horowitz and Debur question 321: and at each time of one's life one can speak [with] one's Heavenly Father.[‡]

Finally, in the Holy Scripture there are no formal references to the place and time of prayer apart from those in Deut. 26: 5–10 concerning first offerings.

Ad 2.  That by holding services in various places they cannot be informed about different governmental directives through announcements.

This is a very insubstantial reason because, if the board of the synagogue in Łask orders the so-called *minyanim* (that is, a gathering consisting of 10

Jews over 13 years of age, who are entitled to pray in any place), I say, if the elders order this *minyanim* to advertise *publicanda*, they will hasten to publicize them all at once.

Besides, I should be glad to know whether these elders also treat the *minyan* in the first seven days of mourning (*shivah*) in the same scrupulous manner?

**Ad 3.** That even the main synagogue suffers considerable losses of income, namely:

**Ad A.** 'for the maintenance of the hospital and the poor from the alms put in the collection box at the entrance to the synagogue'

Indeed, one cannot bear a grudge against a Jew who prefers to give his charitable alms directly into the hands of the poor or ill, rather than putting the money into a collection box so unscrupulously managed by the elders. As far as putting alms into the collection box is concerned, each of the *minyanim* may organize such a collection separately and they will surely dispose of it better and more generously than the Jewish community board.

Finally, how Jewish hospitals in our province are managed (as *exemplum rem demonstrat*) can be learned from the poor administration of the Jewish hospital in Kalisz, which surely serves as a model for others.

**Ad B.** 'that it is to the detriment of the synagogue when the income from the reading of the Pentateuch, that is the Ten Commandments (the Torah), is depleted'

This is one of the most shameful and demoralizing abuses that this so-called *mitsvah* permits itself by way of auctioning, and scandalous bidding for a service, which is given only to the one who offers the most! Indeed, this practice exceeds all limits of honesty and piety, because in these circumstances in such a holy place a poorer Jew is subjected to the most deeply felt humiliation and affronts. Just imagine this dishonesty and stupidity—whoever offers more, has access to the Torah? Which peace-loving Jew with a sense of honour would not rather pray in solitude to the Heavenly Father whom we all share? Or go to the hall of prayer in private and pray there in a *minyan*, rather than in the synagogue, where God can only be reached through higher fees! O Heavenly Father! Promptly grant Israel services free of stupidity and filth!

**Ad C.** It is now obvious what the spirit of the elders of Łask is, because these elders demand that each private act of praying be dependent upon their synagogue. And this all falls into place because they say in Ad 1 that Jews can celebrate services only in the main synagogue and here they surely want (which is self-evident) to be granted fees and a fee for their permission, and so it would be a *status in statu* situation.

The members of the board became illogically entangled, because, having written enough nonsense, they made known their intention of making the faithful pay money; that is, contributions. Yet, if strict religious laws have been handed down, such persons as the superiors in Łask should not disrespect them, and for that they deserve to be rebuked soundly and ordered to read the following chapters by the Divine Psalmist David—Psalm 15, Psalm 101: 4, 5–7, and Psalm 13, and to communicate the decision to the accusing party.—

OPINION

It clearly results from the above-described laws of the Jewish religion that the Israelites, not only according to the Mosaic faith, but also according to talmudism, are permitted to establish their own halls of prayer and have them located as they wish and where they wish. And that the Jews choose no inappropriate place for such a practice is upheld by the care with which they celebrate even the smallest ceremony.

In this respect, in all conscience according to my beliefs, knowledge and belief in the Mosaic faith and Judaism, in accordance with justice I hereby submit my opinion.

Kalisz, this 13th day of June 1820.

[Schönfeld]

Certified by
Secretary General of the Commission of Kalisz Voivodeship Jałowiecki

---

\* Hagai, which should be *Hegeh*; refers to the comment by Moses Isserles. MW.

† The source is corrupted in what follows. It possibly refers to a discussion concerning the saying of prayers in languages other than Hebrew in *Shulḥan arukh*, *Sotah* 33, and in the commentary by Rashi (corrupted to Yashi). MW.

‡ Another fragment probably corrupted by a copyist. 'Horowitz and Debur' possibly refers to Isaiah Horowitz, *Shenei luḥot haberit*, ch. 4 (*dalet*, which stands for '4', was misunderstood by the copyist as an abbreviation for 'debur'), where the author discusses the languages in which prayers can be said. MW.

## 6. SCHÖNFELD'S REPORT ON THE BATHS IN CZĘSTOCHOWA (1820)

This report by Dr Schönfeld was commissioned by the Voivodeship Commission of Kalisz, which had been prompted to investigate hasidism by the conflict between the hasidim and their opponents over the use of the ritual baths in Częstochowa in 1820. This lengthy report was delivered to the Voivodeship Commission in German and was never forwarded to any central authorities. The translation is taken from AGAD, KWK 702, pp. 73–86.

## MAY JEWISH MEN—AND ESPECIALLY HASIDIM—USE THE BATH FOR JEWISH WOMEN?

*A special report by Schönfeld published by the Kalisz Provincial Commission on 29 October of this year under No. 2497.*

Kalisz, November 1820

CONTENTS

*Motto*
Think your beliefs ten times in earnest over
Ere you rush in. Stand still and do not run but hover.—
No ancient prejudice uphold forsooth.
The oldest often is the weakest truth
Born of great error, for its looks alone extolled
Silvered by time but never good as gold.

                                                        DUSCH

### §1 INTRODUCTION

All customs, commandments, and ceremonies of the Jews that are not found in the Pentateuch are contained in the Talmud, and derive their authority from it. However, at different times and in different countries, the Israelites have introduced special customs, ceremonies and liturgies.

Thus German, Polish and Russian Jews have one custom (*minhag*), but the Spanish and Portuguese have another, which again differs from that of the Italian and Levantine Jews. Those in China and in Indian lands have yet another custom. *Only on the main points of their faith and customs do all Israelites agree.*

### §2 AN EARLY HISTORY OF HASIDISM

In 1760 and 1765 Israel Löbel of Międzyworz [*sic*] first became known in the Ukraine. This Israel, a man of great ambition but not very well versed in the Talmud and hence unlikely to achieve fame among his co-religionists, yet filled with vain delusions of achieving fame, followed the path of Cagliostro and became an exorcist: 'My spirit', he said, 'often tears itself from my body, the better to gather news of the spirit world. It tells me what happens there and keeps me informed about the many evils with which the spirit world threatens our earth.'

Israel Löbel adopted the title of hasid. That word meant 'pious' in the original language, but among the hasidim it refers to someone who is not content to follow the ceremonial rites of Moses and the talmudists, but is determined to bind himself closer to God by righteous deeds.

By attracting wealthy Jews, Israel Löbel helped his sect to expand in size and in power.

### §3 ON HASIDIC RITES

Apart from the usual host of laws enforced by the ritual police of the Jews, and over and above the ceremonial customs, which the hasidim observe most scrupulously, they also have a number of special prayers composed of an incomprehensible mixture of kabbalistic, Neoplatonic, and Habad mysteries, whose origins may well go back to the Talmud. These mysteries do not constitute an independent system, nor are they recorded in specially printed prayer books or in other sacred writings. They may, of course, have been put down in secret and handwritten manuscripts. The hasidim do not have an official leader, but the most pious and learned among them, whom they call *magid* (orator) or *ba'al shem* (kabbalistic exorcist), is, so to speak, the *first* among them, and he appoints his favourite disciple as his successor on his deathbed. This *first* among equals (whom they usually call rabbi) is a miracle-worker, a dispenser of amulets, and is allegedly in touch with the dead. The mystical book called the Zohar (written in Syro-Chaldaic) is their Delphic oracle. The hasidim are hated by other Jews, although they cannot charge them with immoral behaviour. The talmudists probably fear them as a growing band of rivals.—That no objections to them can be raised is due—according to David Friedländer's apt observation—partly to the fact that they cannot be accused of particular transgressions, and partly to the unfortunate failure of our authorities to take cognizance of internal hatreds among the Jews. No hasidim can be found outside the Kingdom of Poland or Austrian and Russian Poland.

### §4 THE PURIFICATION OF THE JEWS, WITH SPECIAL REFERENCE TO HASIDIC BATHING PRACTICES

With the dissolution of the Jewish state, many of the laws laid down in the Pentateuch and interpreted in the Talmud ought to have been scrapped, inasmuch as these laws—and especially the purification laws—are based on local and temporal conditions. Of these, particularly relevant to our discussion are the laws governing washing and bathing, together with bodily cleanliness in general, which still prevail in the East. These are enjoined upon Jews as police-enforceable ritual laws, by the Bible as well as by the commentaries, especially by the Talmud. (Something our Jews in Poland unfortunately often fail to take into account.) Inasmuch as the hasidim consider it their duty to heed the least ceremonial law of their religion—which is particularly commendable when it comes to cleanliness—there can be no doubt that they are also scrupulous in this respect, and that bathing '*must rightly be considered an integral part of their rite*'.

### §5 MAY MEN AND WOMEN OF THE MOSAIC FAITH MAKE USE OF ONE AND THE SAME BATH?

The talmudists have fixed the time when Jewish women must take their bath (after every menstrual period), namely at dusk, when daylight makes way for night. The bath (*mikveh*) must be a cistern the height of a man, filled with spring water. *Whether Jewish men may or may not bathe in such mikvehs is laid down neither in the Talmud nor in rabbinical writings.*

### §6 HENCE MAY THE HASIDIM USE THE LOCAL WOMEN'S BATH IN STARA CZĘSTOCHOWA?

For the cogent reasons mentioned above, I can conscientiously answer the above question *in the affirmative*. However, the times set aside for this purpose must be fixed in such a way that decency and morality are not offended in any way, something the local hasidim are bound to accept.

The precise bathing time is best fixed locally by an expert committee.

### §7 CONCLUSION

This may be the right place to say a few words more about public baths (*mikvehs*) for Jewish women.—In his book on forensic medicine, Wildberg states (on page 4, §3):

> Since the individual inhabitant has neither the knowledge nor the opportunity to assess the true condition of the whole and of the individual parts, lacking as he does the ability to remove obstacles to his well-being, and hence to help himself as best he can; since he is unable to fathom the consequences of unavoidable past effects, or even to diminish them, he must resolve not only to protect himself against acts of public violence but also to take care of his physical well-being, or entrust bodies or institutions with the implementation of what is beyond his individual understanding and power.

Do not the words taken from this excellent scholar apply quite particularly to the baths (*mikvehs*) for Jewish women? Why have these baths (as public institutions) not been placed under medical and police supervision? Has Dr Wolff from Hamburg not demonstrated convincingly—in his work entitled *The Diseases of Jewish Women*—what deleterious effects a *mikveh* (without medical installation and without medical knowledge) can have on the health of Jewish women?

No matter if Jews are treated as *guests* (*hospites*), as *vassals* (under the *jus incolatus*) or as citizens (*civitate donare*), I believe that they understand the importance of maintaining good health.

May our humane and wise government continue, as it has already begun to do, to take a growing interest in the ritual of the Jews, so that Jews may no longer be looked down upon as Jews, but treated honourably as Poles of the Mosaic (Jewish) religion, and respected for their sacred and thoughtful . . .

No more hounded for what is in their mind
No longer for their faith despised
Love does all churches fuse and bind
Temples and mosques like them are prized.

*Schönfeld*

# 7. ADVISORY CHAMBER OF THE JEWISH COMMITTEE ON THE HASIDIC RABBI IN PŁOCK (1829)

The opinion of the Advisory Chamber of the Jewish Committee, responding to the enquiry whether a hasid and a usurer can be a rabbi, was commissioned by the Jewish Committee, which had reacted to a query from the Government Commission for Religious Denominations and Public Enlightenment. The issue was raised during a conflict between supporters of Alexander Zusya Kahana (1795–1837), rabbi of Siedlce and a close associate of the tsadik Simha Bunim of Przysucha, accused of usury, and those supporting Abraham Rafael Landau (1789–1875), the rabbi of Ciechanów, also a follower of hasidism. The document is in Polish; the translation is from AGAD, CWW 1666, pp. 268–9.

Copy
Re: Register of Petitions, item No. 130.
Warsaw, this 21st day of September 1829
To the Jewish Committee in the King[dom] of Pol[and]
From the Advisory Chamber

The Advisory Chamber has read the request of the inhabitants of Płock of the 20th day of the previous month brought to its notice, together with the call from the Committee, and is honoured, in accordance with the minutes of the meeting held on the 18th day of this month, to reply as follows:

1. Religious laws do not clearly forbid the hasidim to be rabbis. Yet this is based on the fact that hasidism was established after the time in which the religious laws, that is, the books of the *Shulḥan arukh*, were collected and published, and so it is natural that they make no mention of it, as this was an unforeseen case. Yet because

the hasidim have introduced changes into some religious rites, it is inappropriate for a hasid to be appointed rabbi in a town where a majority of the Jewish community does not belong to the hasidim. Thus, it is very inappropriate when, in the celebration of some religious rites, the Jewish community and its rabbi behave in a different manner. That this Kohen Alexander is a hasid is beyond a shadow of a doubt.

2. As for Alexander Kohen's conduct, in relation to which the supplicants request that the Advisory Chamber be consulted, its members reply that, to date, no longer being in close contact with him, they know nothing specific of his behaviour, apart from a certain fact that there has been a rumour that he has committed usury. As it is clearly stated in point 2 of the rules governing the election of rabbis that a rabbi should be a person of integrity and one who *has never committed usury*, it would appear to the Advisory Chamber that although the above rule concerning an examination is not binding on Kohen as an ex-rabbi, any proof that he has not committed usury should relate to both Kohen and all others, even former rabbis, as he is only moving from one place to another. Nevertheless, in the case in question, if a person applying to be a rabbi has ever been accused of an act such as usury, even if he has been excused from court-administered punishment for want of evidence, this already tarnishes his reputation and he should not become a rabbi. Annexes to be returned.

Governor [signed] *de Müller*
Secretary [signed] *J. Glücksberg*
Certified by Secretary of the Committee Józef Augustynowicz

## 8. THE HASIDIM IN PILICA (1830)

**The Jewish Community Board of Pilica petitioned the Government Commission for Religious Denominations and Public Enlightenment to force the local hasidim to contribute to the restoration of the synagogue closed because of its run-down condition. The Government Commission in turn requested the Jewish Committee for its opinion. The petition was written and signed in Polish, as were both (contradictory) opinions of the Jewish Committee. The broader context of the conflict is unknown. The translation is from AGAD, CWW 1472, pp. 16–18.**

To the High Government Commission for Religious Denominations and Public Enlightenment

Pilica, this 14th day of July 1830.

In the district town of Pilica by order of His Ex[cell]ency Commissioner of Olkusz District, the synagogue of the Israelites was sealed, because of the threat of imminent collapse. In this town, there dwells among the Mosaic inhabitants of the first and second [fiscal] class a sect of hasidim who pray in private homes and thus have refused to make any voluntary contribution to the restoration of the synagogue, stating as their reason that they do not attend it. The Jewish community board, deeming the hasidim's behaviour pernicious, requests that similar clandestine meetings and gatherings of the rabble in improper places be prohibited by the authorities. Therefore, the Board addresses its request to the High Government Commission, that the Commission order the local administrative authorities to forbid the hasidic sect to hold prayers or services under any pretext in any hall other than the synagogue as their proper place and, in this way (with the contribution of the aforementioned hasidim from the first and second class), the synagogue may be restored without the need for the poorer inhabitants to contribute. In renewing my request, I earnestly implore the swiftest possible outcome.

*Eyzyk Herszberg* Com[munity] B[oard] Mem[ber]
*Kalman Weingarten* Com[munity] B[oard] Mem[ber]

[in the margin:] *Opinion of the Jewish Committee.*

Addressing the General Directorate for Denominations with the request of the Jewish community board members from the town of Pilica in which they petition to have an order issued to force the local hasidim to pay contributions for the restoration of the synagogue and to prohibit them from holding prayers in private homes instead of the synagogue, the Committee, invoking its previous replies in this respect given to the General Directorate for Denominations, namely those of 7th June 1827 and of 12th August 1829, begs to reiterate that, according to religious law, Israelites are entitled hold all prayers not only in the synagogue, but in private homes as well, provided their gathering numbers ten or more persons. On the other hand, there is some proof in its documents that, under Prussian and Austrian government, Jews were forbidden to use *minyanim*, that is, private prayer halls.

Warsaw, this 23rd day of August 1830.
On behalf of the Director: Assessor of the Committee *S. Witwicki*
Secretary *J. Jakobkowski*[?]

[in the margin:] *Pending Decision*

In the opinion of the Jewish Committee, religious law grants people of this faith the right to pray both in private homes and in synagogues if 10 persons gather. However, as the issue concerns the renovation of the synagogue, which has been closed for reasons of safety, and because exempting the sect of the hasidim would make such a difference that the poorer classes would be unable to afford to pay their required contributions, it would seem necessary to make all Jews without exception contribute to the costs, but to allow them the freedom to choose whether they pray in the synagogue or in private houses. Surely both the Prussian and Austrian authorities forbid Jews to pray in private homes for no other reason than to ensure that everybody, without exception, pays their contribution in similar cases.

Warsaw, 24 August 1830
  *M. Zaleski*
  *Stern*


## 9. THE MASKILIC PRAYER HALL IN SUWAŁKI (1833)

This petition, asking in good Polish for the right to establish a maskilic prayer hall, was submitted to the Government Commission for Internal and Religious Affairs and Public Enlightenment by an otherwise unknown maskil from Suwałki, Anszel Flatau. The circumstances of the petition are unknown. The translation is from AGAD, CWW 1818, pp. 70–1.

To the High Government Commission for Internal and Religious Affairs and Public Enlightenment.

Warsaw, this 27th day of September 1833

Anszel Flatau, an inhabitant of the town of Suwałki, submits the enclosed request.

When the author is subjected to various vexations and insults by Mosaic inhabitants of the local parish, particularly in the synagogue, in the name of achieving civilization, both for my attire and for all other customs which distinguish my house from others of that denomination; for this reason, in order to avoid distress, I have resolved to appoint my own house as a place for celebrating services with my family and selected persons. Anticipating obstacles on the part of the Jewish community board, I apply to the High Government Commission with a humble request that I graciously be granted such permission.

In anticipation of a prompt hearing of my request, I remain your humble servant

  *Anszel Flatau*


## 10. TUGENDHOLD'S REPORT ON SMOKING TOBACCO IN THE *BEIT MIDRASH* (1840)

This report was delivered by Jakub Tugendhold (1794–1871), one of the key figures among the Polish maskilim, at the demand of the Government Commission for

Internal and Religious Affairs after a resident of Międzyrzec Podlaski, Moszko Tajtelberg, had submitted a proposal to the Commission to have tobacco-smoking by the hasidim in the area of the *beit midrash* prohibited. At the same time the Commission received a letter from Rafał Goldman, who represented the hasidim of Międzyrzec, demanding the legalization of smoking in the *beit midrash*. The Tugendhold report was to comment on both petitions. It was delivered in Polish. In the appendix a long section of the report discussing religious laws on the synagogue and *beit midrash* has been omitted. The translation is from AGAD, CWW 1780, pp. 38–45.

To the High Government Commission for Internal and Religious Affairs

In response to the rescript of the Denominations Department of 21st September/ 3rd Octob[er] of this year, No. 5917, I am pleased to present the following: that after careful consideration of the two jointly addressed requests so communicated to me, one of which advocates prohibition while the other favours permission being granted to smoke tobacco in the so-called *beit midrash* in the town of Międzyrzec, as well as serious Hebrew works, which are related to the issue in question, I wish, above all, to state the following.

Although at first glance the entire affair, particularly in individual terms, appears to be a matter of inconsiderable weight, it nevertheless deserves the consideration of the High Authorities when seen in general terms as relating to the Israelites of this country and when it is perceived in terms of the influence it can have on curbing the fanatical liberty of this so-called sect of hasidim, which is spreading in Poland, and thereby on the prevention of conflicts and arguments which oftentimes have taken place between the supporters of this sect and other Israelites who do not belong to it. Having such a standpoint and acknowledging with deep-felt gratitude (with which all enlightened and right-thinking Israelites are surely filled) the benevolent tolerance of the High Government Commission for Internal and Religious Affairs, which seeks to solve issues arising in the Mos[aic] faith in accordance with the laws of this religion, I shall begin to clarify the matter in the following manner:

 . . . It appears to be clear

1. That, according to the binding religious work *Shulḥan arukh*, 'Oraḥ ḥayim', the sanctity of the *beit midrash* surpasses the sanctity of the synagogue itself and anything which savours of disrespect or an insult to the sanctity of the place is forbidden equally in synagogues and in *beit midrash*.

2. Although teachers and their students in the *beit midrash* may eat and drink if need be, pipe-smoking cannot be regarded as a necessity of life. Moreover, one should distinguish between a *beit midrash* designed only for religious instruction, which could be called a theological school, and those *batei midrash* in which services also are regularly held and which thereby acquire the character of a synagogue.

3. That common religious and moral norms recommend each nation to accord the highest regard to any place reserved for the glory of God or religious instruction and that, even in places of no religious significance that are, nevertheless, frequented by the public, the smoking of tobacco is usually prohibited.

4. That the aforementioned Israelite theologian places smoking tobacco among those worldly desires that should be avoided.

5. That the smoke and smell of the pipe can be harmful to persons afflicted by old age or weakness (as Israelite Mojżesz Teitelbaum rightly complains).

Therefore, the warning issued by the Podlasie Provincial Authority prohibiting pipe-smoking in the *beit midrash* in Międzyrzec, not being contrary to important religious laws, does not in the least need to be revoked, but indeed should be upheld.

However, in order to forestall groundless complaints which could be made by the hasidim in particular, and which could be unnecessarily vexatious to the High Government Commission, and, moreover, in order to place, in the country as a whole, something of a restraint upon the fanatical liberty and conceit of this sect, which oftentimes vexes the simple pious class of Isra[elites] and disturbs the peace in communities, and whose supporters, even those youthful in years, so compulsively smoke tobacco that oftentimes they enter the *beit midrash* during a service with a pipe, I make bold to suggest that it would be of great service, were the High Government Commission for Internal and Religious Affairs to resolve to pass a general order to the following effect:

> The Government Commission for Internal and Religious Affairs, extending its care to all denominations in the Kingdom and wishing to prohibit all things which might be insulting to the sanctity of a place dedicated to the glory of God, having learnt that some Israelites indulge in the smoking of tobacco in the so-called *beit midrash*, against which violation of law complaints to the authorities have been lodged by Israelites themselves, hereby resolves to prohibit the smoking of tobacco in such *batei midrash* as are the common property of the respect[ive] communities and in which, apart from religious instruction, morning and evening services are regularly held, both on weekdays and on Saturdays and Jewish holidays.

Finally, I am pleased to inform you that, prior to making this reply, I consulted with both Mr Abraham Stern, who, as a member of the presiding Censorship Committee for Hebrew Books, is very thoroughly acquainted with literature and erudition in the Hebrew language, and also the rabbi of Warsaw, and that both these persons are satisfied with my present labours, which is corroborated by Mr Stern's letter enclosed herein.

Warsaw, this 3rd/15th day of October 1840.

*Jakub Tugendhold*

# 11. MOSZKOWSKI'S MEMORANDUM (1845)

A memorandum concerning improvements to the situation of Jews in Poland was delivered to the Government Commission for Internal and Religious Affairs by Eliasz Moszkowski, an influential entrepreneur and maskil from the small provincial town of Działoszyce. It was written in Polish. The appendix gives only sections dealing with hasidism. The translation is from AGAD, CWW 1436, pp. 215–33 (fragments).

## ON THE NEED TO REFORM JEWS AND THE MEANS THEREOF

. . . 2. The sect of the hasidim, whose number is increasing in greater abundance and gaining in strength and submerging the whole country in backwardness, superstition, and prejudice, thwarts and condemns to the greatest extent all beneficial resolutions of the authorities aiming at the enlightenment of Jews; they, and especially their leaders, that is, the *rebbe*s, prevent children or adolescents from being sent to Christian schools or to enlightened Jewish teachers. These leaders, who possess neither any serious religious instruction nor a good knowledge of any language, including Hebrew, when they manage to win a certain number of supporters, mediators, and assistants immediately assume the title of *rebbe*, that is, leader [*naczelnik*], and, using their devious and allegorical teachings, try to instil in them the worst ignorance, superstitiousness, and religious hatred, because this gives them the power to inveigle money, and to spread and strengthen their ruses with fortune-telling, magic spells, and their ability to treat illnesses, chronic ailments, and mental disorders, and also with claims that their machinations can nullify government decisions, delivering culprits and frauds from punishment, and all this allegedly through the use of talismans, etc.; and they do not allow parents to send their children to Christian schools to gain knowledge and learn [Polish] manners, or even the Russian and Polish native languages, as they are well aware that the more enlightenment spreads among Jews, the more their wicked sect will decline and disappear. It will be like in Germany and other countries, where there is no trace of them.

And to these leaders, that is, the *rebbe*s, flock men, women with children, and even whole families from distant places in the Kingdom, several hundred people for the sabbath and thousands for holidays, showering them with money and seeking help and advice from them concerning all commercial and domestic affairs, even staying there for several weeks, indulging in all kinds of idleness, debauchery, drunkenness, and depravity, neglecting their domestic and family duties; and the young people there, deceived by persuasion and the hope of prosperity, sell and squander whatever they have and what they steal and take of even their parents' or wives' valuables and clothes, carousing there, in the hope of finding favour with the *rebbe*, who promises to oversee all their business and affairs. And all this wickedness takes place with the acquiescence of the local mayor, who willingly suffers such debauchery and lawlessness and regards them favourably, because wherever leaders such as these live, the mayors in those places make considerable profits, both from the fraudulent leaders themselves, that is the *rebbes*, whom they allow to engage in their ruses as they please and to entertain a host of people for no particular purpose, and, even more so, from the hasidim who arrive each day, from whom they obtain various contributions due to the fact that they do not possess certain certificates or because they are runaway frauds, or are accused of committing crimes, or of forging certificates, mainly for permitting them to loiter at will and live lawlessly.

. . . One should . . . put an end to the sect of the hasidim, and expressly forbid them to have separate halls for holding services in towns or villages, the so-called *chasydem sztybeł* [hasidic *shtiblekh*], and to organize clandestine meetings there, because it is there that all debauchery, over-indulgence and drunkenness take place, it is there that one can learn all manner of impertinence, disobedience and idleness, and how to avoid punishment, as well as hatred and loathing for any learning or work and, above all, and as soon as possible, all leaders, that is *rebbes*, should be forbidden, on pain of punishment fitting frauds and debauchers, to extend invitations to local or unknown Jewish men and women, whether on the pretext of holding a service, offering advice in various undertakings and trades, or fortune-telling and treating illnesses or mental disorders, or other trickery. Neither should they be permitted to collect contributions, as they often do, with a view to thwarting the beneficial resolutions of the authorities, nor to accept the smallest gift of money or effects on pain of being punished in person, with the punishment administered by the High Government Commission, and on pain of having these donations confiscated for the benefit of the hospital. Any mayor who has such a *rebbe* or gatherings and meetings of alien Jews of both genders and of a variety of ages in the town under his administration, or any such mayor who dares to issue certificates authorizing visits to the leader or other hasidim, or allowing them to hold services in separate halls, and not in synagogues quietly and reverently together with other Jews, or permitting clandestine meetings, or letting them interfere in or criticize those school, trade, and agricultural matters, which are so abhorrent to them, shall be dismissed from his office and punished in person according to the seriousness of the offence and the degree of obstruction of the beneficial resolutions of the authorities. . . .

*Eliasz Moszkowski*

## 12. ROSEN'S OPINION ON MOSZKOWSKI'S MEMORANDUM (1845)

Mathias Rosen (1804–65), the most influential leader of Warsaw Jewry in the mid-nineteenth century, was commissioned by the Government Commission for

Internal and Religious Affairs to deliver an opinion about proposals of Eliasz Moszkowski's memorandum (Appendix 11 above). The following contains only those sections commenting on Moszkowski's proposals concerning hasidism. The translation is from AGAD, CWW 1436, pp. 242–4 (fragment).

. . . It is evident (*a*) that the sect of the hasidim exists and that on sabbaths and holidays their clandestine meetings and gatherings take place. It is equally certain that (*b*) the aims of this sect are not of a civilizing nature, and thus are also detrimental to the general designs of the authorities. But Ad (*a*), gatherings and clandestine meetings of persons belonging to this sect are purely religious in nature and it is beyond any doubt that a great number of these persons are of quite strong faith. These clandestine meetings can be compared to indulgence pilgrimages, in which a great many people also lack the good faith proper to all religious observations and yet which have never been banned by the government. Thus there is no serious reason for forthrightly forbidding the hasidim to hold such meetings.

Only the empowered authorities should be ordered to ensure that those same policing formalities that are observed in relation to Christians on indulgence pilgrimages are observed in relation to Jews visiting persons calling themselves *rebbe*s (rabbis). Moreover, that they remain calm and do not stay in one place for longer than 14 days, neither should they gather in the prayer hall outside the times at which prayers are held. And, most importantly, persons who have not been appointed by the authorities should be forbidden on pain of a high fine to call or make themselves *rebbe*s, that is, rabbis.

Ad (*b*), an official acknowledgement of the influence of this sect on the population could endow it with a strength which it does not as yet possess, while persecution of this sect would only make martyrs of its adherents, which would be most detrimental.

History teaches that each persecuted society finds supporters and spreads even further. Thus by the very recommendation that we ensure—*really ensure*—that those people coming to the *rebbe*s are supplied with the appropriate identity cards and are registered according to police regulations, and that nobody assumes a title to which he has no right, I say, one such recommendation will put a halt to these tendencies because it will not be aimed against the hasidim only but will be a consequence of enforcing the long-standing regulations governing the registration and identification of persons moving from place to place, or those assuming titles without any right to them.

These are external measures aimed against this group; yet, with a view to its radical improvement, it is necessary to establish schools and encourage the young people to attend them, and, as a result, this sect will, over time, disappear.

# 13. PROTOCOL OF THE INQUIRY INTO HASIDIC PERSECUTIONS IN ŁÓDŹ (1848)

In 1848 eleven individuals from Łódź, led by Icek Seidenman, a wealthy cotton merchant, applied to the Government Commission for Internal and Religious Affairs to have their own prayer house legalized and to be protected from persecution by the local hasidim. The Warsaw provincial authorities ordered the city council of Łódź to investigate the matter, which resulted in the inquiry recorded in these protocols. The protocols and all the signatures are in Polish. The translation is from AGAD, CWW 1712, pp. 52–65. From the 1830s the administrative documents in the Kingdom of Poland were given two dates, one in the old (Julian) style, used in Russia, and second in the new (Gregorian) style, common in Poland and central-western Europe. The dates in this and subsequent appendices reflect this practice.

It transpired in the town of Łódź this 9th/21st day of November 1848.

Israelite Icek Sejdeman, a merchant running a cotton store in this town, on 1st/13th February this year submitted on his own behalf and on behalf of other co-believers a petition to the Government Commission for Internal and Religious Affairs, in which petition he states the following:

That the community of all Israelites who, in accordance with the wishes of the authorities, have changed their Jewish attire and have accepted the norms of civilized behaviour, and who send their children to public schools, suffer persecution under various pretexts at the hands of the fanatical, that is, superstitious, sect of the hasidim, namely:

(*a*) Students of the Mosaic faith attending the district *Realschule* are variously teased and mocked in the synagogue, with the effect that these young persons have had to cease to attend prayers.

(*b*) Adult persons dressed in the attire customary for their fellow countrymen, and not wearing an overgrown beard or ringlets, are teased in a similar manner during services, insulted in a way which could lead to an incident, pushed around, made the objects of various sarcastic jokes, as a result of which they, just like the young people, have had to cease to attend the synagogue.

(*c*) In addition to this, the small size of the aforementioned prayer hall does not accommodate all Israelites and some unfortunate accident may occur as the result of the overcrowding typical of holiday time.

(*d*) Civilized Israelites are overburdened with religious contributions.

(*e*) The Jewish community board disproportionately distributes among the poor the funds for the poor as well as donations made during religious festivals.

For such reasons, the petitioner requests the following facilitations and help, namely:

1. To permit civilized Israelites to retain the established prayer hall, in which they can freely hold prayers.

2. To elect two members of the Jewish community board from among the civilized Israelites.

3. To introduce greater order in the activities of the Jewish community board, especially in supporting the poor.

4. To have a few persons present from each class and acquainted with the financial situation of other inhabitants when decisions are being passed which concern community taxes.

Upon delivery of the aforementioned petition, the Warsaw Provincial Authorities ordered in the rescript of 14th/26th June this year No. 50208/2446 that the circumstances be verified and endorsed, and as the result of this and of a handwritten instruction of the high governor of the district of 7th/19th September of this year, No. 19,724, today the Magistrate of the town of Łódź set about investigating the particulars in question in greater detail. For this reason the Israelite Iciek Sejdeman was summoned to substantiate his request, and testified upon being questioned.

My name is, as stated above, Icek Sejdeman, of the Mosaic faith, 49 years of age, I have a wife and children and I am a merchant, I live in my own house in this town, I have had no convictions.

I acknowledge that the petition currently presented to me, which I submitted to the Government Commission for Internal and Religious Affairs on 1st/13th February this year, is my own and such in all details. With a view to clearer elucidation of my request, I testify that the persecution described therein which we suffer from the hasidic sect is genuine, as can be explained in more specific detail by:

1. Morytz Sandt

2. Izrael Wejlandt

3. Adolf Likiernik

Thus, this deviousness of the aforementioned sect and their constant harassment forced us to establish a separate, new prayer hall in which we could pray freely, and forced us to approach the superior authorities to request their permission. Although I wrote in the aforementioned petition that we are overburdened with religious contributions, and that funds are unevenly distributed among the poor, not having at present further proof which could serve to substantiate these circumstances, I withdraw my claims entirely and do not wish to pursue them.

Because now a new election of members of the Jewish community board will also take place, greater order will prevail, order that has been neglected by the incumbents, and thus our wish will be completely fulfilled in this respect.

On this, I close, having read this protocol I acknowledge it and sign

*I. Seidenmann*

This transpired in the town of Łódź this 16th/28th day of November 1848.

Then, Adolf Likiernik was summoned and testified to questions asked in this respect:

My name is Adolf Likiernik, of the Mosaic faith . . . years of age. I am a dyer and this is my trade, I am a widower, I have had no convictions, and I reside in the town of Łódź.

The petition submitted by the Israelite Iciek Sejdeman to the Government Commission for Internal and Religious Affairs was submitted also with my knowledge and in consultation with me. The persecution described in this petition, that civilized Israelites suffer from the superstitious hasidic sect, did in fact take place and to the present day is still taking place. When we gather for prayers in the synagogue, we are always the object of various hasidic jokes; we are pushed around, taunted and subjected to other similar unruly behaviour, which not only disrupts prayer, but also potentially may lead to incidents or arguments. Moreover, they often refuse to celebrate services with us, citing various falsehoods hostile to our faith.

Because my abode in this town is outside the Jewish district, in a new factory district, this circumstance has also caused me to be persecuted. As a result of such alleged separation from other Mosaic families, I encountered numerous difficulties in the burial of my deceased wife's remains, which involved considerable costs being incurred.

The various forms of harassment to which we are subjected have forced us, for the sake of protection against further abuse, to establish our own, separate prayer hall, the continuation of which Sejdeman has requested on our behalf.

As for malpractices committed by the Jewish community board in decisions concerning community taxes and in the distribution of aid for the poor, nothing is known to me and in this respect I cannot offer any elucidation.

Having read this protocol, I acknowledge it and sign.

*Adolf Likiernik*

Then Morytz Zandt was summoned and testified as follows:

My name is Morytz Zandt, of the Mosaic faith, I am 21 years of age, I have a wife and children, I earn my living by trading in goods produced in the Kingdom of Poland, I have had no convictions, and I swear to testify the truth.

As I belong to those Israelites who have changed their Jewish attire to that worn by other countrymen and are more concerned with norms closer to those of civilization, I have also suffered persecution at the hands of the superstitious sect of the hasidim. I am aware that the Israelite Iciek Sejdeman has submitted a petition to the Government Commission for Internal and Religious Affairs in which he requested permission for us to retain our separate prayer hall and this was also done with my consent.

Once, during a service, other Israelites belonging to the hasidic sect, having surrounded me in the synagogue, knocked the hat off my head, and insulted me with various expressions. On another occasion, when I was to say Kaddish in the synagogue, some forbade the others to pray together with me. In addition to that, at each meeting I become the object of various jokes and derisive remarks. Such constant harassment of us by the hasidim has forced all civilized Israelites to open another prayer hall, in which we can hold prayers with decency and in peace.

As I have no knowledge of malpractices by the Jewish community board in making decisions concerning community taxes and in the distribution of aid for the poor and I have formed no opinion concerning this, I therefore cannot testify to anything certain in this respect.

Having read this protocol, I acknowledge it and sign
*Moritz Zandt*

Izrael Wejlandt was summoned and testified to the questions asked of him as follows:

My name is as specified above, I am of the Mosaic faith, I am 36 years of age, I have a wife and children, I earn my living by trading in goods produced in the Kingdom of Poland, I have had no convictions, and I swear to testify to the truth.

Iciek Sejdeman submitted his request to the Government Commission for Internal and Religious Affairs with our knowledge and in consultation with us. The hasidic persecution described in the aforementioned request truly takes place and this has forced us to establish our own, separate prayer hall. Not only have I, dressed in clothes worn by my countrymen, become the object of frequent jokes by the superstitious sect; my son, attending the German–Russian *Realschule*, has suffered even greater persecution: when he went in his uniform to pray in the prayer hall, he was insulted, pushed around and humiliated in various ways, and once, when he was wearing an overcoat, he had the tassel from the uniform cut off and the lace destroyed.

Such and other various kinds of nonsense force us to establish and run a separate prayer hall, in which we can pray in decency and in peace.

Having read this protocol, I acknowledge it and sign,

*Israel Weylandt*


## 14. REPORT ON TSADIK ABRAHAM TWERSKY OF TURISK (1857)

The report on the activities in the Lublin province of the Volhynian tsadik Abraham Twersky of Turisk was delivered to the Government Commission for Internal and Religious Affairs by the Civil Governor of the Lublin Province. The immediate reasons for delivering this report, which resulted in a major investigation, are unknown. It was written in Polish and is translated from AGAD, CWW 1446, pp. 134–6.

To the Government Commission for Internal and Religious Affairs

Report of the Civil Governor of Lublin

Having learned that a certain rabbi from the Russian empire travelling from town to town in this province and deceiving its Mosaic inhabitants, had inveigled considerable sums of money out of them, in my rescript of 21st May/2nd June of this year No. 37155/7618, I ordered that the subordinate executive authorities should endeavour to capture him, and then, together with any documents found on him, to deliver him to the office of the local Provincial Authorities so that further proceedings might be brought against him.

Of late, the Jewish community boards and inhabitants of some towns in the Lublin Province, namely Hrubieszów, Chełm, Izbica, and Bychawa, have approached me with a petition in which they claim that the person mentioned in the above-mentioned directive is called *Abram Tweryskier*, and that he comes from the town of Turisk in the Russian empire, is a rabbi and also a merchant of the second guild and that the Mosaic inhabitants of some of the towns in this province invited the aforementioned rabbi, who is called a *magnet* [*magid*], as one better acquainted with spiritual and religious laws, to hold religious services; first during a raging epidemic of cholera where he could entreat God to reverse this plague, and then during the more important holidays, reimbursing him only for travel expenses. If one of the wealthier inhabitants offered the rabbi some voluntary donation for a religious rite or for a particular service at his own request, the latter distributed the whole sum among the town's poor inhabitants of the same faith, and he himself never demanded or took any money from anyone; as a result of the same, they petition for instructions to be issued to the executive powers ordering that the sojourn of the aforementioned rabbi, Abram Tweryskier, remain unobstructed in the Lublin Province, provided he holds a valid passport from the empire's authorities.

However, from the accounts of the executive authorities, namely the reports of the magistrates of the towns of Chełm, Rejowiec, Turobin, Wojsławice, Tarnogóra, and Izbica of 13th/25th July this year No. 10145, presented by the governor of the Krasnystaw district, and also from the report of the governor of the Zamość district of 9th/21st July this year [referring] to [Report] No. 10417, it is evident that the Isra[elite] rabbi Abram Tweryskier, having come from the empire to the aforementioned towns as a rabbi summoned by the inhabitants themselves with a passport valid for one year which was issued on 23rd October 1856 No. 107, performed only those religious rites with which he is allegedly more familiar than the others, and that he did not demand or take any remuneration for it, but that the inhabitants reimbursed him only for travel expenses, before passing . . . instructions to the executive authorities, as petitioned, to revoke the previous one quoted at the beginning; at the same time I appealed to the Kovel District Court to inform me promptly as to the demeanour and the manner of thinking of the aforementioned rabbi, Abram Tweryskier, and, having notified the Government Commission of this, I have the honour to request a decision to the effect that, in the event of receiving a favourable opinion from the authorities of the empire, Rabbi Abram Tweryskier; that is, the *magnet*, be allowed to travel freely in this province with legal passports obtained to this end from the authorities of the empire.

Deputy Civil Governor
Collegial Counsellor *H. Sermanerczak*
Head of the Office *E. Inatowicz*

This 9th/21st day of August 1857
The town of Lublin

# 15. TUGENDHOLD ON ABRAHAM TWERSKY OF TURISK (1857)

**This opinion on Abraham Twersky of Turisk was commissioned from Jakub Tugendhold by the Government Commission for Internal and Religious Affairs as the response to the report by the Civil Governor of the Lublin Province (see Appendix 14). The opinion is in Polish, and is translated from AGAD, CWW 1446, pp. 137–8.**

To His Excellency, Counsellor of State, Head of the Denominations Department of the Government Commission for Intern[al] and Religious Affairs

Returning the enclosed paper sent to me, I have the honour to reply as follows:

That after lengthy enquiries and careful questioning of some Israelites familiar with the vicinity of Hrubieszów and having heard of the person in question, I can in all conscience announce that Abraham Tweryskier is one of those roguish fanatics who, pretending to work wonders, take advantage of the credulousness of unenlightened persons of the Mos[aic] fai[th] and inveigle contributions out of them under the pretext of interceding with the Heavenly Lord to alleviate some ailment or to cure infertility, etc.

In the Kingdom of Poland, there are a few such fanatical leaders, but, living a pious life and not imposing themselves with their demands, they are far less pernicious than strangers such as Tweryskier, who usually practise their art with brazenness.

Therefore, I am of the opinion that the Lublin Provincial Authorities should be advised to make an order to have the aforementioned itinerant promptly expelled from the country and an order to counsel Jewish community boards to refuse similar guests a friendly welcome in Jewish communities.

It would be also appropriate to notify other provincial authorities of this matter.

Warsaw, this 24th/6th day of September/October 1857.

*J. Tugendhold*

## 16. AEOLUS AND PHOEBUS (A FABLE) (1863)

'Eol and Phoebus (A Fable)', *Jutrzenka*, 3 (1863), 1–2.

This fable, written in Polish, was published in early 1863 in *Jutrzenka*, a Polish Jewish weekly promoting Jewish integration. It was intended as a contribution to a debate on the reform of the hasidic movement in Poland. Its author is unknown, but was probably the editor in chief of the weekly, Daniel Neufeld (1814–74).

The gods sat on Mount Olympus, in council over the good of the inhabitants of the planet. Great reforms were analysed: how to make humanity happy, how to protect people from a fall, how to eradicate religious, national, and caste envy, how to turn selfishness into the love of others; in a word, how to restore the golden age for which the world so longs.

Suddenly, the dignified circle of the Olympian parents resounded with Homeric laughter, as they spied in Grzybów, in the country of Poland, the figure of a young man dressed so strangely that even the most serious senators relaxed their brows. Despite the heat of the summer sun, he wore a large fur cap, beneath which his head was nearly completely shaven save two locks of hair which hung from his temples and reached his shoulders; his beard, the adornment of the human species, was in complete disarray: uneven, misshapen and matted, it resembled a tangle that marred the human face rather than acting as a decoration of the chin; the moustache, in whose honour so many songs are sung in the country of the Poles, grew wildly over his lips like weeds in an overgrown garden. The body of this curious figure was covered with a long black cloak, from which a kind of apron of dubious whiteness showed, seemingly for the sake of contrast, covering his stomach and hanging down to his knees; short trousers and tights seemed reminiscent of the times of the knights, but the shoes on his feet and his bare heels revealed some mysterious costume, unknown even to the omniscient gods.

When the derisive laughter of the debaters had subsided, Jupiter spoke thus: 'Man's internal worth undoubtedly surpasses his external form. You have been so greatly entertained by this phenomenon from the country on the banks of the Vistula that you have not noticed that his brow is full of thought, his eyes are burning with fire, his countenance reveals the play of elevated thoughts. However, aesthetics, too, have their place, and mankind should, above all, avoid provoking ridicule for there is nothing more humiliating than acting in a ridiculous manner. Which of you, my advisers, shall endeavour to persuade this young man to discard this caricature of Eastern, knightly and old-Polish dress?' To which Aeolus thus replied: 'Lord of Heaven! Let it be given to me to fulfil Your high order!' And Jupiter agreed. Aeolus freed the winds held captive in a cavern, which

> . . . velut agmine facto
> Qua data porta, ruunt et terras turbine perflant.
>
> (*Aeneid*, Book I)

He expected to tear off the robes of the young man with a powerful gust; but the more the winds blew, the more the youth enveloped himself in his clothes, the more tightly he held his cap, the more firmly he clutched his cloak.

These attempts being of no avail, Aeolus, who had destroyed so many ships, carried off so many roofs, crushed and uprooted hundred-year-old oaks like reeds, was unable to overcome obstinate *fanaticism*, and, enraged, announced on Olympus that the young man whom he had endeavoured to improve did not wish to comprehend his designs, thus there was no hope of his being cured.

Then Phoebus spoke: 'Violent means can sometimes have an effect, but only on weak minds. The youth whom we endeavour to improve has an unyielding character and that is why Aeolus did not defeat him. Is it possible to forbid him to look ridiculous on the outside if he so wishes, as long as his inner qualities command respect? Lord of Heaven, let me exert my power over him, and I guarantee a favourable result.'

And so in the high circle of the skies Phoebus drove out in his golden chariot, and his steeds galloped through space belching out reviving fire; the flames of this fire fell on to the youth from Grzybów, who still was gasping for breath from the roar of the winds and he, warmed with the benevolent heat of *enlightenment*, threw off both the fur cap and the silk cloak, cut his long hair, trimmed his beard and moustache, looked around and saw all nature smiling at him; he no longer heard the roar of Boreas over his head, the light breezes from the West cooled the heat of the sun and he finally saw the true light—And on Olympus, the laughter of derision became appreciative applause, and Grzybów was Grzybów no more!

# 17. TSADIK BRUKMAN AND THE DOCTORS IN PIOTRKÓW (1870)

This petition was delivered in 1870 to the General Governor of Warsaw by putative Galician followers of the tsadik Moses Brukman (1794–1881) of Piotrków Trybunalski. The hasidim accused local Jewish physicians and the governor of Piotrków province of persecuting the tsadik, and demanded the right to re-establish his *shtibl*. The petition is written in inexpert Polish with numerous errors of grammar and spelling, and it is sometimes barely comprehensible. All the signatures are in Hebrew. The translation is from AGAD, CWW 1411, pp. 550–7.

The Kingdom of Austrian Galicia
This 24th/5th day of December/January 1869/70

Your Excellency, Magnanimous and Mighty Sir!

From time immemorial there has been a tradition among the Mosaic people that learned men known for their exceptional piety have had their supporters, whom we call hasidim, coming to them. Thus, certain people choose certain rabbis for their ideals and their leaders, and it is customary for them to disclose to their rabbi all their ailments and needs, both of a material and of a spiritual nature, and to request their advice and their prayers to God on their behalf; and the advice given in such a manner is in the spirit of the Holy Scripture (the Talmud) and stems from the practical experience of the rabbi concerned.

These rabbis bring conciliation to the parties in conflict, humble the proud and the impassioned, and take pains to put an end to evil.

Persons of this kind require an income appropriate to the desired aim if their prayers and services are to be effective, if their thoughts are to take wing, and if the rabbis are to be predisposed to commune in their souls with the Highest Being in fervent prayer.

Thus they cannot attend services together with ordinary folk, but can do so only at times that they deem appropriate; therefore rabbis have in their homes their own separate halls of prayer, and those supporters who come to them with such intentions adjust their daily prayers to the time appointed by the rabbi, so that the service may take place in a congregation with him, as the religion prescribes.

It is also accepted as a common custom at such meetings with the rabbi that voluntary donations be made, according to the offerer's will and prosperity, and there is no obligation here or any imposition of will on the part of the rabbi in this respect, because even if a person makes no offering, the rabbi will not demand one.

Thus, in the town of Piotrków, apart from the local rabbi, there is a rabbi similar to those described above, one Mosiek Brukmann, who was appointed a minister of the Mosaic faith 24 years previously by the Russian authorities. In his youth, this Brukmann earned his living as a cobbler in various towns, and by building a road.

In 1820 he was employed as a trustee and manager by entrepreneurs building the road from Lublin to Zamość; because of his skill and trustworthy dealings with people in financial and other affairs, he found great favour with the then president of the Voivodeship Commission (now the governor). He was presented to HRH Alexander I when the latter passed through Lublin, conversed with him for 16 minutes, and was awarded a gold medal and 150 ducats.

At the age of 34, he moved to the town of Szydłowiec, in Radom Province, where he left his profession and dedicated himself to the service of God alone; he scrupulously avoided all luxuries and renounced all the comforts of worldly life; then people began to flock to him—even from distant lands—with business as to a rabbi in the manner described above.

Later, in 1832, the Jewish community board, together with the notables of the town of Piotrków, persuaded him to come to Piotrków as a religious leader and to instil in the Israelite people the fear of God in the aforementioned manner, and thus visitors to him from Poland, Prussia, Galicia, and Hungary became more frequent.

This Brukmann is so liberated from all worldly luxuries that every day, for the last 38 years, he has observed a complete fast, neither eating nor drinking until 10 p.m., and then he does not even eat bread or meat—with the exception of holidays and sabbaths; and never once in his entire life has he drunk alcohol.

Many of those who are infertile have regained their fertility and many of the sick have recovered as a result of their praying with him to God, as have many of those afflicted with mental and chronic illness, and there are many whom he has made rejoice; he has aided many of the poor, he has uplifted many of those who lost their property from collapse and despair; because he has given the greater part of his own income—which he has received from those who came to him—to a charity for the poor and the needy.

This Brukmann—in addition to bringing his followers to God's ways, has always instilled in them the love of the emperor and, even more, warned all his followers in the country throughout the entire uprising in Poland to retain their loyalty and respect towards Emperor Alexander II of All Russia and not to join the insurgents in the country, as they would not succeed. In addition, on each holiday, right after the service in the prayer hall in his home, he has preached forceful sermons when people have been gathered and he has persuaded them, using religious laws from the Bible (the Talmud), etc., that they must not renounce their loyalty to the empire; he also has held services and prayers for the emperor of All Russia and his family; in addition, he has made copies of his sermons and speeches and hung them on walls, enclosed in glass; also, he has given similar replicas to his followers with a recommendation that they pray every day just as he does.

For 20 years we, in this country, together with other men of our faith, have gone to the aforementioned Brukmann for religious instruction at least once a year, and sometimes twice or three times; but, unfortunately, since 1867, we have no longer gone to him because the Governor of Piotrków, Mr Kochanów, forbade visits to the same Brukmann on pain of being fined and arrested for reasons puzzling to all, and these are as stated below:

In 1869 in Piotrków, two constables from the local military police station, i.e. Piotr Nowaków and Jakób Choromiejów, became deranged. For eight months their superintendent consulted local doctors and endeavoured to restore them to health, but it was all in vain; thus he sent them to Brukmann, who restored them to health within eight [*sic*] using only his prayers, and they immediately returned to work.

The superintendent mocked the doctors from Piotrków, and the latter began to slander and persecute Brukmann, particularly Doctors Sztein and Szancer—who, being German Jews, already nurtured a great hatred for a religion that was fervently observed and maintained by all believers coming to such rabbis—because whoever has no religion in his heart and soul surely cannot be expected to display honesty in relation to mankind, or loyalty towards the monarchy, or obedience to the official authorities.

In 1864, when the aforementioned Doctor Sztein came to Brukmann with other doctors and demanded several thousand roubles of him for a donation for the uprising—and Brukmann refused and even pointed out to them their improper behaviour towards the monarch and advised them to refrain from undertaking such an irreligious action, these doctors gathered together with other organizers of the uprising in Piotrków to debate Brukmann's case; and, having sentenced him to death, they appointed secret guards whose task was to capture Brukmann during his journey for recreational purposes or to attend some religious business in the vicinity of Piotrków and to either hang him or stab him to death. For this reason, Brukmann did not leave his home during the uprising for fear of losing his life.

Upon seeing that it was impossible to capture Brukmann, these same doctors reported him to General Trepów, claiming that he was a depository of supplies for the uprising and that he kept weapons and ammunition in his house. Brukmann's place was searched by the army, but nothing forbidden was found there; yet his enemies were content even to stir up the smallest trouble. At that same time, Russian soldiers who were ill or wounded in battle were brought to Piotrków from smaller field hospitals, for which there was no room in Piotrków. It was autumn. So Brukmann, with one house still unfinished, temporarily took in these sick people to his and his children's home, taking care of them along with the restoration of that house, sparing no expense for the materials and the foreman, and once the building had been completed and fitted with all the necessary facilities, Brukmann donated it to serve as the state hospital, which still exists today.

For this reason, the doctors persecuted him even more, calling him 'Hospitaller'. Nevertheless, Brukmann did not refrain from holding services and prayers for his emperor and lord, and he still warned his followers gathered at his place in the prayer hall not to join the insurgents, etc.

The doctors from Piotrków and other insurgents, upon seeing that they had already lost and that they were on the brink of being handed over to the government's justice, entered into a close alliance with Oleksejów, the head of police from Piotrków, in order to gain protection and safety if their doings were discovered, and they fêted him and entertained him socially as if they were his friends. At this time, Brukmann had a servant, one Fiszel Szytenberg, who had served him for 28 years; because this Szytenberg led an increasingly wicked, immoral and irreligious life and did not respond to admonitions or attempts to restore him to righteousness, Brukmann was forced to dismiss him. As a result, Szytenberg joined his enemies, and once, when the head of police, Oleksejów, was in financial difficulties and insisted on a financial loan from Dr Sztein in his presence, this Szytenberg said: 'You would be better to send someone to Brukmann, he is moneyed, you can borrow from him without paying him back.' This idea was to Oleksejów's liking and at once he sent his agent, Abraham N., to Brukmann, with a demand for a loan of 3,000 roubles. But when Brukmann refused his wish and indeed hesitated over such a sum of money, because at that stage he had not paid off his mortgage to the Polish Bank, Oleksejów, incited by his desire for money, sought revenge on Brukmann.

Thus, Dr Sztein and his companions, the head of police, Oleksejów, and Fiszel Szytenberg (an ex-servant of Brukmann's), all gathered and wrote a petition to Governor Kochanów in Piotrków in which they falsely denounced Brukmann, accusing the latter of posing as a miracle-worker and a prophet, who cheated people and inveigled money out of them, that he treated the sick illegally, placing their lives at risk, and that his wealth amounted to 2 million roubles.

This denunciation was brought to Governor Kochanów by the head of police, Oleksejów himself, who supplied further accounts of other untrue and imagined circumstances.

The governor gave no consideration whatsoever to this false denunciation, but returned the petition to Oleksejów and permitted Oleksejów to deal with Brukmann as he wished and liked. So Oleksejów instantly gathered several members of the civil guard, the superintendent of the military police and the mayor of Piotrków, who rushed in to search Brukmann's place, shouting, bringing disgrace upon him and insulting him, in every room scattering all the furniture, dishes, clothing, etc. They took from him some 600 roubles in cash, Hebrew books, talismans, petitionary notes, papers—among which there were 18 sermons and prayers for the Russian emperor and his family (the latter written in Hebrew by Brukmann himself)—and simultaneously he ordered the guards not to let in those who normally came to him on religious business, and he closed the aforementioned prayer hall at his place, in which no services have been held since that time.

This latter action is highly disagreeable to a God-fearing man such as Brukmann, a 76-year-old man, because, for reasons quoted above, he cannot hold his services in another place, and it is still more painful and vexing for those who used to come to him seeking solace in religion and who, by this action, have been deprived of any opportunity to reverently hold their religious services with Brukmann.

The above-mentioned papers which were taken from Brukmann were faithfully translated into Russian upon the order of the governor of Piotrków, and this governor, having read them, became convinced that Brukmann was a God-fearing elderly man who was law-abiding and occupied with his religious business and that there was nothing suspicious proven against him, but only that he was a well disposed and faithful servant of the tsar and his lord. On the other hand, he [the governor] became convinced that the doctors making the denunciation and other persons from Piotrków had participated in the last uprising and thereby were enemies of the Russian throne. Nevertheless, he complied with the wishes of those conniving and devious persons, dismissed their vile doings and, ill-treating the kind-hearted old man and insulting the ancient religion, he forbade the holding of services and prayers to One God Almighty for their emperor, a practice that once was a model for all to emulate!!!

Moreover, he ordered Oleksejów to conduct an administrative inquiry. Oleksejów interviewed those persons visiting Brukmann as to the number of times they had visited him, how much money they had given him and on what business, while Szytenberg and Sztein persuaded people to seek compensation for the money given, claiming that the governor would force Brukmann to pay it back; but not one of them made a claim, as their donations had been made voluntarily.

As if this were not enough, the governor then referred the entire inquiry, together with the denunciation, to the criminal court with an order that the case be closely investigated and that Brukmann be punished. In turn, the Warsaw Criminal Court, once it had gathered all the evidence, resumed the investigation, heard the testimony of many witnesses and consulted the Warsaw rabbinate, after which it passed sentence—clearing Brukmann completely—which was approved by the Court of Appeal of the Kingdom of Poland on the day of 3rd/15th March 1869, namely: 'that Brukmann as a rabbi renowned for his piety followed the example of other rabbis in accordance with talmudic laws, did only what was sanctioned by the office of rabbi, the notion of religion and the faith of his co-believers and availed himself of those rights founded in religious beliefs, and such beliefs should be respected, because the Mosaic faith in this country is guaranteed tolerance; thus the giving away of talismans for money cannot on any account be considered fraud or breach of law, and as for the illegal treatment of ill persons, those denouncing Brukmann could not prove it to be a criminal act by nature—their denunciation had been fuelled by hatred alone'.

The pronouncement was communicated to the governor of Piotrków by Brukmann with an enclosed request that the prayer hall be opened.

We, living in this country, also submitted a request to the governor for Brukmann's prayer hall to be opened and for entrance to it on religious business to be permitted; a request in which we explained the sources of the hatred towards this man; yet the governor refuses to change his order. This case will be unpleasant to the ears of any person who comes to hear of it; for should this prayer hall, which has been maintained in this place at Brukmann's expense for 38 years with no contribution from other persons, and which was founded for a good cause—as stated above—should this prayer hall be closed down by Brukmann's enemies and god-less Hebrews—and, what is more, with the help of the governor of Piotrków? This would be immoral, in addition to being an insult to the monarch on the part of the governor, whom no other than this monarch elevated to such a position, bidding him to do justice in his office, and not to tolerate the false denunciations of rascals!

The truth of this affair can be verified at any time by Brukmann himself if he is questioned separately; surely, as an old man at death's door he cannot lie.

Thus we fall at the feet of Your Excellency, requesting and beseeching that Your Excellency pass an order to open Brukmann's prayer hall in Piotrków, for the reinstatement of God's free service to its original state in accordance with the old Hebrew custom glorifying God, for the good of the emperor and his family and for the good of all, and also we humbly request Your Excellency to kindly permit us, Galician Israelites of this country, to visit Brukmann on purely religious business.

We await a favourable decision, placing this request, made from our hearts, in the hands of Mendel Bibelmann in Tarnów in Austrian Galicia.

Namely Lebusch Beker
     Jakub Weisman
     Herschly Treitel
     Herschly Neuman
     Baruch Goldberg

[signed by all in Hebrew]


# 18. SEGEL ON HASIDISM (1897)

B. W. Segel, 'Z piśmiennictwa' [From the Writings], *Izraelita*, 32 (1897), 96–7 (fragment).

Beniamin Wolf Segel (1866–1931) was one of the first Jewish folklorists in Poland and a journalist. This essay on the historiography of hasidism was written in Polish and published in *Izraelita*, a weekly for Polish Jewish integrationists.

I have always wished that one day there would come a teacher/historian in whose soul there was at least a spark of Renan's spirit, who would tell us the *inside* history of hasidism and its many directions, and who would depict for us the most prominent people in this movement. Because everything that has been written to date—including my offering in *Wisła* in 1894—skims the surface to a greater or lesser extent, never penetrating to the very core of the matter. New Hebrew literature possesses a whole range of skilful and even artistically executed satires on hasidism and the hasidim—beginning with Perl's *Revealer of Secrets* and ending with the masterly scenes from the lives of the hasidic luminaries who are found here and there in the stories of Smolenskin. But we do not possess a single book that attempts, objectively and without bitterness or sarcasm, to reveal what was and still is the life-giving force of that movement; what force it was that enabled it to exercise such influence over the masses and drew to it so many minds, even those of brilliant and outstanding individuals. It is easy to understand why. Let us consider: Hebrew literature came to the fore at a time when the degradation of hasidism was already well under way, so, perceiving in it nothing but an obstacle to the enlightenment of the general masses, literature assumed a hostile attitude towards hasidism. However, our approach to hasidism should be one of understanding and explanation rather than hostility. Graetz, who devoted an entire chapter of the eleventh volume of his history to hasidism,* dismissed it with a single, unflattering label which has been widely repeated: *hässlich*. But can this [dismissive attitude] truly explain the tremendous popularity and nearly hundred-and-fifty-year existence of a movement which, unfortunately in such a terribly deviant form, has become so deeply ingrained in the spiritual organism of the Jewish people in eastern Europe?

The treatises of Simon Dubnow on this subject are very thorough, and drawn from a broader viewpoint. In my opinion, however, they are strictly historical; they deal more with the external manifestations and development of hasidism than with its internal substance . . . However, if somebody was able to explain this movement in its entirety, from its embryonic state through the epoch of its growth, to its later distortion and present collapse; if somebody could unearth the great wealth of philosophical and ethical ideas which hasidism, along with a vast web of nonsense and superstition, has produced; if somebody could depict artistically just a few outstanding individuals from the great and varied gallery of personalities who have led the hasidim—ascetics and frauds, philosophers and simpletons, people with astonishing strength of will and fantastic dreamers—that person would create a work that could easily stand alongside that of Sabatier on St Francis of Assisi, to whom, incidentally, a number of the most prominent 'heads' of hasidism have borne a striking similarity.

Not only for the historian/psychologist, but equally for the poet, hasidism is a pleasing and attractive subject. It is an interesting phenomenon that the present generation is far more objective and, in some cases, even sympathetic in its approach to this Jewish movement, a movement that has, after all, been deviant, and which has had disastrous effects. *Was im Liede soll auferstehen, muss im Leben untergehen.*† At present, when hasidism is nearing its end, when it holds on only by force of tradition and intellectual inertia, we, the younger ones, have begun to be interested in its poetic aspect, which has eased the lives of innumerable poor people, and in the contemplative and ethical elements which it contains and which even developed within it; we have begun to recall just how many powerful minds and astute personalities were caught up in its vicious circle, and that at its beginning hasidism was only a reaction against decaying rabbinism. It is child's play to ridicule it today; there is no need to fight it, because it is dying by sheer force of circumstance. Thus, viewing it as a historical necessity and a thing of the past, we prefer to *understand* its substance and its essence.

* H[einrich] Graetz, *Geschichte der Juden von den ältesten Zeiten bis auf die Gegenwart. Aus den Quellen neu bearbeitet*, 11 vols. (Leipzig, 1853–76), xi. 102–26.
† Whatever is resurrected in song must die in life.


# 19. SOKOŁÓW ON HASIDISM (1898)

N.S., 'Zanik misnagdyzmu' [The Disappearance of Mitnagedism], *Izraelita*, 33 (1898), 449.

Nahum Sokołów (1859–1936), journalist, ideologist, and politician, was one of the most prolific Jewish writers of his age. From 1896 he edited the Polish Jewish integrationist weekly *Izraelita*, and advocated a rapprochement between traditional Jewish Orthodoxy and the integrationist Jewish intelligentsia. One of his main aims in doing this, also advocated in this essay, was to form a coalition against the political aspirations of hasidism. The essay is in excellent Polish.

A significant transformation is taking place in the development of Jewish political parties in our country. The party of the 'misnagdim' [mitnagedim], once the most numerous, is now gradually disappearing from sight. Who were the 'misnagdim' in the past, and who are they today? Once, they were the intellectual aristocracy, the backbone of orthodoxy, the solid core of the masses; today they are a party few in number and obsolete, a party with no influence or meaning. The name 'misnagdim' goes back to the time when the new sect of the hasidim began to form in the bosom of Judaism. Its beginnings were insignificant: a few miracle-workers, a small crowd of adherents, vagabond gatherings of ardent dreamers, sincere and inspired ascetics—and a few charlatans. Their principles were woven from various threads: from the mystical studies of kabbalah in its most backward form, from the cult of personalities somewhat reminiscent of the period of pseudo-messianism, from reformatory whims imperfectly formulated and explained. Their ritual departed somewhat from recognized codes, and in addition the text of their prayers was a 'German–Hispanic' conglomeration. All of this heralded an innovation, which only a fragment of Jewry can comprehend, but never its entirety. Orthodox Judaism in its official form, as it were, came out in full force against this insignificant handful. The 'misnagdim' who protested against them from the outset were more numerous than their own party; they constituted almost the whole of orthodox Jewry. The differences [among the mitnagedim] lay only in the volume of their protests. While such an outstanding talmudic personality as Rabbi Elijah, the Gaon of Vilna, cursed the renegades with the full dreadfulness of religious prophecy, others contented themselves with plaintive cries or ignored the new group as being the product of empty and useless propaganda. Neither the storm of indignation nor indulgent indifference was to any avail. The bright rays of hasidism were not lost in the haze of faith and pious desires; the dream took shape in the body, the small sect grew little by little. Already in the first decades of our century we were dealing with a serious sect that was divided into the various branches of the dynasties of the miracle-workers. In Volhynia and in Podolia there was a whole procession of 'grandchildren'; here we had a number of centres of hasidism. Primitive, supposedly liberal, impulses still throb here and there in Przysucha, in Kock, but they die in the more distant embranchments. Hasidism exerts an overpoweringly attractive influence, and its nebulous, undefined principles seduce, capture, and arouse. Already there are *shtiblekh* along the lanes in every town alongside the synagogues and houses of prayer, already in some places hasidism exhibits a certain defiance and pugnacity, discord and agitation, but in comparison with the general community it is still small.

Not so many decades ago, the 'misnagdim' waved the sceptre of leadership. To define it geometrically, it was at the centre of local Judaism. The hasidim were the right wing, the 'maskilim' the left, and a further outlying post was occupied by the progressives, or 'Germans' as the masses called them. But the centre was made up of the orthodox, the rigorous, the pious, the learned and the sober-minded, those who did not go to miracle-workers, those who did not pray in the *shtiblekh* but only in the synagogues, those drawing the chariot of the community, those who busied themselves in different fields of public activity. There was not much enlightenment there, but at least there was a certain notion of order, a certain cohesion in the structure, a certain authority in the system, all of which is in its own way a bridge to civilization. The rabbi/hasid was a rarity; a hasidic house of prayer was almost an impossibility. The representatives [the Jewish elders] were mainly misnagdim; the lower strata, artisans, workers, etc., felt no attraction to hasidism.

It has only been in the last few dozen years that hasidism has started to grow so rapidly before our very eyes. It is possible to say without exaggeration that misnagdism has completely turned to dust. All that is conservative—and after all, with the exception of a few of the larger towns, which already have a progressive party, nearly all of our Jews [are conservative]—is crossing over to the hasidic camp. One only has to look at the provinces, at those small towns that are crowded with Jews, to convince oneself that the synagogues are emptying but the *shtiblekh* are increasing in number and that there are few rabbis who do not go to some miracle-worker. Thus the institution of the rabbinate has lost its former influence, because its centre of gravity has moved to the capitals of the tsadikim.

Here we are not writing a criticism of hasidism. This is not the place for it, nor do we wish to elevate the merit or measure of misnagdism. We merely emphasize a social symptom and wish to penetrate to the heart of its causes. And so, one of the reasons for the decline of the misnagdim has been the failure of the Haskalah, that third option, which heralds the dawn of Jewish civilization, to grow. Elsewhere—for example, at the scene of the activities of the above-mentioned Gaon Rabbi

Elijah—misnagdism continues to be abundantly aided by the revival of the Hebrew language and by a Haskalah of solemn Israelite aspirations, making the growth of hasidism impossible. Our misnagdism, though, has been encrusted and embalmed in orthodoxy, whereas hasidism comes equipped with incentives and slogans. The mystical *rebbe*, the democratic *shtibl*, the congregating of the masses—all have an enlivening and arousing quality, particularly as there is no other collective impulse or idea that appeals to the masses. It is necessary to impress on the minds of our contemporaries an awareness of this symptom and an understanding of its causes. The dispersal and the helplessness of the misnagdim summon us to bring into play new, more progressive ways of thinking and acting, because, without a new programme, the usual criticisms of hasidism will become pointless moralizing.

# Bibliography

## ARCHIVAL SOURCES

*American Jewish Archives, Cincinnati*
Marcus Jastrow biographical notes; letter from Marcus Jastrow to Jacob Raisin (n.d.); Marcus Jastrow nearprint file.

*Archives of the YIVO Institute for Jewish Research, New York*
RG 87: Simon Dubnow Collection, 996.

*Archiwum Główne Akt Dawnych (AGAD), Warsaw*
Centralne Władze Oświatowe, 33.
Centralne Władze Wyznaniowe (CWW), 1408, 1409–11, 1416–17, 1419, 1424, 1431–6, 1439, 1441, 1445–6, 1448, 1456–8, 1470, 1472, 1501, 1508, 1542, 1555, 1557, 1562, 1571, 1602, 1610–11, 1613, 1617, 1632, 1661, 1663, 1666, 1684, 1696, 1708, 1712, 1716, 1723–31, 1734, 1779, 1780, 1784, 1786, 1788, 1800, 1818, 1827, 1869, 1871.
Komisja Rządowa Spraw Wewnętrznych (KRSW), 6630, 6634, 6635.
Komisja Województwa Kaliskiego (KWK), 699, 700, 702, 704, 710, 713, 3224.
Protokoły Rady Administracyjnej Królestwa Polskiego, vol. 12.
Rada Ministrów Księstwa Warszawskiego, 165.
I Rada Stanu Królestwa Polskiego, 283–5, 436.
Rada Stanu i Rada Ministrów Księstwa Warszawskiego, 216.

Sekretariat Stanu Królestwa Polskiego, 199.

*Archiwum Państwowe w Kielcach (APK)*
Rząd Gubernialny Radomski (RGR), 4008, 4010, 4399, 4405, 4411.

*Archiwum Państwowe w Lublinie (APL)*
Akta miasta Lublina (1809–1874) (AmL), 2158, 2258, 2415, 2419.

*Archiwum Państwowe w Radomiu (APR)*
Rząd Gubernialny Radomski (RGR), I. 4359.
Rząd Gubernialny Radomski (RGR), II. 4130.

*Central Archives for the History of the Jewish People in Jerusalem (CAHJP)*
PL/82: Tugendhold letters.
Microfilms HM2/6010, HM2/6012, HM2/6014, HM2/6863, HM2/6874, HM2/8248.1, HM3635, HM3636, HM3667, HM7426.

## JOURNALS AND NEWSPAPERS

*Allgemeine Zeitung des Judentums (AZJ)*, Berlin, 1837–64.

*Dostrzegacz Nadwiślański*, Warsaw, 1823–4.

*Gazeta Codzienna*, Warsaw, 1832–61.

*Gazeta Polska*, Warsaw, 1826–31.

*Gazeta Warszawska*, Warsaw, 1794–1864.

*Hatsefirah*, Warsaw, 1862–1906.

*Israelitische Annalen*, Frankfurt am Main, 1839–41.

*Izraelita (Izr.)*, Warsaw, 1866–1913.

*Jewish Expositor and Friend of Israel (JE)*, London, 1816–31.

*Jewish Intelligence (JI)*, London, 1835–60.

*Jutrzenka (Ju.)*, Warsaw, 1861–3.

*Korespondent Warszawski [Gazeta Korespondenta, Korespondent]*, Warsaw, 1797–1839.

*Kurier Warszawski*, Warsaw, 1821–64.

*Monthly Intelligence (MI)*, London, 1830–4.

*Der Orient*, Leipzig, 1840–51.

*Pamiętnik Warszawski*, Warsaw, 1815–23.

*Varshoyer Yidishe Tsaytung*, Warsaw, 1867.


## BOOKS, ARTICLES, AND THESES

AESCOLY, AHARON ZE'EV, *Haḥasidut bepolin* [Hasidism in Poland], ed. David Assaf (Jerusalem, 1998).

AGES, ARNOLD, 'Luigi Chiarini: A Case Study in Intellectual Anti-Semitism', *Judaica*, 37/2 (1981), 76–89.

ALFASI, ITSHAK, 'Toledot yehudei opotsno' [History of the Jews in Opoczno], in id. (ed.), *Sefer opoczno: Yad vashem lakehilah sheharvah* [Book of Opoczno: In Memory of the Destroyed Community] (Tel Aviv, 1989), 23–36.

'Analekten und Monatsbericht', *MGWJ* 18 (1869), 191–2.

ARON, 'Zur Lage der Juden in Polen', *Neuzeit*, 29/23 (1889), 223–4.

ASSAF, DAVID, *Derekh hamalkhut: R. yisra'el miruzhin umekomo betoledot haḥasidut* [The Regal Way: The Life and Times of Rabbi Israel of Ruzhin] (Jerusalem, 1997).

—— '"Money for Household Expenses": Economic Aspects of the Hasidic Courts', *Scripta Hierosolimitana*, 38 (1998), 14–50.

—— *The Regal Way: The Life and Times of Rabbi Israel of Ruzhin*, trans. David Louvish (Stanford, Calif., 2002).

——and ISRAEL BARTAL, 'Shetadlanut ve'ortodoksiyah: Tsadikei polin bemifgash im hazemanim haḥadashim' [*Shtadlanut* and Orthodoxy: Polish Tsadikim Facing New Times], in Rachel Elior, Israel Bartal, and Chone Shmeruk (eds.), *Tsadikim ve'anshei ma'aseh: Meḥkarim ḥasidut polin* [Hasidism in Poland] (Jerusalem, 1994), 65–90.

BACON, GERSHON, *The Politics of Tradition: Agudat Yisrael in Poland, 1916–1939* (Jerusalem, 1996).

BAKER, MARK, 'The Reassessment of Haskala Ideology in the Aftermath of the 1863 Polish Revolt', *Polin*, 5 (1990), 221–49.

BAŁABAN, MAJER, 'Polnische Übersetzungen und Editionen der Werke Moses Mendelssohn', *Zeitschrift für die Geschichte der Juden in Deutschland*, 1 (1929), 262–8.

—— 'Żydzi w powstaniu 1863 r. (Próba bibliografii rozumowanej)' [Jews in the 1863 Uprising (A Tentative Bibliography)], *Przegląd Historyczny*, 34 (1937–8), 564–99.

BAR-TAL, DANIEL, 'Delegitimization: The Extreme Case of Stereotyping and Prejudice', in Daniel Bar-Tal, Carl F. Grauman, Arie W. Kuglanski, and Wolfgang Stroebe (eds.), *Stereotyping and Prejudice: Changing Conceptions* (New York, 1989), 169–88.

BARTAL, ISRAEL, 'From Traditional Bilingualism to National Monolingualism', in Lewis Glinert (ed.), *Hebrew in Ashkenaz: A Language in Exile* (New York, 1993), 141–50.

—— 'Le'an halakh tseror hakesef? Habikoret hamaskilit al hebeteiha hakalkaliyim shel haḥasidut' [Where Did the Money Go? Maskilic Criticism of the Economic Foundations of Hasidism], in Menahem Ben-Sasson (ed.), *Dat vekalkalah: Yaḥasei gomelin. Shai leya'akov kats bimelot lo tishim shanah. Kovets ma'amarim* [Religion and Economy: Connections and Interactions] (Jerusalem, 1995), 375–85.

BARTOSZEWICZ, KAZIMIERZ, *Wojna żydowska w roku 1859: Początki asymilacji i antysemityzmu* [The Jewish War in 1859: The Beginnings of Assimilation and Anti-semitism] (Warsaw, 1913).

BARZILAY, ISAAC E., 'Acceptance or Rejection: Manasseh of Ilya's (1767–1831) Ambivalent Attitude toward Hasidism', *Jewish Quarterly Review*, 74 (1983–4), 1–20; repr. in id., *Manasseh of Ilya: Precursor of Modernity among the Jews of Eastern Europe* (Jerusalem, 1999), 114–36.

—— 'The Ideology of the Berlin Haskalah', *Proceedings of the American Academy for Jewish Research*, 25 (1956), 1–37.

—— *Manasseh of Ilya: Precursor of Modernity among the Jews of Eastern Europe* (Jerusalem, 1999).

BAUER, ELA, 'Nahum Sokolow and the Problematics of the Polish Jewish Intelligentsia', Ph.D. thesis (New York University, 2000).

BAUMAN, ZYGMUNT, *Globalization: The Human Consequences* (London, 1999).

BEATUS, EDWARD, *Rys historyczny oraz stan obecny Szpitala Starozakonnych w Kaliszu* [Historical Sketch of the Jewish Hospital in Kalisz] (Warsaw, 1904).

BEER, PETER, *Geschichte, Lehren und Meinungen aller bestandenen und noch bestehenden religiösen Sekten der Juden und der Geheimlehre oder Kabbalah*, 2 vols. (Brünn, 1823).

'Berichte und Correspondenzen', *Israelitische Wochenschrift*, 5/16 (1874), 126.

BERO, JÓZEF, 'Z dziejów szkolnictwa żydowskiego w Królestwie Kongresowym 1815–1830' [History of Jewish Education in the Congress Kingdom, 1815–1830], *Minerwa Polska*, 2/1–4 (1930), 77–106.

BET-HALEVI, ISRAEL DAVID, *Toledot yehudei kalish* [History of the Jews in Kalisz] (Tel Aviv, 1961).

BIALE, DAVID, *Gershom Scholem: Kabbalah and Counter History* (Cambridge, Mass., 1979).

—— *Power and Powerlessness in Jewish History* (New York, 1986).

BIDERMAN, ISRAEL M., *Mayer Balaban, Historian of Polish Jewry: His Influence on the Younger Generation of Jewish Historians* (New York, 1976).

BLEJWAS, STANISLAUS A., 'Polish Positivism and the Jews', *JSS* 46/1 (1984), 21–36.

BLOCH, JOSEPH S., *Erinnerungen aus meinem Leben*, ii: *Schwurgerichstprozess kontra Pfarrer Dr. Joseph Deckert und Paulus Meyer* (Vienna, 1922); trans. A. Z. I. Jessie and L. Smith as *My Reminiscences* (New York, 1973).

BOIM, YEHUDA MENAHEM, *Harabi rebe bunem mipeshishah: Toledot hayav, sipurim, minhagim, sihot* [Rabbi Bunem of Przysucha], 2 vols. (Benei Berak, 1997).

BORODIANSKI, KHAIM, 'Araynfir-shtudye tsum *Teater fun khsidim*' [An Introductory Study of the *Theatre of the Hasidim*], *Historishe Shriftn fun YIVO*, 1 (1929), 627–44.

BOROWY, WACŁAW, 'Z historii równouprawnienia Żydów w powieści polskiej' [History of the Emancipation of the Jews in the Polish Novel], *Pamiętnik Literacki*, 22–3 (1925–6), 394–403.

BORZYMIŃSKA, ZOFIA, *Dzieje Żydów w Polsce: Wybór tekstów źródłowych, XIX wiek* [History of the Jews in Poland: Source-Book, Nineteenth Century] (Warsaw, 1994).

——*Szkolnictwo żydowskie w Warszawie 1831–1870* [Jewish Education in Warsaw 1831–1870] (Warsaw, 1994).

BRANDSTAETTER, ROMAN, 'Moszkopolis', *Miesięcznik Żydowski*, 2/2 (1932), 26–41.

BROMBERG, ABRAHAM I., *Harav eliyahu gutmakher migraidits* [Rabbi Elijah Guttmacher of Grodzisk] (Jerusalem, 1969).

BRONIEWICZ, LUCJAN, '*Jutrzenka, tygodnik dla Izraelitów polskich* (1861–1863): Propozycje reformy oświaty i wychowania Żydów w Królestwie Polskim jako głos w dyskusji nad sposobami rozwiązania kwestii żydowskiej' [*Jutrzenka, Weekly of the Polish Israelites* (1861–1863): Reform Projects for the Education of the Jews in the Kingdom of Poland as a Voice in a Debate on the Jewish Question], in *Acta Universitatis Nicolai Copernici: Nauki Humanistyczno-Społeczne*, 253: *Pedagogika*, no. 18 (Toruń, 1992), 113–28.

BUBER, MARTIN, *Die Geschichte des Rabbi Nachman* (Frankfurt am Main, 1906).

BUCHNER, ABRAHAM, *Doresh tov kolel musar heskel hameyusad al divrei hatorah uma'amarei hazal lehorot et bahurei yisra'el* [A Thorough Examination Containing the Rational Ethics Based on the Torah] (Warsaw, 1822).

——*Hamoreh letsedakah kolel pirkei sefer hamoreh hamelamedim tuv ta'am al hamitsvot* [The Teacher of Charity, Containing Chapters of the Teacher's Book for Good Deeds] (Warsaw, 1838).

——*Katechizm religijno-moralny dla Izraelitów—yesode hadat umusar haskel* [A Religious and Moral Catechism for Israelites], trans. J. Rosenblum (Warsaw, 1836).

——*Kwiaty wschodnie: Zbiór zasad moralnych, teologicznych, przysłów, reguł towarzyskich, alegorii i powieści, wyjęte z Talmudu i pism ówczesnych* [Flowers of the East: A Collection of Theological and Moral Sayings from the Talmud and Other Writings] (Warsaw, 1842).

——*Otsar leshon hakodesh* [Thesaurus of the Sacred Language] (Warsaw, 1829).

——*Prawdziwy Judaizm czyli zbiór religijno-moralnych zasad Izraelitów, czerpany z klasycznych dzieł rabinów* [True Judaism; or, A Collection of the Religious-Ethical Principles of the Israelites Based on the Classical Books of the Rabbis] (Warsaw, 1846).

——— *Der Talmud in seiner Nichtigkeit*, 2 vols. (Warsaw, 1848).

CAŁA, ALINA, *Asymilacja Żydów w Królestwie Polskim (1864–1897): Postawy—Konflikty—Stereotypy* [Assimilation of the Jews in the Kingdom of Poland (1864–1897): Opinions, Conflicts, Stereotypes] (Warsaw, 1989).

——— 'The Cult of Tzaddikim among Non-Jews in Poland', *Jewish Folklore and Ethnology Review*, 17/1–2 (1995), 16–19.

——— 'The Question of the Assimilation of Jews in the Polish Kingdom (1864–1897): An Interpretative Essay', *Polin*, 1 (1986), 130–50.

[CALMANSON, JACQUES], *Essai sur l'état actuel des Juifs de Pologne et leur perfectibilité* (Warsaw, 1796).

——— *Uwagi nad niniejszym stanem Żydów polskich i ich wydoskonaleniem*, trans. J[ulian] C[zechowicz] [Essay on the Current State of the Polish Jews and their Betterment] (Warsaw, 1797).

CHAJES, CHIL, 'Baal-Szem-Tow u chrześcijan' [Baal Shem Tov and Christians], *Miesięcznik Żydowski*, 4 (1934), 440–59, 550–65.

CHIARINI, LUIGI, *Théorie du Judaisme, appliquée a la réforme des Israélites de tous les pays de l'Europe*, 2 vols. (Paris, 1830).

CHODŹKO, IGNACY, *Nowe pamiętniki kwestarza* [New Memoirs of the Collector of Funds], in id., *Obrazy litewskie* [Lithuanian Pictures], ser. 6 (Vilna, 1862).

——— *Pustelnik w Proniunach: Podania litewskie* [An Eremite in Proniuny: Lithuanian Stories], ser. 3 (Vilna, 1858).

CHWALBA, ANDRZEJ, *Historia Polski 1795–1918* [History of Poland 1795–1918] (Kraków, 2000).

CORRSIN, STEPHEN D., 'Aspects of Population Change and of Acculturation in Jewish Warsaw at the End of the Nineteenth Century: The Censuses of 1882 and 1897', *Polin*, 3 (1988), 122–41.

CZACKI, TADEUSZ, *Rozprawa o Żydach i karaitach* [Treatise on Jews and Karaites] (Vilna, 1807).

DANIŁOWICZ, BARBARA, '*Jutrzenka—tygodnik Izraelitów polskich*' [*Jutrzenka—Weekly of the Polish Israelites*], in Stefania Walasek (ed.), *Studia o szkolnictwie i oświacie mniejszości narodowych w XIX i XX wieku* [Studies in the Education of National Minorities in the Nineteenth and Twentieth Centuries] (Wrocław, 1994), 23–62.

DINUR, BENZION, 'The Origins of Hasidism and its Social and Messianic Foundations', in Gershon D. Hundert (ed.), *Essential Papers on Hasidism: Origins to Present* (New York, 1991), 86–208.

DOKTÓR, JAN, 'Mesjańskie widzenie Beszta (Przyczynek do dyskusji na temat stosunku Baal Szem Towa do sabbataizmu)' [The Messianic Vision of the Besht (A Voice in a Discussion on the Besht's Attitude towards Shabbateanism)], *BŻIH* 51/4 (2000), 526–31.

——— *Początki chasydyzmu polskiego* [The Beginnings of Polish Hasidism] (Wrocław, 2004).

——— 'Warszawscy frankiści' [Warsaw's Frankists], *Kwartalnik Historii Żydów*, 1 (2001), 194–209.

DUBNOW, SIMON, *History of the Jews in Russia and Poland from the Earliest Times until the Present Day*, 3 vols. (Philadelphia, 1918).

DUBNOW, SIMON, *Toledot haḥasidut* [History of Hasidism] (Jerusalem, 1930–1).

DYNNÉR, GLENN, '"Men of Silk": The Hasidic Conquest of Polish Jewry, 1754–1830', Ph.D. thesis (Brandeis University, 2002).

EISENBACH, ARTUR, *Emancypacja Żydów na ziemiach polskich 1785–1870 na tle europejskim* [The Emancipation of the Jews in Poland, 1785–1870] (Warsaw, 1989).

—— *Kwestia równouprawnienia Żydów w Królestwie Polskim* [The Question of the Emancipation of the Jews in the Kingdom of Poland] (Warsaw, 1972).

—— 'Nussbaum, Hilary', in *PSB* xxiii. 416–17.

—— *Z dziejów ludności żydowskiej w Polsce w XVIII i XIX wieku: Studia i szkice* [History of Jewish Society in Poland in the Eighteenth and Nineteenth Centuries] (Warsaw, 1983).

—— and ELIGIUSZ KOZŁOWSKI, 'Jastrow, Marcus', in *PSB* xi. 70–1.

—— DAWID FAJNHAUZ, and ADAM WEIN (eds.), *Żydzi a powstanie styczniowe: Materiały i dokumenty* [Jews and the January Uprising: Sources and Documents] (Warsaw, 1963).

—— JERZY MICHALSKI, EMANUEL ROSTWOROWSKI, and JANUSZ WOLAŃSKI (eds.), *Materiały do dziejów Sejmu Czteroletniego* [Sources for the History of the Four-Year Sejm], vi (Wrocław, 1969).

ELSENBERG, JAKUB, *Droga wiary albo Przewodnik religijny dla młodzieży wyznania mojżeszowego* [The Path of Faith; or, A Religious Guide for Young People of the Mosaic Faith] (Warsaw, 1846; 4th edn. Warsaw, 1860).

—— *Modlitwy dla dzieci wyznania mojżeszowego ułożone* [Prayers for Children of the Mosaic Faith] (Warsaw, 1848).

—— *Przewodnik religijny dla młodzieży wyznania mojżeszowego* [Religious Guide for Young People of the Mosaic Faith] (Warsaw, 1863).

ELUKIN, JONATHAN M., 'A New Essenism: Heinrich Graetz and Mysticism', *Journal of the History of Ideas*, 59/1 (1998), 135–48.

*Encyclopaedia Judaica*, 16 vols. (Jerusalem, 1971).

ENDELMAN, TODD M., 'Jewish Converts in Nineteenth-Century Warsaw: A Quantitative Analysis', *JSS* 4/1 (1997–8), 28–59.

ERIK, MAX, *Etyudn tsu der geshikhte fun der haskole 1789–1881* [Essays on the History of the Haskalah 1789–1881] (Minsk, 1934).

ETKES, IMMANUEL, 'Darko shel rabi shneur zalman miliyadi keminhag shel ḥasidim' [Rabbi Shneur Zalman of Lyady as a Hasidic Leader], *Zion*, 50 (1995), 321–54.

—— 'The Gaon of Vilna and the Haskalah Movement: Image and Reality', *Binah*, 2 (1989), 147–75.

—— 'Leshe'elat mevasrei hahaskalah bemizraḥ eiropah' [The Question of the Harbingers of the Haskalah in Eastern Europe], in id. (ed.), *Hadat vehaḥayim: Tenuat hahaskalah hayehudit bemizraḥ eiropah* [Religion and Life: The Jewish Haskalah Movement in Eastern Europe] (Jerusalem, 1993), 25–44.

—— *Yaḥid bedoro: Hagaon mivilna—demut vedimui*, 2nd edn. (Jerusalem, 1999); trans. Jeffrey M. Green as *The Gaon of Vilna: The Man and his Image* (Berkeley, 2002).

ETTINGER, SOLOMON, *Ale ksovim fun dr. Shloyme Etinger* [Collected Writings], ed. Max Weinreich (Warsaw, 1925).

E.Z., 'Cudotwórca' [The Miracle-Worker], *Krytyka*, 2/12 (1900), 776–7.

FEINER, SHMUEL, 'Hamifneh beha'arakhat haḥasidut: Eli'ezer tsveifel vehahaskalah hametunah berusiyah' [The Turning Point in the Evaluation of Hasidism: Eliezer Zweifel and the Moderate Haskalah in Russia], *Zion*, 51/2 (1986), 167–210.

——*Haskalah vehistoriyah: Toledoteiha shel hakarat-avar yehudit modernit* [Haskalah and History] (Jerusalem, 1995).

——*Haskalah and History: The Emergence of a Modern Jewish Historical Consciousness*, trans. Chaya Naor and Sondra Silverston (Oxford, 2002).

——'"Kayonek hanoshekh shadei imo": Post-haskalah bekets hame'ah hatesha-esrei' [Like an Infant Biting its Mother's Breast: Post-Haskalah at the End of the Nineteenth Century], *Alpayim*, 21 (2001), 59–94.

——'Nineteenth-Century Jewish Historiography: The Second Track', in Jonathan Frankel (ed.), *Reshaping the Past: Jewish History and the Historians, Studies in Contemporary Jewry. An Annual*, 10 (1994), 17–44.

——'The Pseudo-Enlightenment and the Question of Jewish Modernisation', *JSS* 3/1 (1996–7), 62–88.

——'Solomon Maimon and the Haskalah', *Aschkenas*, 10/2 (2000), 337–59.

——'Towards a Historical Definition of the Haskalah', in id. and David Sorkin (eds.), *New Perspectives on the Haskalah* (London, 2001), 184–219.

FEINKIND, MOJŻESZ, *Dzieje Żydów w Piotrkowie i okolicy od najdawniejszych czasów do chwili obecnej* [History of the Jews in Piotrków] (Piotrków, 1930).

——*Gute Yuden in Poylen* [The Tsadikim in Poland] (Warsaw, 1936).

FELDMAN, WILHELM, *Cudotwórca. Sztuka w 4. aktach* [The Miracle-Worker] (Warsaw, 1901).

FIJAŁEK, JAN, 'Do zagadnienia szpitalnictwa żydowskiego w Piotrkowie Trybunalskim w połowie XIX w.' [The Jewish Hospitals in Piotrków Trybunalski in the Mid-Nineteenth Century], *BŻIH* 10/3 (1959), 28–56.

[FISCHELSOHN, EFRAIM FISHL], 'Teater fun khsidim' [The Theatre of the Hasidim], *Historishe Shriftn fun YIVO*, 1 (1929), 645–94.

FISHMAN, DAVID, *Russia's First Modern Jews: The Jews of Shklov* (New York, 1995).

FRANKEL, JONATHAN, *The Damascus Affair: 'Ritual Murder', Politics, and the Jews in 1840* (Cambridge, 1997).

FRENK, EZRIEL N., 'Yekhezkel Hoge oder "Haskel Meshumad"' [Ezechiel Hoge; or, 'Haskel the Apostate'], in id., *Mushumodim in Poyln in 19tn yorhundert* [Converts in Poland in the Nineteenth Century] (Warsaw, 1923), 38–110.

——and J. H. ZAGORODSKI, *Di familie Dawidsohn* [The Dawidsohn Family] (Warsaw, 1924).

FRIEDLAND, ERIC L., 'Marcus Jastrow and *Abodath Israel*', in Michael A. Fishbane and Paul R. Flohr (eds.), *Texts and Responses: Studies Presented to Nahum N. Glatzer on the Occasion of his Seventieth Birthday by his Students* (Leiden, 1975), 186–200.

FRIEDLÄNDER, DAVID, *Über die Verbesserung der Israeliten im Königreich Pohlen. Ein von der Regierung daselbst im Jahr 1816 abgefordertes Gutachten* (Berlin, 1819).

FRIEDLANDER, YEHUDA, 'Hasidism as the Image of Demonism: The Satiric Writings of Juda Leib Mieses', in Jacob Neusner, Ernest S. Frerichs, and Nahum M. Sarna (eds.),

*From Ancient Israel to Modern Judaism: Intellect in Quest of Understanding. Essays in Honor of Marvin Fox*, iii (Atlanta, Ga., 1989), 159–77.

FRIEDLANDER, YEHUDA, 'The Struggle of the Mitnagedim and Maskilim against Hasidism: Rabbi Jacob Emden and Judah Leib Mieses', in Shmuel Feiner and David Sorkin (eds.), *New Perspectives on the Haskalah* (London, 2001), 103–12.

FRIEDMAN, FILIP, *Dzieje Żydów w Łodzi od początków osadnictwa Żydów do r. 1863* [History of the Jews in Łódź from its Beginnings until 1863] (Łódź, 1935).

FRIEDRICH, AGNIESZKA, 'Bolesław Prus: Toward Zionism', in Wolf Moskovich, Shmuel Shvarzband, and Anatoly Alekseev (eds.), *Jews and Slavs*, viii: *Oh, Jerusalem!* (Jerusalem, 1999), 105–10.

FRÜHLING, ZYGMUNT, *Klątwa galicyjskich rabinów i cudotwórców* [The Ban on the Galician Miracle-Workers] (Lwów, 1883).

FUKS, MARIAN, 'Neufeld, Daniel', in *PSB* xxii. 682–3.

—— 'Peltyn, Samuel Henryk', in *PSB* xxv. 564–5.

—— *Prasa żydowska w Warszawie 1823–1939* [The Jewish Press in Warsaw 1823–1939] (Warsaw, 1979).

—— 'Prasa żydowska w Warszawie XIX w. *Izraelita*' [The Jewish Press in Warsaw in the Nineteenth Century: *Izraelita*], *BŻIH* 25/3 (1974), 17–36.

—— 'Prasa żydowska w Warszawie XIX w. *Jutrzenka* (1861–1863)' [The Jewish Press in Warsaw in the Nineteenth Century: *Jutrzenka* (1861–1863)], *BŻIH* 25/2 (1974), 25–46.

—— *Żydzi w Warszawie: Życie codzienne, wydarzenia, ludzie* [Jews in Warsaw: Everyday Life, Events, and People] (Poznań, 1992).

GARTNER, LLOYD P., *The Jewish Immigrant in England, 1870–1914* (London, 1960).

GELBER, NATAN M., 'Dr mordekhai (markus) yastrov (miyozemei ha'ahavah hapolanit hayehudit erev mered 1863' [Dr Marcus Jastrow: One of the Leaders of the Polish Jewish Brotherhood on the Eve of the 1863 Uprising], *Ha'avar*, 11 (1963), 7–26.

—— *Hayehudim vehamered hapolani: Zikhronotav shel ya'akov halevi levin miyemei hamered hapolani bishenat 1830–1831* [Jews and the Polish Uprising: Memoirs of Jacob Halevi Levin from the Polish Uprising of 1830–1831] (Jerusalem, 1953).

—— *Die Juden und der Polnische Aufstand 1863* (Vienna, 1923).

—— 'Mendel lefin-satanover vehatsaotav letikun orah hahayim shel yehudei polin bifnei haseim hagadol (1788–1792)' [Mendel Lefin Satanower and his Projects to Reform the Polish Jews at the Four-Year Sejm (1788–1792)], in *Sefer yovel likhevod harav dr avraham veis* [Jubilee Volume for Abraham Weiss] (New York, 1964), 275–83.

—— 'Mendel Satanower der Verbreiter der Haskala in Polen und Galizien. Ein Kulturbild aus dem jüdischen Polen am der Wende des XVIII. Jahrhundert', *Mitteilungen zur Jüdischen Volkskunde*, 16 (1914), 41–55.

—— 'She'elat hayehudim bepolin bishenot 1815–1830' [The Jewish Problem in Poland, 1815 to 1830], *Zion*, 13–14 (1948–9), 106–43.

—— *Toledot yehudei brodi* [History of the Jews in Brody] (Jerusalem, 1945).

—— 'Żydzi a zagadnienie reformy Żydów na Sejmie Czteroletnim' [Jews and the Question of the Reform of the Jews during the Four-Year Sejm], *Miesięcznik Żydowski*, 1 (1931), 326–44, 429–40.

GLATSTEIN, JACOB, 'Peretz and the Jewish Nineteenth Century (Fragments from a Larger Study)', in Eliezer Greenberg (ed.), *Voices from the Yiddish: Essays, Memoirs, Diaries* (Ann Arbor, 1972), 51–63.

[GLÜCKSBERG, JAN], *Rzut oka na stan Izraelitów w Polsce, czyli Wykrycie błędnego z nimi postępowania, na aktach rządowych oparte* [A Cursory Glance at the State of the Israelites in Poland] (Warsaw, 1831).

GOLCZEWSKI, FRANK, *Polnisch-jüdische Beziehungen 1881–1922. Eine Studie zur Geschichte des Antisemitismus in Osteuropa* (Wiesbaden, 1981).

GOLDBERG, JAKUB, 'Jewish Marriage in Eighteenth Century Poland', *Polin*, 10 (1997), 3–39.

——'Julian Ursyn Niemcewicz wobec polskich Żydów: Krytyka, chasydyzm, zbliżenia' [Julian Ursyn Niemcewicz and the Jews: Criticism, Hasidism, Rapprochement], in Jacek Wójcicki (ed.), *Julian Ursyn Niemcewicz pisarz, historyk, świadek epoki* [Julian Ursyn Niemcewicz: Writer, Historian, and Witness of an Epoch] (Warsaw, 2002), 145–58.

GOLDBERG-MULKIEWICZ, OLGA, *Ethnographic Topics Relating to Jews in Polish Studies* (Jerusalem, 1989).

GRAETZ, H[EINRICH], *Geschichte der Juden von den ältesten Zeiten bis auf die Gegenwart. Aus den Quellen neu bearbeitet*, 11 vols. (Leipzig, 1853–76).

GREŃ, ZYGMUNT, *Rok 1900: Szkice o dramacie zapomnianym* [The Year 1900: Outline of a Forgotten Drama] (Kraków, 1969).

GROCHOWSKA, HELENA, 'Srul Rabi Bal-Szim' [Israel Ba'al Shem], *Lud*, 10 (1903), 51–8.

GROSSGLÜCK, ABRAHAM, *O powadze majestatu/Sefer godel yikrat hamalkhut* [On the Greatness of Majesty] (Warsaw, 1856).

GRUSZCZYŃSKA, MARIANNA, 'Początki osadnictwa żydowskiego we Włocławku (1800–1845)' [The Beginnings of the Jewish Settlement in Włocławek (1800–1845)], in Mirosław Krajewski (ed.), *Byli wśród nas: Żydzi we Włocławku oraz na Kujawach Wschodnich i w Ziemi Dobrzyńskiej* [They Were in our Midst: Jews in Włocławek, Eastern Kujawy, and the Region of Dobrzyń] (Włocławek, 2001), 12–36.

GRYNSZPAN, SHLOMO, 'Rabanim: Kovets masot al rabanei plotsk' [Rabbis: Essays on the Rabbis of Płock], in Eliahu Eizenberg (ed.), *Plotsk: Toledot kehilah atikat-yomin bepolin* [Płock: History of the Old Polish Community] (Tel Aviv, 1967), 89–145.

GUESNET, FRANÇOIS, *Polnische Juden im 19. Jahrhundert. Lebensbedingungen, Rechtsnormen und Organisation im Wandel* (Cologne, 1998).

GUTERMAN, ALEXANDER, *Mehitbolelut lele'umiyut: Perakim betoledot beit-hakeneset hagadol hasinagogah bevarsha* [From Assimilation to Nationalism: Chapters in the History of the Great Synagogue in Warsaw 1806–1943] (Tel Aviv, 1997).

——'The Origins of the Great Synagogue in Warsaw on Tłomackie Street', in Władysław T. Bartoszewski and Antony Polonsky (eds.), *The Jews in Warsaw: A History* (Oxford, 1991), 181–211.

——*Perakim betoledot yehudei polin ba'et hahadashah* [Chapters in the History of the Jews in Poland in the New Era] (Jerusalem, 1999).

——'Hapulmus bekhitvei-et yehudiyim bepolin bidevar tikunim bedat (1861–1885)' [The Debate over Religious Reform in the Polish-Language Jewish Press], *Gal-ed*, 10 (1987), 41–62.

GUTERMAN, ALEXANDER, 'Yaḥasam shel mitbolelei varsha—dorot rishonim ve'aḥaronim (1820–1918)—lehamarat hadat' [Three Generations of Warsaw Assimilationists and their Attitudes towards Conversion, 1820–1918], *Gal-ed*, 12 (1991), 57–77.

HASDAI, YAACOV, 'The Origins of the Conflict between Hasidim and Mitnagdim', in Bezalel Safran (ed.), *Hasidism: Continuity or Innovation?* (Cambridge, Mass., 1988), 27–45.

HASS, LUDWIK, *Wolnomularstwo w Europie Środkowo-Wschodniej w XVIII i XIX wieku* [Freemasonry in Central Eastern Europe in the Eighteenth and Nineteenth Centuries] (Wrocław, 1982).

——'Żydzi i "kwestia żydowska" w dawnym wolnomularstwie polskim do lat dwudziestych XIX w.' [Jews and the 'Jewish Question' in Old Polish Freemasonry up to the 1820s], *BŻIH* 28/4 (1977), 3–26.

HENDERSON, E., *Biblical Researches and Travels in Russia* (London, 1826).

HERTZBERG, ARTHUR, *The French Enlightenment and the Jews: The Origins of Modern Anti-Semitism* (New York, 1968).

HILBERG, ARNOLD, 'Der Rabbi von Sadagóra', *Die Gartenlaube*, 28 (1876), 471–5.

HIRSZHORN, S., *Historia Żydów w Polsce od Sejmu Czteroletniego do Wojny Europejskiej (1788–1914)* [History of the Jews in Poland from the Four-Year Sejm until the European War (1788–1914)] (Warsaw, 1921).

H[OGE], E[ZECHIEL], *Nauka religii dla młodzieży Izraelitów* [Religious Studies for Israelite Youth] (Warsaw, 1822).

—— *Tu Chazy czyli Rozmowa o Żydach* [Tu Chazy; or, Dialogue about Jews] (Warsaw, 1830).

HOMA, BERNARD, *A Fortress of Judaism in Anglo-Jewry* (London, 1953).

[HOMBERG, HERZ], *Ben yakir (gelibte sohn)/Ben Jakir czyli Syn ulubiony: O prawdach religijnych i nauce obyczajów dla młodzieży Izraelskiej przez zapytania i odpowiedzi* [Ben Yakir; or, Beloved Son: Questions and Answers about Religion and Morality for Israelite Youth], trans. Jakub Tugendhold (Warsaw, 1824).

HORODEZKY, SAMUEL ABBA, *Haḥasidut vehaḥasidim* [Hasidism and the Hasidim] (Tel Aviv, 1953).

HOROWITZ, J., 'Chassidäische Silhouetten', *Jahrbuch für Israeliten 5626*, 1 (1865–6), 170–207.

HUNDERT, GERSHON, *Jews in Poland-Lithuania in the Eighteenth Century: A Genealogy of Modernity* (Berkeley, 2004).

HURWICZ, ZALKIND, 'Usprawiedliwienie czyli Apologia Żydów' [Justification or Apology of the Jews], in Artur Eisenbach, Jerzy Michalski, Emanuel Rostworowski, and Janusz Wolański (eds.), *Materiały do dziejów Sejmu Czteroletniego* [Sources for the History of the Four-Year Sejm], vi (Wrocław, 1969), 113–18.

IDEL, MOSHE, 'Martin Buber and Gershom Scholem on Hasidism: A Critical Appraisal', in Ada Rapoport-Albert (ed.), *Hasidism Reappraised* (London, 1996), 389–403.

INGLOT, MIECZYSŁAW, *Postać Żyda w literaturze polskiej lat 1822–1864* [The Image of the Jew in Polish Literature 1822–1864] (Wrocław, 1999).

JACOBS, LOUIS, *Hasidic Prayer* (London, 1972).

JANCZAK, JULIAN K., 'Struktura narodowościowa Łodzi w latach 1820–1939' [The National Structure of Łódź in 1820–1939], in Wiesław Puś and Stanisław Liszewski (eds.), *Dzieje Żydów w Łodzi 1820–1944: Wybrane problemy* [History of the Jews in Łódź 1820–1944: Selected Issues] (Łódź, 1991), 42–54.

JANION, MARIA, *Do Europy tak, ale razem z naszymi umarłymi* [To Europe, but with our Forefathers] (Warsaw, 2000).

J[ANOWSKI, LUDWIK], *O Żydach i judaizmie czyli Wykrycie zasad moralnych tudzież rozumowania Izraelitów* [On Jews and Judaism; or, The Revealing of the Moral Principles and Thinking of the Jews] (Siedlce, 1820).

JASTROW, MARCUS, 'Bär Meisels, Oberrabbiner zu Warschau. Ein Lebensbild auf historischem Hintergrunde, nach eigener Anschauung entworfen', *Hebrew Leader*, 15/25–6 (1870); 16/1–10 (1870); 17/1 (1870).

—— *Kazania miane podczas ostatnich wypadków w Warszawie w r. 1861* [Sermons Delivered during the Recent Events in Warsaw in 1861] (Poznań, 1862).

JOST, ISAAK MARCUS, *Geschichte der Israeliten seit der Zeit der Maccabäer bis auf unsere Tage nach den Quellen bearbeitet* (Berlin, 1828).

JUDAITA [SAMEL HENRYK PELTYN], *Projekt reformy w judaizmie ze szczególnym uwzględnieniem jego strony etycznej* [Project for Reform in Judaism with a Focus on Ethics] (Warsaw, 1885).

KANDEL, DAWID, 'Abraham Stern a Szkoła Rabinów w Warszawie' [Abraham Stern and the Warsaw Rabbinical School], *KŻP* 1/1 (1912), 120–5.

—— 'Kariera rabiniczna cadyka Icie-Majera' [The Rabbinical Career of Isaac Meir Alter], *KŻP* 1/2 (1912), 131–6.

—— 'Komitet Starozakonnych' [The Jewish Committee], *KŻP* 1/2 (1912), 85–103.

—— 'Napisy nagrobkowe polskie na cmentarzu żydowskim w Warszawie' [Tombstone Inscriptions in the Jewish Cemetery in Warsaw], *KŻP* 1/2 (1912), 142–3.

KATS, F., 'Varshe der tsenter fun haskole' [Warsaw: Centre of the Haskalah], in *Pinkas Varshe*, i (Buenos Aires, 1955), 187–94.

KATZ, JACOB, *Jews and Freemasons in Europe 1723–1939*, trans. Leonard Oschry (Cambridge, Mass., 1970).

—— *Tradition and Crisis: Jewish Society at the End of the Middle Ages*, trans. B. D. Cooperman (New York, 1993).

—— (ed.), *Toward Modernity: The European Jewish Model* (New Brunswick, NJ, 1987).

KEMPNER, GABRIEL, 'Ze scen letnich' [Open-Air Theatres], *Przegląd Tygodniowy*, 35/29 (1900), 296–7.

KHITERER, VIKTORIYA, 'Tsensory i tsensura evreyskikh religyoznykh knig v Rosii' [Censors and Censorship of Jewish Books in Russia], *Yerusalimskiy bibliofil Almanach*, 1 (1999), 7–16.

KIEL, MARK W., '*Vox populi, vox dei*: The Centrality of Peretz in Jewish Folkloristics', *Polin*, 7 (1992), 88–120.

KIENIEWICZ, STEFAN, 'Assimilated Jews in Nineteenth-Century Warsaw', in Władysław T. Bartoszewski and Antony Polonsky (eds.), *The Jews in Warsaw: A History* (Oxford, 1991), 171–80.

KIENIEWICZ, STEFAN, *Historia Polski 1795–1918* [History of Poland 1795–1918] (Warsaw, 1976).

——(ed.), *Polska XIX wieku: Państwo, społeczeństwo, kultura* [Poland in the Nineteenth Century: State, Society, and Culture] (Warsaw, 1982).

KIRSZROT, JAKUB, *Prawa Żydów w Królestwie Polskim: Zarys historyczny* [Jewish Laws in the Kingdom of Poland: Historical Outline] (Warsaw, 1917).

KLAUSNER, ISRAEL, 'Hagezerah al tilboshet hayehudim, 1844–1850' [The Decree on Jewish Attire, 1844–1850], *Gal-ed*, 6 (1982), 11–26.

KLAUSNER, JOSEF, *Historiyah shel hasifrut ha'ivrit haḥadashah* [History of Modern Hebrew Literature], 2nd edn., 6 vols. (Jerusalem, 1952–8).

KLIER, JOHN D., *Imperial Russia's Jewish Question, 1855–1881* (Cambridge, 1995).

——*Russia Gathers her Jews: The Origins of the Jewish Question in Russia, 1772–1825* (DeKalb, Ill., 1885).

[KOHN, ABRAHAM], 'Briefe aus Galizien', *Kalender und Jahrbuch für Israeliten auf das Jahr 1847* (1846), 197–202.

KONECZNY, FELIKS, 'Teatr krakowski' [Kraków Theatre], *Przegląd Polski*, 35/3 (1900–1), 144–6.

KOTIK, YEKHEZKEL, *A Journey to a Nineteenth-Century Shtetl: The Memoirs of Yekhezkel Kotik*, ed. David Assaf, trans. Margaret Birnstein (Detroit, 2002).

KOZIŃSKA-WITT, HANNA, 'Żydzi—polscy? niemieccy? Szkic o tożsamości Żydów postępowych w latach sześćdziesiątych i siedemdziesiątych XIX w.' [Polish Jews or German Jews? The Identity of the Progressive Jews in the 1860s and 1870s], *Teksty Drugie*, 6 (1996), 71–81.

KOZŁOWSKA, TERESA, 'Z dziejów przedsiębiorczości żydowskiej w Małopolsce: Eliasz Moszkowski i jego kariera' [Jewish Enterprises in Małopolska: Eliasz Moszkowski and his Career], *BŻIH* 50/3 (1999), 49–54.

KR[AKOW]SKI, J., 'O cmentarzu i służbie pogrzebowej tutejszej Gminy Starozakonnych' [The Cemetery and Funeral Services of the Local Jewish Community], *Kalendarz dla Izraelitów na rok przestępny 5638 1877–1878 od stworzenia świata* (1878), 55–62.

KRAMSZTYK, IZAAK, *Kazania* [Sermons], 2 vols. (Kraków, 1892).

KRASZEWSKI, JÓZEF IGNACY, *Wilno* [Vilna], vol. iii (Vilna, 1841).

——*Wspomnienia Polesia, Wołynia i Litwy* [Memoirs from Polesie, Volhynia, and Lithuania] (Vilna, 1840).

KUPFER, EFRAIM, 'Meraḥok umikarov' [From Near and Far], in Israel Klausner, Raphael Mahler, and Dan Sedan (eds.), *Sefer hayovel mugash likhevod dr n. m. gelber leregel yovel hashivim* [Jubilee Volume for N. M. Gelber on his Seventieth Birthday] (Tel Aviv, 1963), 217–19.

LANDAU, J. L., *Short Lectures on Modern Hebrew Literature from M. H. Luzzatto to S. D. Luzzatto* (Johannesburg, 1923).

LASK ABRAHAMS, BETH-ZION, 'Stanislaus Hoga—Apostate and Penitent', *The Jewish Historical Society of England: Transactions*, 15 (1939–45), 121–49.

ŁASTIK, SALOMON, *Z dziejów oświecenia żydowskiego: Ludzie i fakty* [History of the Jewish Enlightenment: People and Events] (Warsaw, 1961).

LEDERHENDLER, ELI, *The Road to Modern Jewish Politics: Political Tradition and Political Reconstruction in the Jewish Community of Tzarist Russia* (New York, 1989).

[LEFIN, MENAHEM MENDEL], *Essai d'un plan de réforme ayant pour objet d'éclairer la nation juive en Pologne et de redresser par là ses mœurs*, in Artur Eisenbach, Jerzy Michalski, Emanuel Rostworowski, and Janusz Wolański (eds.), *Materiały do dziejów Sejmu Czteroletniego* [Sources for the History of the Four-Year Sejm], vi (Wrocław, 1969), 409–21.

LEVINE, HILLEL, 'Bein ḥasidut lehaskalah: Al pulmus anti-ḥasidi musveh' [Between Hasidism and Haskalah: A Concealed Anti-Hasidic Polemic], in Immanuel Etkes and Joseph Salmon (eds.), *Perakim betoledot haḥevrah hayehudit biyemei habeinayim uve'et haḥadashah* [Studies in the History of Jewish Society in the Middle Ages and the Modern Period (Presented to Professor Jacob Katz on his Seventy-Fifth Birthday by his Students and Friends)] (Jerusalem, 1980), 182–91.

—— 'Menahem Mendel Lefin: A Case Study of Judaism and Modernization', Ph.D. thesis (Harvard University, 1974).

LEVINSON, ABRAHAM, *Toledot yehudei varsha* [History of the Jews in Warsaw] (Tel Aviv, 1953).

LEWIN, SABINA, 'Beit hasefer lerabanim bevarsha bashanim 1826–1863' [The Warsaw Rabbinical Academy, 1826–1863], *Gal-ed*, 11 (1989), 35–58.

—— 'Beit hayetomim vehazekenim hayehudim harishon bevarsha' [The First Jewish Orphanage and Old People's Home in Warsaw], *Gal-ed*, 4–5 (1978), 55–78; repr. as 'Warszawski Dom Sierot (Dom Schronienia) w XIX w.', *BŻIH* 33/3–4 (1982), 31–49.

—— 'Pierwsze szkoły elementarne dla dzieci wyznania mojżeszowego w Warszawie w latach 1818–1830' [The First Elementary Schools for Children of the Mosaic Faith in Warsaw 1818–1830], *Przegląd Historyczno-Oświatowy*, 8/2 (1965), 157–96; repr. as 'Batei hasefer ha'elementariyim harishonim liyeladim benei dat mosheh bevarsha 1818–1830', *Gal-ed*, 1 (1973), 63–100.

LIBERMAN, HAYIM, 'Keitsad ḥokerim ḥasidut beyisra'el' [Research into Hasidism], *Bitsaron*, 16/33, no. 1 (5715 [1954/5]), 113–20.

LIBRETT, JEFFREY S., 'Stolen Goods: Cultural Identity after the Counterenlightenment in Salomon Maimon's "Autobiography" (1792)', *New German Critique*, 72 (2000), 36–66.

LICHTEN, JOSEPH, 'Notes on the Assimilation and Acculturation of Jews in Poland 1863–1943', in Chimen Abramsky, Maciej Jachimczyk, and Antony Polonsky (eds.), *The Jews in Poland* (Oxford, 1986), 106–29.

LIEBES, YEHUDA, '"Ha-Tikkun ha-Kelali" of R. Nahman of Bratslav and its Sabbatean Links', in id., *Studies in Jewish Myth and Jewish Messianism* (Albany, NY, 1993), 115–50, 184–210.

LIEBKIND, HENRYK, *Modlitwy dla Izraelitów na dni zwyczajne i uroczyste wraz z przekładem polskim* [Prayers for the Israelites] (Warsaw, 1846).

[LIPSZYC, PINKUS ELIAS], *Prośba czyli Usprawiedliwienie się ludu wyznania Starego Testamentu, w Królestwie Polskiem zamieszkałego* [Petition; or, Self-Justification of the People of the Old Testament Faith] (Warsaw, 1820).

LITVAK, OLGA, 'The Literary Response to Conscription: Individuality and Authority in the Russian-Jewish Enlightenment', Ph.D. thesis (Columbia University, 1999).

Löbel, Israel, 'Glaubwürdige Nachricht von der in Polen und Lithauen befindlichen Sekte. Chasidim genannt', *Sulamith*, 1/2, no. 5 (1807), 308–33.

Loewenthal, Naftali, *Communicating the Infinite: The Emergence of the Habad School* (Chicago, 1990).

Lowenstein, Steven M., *The Berlin Jewish Community: Enlightenment, Family, and Crisis, 1770–1830* (New York, 1994).

Lubliner, O. Ludwik, *Obrona Żydów zamieszkałych w krajach polskich od niesłusznych zarzutów i fałszywych oskarżeń* [Defence of the Jews Living in the Polish Lands against False Accusations] (Brussels, 1858).

Lurie, Ilia, and Arkadii Zeltser, 'Moses Berlin and the Lubavich Hasidim: A Landmark in the Conflict between Haskalah and Hasidism', *Shvut*, 5 (1997), 32–64.

Mahler, Raphael, *Divrei yemei yisra'el: Dorot aharonim* [History of the Jews in Modern Times], 6 vols. (Merhavyah, 1952–1976).

——*Hahasidut vehahaskalah (begalitsiyah uvepolin hakongresayit bamahatsit harishonah shel hame'ah hatesha-esrei, hayesodot hasotsiyaliyim vehamediniyim)* [Hasidism and the Haskalah in Galicia and Poland in the First Half of the Nineteenth Century] (Merhavyah, 1961).

——*Hasidism and the Jewish Enlightenment: Their Confrontation in Galicia and Poland in the First Half of the Nineteenth Century*, trans. Eugene Orenstein, Aaron Klein, and Jenny Machlowitz Klein (Philadelphia, 1985).

——*A History of Modern Jewry, 1780–1815* (New York, 1971).

——'R. Khayim Halbershtam un zayn dor' [Rabbi Hayim Halberstam and his Times], in id. (ed.), *Sefer Sants* [Book of Nowy Sącz] (Tel Aviv, 1970), 291–341.

——*Yidn in amolikn Poyln in likht fun tsifern* [Jews in Old Poland in the Light of Numbers] (Warsaw, 1958).

Maimon, Salomon, *Autobiografia* [Autobiography], trans. Leo Belmont, 2 vols. (Warsaw, 1913).

——*The Autobiography of Solomon Maimon*, trans. J. Clark Murray (London, 1954).

——*Salomon Maimons Lebensgeschichte*, 2 vols. (Berlin, 1792).

Majmon, Salezy, 'Luźne kartki: Z dziejów rozkrzewienia się u nas chasydyzmu' [History of the Expansion of Hasidism], *Izr.* 29/40 (1894), 329.

Malts, Ya'akov, and Naftali Lau (eds.), *Piotrkov tribunalski vehasevivah: Sefer zikaron/Pietrkov Tribunalski un umgegent* [Piotrków Trybunalski: Memorial Book] (Tel Aviv, n.d.).

*Me'ir einei hagolah*: see *Sefer me'ir einei hagolah*

Mendelsohn, Ezra, 'Jewish Assimilation in Lvov: The Case of Wilhelm Feldman', *Slavic Review*, 28 (1969), 577–90.

——'A Note on Jewish Assimilation in the Polish Lands', in Bela Vago (ed.), *Assimilation in Modern Times* (Boulder, Colo., 1981), 145–9.

——*On Modern Jewish Politics* (New York, 1993).

[Mendelssohn, Moses], *Fedon, o nieśmiertelności duszy z Platona w trzech rozmowach przez sławnego filozofa* [Phaedon; or, On the Immortality of the Soul], trans. Jakub Tugendhold (Warsaw, 1829; 2nd edn. Warsaw, 1841).

MICHAEL, REUVEN, 'R. yisra'el lebel vekuntreso hagermani' [Rabbi Israel Löbel and his German Pamphlet], *Kiryat sefer*, 51 (1976), 315–23.

MICHALSKI, JERZY, 'Sejmowe projekty reformy położenia ludności żydowskiej w Polsce w latach 1789–1792' [Projects to Reform the Status of the Jewish People in Poland in the Years 1789–1792], in id. (ed.), *Lud żydowski w narodzie polskim: Materiały z sesji naukowej w Warszawie 15–16 wrzesień [sic] 1992* [Jewish People in the Polish Nation: Proceedings of the Conference in Warsaw, 15–16 September 1992] (Warsaw, 1994), 20–44.

MICHELSON, TSEVI YEHEZKEL, 'Kuntres mareh kohen vehu toledot rabenu hameḥaber' [History of the Writer], in Alexander Zusya Hakohen, *Sefer torat kohen* [Book of the Priestly Torah], 2 vols. (Warsaw, 1939), ii, separately paginated.

MIESES, MATEUSZ, *Z rodu żydowskiego: Zasłużone rodziny polskie krwi niegdyś żydowskiej* [Distinguished Polish Families of Jewish Origin] (Warsaw, 1991).

'Mikhtav galui' [An Open Letter], *Hamagid*, 13/8 (1869), 10.

MISSALOWA, GRYZELDA, *Studia nad powstaniem łódzkiego okręgu przemysłowego* [Studies in the Development of the Łódź Industrial Area], 3 vols. (Łódź, 1964–75).

NADAV, MORDECAI, 'Toledot kehilat pinsk 1506–1880' [History of the Pinsk Community 1506–1880], in *Pinsk: Sefer edut vezikaron lekehilat pinsk-karlin* [Pinsk: Memorial Book for the Jewish Community of Pinsk-Karlin], i (Tel Aviv, 1973), 15–334.

NADLER, ALLAN, *The Faith of the Mithnagdim: Rabbinic Responses to Hasidic Rapture* (Baltimore, 1997).

NEUFELD, DANIEL, 'Chassyd' [Hasid], in *Encyklopedia Powszechna*, v (Warsaw, 1861), 169–77.

——*Or Torah: światło Zakonu: Uwagi i objaśnienia gramatyczne, leksykograficzne, history-czne, geograficzne i obrzędowo-religijne do tłumaczenia polskiego Pięcioksięgu Mojżesza*, i: *Księga Rodzaju* [The Light of the Torah: Grammatical, Historical, Geographical and Ceremonial Notes and Comments on the Polish Translation of the Pentateuch, i: Genesis] (Warsaw, 1863).

NIEMCEWICZ, JULIAN URSYN, *Lejbe i Sióra czyli Listy dwóch kochanków. Romans* [Leibe and Siora; or, Letters of Two Lovers. A Novel], 2 vols. (Warsaw, 1821).

NIGER, SHMUEL, *I. L. Perets: Zayn lebn, zeyn firndike perzenlekhkeyt, zayne hebreishe un yidishe shriftn, zayn virkung* [I. L. Peretz: His Life, Personality, Hebrew and Yiddish Works, and Activities] (Buenos Aires, 1952).

NIRNSTEIN, JOACHIM, *Proverbia Salomonis: Przysłowia Salomona. Wyjątek z Pisma świętego z hebrajskiego tekstu spolszczył wierszem* [Proverbs: Fragments of the Bible in the Polish Translation in Verse] (Warsaw, 1895).

NOSEK, BEDŘICH, 'Shemuel Shmelke ben Tsvi Hirsh ha-Levi Horovits: Legend and Reality', *Judaica Bohemiae*, 21/2 (1985), 75–94.

NUSSBAUM, HILARY, *Historia Żydów od Mojżesza do epoki obecnej*, v: *Żydzi w Polsce* [History of the Jews from Moses to the Present, v: The Jews in Poland] (Warsaw, 1890).

——*Jakub Izraelowicz: Szkic powieściowy z życia Żydów* [Jakub Izraelowicz: A Novel Based on the Life of the Jews] (Warsaw, 1886).

——*Kol-nehi: Elegia na skon Matiasa Rosen* [Voice of Lamentation: Elegy on the Death of Mathias Rosen] (Warsaw, 1865).

Nussbaum, Hilary, *Leon i Lajb: Studium religijno-społeczne* [Leon and Laib: A Socio-Religious Treatise] (Warsaw, 1883).

——*Szkice historyczne z życia Żydów w Warszawie od pierwszych śladów pobytu ich w tym mieście do chwili obecnej* [Historical Essays on the Jews in Warsaw] (Warsaw, 1881).

——*Z teki weterana warszawskiej gminy starozakonnych* [From the Files of a Veteran of the Jewish Community of Warsaw] (Warsaw, 1880).

Opalski, Magdalena, and Israel Bartal, *Poles and Jews: A Failed Brotherhood* (Hanover, NH, 1992).

Panas, Władysław, *Pismo i rana: Szkice o problematyce żydowskiej w literaturze polskiej* [Essays on Jewish Themes in Polish Literature] (Lublin, 1996).

Paprocki, A[braham], *Krótki rys dziejów ludu izraelskiego od jego początku aż do naszych czasów (dla Izraelitów)* [An Outline History of the Jews from the Beginnings to the Present (for Israelites)] (Warsaw, 1850).

Patterson, David, *The Hebrew Novel in Czarist Russia: A Portrait of Jewish Life in the Nineteenth Century*, 2nd edn. (Lanham, Md., 1999).

——'Israel Weisbrem: A Forgotten Hebrew Novelist of the Nineteenth Century', *Journal of Semitic Studies*, 4/1 (1959), 37–58.

Penkalla, Adam, 'Rabbis in the Radom Province in the 19th Century (1815–1914)', *Acta Poloniae Historica*, 76 (1997), 75–84.

Perl, Joseph, *Uiber das Wesen der Sekte Chassidim*, ed. Avraham Rubinstein (Jerusalem, 1977).

Petrovsky-Stern, Yohanan, 'Hasidism, Havurot, and the Jewish Street', *Jewish Social Studies*, 10/2 (2004), 20–54.

Piekarz, Mendel, *Bimei tsemiḥat haḥasidut* [The Beginnings of Hasidism: Ideological Trends in Derush and Musar Literature] (Jerusalem, 1978).

——'Meni'ei hamaḥalokot harishonot al haḥasidut' [The Impetus of Early Anti-Hasidic Polemics], in Immanuel Etkes, David Assaf, Israel Bartal, and Elchanan Reiner (eds.), *Bema'agelei ḥasidim: Kovets meḥkarim lezikhro shel profesor mordekhai vilenski* [Within Hasidic Circles: Studies in Hasidism in Memory of Mordecai Wilensky] (Jerusalem, 2000), 3–20.

*Pinkas hakehilot polin* [Encyclopaedia of Jewish Communities: Poland], iv (Jerusalem, 1989).

Piotrowski, Wojciech, 'Kwestia żydowska w twórczości Juliana Ursyna Niemcewicza' [The Jewish Question in the Works of Julian Ursyn Niemcewicz], in Jacek Wójcicki (ed.), *Julian Ursyn Niemcewicz pisarz, historyk, świadek epoki* [Julian Ursyn Niemcewicz: Writer, Historian, and Witness of an Epoch] (Warsaw, 2002), 159–75.

Poliakov, Léon, *The History of Anti-Semitism*, 4 vols. (London, 1974–85).

Polonsky, Antony, 'Warszawska Szkoła Rabinów: Orędowniczka narodowej integracji w Królestwie Polskim' [The Warsaw Rabbinical School: A Centre of National Integration], in Michał Galas (ed.), *Duchowość żydowska w Polsce: Materiały z między-narodowej konferencji dedykowanej pamięci Profesora Chone Shmeruka. Kraków 26–28 kwietnia 1999* [Jewish Spirituality in Poland: Conference Materials] (Kraków, 2000), 287–307.

*Polski Słownik Biograficzny* [Polish Biographical Dictionary], 42 vols. to date (Kraków, 1935– ).

PORTER, BRIAN, *When Nationalism Began to Hate: Imaging Modern Politics in Nineteenth-Century Poland* (New York, 2000).

PRUS, BOLESŁAW, *Kroniki* [Chronicles], 20 vols. (Warsaw, 1956–70).

PUŚ, WIESŁAW, *Żydzi w Łodzi w latach zaborów 1793–1914* [Jews in Łódź during the Period of the Partitions 1793–1914] (Łódź, 1998).

RABINOWICZ, TSEVI M., *Bein peshishah lelublin: Ishim veshitot beḥasidut polin* [Between Przysucha and Lublin: Personalities and Ideas in Polish Hasidism] (Jerusalem, 1997).

—— (ed.), *The Encyclopedia of Hasidism* (Northvale, NJ, 1996).

[RADOMIŃSKI, JAN ALOJZY], *Co wstrzymuje reformę Żydów w kraju naszym i co ją przyspieszyć powinno?* [What is Hampering the Reform of the Jews in our Country and What Could Hasten It?] (Warsaw, 1820).

RAPOPORT-ALBERT, ADA, '"Eizeh she'elot uteshuvot al derekh she'alti'el veyehuyada". Sanegoriyah maskilit al haḥasidut bikhtav yad alum shem mibeit midrasho shel eli'ezer tsveifel' [A Maskilic Tract in Defence of Hasidism in an Anonymous Manuscript from the Circle of E. Z. Zweifel], in David Assaf *et al.* (eds.), *Mivilna liyerushalayim: Meḥkarim betoledoteihem uvetarbutam shel yehudei mizraḥ eiropah mugashim leprofesor shmuel verses* [Studies in East European Jewish History and Culture in Honour of Professor Shmuel Werses] (Jerusalem, 2002), 71–122.

RASKIN, DWOJRA, *Ks. profesor Alojzy Ludwik Chiarini w Warszawie (ze szczególnym uwzględnieniem jego stosunku do Żydów)* [Luigi Chiarini in Warsaw: His Attitude towards Jews], AŻIH, Majer Bałaban Collection, 47 (copy in CAHJP, HM7426).

RASZEWSKI, ZBIGNIEW, 'Zapolska—pisarka teatralna' [Zapolska—Dramatist], in Gabriela Zapolska, *Dramaty* [Dramatic Works], ed. Anna Raszewska, 2 vols. (Wrocław, 1960–1), vol. i, pp. ix–cxxiv; vol. ii, pp. ix–lxxx.

RINGELBLUM, EMANUEL, 'Baytrogn tsu der geshikhte fun di doktoyrim in Poyln' [Studies in the History of Physicians in Poland], *Sotsyale meditsin*, 4/9–10 (1931), 127–31; repr. in id., *Kapitlen geshikhte fun amolikn yidishn lebn in Poyln* [Chapters in the History of Jewish Life in Old Poland], ed. Yakov Shatzky (Buenos Aires, 1953), 183–94.

—— 'Khsides un haskole in Varshe in 18–tn yorhundert' [Hasidism and the Haskalah in Warsaw in the Eighteenth Century], *YIVO Bleter*, 13 (1938), 124–32.

—— 'Projekty i próby przewarstwienia Żydów w epoce stanisławowskiej' [Projects and Attempts to Reform the Jews in the Period of Stanisław Poniatowski], *Sprawy Narodowościowe* (1934), 1–30, 181–224.

—— 'Reshime fun yidishe doktoyrim, mediker un farmatsevtn, bateylikte inem oyfshtand fun yor 1863' [List of Jewish Doctors and Pharmacists in the 1863 Uprising], *Sotsyale Meditsin*, 10/1–2 (1937), 23–9; 10/3–4 (1937), 23–7; repr. in id., *Kapitlen geshikhte fun amolikn yidishn lebn in Poyln* [Chapters in the History of Jewish Life in Old Poland], ed. Yakov Shatzky (Buenos Aires, 1953).

—— 'Yidishe doktoyrim un mediker in oyfshtand fun yor 1863' [Jewish Doctors in the 1863 Uprising], *Sotsiale Meditsin* 9/1–12 (1936), 23–6; repr. in id., *Kapitlen geshikhte fun amolikn yidishn lebn in Poyln* [Chapters in the History of Jewish Life in Old Poland], ed. Yakov Shatzky (Buenos Aires, 1953).

ROBERTSON, RITCHIE, 'From the Ghetto to Modern Culture: The Autobiographies of Salomon Maimon and Jakob Fromer', *Polin*, 7 (1992), 12–30.

[ROSENBLUM, BENJAMIN], *Uwagi nad teraźniejszym stanem starozakonnych pod względem policyjno-lekarskim przez B. R. Lekarza praktykującego w Warszawie* [Essays on the Current State of the Jew] (Warsaw, 1842).

ROSKIES, DAVID G., 'Rabbis, *Rebbes* and Other Humanists: The Search for a Usable Past in Modern Yiddish Literature', in Ezra Mendelsohn (ed.), *Literary Strategies: Jewish Texts and Contexts, Studies in Contemporary Jewry: Annual*, 12 (1996), 55–77.

ROSMAN, MOSHE, *Founder of Hasidism: A Quest for the Historical Baal Shem Tov* (Berkeley, 1996).

—— 'Social Conflicts in Międzybóż in the Generation of the Besht', in Ada Rapoport-Albert (ed.), *Hasidism Reappraised* (London, 1996), 51–62.

RÓŻAŃSKI, ADOLF, 'Dzieje osad żydowskich we wsi Kuchary: Przyczynek do dziejów rolnictwa żydowskiego w Polsce' [History of the Jewish Settlement in the Village of Kuchary], *BŻIH* 9/1 (1858), 31–49.

RUBINSTEIN, ABRAHAM, 'Bein ḥasidut leshabta'ut' [Between Hasidism and Shabbateanism], in id. (ed.), *Perakim betorat haḥasidut uvetoledoteiha* [Chapters in the History and Ideas of Hasidism] (Jerusalem, 1978), 182–97.

—— 'Hahaskalah vehaḥasidut: Pe'iluto shel yosef perl' [The Haskalah and Hasidism: Joseph Perl's Activities], *Bar Ilan*, 12 (1974), 166–78.

—— 'Reshitah shel haḥasidut bepolin hamerkazit' [The Beginnings of Hasidism in Central Poland], Ph.D. thesis (Hebrew University of Jerusalem, 1960).

RYDEL, LUCJAN, 'Z teatru' [From the Theatre], *Czas*, 53/301 (1900), 1–2.

SALMON, YOSEPH, 'Al pulmus keneged haḥasidut behakdamat r. barukh mishklov le"Sefer oklidos"' [The Anti-Hasidic Polemic in Rabbi Barukh Schick of Shklov's Introduction to Euclid], in Immanuel Etkes, David Assaf, and Josef Dan (eds.), *Meḥkarei ḥasidut* [Studies in Hasidism], *Meḥkarei yerushalayim bemaḥshevet yisra'el*, 15 (Jerusalem, 1999), 57–64.

SAPHIRSTEIN, HERMANN, *Mowa w dniu uroczystego obchodu w Lublinie, z okazji ogłoszenia bytu Królestwa, i Najjaśniejszego Aleksandra Pierwszego, Imperatora Wszech Rosji, Królem Polskim; przed wykonaniem solennej przysięgi na wierność w Bóżnicy Synagogi Lubelskiej* [Speech on the Day of the Celebration in Lublin of the Declaration of the Resurrection of the Kingdom of Poland by Emperor Alexander I] (Lublin, [1815]).

SARNECKI, ZYGMUNT, 'Teatrzyki letnie' [Open-Air Theatres], *Wiek Ilustrowany*, 27/190 (1900), 2.

SAWICKI, ARON, 'Szkoła Rabinów w Warszawie (1826–1862) (na podstawie źródeł archiwalnych)' [The Warsaw Rabbinical School (1826–1862)], *Miesięcznik Żydowski*, 3/1 (1933), 244–74.

SCHAPIRO-MEMEL, H., 'Ein jüdischer Pater Loyola', *Das Jüdische Literaturblatt*, 22/26–30 (1893), 99–100, 103–4, 107–8, 111–12, 115–16.

SCHECHTER, SALOMON, *Die Chassidim. Eine Studie über jüdische Mystik* (Berlin, 1904).

SCHIPER, IGNACY, *Cmentarze żydowskie w Warszawie* [Jewish Cemeteries in Warsaw] (Warsaw, 1938).

—— 'Początki haskali na ziemiach centralnej Polski' [The Beginnings of the Haskalah in Central Poland], *Miesięcznik Żydowski*, 2/1 (1932), 311–27.

—— *Przyczynki do dziejów chasydyzmu w Polsce* [Studies in the History of Hasidism in Poland], ed. Zbigniew Targielski (Warsaw, 1992).

—— 'Samorząd żydowski w Polsce na przełomie wieku 18 i 19-go (1764–1831)' [Jewish Self-Government at the Turn of the Eighteenth Century], *Miesięcznik Żydowski*, 1 (1931), 513–29.

—— *Żydzi Królestwa Polskiego w dobie powstania listopadowego* [The Jews of the Kingdom of Poland at the Time of the November Uprising] (Warsaw, 1932).

SCHOCHET, ELIAH J., *The Hasidic Movement and the Gaon of Vilna* (Northvale, NJ, 1994).

SCHOLEM, GERSHOM, 'Hapulmus al haḥasidut umanhigeiha besefer "Nezed hadema"' [The Polemic on Hasidism and its Leaders in *Nezed hadema*], *Zion*, 20 (1955), 73–81.

—— 'Hatenuah hashabta'it bepolin' [The Shabbatean Movement in Poland], in id., *Meḥkarim umekorot letoledot hashabta'ut vegilguleiha* [Studies and Texts on the History of Shabbateanism and its Metamorphoses] (Jerusalem, 1974), 68–140.

—— 'Martin Buber's Interpretation of Hasidism', in id., *The Messianic Idea in Judaism and Other Essays on Jewish Spirituality* (New York, 1971), 228–50.

*Schreiben eines Krakauer Israeliten an seinen Christlichen Freund auf dem Lande, die Chassidim betrefend* (Breslau, 1832).

SCHULTE, CHRISTOPH, 'Kabbala in Salomon Maimons Lebensgeschichte', in Eveline Goodman-Thau, Gert Mattenklott, and Christoph Schulte (eds.), *Kabbala und die Literatur der Romantik zwischen Magie und Trope* (Tübingen, 1999), 33–66.

—— 'Salomon Maimons Lebensgeschichte. Autobiographie und moderne jüdische Identität', in Karl E. Grözinger (ed.), *Sprache und Identität im Judentum* (Wiesbaden, 1998), 135–49.

*Sefer me'ir einei hagolah* [The Book of Enlightening the Eyes of the Diaspora], 2 vols. (Brooklyn, 1970).

SEGEL, BENJAMIN WOLF, 'Materiały do dziejów etnografii Żydów wschodnio-galicyjskich' [Materials on the Ethnography of the East Galician Jews], *Zbiór Wiadomości do Etnografii Krajowej*, 17 (1893), 261–331.

—— 'O chasydach i chasydyźmie' [The Hasidim and Hasidism], *Wisła*, 8 (1893), 304–12, 508–21, 677–89.

—— 'Wierzenia i lecznictwo ludowe Żydów' [Jewish Beliefs and Healing Practices], *Lud*, 3 (1897), 49–69.

SELTZER, ROBERT M., 'The Secular Appropriation of Hasidism by an East European Jewish Intellectual: Dubnow, Renan, and the Besht', *Polin*, 1 (1986), 151–62.

SHALOM HAKOHEN, *Koreh hadorot* [History] (Warsaw, 1838).

—— *Pierwsza wskrzeszona myśl o istnieniu Boga, legenda starożytna z hebrajskiego* [First Thoughts on the Existence of God: Ancient Hebrew Legend], trans. Jakub Tugendhold (Warsaw, 1840).

SHATZKY, JACOB, 'Arkhivalia' [Archival Materials], *Historishe Shriftn fun YIVO*, 1 (1929), 713–38.

—— 'Avraham Ya'akov Stern (1768–1842)', in *The Joshua Starr Memorial Volume: Studies in History and Philology* (New York, 1953), 203–18.

—— *Geshikhte fun Yidn in Varshe* [History of the Jews in Warsaw], 3 vols. (New York, 1947–53).

—— 'Haskole in Zamoshtsh' [The Haskalah in Zamość], *YIVO Bleter*, 36 (1952), 24–62.

SHATZKY, JACOB, 'Der kamf arum geplante tsaytshriftn far Yidn in Kongres Poyln' [The Fight over Plans for Periodicals for Jews in Congress Poland], *YIVO Bleter*, 6 (1934), 61–83.

——'A tsushtayer tsu der biografye fun Daniel Neufeld' [On the Biography of Daniel Neufeld], *YIVO Bleter*, 7 (1934), 110–16.

—— *Yidishe bildungs-politik in Poyln fun 1806 biz 1866* [Jewish Educational Politics in Poland 1806–1866] (New York, 1943).

——'Yidn un der Poylisher oyfshtand fun 1831' [Jews and the Polish Uprising of 1831], *Historishe Shriftn fun YIVO*, 2 (1937), 355–89.

SHAVIT, YAAKOV, 'The "Glorious Century" or the "Cursed Century": Fin-de-Siècle Europe and the Emergence of Modern Jewish Nationalism', *Journal of Contemporary History*, 26 (1991), 553–74.

SHIFFER, FAIVEL, *Devar gevurot* [Words of Power] (Warsaw, 1845).

SHMERUK, CHONE, 'Al ekronot ahadim shel tirgum mishlei lemendel lefin' [Principles Employed by Mendel Lefin in his Yiddish Translation of Proverbs], in id., *Sifrut yidish bepolin: Mehkarim ve'iyunim historiyim* [Yiddish Literature in Poland: Historical Studies and Perspectives] (Jerusalem, 1981), 165–83.

——'Mashma'utah hahevratit shel hashehitah hahasidit' [The Social Significance of Hasidic *Shehitah*], *Zion*, 20 (1955), 47–72.

SIENKIEWICZ, JULIA, 'Między romansem a rozprawą: *Lejbe i Sióra* Juliana Ursyna Niemcewicza' [Between a Novel and a Treatise: *Leibe and Siora* by Julian Ursyn Niemcewicz], in Jacek Wójcicki (ed.), *Julian Ursyn Niemcewicz pisarz, historyk, świadek epoki* [Julian Ursyn Niemcewicz: Writer, Historian and Witness of an Epoch] (Warsaw, 2002), 177–87.

SINKOFF, NANCY B., 'Benjamin Franklin in Jewish Eastern Europe: Cultural Appropriation in the Age of the Enlightenment', *Journal of the History of Ideas*, 61 / 1 (2000), 133–52.

——'Strategy and Ruse in the Haskalah of Mendel Lefin of Satanow', in Shmuel Feiner and David Sorkin (eds.), *New Perspectives on the Haskalah* (London, 2001), 86–102.

——'Tradition and Transition: Mendel Lefin of Satanów and the Beginning of the Jewish Enlightenment in Eastern Europe, 1749–1826', Ph.D. thesis (Columbia University, 1996).

SŁONIMSKI, CHAIM ZELIG, *Malshinai beseter* [My Secret Informers] (Odessa, 1893).

SOKOŁÓW, NACHUM, *Zadania inteligencji żydowskiej: Szkic programu* [Responsibilities of the Jewish Intelligentsia: Outline of the Programme] (Warsaw, 1890).

SORKIN, DAVID, *The Transformation of German Jewry, 1780–1840* (New York, 1987).

STAMPFER, SHAUL, 'Lekorot mahaloket hasakinim hamelutashot' [The Dispute over Polished Knives and Hasidic *Shehitah*], in Immanuel Etkes, David Assaf, and Josef Dan (eds.), *Mehkarei hasidut* [Studies in Hasidism], *Mehkarei yerushalayim bemahshevet yisra'el*, 15 (Jerusalem, 1999), 197–210.

——'The 1764 Census of Polish Jewry', *Bar-Ilan: Annual of Bar-Ilan University*, 24–5 (1989), 41–59.

STANISLAWSKI, MICHAEL, *Tsar Nicholas I and the Jews: The Transformation of Jewish Society in Russia 1825–1855* (Philadelphia, 1983).

STEINLAUF, MICHAEL C., 'Mark Arnshteyn and Polish-Jewish Theater', in Yisrael Gutman, Ezra Mendelsohn, Jehuda Reinharz, and Chone Shmeruk (eds.), *The Jews of Poland between Two World Wars* (Hanover, NH, 1989), 399–411.

——'Polish-Jewish Theater: The Case of Mark Arnshteyn, a Study of the Interplay among Yiddish, Polish, and Polish-Language Jewish Culture in the Modern Period', Ph.D. thesis (Brandeis University, 1988).

STĘPNIEWSKA-HOLZER, BARBARA, 'Ruch chasydzki na Białorusi w połowie XIX wieku' [The Hasidic Movement in Belarus in the Mid-Nineteenth Century], *Kwartalnik Historii Żydów*, 3 (2003), 511–22.

STERN, ABRAHAM, *Hymn i modlitwa w dniu szczęśliwej Koronacji Najjaśniejszego Mikołaja Pierwszego Cesarza Wszech Rosji, Króla Polskiego i Jego dostojnej małżonki cesarzowej Aleksandry dnia 24 maja 1829 r. w Warszawie odbytej śpiewane we wszystkich świątyniach starozakonnych w Królestwie Polskiem. Na żądanie tychże wyznawców napisał* [A Hymn and a Prayer on the Day of the Coronation of Nicholas I], trans. J. Glücksberg as *Ranah utefilah asher ranenu benei yisra'el hayoshvim bemalkhut polin bekhol batei hakenesiyot shelahem beyom asher natan keter malkhut polin berosh mikolai harishon* (Warsaw, [1829]).

[——and JAKUB TUGENDHOLD], *Recenzja dzieła pod tytułem: 'Słownik hebrajski i pokrew. dialektami arab. chald. i syriackim pokrótce objaśniony'* [Review of the Dictionary of the Hebrew Language] (Warsaw, 1830).

STIFTEL, SHOSHANA, 'Sokolov veha'*Izraelita*: Perek alum bedarko ha'itona'it shel hamanhig hatsiyoni hanoda ve'orekh *Hatsefirah*—ketivah ve'arikhah be'iton mitbolelim bepolin' [On Sokołów and *Izraelita*], *Kesher*, 17 (1995), 5–18.

SZANTÓ, SIMON, 'Der Bescht und seine Nachfolger', *Jahrbuch für Israeliten, 5627*, 2 (1866–7), 107–78.

SZCZEŚNIAK, JANINA, 'Kreacje bohaterów żydowskich w twórczości Bolesława Prusa' [Jewish Characters in the Writings of Bolesław Prus], in Eugenia Łoch (ed.), *Literackie portrety Żydów* [Literary Portrayals of the Jews] (Lublin, 1996), 263–71.

TALGRÜN, ELEAZAR, *Tokhahat musar hu sefer tehilim im tirgum ashkenazi uvi'ur latirgum* [An Ethical Reproach; or, Book of Psalms with a German Translation and Commentaries] (Warsaw, 1854).

TANNENBAUM, MOSES, *Mata'ei mosheh* [The Plantations of Moses] (Warsaw, 1838).

TATARZANKA, WŁADYSŁAW, 'Przyczynki do historii Żydów w Królestwie Kongresowym, 1815–1830. I' [Studies in the History of the Jews in the Kingdom of Poland, 1815–1830], *Przegląd Judaistyczny*, 1/4–6 (1922), 271–94.

TAZBIR, JANUSZ, 'Conspiracy Theories and the Reception of *The Protocols of the Elders of Zion* in Poland', *Polin*, 11 (1998), 171–82.

——'Żydzi w opinii staropolskiej' [Old Polish Views of Jews], in id., *Świat panów Pasków: Eseje i studia* [Essays and Studies of Old Poland] (Łódź, 1986), 213–41.

TOMASZEWSKI, JERZY, 'The Jews of Poland, 1918–1939: An Emerging National Minority', in Yisrael Gutman and Avital Saf (eds.), *Major Changes within the Jewish People in the Wake of the Holocaust: Proceedings of the Ninth Yad Vashem International Historical Conference, Jerusalem, June 1993* (Jerusalem, 1996), 111–27.

TRZEŚNIOWSKI, DARIUSZ, 'Biografia ideowa polskiego inteligenta: od filosemityzmu do antysemityzmu. Andrzej Niemojewski', in Grażyna Borkowska and Magdalena

Rudkowska (eds.), *Kwestia żydowska w XIX wieku: Spory o tożsamość Polaków* (Warsaw, 2004), 319–29.

TUGENDHOLD, ISAIAH, *Divrei yeshayahu* [The Words of Isaiah] (Kraków, 1896).

[———], *Rzecz w języku Hebrajskim przez starego Izraelitę w małem miasteczku Polskiem osiadłego wypracowana, a przez syna tegoż w języku Polskim przerobiona* [A Treatise Written in Hebrew by an Old Israelite Living in a Small Polish Town, Translated into Polish by his Son], [trans. Jakub Tugendhold] (n.p., [1825]).

TUGENDHOLD, JAKUB, *Der alte Wahn vom Blutgebrauch der Israeliten am Osterfeste* (Berlin, 1856).

——— *Dumania Izraelity na warcie w pierwszych dniach grudnia 1830 roku* [Reflections of an Israelite Standing Guard at the Beginning of December 1830] (Warsaw, 1831).

——— *Jerobaał czyli mowa o Żydach, napisana z powodu wyszłego bezimiennie pisemka pt. 'Sposób na Żydów'* [Jerobaal; or, Treatise on the Jews in Reply to an Anonymous Brochure *A Means of Dealing with the Jews*] (Warsaw, 1818).

——— 'Krótki rys historii języka i literatury hebrajskiej' [An Outline History of the Hebrew Language and Literature], in [Jedaiah ben Abraham Bedersi], *Beḥinot olam / Rozmyślania o świecie* [Reflections on the World], trans. Jakub Tugendhold (Warsaw, 1846), 1–46.

——— *Modły, krótkie rozpamiętywania religijno-moralne dla młodzieży szkolnej wyznania mojżeszowego* [Prayers, Short Religious-Ethical Reflections for Young People of the Mosaic Faith] (Warsaw, 1837).

——— *Obrona Izraelitów, czyli odpowiedź dana przez Rabbi Manasse ben Izrael uczonemu i dostojnemu Anglikowi na kilka jego zapytań względem niektórych zarzutów Izraelitom czynionych* [A Defence of the Israelites; or, A Reply Given by Rabbi Manasseh ben Israel to a Learned and Honourable Englishman Concerning Some Accusations Made against the Jews] (Warsaw, 1831).

——— *Skazówki prawdy i zgody pod względem różnicy wyznań, ze starożytnych dzieł hebrajskich, powagę religijną mających, zebrane, tłumaczone i uwagami powiększone przez . . . Koshet imre emet* [Admonitions about Truth and Harmony among Religions Based on Ancient Hebrew Books] (Warsaw, 1844).

——— *Słowo w swoim czasie czyli Rzecz na uczczenie dnia, w którym założony został kamień węgielny nowej budowli rozprzestrzeniającej Dom Przytułku Sierot i Ubogich Wyznania Mojżeszowego w Warszawie* [Celebration of the Foundation Stone Donated to the Jewish Orphanage in Warsaw] (Warsaw, 1847).

VAN LUIT, RIETY, 'Hasidim, Mitnaggedim and the State in M. M. Lefin's *Essai d'un plan de réforme*', *Zutot*, 1 (2001), 188–95.

'Vermischte und neueste Nachrichten. Beuthen O/S', *Israelitische Wochenschrift*, 5/11 (1874), 88.

WACHSTEIN, BERNHARD, *Hebräische Publizistik in Wien* (Vienna, 1930).

WALICKI, JACEK, *Synagogues and Prayer Houses of Łódź (to 1939)*, trans. Guy Russel Torr (Łódź, 2000).

'Die Wallfahren nach Grätz', *Israelitische Wochenschrift*, 5/14–15 (1874), 108–9.

WARSCHAUER, JONATAN, *Agitacje stowarzyszenia 'Machsike Hadas'* [The Propaganda of the Mahzikei Hadas Association] (Kraków, 1883).

—— *W sprawie wiecu rabinów: Odb. z 'Reformy'* [On the Gathering of the Rabbis] (Kraków, 1882).

WASIUTYŃSKI, BOHDAN, *Ludność żydowska w Polsce w wiekach XIX i XX: Studium statystyczne* [The Jewish Population in Poland in the Nineteenth and Twentieth Centuries: Statistical Analysis] (Warsaw, 1930).

WASTRAKÓWNA, CECYLIA, '*Lejbe i Sióra czyli Listy dwóch kochanków* Juliana Ursyna Niemcewicza (Kwestia żydowska w epoce Sejmu Czteroletniego)' [*Leibe and Siora* by Julian Ursyn Niemcewicz: The Jewish Question in the Period of the Four-Year Sejm], MA thesis (Warsaw University, 1932); copy in AŻIH 117/6.

WEEKS, THEODORE R., 'Poles, Jews, and Russians, 1863–1914: The Death of the Ideal of Assimilation in the Kingdom of Poland', *Polin*, 12 (1999), 242–56.

—— 'Polish "Progressive Antisemitism", 1905–1914', *East European Jewish Affairs*, 25/2 (1995), 49–68.

WEIN, ADAM, 'Kramsztyk, Izaak', in *PSB* xv. 133.

WEINFELD, DAVID, '"Ish ḥasidi" shel re'uven asher brodes vehatemurah beyaḥas kelapei haḥasidut bishenot ha-70 shel hame'ah ha-19' [R. A. Brodes's *The Pious Man* and the Changed Attitude towards the Hasidic Movement in the 1870s], in Immanuel Etkes, David Assaf, Israel Bartal, and Elchanan Reiner (eds.), *Bema'aglei ḥasidim: Kovets meḥkarim lezikhro shel profesor mordekhai vilenski* [Within Hasidic Circles: Studies in Hasidism in Memory of Mordecai Wilensky] (Jerusalem, 2000), 237–44.

WEINIG, N., 'Beniamin Wolf Segel', *YIVO Bleter*, 3 (1932), 91–3.

WEINLOS, ISRAEL, 'Mendel Lefin-Satanower (biografishe shtudye oyfn smakh fun hant-shriftlekhe materyaln)' [Mendel Lefin-Satanower: A Biographical Study], *YIVO Bleter*, 2 (1931), 334–57.

WEINREICH, MAX, 'Mendele-dokumentn' [Mendele Mokher Seforim's Documents], *YIVO Bleter*, 10 (1936), 364–75.

WEINRYB, BERNHARD, 'Aus Marcus Jost Briefwechsel', *Zeitschrift für die Geschichte der Juden in Deutschland*, 4 (1932), 202–4.

—— *The Jews of Poland: A Social and Economic History of the Jewish Community in Poland from 1100 to 1800* (Philadelphia, 1972).

—— 'Letoledot hade'ot hakalkaliyot vehaḥevratiyot etsel hayehudim bame'ah hatesha-esrei' [History of the Economic and Social Views of the Jews in the Nineteenth Century], *Tarbiz*, 7 (1936), 57–73.

—— 'Toledot ribal' [History of Isaac Beer Levinsohn], *Tarbiz*, 5 (1934), 199–207.

—— 'Tsu der geshikhte fun der Poylish-Yidisher prese' [History of the Polish Jewish Press], *YIVO Bleter*, 2 (1931), 73–9.

—— 'Zur Geschichte der Aufklärung bei den Juden', *MGWJ* 76 (1932), 139–52.

—— 'Zur Geschichte des Buchdruckes und der Zensur bei den Juden in Polen', *MGWJ* 77 (1933), 273–300.

WEISSBREM, ISRAEL, *Israel Weissbrem and his Work: Novels and Poems*, trans. Alan D. Crown (Tel Aviv, 1983).

WERSES, SHMUEL, 'Be'ikvotav shel haḥibur *Maḥkimat peti* ha'avud' [On the Trail of the Lost Book *Maḥkimat peti*], in id., *Megamot vetsurot besifrut hahaskalah* [Trends and Forms in Haskalah Literature] (Jerusalem, 1990), 319–37.

WERSES, SHMUEL, 'Bein metsiut lebidyon: *Megalei temirin* shel yosef perl be'einei maskilim vehasidim' [Between Reality and Fiction: Joseph Perl's *Megaleh temirin* [Revealer of Secrets] in Maskilic and Hasidic Eyes], in Immanuel Etkes, David Assaf, Israel Bartal, and Elchanan Reiner (eds.), *Bema'aglei hasidim: Kovets mehkarim lezikhro shel profesor mordekhai vilenski* [Within Hasidic Circles: Studies in Hasidism in Memory of Mordecai Wilensky] (Jerusalem, 2000), 209–35.

—— 'Bein shenei olamot: Ya'akov shemu'el bik bein haskalah lehasidut. Iyun mehudash' [Between Two Worlds: Ya'akov Shmuel Bik between the Haskalah and Hasidism. A New Scrutiny], *Gal-ed*, 9 (1986), 27–76.

—— 'Hahasidut be'einei sifrut hahaskalah: Min hapulmus shel maskilei galitsiyah' [Hasidism in the Eyes of Haskalah Literature: From the Polemic of the Galician Maskilim], in id., *Megamot vetsurot besifrut hahaskalah* [Trends and Forms in Haskalah Literature] (Jerusalem, 1990), 91—109; repr. in Immanuel Etkes (ed.), *Hadat vehahayim: Tenuat hahaskalah hayehudit bemizrah eiropah* [Religion and Life: The Jewish Haskalah Movement in Eastern Europe] (Jerusalem, 1993), 45–63].

—— 'Hahasidut be'olamo shel berditshevski' [Hasidism in the View of Berdyczewski], *Molad*, NS 1/4 (1967–8), 465–75.

—— '*Hakitsah ami*': *Sifrut hahaskalah be'idan hamodernizatsiyah* ['Awake, my People': Hebrew Literature in the Age of Modernization] (Jerusalem, 2001).

—— [Wilnai], '"Ma'i hanukah": Letoledot hapulmus al mahutah shel hanukah basifrut ha'ivrit' ['What is Hanukah?' History of the Debate over Hanukah in Hebrew Literature], *Hatsofeh*, 4/1208 (1941), [6].

—— 'Hasefer *Penei tevel* bezikato lamasoret hamakamah besifrutenu' [The Book *Penei tevel* in Relation to the Tradition of Maqamah in our Literature], in id., *Megamot vetsurot besifrut hahaskalah* [Trends and Forms in Haskalah Literature] (Jerusalem, 1990), 207–22.

—— 'Hasifrut ha'ivrit bepolin: Tekufot vetsiyunei derekh' [Hebrew Literature in Poland: Periods and Directions], in Israel Bartal and Israel Gutman (eds.), *Kiyum veshever: Yehudei polin ledoroteihem*, ii: *Hevrah, tarbut, le'umiyut* [The Broken Chain: Polish Jewry through the Ages, ii: Society, Culture, and Nationalism] (Jerusalem, 2001), 161–90.

—— 'Ketav pulmus maskili ganuz bigenutah shel hahasidut' [An Unknown Maskilic Polemical Treatise against Hasidism], in Immanuel Etkes, David Assaf, and Josef Dan (eds.), *Mehkarei hasidut* [Studies in Hasidism], *Mehkarei yerushalayim bemahshevet yisra'el*, 15 (Jerusalem, 1999), 65–88.

—— 'Tofaot shel magiyah vedemonologiyah be'aspaklariyah hasatirit shel maskilei galitsiyah' [The Phenomena of Magic and Demonology in the Satirical Approach of the Galician Maskilim], *Mehkarei yerushalayim befolklor yehudi*, 17 (1995), 33–62.

WERTHEIM, AARON, *Law and Custom in Hasidism*, trans. Shmuel Himelstein (Hoboken, NJ, 1992).

WIEDERKEHR-POLLACK, GLORIA, *Eliezer Zweifel and the Intellectual Defence of Hasidism* (Hoboken, NJ, 1995).

WIERZBIENIEC, WACŁAW (ed.), *Judaika polskie z XIX wieku: Materiały do bibliografii*, i: *Druki w językach nie-żydowskich* [Polish Judaica of the Nineteenth Century: Bibliographical Materials, i: Publications in Non-Jewish Languages] (Kraków, 1999).

Wilensky, Mordecai, *Ḥasidim umitnagedim: Letoledot hapulmus shebeinehem 1772–1815* [Hasidim and Mitnagedim: A Study of the Controversy between them in 1772–1815], 2 vols. (Jerusalem, 1970).

—— 'Hassidic Mitnaggedic Polemics in the Jewish Communities of Eastern Europe: The Hostile Phase', in Gershon D. Hundert (ed.), *Essential Papers on Hasidism: Origins to Present* (New York, 1991), 244–71.

Wisse, Ruth R., *I. L. Peretz and the Making of Modern Jewish Culture* (Seattle, 1988).

[Witowski, Gerard], *Sposób na Żydów czyli środki niezawodne zrobienia z nich ludzi uczciwych i dobrych obywateli: Dziełko dedykowane posłom i deputowanym na Sejm 1818 r.* [A Means of Dealing with the Jews; or, Sure Methods by which they Can be Made into Honest People and Good Citizens] (Warsaw, 1818).

Wodzicki, Stanisław, *Wspomnienia z przeszłości od roku 1768 do roku 1840* [Memoirs of the Past from 1768 until 1840] (Kraków, 1873).

Wodziński, Marcin, 'Dybuk: Z dokumentów Archiwum Głównego Akt Dawnych w Warszawie' [Dybbuk: From the Central Archives of the Old Files in Warsaw], *Literatura Ludowa*, 6 (1992), 19–29.

—— 'Hasidism, *Shtadlanut*, and Jewish Politics in Nineteenth Century Poland: The Case of Isaac of Warka', *Jewish Quarterly Review*, 95/2 (2005) [forthcoming].

—— 'Jakub Tugendhold and the First Maskilic Defence of Hasidism', *Gal-ed*, 18 (2001), 13–41.

—— 'Rząd Królestwa Polskiego wobec chasydyzmu. Początki "polityki chasydzkiej" w Królestwie Kongresowym (1817–1818)' [The Beginnings of the 'Hasidic Politics' in the Congress Kingdom, 1817–1818], in Krzysztof Pilarczyk (ed.), *Żydzi i judaizm we współczesnych badaniach polskich* [Jews and Judaism in Contemporary Polish Research], iii (Kraków, 2003), 65–77.

—— '"Sprawa chasydymów": Z materiałów do dziejów chasydyzmu w Królestwie Polskim' ['The Case of the Hasidim'. From Materials on the History of Hasidism in Central Poland], in Krystyn Matwijowski (ed.), *Z historii ludności żydowskiej w Polsce i na Śląsku* [History of the Jews in Poland and Silesia], Acta Universitatis Wratislaviensis, 1568 (Wrocław 1994), 227–42.

Wróbel, Józef, 'Twórczość Wilhelma Feldmana—świadectwo podwójnej tożsamości', in Grażyna Borkowska and Magdalena Rudkowska (eds.), *Kwestia żydowska w XIX wieku: Spory o tożsamość Polaków* (Warsaw, 2004), 343–54.

[Yedaiah ben Abraham Bedersi], *Beḥinot olam/Rozmyślania o świecie* [Reflections on the World], trans. Jakub Tugendhold (Warsaw, 1846).

Yerushalmi, Yosef H., *The Lisbon Massacre of 1506 and the Royal Image in the Shebet Yehuda* (Cincinnati, 1976).

Zachariasiewicz, Jan, *W przededniu* [On the Day Before] (Lwów, 1863).

Zalkin, Mordecai, *Ba'alot hashaḥar: Hahaskalah hayehudit be'imperiyah harusit bame'ah hatesha-esrei* [A New Dawn: The Jewish Enlightenment in the Russian Empire— Social Aspects] (Jerusalem, 2000).

—— 'Economic and Occupational Aspects of the Jewish Enlightenment in Russia in the First Half of the Nineteenth Century', in Richard Hovannisian and David N. Myers (eds.), *Enlightenment and Diaspora: The Armenian and Jewish Cases* (Atlanta, 1999), 223–240.

ZALKIN, MORDECAI, 'Hahaskalah hayehudit bepolin: Kavim lediyun' [The Haskalah in Poland: An Outline], in Israel Bartal and Israel Gutman (eds.), *Kiyum veshever: Yehudei polin ledoroteihem*, ii: *Ḥevrah, tarbut, le'umiyut* [The Broken Chain: Polish Jewry through the Ages, ii: Society, Culture, and Nationalism] (Jerusalem, 2001), 391–413.

—— 'Hahaskalah hayehudit bekrakov bame'ah hatesha-esrei' [The Haskalah in Kraków in the Nineteenth Century], in Elchanan Reiner (ed.), *Kruke, kazimierz, krakov: Meḥkarim betoledot yehudei krakov* [Kraków: Studies in the History of the Jews in Kraków] (Tel Aviv, 2001), 131–53.

'ZAST', 'Przegląd dramatyczny' [A Survey of Drama], *Echo Muzyczne, Teatralne i Artystyczne*, 28 (1900), 331–2.

*Z dziejów gminy starozakonnych w Warszawie w XIX stuleciu*, i: *Szkolnictwo* [History of the Jewish Community in Warsaw in the Nineteenth Century, i: Education] (Warsaw, 1907).

ZIENKOWSKA, KRYSTYNA, 'Citizens or Inhabitants? The Attempt to Reform the Status of the Polish Jews during the Four Years' Sejm', *Acta Poloniae Historica*, 76 (1997), 31–52.

ZILBERTSVEIG, ZALMAN, *Leksikon fun yidishn teater* [Lexicon of the Jewish Theatre], 6 vols. (New York, 1931–69).

ZILBERSZTEJN, SARA, 'Postępowa synagoga na Daniłowiczowskiej w Warszawie (przyczynek do historii kultury Żydów polskich XIX stulecia)' [The Progressive Synagogue on Daniłowiczowska Street in Warsaw], *BŻIH* 21/2 (1970), 31–57.

ZINBERG, ISRAEL, *A History of Jewish Literature*, trans. Bernard Martin, 12 vols. (New York, 1972–8).

ZWEIFEL, ELIEZER, *Shalom al yisra'el* [Peace to Israel], ed. Abraham Rubinstein (Jerusalem, 1972).

ŻYGA, ALEKSANDER, 'Problem żydowski w twórczości J. I. Kraszewskiego' [The Jewish Question in the Works of J. I. Kraszewski], *Rocznik Komisji Historycznoliterackiej* [*PAN, Oddział w Krakowie*], 2 (1964), 139–226.

# Index of Persons

# Subject Index

Printed and bound by CPI Group (UK) Ltd, Croydon, CR0 4YY

13/04/2025

14656571-0005